BEGGING
PARDON
AND FAVOR

BEGGING PARDON AND FAVOR

Ritual and Political Order in Early Medieval France

GEOFFREY KOZIOL

CORNELL UNIVERSITY PRESS

Ithaca and London

First published 1992 by Cornell University Press.
First printing, Cornell Paperbacks, 2011
International Standard Book Number 978-0-8014-7753-9
Library of Congress Catalog Card Number 91-55073

Portions of Chapter 7 were originally published as "Lord's Law
and Natural Law" in *The Medieval Tradition of Natural Law*,
ed. Harold J. Johnson (Kalamazoo: Medieval Institute
Publications, 1987).

Printed in the United States of America

*Librarians: Library of Congress cataloging information
appears on the last page of the book.*

⊗ The paper in this book meets the minimum requirements of the
American National Standard for Information Sciences—
Permanence of Paper for Printed Library Materials, ANSI Z39.48-1984.

To Leslie

Contents

PART THREE   BEGGING PARDON

PART FOUR   RITUAL AND REALITY

Illustrations

Preface

Writing this book has been full of surprises, not the least of which is that it became a book about ritual. Power, not ritual, was my original interest. In the early Middle Ages there was either too much of it or not enough: too much because all lords had access to some degree of military force and were not afraid to use it; not enough because no overarching ruler or ruling group had the resources to deter them. What could rituals have to do with order in this kind of society? A king's anointing might provide a moment of splendid ceremony, and vassals might kneel in homage to a count and swear their loyalty on a saint's relics; but the historian should not mistake these theatrics for the reality of power. If there was order in such a strife-riven society, it could only be studied as the interplay of competing or coordinating self-interests.

It was with these thoughts in mind that I began some years ago to study eleventh- and twelfth-century disputes in northern France, believing that the surest test of social and political order was the ability of a lord or a community to compel or convince powerful individuals to renounce all or part of a claim against their will. I had assumed that such an analysis would isolate the determinants of power and consensus: kinship, landholding, and patronage, for example. Instead, the first thing that caught my eye was a sea-change in the language contemporaries used to write of dispute settlement. Beginning in the 1120s, charters from northern France habitually described the disputing process in bilateral terms. Disputes arose between two parties, mediators passed back and forth between them to arrange a settlement, judges listened impartially to each side's story, and the final outcome was usually some sort of compromise in which both parties surrendered part of what they had claimed. The few eleventh-century accounts I had gathered differed in every respect. These narratives began by announcing that one party had approached a lord and "made clamor" against an enemy over some heinous misdemeanor. The lord summoned the accused into court and demanded to know how he dared commit such acts. And instead of leading to a compromise, the process ended with the court's formally censuring the guilty party for his misdeeds. Whereas twelfth-century disputes were depicted as a sequence of bilateral acts in which two parties once at peace were restored to peace, eleventh-century disputes were imagined as a sequence of unilateral and antagonistic actions by which the virtuous defeated the wicked.

A little research convinced me that the earlier formulas in which an accuser "made clamor" against an enemy constituted a variation on the language of ordinary charters, which normally began with a statement that a petitioner had come before a lord to "supplicate" a favor. More digging revealed that this language denoted a set of gestures, since the petitioner was supposed to assume a posture of deference when making an entreaty. Still more research showed that this language and these gestures of supplication—more accurately, the thought structure underlying them—echoed throughout the culture of early medieval Europe, from its devotional prayer to its litigation. Having begun with power, I had ended with a ritual. But unlike the rituals medieval historians have usually studied, these ritual supplications were not routinized, like homages, or highly choreographed, like anointings and entries. More important, they could not be isolated as special ritual moments cut off from the power plays of ordinary political life. Supplication and its attendant symbology manifested themselves throughout early medieval culture. In other words, I found myself dealing not just with a ritual but with a discourse that so permeated social beliefs that it shaped beliefs about power, and therefore shaped the exercise of power.

Having begun with the belief that understanding power required analyzing measurable quanta of resources, I ended believing that the quanta themselves represented culturally distinctive categories of cognition, and that before we could measure them we had to recognize what they should be. Furthermore, these cognitive categories in turn shaped the beliefs and ideals of individuals to such an extent that belief itself could become a significant historical force, for example, by making certain kinds of conflict inevitable or certain kinds of actions unthinkable. To be sure, such mental categories do not transcend social and economic realities. A large part of this book is in fact devoted to specifying the relationship between them. But I no longer thought it was even heuristically valuable to reduce collective social action to some fundamental structure of material reality. Beliefs, in and of themselves, mattered. Values mattered. Virtue and vice mattered (or, more accurately, beliefs about virtue and vice mattered). Rituals therefore mattered, but only if we jettisoned the idea that rituals comprise some prescribed and static set of routine actions performed time out of mind and therefore without respect for either changing times or learning minds.

This serendipitous evolution of my project explains what even I regard as its flaws. My conception of its scope and purpose, of the society I was studying, of what and how historians should study—all these have changed over the years I have been writing. The organization both of the book and of the chapters is consequently somewhat ungainly. In particular, if I had known when I began this study what I know now, I would have seen that my ritual in the form I have described it was essentially Carolingian. Not that the Carolingians invented it. The language of prayer, the gestures of public penance, the belief in the intercession of saints, the habit of showing deference to superiors—all these components of the developed ritual complex I call supplication were quite old. But it was the Carolingians—specifically, Louis the Pious and his Aquitainian advisers—who consciously, purposively coordinated these components and gave them an overtly political meaning. Had I known all this when I began, I would have written a book on the history of supplication. I would have written of its transmission from Rome to the fifth- and sixth-century kingdoms that tried so

hard to maintain Roman trappings of government. I would have
written of its decline in the face of Frankish attitudes toward
kingship and of its recovery in the later eighth century, as the
Carolingians' expansion into Spain and Italy forced the Franks
to accept Mediterranean patterns of rulership. Most of all I
would have written of Louis and Charles the Bald, of how in
their reigns supplication came to represent an ideal of government in which church and state became one.

Unfortunately, it proved impossible to incorporate the material I had gathered on those subjects into this book. There were
simply too many gaps to fill, too many treacherous, shape-shift-
ing sources to be mastered. Perhaps that is just as well. Writing
the history of a ritual does not necessarily bring us any closer to
understanding its use in any given community. Concentrating
on supplication to kings easily diverts attention from fundamental beliefs about power and habitual displays of deference
that make deference to kings natural. Finally, this was never
intended to be a book about the Carolingians. It remains what it
always was, a book about political order in a kingdom so martial and competitive that one wonders why it remained a kingdom at all.

In writing about this culture I have chosen a style that is not
only, so far as possible, free of the technical language beloved of
specialists (in particular, diplomatists and semiologists) but also
unashamedly rhetorical. One reason is that I want to write for
readers who are not specialists, another that I distrust jargon,
believing that such language too often redefines the obvious instead of explaining the unusual. The most important reason,
however, concerns the nature of my subject matter. I am describing a ritual and a way of seeing the world. Part of my task
as a historian, then, is the task of rhetoric: to persuade the
reader, to conjure up an alien world so vividly that it begins to
make sense, begins to seem natural. This is not the only task of
history, and not the only task of this book. But it is a respect-
able one.

When I began this was also a solitary project. It ended with
friends and colleagues scattered across this and other countries
and a deep sense of gratitude toward them. Some will disagree
with what I have written, having already disagreed with what I
tried to write. Others will disagree with the way I have chosen

to write it, with inadequate regard for the origins of supplication and too much talk of "discourse" and "root metaphors." But I could not have finished without their learning, selflessness, and support. Janelle Rohr and Sarah Chayes were research assistants who anticipated my every need. Working with them was a delight. Joan Fearing, the interlibrary loan officer at Hamline University in St. Paul, Minnesota, accepted even the most obscure references as a challenge and said not a word when I single-handedly broke her annual budget. Also at Hamline, David Lukowitz and Jerry Gaff graciously allowed me a leave that I had done nothing to deserve. And without the tremendous resources and great kindness of the staff at the Institut de Recherche et d'Histoire des Textes at Paris and Orléans, I would never have thought this project possible. I owe special thanks there to Mme Annie Dufour and Mlle Anne-Marie Legras, not least for saying nothing about my atrocious accent, as flat as the Midwest plains. Raymond Kierstaed and Marvin Becker gave me moral support when it was needed even more than financial. But financial support was needed, too, and I thank the institutions that provided it: the Mabelle McLeod Lewis Memorial Trust; the Whiting Foundation; the Georges Lurcy Trust; the American Council of Learned Societies; and the College of Letters and Sciences at Harvard University, which administered a second grant from the Lurcy Foundation.

Many colleagues shared unpublished work with me which they thought might be relevant. Carol Lanham and the late John Benton criticized the very earliest versions of this book so incisively that they completely changed its orientation. Thomas Bisson, Patrick Geary, Gavin Langmuir, Richard Landes, Frederick Paxton, Brigitte Bedos Rezak, and Bernard Bachrach read one or more of its versions carefully and insightfully. And there are others, too many to thank individually, who shaped this book, from friends who offered passing references to anonymous readers with biting commentaries. I am grateful to all. One often hears that scholars are distant and aloof, reluctant to spend their time on anything not directly relevant to their own research. It is not true.

GEOFFREY KOZIOL

Orinda, California
December 1990

Abbreviations

The titles of all but infrequently cited works are abbreviated in the notes. Complete citations may be found in the bibliography. Special abbreviations are listed below.

AASS   *Acta Sanctorum quotquot toto orbe coluntur*, ed. Jean Bolland, Jean Carnandet, et al. (Paris/Rome, 1863–).

AD   Archives Départementales.

Amiens   *Cartulaire du chapitre de la cathédral d'Amiens*, ed. J. Roux and E. Soyez, vol. 1 (Amiens, 1905).

AN   Paris, Archives Nationales.

Angély   *Le cartulaire de l'abbaye royale de Saint-Jean d'Angély*, ed. G. Musset, vol. 1 (Paris, 1901).

Angers   *Cartulaire noir de la cathédrale d'Angers*, ed. C. Urseau (Angers, 1908).

Autun   *Cartulaire de l'église d'Autun*, ed. A. de Charmasse, 2 vols. (Paris, 1865, 1900).

Bm   Bibliothèque municipale.

BN   Paris, Bibliothèque Nationale.

Charles II   *Recueil des actes de Charles II le Chauve, roi de France*, ed. Arthur Giry, Maurice Prou, and Georges Tessier, 3 vols. (Paris, 1943–55).

CLA   *Chartae latinae antiquiores*, ed. Hartmut Atsma et al., vols. 13–17, 19 (Zurich, 1981–87).

Cluny	*Recueil des chartes de l'abbaye de Cluny*, ed. A. Bernard and A. Bruel, 6 vols. (Paris, 1876–1903).
Corbie	Léon Levillain, *Examen critique des chartes mérovingiennes et carolingiennes de l'abbaye de Corbie* (Paris, 1902).
Dipl. Belg.	*Diplomata belgica ante annum millesimum centesimum scripta*, ed. M. Gysseling and A. C. F. Koch, 2 vols. (Tongres, 1950).
Fauroux	*Recueil des actes des ducs de Normandie (911–1066)*, ed. Marie Fauroux (Caen, 1961).
Fleury	*Recueil des chartes de l'abbaye de Saint-Benoît-sur-Loire*, ed. Maurice Prou and Alexandre Vidier, vol. 1 (Paris, 1900).
GC	*Gallia christiana in provincias ecclesiasticas distribuata*, 16 vols. (Paris, 1715–1865).
Guillot, Cat.	Olivier Guillot, *Le comte d'Anjou et son entourage au XIe siècle*, vol. 2, "Catalogue d'actes" (Paris, 1972).
Guimann	*Cartulaire de l'abbaye de Saint-Vaast d'Arras rédigé au XIIe siècle par Guimann*, ed. E. Van Drival (Arras, 1875).
Hariulf	Hariulf, *Chronique de l'abbaye de Saint-Riquier*, ed. Ferdinand Lot (Paris, 1894).
Homblières	*The Cartulary and Charters of Notre-Dame of Homblières*, ed. Theodore Evergates (Cambridge, Mass., 1990).
Jumièges	*Chartes de l'abbaye de Jumièges*, ed. J.-J. Vernier, vol. 1 (Paris/Rouen, 1916).
Lex	L. Lex, *Eudes, comte de Blois, de Tours, de Chartres, de Troyes et de Meaux (995–1037), et Thibaud, son frère (995–1004)* (Troyes, 1892).
Livre des serfs	*Le "Livre des serfs" de l'abbaye de Marmoutier*, ed. André Salmon (Tours, 1865).
Lothaire	*Recueil des actes de Lothaire et de Louis V, rois de France (954–987)*, ed. Louis Halphen and Ferdinand Lot (Paris, 1908).
Marmoutier, Blésois	*Marmoutier. Cartulaire blésois*, ed. Charles Métais (Blois, 1889–91).
Marmoutier, Dunois	*Cartulaire de Marmoutier pour le Dunois*, ed. Emile Mabille (Châteaudun, 1874).

MGH	Monumenta Germaniae Historica. Capit.: Capitularia regum Francorum; Dipl. Karol.: Diplomata Karolinorum; Epist.: Epistolae; SRG: Scriptores rerum Germanicarum in usum scholarum; SS: Scriptores.
Mir.	*Miracula.*
Montierender	*Chartes de Montierender*, ed. Charles Lalore (Paris/Troyes, 1878).
MSB	*Les miracles de saint Benoît*, ed. E. de Certain (Paris, 1858).
MSQ	"Charters of Mont-Saint-Quentin of Péronne," ed. William Mendel Newman (Cambridge, Mass.: Medieval Academy of America, n.d.), typescript. Quoted here with indications to primary manuscript locations.
ND Chartres	*Cartulaire de Notre-Dame de Chartres*, ed. E. de Lépinois and Lucien Merlet, vol. 1 (Chartres, 1862).
ND Noyon	Cartulary of the cathedral chapter of Notre-Dame of Noyon, Beauvais, AD Oise, G 1984.
ND Paris	*Cartulaire de l'église de Notre-Dame de Paris*, ed. Benjamin Guérard, 4 vols. (Paris, 1850).
Newman, *Cat.*	William Mendel Newman, *Catalogue des actes de Robert II, roi de France* (Paris, 1937).
Nouaillé	*Chartes de l'abbaye de Nouaillé de 678 à 1200*, ed. P. de Monsabert (Poitiers, 1936).
Philippe Ier	*Recueil des actes de Philippe Ier, roi de France (1059–1108)*, ed. Maurice Prou (Paris, 1908).
PL	J.-P. Migne, ed., *Patrologia cursus completus*, Series latina (Paris, 1878–90).
Pontieu	*Recueil des actes des comtes de Pontieu (1026–1279)*, ed. Clovis Brunel (Paris, 1930).
Pontoise	*Cartulaire de l'abbaye de Saint-Martin de Pontoise*, ed. J. Depoin (Pontoise, 1895–1904).
PUF	*Papsturkunden in Frankreich.*
Redon	*Cartulaire de l'abbaye de Redon en Bretagne*, ed. Aurélien de Courson (Paris, 1863).
RHF	*Recueil des historiens des Gaules et de la France*, 13 vols. (Paris, 1738–86).
Robert Ier	*Recueil des actes de Robert Ier et de Raoul, rois de France (922–936)*, ed. Jean Dufour (Paris, 1978).

Ronceray	*Cartulaire de l'abbaye du Ronceray d'Angers (1028–1184)*, ed. Paul Marchegay (Paris/Angers, 1900).
St-Amand	Cartulary of Saint-Amand. Lille, AD Nord, 12 H 1 and 2.
St-Aubin	*Cartulaire de l'abbaye de Saint-Aubin d'Angers*, ed. Bertrand de Broussillon, 3 vols. (Angers, 1896–99).
St-Bénigne	*Chartes et documents de Saint-Bénigne de Dijon (900–1124)*, ed. Georges Chevrier and Maurice Chaume (Dijon, 1911).
St-Bertin	*Cartulaire de l'abbaye de Saint-Bertin*, ed. B. Guérard (Paris, 1841).
St-Corneille	*Cartulaire de l'abbaye de Saint-Corneille de Compiègne*, ed. E.-E. Morel, 2 vols. (Paris/Montdidier, 1904, 1909).
St-Cyprien	*Cartulaire de l'abbaye de Saint-Cyprien de Poitiers*, ed. L. Redet (Poitiers, 1874).
St-Eloi	Cartulary of Saint-Eloi of Noyon. BN, ms. lat. 12669, ff. 105–25v.
St-Etienne	*Chartes de l'abbaye de Saint-Etienne de Dijon (VIIIe, IXe, Xe et XIe siècles)*, ed. J. Courtois (Paris/Dijon, 1908).
St-Florent	"Livre noir" of Saint-Florent of Saumur. BN, n.a.l. 1930.
St-Germain	*Recueil des chartes de l'abbaye de Saint-Germain-des-Prés des origines au début du XIIIe siècle*, ed. René Poupardin, vol. 1 (Paris, 1909).
St-Hilaire	*Documents pour l'histoire de l'église de Saint-Hilaire de Poitiers*, ed. L. Redet (Poitiers, 1848).
St-Jouin	*Cartulaire de Saint-Jouin-des-Marnes*, ed. Charles L. de Grandmaison (Niort, 1854).
St-Maixent	*Chartes et documents pour servir à l'histoire de l'abbaye de Saint-Maixent*, ed. Alfred Richard (Poitiers, 1886).
St-Maur	*Cartulaire de Saint-Maur-sur-Loire*, ed. Paul Marchegay, Archives d'Anjou 1 (Angers, 1843).
St-Père	*Cartulaire de l'abbaye de Saint-Père de Chartres*, ed. B. Guérard, 2 vols. (Paris, 1840).
St-Remi	Cartularies of Saint-Remi of Reims. Reims, Bm, fonds départementales. A: H1413; B: H 1411; C: H 1412; D: H 1414.

St-Thierry	Cartulary of Saint-Thierry-les-Reims. Reims, Bm, ms. 1602.
St-Vincent	*Cartulaire de Saint-Vincent de Macon*, ed. M.-C. Ragut (Macon, 1864).
Schramm, *KKP*	Percy Ernst Schramm, *Kaiser, Könige und Päpste: Gesammelte Aufsätze zur Geschichte des Mittelalters*, 4 vols. (Stuttgart, 1968–70).
Soehnée	Frédéric Soehnée, *Catalogue des actes d'Henri Ier, roi de France (1031–1060)* (Paris, 1907).
SQB	Cartulary of Saint-Quentin of Beauvais. BN, n.a.l. 1921.
Vendôme	*Cartulaire de l'abbaye candinale de la Trinité de Vendôme*, ed. Charles Métais, vols. 1 and 2 (Paris, 1893, 1894).
ZSSRG	*Zeitschrift der Savigny-Stiftung für Rechtsgeschichte.* Germ. Abt.: Germanistische Abteilung; Rom. Abt.: Romanistische Abteilung.

Author's Note

I have generally Anglicized proper names in Latin (thus William instead of Guillelmus, Theobald for Tetbaldus). When no close English equivalent exists I have used a truncated form of the Latin nominative (Lothar in place of Lotharius). Exceptions are a few Latin names such as Radulphus, for the perfectly idiosyncratic reason that I cannot imagine calling anyone Radulph and cannot think of an ancestor of the French as Ralph. I have therefore translated this name as Raoul, the form in any case most familiar to medieval historians.

Because I hope that this work will be read by nonmedievalists, I have translated Latin passages quoted in the text, save for short phrases that are untranslatable or whose meaning is apparent from the context. When the precise wording of the original is important, I have given it in the notes. This practice is especially common in chapter 2, whose notes provide numerous though shortened instances of the Latin formulas of supplication in order to give the reader a sense of their variety and, by implication, of the living nature of this language.

BEGGING
PARDON
AND FAVOR

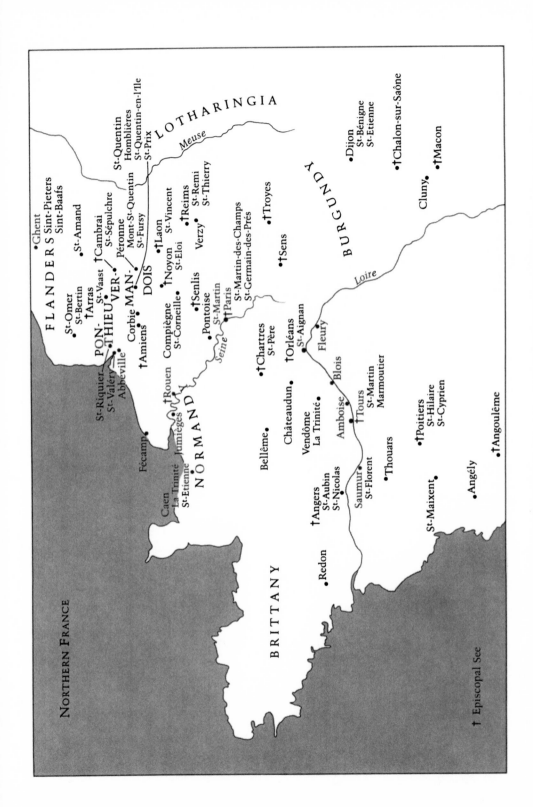

Introduction

In June 991 thirteen bishops, along with a number of abbots and other ecclesiastical dignitaries, gathered in the church of Saint-Basle of Verzy to try the archbishop of Reims for treason.[1] The facts of the case were beyond dispute. Promoted to the archbishopric by Hugh Capet, Arnulf had betrayed the city to his own half brother, Charles, who was then asserting his own claim to the throne. But the certainty of Arnulf's guilt was offset by a morass of difficult jurisdictional and political issues. The most troubling was that the pope appeared to have been bought for Arnulf's side. His open displeasure with the proceedings gave added force to the argument of some of the attending abbots that the bishops had no right to hear a case that should be reserved for Rome.[2] The pope's attitude also guaranteed that an episcopal sentence against Arnulf would not end the issue once and for all, but only set the stage for an appeal to his friendlier court, where this ugly and divisive issue would be used to discredit both the bishops and the king. Yet for the bishops to abnegate responsibility would make it appear that they were protecting a traitor; besides, Hugh would still take action against Arnulf and thereby intrude upon the sanctity of the episcopal order. Better, said some, for the bishops to act for themselves.

Such profound uncertainty meant that the participants in the council proceeded with unusual caution, trying to avoid an explicit judgment against Arnulf and instead to work out a compromise by which the archbishop would voluntarily admit his guilt and resign his office. After deliberating about its competence, the council proceeded to hear the evidence against him, evidence that consisted of depositions by his accomplices. The bishop of Orléans, who had led the case against the archbishop, then rebuked him for his treachery and demanded that he confess his sin, so that he might at least save his soul if he could not save his body and, what was equally important, so that those outside the council who doubted his guilt (or the bishops' competence) might learn the truth from his own mouth. At this point in the proceedings the abbots attending the council asked that Arnulf be given leave to discuss his options in private. It was therefore agreed that he should retire to the crypt of the church with the leading bishops. There Arnulf prostrated himself, and crying and sighing confessed his guilt and stated his desire to be divested of an office he had abused.[3] The other bishops were then summoned to hear Arnulf's confession, and finally a large group of abbots and clerics, presumably including those who had objected to the trial in the first place.

The bishops still had to decide exactly what to do. This discussion also took place in the crypt. There, safe from public view, it was agreed that Arnulf should be divested of his office. It was also there that the various models for deposition were discussed, until the group settled on the ninth-century case of Ebbo of Reims, himself deposed for treason against a king. After all this had been decided upon, in secret, in the crypt, safe from public scrutiny behind locked doors, the group finally dispersed, the deposition being scheduled for the next day.

As it happened, on that day Hugh and his son, Robert, already crowned king, unexpectedly appeared at the council, impatient for the affair to be ended quickly and satisfactorily; but Arnulf refused to give them the incontrovertible admission of treason they wanted. Perhaps a night's reflection had convinced him that his best course of action lay in following the bishops' plan to the letter. Having confessed to a sin in private, he had made the facts of his guilt a privileged secret. Now no one could force him to admit anything publicly; and having admitted nothing, he could still hope that the pope would quash the entire proceedings. Pressed by the kings, Arnulf evaded, trying to return responsibility for his deposition onto the bishops. Thus when the bishop of Orléans invited him to speak, Arnulf only mumbled a response. The bishop cued him, asking if he agreed with the previous day's sentence and if he was willing to abdicate the office he had abused. "Yes," Arnulf replied. "It is as you say."

The bishops may not have been entirely satisfied with this reply, but they were willing to live with it. However, its ambiguity, its innuendo that his confession had been coerced, exasperated the kings. A nasty interchange ensued between the bishop of Orléans and one of Hugh Capet's leading counselors, Burchard of Vendôme. Burchard wanted Arnulf to confess his treason then and there; but the bishop asserted that it was enough for Arnulf to confess to the bishops and kings "in the sight of the church" and to have volunteered to resign his office. It is important to realize the source of the two men's disagreement. It was not, as the bishop himself acknowledged, a question of Arnulf's guilt. Of that he had no doubt. But Burchard and the kings were intruding into an affair which the bishops wanted to control; and Burchard's insistence on a detailed admission of guilt was endangering the tedious negotiations which had finally led to a successful outcome, successful in that the bishops had obtained Arnulf's deposition while steering between the political obstacles that had threatened to wreck the trial. The essence of this success was that Arnulf had confessed his sinfulness and his unworthiness to be a priest to the bishops and would make the same confession to the kings. "It is not pertinent," the bishop of Orléans concluded, "whether he is deprived of his priestly office for this crime or that."

Then seizing the initiative, the bishop immediately turned to Arnulf and demanded that he prostrate himself before the kings (as he had formerly prostrated himself before the bishops in the crypt).

"Prostrate yourself," he said, "before your lords and before your kings, whom you have unforgivably offended, and confessing your own guilt beseech them for your life." And prostrating himself in the form of a cross and crying aloud, he so supplicated for his life and limbs that he reduced the entire synod to tears and sighs.[4]

The affair was not over yet, however. Arnulf's confession of guilt made him liable to execution; were that to happen, the bishops' role in obtaining his confession would expose them to the charge that they had stained their own priestly hands with his blood. To prevent this, they still needed to obtain the kings' promise that Arnulf would not be executed. And so upon Arnulf's prostration, the archbishop of Bourges immediately cast himself at the knees of the kings, "offering the most humble prayers of all for the life of this man." Sensitive to their prayers, but also, like the bishops, aware of the political fallout that would come from executing their enemy, the kings granted Arnulf not only his life but also limited freedom.[5]

All events are not equal. Some seem almost charismatic in their ability to absorb the opposing charges of competing ambitions and ideas and then spin them off again, organized and hence powerful. In just this way, the council of Saint-Basle organized the political flux surrounding the collapse of the Carolingian dynasty in the kingdom known to historians as Francia, and catalyzed its transformation into a new and stronger political order—not France, but certainly a step toward it.[6] Since this transformation is central to the present study, the council also embraces its varied but related themes and serves to introduce them. The first is the importance attributed to ritual dramas of political order—what Germans succinctly call *Schauspiele*—in late tenth- and eleventh-century northern France.[7] Arnulf's guilt was a foregone conclusion, and the evidence and testimony presented against him were summary, though convincing. What most preoccupied the bishops were questions of public image, to the point that they refused to condemn Arnulf, preferring the illusion of his spontaneous renunciation of his see. Even the kings satisfied themselves with a public show of humiliation and entirely sidestepped the more problematic issue of punishment. Everything possible was also done to make sure that the trial presented a facade of unanimity and consensus. To create that facade, the mechanics of the trial were actually hammered out not in the publicity of the council itself but inside the church's crypt. Only when the bishops and abbots had privately agreed what had to be done did they proceed to do it in public.

We should not be surprised that the kings and their bishops paid such attention to image, since that has been a concern of political leaders in all societies.[8] The rulers of the early Middle Ages were no exception. The Carolingians cultivated a wide range of rituals, from anointings and ceremonial donnings of regalia to hunting and the giving of tribute.[9] During the period covered by this book the Saxon emperors who ruled east of the Meuse were bringing rites of royalty to such a high degree of articulation that historians have described the result as "liturgical kingship."[10] What, then, would be more natural than for the kings of the Franks to have done the same?

In fact, given our understanding of West Frankish politics, it has not seemed natural. The Carolingians and Saxons were emperors in both power and name. Drawing on Roman, Byzantine, and ecclesiastical models made familiar to them by their rule in Italy, they defined their authority in expressly imperial terms and used imperial emblems and ceremonies to project that authority.[11] The situation in Francia was quite different. Whereas the two empires are known for the strength of their rulers, the tenth century in the western kingdom is known primarily as a period of civil wars, wars so endless and seemingly without purpose that Philippe Lauer, their leading modern chronicler, complained that just reading about them wearied him.[12] Toward the end of the century contemporaries tired of them as well, lamenting that the previous decades had been a time "when justice slept in the hearts of the kings and princes."[13] Yet their attempts to remedy the situation were largely unsuccessful. Not only did the next century continue to be plagued by wars; the number of small-scale conflicts also increased, as castellans, advocates, knights, and petty officials tried to expand their resources at the expense of counts, churches, peasants, and each other. As a result, historians long characterized the eleventh century as a time of "feudal anarchy," when subjects obeyed their rulers only insofar as it suited their interests to do so.[14]

Given this interpretation of late Carolingian and early Capetian history, historians had little incentive to study its royal and princely rituals, for these could reveal nothing about the real nature of power. In consequence, whereas high Carolingian and Ottonian rituals have been the subject of intensive study, little work has been done on the corresponding rituals of tenth- and eleven th-century Francia. The one exception is homage; and even here historians have been less impressed by the protestation of loyalty demanded in the ordinary ritual than by the egalitarianism of *hommage de paix*, which was little more than a peace treaty between warring rulers that solved the problem of obtaining a vassal's loyalty by requiring none.[15]

Certainly one should not deny the easy recourse to violence in tenth- and eleventh-century Francia or underestimate the difficulties rulers had in commanding obedience from their more powerful *fideles*. Nor can one deny that the competitiveness of West Frankish politics translated into rituals that emphasized the independence of counts from kings and castellans from counts. *Hommage de paix* was only one of these rituals. There were also the kisses, oaths, and exchanges of gifts associated with the establishment of pacts—rituals that underscored the de facto equality of the parties, no matter what the disparities in their titles.[16]

Yet just as important as the anarchy is the fact that the anarchy had its limits. Even the most embattled rulers were far from helpless. To put the issue in Olivier Guillot's fine terms, kings and counts may not have been able to rule, but they could govern; that is, they may not have possessed such a monopoly of power that they could unilaterally impose their will on their *fideles*; but they did control enough resources that they could dominate their dominions and shape a consensus among their more powerful subjects to suit their ends.[17] Recent historians have also found that the traditional categories of political authority were surprisingly resilient. In the course of the tenth century kings may have lost much of their power to the great counts, yet the counts themselves conceived of their authority in explicitly regal terms. The result was not the abandonment of traditional Carolingian ideals of authority but their transposition to a lower level of rulership.[18] Still more recent studies have documented a concerted effort, beginning in the 960s, to restore the dignity of monarchy itself, as the kings tried to assert their independence from the Ottonians and their supremacy over the magnates, while the episcopate began to look upon cooperation between kings and magnates as the best hope for lasting peace.[19]

In this climate of competition and consensus, rituals became more important than ever, and not just rituals of equality like pacts and *hommage de paix*. In the late ninth century, as a handful of great counts asserted their control over nascent principalities, their appropriation of royal rites and epithets declared their new status.[20] In the tenth century, when loyalties shifted quickly and the news of an alliance (or its repudiation) could be as effective a political weapon as the allies' actual appearance in the field, ritual displays of favor or allegiance became tactical moves in the political contest.[21] Most important of all was the quickening interest in rituals, royal and princely alike, that began in the late tenth century and continued into the 1030s, with festal coronations, lavish burials of kings, joyous entries into cities, and translations of saints and assemblies of peace presided over by kings, counts, and prelates.[22] Seen against this background, the council of Saint-Basle was neither an anomaly nor business as usual. It was at the center of a conscious program, developed by the Capetians and their bishops, that used pageantry to communicate their vision of a society restored to peace by a new spirit of cooperation among its leaders.

To be sure, the council was not immune to conflict. The bishops' intransigence in the face of Count Burchard's demand for Arnulf's public admission of treason revealed the kings' imperfect control over the episcopacy. The dissension between bishops and abbots over the validity of the trial reflected current tensions over rights of monastic exemption.[23] And the conscious staging of the trial—the bishops' formalism in trying Arnulf and the kings' leniency toward him—reflected their joint concern with possible Ottonian reprisals.

Yet these hints of dissension and struggle do not indicate the failure of the ritual. Far from it, they illustrate a recurring theme of this study: the openness of ritual to the ongoing concerns of ordinary life. However hard rulers may try, they cannot seal off their rituals from political reality; and the historian should not try to do what even they cannot.[24] Too often we imagine rituals as designed to conceal conflict or gloss over ambiguities. Or we study them for what they can tell us about cultural ideals.[25] But in the one case rituals become shams, masking, not revealing, reality. In the other, they become an adjunct to the history of ideas, of uncertain import in the struggle for power. Rather than think of conflict and ambiguity as enemies of ritual, it is more fruitful to regard them as essential to it. Indeed, these qualities are the source of rituals' capacity to elicit strong emotions, the sign of their relevance to existing needs and struggles. Where there is no conflict, no ambiguity, we have not ritual but ceremony—beautiful, comforting, but lacking a darkness that makes it explosive, and consequently emotionally powerful.[26]

This book is therefore about rituals *of* political order in tenth- and eleventh-century France, and our first task is to decipher the meaning of these rituals—to write their exegesis. It is also, however, a book about rituals *and* political order—about how rituals were used by political elites, and what their use tells us about the momentous changes in the nature of political power in Francia over the course of the tenth and eleventh centuries.

Although many rituals are discussed in this book, it is concerned with one ritual in particular: supplication. Supplication is simply the act of begging a favor or forgiveness in a formal language of entreaty. A close synonym in our period would be "prayer." The prayer was often made by a dependent to a lord, and usually entailed some physical gesture of subordination, ranging from a simple bowing of head or torso to a complete prostration. But the ritual was very flexible. Subordinates usually supplicated lords; but lords often supplicated their equals, and occasionally even their inferiors. Similarly, though humiliating gestures were common, they were not essential to the act. All that was essential was a formal language of entreaty that communicated two facts: the petitioner's humility and the benefactor's graciousness.

The range of supplicatory behavior was therefore quite broad within northern France as a whole during the tenth and eleventh centuries; but at various times and places, one kind or another appears more or less prominently in the sources. Such variations point to crucial differences in attitudes toward political authority, and, still more fundamentally, crucial differences in the distribution of political power. They will therefore be studied in considerable detail. Yet one kind of supplication was of particular importance: that in which individuals begged pardon or favor from lords who were believed to hold their authority from God. These lords were not only addressed deferentially. They were also entreated with language and gestures that assimilated their authority to God's. We will call this kind of supplication "theophanic" or "regalian": "theophanic" because the individual who supplicated a lord in this way recognized the divine grace that infused the lord's office; "regalian" because the model for this kind of supplication was the supplication of kings and the King of kings.

Once more the council of Saint-Basle provides a good illustration of the practice, at least as it occurred in trials. Twice Arnulf prostrated himself, first supplicating the bishops to confess his guilt, then supplicating the kings to beg pardon; and the archbishop of Bourges prostrated himself before the kings to supplicate Arnulf's pardon. From Arnulf's confession of wrong to the archbishop's intercession on his behalf, these supplications simply applied the model of penance to the political sphere. And just as penance was intended to restore Christians to a correct relationship with God, so Arnulf's confession and the archbishop's intercession restored a Christian subject to a correct relationship with those who ruled on earth in God's place. In a spectacle intent upon projecting the correct image, the prostration of the archbishops of Reims and Bourges, the one confessing his guilt, the other interceding for him, made a statement as clear as the return to tonic at the end of a symphonic movement. A crisis had ended. Order had been restored.

Once sensitized to the language and gestures of theophanic supplication, one can hardly avoid them in the sources of the period. They could occur at the beginning of trials, when plaintiffs solemnly beseeched their lord's intervention on their behalf. Or they could occur at the end of trials, when the condemned confessed their fault and begged forgiveness. Vanquished rebels came into the presence of a prince to acknowledge his supremacy and their subordination by groveling at his feet and imploring pardon. Supplications also occurred in less trying settings. Charters and diplomas were petitioned from lords in the language of supplication; and as we shall see, iconographic depictions of these solicitations portray the petitioner kneeling before the lord to beg his favor. In religious life supplication was positively ubiquitous. Of course, monks were professional suppliants, praying God to forgive their sins and, as intercessors, begging him to forgive the sins of their clients. It is therefore in monastic sources that we find the most conscious articulation of the ritual. But supplication was equally common in religious settings outside the cloister. In both private and public confession penitents supplicated God and his priests to absolve and forgive their sins. The lame, the sick, and the deaf all knelt before holy men or the relics of saints to beg miraculous cures through their intercession with God. Even ordinary prayer was nothing but the supplication of God and his saints, accompanied by gestures expressing devotion.

Not only ubiquitous, supplication was also an ancient, almost timeless ritual, characteristic of all societies strongly imbued with a spirit of deference. It is thus found in all ancient civilizations, even in democratic Athens and republican Rome. Indeed, some Romans believed that knees were infused with their own distinctive *numen*, that of mercy, so common was it for clients to grasp the knees of their patrons while beseeching a favor. The ritual was of course taken over by the emperors and their agents; but in this context it was often performed less as a spontaneous act of entreaty than as a deliberate act of veneration.[27]

It was also taken over by the early church, which readily borrowed from Judaism the habit of addressing prayer to God as a supplication. To be sure, in this early period the ordinary posture for Christian prayer was the standing *orans* position rather than kneeling or full prostration; yet the language of prayer was still supplicative; and kneeling and prostration remained common, particularly (though not exclusively) in penitential liturgies.[28] The early church did reject offerings to the emperor made in supplication. Most historians believe that it also frowned on supplication to bishops, since that was too redolent of the imperial cult; but this attitude soon changed. When imperial patronage was accepted by the church in the fourth century, the ritual supplication of emperors was accepted along with it. Imperial favor also capped a long trend within the church toward greater episcopal authority by awarding bishops a recognized place in the hierarchy of state offices. As a result, the supplication of bishops also came to be part of the ordinary ceremonial of the church.[29]

Merovingian society inherited ritual supplication along with other parts of late antique culture, and passed it on to the Carolingians. A detailed study of this reception and transmission would be well worth the effort. Certainly it would help clarify many issues in the cultural history of the period: the precise relationship between imperial and ecclesiastical influence on the Frankish kingdoms; the extent to which Merovingian elites anticipated the Carolingians in consciously elaborating political liturgies; and the Carolingian genius in organizing and focusing the liturgical apparatus they had inherited. These problems, however, are outside the scope of this book and must await their own historian. For our purposes it is enough to point out that by the reign of Louis the Pious in the early ninth century, the various strands of supplication received from late antiquity had been gathered together and organized into a coherent paradigm of political order. Thereafter supplication remained an ordinary part of the ritual life of both church and state, for the Ottonians as for the Capetians. Nor did the history of supplication end with the early Middle Ages. In the fourteenth century, petitions to the English Chancery and Parliament were still written in the time-honored formulas that asserted the majesty of the crown and the humility of the supplicant, who begged for favors that only a gracious majesty could grant.[30] And in six-teenth-century France, petitioners still fell to their knees to implore kings to pardon imprisoned friends or relatives.[31]

It is perhaps the very ubiquity of supplication that has caused medieval historians to ignore the full range of its meaning, as if such a pervasive ritual becomes cheapened through a kind of semiotic inflation. A clear sign of its neglect is that an article surveying imperial rituals in medieval and early modern Germany discusses sacrings and crownings, banquets, acclamations, royal tours and entries, even the reception of diplomats, but mentions prostration only in passing, and supplication not at all.[32] The omission accurately reflects the state of earlier scholarship.[33] To be sure, there have been excellent studies of various aspects of supplication in limited settings. The meaning of prostration in the Roman Republic and Empire received magisterial treatment from Andreas Alföldi, while several historians, most notably Otto Treitinger, examined the practice of *proskynesis* in the Byzantine court; but these studies do not cover any part of the Latin Middle Ages.[34] Lothar Bornscheuer discussed royal supplications of God in his insightful study of Ottonian kingship; but he did not discuss the supplication of kings by others, and thereby missed much of the ritual's significance.[35] Percy Schramm, Ernst Kantorowicz, and Janet Nelson, among others, have also discussed royal and episcopal prostrations, but only incidentally, within the relatively circumscribed context of special liturgical and iconographic settings and, like Bornscheuer, without relating the prostrate supplications by kings and bishops to God with those habitually made by their subordinates to them.[36]

Heinrich Fichtenau and Ruth Schmidt-Wiegand have done much to balance this concentration on royal rituals by uncovering the rich lexicon of gestures employed in ordinary social and political interactions. Among the gestures they discuss are displays of humility, such as kneeling and prostration. Yet neither examines the language associated with these actions, and it is the language of entreaty that identifies a supplicant's act of humility as prayer. The full evocative range of the gestures consequently remains unrealized.[37] As for this language, several scholars have studied its use in the formulas of royal diplomas, but without addressing its wider cultural context. At best they regard a supplicant's petition for a diploma as a simple expression of humility.[38] At worst they misread the meaning of the action by ignoring its liturgical echoes, which allows them to argue that formulas of petition and intercession reflected a diminution of royal authority rather than an effort to glorify it.[39]

It is of course these liturgical and religious aspects of supplication that have received the most treatment, most recently in François Garnier's *Langage de l'image au Moyen Age* and Rudolf Suntrup's *Bedeutung der liturgischen Gebärden*. These authors successfully capture the spiritual meanings of prostration and supplication.[40] But if diplomatists have ignored the gestural and liturgical accompaniments of their formulas, liturgists and art historians have tended to overlook the extent to which the language and gestures of the liturgy penetrated even ordinary political and legal affairs.

Of all historians, only Otto Treitinger and Peter Willmes capture something of the semiological complexity of prostration, since both realize that prostration in the Middle Ages was essentially an act of prayer that assimilated earthly rule to an eternal archetype.[41] Yet in writing of prostration (*proskynesis*) in Byzantium, Treitinger examined only the practice of the imperial court, partly because of his and his generation's emphasis on rulers, but also because that is the emphasis of Byzantine sources. The first consequence is that it remains to be proved whether and to what extent his findings are applicable to the Latin West. The second is that we see nothing of the wider uses of supplication which were certainly current in the West and which must also have informed gestures of self-abasement before the Greek emperor. As for Peter Willmes, while pleading eloquently for a greater awareness of the political dimensions of liturgical acts, he applies this insight only to a single ritual transaction—the ceremonial reception of kings by churches—so that its full implications remain to be worked out.[42]

Thus we are left with excellent liturgical studies of supplication which omit its political dimension, political studies that ignore its liturgical aspects, and no studies at all of its role in ordinary social intercourse. The result is a fractured image of supplication, in which the sum of the parts does not equal a whole. Our primary task, then, is to establish that in tenth- and eleventh-century northern France, all facets of supplication, whether diplomatic, liturgical, legal, or political, did form a coherent whole and that they were perceived as such by contemporaries.

This is the purpose of the first part of this book. To accomplish that purpose, however, requires a kind of synchronic analysis of the ritual and its symbolic matrix more customary in ethnography than historiography. Late Carolingian and early Capetian usages are first dealt with as a whole, with only passing allusions to their differences, and sources from many regions of France contribute to the overall picture of the ritual as a paradigm of political order. The justification for this kind of presentation is partly the well-known dearth of early medieval evidence, which makes it necessary to coax information out of all available sources if we are to say anything useful about any given topic; but there are also more positive rationales. The first is that before we can discuss variations and changes in the meaning of supplication, it is necessary to establish that it had a meaning, since this is precisely what historians have not recognized. Defining supplication, then, and demonstrating the coherence of its many facets require that we begin with an exegesis of the ritual in which variations and subtleties are subordinated to the whole. Second, the power of the ritual and its symbolic matrix derived precisely from the overlapping, occasionally contradictory, but always mutually reinforcing evocations of a single set of gestures and symbols. Only a presentation that juxtaposes these different usages will allow the reader to discover something of this resonance. Finally, only by moving back and forth between Carolingian and Capetian sources, sources from Burgundy and Poitou as well as sources from Normandy and Flanders, can we grasp how fundamental the paradigm of supplication was to the early Middle Ages. It was, in effect, a common discourse of early medieval Francia, shared by a ninth-century bishop like Hincmar of Reims and an eleventh-century Cluniac like Raoul Glaber, and common to kings, counts, and *fideles* alike.

Still, the problem with synchronic analysis—in ethnography as in historiography—is its tendency toward artificiality, since it produces an abstract paradigm that can seem out of touch with the incorrigible untidiness of historical reality. One is left with an ideal image of order, with no sense whether the image was believed in, how it affected behavior, or how the ideal itself changed in response to changes in the society.[43] These are the issues taken up in the more properly historical analysis of Part Two, first with respect to rituals of political order in general and then with respect to supplication in particular.

Here we will discover the adaptability of rituals like supplication—how they were used creatively to cope with change rather than thoughtlessly repeated in blind disregard of it. Indeed, I shall argue that rituals were central to the great political changes of this period, for it was through the cultivation of great public spectacles such as the council of Saint-Basle that the king and the bishops of northern France asserted a vision of order and consensus that might inspire an end to a century of wars. And when the rise of castellans began to undermine the free exercise of comital power, many counts reacted by sponsoring rituals that accentuated the gulf between their own unique, sacred authority and the derivative and profane powers of their subalterns.

Never was this need to display authority greater than when it had been openly defied. For that reason, defeated rebels or convicted traitors like Arnulf of Reims were required to perform an especially abject supplication by prostrating themselves before their lord and begging him for mercy. These acts form the subject of Part Three. To establish the contours of their meaning, the exposition again draws on a wide variety of sources from late Carolingian and early Capetian France as a whole; but the focus falls on one particular set of sources. These are records of disputes in which lesser lords and knights asserted rights of jurisdiction and taxation over the lands and peasants of neighboring churches. To the monks and canons who wrote these narratives, their enemies' claims against them were just as much acts of defiance against a divinely established order as were acts of overt rebellion against kings or counts. They therefore applied the model of penitential supplication to the entire disputing process. The idea that litigation should occur within an impartial forum of distributive justice was unknown to them, the belief that peace might require them to negotiate and compromise intolerable. Instead, from the accuser's initial demand for justice to the final prostrate penance of the vanquished, litigation became a public ritual of political order.

To use a well-worn analogy, if rituals like supplication and peacemaking formed a common language throughout northern France, then different regions spoke different dialects. These variations form the subject of Part Four. To take just one example, the use of rituals to project the validity of traditional categories of rule occurred throughout much of early eleventh-century France, from such relatively cohesive principalities as Normandy to ones such as Poitou, where comital authority was weakened by attack from without and decay from within. Yet the hostile reaction of churches to the claims of castellans and knights was not uniform across early eleventh-century France; nor was a penitential model for litigation everywhere equally common. These characteristics were most pronounced in the ecclesiastical province of Reims.[44] In the tenth century this territory contained the domains of the last Carolingians; after their accession the Capetians appropriated these holdings, thereby increasing their already considerable influence in the region. The province was also particularly susceptible to Ottonian influence, since several bishops whose sees bordered the empire—most notably the archbishops of Reims themselves—came from imperial territories. It was only natural that in the late tenth

century these bishops would seek a remedy for disorder in the
sophisticated rites and ceremonies of the Ottonian emperors.
The proximity of kings consequently made archaic models of
rulership of continued relevance here, even as the rise of the
castellans was undermining them in other parts of France. It
was here that supplication and other rituals of political order
were most conservative, that is, most insistent on communicating the sacred attributes of rulership, and here that they were
most consistently applied to the judicial sphere. When in the
following pages I speak of the "core" area of this study, this is
the region I have in mind.

In most other parts of France royal and imperial influence was
much less immediate, comital authority less well established,
the power of castellans correspondingly more entrenched.
Where this was the case, political relations and judicial transactions tended to be established through pacts (*convenientiae,
amicitiae, concordiae, foedera*, etc.). In many ways pacts formed
a paradigm of political order distinct from and opposed to supplication. Whereas a supplicant who begged his lord's favor recognized his dependence on him, pacts were bilateral accords
that assumed the effective autonomy of the parties, irrespective
of their titular differences in status or the theoretical rights of
their lords.[45] Indeed, lords themselves often negotiated *convenientiae* with their subordinates in order to fix their respective
rights and obligations.[46] Pacts also had their own complex of
rituals, and these, too, differed from supplication; for instead of
displaying deference, pacts signaled the autonomy and equality
of the partners by the mutual exchange of rough equivalents: for
example, gifts, kisses, oaths, or hostages.[47]

Yet even in regions where pacts were used frequently, kings,
bishops, and sometimes counts could still be beseeched with
language and gestures also used for God and the saints. Why?
Where was there room for displays of deference in openly combative and pluralistic communities? In regions where rule was
founded on consensus rather than command and where disputes
were resolved by negotiation, were not supplications of kings
and counts nothing but harmless, routinized gestures without significant political meaning? In fact they were not, and in
explaining why they were not we will see how supple these rituals were, as they adapted to accommodate different political
realities.

Although a wide distribution of power and resources characterized much of northern France, it is impossible to know every such region in the detail necessary for correlating ritual forms and political structure. But in the course of research one region proved especially suitable for thorough analysis: this is a group of counties that, politically and economically, were oriented toward the Loire—Anjou, Chartres, Blois, and Tours. Their history in the tenth century overlapped that of the province of Reims, for the rulers of both regions were engaged in the same wars and belonged to a common network of allegiances; but there the similarity ends. Whereas the elite of the province of Reims remained attached to theophanic and regalian models of rulership inherited from the Carolingians, revived by the Ottonians, and borrowed by the Capetians, the counties of western France are notable for the precocity with which they developed a more pluralistic model of political order, one in which counts, castellans, and knights ultimately came to form a single nobility, knit together by a common ethos, bound in *amicitia*, and, most important in the present context, claiming similar signs of deference.

This study is therefore as multilayered as rituals themselves. It is an analysis of supplication; but because one ritual cannot be studied in isolation from others that complement and reinforce its meaning, it is also an examination of the importance of rituals as a whole. Rituals, in turn, cannot be studied apart from the context in which they occur, for the immediate setting of any given ritual affects the interpretation of it held by actors and audience, while over the long term participants vary their rituals to suit their own worlds. The study of ritual therefore requires the study of these different contexts. Finally, a study of rituals that merely "decodes" them, explaining their "meaning" without asking whether they are "meaningful," evades the most important questions of all. How can formal, often repetitive behavior reveal anything at all about actual beliefs? What is the relationship between a society's ideals, as expressed in its rituals, and the struggle for power that often seems to be systematically excised from them? How can we move from the individuals who perform and witness rituals to the collectivity whose values rituals purport to express? So difficult are these questions that their full discussion has been reserved for the final chapter, after a body of data has been presented which can serve as a basis for reflection. Though postponed, this discussion is still integral to the book as a whole. And while it is in the nature of books about ritual that many readers will be dissatisfied with the answers suggested, the answers will have succeeded if they lead others to think more creatively about the questions.

One final caveat is in order. Because the sources used for this study were produced entirely by ecclesiastics, they naturally speak of lordship and litigation largely from the church's point of view. A problem in all areas of medieval history, this inherent bias is particularly pronounced in the case of a ritual that had such a prominent part in liturgies and sacraments. Inevitably, then, this study tends to become an analysis of the recorded perceptions and public pronouncements of the church, and of one group within the church at that—the conservative ecclesiastics who held power in the province of Reims during the late tenth and early eleventh centuries. Yet the study is no less valuable for that, since the convictions of these ecclesiastics shaped the political agenda. It was, for example, their fatigue with the last Carolingians' Lotharingian policy and their demand for a stable government that knew how to seek and respect consensus which paved the way for the Capetian accession in 987.[48] Conversely, the antagonism of monks and canons to the claims of castellans, knights, and insurgent peasants gave the litigation of the period the harsh flavor that will be so evident in Part Three. In these ways the perceptions of ecclesiastics molded events, and to that extent, the study of the rituals by which they tried to inculcate their values is absolutely essential for a proper understanding of the period.

Even apart from this consideration, the ecclesiastical bias of our sources should not completely deter us from trying to understand the laity's attitude toward a ritual like supplication. In the first place, the performance of the ritual was not a fiction devised by clerical authors. When a chronicler tells us that a powerful noble fell to the ground to beg forgiveness from a king or count, we should not doubt him. And if a sketch, without iconographic precedent, shows a king granting a diploma to a prostrate supplicant, there is no reason not to believe that the illustrator was recording a common occurence.[49] Nor is the laity's understanding of the ritual beyond an informed guess.

Quite the contrary, supplication is important precisely because its liturgical and sacramental usages made it the ecclesiastical ritual most frequently performed by the laity. Laymen and laywomen knew what it meant to prostrate themselves and beg God's grace in prayer or his forgiveness in penance. They therefore understood that when they knelt to beg favor or forgiveness from a lord who claimed to hold his authority "by the grace of God," they were countenancing that claim by approaching him as they approached God.

PART ONE

Begging Favor

But Cornelius was expecting them, and called
together his relatives and closest friends; and
when Peter arrived Cornelius came to meet him,
and casting himself at his feet adored him.
But Peter raised him up saying, "Arise, for I
myself am also a man."

Acts 10:25–26

In no society is the distribution of political power regarded simply as a matter of force. Power is always legitimated with reference to an ideology that justifies its distribution among certain individuals, statuses, or classes. Among the conservative intellectuals of tenth- and early eleventh-century France the justification for the traditional Carolingian forms of earthly power was that they reflected the divine order. The axiom of political theory was the belief in "a coherence between heaven and earth, two aspects of a homogeneous world, each built according to a single plan and each therefore in correlation with the other."[1] Established by God and reflecting facets of the Godhead itself, political order was essentially a moral order, and therefore the right order.

If it were true that government represented the incarnation of divine principles, then as a corollary it should have been possible to find embodiments—visible signs—of those principles on earth. This was not simply true of political order in the narrow sense. It was true of all aspects of earthly order. Thus the fragments of bones and teeth venerated by men and women furnished tangible proof that the saints in heaven still lived and exercised power on earth. And sacraments were visible signs of membership in an invisible community, while excommunication was, conversely, a sign of exclusion. In the same way visible signs of political authority linked legitimate earthly lordship with its heavenly model. The most famous is the ceremony for the anointing of a king, an act in which the bishop fulfilled the role of an Old Testament prophet and the christened king (*christus*) was transformed into God's anointed one.[2] But the ritual supplication of a lord was arguably even more important in linking earthly and heavenly lordship, since it occurred much more frequently than unction and played on sacramental themes familiar to a larger number of persons.

The act of supplication can be defined as the presentation of an entreaty, announced in a formal language of petition and accompanied by some gesture of humility, if only a simple bowing of the head or extension of the hands. Of these two components, gesture is the more immediately striking; but language was in fact the more important, for it was the words of the petition that identified the act of humility as something more than mere subjection to a lord. They identified it as an act of prayer. And in ascribing a contrasting set of virtues and capacities to lord and supplicant, the petition encapsulated a distinctive ideal of political order which remained important throughout the entire Carolingian and post-Carolingian period. We therefore begin with an analysis of this language.

I   The Language of Petition

The ritual of supplication was common in a wide variety of settings in tenth- and eleventh-century France; but the attitudes expressed by the ritual are probably most familiar to historians through the formulas of petition used in royal *praecepta*, the written acts issued in the name of a king to record a privilege, donation, or other transaction.[1] For example, in 955, the first year of his reign, King Lothar approved the reform of Saint-Basle of Verzy by Archbishop Artald of Reims at the entreaty of the archbishop himself:

> He approached our royal highness and humbly petitioned that we authorize his desire. Hearing this with favor and approving it with greatest speed, we confirm and establish by a lasting decree of our royal precept. . . .[2]

Continuity of diplomatic expression was important in European countries before the Age of Revolution, since it demonstrated the stability of the political system. Rulers might change, even dynasties, but order would continue.[3] So here the next-to-last Carolingian king was using formulas that his ancestors had used and that the Capetians would use after him. These royal formulas of petition consisted of four parts. The first was a statement recording the petitioner's accession into the king's presence, a kind of inverted *adventus*, implying that the king was the fixed center of the political universe, the *auctor ac stabilator* of the polity[4] and its penultimate source (beneath God) of legitimate wealth and power. The king did not need to give a favor; others needed to receive one; and so he did not go to his subjects; they came to him. Second, the formula ascribed a distinctive set of attributes to each figure. The petitioner made his request humbly or devotedly (or the request itself was humble or devout). Conversely, the king was either personified or characterized by a typically royal virtue, such as clemency, excellency, or serenity (or its adjectival equivalent). In other words, he was as exalted as the petitioner was humble. Then there were the words used to describe the petition itself. Until the last years of Charlemagne's reign, these were usually *suggerere* or *petere*, words taken over from the language of Roman imperial rescripts which implied that though the ruler acted with the advice and for the benefit of others, the responsibility for decisions was his alone.[5] Thereafter, the petition was increasingly assimilated to prayer, as the petitioner was said to "beseech," "implore," or "supplicate" the king (*deprecare, obsecrare, supplicare*). Appropriate for entreaties to God, such words were also appropriate for entreaties addressed to God's anointed ruler. *Suggerere*, though still appropriate, became much rarer; *petere*, however, remained common because it too had an important place in the liturgy.[6] Finally, there were the phrases describing the king's actual acceptance of the petition. Usually he did so "most willingly" (*libentissime*) or "benevolently" (*benigne*). Often his language was strongly marked by tokens of condescension or command, as when the king "accorded a benevolent ear to the prayers of our princes," or "ordered" or "decreed" the requisite precept to be issued.

The Devolution of Regalian Prerogatives

The meanings of these phrases, the way in which they combined to project a particular ideal of political order, will be discussed shortly. A more immediate question concerns the protocols governing the use of petition: in other words, who in tenth- and eleventh-century France could be petitioned? Certainly the formulas were closely associated with royal authority: to hear and grant petitions was in fact described as "a royal custom."[7] Yet in practice kings were not the only political figures to receive petitions. Bishops of course did, having presumably received the right to be supplicated during the late empire, when emperors granted them a recognized place within the official hierarchy of titles. The tendency of the ninth-century Carolingians to assimilate royal and episcopal offices, granting each the other's epithets, insignia, and ceremonial privileges, reinforced the usage. As a result, bishops not only accepted suppliant petitions; they also assumed royal epithets, as petitions were made to their "gentleness," "serenity," "highness," "clemency," and even "magnificence."[8] More frequently, however, episcopal formulas emphasized a prelate's distinctive spiritual traits. Thus petitioners usually beseeched a bishop's "fatherhood," "piety," or "smallness" rather than his excellency.[9] Abbots, deans, and monastic and secular chapters also received petitions; and they applied the same epithets of exaltation and humility to themselves, although to a lesser extent than bishops.[10]

More varied and interesting is the broad application of the formulas to the laity. It is also more difficult to explain. At first glance the pattern seems straightforward enough, since the use of petitionary formulas among the lay nobility appears to confirm a trend long familiar to historians: that of the devolution of regalian prerogatives in tenth- and eleventh-century France, as kings lost their authority to the great princes, who in turn lost it to counts, who themselves lost it to viscounts and castellans; and with the loss of authority went a loss of control over regalian insignia.[11] The most famous such prerogative was of course the devotional epithet *Dei gratia*, which filtered down from kings to marquesses and dukes, and from them to ordinary counts, and which, when assumed, implied that the lord was responsible for his office to God alone, and not to any earthly superior.[12]

A cursory study of charters suggests that petitionary formulas underwent a similar devolution; for they were used not only by kings but also by dukes and marquesses, counts and viscounts, and even ordinary knights; and in general, the chronology of their use by each group corresponds to its increasing political autonomy. Thus the formulas began to be common in ducal and marquisanal acts during the late ninth and early tenth centuries, and their use differed from kings' even less than bishops'. All four elements of the supplication were often present; and here too the princes were lauded with royal attributes such as excellency and clemency.[13] The only difference was the technical one that princes who were also lay abbots might call themselves "venerable" or "our fatherhood" by virtue of that office.[14] After the middle of the tenth century petitionary formulas also became common in comital acts; and again all elements of the royal model might be present, including (though somewhat irregularly) the attribution of royal virtues.[15] The formulas were also used in the acts of some viscounts, though always without the mention of royal virtues.[16] Finally, during the second half of the tenth century in the vicinity of Chartres, even *milites* began to issue acts in their own name that recorded the accession and humble entreaties of abbots and monks, though like viscounts they did not appropriate royal attributes for themselves.[17]

The pattern, then, seems obvious enough; but its simplicity is deceptive. In the first place, the model of an unchecked devolution of regalian rights has recently come under attack, as several historians have argued that insignia and prerogatives of lordship did not proliferate as anarchically as had once been thought. Ducal, marquisanal, and comital titles devolved according to discernible patterns—viscounts, for example, usually taking the title of count only when their count had himself assumed higher status.[18] The profits of coinage may have been doled out to vassals or ministers; but the mint itself remained under the control of kings, counts, or the few monasteries and bishoprics important enough to be favored with the privilege.[19] Sealing documents appears to have remained a royal prerogative, at least until the mid–eleventh century; and when other lords did finally begin to employ seals, their iconography and inscriptions respected a fairly strict protocol. The seals of dukes and lesser lords, for example, gave their names in the genitive (in contrast to the royal nominative), expressing the derivative nature of their power. More important, not even ducal seals showed princes in the quintessential royal pose, enthroned in majesty and holding a baton. If they did sit, they held a sword, the emblem of delegated judicial and military authority. More often they were portrayed wielding those swords on horseback—in other words, in motion, without the serene immobility appropriate to sitting kings, emblematic of the stability required at the center of the political order and itself a reflection of the Godhead's constancy.[20]

The idea of an uncontrolled usurpation of regalian prerogatives may also be criticized from another angle, insofar as it exaggerates the degree of control that even the most powerful Carolingian kings had exercised over their agents. Royal capitularies and royalist political tracts did try to present an image of regular *missatica* and *placita* through which counts served the king; but the reality was somewhat less orderly. The *missatica* were never as evenly distributed throughout the empire as historians once thought; nor had the kings ever been consistently able to supervise or enforce obedience by counts, who for good and ill were the real rulers of their localities, in the ninth century as in the eleventh. The counts were simply too powerful, the infrastructure required to support centralized government too primitive. But out of necessity came cooperation, as the Carolingians accepted the principle that their aristocracy was powerful and important to their rule, and therefore deserved to be treated with due honor and deference.[21]

The history of the epithet *Dei gratia* is particularly instructive in this regard. More than any other regalian attribute, the use of this epithet by tenth-century counts has often been seen as a usurpation from kings, and therefore as a testimony to their new-found power; yet in fact the usage may not have been new at all. Counts had always been impressive figures, even in the eighth and ninth centuries. They ruled their *pagi* on behalf of the king, and to execute their duties they possessed the king's ban, that concentration of military and judicial authority which was as close as the early Middle Ages ever came to a notion of sovereign authority. Agents of the king, ruling not only for him but in his image, they were naturally regarded as possessing something akin to his grace (*gratia*), a word whose theological allusions accurately convey its essence, as arbitrary as it was necessary. Thus a Bavarian formulary from the first decade of the ninth century has a bishop writing a count to request clemency for some criminals formerly in the count's service. Specifically, the bishop requests that the count suspend a sentence of mutilation and receive them back into his service, "so that they

be allowed to remain faithfully in your grace."[22] Counts themselves decked their authority in this language, as in a somewhat
earlier formula from Neustria in which a count ordered one of
his vicars to do justice responsibly. "As much as you strive to
do this, so we will know how much you desire our grace."[23]

It was a short and easy step from speaking of a count's grace
to thinking of that grace as analogous to God's. This step had
already been taken by the late eighth century at the latest—
nearly contemporary with the first attested use of the epithet by
the Carolingians themselves. At that time the "Formulae Marculfinae" recorded two letters, one saluting a count as *comes
gratia Dei*, the other lauding him *comes dono Dei*.[24] It is of
course possible that these epithets, or the letters as a whole,
represent later interpolations. But not only is this unlikely;[25] it
is also irrelevant, since the editor of the manuscripts that include the formulas dated them to the ninth century. In other
words, even if the formulas had been interpolated, the date of
the interpolations would still be too early to accommodate the
notion that use of *Dei gratia* formulas by tenth-century counts
was a novelty occasioned by the decline of royal authority.
Moreover, the fact that these two salutations occur in letters
sent by a bishop and a count indicates that the protocol represented no illegitimate usurpation of a royal prerogative imposed
on cowering vicars or hapless clerical scribes. It was a norm
accepted at the highest levels of the imperial aristocracy.

If counts' use of devotional formulas in the tenth century was
no novelty, neither was their use of petitionary formulas. Indeed, the formularies prove that the custom of petitioning lords
and patrons was even more ancient and widespread than that of
attributing devotional formulas to them. In the earliest collections, for example, which record sub-Roman usages, urban magistrates are habitually lauded and entreated as *viri magnifici*,
while counts, like kings and bishops, received *suggestiones*.[26]
Gregory of Tours, writing in the late sixth century, confirms
this evidence, for his *History of the Franks* records not only
supplications to kings, bishops, and abbots but also supplications to counts and even to lesser officials (*minores*)—many of
them accompanied by prostrations.[27] Even before they were
kings the Carolingians themselves had received letters of entreaty: "Do not despise my entreaty nor close your ears to my

request," wrote Gregory III to Charles Martel in 740. Granted, the pope had intended the phrase to suggest Charles's royal status, since he addressed him as *subregulus*. Still, the precedent remained, perpetuating the late antique protocol: the formulas were not only for kings but also for those who ruled on their behalf.[28]

With a few variations, Carolingian formularies continue these usages; but commensurate with the still greater prominence of bishops and abbots in local government (and reflecting the ecclesiastical origins of the formularies), they give many more examples of petitions to prelates. These petitions are also more elaborate, as bishop or abbot is often characterized as *magnificientia, pietas, benivolencia,* or *almitas,* while the petitioner occasionally calls attention to the humility with which he made his entreaty.[29] Carolingian counts, *illustres viri,* were petitioned in much the same way, partly because they were peers of bishops and therefore merited analogous honors, but mostly because they possessed the king's ban and people needed to beg to remain in their grace. Thus the bishop who asked a count to spare his men formulated his request as a supplication that not even a king would have disdained: "We humbly ask your prudence that they may merit receiving forgiveness before your clemency. . . . With fervent prayer we beseech you to agree to and consent to our request."[30]

Although the formularies' evidence for the application of petitionary language to counts seems strong, it is not immune to the problems inherent in these kinds of sources. The purpose of the formularies was to provide exemplars for the drafting of a wide range of documents. To that end their compilers usually excised all references to specific persons or places, giving their samples a rather abstract air and making it difficult to know whether a given model was actually in current use or had simply been copied for the sake of completeness. This is not a difficulty with the formularies' petitions. The fact that the language evolves in a consistent and plausible pattern from the simple usages of late Roman provincial administration to the sonorous liturgical prayers of the Carolingian empire argues in their favor. What erases all doubt, however, is the formulas' presence in letters that actually circulated among the Carolingian elite during the reign of Louis the Pious. Indeed, they are so common at all levels of the ruling hierarchy that the usage warrants only one conclusion. Far from representing a derogation from imperial authority, the diffusion of supplicatory language was intentionally cultivated by Louis's court as a prerogative that identified bishops, abbots, and counts as a single, united ruling elite, exalted under the emperor as sharers in his authority.[31] Within this group deferential petitions were therefore an essential part of epistolary etiquette, differences in rank and personal affection being marked by more or less arabesque language. Letters to the emperor and to kings incorporated the most grandiloquent petitions, the monarch being beseeched as *piissime, excellentiae, magnitudini, clementiae, sanctitati,* and the like, while petitioners protested their humility and devotion and described themselves as *mea parvitas,* "the least of your servants," "the most wretched of the wretched."[32] Although bishops and abbots were also petitioned, they received much less august treatment, at least in Einhard's letters, his requests to them being couched as simple entreaties to *benignitatem* or *sanctitatem vestram.* But these were letters written by Einhard to his peers, and expressions of abject self-abasement may have been regarded as unseemly.[33] Rather than the humility and devotion with which petitioners ordinarily addressed their superiors, Einhard therefore emphasized the friendship that bound him and his correspondents. "I beseech your beloved," he wrote to the abbot of Fontanelle, "that not harshly but with mercy and friendship you deign to accept my intercession before you on behalf of N., our former dependent."[34] In contrast, petitions by other writers were more extravagant, particularly when lesser persons wrote to request special favors from prelates whose court position gave them something approaching vice-regal authority. Thus the clergy and people of Sens wrote to Hilduin, the archchaplain, requesting his intercession with imperial *missi* on their behalf. He was their "most holy and worthy lord," "excellence," "highness," and "piety," while the petitioners wrote him in "most humble devotion." We would not, they said, have "presumed to disturb the ears of your highness were we not compelled by need."[35]

Since counts also wielded delegated royal authority, they were entreated in the same way, not exceptionally or wrongfully, but regularly and legitimately. Einhard beseeched them (*precor, obnixe deprecor*), like bishops and his fellow abbots, as *dilectionem tuam, benignitatem vestram*, asking that they "deign" (*dignemini*) to grant his petitions; and he was notably restrained by the standards of the period.[36] Archbishop Agobard of Lyons wrote to Count Matfred—*prestantissimo atque inlustrissimo Matfredo*—beseeching "your unsurpassed splendor that you deign to listen, patiently and beneficently, to what a faithful little servant advises." In sending a book to Count Hatto, a chorbishop of Trier recalled the count's past "beneficence" (*benignitas*) toward him. He had therefore thought long about "what I, poor in means, might send to your serene presence," desiring to "commend the memory of my name to your piety." Later in the century, an anonymous Ghentish church thanked two counts for having earlier granted petitions, addressing them as *vestra celsitudo, vestra excellentia,* and *vestra sublimitas.*[37]

In light of these facts, the appearance of petitionary formulas in the charters of dukes and counts in tenth-century France cannot indicate a radical break in ordinary usage. It is true that these formulas, like the phrase *Dei gratia,* do not appear in extant princely charters before the late ninth century; but earlier comital acts are primarily private documents (testaments, for example, or notices of sales) in which the lord did not act in an official capacity.[38] There was therefore no place for the deference and honor conveyed by petitionary formulas and devotional epithets. Significantly, the same pattern held true even in the tenth and eleventh centuries: charters recording a ruler's private acts of devotion usually omit the formulas.[39]

The princely "diploma," fully evolved only late in the ninth century, was quite different. Here a lord confirmed his own or another's transaction by virtue of the authority that inhered in his office. And here he acted as *princeps* within his own territory, a ruler in his own right.[40] These circumstances demanded the special formulas associated with the subjection of dependents to regal authority. In other words, it is likely that devotional epithets and petitionary formulas had been used when addressing great lords, whether in person or by letter, even in the late eighth century, but that they took on an entirely new meaning when they were used in princely diplomas a century later.

One might make a similar argument with respect to the formulas' appearance in acts of viscounts and knights during the tenth century. Merovingian and Carolingian formularies include numerous petitions made to persons who cannot be positively identified with any particular rank.[41] And though Einhard did not usually beseech his own *vicedomini* (he simply announced what they were to do for him), he did once ask a *vicedominus* to allow a slaying to be amended with compensation: *rogamus dilectionem tuam, ut . . . ei parcere digneris.* (In this case, however, it appears that the *vicedominus* was in fact a personal friend. For that reason Einhard not only asked rather than commanded; he also addressed him with the familiar *te* instead of the more formal *vos*. Even so, in making his request Einhard used the one word [*rogare*] that had no role in liturgical prayer and implied no deference.)[42]

Given these precedents, when we later find petitions addressed to knights and lesser lords we cannot be certain that this, too, did not simply continue ordinary practice, only now made visible to us by the greater diversity of sources. One should also note another phenomenon: the earliest occurrence of these formulas in the extant charters of viscounts and knights does not correlate with the dissolution of ducal and comital authority, since the practice first appears not when the overlord's power was weakening but precisely when it was strongest. Thus Hugh the Great's control over his viscounts was perhaps greatest in the 920s and early 930s, and it was certainly as strong at Paris as anywhere else. But in 925, precisely during this period, his viscount at Paris received an accession and humble entreaty from the abbot of Saint-Maur. Moreover, Hugh himself subscribed and approved the viscount's act.[43] In fact, viscomital acts that incorporated petitionary formulas were often subscribed or approved by the appropriate count.[44] So were formal petitions addressed to men of lesser status, including knights.[45] In all these cases we must conclude that the counts saw nothing untoward in the application of the formulas to their subalterns and accepted it. A viscount wielded a count's ban, just as a count wielded a king's. Interpreted from this perspective, petitions to a subordinate did not derogate from his superior's authority. They appealed to it as the avowed model and source of legitimacy for the inferior's office.

The Habit of Deference

The widespread use of petitionary formulas in tenth- and eleventh-century charters will indicate the dissolution of royal and episcopal prerogatives only if we assume that petitions to kings and bishops were the model for other supplications. It may be more accurate to believe that they were only one pole in a range of deferential language, which was common at all levels of this society. Thus a charter from Poitou shows a wife beseeching her husband.[46] In the charters of Redon, in Brittany, we find that ordinary priests were beseeched, since their office made them *viri magnifici*.[47] At the lowest levels of the nobility of Blois and Anjou, vassals were described as beseeching their lords, even when these lords appear to have been neither count, viscount, nor castellan.[48]

Deference could also be shown to peers, or even to inferiors, as a means of honoring them. If wives beseeched their husbands, husbands beseeched their wives and their in-laws, while brothers and cousins entreated each other.[49] Counts begged each other for favors;[50] so did knights. This last custom is particularly noticeable in those regions, such as the Chartrain, where the creation of a distinctive chivalric ethos of brotherhood and honor was precocious. At Brou, for example, near Chartres, a *cummilitio* donated a church to Saint-Père, acting at the "prayers" of the other *milites* guarding the castle, while a knight holding the castle of Timer summoned his in-laws and "begged" them to go to a monk of Saint-Père to obtain his absolution.[51]

We should also remember that if the writing of these acts conformed to ordinary practice, then they were drawn up by the monasteries and chapters that benefited from the transactions. When the formulas were applied to a viscount or knight, then, the usage represented less that person's illegitimate usurpation of an honor than the monastery's decision to grant the honor. We see this clearly in a mid-eleventh-century act from Jumièges, in which the abbot is said to have approached a knight named Peter of Paris and begged him to make his ministers stop their intrusions on a farm Peter's father had given the monastery. Though called only a knight, Peter deserved the honor of an entreaty, for his father had been an honorary member of the

monastery's brotherhood and Peter himself was a prominent figure at the royal court—*summus apud proceres*, his epitaph
read.[52] Similarly, the viscounts of Chartres may have merited
formal supplication by the abbots of Saint-Père not because of
their office but rather because they were important men, their
family as old as the counts', their family connections nearly as
extensive. The fact that they were viscounts was so secondary
that it could be omitted from the texts.[53]

Of all sources, however, the cartulary of Redon affords perhaps the best example of begging as an ordinary way of granting
honor; for the power structure of Breton villages was quite diffuse and never entirely conformed to the Frankish insistence on
hierarchy. Priests, for example, were more important political
figures in Breton communities than in Frankish; and the au-
tochthonous power of the local chiefs known as machtierns required acknowledgment.[54] This relatively pluralistic power
structure found its reflection in frequent displays of deference.
Hence a priest "prayed" his brothers to redivide their inheritance.[55] Machtierns begged priests and peasants begged machtierns, while suitors in court requested the attending *boni viri*
to confirm their transactions.[56] For the laity and lesser clergy,
etiquette was an essential part of negotiation, and marks of
honor were an essential part of etiquette. The monks of Redon
conformed to the custom. Of course they regularly supplicated
the duke, counts, and bishops of Brittany (as they were beseeched by them); but they also occasionally beseeched machtierns, castellans, and highly placed nobles for benefactions—
again just as these men regularly entreated the abbot and
monks.[57]

Several petitions addressed by the monks of Redon to local
notables were clearly conceived as special signs of honor appropriate for unusual circumstances. They therefore offer useful illustrations of the way the monks adapted the language of entreaty to specific exchanges. In 1100, for example, the abbot of
Redon found himself at odds with a local *dominus terrae* over
his exaction of customs. The record notes that this particular
lord had never before been one of the monks' benefactors; and
so the abbot had no reason to expect favors from him now. That
was doubtless the reason that the abbot proceeded rather deli-
cately, trying to "soothe" the lord by presenting his claim "with

humility."[58] Even more telling is the supplication, some sixty years earlier, of one Gurk, a Norman warlord who had apparently set himself up as a petty chieftain in the region and built a castle on a peninsula near Vannes. Redon's scribe was clearly fascinated by Gurk's odd blend of ferocity and culture. He described him, for instance, as "a savage man" (and implied that in this he was just like all Normans); but he was also intrigued by his habit of dressing only in white robes (*albis*) woven entirely of wool. If Gurk was a savage, he was a savage with pretensions. All the more reason, then, to approach him cautiously; nor would it hurt to flatter him. And so, wishing to have control over the peninsula restored to Redon's control, the abbot made his request by approaching him "humbly, and with all mildness."[59]

Of course, Gurk would have received the abbot's show of humility as an honor all the greater because kings and dukes were approached in a similar way. But it is unlikely that the habit of petitioning men like Gurk was a corruption of a royal prerogative. Quite the contrary, the entreaty of powerful men was the norm. What distinguished entreaties to the greatest men was their greater lavishness.

The Supplication of Great Lords

The vocabulary of petition was remarkably consistent over time; but the consistency cannot have been due to the rote copying of ancient formulas, since the formulas do vary significantly according to period, region, and the status of the benefactor.[60] Rather, the durability of the formulas is a sign of the continuing importance of etiquette in medieval society, and of the formulas' flexibility, their ability to shift meanings to accommodate a variety of interactions. Thus at all levels of society inferiors beseeched superiors; to refuse this token of honor would have been seen as an act of intolerable arrogance and insubordination. But great men would also beseech their equals, since to do otherwise would have been rude.[61] As a demonstration of their magnanimity they might even beseech inferiors.

Yet it is quite clear that the greatest lords placed the greatest emphasis on the formulas, since the language of petition in their diplomas was consistently and consciously embellished in order to present a fitting image of their more exalted authority. The development can be seen quite clearly in the charters of late ninth- and early tenth-century dukes and marquesses like Robert of Neustria and William the Pious of Aquitaine. In 904, for example, Robert, count of Paris but choosing to call himself abbot of Saint-Martin of Tours, recorded the accession to "the familiarity of our rulership" of a vassal and his wife, who sought a precarial grant by "begging our charity in supplication."[62] Such lofty, even florid language was common in Robert's acts. He was Robert, "by the grace of the omnipotent God abbot of the flock of St. Martin and count," or "abbot of the possessions and flock of the glorious confessor of Christ, the blessed Martin"; and as Saint-Martin's lay abbot he received his monks' accession "to the grace [*mercedem*] of our piety and paternity" and listened as they "humbly and tearfully" recounted their ills and sought redress from their lord and father.[63]

Again, it was not the custom of supplicating such lords that was new but the lavishness and frequency of the entreaties, along with the fact that these entreaties were embedded in authoritative diplomas. What is new, then, is the princes' conscious attention to image in public documents, and signs of this pervade the language of their charters. We see it, for example, in the inflated titles many of them took—not only *dux* and *marchio* but also *primarchio* and *trimarchio*—often joined with such hyper-superlatives as *inclytissimus, illustrisimus, gratissimus,* and *praeexcellentissimus*: singular honorifics appropriate to princes of singular prestige.[64] There were also more frequent allusions to the special divine favor that sanctioned and protected a prince's authority. The insistent iteration of the *Dei gratia* epithet is one example. Another is Arnulf of Flanders' wondrous temerity in comparing himself to Judas Maccabeus, since he had restored Sint-Pieters at Ghent as Judas had restored the Temple of Jerusalem.[65] The elaboration of petitionary formulas worked to the same end; for as we will see, these formulas had no other purpose in this context than to call attention to the divine basis of princely authority.

In this connection it is significant that so many of the early supplications call attention to the prince's position as lay abbot: to Robert, for example, as abbot of Saint-Martin of Tours; to

William the Pious as abbot of Saint-Julien of Brioude; to William Towhead as abbot of Saint-Hilaire of Poitiers. The title did not simply give the princes control over these monasteries' estates. It also allowed them to insert themselves into a liturgical setting where their theoretically distinct offices of abbot and count could be quietly conflated so that the holy authority of the one flowed into the other. Thus William the Pious, "by the grace of God count, duke, and *rector* of the assembly of St. Julian," sat in the chapter of Brioude as abbot to receive petitions from laymen. Similarly, it was as lay abbot of Saint-Martin that Robert received petitions from laymen for grants from the church's estates.[66] In this way the lay abbacy showed the way to the liturgification of ducal authority.

To a certain extent this process of liturgical exaltation was directed against the king. On the other hand, the princes' appropriation of regalian attributes was not without some justification. Dukes and marquesses could at least pretend to rule territories that either descended from former national units or corresponded to perceived quasi-ethnic ones. Thus Normandy, Aquitaine, Brittany, even Flanders were sometimes styled *monarchiae*.[67] Those who ruled these territories could therefore legitimately depict themselves as viceroys, and even wear viceregal insignia, such as crowns.[68] Their use of royal formulas of supplication, including the assumption of royal epithets (*clementissimus, excellentissimus*), and their use of liturgical formulas were equally appropriate.

There is also good reason to believe that the assumption of these honorifics was directed as much against lesser counts as it was against the king. As Karl Brunner has pointed out, the political status of these princes was ambiguous.[69] Like the pope, who for all his prestige remained essentially bishop of Rome, the early tenth-century dukes and marquesses were largely great counts, their duchies agglomerations of counties held together by an individual's personal power and reputation. Carolingian political theory had given them neither an institutional nor a theoretical basis for their power any different from that of the ordinary counts whom they ruled. Hence they tried to distinguish their authority by cultivating special marks of honor, of which extravagant formulas of supplication were one.

Yet we have seen that ordinary counts and viscounts had also

long had the right to receive entreaties. The differences among
these petitions were therefore differences in degree, as were the
differences in the lords' powers. For that reason, it would have
been no more possible for the princes to monopolize liturgical
formulas of supplication than for kings and bishops. Moreover,
as time went on the lines between greater and lesser counts
became even more fluid than they had been in the ninth century. During the tenth century, some princes (those of Auvergne
and Poitou, for example) kept their titles and dignities while
losing much of their authority. Conversely, some counts and
viscounts gained in stature and assumed higher titles and prerogatives. There could be no clear line between the petitionary
formulas of these various rulers when no clear distinction could
be drawn in the nature of their authority. One could only admit
that petitionary formulas were appropriate for all, variations being largely a matter of scriptorial traditions and the cultural and
political contexts of a region.[70]

The interesting thing, however, is the way the most lavish
formulas of entreaty generally stopped with the counts. Even
viscounts only rarely had the formulas applied to themselves,
save for those from the most powerful and noble families, such
as the Breteuils. For the most part, the fully developed formulas
of petition were a prerogative of the greatest lords. The surviving charters of Saint-Hilaire of Poitiers, for example, record
thirty-seven petitions between 800 and 1100. All were made to
kings, dukes, bishops, or canons, twenty-three of them to the
duke of Aquitaine alone. The same can be said of acts from
many other churches—Fleury, Homblières, Montierender,
Saint-Amand, Fécamp, Saint-Florent of Saumur (at least in the
tenth century), Saint-Etienne of Dijon, Sint-Pieters at Ghent,
Saint-Quentin and Saint-Quentin-en-l'Ile: kings, popes, counts,
bishops, abbots, canons, and monks received petitions. Lesser
figures either petitioned these lords to confirm their transactions or issued charters recording them as simple donations,
sales, or exchanges.[71]

Furthermore, even those scriptoria that sometimes mentioned the beseeching of lesser men and women did so quite
infrequently, tending to reserve such language for the great
lords. In the tenth- and eleventh-century charters of Saint-Maixent, 80 to 100 percent of all mentions of beseeching were ap-

plied to dukes, bishops, and abbots and monks, with no significant change in the proportion over time. In the cartulary of Redon, beseechings to these lords accounted for 90 to 100 percent of the total.[72] Such scriptoria also reserved the most extravagant supplications for the great. Only their diplomas habitually record at least three of the four constituent parts of the fullest formulas: formal accession; attribution of distinctive attributes to petitioner and benefactor; liturgical terms for the entreaty (for example, *deprecans* or *supplicans*); and condescending acceptance or authoritative mandating of the request. Viscounts might receive accessions and humble petitions, but they are never described as possessing those regal attributes that distinguished them from their superiors.[73] As for other individuals, whether castellans or simple knights, petitions to them are usually recorded only incidentally, by a brief phrase (such as *per deprecationem*) set in the middle of an act or notice. Neither a statement of accession nor the ascription of special attributes is common. Even when the petition is enunciated at the outset, it still usually lacks these signs of emphasis.[74]

Petitions to others besides traditional authorities are also often tempered in a way that undercuts the exaltation inherent in the regalian formulas. In addressing the Norman mercenary and the lord of Fruzai, for example, the abbot of Redon approached them humbly but announced his petition as a warning or legal claim.[75] Similar subtlety is shown the abbot of Jumièges's petition to Peter of Paris; for if the abbot's petition is described with the usual terms of accession and entreaty, in this case humility is attributed not to the petitioner, as was normally the case, but to the knightly benefactor.[76] The formulas of supplication used for kings and bishops may not have provided the model from which others derived; but they did set a standard of perfection against which other beseechings could be measured. Had it been otherwise, there would have been no honor at all in applying such language to a castellan, knight, or mercenary. Petitioning would have degenerated into a ubiquitous and therefore largely meaningless etiquette.

The restrictive standard was obeyed with particular rigor in the more conservative regions of northern France. In this heartland of the West Frankish Carolingians, lavish petitionary formulas long remained the prerogative of traditional authorities,

first and foremost the kings themselves. To take only the acts
of the eleventh-century Capetians: of the forty-six acts issued
by Robert the Pious for the northern ecclesiastical provinces
(Sens, Tours, Reims, and Rouen), forty were granted in response
to some form of petition addressed to the king. Of Henry I's
twenty-six acts for the same provinces, twenty-two were petitionary. Of Philip I's forty-two acts for institutions and persons
of the province of Reims, thirty-four incorporated some element
of the formulas.[77] So constant was their use that the earliest
mandate issued by Philip was given in response to a petition
made by Ivo of Chartres, even though the mandate is supposed
to represent a radically new diplomatic form.[78]

Petitionary protocols also prevailed in the charters of counts,
especially those from the province of Reims. The most striking
illustration of their use is found in the acts of the counts of
Vermandois, who of all regional lords apart from the kings have
left the largest number of surviving diplomas. Between 950 and
1075 these counts issued some twenty-one surviving acts, sixteen of them in response to petitions from their dependents.[79]
Other counts either left fewer records or left records scattered
throughout many depositories, but what has been examined of
the surviving material falls into the same pattern: the counts of
Ponthieu, Flanders, and (to a lesser extent) Valois all issued acts
as responses to petitions.[80] Indeed, most eleventh-century charters issued by a regional lord with any pretense to legitimate
authority were written in the petitionary form, as were most of
those issued by bishops and abbots.

Thus, in the areas of France most suceptible to Carolingian
influence, not every lord received and granted petitions according to the regalian model. Kings did, of course. Dukes and
counts did. So did bishops, abbots, and certain of the oldest
chapters of secular canons in the region, such as Saint-Corneille
of Compiègne and Saint-Quentin in the Vermandois.[81] But other
figures did not, neither castellans nor knights nor individual
clerics.

The key to this more restrictive use of the formulas lies in a
crucial difference between the two groups: lords who received
extravagant supplications were considered or considered themselves either to hold authority from God or in some way to specially represent God on earth. Kings, counts, and bishops

claimed to hold their offices "by the grace of God" or by his "clemency" or "mercy." The monastic rule proclaimed that an abbot acted in his monastery as "the vicar of Christ."[82] And chapters and monasteries were, collectively, the intercessors through which God and his saints were approached. No others could make such claims.

The distinction was rigorously applied. In charters from the Vermandois, for example, the count of Vermandois is regularly petitioned. The second most powerful layman in the county, the lord of Péronne, is never petitioned, even though the family had descended from the counts.[83] But then, the counts held their authority "by the grace of God," a claim never made for their relatives.[84] The charters of Saint-Riquier follow the same pattern. The duke of Normandy, the count of Ponthieu, the bishops of Liège and Amiens, the abbot of Saint-Riquier, all receive petitions from knights and *fideles*, who do not even issue their own charters, much less issue them in response to petitions.[85] In other words, those who rule on behalf of God receive petitions from those who are ruled by them.

The acts of the counts of Ponthieu are especially revealing, since their evolution suggests that contemporaries were conscious of this protocol. Sometime before 1027 Angelran, the advocate of Saint-Riquier, killed the count of Boulogne in combat and married his widow. At that point he took the title of count, a title his successors retained.[86] But at first Angelran's county was conceived of in the traditional way, as a subordinate office dependent on the acquiescence of the king; for in 1027, when Angelran issued a charter for Saint-Riquier, he introduced himself only by his name, without appending any title; and his subscription at the end of the act styles him only *Angelrannus comes*, without mentioning the territory of Ponthieu over which he exercised power, and, more important, without ascribing any divine approval to his authority. In 1027 Angelran was not yet considered a count "by the grace of God," and significantly, he issued his act as a memorandum recounting that he had made his donation in the presence of the king and with the king's confirmation. There was no petition.[87]

By the time his grandson, Angelran II, issued the next surviving comital act, the image of the count's power had grown loftier. Angelran II called himself (or the scribe of Saint-Riquier

called him) *gratia Dei comes* and now recorded his donation to
Saint-Riquier "at the petition of Abbot Gervin."[88] Yet the petition is included only incidentally, toward the end of the act.
The count's office was still too recent to merit the fully developed formula. That step was taken sometime after 1053, in another act for Saint-Riquier, this one issued by Count Gui,
brother of Angelran II. Here Gui was titled *gratia Dei Pon-
tivorum comes*. And at the head of the charter, immediately
after the notification and introducing the dispositive, came a
fully articulated entreaty, as the abbot of Saint-Riquier formally
approached the count (*nostram praesentiam adierit*), "fervently
beseeching" (*magnopere deprecans*) a favor that would demonstrate the count's magnanimity: that he lighten the customs
owed by villagers of Saint-Riquier.[89] In this way, the monks of
Saint-Riquier acknowledged the evolving power and prestige of
their counts by accepting first their use of the title of count,
then that of count by the grace of God; and always the presence
or absence of petitionary formulas and gradations in their pro-
lixity and placement within the charter worked to convey the
legitimacy and scope of their title. In the beginning, simple advocates who had made good by the favor of the king, who confirmed their actions; two generations later, potentates whose
prestige was a matter of fact. The language of petition measured
the difference.

The Virtues of the Suppliant

As we have seen, the use of petitionary formulas was extremely flexible. It could encompass a variety of social relations, not only the deference owed by wives to husbands but
also the honor husbands owed their wives. Phrasing demands
as humble requests was a relatively painless way for the abbots
of Redon to flatter the egos of overmighty lords. In Blois and
Chartres toward the end of the tenth century, the beseeching
of knights by other knights (or even by their lords) reflected a
new pride in knightly status. Finally, as the charters of the
counts of Ponthieu demonstrate, the simple fact that monastic
or clerical scribes chose to apply petitionary formulas to a given
individual could in itself make an important statement about

that individual's political or social standing. When scribes applied the most developed formulas to one of the great lords, however, they were not only acknowledging that individual's sacred office. They were also using the formulas to make a special statement about the nature of political order.

The strength of petition was that it encapsulated the relation of lordship and dependence that was the core of ideal political relations in a single, concise formula. The dependence of a petitioner on his lord was inherent in the act of petition itself, since an individual was forced to request his lord's favor in order to achieve his goals. To come before a lord and petition his favor was to accept his lordship and to express one's dependence. As described by Fulbert of Chartres, it was nothing short of an act of "subjection."[90] But a petitioner's subjection was not a coerced response to superior power. It was (or was supposed to be) a willing subjection, a product of the petitioner's own virtues. Chief among these virtues was his or her humility; for whatever word was used to denote the petition, that petition was made "humbly." *Humiliter rogitante, humiliter obsecrans, humiliter expetiit, expetierunt humillime, humiliter deprecatus*: humility was the moral virtue expressed by the act of petition.[91] The very act of coming into a lord's presence in the first place was done "humbly" (*humiliter adiise*), and the words of the petition were declared "with humble voice" (*humile voce*).[92]

Humility was not the only attitude conveyed by the act of petition. The supplication of Philip I, for example, was equally an act of "devotion" by which even the queen mother had to recognize the "sublimity" of her son. Philip also entertained petitions that were made "faithfully and religiously."[93] Such religious attributes had perhaps originally been prerogatives of the Carolingian kings, whose diplomas and annals had fixed the model of petition. When the Saxons, for example, had been vanquished by Charlemagne, they appeared before him "devout and supplicating, begging forgiveness."[94] By the tenth century, however, all those who were lords by the grace of God had assumed such religious attributes, or been given them by their ecclesiastical propagandists. The attributes were of course accorded ecclesiastical figures such as the archbishop of Tours, who received a petition made by the chapter of Chartres "in the devotion of fidelity."[95] They were also accorded lay lords, as when the duke of Normandy was petitioned by a "supplicating and devout" count of Flanders.[96] No less than kings and bishops, counts expected petitions for their favor to be "religious" and to be made "piously" and "with devotion."[97]

The use of such overtly religious terms transformed the humility of political dependence into the humility of religious reverence. The transformation was easily made since supremacy in the two realms—political and religious—passed through the same men. Bishops were counts or held comital powers, presiding over courts, issuing coinage, and building and razing castles.[98] And counts were often lay abbots, by virtue of which office they styled themselves "venerable" and spoke of their "fatherhood," attributes usually reserved for prelates. This had been true of tenth-century princes, like the dukes of Francia and Aquitaine and the counts of Flanders. Until 1075 it remained true of the count of Vermandois. Calling himself count "by the mercy of God" and claiming to hold "the office of our power from God," the count was also "abbot and rector of the monastery of Saint-Quentin in the name of God."[99] With such a lofty conception of their responsibilities the counts understandably regarded themselves as the protectors of their monasteries' interests and appropriated royal and papal formulas for their own charters, approving the "just petitions" (*iustis petitionibus*) of the abbots of Homblières in the same terms as did king and pope.[100]

If religious and secular attributes were merged in bishops and counts, they were, a fortiori, merged in the king of France. Anointed with chrism, the protector of churches, he approved the translation of relics and the founding of chapels; and he appointed bishops to their sees, sometimes calling them to council to judge their brethren.[101] By his unction and coronation he was made "a sharer of the ministry" of bishops and established as the *auctor ac stabilitor* of Christianity and the Christian faith.[102] And this coronation was made "in suppliant devotion," an act of primal reverence recalled in all subsequent supplications of the king, when his dependents again acted "in suppliant devotion" to petition "faithfully and religiously" his "piety" and "clemency."[103]

One specific indicator of the confluence of political and religious authority is the ambiguity inherent in the Carolingian and early Capetian notion of fidelity. All Christians who were faithful to God, his sacraments, and his earthly vicars were *fideles*. *Fideles* were also the vassals of a lord who had sworn their faith to him. The two were easily and consciously conflated.[104] Both types of *fideles*, the ecclesiastical and the secular, were said to owe "reverence" to their lord. Dudo of Saint-Quentin even spoke of the "cult of reverence" shown to a lord by his followers.[105] The phrase implies that a lord should receive the same kind of veneration from his dependents that monks—familiars of the saints—paid to their heavenly patrons.

In the same way, diplomas frequently left the two meanings of "faithful" ambiguous, if they distinguished them at all. Eleventh-century kings, imitating their Carolingian predecessors, still addressed their acts to *posteritati fidelium sancte Dei ecclesie et nostrorum*, a phrase which deliberately blurs the two sets of "faithful."[106] Bishops, who were both spiritual lords of Christians and temporal lords of Christian vassals, were masters at highlighting the ambiguity of "faith," addressing their acts to "all our faithful of the church of God," or, more simply, to "our faithful."[107] The charters of the counts of Vermandois also play the two faiths off one another, as when Otto addressed an act to "all the faithful of Holy Church" immediately after stating that it was his duty to grant "the petitions of our faithful." If the latter usage denoted the count's vassals, the former introduced an ambiguity which can only have been intentional.[108] After all, in charters from the Vermandois mention of "the faithful" was left to counts, and occasionally bishops. The monks of Hombliéres, castellans, and knights addressed their charters to "posterity" or made no formal notification at all.[109]

The Attributes of the Lord

A petitioner's humility, devotion, and faithfulness were only half of the dyadic relationship that expressed the right political order, for the humility of the dependent merely confirmed the greatness of the lord. The contrast was particularly marked in royal acts. Thus Philip I had it written that "our highness was humbly prayed through several of our best men," while another charter recorded that Gervais, archbishop of Reims, had come before him "to postulate assiduously our royal serenity."[110] Such lauding phrases were used constantly in royal acts. The count of Dreux "approached the mildness of our majesty in supplication, beseeching" a confirmation from Robert the Pious. According to another of Robert's acts, the count of Troyes "humbly entered the magnificence of our highness," devoutly making a petition to "the ears of our serenity."[111] "Magnificence," "highness," "majesty," "serenity," "piety," "sublimity"—all were used as epithets for the king;[112] and all served to contrast the self-abasing unworthiness of the petitioner with exalted royal majesty. The king's excellence was the necessary counterpart to the petitioner's humility.

It was not only these contrasting virtues that established a gulf between king and supplicant. The accession formula (*ad nostram presentiam accessit*) did that as well by conjuring an image of a public, even sacred space, dominated by the king, which the petitioner had to cross in order to present his request.[113] The formulas also occasionally included an interesting synecdoche that further removed the supplication from the realm of ordinary private communication; for one presented a petition not to the king but to his "ears."[114] Whether he heard it or not was left to his own discretion.

Discretion was, in fact, one of the most important prerogatives these formulas attributed to the king, because the distance between humble supplicant and majestic lord could be bridged only by the king's own condescending action. Royal formulas therefore consistently emphasized the king's graciousness in responding to petitions. If petitioners addressed their prayers to the ears of the king, even more frequently the king accepted them by "kindly lending an ear to their desire."[115] He might confirm them by an act of "royal authority and indulgence" or by "offering his gracious assent" to them, perhaps because "it pleased our royal highness."[116] But the king did not just graciously accept petitions. The last component of the formulas instituted the desired favor by an act of royal authority, as the king "ordered" or "decreed" its enactment "by a command [*praeceptum*] of our authority" or "established [it] by lasting decree."[117] Of course, the king did not possess any real power to enforce his commands; but that did not matter. The formulas spoke to an ideal of political order, not the reality. They sought to underscore the need for some overarching authority that could establish the rightness of donations, immunities, and monastic reforms, that could anchor them (*stabiliendus, stabilire*) in a sacred, and therefore sempiternal, political order.[118] So a group of *primates* came before Robert the Pious, "before the knees of our serenity," begging on behalf of the chapter of Châlons that the king issue a *sempiternum regalis praecepti stabilimentum*.[119] To make a petition to the king in this context was to recognize the legitimacy of royal lordship—not its material power but its moral necessity, its *auctoritas*.

These same qualities are found in the formulas of ecclesiastical dignitaries, particularly bishops. We have already noted that they might be honored with any of the royal epithets that contrasted the lord's greatness with the piety and humility of the supplicant. Bishops were also assumed to have the same discretionary grace that characterized kings. Thus a ninth-century bishop of Angers accepted a monk of Prüm's petition "that we concede a plot of land through the grace of our generosity," while a tenth-century bishop of the same city granted a vassal's request for a benefice, "not disdaining his petition."[120] Analogous formulas continued to be common in the eleventh century, the bishop of Noyon, for example, "benevolently condescending" to an abbot's "prayers," or the bishop of Cambrai looking with "indulgence" on the petition of the count and countess of Flanders.[121] Episcopal acts might also use more specifically royal formulas of condescension, as when tenth-century Burgundian bishops were said to "bend an ear" to their supplicants.[122] Finally, bishops, like kings, called attention to the authority inherent in their offices, "ordering" requests to be implemented (*decrevimus*), "ordaining" their observance (*statuimus*), or confirming requests "by our authority."[123] So clearly were episcopal confirmations conceived as an act of authority that the charter itself was even referred to as an *auctoritas*.[124]

The rhetorical conventions that applied to bishops also applied to other high-ranking prelates, whether abbots or the dignitaries of chapters, though as always to a lesser extent.[125] This was not only the case when they confirmed ordinary donations. The act of offering oneself or one's child to a monastery was performed as a petition to the abbot and monks, as were requests for prayer fellowships and precarial grants.[126] Indeed, requests for *precaria* were in some sense archetypal petitions, since by definition the precarium (from *prex*, for "prayer") was lands or revenues to which an individual had no right. He could only request their temporary use as an act of free grace from the lord who disposed of the resources at his discretion. Precarial petitions were therefore among the oldest formulas, and the most enduring.[127]

These expressions of exaltation and condescension were equally appropriate for the great counts. The quasi-royal rulers of Francia, Brittany, Normandy, and Aquitaine could all speak of petitions addressed to their "magnificence," "sublimity," "clemency," "highness," and "piety."[128] Like the king exalted above his supplicants, they also accepted petitions with a measure of condescension, "deigning" to grant them, "recognizing the entreaty as not unworthy," "kindly accepting" it, or simply granting the request because "it pleased us."[129] Also like kings and bishops, dukes and marquesses possessed a special authority—not the power that could enforce respect for a privilege or donation but the authority that would give it sempiternal standing as part of the right order of things. These lords therefore responded to just and devout petitions by issuing "decrees" or by corroborating the acceptance of a request "by a testament of this our authority."[130]

Yet the nature of comital and princely authority differed in important ways from that of kings and prelates, and these differences affected their respective use of the formulas. For one thing, the petitionary formulas for magnates appear to have been more susceptible to the forces of change. The arabesque phrases of exaltation and condescension of princely diplomas, for example, were most pronounced in the early stages of the process by which a given dynasty established its power, since it was then that its members most needed to cloak their authority in an aura of majesty—and then that they had the most power to do so. We see such a pattern during the early tenth century among the dukes of Aquitaine and Francia, in the early eleventh century among the dukes of Normandy. After the middle of the tenth century, in Aquitaine and Francia, formulas of exaltation and condescension became somewhat less common in ducal acts. In their place came more streamlined formulas mentioning a petitioner's accession, entreaty, and humility but no special marks of exaltation or any expressions of condescension and command.[131] Similarly, in Normandy lavish petitionary formulas, quite common in ducal acts of Richard II (996–1026) and Robert (1027–35), became significantly less so under William II (1035–87).[132]

This trend away from ornateness affected lesser counts as well as greater. Letters and the few extant comital acts show that in the ninth and tenth centuries petitioners had addressed them, like kings and dukes, as "clement" or "most serene."[133] In the more numerous acts of eleventh-century counts such attributes are relatively uncommon, as are expressions of condescension. Instead, an act might record a word of petition (usually *deprecatus*) without mentioning any accession and without ascribing any attributes to either lord or supplicant.[134] And far from providing an occasion to propound a lord's graciousness, the acceptance of a petition could be noted by a terse *quod et fecimus*, if there was any special statement of acceptance at all.[135]

These developments hint at a profound change in the way political authority was conceived. The issue is complex, and requires separate discussion.[136] For the moment, one need only suggest its fundamental cause: the evolution of a more pluralistic political order, in which military and judicial power and economic resources were widely diffused across the spectrum of leadership, encompassing not only counts but also castellans and knights. With this development, appeals to a lord's "excellence" and references to his "gracious assent" came to seem oddly dissonant with a world in which lords and their former dependents had to negotiate conventions in order to establish their mutual obligations.

To a lesser extent the same evolution occurred in royal diplomas—part of a process one might call the "seigneurialization" of royal diplomatics. Though the Capetians began by closely imitating Carolingian diplomatics, their diplomas soon took on some of the aspects of ordinary private charters. Robert the Pious (996–1031) initiated the trend by appending the names of subscribers to his acts. The trend continued under Henry I (1031–60).[137] Whereas royal diplomas had invariably been written in a decorative chancery script on oversized membranes, some of Henry's surviving originals were written in a homely minuscule on small pieces of parchment and scarcely

differed at all from ordinary private charters. As part of the
same phenomenon, the petitionary formulas drafted by Henry's
chancery themselves became somewhat simpler and more rigid.
Toward the end of his reign, and even more under Philip I
(1060–1108), yet simpler forms were introduced. The mandate
is the best known; but long before mandates appeared, the chancery was occasionally issuing charters with the same kind of
truncated, incidental petitionary phrases that occur in eleventh-
century comital acts from Blois and Anjou.[138]

All the same, royal charters remained quite distinctive. Even
the simpler petitionary formulas created by Baldwin, Henry's
innovative chancellor, were more elaborate than ordinary comital petitions. The king was still clement and serene. Petitioners
still made a formal accession into his presence; and they still
made their petitions "fervently."[139] One must also realize that
the chancery did not limit itself to the new style. Baldwin used
more intricate formulas, and Philip's chancery issued diplomas
whose petitionary clauses were as lavish as ever.[140] A reasonable
conjecture is that the chancery developed a core formula to be
used for simple awards, but felt free to compose special formulas for great ceremonial occasions.[141]

Most important of all, diplomas drafted outside the chancery
by beneficiaries—that is, the vast majority of diplomas—often
remained extravagant and eccentric. In other words, even if the
more streamlined formulas do indicate a deemphasis of traditional ideology within the royal chancery, beneficiaries resisted
the change.[142] To them there was something axiomatic, and
therefore untouchable, about the authority of a king which
made it impossible to conceive of him as one lord among many,
his *acta* as no different from a count's. Even if the king was
only a figurehead, his mere existence as God's anointed gave
legitimacy to the political order. By this is not meant the legitimacy of the magnates' titles and honors; they held these as
much from God as from the king. Rather, what kingship justified was the far more fundamental principle of political stratification. Monarchical rule, an image of the rule of the *kosmo-
krator*, was the embodiment of the God-given rightness of a
political system in which a select group of men claimed to
wield viceregal authority over their subjects. It is the durability
of this system that perhaps explains the equal durability of

royal petitionary formulas, applied to the weakest and strongest kings alike as long as kings ruled at all.

These factors guaranteed that there would always be a greater *ritual* distance between kings and their dependents than there was between counts and theirs. An axiomatic belief in the need for authority was also part of ecclesiastical tradition; perhaps for this reason, the formulas of episcopal charters were nearly as changeless as those of royal diplomas. The formulaic continuity of prelatial acts was further reinforced by two other considerations: the enduring strength of the ecclesiastical conception of public ministry and the prelates' familiarity with liturgical supplication, which constantly refreshed the grandiloquence of entreaties made to them.

Still, one should not make too much of these differences. An occasional narrative describing a princely donation proves that even in those regions where grandiloquent formulas of petition were not customarily used in comital charters (Anjou, for example, and Normandy under William II), the event still sometimes conformed to the actions and values of supplication, as when an abbot kissed William's knee in thanks for a gift.[143] The exaltation of God-given authority therefore remained latent in petitions to all great lords; and if these phrases were less commonly applied to them in the eleventh century, they were still frequent enough. Thus a monk of Marmoutier "poured forth a prayer before that most glorious count," Odo II of Blois, which he "most graciously granted."[144] And at the very end of the eleventh century the monks of Saint-Maur spoke of the "highness" of Fulk le Réchin's "dignity," and beseeched his aid. Like the great count he so wanted to be, Fulk took his place in their chapter and accepted their entreaties, "acquiescing in their pious petitions."[145]

Any count, then, could step into the traditional role of the excellent lord who graciously accepted the entreaties of his dependents. Once more, however, the role was especially common in the counties of the province of Reims. Far from losing interest in these emblems of authority, the counts of Ponthieu did not even begin to use the formulas until the middle of the eleventh century.[146] And whereas in the tenth century Count Arnulf of Flanders (918–964/65) had completely ignored the formulas, his eleventh-century successors, from Baldwin IV (988–1035) to

Robert II (1087–1111), used them consistently, if intermittently, "condescending in the just petitions" of an abbess who "came into our presence, fervently begging" a favor, and recording the petition of the count of Hesdin, who "came before me suppliantly and by the grace of God easily obtained what he piously beseeched from me."[147]

Above all the formulas retained their importance in the county of Vermandois, at least up to 1075.[148] To be sure, the counts' petitioners never called attention to their lords' quasi-royal virtues; but they still acknowledged their special authority. Thus Otto of Vermandois spoke of the "office of our power" and validated his acts with his "sign of authority." Petitioners sought acts which were thought to require and manifest that authority, as when the count recorded that the abbot of Homblières had "petitioned a charter of my authority."[149] The counts' formulas also retained something of the sense of discretion inherent in this regalian conception of lordship, as they granted petitions "by our grace" (*ex beneficio nostro*) or confirmed a donation by a vassal who had "humbly petitioned that we might show him favor in this matter."[150] Even in the early twelfth century, when use of the formulas had declined in most areas of France, the countess of Vermandois was still perpetuating its ideal of discretionary lordship when she confirmed a donation to Saint-Corneille made by one of her knights. He had come before her, "humbly beseeching" her approval for his action. She gave that approval spontaneously, graciously, condescendingly, "benevolently acquiescing in his petition because it is very pleasing to us."[151]

A Language of Ceremony

Whether addressed to kings and counts or to bishops and abbots, this kind of language did not simply vaunt the petitioners' humility in order to glorify their lords. The purpose of the formulas, if one can speak of the "purpose" of what was really a cultural paradigm, was to present an image of right order; and the dictates of that order obliged the benefactor as much as the beneficiary. True, when scribes wrote that a lord had "acquiesced" in a petition or "deigned" to grant one (*adquiescere, con-*

descendere), they implied that he had the freedom to refuse it.[152] But their formulas also implied that he would not; for when a petitioner approached a lord with the humility, devotion, and reverence which were the lord's due, the lord was called upon to act his part by giving his assent to the petition. The acts of the counts of Vermandois are again instructive. Petitioners beseeched the count's intervention with all the humility that was fitting for God's protector of earthly order. As for the count, as a ruler by the grace of God he had to fulfill his own obligations to God. Most prominent among them was the duty to use his authority in the service of the divine institutions he protected, insofar as they showed due respect by petitioning acts from him. "If we would execute the office of our power, conceded to us by God in this world, for the salvation of the soul, then it is proper to offer ceaseless assent to just petitions, especially when they concern ecclesiastical affairs."[153]

"It is proper" (*oportet*): the phrase reveals an element of ethical constraint, for the appropriate accession by a petitioner demanded an appropriate response. When a petitioner approached a lord in humble supplication, "it was fitting" (*dignum erat*) that the lord receive the petitioner "reverently."[154] The same point was made when chroniclers and scribes described lords as "constrained" (*coactus*) to grant a request because of its humility, piety, or justice.[155]

Many considerations might be said to limit the lord's freedom of action. As in Einhard's time, a lord petitioned by a peer might call attention to the requirements of friendship that constrained him, as when the bishop of Angers wrote that he could not refuse the request of some monks because he was "obligated and bound by the tight bond of friendship and love."[156] If there was reciprocity among peers, there were also reciprocal obligations between lords and followers. The dean of the count of Vermandois's own church at Saint-Quentin rehearsed this ancient ideal when he described the relationship between Duke Richard I of Normandy and his followers: "They loved him with all their hearts and served him in the highest cult of reverence, humbly obeying his orders and edicts and obediently executing his commands. He, for his part, ruled them mildly, as the head of a household does his servants, and nourished them sweetly with the food of kindness, as does a father his sons."[157] The protocol of petition conformed to the same ideal of reciprocity. The etiquette that required petitioners to address their lords with humility required the lords to receive their entreaties with grace.

Friendship and patronage spoke to the personal responsibilities lords had toward their petitioners. But a lord might also be constrained by a more august consideration. The count of Vermandois, for example, said that he was obliged to accept just petitions because of God's demands upon him; in other words, because of the moral demands imposed on him by his divinely ordained office. Here again the model of petition perpetuated Carolingian ideas of authority—in this case, the idea of public office as a *ministerium* whose moral responsibilities bound king or count more straitly than any accountability to public wishes.[158]

These variations show once more that the language of petition, though formulaic, was not out of step with the reality of everyday life. In fact, the language of petition was the language of everday life, as shown by the occasional notice that purports to give us the petitioner's own words. When Geoffrey Martel requested that the bishop of Le Mans restore two churches to Saint-Aubin, he addressed the prelate as a supplicant: "Lord Bishop," he was remembered as saying, "we greatly beseech your clemency, I and the monks of Saint-Aubin, that for the sake of the friendship we should have for each other . . . you restore to Saint-Aubin the churches of Bousée and Arthèze."[159] An archbishop of Bourges closed his testament with an admonition addressed to all kings, prelates, counts, and Christian faithful that they respect his will: "I ask, on bended knee I beseech . . . , by the indivisible and inseparable majesty of the Trinity I fervently entreat and entreatingly adjure. . . ."[160]

Given the power of the liturgy in early medieval Europe, one would expect this kind of liturgical language to have entered conversational speech. But its basis was not only familiarity with the liturgy. "One of the princes of our kingdom . . . came humbly before the magnificence of our highness, and with devotion announced to the ears of our serenity":[161] the formula echoes the liturgy, but it makes sense only within a governmental system that is public, oral, and ceremonial. Hence many, if not most, of these entreaties were made within formal public assemblies: a king's coronation assembly, a diocesan synod, a special meeting of a monastic chapter in the rare presence of its powerful lay abbot.[162] These gatherings provided opportunities to renew allegiances and exchange information, to plot and to plan; but they also provided an arena for display, and a special, ceremonial language was part of the display.

In none of these respects was early medieval France unusual among traditional societies. On the contrary, the evolution of a special language for formal occasions has been quite common. In Madagascar, for example, it was known as *kabary*, defined as "winding one's words." On requesting a wife, burying the dead, or circumcising those who were to become adults, a chosen speaker would purposely adopt a formal style of speech, limited in its vocabulary and repertory of ideas but able to communicate the specialness of the moment. Indeed, simply to adopt *kabary* in an ordinary encounter solemnified the exchange and honored the respondent. In many societies that have used such rhetoric, ceremonial address not only honored the recipient; like a petition, it also coerced his response, for to be addressed with honor pressured him to live up to the virtues expected of honorable men. Again as in a petition, the constraints of this kind of speech in no way precluded innovation or sincerity. Rather, skill was measured by the quality of a speaker's verbal arabesques around the stock themes, while the fixed patterns made innuendo by omission or excess all the more noticeable.[163]

Finally, like the rhetoric of petition and grace, such ceremonial styles of speech placed a high value on tradition. This was expressed overtly, through the virtues a speaker openly praised and associated with honored ancestors. But convervatism was inherent in the very choice of language, simply because the rhetoric was traditional, in the case of *kabary*, for example, believed to have been handed down by these same ancestors. In being repeated the rhetoric did not become stale. Rather, it was repeated because it was solemn, even sacred language, appropriate as a means of showing honor to superiors—particularly in settings like betrothals and assemblies, where it was important to demonstrate the continuing vitality of traditional values and the enduring legitimacy of traditional social order.

When, therefore, a diploma repeated the language of petition, its author was not simply following a scribal formula. He was recapturing the words used in the event itself. And this realiza-

tion offers insight into the purpose of diplomas and their liturgical language. Besides providing a useful catalogue of lands and
immunities, a diploma was a token of the original act of authority that guaranteed them. It was a kind of textual *festuca*. In
other words, a diploma did not just record a church's rights and
privileges. Like the pieces of wood or bags of dirt used by donors
in rituals of conveyance and retained by the beneficiaries, it also
recalled the public ceremony in which they had been granted
and which alone legitimated their possession.[164] But most of all,
it recalled the mutual demonstrations of devotion and favor
that maintained political stability among the powerful. The
supplicant displayed his humility in order "to find grace in the
eyes" of his lord.[165] He did not demand what was his by right;
rather he approached his lord as the church dignitaries of Autun
approached Duke Odo of Burgundy late in the eleventh century:
they "came into our presence fervently beseeching that . . . we
might deign to make a gift." As for Odo, he wanted to "extend
the ear of our serenity to the petitions of the faithful," because a
gracious magnanimity was the hallmark of those whom God
had graced. "And so it pleased our sublimity to acquiesce in
their more useful petitions."[166] True, the language was formulaic, and it did not correspond to the way the world really was;
but it was the way people really spoke when trying to represent
the way the world should be.

2 The Act of Supplication

In a society riven by war and possessing few if any permanent institutions, power was extremely fluid. A ruler's prestige, the loyalty of his dependents, and the allegiance of his friends and kin counted for more in maintaining power than any official position. Hence the supreme importance of rituals, great and small, rare and frequent, throughout the early Middle Ages, for loyalty, dominance, and friendship had to be recast, tested, and affirmed for each new alliance, every new generation.[1] Feudal homage, royal coronations, and crown-wearings are the most familiar of these ceremonies. There were many others. Partners to pacts exchanged kisses (or, less trustingly, oaths or hostages).[2] Lords acted as grooms to other lords to show them reverence or waited at their tables.[3] Counts demanded processions of *occursus* from monasteries they suspected of disloyalty.[4]

Given this need to give physical expression to social and political relations, it is not surprising that there was also a *forma humilitatis* considered appropriate to the humility of petition.[5] The language of petition was itself part of the proper form. Chroniclers often wrote that a dependent approached a lord and made his petition "with humble voice."[6] The phrase may simply refer to the language of the petition, for it is frequently followed by just that kind of formal petition I have described, as the petitioner drew attention to his own humility while begging

the lord's "mercy" and "authority" and lauding him as "clement," "unconquered," and "gentle."⁷ More likely, however, *vox
humilis* refers to the way the petition was delivered—dolefully,
tremulously, or with tears.⁸ Of course, these descriptions are
highly formulaic since they were taken straight from the lit-
urgy.⁹ Whether they corresponded with reality is difficult to determine; but one can easily imagine a petitioner using a special
tone to address his lord in a formal assembly. The tears may not
have been real, but the wailing may well have been. It would in
any case be quite wrong to imagine the petition delivered in a
monotone, since understatement was not particularly valued at
the time. One recalls the loud wailing (*clamore et ululatu*) with
which the followers of Duke William Longsword mourned the
treacherous murder of their lord before their very eyes.¹⁰ The
Miracula sancti Benedicti tells the story of a woman who grew
angry at Saint Benedict for failing to protect her from an evil
lord. She finally went to church and threw herself on the saint's
altar, pummeling it and shouting invective at the saint.¹¹ In the
Middle Ages, devotion did not require diffidence. And so there
is no reason not to believe that a petitioner may well have addressed his lord literally *à haute voix*—a public ritual voice for
a public ritual action.¹²

Along with humble words and the adoption of a liturgical
tone, a petitioner's physical bearing also gave proof of his humility, for as Peter the Chanter later said, "The gesture of the
body is an argument and proof of the devotion of the mind."¹³ A
lord could not see the humble mind, but he could see the gestures by which a petitioner exhibited his humility. These were
the gestures of supplication which frequently accompanied a petition.

It is important to realize that supplication was less a specific
posture than a prayer addressed to a lord accompanied by some
physical sign of deference. As is evident in Peter's statement, it
was the attitude that remained essential to supplication, the
suppliant gesture only providing evidence of the attitude. There
was therefore no single gesture by which the supplicant demonstrated his or her devotion. One of the most common gestures
of supplication, in fact, seems to have been no more than standing with head slightly bowed and hands stretched out toward
the lord, palms up;¹⁴ but there were many other postures. In

fact, supplicants had considerable latitude to modulate the impression of their humility, ranging from simple deference in the case of an ordinary petition to abject self-abasement in penitential atonement for wrong. Such flexibility helped prevent these recurring gestures from degenerating into rote etiquette. If the physical attitude were to be convincing as a sign of the inner attitude, then variation in posture was essential to permit expression of a full range of emotional states.[15]

Latitude was also necessary because the supplication of a lord took place in a specific physical environment whose structure actors automatically took into account. Thus to stand in the presence of a sitting lord was considered a posture of deference—save in the case of those condemned by sitting judges, when to stand was regarded as a mark of arrogance and rebellion.[16] Conversely, for a lord to stand at the accession of a dependent was an unusual mark of favor. When Archbishop Lanfranc of Canterbury had an audience with Pope Alexander II, the pope actually rose when the archbishop entered, reportedly explaining, "I have not stood up for him because he is archbishop of Canterbury, but because I was at his school of Bec, and I sat at his feet together with other listeners." "As an indication of his love," Alexander also handed Lanfranc two palls with his own hands rather than let him take them from the altar as was customary—so much did small gestures count in the Middle Ages.[17]

Alexander mentioned what was in fact the most common sign of subordination: to place oneself beneath a superior, as Alexander had sat at the feet of his master, Lanfranc. So at a gathering of the court of Henry II of Germany, Frederick, one of the great nobles of Lorraine, chose to sit at the feet of his abbot, Richard of Saint-Vanne, rather than take his place "higher up" (*eminentiori loco*) among the king's counselors, as his birth permitted. (As often happened, the demonstration of humility was so impressive a declaration of a "faithful" spirit that it brought exaltation through the lord's favor: Henry summoned Abbot Richard to his side and had Frederick—still sitting at his abbot's feet—join him there. And that was the beginning of Richard's illustrious diplomatic career.)[18] In ecclesiastical councils, the prelates sat on raised benches, above those who approached them.[19] Within this overall structure, details in the arrangement of dignitaries articulated fine points of ecclesiastical organization, so that the very setting of these tribunals replicated political order. Those who presided over a council—whether emperor, king, or archbishop—might sit at the head of the assembly, while suffragan bishops arranged themselves arround the president by seniority, the attending but subordinate dignitaries—priests, deacons, and abbots—standing behind them all. Honored individuals might be treated specially, as when in local synods the abbot of Saint-Martial, vicar of the purported apostle of the Gauls, was allowed to sit across from the bishop's cathedra, *in corona episcoporum*, the other ecclesiastical dignitaries sitting around them.[20] Nor were such considerations limited to ecclesiastics. Richer passes off as history a legend about a meeting between Otto I and Louis d'Outremer, where a considerable tumult was caused because Louis had sat beneath Otto. Even if apocryphal, the story still reveals the importance of such protocols in the minds of contemporaries. Besides, Flodoard, a more reliable source, writing about another meeting between the two kings, was careful to point out that they had sat down simultaneously.[21]

As these examples show, the physical arrangement of public gatherings could force social interactions into patterns of deference. At least in Germany, even burial corteges were structured to require signs of deference to the dead, as the son who acted as pallbearer placed himself beneath his father, who demanded subservience even in death. Contemporaries were quite aware of this meaning, as we see in the *Vita Chuonradi*'s account of Conrad's burial, at which the young King Henry served as pallbearer. Henry "bent his shoulders under the body of his father with very humble devotion at every entry into a church and finally at the entombment. And the King showed most zealously to his dear father all this—not only what the son owes to the father in perfect love, but what the servant owes to his lord in fear."[22]

In these cases deference was imposed by the nature of the setting. Supplication, in contrast, required a conscious act of deference, as the petitioner willingly and purposely assumed a humble posture. Most commonly this entailed his kneeling or prostrating himself before his lord. Prostration was certainly the posture most closely identified with humility, as shown by an illustration in an eleventh-century penitential from Moissac (figure 1). As a loose model the illustrator chose the theme of the *Conflictus virtutum et vitiorum*. Usually the iconography of this allegory continued a late-antique tradition; but the Moissac illustrator broke with that tradition, perhaps in order to portray the allegory in a style more appropriate to the world he saw around him. In any case, Pride, the chief vice, he showed cast headlong down from the feast table where she and her harpies had been sating themselves. Humility, the chief virtue of supplication and petition, he showed curled up on the ground, her hands to her knees and her forehead touching the ground in a supplicatory pose.[23]

Iconography, literature, and chronicles provide numerous associations of humility with gestural acts of deference. Two eleventh-century notices describe individuals prostrating themselves to a bishop or kissing the knee of a count in thanks for a benefaction.[24] And Archbishop Arnulf's prostration to his kings, the incident with which this book began, shows the practice in a penitential request for mercy, a special type of petition discussed in later chapters. For the moment, however, the question is whether such physical expressions of humility ordinarily accompanied the seeking of favors from a temporal lord— whether, that is, the formulas of petition found in charters and diplomas denoted a ritual. Of that there is little doubt. As already mentioned, a petitioner might stand when announcing his request, and liturgical practices suggest that in such cases humility would have been expressed by the supplicant's hands, held outward in the *orans* position.[25] But genuflection, kneeling, and prostration were also favored postures for beseeching a lord's grace because they provided such a clear demonstration of deference.

Usually postures are not mentioned in the charters, which normally are silent about every aspect of the physical environment within which a petition was made. There are enough exceptions, however, to prove that kneeling or prostration was the normal position for making supplications. In the 880s, for example, Carloman's chancellor began to expand on the traditional formulas of Carolingian diplomatics by describing petitioners as kneeling before the king to make their request.[26] Jacques de Font-Réaulx, who briefly discussed the new formulas,

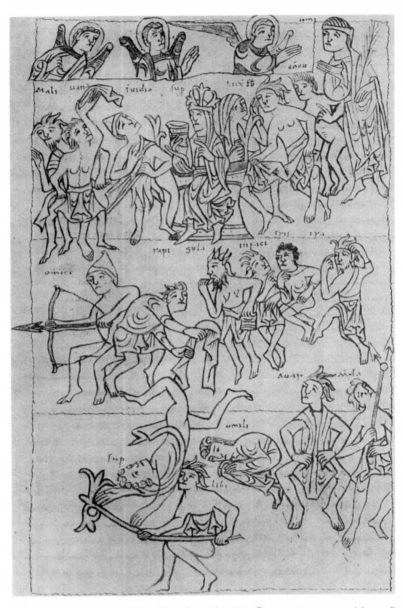

1. Images of Pride and Humility, from the "Conflictus virtutum et vitiorum" (Moissac, late eleventh century, from an early eleventh-century original). Paris, Bibliothèque Nationale, ms. lat. 2077, f. 163r.

called them a "cliché" and related their introduction to the decline of royal power.[27] He may well be correct that the formulas
were introduced into royal diplomas at this particular time to
counteract the king's weakness. Yet the postures themselves
were not new. Kneeling and prostration are attested in a wide
range of petitions long before Carloman's time. And though descriptions of these postures were formulaic, they were not clichés. On the contrary, writers constantly embroidered the formulas precisely in order to present an image of sincerity.

There is some diplomatic evidence for these assertions. A
charter from Brioude written shortly after Carloman's death
mentions a petitioner's prostration before the archbishop of
Bourges. It describes the prostration quite matter-of-factly, using no traditional formula at all.[28] Two decades before Carloman's accession, in a charter for Beaulieu, the archbishop of
Bourges requested future generations to respect his testament,
writing that he did so "humbly, on bended knee."[29] As with
other aspects of petition, however, the best early evidence comes
from letters. We have already seen that epistolary and diplomatic petitions were quite similar in both language and usage.
The major difference was this: Since a lord could not see a letter
writer offering his petition, the supplicant often described the
gestures that the lord would have seen had the petition been
made in his presence.[30] Thus the "Salzburg Formulary," compiled in the early ninth century, includes several letters referring to the petitioner's complete prostration at the feet of
bishops.[31] Later writers varied these exemplars and sought out
grander models, as if the novel expression of self-effacement
presented a delightful challenge. "Groveling in spirit at the feet
of your piety," wrote the people of Sens, entreating aid from
Hilduin of Saint-Denis. Letters to the emperor were, suitably,
more lavish still, as when the people of Mainz beseeched Louis
the Pious to release their archbishop from burdensome court
service: "Most clement lord, we pray one, we pray all, as if
bodily cast down before your most kind feet, that we may re-
joice in again receiving the shepherd whom we formerly received by the concession of your most generous grace."[32] In 871
the duke of Brittany addressed a request to the pope "on bended
knees and with bowed head."[33]

Prostrate supplications of kings, bishops, and princes remained common throughout the tenth century. In fact, at the end of the century Richer was taking their performance for granted, as we see in the speech he attributed to Adalbero of Reims on the occasion of Hugh Capet's election as king. As Hugh's supporter, the archbishop spoke out eloquently against the alternative election of Charles of Lorraine. One of his many arguments was that Charles's election would dishonor the duke of the Franks by requiring his subordination to Charles's low-born wife, a woman whose equals and even superiors were accustomed to kneel before the duke and place their hands at his feet. Because the supplicants placed their hands at the duke's feet and not within his hands, no homage is meant here. This is a regal *proskynesis*, which Richer assumes to be a frequent and customary token of subjection.[34] Richer's evidence is confirmed by tenth-century charters. Acts from Burgundy regularly describe petitioners as kneeling or as addressing their entreaties to bishops' knees. Around 949, for example, a *fidelis* of Saint-Vincent named Vislemar entered the cathedral where the bishop of Macon was holding court with his canons and faithful. Vislemar "approached the knees of his humility, begging in all supplication that something from the property of the said martyr be conferred on him." In 968 a knight and an archpresbiter presented an entreaty to the bishop of Langres, "beseeching our gentleness on bended knees."[35] Again, however, prostration, kneeling, and genuflection were not absolutely necessary for making the petition: another act from Saint-Vincent describes an *illustris vir* entreating the bishop, approaching "the clemency of his serenity with bowed head."[36]

Though less frequent, such statements still occur in charters of the next century, as in one recording a request by a monk of Beaulieu to the bishop of Cahors: "Falling at your feet I beseech your benevolence, my lord bishop, with complete devotion of body and soul."[37] Petitioners also knelt to present their entreaties to Robert the Pious—"approaching the knees of our serenity," as the king said—whether they were faithful vassals like Ansold the Rich or magnates like the count of Chalon and the bishop of Auxerre.[38] Where the charters are silent, epistolary petitions again provide corroborating evidence for the suppliant gestures of ordinary petitions to great lords. Early in the twelfth century Ivo of Chartres wrote to Louis VI, requesting that he not avenge the murder of a man slain by the clergy and people of Beauvais but leave the affair to ecclesiastical judges. The letter begins with a phrase clearly modeled on the standard petitionary formulas of royal diplomas; but to this core Ivo added a description of the physical signs of sincerity and devotion that were supposed to accompany an entreaty: "I supplicate your royal excellency, from my heart on bended knees, that in this matter it might happen that I obtain grace in the eyes of your royal majesty."[39] A century earlier Fulbert of Chartres had written to Robert the Pious in behalf of the king's miscreant son, "to beseech your piety on bended knee, with weeping heart and mind." Around the same time the canons of Chartres sought the aid of the archbishop of Tours, to whom they wrote as suppliants, "prostrate and devout," offering "the service of our faithfulness" (*prona atque devota fidelitatis obsequium*).[40]

The wide variation of these phrases shows that writers were not slavishly imitating older models. It is also significant that the elaborate descriptions of kneeling or prostration found in charters and letters have no equivalent in extant formularies.[41] Like the Moissac illustrator of the *Conflictus virtutum et vitiorum*, scribes and letter writers were varying their inherited models to conform to their own needs—and to contemporary reality. There is no possibility that the formulas were only literary conventions without relevance to actual behavior. In any case, chroniclers of the period assumed that prostration really did accompany petitions. Thus Richer, William of Jumièges, and William of Poitiers used *supplex* and its derivatives in contexts that suggest their classical and ecclesiastical meanings of kneeling and prostration, since an individual's "supplication" is treated as an action distinct from his or her petition and entreaty.[42] But the most explicit evidence for the gestures of supplication comes from Dudo of Saint-Quentin's history of the Norman dukes, which is, we will see, entirely organized around the theme of supplication. Thus according to Dudo, Bernard of Senlis sought aid from Duke Hugh the Great by "adding prayer upon prayer [and] falling in supplication at his feet." The count of Montdidier and Cono of Saxony prostrated themselves before William Longsword, as did a knight of Rouen before Count Bernard of Rouen—all in order to "beseech," "pray," or "beg" favors of their lords.[43]

Paradoxically, two of the most explicit proofs that the formulas of petition found in later charters denoted a ritual action
come from forgeries. Though not authoritative acts, they are all
the more valuable insofar as they reveal how contemporaries
imagined petitioning ought to occur. One, from Saint-Père of
Chartres, was attributed to 987 though it was probably written
sometime after 1078. In it King Lothar proclaims that the
bishop, count, and countess of Chartres "came suppliantly before the knees of our magnificence" to beseech immunity for
Saint-Père.[44] The second is an act drawn up at Marmoutier in
the late tenth century but attributed to the ninth-century
count Odo of Paris. While I was at Tours, announces Odo,
"suddenly the flock of the said monastery came before me, and
striking greater dread in me they prostrated themselves together
at my feet, beseeching that they might be aided by our mercy."[45]
None of Lothar's extant diplomas (or those of Louis IV or Louis
V) use such phrases; nor do other charters from the scriptoria of
Saint-Père and Marmoutier speak of prostration. If the scribes of
these institutions did so here, it can only have been to give their
forgeries greater verisimilitude for their own age—verisimilitude not in the sense of what would have been diplomatically
correct, but in the sense of what they believed would have been
the most perfect representation of an ideal supplication. Moreover, the fact that these forgeries come from Saint-Père and
Marmoutier shows that even scriptoria whose extant notices
frequently mention the beseeching of viscounts, castellans, and
knights still reserved special forms of behavior for begging favors from the greatest lords.

One other example, the most important of all, presents a final
archetypal image of supplication. The eleventh-century manuscript of the "Chronicle of Saint-Martin-des-Champs" includes
a diploma of Henry I recording his restoration and endowment
of Saint-Martin, accompanied by a sketch depicting the award.
The diploma itself mentions no petition—most charters of endowment do not, for here a lord acted on his own initiative. It
does, however, say that the endowment included lands originally received by Henry from a disgraced familiar as the price
for restoring him to favor. It further specifies that this reconciliation had been achieved through the prayer (*prece*) of Bishop
Imbart of Paris. Perhaps this is the entreaty portrayed in the
accompanying sketch (figure 2), the illustrator misreading his

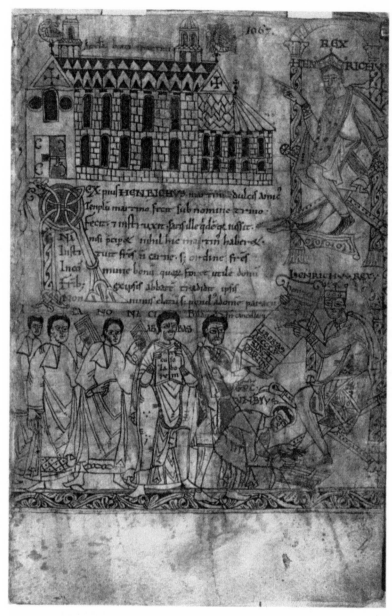

2. King Henry I grants a charter of liberty to Saint-Martin-des-Champs at the petition of Bishop Imbert of Paris. Chronicle of Saint-Martin-des-Champs (1067–79). London, British Museum, ms. addit. 11662, f. 4r.

text or telescoping events; perhaps Imbert actually had played a role in restoring the college, as well as in assuaging the king's anger against his knight. Whatever the truth, the sketch depicts a model supplication. The king, crowned and sitting on an ae-dile's chair, is shown presenting a charter to his chancellor, Baldwin. Interceding for the canons and ready to receive the diploma, Bishop Imbert (identified by a caption) kneels before Henry's feet, his shoulders and head bowed toward the ground in a gesture of humility.[46] Not only does this sketch show that kneeling or prostration ordinarily accompanied petitions; it also suggests that even the tersest references to "prayers" and "entreaties" in charters and notices may sometimes denote such gestures, at least in the case of great lords. How often they were preferred to other supplicatory postures and whether the gestures tended to change over time are questions that cannot be answered; but certainly acts of self-abasement often accompanied petitions throughout our period. More important, the cultural associations of petition were such that to seek an act from those who were lords by the grace of God was to assume an attitude of deference, if only that of a lowered visage. By humbling themselves they exalted their lords.

Intercession

The sketch from the "Chronicle of Saint-Martin-des-Champs" has one more feature worthy of note: although the royal privilege was intended for the canons of Saint-Martin, it was the bishop of Paris who knelt before the king to make the petition and receive the benefaction. This, too, was part of the archetype of supplication. Throughout our period it was necessary for petitioners to approach great lords "in the proper manner" (*modo quo decuit*), which meant not only addressing them with humble voices and gestures but also indirectly, through the intercession of their own lords or protectors or that of individuals who were close to the overlord who would grant the privilege.[47] It was this intermediary who actually presented the petition on behalf of his subordinate or client. The durability of this practice resulted from an equally durable fact of political life: if one wanted to obtain something from a lord, one needed to win over those whom the lord trusted. This explains the efforts of the abbot of Redon in 1108 to learn from his friends at court just what gifts would be needed to induce the count of Brittany to accept his petition. Not only did his contacts tell him that the count would be most pleased with one of the abbot's prize horses; they also told him when he should appear before the count; and when the count asked for their advice about the abbot's request, they counseled him to accept the petition which they themselves had helped formulate.[48] The situation had been essentially no different 170 years earlier, when a vassal of the count of Autun named Ingrann petitioned the canons of Autun for a precarial grant. The chapter refused until Ingrann sought support from the count and from the newly consecrated bishop of Autun, who had been raised within the chapter. Only when count and bishop repeated Ingrann's petition on his behalf did the chapter acquiesce.[49]

Although these examples show the dynamics of intercession with unusual clarity, many charters and notices assume its importance. The custom and its subtle changes are most visible in the continuous record of royal diplomas. The ninth-century Carolingians had been careful to project an image of a power accessible to men and women of all stations; as a result, even smallholders could approach the king to make requests, while monks and canons collectively sought the confirmation of donations made to their houses.[50] For the most part, however, only the politically influential petitioned the king: the queen, for example, or the palace cantor, or well-regarded *fideles*, who might request confirmation of conveyances involving their benefices.[51] But the most frequent intercessors of all were those who held recognized *ministeria*. If monks often petitioned the king directly, they relied on their abbots to do so even more frequently.[52] Bishops not only sought diplomas for their chapters; they also requested the king to confirm their donations to favored monasteries, or to make his own donations to them.[53] Counts petitioned the king on a wide range of business. Most often recorded are their requests on behalf of churches of which they were lay abbots, advocates, or benefactors; but they also interceded for vassals, whether their own or the king's.[54] Since conveyances of lands attached to their honors had to be approved by the king, it was counts, not the beneficiaries, who requested

this approval, even when the transfers appear to have been instigated by others.[55]

The custom in the ninth century, then, was that those who
had the king's ear presented petitions for either themselves,
their charges, or their favorites. Subsequent political developments only accentuated the trend. Queens, for example,
(whether wives or mothers), appear as petitioners much more
frequently in the diplomas of Lothar than in earlier royal diplomas, begging the king to reform and restore lands to monasteries, to grant them immunities, even to grant lands to favored
counts.[56] Their increasing prominence in the tenth century
probably reflected their greater political importance, given the
queens' close connections to the Ottonian emperors who protected the West Frankish kings. It is also possible that the intercession of queens was felt to convey an image of a well-run
palace household, where the king distributed favors at the petition of the women who ruled the household and guarded its
spiritual interests.

Queens were not the only intercessors, however. Just as
prominent were the princes, who at this time were trying to
consolidate their power over the territories subject to them.
Part of this process required them to control the flow of royal
favors to their clients, who no longer approached the king directly but only through their immediate protectors. The dukes
of Normandy, Burgundy, and Francia and the count of Flanders
all therefore petitioned Lothar to confirm donations, reforms, or
grants of immunity for monasteries within their spheres of influence.[57] At the same time, political struggles among the
princes came to be played out around the king's person. Against
this backdrop, proximity to the king came to be seen as both a
sign and a source of power, and a prince's ability to intercede
with the king was one of its indicators. Thus in the reign of
Charles the Simple, Robert, the king's "much beloved" and
"most faithful" marquis but also his future supplanter without
whose support he could not hope to rule, frequently presented
petitions to Charles on behalf of others.[58] In the same way Hugh
the Great, together with his wife, Hedwig, sister of Otto I and
maternal aunt of the young King Lothar, interceded with the
newly crowned monarch in 955 to support a petition by the
bishop of Le Puy. Later Herbert the Old, count of Troyes, relied

upon Lothar's ever-faithful bishops of Laon and Châlons to transmit a petition to the king.[59]

The earliest Capetian diplomas remained true to the older usages, as when in the first year of his reign Hugh Capet accepted a petition offered for Abbot Maingaud of Corbie by the archbishop of Reims.[60] Prelate petitions king for prelate: this kind of intercession harked back to an age when the royal court was a gathering place for the greatest magnates and the magnates ruled the kingdom. By the time of Robert the Pious, however, the age of the princes was passing, as lesser counts and local castellans had replaced the great princes as most men's lords of first resort, and political power had grown more territorial and parochial. Increasingly, then, these lesser lords petitioned the kings for their dependents, at least with respect to the lords and institutions of northern France (that is, above the Seine and Marne).[61] Nevertheless, the dynamic driving the need for intercession remained the same. The pattern is most conveniently studied in the court of Philip I, thanks to Maurice Prou's edition of his *acta*. Sometimes ecclesiastical houses, especially the more powerful—that is, the better connected—sought the intervention of powerful lords whose requests in their behalf the king would not want to refuse. Thus when Adelaide, countess of Flanders, presented Saint-Denis with the village of Courcelles, the monks succeeded in getting her to petition Philip for a simultaneous donation of his own rights there. Similarly, Mathilda, queen of England and duchess of Normandy, joined the canons of Saint-Corneille in requesting permission to translate their relics into the new reliquary she had given them.[62]

Apart from these special cases, ecclesiastical houses usually relied on their natural protectors to make their petitions. For the monasteries of the province of Reims, this was the abbot. In charters issued by Philip I for the monasteries of the province, not until 1101 was it said that the king received a petition from the "abbot and monks" of a religious institution.[63] Petition was a rhetoric of lordship, and so it was the lord abbot who presented petitions, not the monks, whom the formulas treated as his subjects. The usage was also sanctioned by the protocols of the papal chancery, which habitually addressed monastic privileges to the abbot of a monastery alone, to the abbot "and his successors," or at best to the abbot "and the brothers committed to him," all phrases that expressed the enduring paternalism inherent in the Benedictine conception of the abbatial office.[64] Only after 1139 were papal privileges regularly addressed to the "abbot and monks" of a monastery together.[65]

As an abbot stood at the head of his monastery, a bishop stood at the head of his cathedral chapter; and so privileges and confirmations for chapters were usually solicited by the bishop alone. There were exceptions. In 1068 Odo, bishop of Senlis, "and all the congregation of Holy Mary" came before Philip I "imploring our clemency" and petitioning a general confirmation of donations. Here the canons were mentioned as participating in the petition; but they did so only with their bishop, and even so the combination was unusual. Elinand of Laon alone petitioned Philip for redress of grievances against the king's sergeants on behalf of his chapter, just as his predecessor, Gebuin, had petitioned Henry I on behalf of one of his clerics. Bishop Baldwin of Noyon petitioned Philip I to transfer the castle of Quierzy to the domain of his chapter on its behalf, as one of his predecessors had petitioned Robert the Pious to confirm his own donations to his chapter.[66]

Would-be beneficiaries also sought out less august figures as intercessors; but these intercessors were still men who were close to the centers of power. Always an important consideration, proximity to the powerful appears to have become even more so under Philip, who increasingly depended on his palatine household for political counsel rather than on the counts and bishops of the realm.[67] For that reason it was often the members of his household—the *optimates*—who petitioned and received privileges from the king, both for themselves and for their protégés. For example, Waleran, Philip's chamberlain, held the cell of Saint-Christophe-en-Halatte as a fief from the abbot of Saint-Pierre of Beauvais; but when immunity was sought for Saint-Christophe, it was Waleran and not the abbot who obtained it from Philip.[68]

Even lords of high status recognized the importance of gaining support for their petitions from the king's counselors. In 1095 Philip issued a charter confirming the donation of any land Ingelran of Coucy or his knights might give to the abbey of Nogent from the fiefs that they held of the king. The charter states that Philip acted "at the request of Ingelran and the best men of the said castle." The witness list appended to the act is more specific; for after the name of Renald of Coucy, the castellan, it mentions that he had "obtained this confirmation" (*hoc obtinuit confirmari*). As we know from the lists of witnesses to Philip's acts, Renald was a more constant member of Philip's entourage than Ingelran. Renald therefore seems to have been given the responsibility of interceding on behalf of his own lord and allies to obtain the royal confirmation.[69]

A bishop like Baldric of Noyon also understood the value of the *optimates'* support, for when he sought the transfer of the castle of Quierzy to his chapter, he did not make this request himself but sought the intercession of the *optimates* of Philip's court. Perhaps it was only the importance of the request that determined Baldric to seek support from men close to Philip. But it may also be significant that although Baldric was a royal bishop, he did not attend Philip's court with any great regularity; nor did Philip possess major holdings in his diocese.[70] The bishops of Laon and Soissons, in contrast, did present petitions to Philip on behalf of the monasteries of their cities; and not only were these two men royal bishops, they were also regular members of Philip's entourage, and each of their sees included areas where the king had important holdings in his own right, often interspersed with episcopal holdings.[71]

Proximity to power was a practical consideration in the use of intercessors, but it was not the only consideration. As in the tenth century, intercession was also a way to formalize the consent of an intermediary lord to a legal transaction—but now those lords were lesser counts and castellans rather than great princes. When the monks of Saint-Vincent of Laon came before Philip to seek rights in woods that formed part of the king's domains, their petition was "humbly" presented not by themselves but by the bishops of Laon and Soissons and by the count of Beaumont-sur-Oise. The bishop of Laon was the diocesan of Saint-Vincent; the woods subject to the transaction were within the diocese of Soissons; and the count of Beaumont shared rights in the woods with Philip himself. In several other instances the intercessor who presented a petition to Philip was the feudal lord of the party actually concerned in the transaction. Amalric of Châteaufort, for example, established canons in the church of the castle that he held from Gui and Hugh, lords of Montlhéry and Rochefort. In seeking Philip's confirmation of this act, Gui and Hugh made the petition on Amalric's behalf.

Similarly, Hugh, a knight of Château-Thierry, held an altar as a fief from the bishop of Soissons. When he sought royal confirmation for his foundation of a college of canons there, both he and the bishop made the petition.[72] By actively associating themselves with these transactions as intercessors, these lords made their consent to the transactions a matter of public knowledge. They also identified themselves with the grants (thereby meriting their spiritual benefits), while becoming their warrantors more directly than they would have done by simply consenting to them.

The pervasiveness of intercession throughout this society could produce interesting nestings of "patron-client" relations. The impulse is most noticeable during disputes, situations that required litigants to behave impeccably and negotiate with those lords who could actually arrange settlements. So in 985, when the abbey of Corbie found itself embroiled in a dispute with two vassals of the count of Amiens, the count took over the claims of his men and settled the dispute in their place.[73] And in 1016 the bishop of Noyon acted for his chapter in accepting the claims of his cleric, Gerard, to a church and six manses held in benefice of the chapter. But Gerard himself was acting on behalf of his two nephews in seeking the revenues, "impetrating" the bishop's charter in order to protect their rights.[74] Most telling of all is a case from 1056, in which the abbot of Saint-Eloi, near Noyon, sought the excommunication of Gerard of Roye, who had abused his rights of advocacy over Saint-Eloi's peasants at Vrély. Because Gerard was a parishioner of the bishop of Amiens, only the bishop could excommunicate him. However, the abbot did not approach the bishop of Amiens directly, but only through the intervention of the bishop of Noyon, his own ordinary. Thus the bishop of Amiens acted upon the intercession of the bishop of Noyon, who acted on behalf of the abbot of Saint-Eloi, who acted for his monastery, which acted to protect both its own rights and those of its peasants at Vrély.[75] Lords approached lords to approach lords: supplication and intercession projected an image of a polity in which lords were the real actors. Without their assent and cooperation, nothing of importance could be done; but they would act only if they were beseeched "in the proper manner"—through the humble prayers of those whose devotion and virtue had earned their trust.

3 The Court of the Heavenly King

In a passage of remarkably condensed insight, J. M. Wallace-Hadrill captured the essence of early medieval political theory: "The Carolingians saw God as King of Heaven. To Him they transferred the essential features, duly magnified, of royal power, and then, as it were, borrowed them back. God thus became not only the source of their power but also their model."[1] It was no different for the early Capetians. Having taken over their predecessors' formulas and rituals, they took over their political theory as well. In the eleventh century as in the ninth and tenth, God was the "Lord of lords," "King of kings," and "Eternal Emperor."[2] To him all the attributes of earthly kingship were applied—or rather, from the medieval point of view, from him all earthly kings received their attributes.[3] Along with those earthly lords who ruled by his grace he was addressed as "clement" and "majesty."[4] And like the great lords on earth, he, too, had his *fideles*. The term meant the body of Christian "faithful," of course; but individuals were also called God's *fideles* in ways that were more reminiscent of vassalage.[5] Thus in the eleventh century those who left the world to become monks were called the *fideles* of God as if they were his special retainers.[6] A similar meaning was conveyed when coronation orders referred to Abraham as God's *fidelis*.[7] Just as the secular fidelity owed to earthly lords took on religious overtones, so secular associations found their way into the religious fidelity owed to the Lord of lords.

77

Supplication gave ritual expression to the essential identity of earthly and heavenly lordship; for even more than an act of deference to king, count, or bishop, supplication was the act by which one sought the grace of God.[8] The idea was familiar enough for Bishop Gerard of Cambrai to use it in a sermon he preached to a group of heretics in Arras in the 1020s. Among other things, the heretics seem to have believed that there was no need to worship God in a church. If God were everywhere, they reasoned, he could surely be worshiped anywhere. Gerard told them that yes, they could worship God wherever they pleased; but they could honor him most fully only in his temple. As he further explained: "No place is absent from the presence of his majesty, yet here more especially and more fully he bestows the favors of his grace on petitioners."[9] Thus for the benefit of the heretics Gerard depicted God as a lord enthroned in majesty, seated in his *aula*, as it were, receiving petitions and distributing his favors. He also denounced the heretics for not showing proper obedience and humility, since they refused to venerate the image of the cross, an act in which Christians "beseech" (*deprecamur*) God for their salvation—a salvation that God would grant them as an act of grace, just as a lord might confer an immunity.[10] Like the king, count, bishop, and abbot whom he favored with authority, the Lord God received petitions from those who were truly humble.

It is important to realize that supplicatory prayer to God was not a ritual hidden within the walls of a cloister. Certainly Gerard must have thought that its characteristics would be familiar enough to the heretics to help return them to obedience. In fact, the image of supplication was familiar, for all men and women prayed to God in order to beseech his grace in times of need. Prayer itself was nothing but "a repeated beseeching and fervent supplication," by which a person "speaks to God, or rather, petitions what he wants from him."[11] Saints were even more accessible to ordinary people, and again the language with which men and women supplicated them was the same as that with which they supplicated lords. A knight, captured and imprisoned, desperate after his entreaties to other saints had failed, finally "with tremulous voice began to implore" Saint Benedict, by whose intervention he was at last set free. A woman too ill to walk was laid in a church, where "she dissolved into tears and spoke with a voice of pious petition" to Saint Benedict, asking to be healed so that she might follow others on a tour of relics.[12] Holy men also received the humble prayers of the faithful. Philip I's own queen sought the aid of the ascetic Arnulf of Saint-Médard in her efforts to conceive an heir for her husband: "She frequently prayed God's familiar [*famulum Dei exoravit*], both herself and through other illustrious men, that he beseech God" to give her a son. The countess of Porcien also beseeched Arnulf when she came into his presence (*accessit*: the term is a formal one used to describe the act of coming before a lord) "leading a woman by her hand who had been blind for fifteen years, and bending the knee said to him: 'Holy lord, have mercy on this miserable little one, and by your holy prayer and by the imposition of your hand clemently restore light to her eyes.'" Of course Arnulf worked the miracle.[13]

Supplication was therefore an act of subjection; but in terms of the theology of supplication, this was almost a secondary meaning. Much more important, supplication was the proper way in which one sought the aid of God and God's familiars. This meaning gave rise to a corollary: whoever humbly petitioned another with prayers and supplications gave formal and public witness to his or her faith that God stood behind that individual. Monks, for example, prostrated themselves before the poor to whom they gave alms, since the poor were the *pauperes Christi*, in whom Christ said he would appear.[14] In early medieval art, a moment of theophany was frequently signaled by some gesture of genuflection or prostration, as the individual to whom God was revealed fell into a posture of veneration. For this reason the Magi were often depicted presenting their gifts to Christ in supplicatory poses, on bended knees and with lowered heads. The image, especially as it came to be rendered in Germany and England during the late tenth and early eleventh centuries, signified their recognition of Christ's imperial majesty, since at this time the Magi came to be represented as crowned kings, on occasion even presenting a diadem to the heavenly emperor[15] (figure 3). Alongside this meaning, however, their suppliant pose also proclaimed their humility before the truth of God's incarnation. Thus God's speaking to Moses was imagined as a theophany by an eleventh-century artist, who accordingly portrayed Moses prostrate on the ground grasping

3. Adoration of the Magi, from the Gospel Book of Poussay (Toul?, second half of the tenth century). Paris, Bibliothèque Nationale, ms. lat. 10514, f. 18v.

God's foot. For the same reason an apostle was represented as prostrate in a twelfth-century depiction of the Transfiguration[16] (figures 4 and 5).

The theophanic implications of supplication were of course known by monks and the secular clergy; but they were also inescapable to the laity, who knew quite well that they were to supplicate God, his saints, his holy men, and his poor when beseeching their favor and intervention. Knowing when, they must also have known why they did so: because God appeared in them. The count of Amiens certainly knew this when he granted the petition of the abbot of Jumièges "lest I offend the man of God, or rather, loving and fearing God in the man."[17] And God was present not only in holy abbots. He was present in kings, bishops, and all those earthly authorities who held their offices "by the grace of God." From all of them petitioners beseeched acts of mercy and grace, just as they beseeched the grace of God. And though supplication manifested subjection, it was not so much subjection to an individual as subjection to an idea, to a "faith"; for when the queen sought a favor from Philip I "in the devotion of supplication," or when the abbot of Homblières requested the intervention of his count against the exactions of one of his vassals, the petitioner acknowledged not only the supremacy of the lord but also the divine authority that was the source of all legitimate earthly authority.

God's Barons

Petition and concession, humility and grace, dependence and dominance: these were the categories that expressed the fundamental political relations of the tenth and eleventh centuries— and not political relations alone, for secular lordship modeled itself on divine lordship. Thus even the most common forms of petition echoed the supremacy of the one true Lord, as both God and his vicars were beseeched in analogous terms that contrasted the lord's capacity for grace with the humble dependence of the kneeling or prostrate petitioner. The ideal of lordship enacted in theophanic supplications did not acknowledge banal lordship, or feudal lordship, or landlordship. There was only one legitimate lordship: that derived from God as the font

E⳰⳰PLICIⱽⱮT CAPITⱽLA·

INCIPIT LIBER ⱽAIEDABER

QⱽENⱷDEM NⱽⱮERⱤ:

O CⱽTUSESTDNS

admorſen indeſerto ſrnai incabnacu
lo ſederiſ·prima die mſiſſcdi·anⱮo
altero egreſſioniſ eoꝛu exaegipto·
dicenſ· Tollite ſumma uniuerſe con
gregationiſ filioꝛu iſrl pcognationeſ
ꝶdomoſſuaſ·ꝶnomina ſinguloꝛum
quicquid ſexuſ÷ maſculini a uceſi
mo anno ꝶſupra omium uirⱷꝛu foꝛ
tⳡ exiſrt·ꝶinumerabitiſ eoſ pᵉmaſ
ſuaſ tu ꝶaaron· Erⳡtq̃· uobiſ cⳡ
principeſtribuⳡ ac domoꝛu incog
nationib·
ſuⳡ·quoꝛu
ꝶ ta ſunt
nomina·

De ruben· heliſur· filuſ ſedeur· De ſŷmeon· ſalami
hel·filuſ ſurıſaddaı· De ıuda·naaſon filuſ amina
dab· De ıſachar· nathanahel filuſſuar· De zabın

4. Moses prostrates himself before the Lord: initial from the Book of Numbers, "Locutus est Dominus ad Moysen" (second half of the eleventh century). Paris, Bibliothèque Mazarine, ms. 1, f. 41v.

5. The Transfiguration, from "Le Bible de Manerius" (second half of the twelfth century).
Paris, Bibliothèque de Sainte-Geneviève, ms. 10, f. 129v.

of all earthly authority; and all such authority was to be venerated.

Medieval historians have long understood the importance of
rituals in communicating the sacredness of ruling offices. The
anointings of kings by bishops replicated the anointing of the
kings of Israel by the prophets and reflected the kingship of
Christ the Anointed. The entry of a king into a city or monastery was attended with hymns and lauds that transformed the
space into an image of heavenly Jerusalem, the king into a figure of the triumphant Christ. What the above discussion shows
is that such typologies, as they are called, were not the preserve
of the literate clergy alone, made visible to the laity in a few
solemn but infrequent events. Through acts of supplication
they also came to inform ordinary political interactions.

It was not only the language and gestures of prayer that communicated the typology. On the contrary, the reason that supplication offered such an elegant expression of ideal political
and social relations was its capacity to be projected onto so
many aspects of early medieval experience. We have noted, for
example, that petitioners relied on intercessors to present their
requests to lords. As on earth, so in heaven: because the divine
majesty was too transcendent to be approached directly in most
cases, one ordinarily sought God's grace through intercessors. In
turn, God ordinarily distributed his favors through intercessors.
The most important were the saints, conceived, of course, as
the *famuli* and *fideles* of the heavenly king, who beseeched the
divine majesty for acts of grace on behalf of their clients. According to a story that emerged during the early eleventh century, Hugh Capet, while still duke of the Franks, had a vision
one night in which Saint Valerius appeared to him, lamenting
that he and Saint Richarius (meaning their relics) had been
taken from their monasteries by the count of Flanders. Valerius
charged the duke to release them from their capitivity. "And
if," said the saint, "you fulfill this, I promise you by the command of God, through the pious merits of St. Richarius and
through my prayer, that you will become king, and your off-
spring after you, and your line will hold the kingdom up to
seven successions."[18]

"By the command of God" (*ex Dei jussu*): mutatis mutandis
the phrase could have been used in an act of any king or count.[19]

However, that command was given not directly, but only through the agency of those whose merits had made them God's familiars. Conversely, those who required God's aid sought the support of one of his familiars to present their prayers, and writers described their supplications in terms taken from the etiquette of the court. In the *Miracula sancti Benedicti* the men and women of a castle struck by the *ignis sacer* "beseeched the glorious confessor [Saint Benedict], that through his pious intervention the Lord might take mercy upon them." During the same epidemic, a monk from the town decided to take action. Gathering the relics of the saints, he and other people of the castle went to a neighboring town where they had heard the disease was worst; and there they sought "a gift of the mercy of God through the prayers of these two barons [*proceres*], that is, the most holy lawgiver Benedict and the glorious Martial."[20]

Contemporaries used such courtly language to describe the intercession of saints quite consciously. They frequently spoke of the "celestial court" or "heavenly hall," and imagined the mother of God as a queen who sat on a "throne set in the midst of many great princes."[21] But if heaven were a court, then it must also have a correct protocol. In 1077 Raginard of Mont-Saint-Jean, brother of the bishop of Autun, enunciated the principle clearly—and what is equally important for our purposes, explained its rationale by referring to the well-known, observable custom that advised the use of intercessors when offering petitions to all lords, whether they resided in heaven or on earth.

> For we often see with respect to earthly princes that whenever someone wants to beseech anything important from a powerful person, he uses an intercessor whom he knows is a familiar to the lord; just so, if we wish to receive eternal salvation from the King of kings, we must strive to acquire as intercessors on our behalf His holy martyrs and His other *fideles* who, we believe, have standing in the court of the heavens.[22]

Though common throughout France, the analogy was especially tenacious in the churches of Reims, since their fate was so closely tied to the kings'. In the late ninth century, for example, Archbishop Hincmar described the Last Judgment as a process of intercession and supplication. We would address a *pa-*

tronus "with great prayers" that he be our defender in a trial before a great lord, he wrote. We should prepare for the day of final judgment in just the same way. "Behold, Jesus, the stern judge, will come to hear our case in that assembly [*conventu*], a great council [*concilii*] of angels and archangels to strike us with terror. . . . And we, unable to rely on any of our works, we shall run to the protection of the saints and fall sobbing upon their holy bodies; for if we are to gain pardon we must beseech through their intercession."[23] Two centuries later the monks of Saint-Remi were still working within the paradigm, applying it to a charter of Raoul of Valois, an important figure at the court of Philip I who would have understood that one needed friends when making a case to a lord. Raoul therefore buried his son at Saint-Remi and made amends for whatever wrongs he and his son had once done to the saint, "so that he [that is, Saint Re-migius] might intercede for his soul and on the day of judgment act as his presenter and advocate [*ductor et advocatus*] before God."[24]

So axiomatic was the need for intercession in this culture that men and women even needed intercessors to approach the intercessors. In other words, they needed monks; for monks guarded the relics of the saints, who had access to God, while the purity of their own lives guaranteed that their prayers would be pleasing to God and so rewarded with his grace. Monks were quite simply the *famuli Dei*, whose acts of faithful "devotion" had earned the Lord's trust and who could be relied upon to make a good case to the Lord; and men and women of all statuses donated lands, rights, or revenues to monasteries in order to gain their favor, and thus their prayers. Thus the count of Valois freed the lands of the monks of Saint-Firmin from vis-comital powers, "in order that I might obtain forgiveness of my sins by their intervention."[25] And even the bishop of Tournai needed the friendship of monks to approach God, giving those of Saint-Bertin the *synodalia* of their altars "so that they might act as intercessors before God on my behalf."[26]

A Typology for Princes

Political historians are often forced to take the meaningful-ness of diplomatic formulas on faith. A formula like *Dei gratia comes*, an epithet like *venerabilis vir*, a phrase of supplication modeled on liturgical prayer: we may want to believe that princes intended these terms to say something about the nature of their authority; but we cannot prove it from the charters alone, because charters were written by the same monks and clerics who wrote mirrors for princes and performed the liturgy.[27] They may have been no more than clerical propaganda, of no real relevance to counts, of still less to their warriors. Perhaps they do not even represent propaganda, but only a calculating desire to flatter. These possibilities seem particularly strong in the case of theophanic supplication, whose neat symmetry makes it difficult to mistake the hand of the clergy. But then where is the mind of the prince?

The heart of the difficulty is that throughout most of the Middle Ages writing was largely a clerical monopoly—in the tenth and eleventh centuries entirely one. If, then, we think of royal diplomas and princely charters primarily as written texts, we logically assume that they were clerical products. But charters and diplomas were not merely texts meant to record information. One need only look at a royal or princely act to know that.[28] With their supple, exquisitely whitened parchment and vast size (ranging from 18 inches to more than two feet on a side), they dwarf the brittle, graying charters of ordinary men and women as the giant image of a king in a bright illumination dwarfs the images of his subjects. The analogy is not farfetched. An ordinary charter is a workaday artifact, written on a scrap of parchment in a squarish, functional minuscule whose cramped lines run to the margins. It is easily read but rarely beautiful (see figure 6). In contrast, diplomas and princely charters from the tenth century are works of high artistry. Far from being readable, their calligraphy is rendered nearly illegible by all the loops and tails flowing from the letters, a decorative impulse found also in the arabesque trellises and chrismons adorning the page. And whereas the scribe of an ordinary charter would parsimoniously fill up the entire scrap of parchment, the charters of kings and princes waste parchment in a display of lordly potlatch, with lavish margins and interlinear spacings and fully a third of the page devoted to the oversized "signs of power" with which a charter ends: in a royal diploma, subscriptions, monogram, and seal (figure 7).[29]

Such acts were not mere administrative records. They were

6. Charter for Sint-Pieters of Ghent by an unidentified Bernard (230 × 140/150 mm). Ghent, Rijksarchief. Archief van der Sint-Baafskathedraal, fonds Sint-Pietersabdij (982–83).

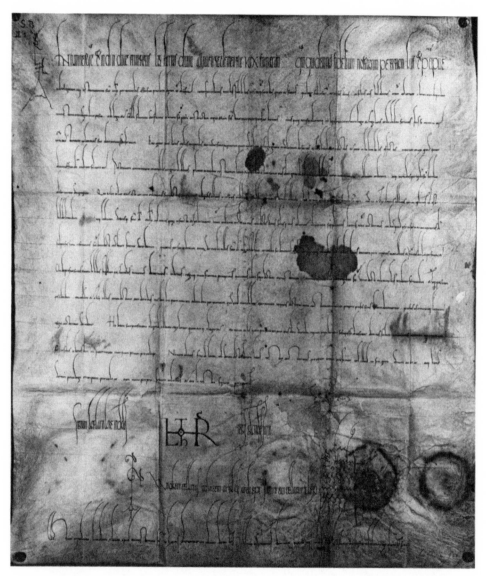

7. Diploma of King Lothar for Sint-Baafs of Ghent (509/507 × 580/578 mm). Ghent, Rijksarchief. Archief van der Sint-Baafskathedraal, fonds Sint-Baafsabdij (954 dec. 11). This particular charter is probably a reworked copy of an authentic diploma, made soon after the original on which it was modeled. Although the seal is no longer extant, its traces remain visible.

just what contemporaries said they were: acts of authority—
auctoritates, precepta, edicta.[30] They were a kind of regalia.
This is the reason so much of a charter's text has nothing to do
with recording information. From the opening invocation of
God and the lord's subscription as *rex, marchisus,* or *comes Dei
gratia* through the solemn preamble to the closing signs of validation, the acts speak of authority. But they do so according to
a discernible structure. The three opening parts of a diploma or
princely charter invoke the sublime: the name of God or the
Trinity, first of all (invocation); the name of the prince with the
Dei gratia epithet (subscription); and the statement of the religious code by which he rules and hopes to triumph in heaven
(preamble). Only after these marks of sublimity does the diploma descend into its banal catalogue of lands, rights, and privileges. Mediating the two, linking the prologue's invocation of
divine authority with the donation or protection of material
goods, is the hinge of it all, the formula of supplication.

This was the purpose of the formula within the text; but it
was also the purpose of the ritual itself. As I have argued, one
cannot be isolated from the other. The formula of supplication
is comprehensible only as the token of a real act of entreaty and
grace in which a subject recognized and a ruler displayed an
authority granted by God. Behind a text written by monks and
clerics lay a regalian, theophanic ritual acted out publicly by
everyone, including the laity.

Because the ritual was common to all members of society,
literate and illiterate, lords and dependents alike, contemporaries cannot have seen supplicatory formulas as a mere clerical
convention. We may not be able to know whether kings and
counts and their lay *fideles* believed in the sacredness of political authority; but the ritual nature of the formulas leaves no
doubt that they countenanced the belief and acted as if it were
true. Indeed, in the case of the tenth-century princes of northern
France one may go further still. They not only countenanced
the sacrality conferred by clerical typologies; they actively cultivated it.

Their partners in this endeavor were the monasteries. We
have already noted their importance to ninth-century magnates,
whose positions as lay abbots offered them opportunities to preside over monastic rites, in effect giving a religious cast to their

secular authority in a way that iterated, on a lesser scale, the emperor's own ambiguous status within the church.[31] Such trends only became more pronounced in the first half of the tenth century, as the great counts began to reform the monasteries in their possession and to renounce their lay abbacies; for the reform of a monastery catapulted a prince into a different realm of authority by showing him acting in place of the king for the benefit of his dynasty, his church, and his people. For that very reason, princely reforms usually did not touch insignificant cells or (as they did in the south) require new foundations. A dynast's monastic reform targeted precisely those formerly royal monasteries with fiscal estates that had become most closely identified with his family's wealth and power: hence Hugh the Great's reform of Fleury and, still more impressive, Arnulf of Flanders's reforms of Saint-Vaast, Sint-Pieters at Ghent, and Saint-Bertin.[32]

In every case, the avowed motive for such patronage was the wish to gain the saints' intercession on behalf of the prince, his family, and his territory. That is, the prince honored the saints so that they would beg for his favor and forgiveness before God, just as his own *fideles* honored him and he honored the king.[33] But monks not only guarded the relics that guarded him and ensured his family's material success and immortal salvation. As emissaries, drafters of charters, and apologists for princely authority, they also put their talent for systematic typologies at the prince's service. At Ghent, for example, the monks of Sint-Pieter's transformed Arnulf of Flanders into an avatar of Judas Maccabeus, because Arnulf had rebuilt their monastery as Judas had rebuilt the Temple.[34] The monks of Fleury who kept the relics of Saint Benedict were no less creative in lauding Hugh the Great, assigning their worldly and otherworldly patrons neatly parallel epithets. Hugh was the *venerabilis vir* (an epithet signifying an abbot's *paternitas*) and *dux Francorum* who had reformed Fleury, where lay the body of Benedict, the *pater et dux monachorum*.[35]

Among their other talents, monks were also impresarios of ritual. They put these skills, too, at the service of their lords and patrons by developing rituals that dramatized the prince's typological identity. Already in the ninth century the dukes of Brittany anticipated the strategy. Though they did not found

Redon, they understood the value of patronizing it. One of the most immediate benefits was that they were integrated into the ritual life of the monastery and honored with the kinds of political liturgies usually reserved for kings, as when Nominoë was received with a formal *occursus*, complete with *laudes* and hymns.[36] Arnulf of Flanders courted such ceremonies even more actively. After reforming Sint-Pieters, for example, he personally led an army of priests, monks, and warriors to Boulogne to demand the restoration of the relics of Wandregisilus and other saints, publicly prostrating himself on the ground to make his request "in humble devotion to the saints." Then, accompanied by the bishop of Tournai and later joined by his wife and son, he led the *adventus* into Ghent, where townspeople and soldiers thronged about him, and monks and clerics sang hymns and burned incense.[37] Were the saints honored by this ceremony? Certainly. Yet the ceremony honored Arnulf still more. It was he who had reformed Sint-Pieters in the first place, choosing its abbot and endowing it, as his charter says, not with all the land to which it had rights but with "whatever I think will suffice."[38] It was his army that had cowed the reluctant people of Boulogne into surrendering the relics. And it was his dynasty, prefigured in the wife and son who accompanied him in triumph, that the saints had been brought to his capital to protect.

Arnulf, Hugh, Nominoë: these were great rulers, Nominoë almost a king, Hugh and Arnulf kingmakers. But lesser lords also needed a source of sacrality, and for them, too, the readiest at hand was the indirect grace that reflected off saints. A nearly contemporary notice from Fleury recalling events of 956 tells us that in that year the "men of Auvergne" invaded Burgundy, and Count Lambert of Chalon and an unidentified Bernard gathered together their men (*potentes*) to head off the incursion. But before setting off, the two men went to Perrecy, a priory of Fleury, prayed to fortify themselves (*gratia sese muniendi*) in the coming battle, and in return for a donation of land received relics from the priory. Then, *sub Dei clementia munitus*, they led their men into battle and defeated the enemy.[39] Praying for the success of their men, protected by relics entrusted to their care, Bernard and Lambert were close to God in a way other laymen were not. Can it be a coincidence that at this very moment Lambert was poised to take over the county of Chalon, the first member of his line to become a count?[40]

Against the backdrop of such rites it is impossible to regard a comital diploma simply as a pastiche of clerical conceits of no real concern to the lord. To award a diploma was rather a symbolic act of authority requiring the participation of ruler and subjects alike. The diploma was the relic, as it were, of this rite of sacred power. But if the supplicatory language of diplomas cannot be understood save in the context of the ceremonial setting in which they were awarded, this ritual in turn can only be understood as one part of a complex of princely rites and initiatives. In isolation a diploma is no evidence of any political beliefs. But return the diploma to its liturgical setting and restore it to the world of political competition from which it issued, and then we can see that the typologies mattered. Through their reforms the princes courted them. By participating in their rituals they dramatized them. Through the liturgical language of diplomas they memorialized them for all time.

The Multivalence of Grace

What the elite of tenth- and eleventh-century France saw as a typology the modern scholar will have no difficulty recognizing as an ideology: in this case, a system of ideas reflective of and supportive of an oligarchical distribution of political power. But in recognizing an ideology we also recognize a familiar problem: How could any system of ideas so transparently political have engaged the loyalty of those who did not rule? How could a mere ideology be convincing?[41]

Part of the answer is that those who articulated the system were not imposing entirely foreign beliefs. The systematization of supplication's typology was new but its component parts were not. Deferential language and gestures, the habit of intercession, and the incorporation of these patterns into liturgical prayer: these elements were old and familiar by the ninth and tenth centuries. One might even argue that the ideology carried all the more weight because it brought all the elements together in a more coherent paradigm, and a truer one, since it did justice to the obvious power of the magnates and their satellites. Furthermore, practice bred belief, because once the magnates began to turn the system to their own ends, it only became more ingrained in ordinary patterns of behavior. Thus the princes' monastic reforms spread the cult of saints throughout their dominions, and with the cult came familiarity with its liturgies, forms of prayer, and cosmological principles, until even peasants knew when and how to beg. Simultaneously, the correct form of address to princes established a standard for other social relations, for if it was obligatory to supplicate magnates, it became wise to beseech lesser lords in less lofty terms.[42]

By the tenth century, then, what we are dealing with is no longer simply propaganda, ideology, or a clerical typology, but a "discourse" common to the entire post-Carolingian period; in other words, a set of axiomatic assumptions that contemporaries brought to their lives and that shaped their experience.[43] The discourse of supplication was especially coherent because the clergy who perfected it had a professional disposition against loose ends; but its unity also resulted from the tendency of all discourses to reshape parts to fit the whole, as individuals, reasoning by analogy, project known relationships onto the unknown in order to comprehend it. In this way a "root metaphor" ramifies throughout a culture, like a motif in a work of art, unifying and strengthening the whole.[44] In the process, the assumptions that originally generated the model also become more plausible, since the endless replication of related motifs makes the entire structure internally consistent and self-reinforcing. The result is a universe linked together by a single matrix of symbols, beyond which one cannot easily think oneself.[45]

It is typical of any such discourse that base and superstructure, template and image become thoroughly blurred. In the case of intercession, for example, we may believe that the protocol of earthly courts was the social reality which men and women then projected onto the cosmos. But in the eyes of contemporaries what was more fundamental was the protocol of the heavenly court, since it justified the etiquette of earthly courts by anchoring it in an eternal archetype. Indeed, that archetype may have contributed to the durability of ordinary intercession by forcing court customs into familiar channels.

As with all discourses, replication of the root metaphor was therefore ultimately self-validating. Customary patterns of human behavior were projected onto the cosmos in all their subtlety and complexity. Then, as part of a morally charged Creation, the behavior was not just legitimated; it was made rationally necessary. To accept this vision of the universe was to accept its implications for earthly rule. The system became hermetic. It did not, however, become static. Far from it, this discourse, like any discourse, was perfectly logical and symmetrical only to the extent that people were—meaning not very. Generated by the way people thought, a reflection of their thought, their use of supplication also revealed the ambiguities and contradictions within their cultural beliefs. And this was another secret of the ritual's success. Supplication did not have a single meaning; but for that very reason it was able to represent the conflicting attitudes toward power and authority that were also characteristic of this society. Far from invalidating the paradigm, its ambiguities only made it "truer."

Inevitably supplication was an act of subjection. That meaning is almost naturally inherent in the act of prostration—and it was recognized by contemporaries, who used the word *prostrati* for those who had been utterly vanquished in battle.[46] Yet supplication to superiors never became a Byzantine-like *proskynesis*, in which king or lord was venerated as the image of God himself. In the west the ritual always remained more supple than this, more ambivalent in its range of attitudes toward authority. We can catch occasional glimpses of a more streamlined meaning, where the ritual seems reduced to a rigorously authoritarian model of political order. Notker the Stammerer, for example, imagined Louis the Pious receiving an *adoratio* of almost oriental scope, as the emperor's subjects acclaimed him as if he were Christ: "The poor . . . would raise their voices to the heavens as they wandered through the great courtyard and the arcades of Aachen . . . and shout '*Kyrie Eleison* to the blessed Louis.' Such of the soldiers as could manage it would embrace the Emperor's feet, and others would worship him from afar as he walked in procession to church."[47]

The story rings true, given Louis's susceptibility to grand interpretations of his office; yet Notker wrote from a cloister, and so long after the event that it is difficult to credit him, the more so because such an openly theocratic reading of supplication is an anomaly. Western rulers were beseeched, not adored; and if kings were depicted as serene and majestic, they were not shown as the absolute masters of their supplicants. Thus, of the sources cited in this study, none describes the *calcatio colli* so common in Byzantium, where the emperor ritually trampled the necks of his enemies.[48] *Adoratio* and *calcatio* went against the reciprocity between lords and followers that was so deeply ingrained in aristocratic culture.[49] Equally important, an authoritarian reading of supplication was tempered by the theological structure within which Latin Christianity embedded the classical ritual it had inherited.

In the first place, the church never managed to control all access to God's grace. Of course there were proper channels through which men and women ordinarily received that grace: the duly ordained clergy whom God had established as mediators between him and his people. But we have also seen the readiness with which ordinary men and women supplicated the aid of their saints and holy men directly, without the intercession of monks and priests. During our period the church actively encouraged this popular piety—within certain limits, of course—since the cult of saints seems to have touched a responsive chord within the laity.[50] As a result, the very popularity of certain saints made it impossible for laymen and laywomen to regard the grace of God as something distant, attainable solely through the mediation of the church's temporal hierarchy.

Perhaps the culture's reluctance to permit a monopoly of grace by prelates carried over into its attitude toward kingship; or perhaps its appreciation for political consensus and power sharing shaped its beliefs about grace. In any case, the temporal and spiritual realms paralleled each other. A king may have been God's temporal vicar, but that position gave him no monopoly on God's grace in political affairs. The material limitations of his power and the cultural attitudes toward grace both conspired against it—the former dictating that princes would seek a basis of their power independent of royal delegation, the latter legitimating their ambition. Thus dukes and counts arrogated the title "by the grace of God" to their own offices and appropriated supplicatory formulas, complete with divine epithets such as "clemency" and "serenity."

The pervasiveness of supplication therefore accurately reflected the pluralism of the late-Carolingian polity.[51] All princes and prelates were supplicated, because all ruled by divine grace. Not only did their dependents obey this rule; lords obeyed it also by supplicating each other. As Richard of Saint-Vanne and his dear friend Simeon, a future archbishop, said farewell, Simeon wept while they "kissed each other's feet and hands and knees, because the grace of the Holy Spirit was in them."[52] Great men could even compete in self-abasement—indeed, they had to compete if they were truly to honor each other. When Archbishop Lanfranc of Canterbury returned to the monastery of Bec and met his former abbot, each tried to prostrate himself to the other, until they became so entangled in each other's arms that they ended by holding each other up.[53]

If such scenes seem to have been particularly common among ecclesiastics, the reason may be only that their actions were more often recorded. There is no reason not to believe that they were also common among the lay nobility. They certainly occurred, as shown by the notice from Fleury—the one that describes the effort of two rising magnates to obtain relics before a battle. The narrative actually begins with a rare account of an election among laymen. After Lambert and Bernard had gathered their armies in anticipation of the battle, the first order of business was to choose one of the two men as leader (*dux*). As soon as Bernard was elected, Lambert immediately signaled his acceptance of Bernard's leadership by personally begging him to lead the combined armies. More, Lambert entreated him as one whose election by the *vox populi* testified to his continuing favor in God's eyes. "Joyfully assenting to their petitions, Lambert entreated Bernard. 'We must go to meet our enemy; but first it is necessary to establish someone of experience who shall carry our standard. Since by the gift of God your nobility has often been proved in such matters, we beg you to be our leader and to aid us in our necessity.'"[54] Bernard would ultimately accept the petition; but he could not do so straightforwardly. He had to show that his virtues made him truly deserving of the honor—meaning in particular that he would not use his position to lord it over Lambert and his men. As for Lambert, who had been passed over for leadership, he had to repeat his petitions in order to show that he really meant what he said. And so the play proceeded, Bernard refusing the position, protesting that his many battles had worn him out, Lambert renewing his entreaties. And when Bernard finally did agree to lead the armies, he still took care to address Lambert with the royal and divine epithet "your highness" (*vestra celsitudo*), and charged him with the sacred trust of ensuring divine favor for their campaign by acquiring relics. In this way great lords acknowledged each other's sacrality. They thereby directly recognized the legitimacy of their peers' and rivals' titles and offices, while indirectly accepting the principle of a pluralistic distribution of power.

There was therefore a collegiality of temporal authority among princes, just as there was of spiritual authority among prelates. Performed in such a context, supplication could not have been perceived as a rigidly authoritarian ritual. Though theophanic, it could not be theocratic, because God's grace could not be restricted to a single ruler, or even to a small group of rulers. God bestowed his grace on all those who exercised legitimate authority.

There were other ways in which the practice of supplication accurately reflected the true state of the tenth- and eleventh-century political order. First, the ritual's liturgical associations meant that a supplicant was subject not to the man but to "God in the man." This was no abject self-abasement of the sort Greek envoys are said to have refused the Persian *autokrator*.[55] However much a prostrate supplication may have represented a person's subjection to a lord, it was primarily a willing recognition of the divine basis of the lord's title and office. A petitioner's gestures of humility did not necessarily represent a personal humiliation, and a ruler's gracious response said nothing about his real power or virtue. Rather, to petition and to accept a petition was a statement about the acceptance of an ideal.

Furthermore, the offices honored in supplication conferred not license but unique responsibilities; for when God gave an earthly lord authority, he intended that lord to act as a mediator between him and his people, not as a barrier. The right of great lords to receive supplication therefore required them to be responsive to their petitioners, as God was responsive to the prayers of those who addressed him humbly and devoutly. Here, too, supplication within a Christian theology left little room for absolutism.

There was one final cultural check on any excessively authoritarian interpretation of supplication. Jacques Le Goff has noticed a pervasive theme in medieval Christianity: its delight in the "inversion of normal social relations," in which the "scandalous" is made "sacred."[56] The possibility—or rather the logical necessity—of such inversion was inherent in the Catholic treatment of grace; for the grace of God was an immanent grace, which could appear everywhere without mediation, and many of its manifestations tended to be just those which inverted ordinary social relations, thereby recalling the great to a truer appraisal of their powers. God's grace thus appeared not only in exalted kings but also in the humble poor; and in recognition of their latent sacrality monks prostrated themselves before the poor when they gave them alms or washed their feet.[57] A count of Flanders was killed in just such a position, prostrating himself on a "humble" stool (*in humili scabello*) as the poor took coins from his outstretched hand.[58] Divine grace also appeared in an ascetic hermit as much as in a bishop: and so all men, however lofty their status, knelt or prostrated themselves before these living saints to beg the grace of a miracle on their behalf. We have already seen the countess of Porcien kneeling to beseech a favor from Arnulf of Saint-Médard; but Helgald of Fleury portrayed King Robert himself prostrate before a holy man to beg his forgiveness for a minor offense.[59] Similarly, the bishop of Tournai fell at the feet of the holy canons of Saint-Martin to beg them not to leave his city—even as the canons were still lying in the dust in front of him, begging his authority to let them leave.[60] Finally, the most powerful sources of sacrality on earth were nothing but bits of bones, fingernails, teeth— the relics of saints who stood far closer to God than any king or bishop. In their presence even the powerful duke of the Franks, soon to be king, knelt and gave thanks that he was worthy to receive such holy remains.[61]

Beneath all these layers of meaning was a simple fact of Christian soteriology: all of the faithful were Christians, even those who ruled Christians. Rulers themselves were therefore subject to God and could be humbled like ordinary Christians. Indeed, the possibility of role reversal was a commonplace of the early Middle Ages. "He shall know the depths of humility so he may rise; but he who knows the proud heights, let him fall"; "The greater thou art, the more humble thyself."[62] These were no mere proverbs. Role reversal lay at the heart of Christian history, as Christ had died and been buried only to rise in triumph; and sinners could expect to receive grace only by imitating his example. "As man fell through pride and disobedience, so through humility and obedience he shall return," wrote Anselm of Laon.[63] Seated on a high throne placed above their petitioners, kings were told to be especially mindful of the lesson. Jonas of Orléans had set the tone in the ninth century. The model of a good king was David, and David had been exalted by God to replace Saul because of his true humility. A king should remember that example; for the king who forgets his essential sinfulness "will return, naked and wretched, to descend to infernal torments."[64]

This Christian gloss on humility further mitigated the harshness of the subjection conveyed by supplication by making its humiliation relative. The bishop of Paris, the people of Bruges, the counts of Senlis and Montdidier, all might prostrate themselves to a king or other great lord in a demonstration of humility;[65] but such great lords would also humble themselves to supplicate the King of kings and Lord of lords. Louis the German, Charles the Bald, Otto II, and Otto III, to list only four prominent examples, were all shown in various attitudes of prostrate supplication to God in reliefs and illuminations.[66] Indeed, a king began his tenure of office by prostrating himself before the altar at his sacring.[67]

Of course, one could read a prince's prostration to God as a further manifestation of the unique and supreme nature of his authority: vassals supplicate him, but he supplicates God. This was perhaps part of the intended meaning of Louis the Pious's penance at Attigny and Otto I's supplication on the Lechfield.[68] But the belief in the rightness of a pluralistic diffusion of power, sanctioned by the widespread effusion of divine grace, undermined such readings.

In fact, the prostration of a king at his coronation and his iconographic portrayal as God's supplicant did not simply (if at all) represent his right to petition God on behalf of his subjects as their patron. Ritual—at least good ritual—is never so straightforward. Rather, the power of ritual derives from the ambiguity of its multivalent symbology, through which cultural paradoxes are objectified as sacred mysteries.[69] Royal supplications, for example, were acts of exaltation; but other meanings were interwoven with this one. Janet Nelson has astutely suggested that a royal coronation followed the classic pattern of a rite of passage. Seen in this light, a king's prostration before his sacring represented the "annihilation of the initiate's former personality in preparation for 'rebirth' into a new status."[70] Coronation supplications also conveyed other meanings far more specifically Christian than this—and also far more political. The prostration of the German kings, for example, made in the form of a cross, was an *imitatio Christi*, through which electors were reminded of the nature of their kings' authority, while kings were reminded of the need for humility and sacrifice in anticipation of triumph on earth and in heaven.[71]

Beneath all these readings lay one other message, the simplest and most fundamental of all: the prostrate supplication of a king before his coronation was a reminder that he was king only by the grace of God. Without that grace he was nothing. And even with that grace he remained a man whose soul must be saved—for all the insignia of his office and for all his responsibility, still Adam's progeny.

The essentially Adamic nature of even the greatest kings always lay just beneath the surface of their exaltation. It was, for example, Notker of St. Gall who described the poor addressing Louis the Pious as *Kyrie* while soldiers embraced his feet or adored him from afar. But in the same passage Notker showed the humility that was the necessary obverse of exaltation by inverting the christomimesis, writing that Louis gave alms to the poor "because he saw Christ in them." He also described the devotions of Louis's son in a quite different manner.

> Louis the German surpassed all men in his zealous devotion to prayer, in his observance of the fasts and in his constant care to attend divine service. He followed the example of Saint Martin in that, whatever else he was doing, he always seemed to pray to God as if he were face to face with him. On the days ordained he abstained from meat and from dainty food. Whenever the litanies were to be used, he would follow the cross barefoot from his palace as far as the cathedral.[72]

Thegan, the biographer of Louis the Pious, recorded that emperor's acts of devotion in similar terms, as Louis prayed with tears, on bended knees, his head touching the ground.[73]

No matter how powerful, kings and counts were sinners, like

ordinary men. Throughout the early Middle Ages this was regarded as a fundamental truth, expressed by a recurring ritual,
as princes who sinned underwent the penitential rites common
to all Christians—rites in which the sinner fell prostrate to the
ground, barefoot and dressed in humble garb, to beg pardon of
the Lord. In just this way Louis the Pious had performed public
penance for his sins, as Theodosius had done before him, as
Robert the Pious did after.[74] Of the German king, Henry III, it
was said that he never "presumed" to wear his regalia before
privately confessing and doing penance.[75] Counts behaved no
differently. Toward the end of the eleventh century, Robert II of
Flanders was supposed to have "come down from his throne
like another king of Ninevah" to make amends to Saint Adalhard for seizing Corbie's Flemish estates. "Approaching barefoot in humility," the count knelt before Adalhard's relics and
"laid down his honor."[76] Though the account is apocryphal,
others are not. Fulk Nerra, for example, really did atone for having violated the sanctuary of Saint Martin at Tours by entering
the chapter with bare feet and prostrating himself in the church.
Other Angevin counts did likewise.[77]

Nor was it penance alone that reduced the powerful to the
level of ordinary Christians. Even their greatest victories recalled to them their dependence on the grace of the Lord of lords.
So Henry III celebrated an important military victory: barefoot
and dressed only in a penitential garment, the king prostrated
himself before a piece of the True Cross, "giving thanks to the
God who gave all."[78] Hugh Capet, while still duke of the Franks,
acted similarly: having intimidated the count of Flanders into
surrendering the relics of Saint Valerius, "the duke, on bended
knees, tears flowing from his eyes, gave thanks to the Lord with
all his knights that he was worthy to receive the bodies of such
saints."[79] Acts neither of pure humiliation nor of unqualified
self-exaltation, such princely supplications expressed both at
the same time.

Supplication was therefore a quintessentially polysemic ritual. Performed by a dependent, it signified his recognition of a
lord's divinely ordained authority and his dependence on that
lord's grace. Yet dependence was relative. The count, bishop, or
abbot who supplicated a king was himself a minister of God and
therefore received supplications from his own dependents. Fur-

thermore, in recognition of their sacrality the humblest men and women and the basest objects received supplications from the powerful, who were in this way recalled to an awareness of their own dependence on the grace of God. Finally, all Adam's heirs—men and women, kings and peasants, bishops and priests—fell to their knees to beg God for forgiveness of their sins, forgiveness which they could not merit but only receive by the Lord's grace. And this knowledge placed those who were lords by the grace of God under a special obligation to give freely to their petitioners, just as God had given freely to them. Far from being rigid and artificial, supplication captured the underlying openness of contemporary attitudes toward power and grace. But then, the one was only a reflection of the other.

PART TWO

Constructing a Political Community

Fair cousin, you debase your princely knee
To make the base earth proud with kissing it.
Me rather had my heart might feel your love
Than my unpleased eye see your courtesy.
Up, cousin, up, your heart is up, I know.

Richard II, 3:3

The mounting Bullingbrook ascends my throne,
The time shall not be many hours of age
More than it is, ere foul sin gathering head
Shall break into corruption. Thou shalt think,
Though he divide the realm and give thee half,
It is too little, helping him to all;
He shall think that thou, which knowest the way
To plant unrightful kings, will know again,
Being ne'er so little urg'd, another way
To pluck him headlong from the usurped throne.

Richard II, 5:1

The foregoing discussion has been devoted largely to a synchronic analysis of supplication in order to present a view of the ritual as a whole. Variations over time and across regions have not been a primary concern. Yet rituals are not static. They do change. Most important of all, the perception of rituals can change. Nothing is more fatal to a high-minded ritual, for example, than apathy or ridicule. Conversely, for a ritual to be taken seriously requires a willingness on the part of at least some participants to take it seriously. The history of ritual is therefore the history of perceptions, not, as is usually thought, because rituals provide a window onto the perceptions of participants, but because their perceptions determine the meaningfulness of their rituals.

Unfortunately, the very nature of rituals tends to conceal these perceptions. Their repetitiveness erodes signs of changing attitudes, leaving a wash of routinized behavior that seems to leave little to the imagination. And their frequent use in shoring up political regimes means that their celebration of legitimacy and political harmony masks—sometimes intentionally—discontent, or simple inertia. A problem in the best of circumstances, these difficulties are especially severe in the early Middle Ages, when sources are few and those few were written by churchmen. Even if we could assume that these writings accurately reflect their authors' beliefs (and we cannot), we still could not assume that they reflect the beliefs of the laity they purport to articulate. Still, to ignore perceptions is to court the greater disaster of not understanding the culture at all. The solution, then, is not to give up the attempt but to undertake it cautiously, trying not to mistake the ritual for the reality.

Luckily, these problems are not so severe in the case of the subject we are about to explore: the rehabilitation of political rituals in late tenth- and early eleventh-century northern France. The reason is twofold. First, our sources, though still written by ecclesiastics, are now consciously propagandistic. There is no possibility of confusing ritual and reality because these clerics were themselves aware of the disparity and wrote to address it. Second, we are no longer studying rituals dumbly transmitted from one generation to the next. We are studying an effort to impose rituals where there were none.

There are still problems: in particular, the inescapable one that our clerical attitudes toward ritual may not correspond with the attitudes of the kings, let alone the magnates, still less the castellans and their followers. Even here, however, we can make some intelligent guesses informed by our knowledge of political history. More important, even if our sources say nothing at all about the attitudes of the laity, what they say about clerical attitudes reveals a fundamental shift in the expectations and hopes of this important social group. Without understanding this change and its causes, we cannot hope to understand one of the great paradoxes of early Capetian history which is indirectly the subject of this section: the fact that kings who had so little power managed to rule for so long.

4 The Rehabilitation of Royal Dignity

By the early tenth century at the latest, the great counts had taken over the liturgical formulas of supplication, in the same way and for the same reasons that they had taken over the care of monasteries and churches within their dominions and arrogated ever more grandiloquent titles: to distinguish themselves from ordinary counts and to underscore the greatness of their power vis-à-vis the king. These dukes and marquesses were no mere counts by royal delegation; they were counts "by the grace of God"; and if the formula conveyed a certain humility, it also conveyed a special relationship with God, who became the protector of their authority and its model.

The princes' use of these formulas did not, however, inaugurate a revolution in political conceptions. It only set the seal on a gathering trend; for the exaltation of the comital office had long been tolerated, even by royal apologists. Formally, then, these developments changed nothing in the paradigmatic role of the king. He continued to be anointed with chrism and heralded at his coronation as a quasi-sacerdotal figure, a "sharer in the ministry" of bishops, the *auctor ac stabilator* of a Christian kingdom.[1] As such he continued to receive the humble prayers of his *fideles*, including the great counts themselves, in this way playing his role as an earthly embodiment of heavenly kingship. Yet in the realm of perceptions everything had changed, because the wars of the tenth century had tarnished the ceremonial luster of kingship. There was little to distinguish the power of a king like Louis d'Outremer from that of his great princes. Even Flodoard had to admit, in a bitterly ironic allusion to Isidorean teaching, that Louis had nothing but "the name of king."[2] Perhaps this was the reason that in chronicling the wars, Flodoard devoted less attention to extolling the royal attributes of his kings than he did to narrating their political intrigues with the princes. Accordingly, his *Annals* gives little space to those ceremonials—anointings, displays of regalia, public assemblies, the giving of gifts—through which ninth-century annalists and historians had conveyed the ideal of royal supremacy.[3]

Supplicating kings had also figured prominently in ninth-century historical writings,[4] but Flodoard neglected these acts as well. It is not that he was unaware of the ritual. Formulas of petition and intercession appear regularly in the correspondence between princes and prelates which he included in his *Historia Remensis ecclesiae*, just as they occur regularly in diplomas of the period, and both here and in his *Annals* he described incidents of petition and intercession in appropriate circumstances. The archbishop of Reims, for example, "beseeched," "supplicated," and "prayed" King Arnulf of East Francia to assume the throne of the West Franks, and beseeched Louis d'Outremer to spare the life of a renegade castellan. Flodoard also recorded instances of prostrate supplication, as when monks prostrated themselves to beseech God for a miracle, and the bishop of Soissons prostrated himself before a papal legate to confess his guilt, only to be absolved by the intercession of the archbishops of Trier and Reims.[5]

For the most part, however, Flodoard slighted both the formulas and the ritual of supplication. In their place comes the language of pact and truce, used to describe agreements not only between princes but also between kings and princes. References to such accords appear frequently in both the *Annals* and the *History*, far more frequently than instances of petition and supplication. In the *Annals* Flodoard used the language of pacts to describe the interactions of political actors at least fifty times but the language of supplication no more than twenty.[6] Along with the language goes a distinctive set of rites: the exchange of gifts or hostages, for example, or the passing back and forth of mediators between two hostile camps, or the mutual swearing of oaths.[7]

The reason for this shift in emphasis is that the language and rites of peace belonged to a paradigm of political order appropriate to conflicts between equals,[8] and this is how Flodoard conceived the wars of the tenth-century kings against the princes: as battles between equals, to be ended by agreements between equals. In 924, for example, King Raoul prepared a campaign against William of Aquitaine, who had not yet recognized his title. Raoul never even made it to the Auvergne. Instead he stopped at the Loire; and while he and his army stayed on one side of the river, William and his camped on the other, as mediators passed back and forth between the two sides trying to negotiate a solution to the impasse. In its subtle ambiguity, the agreement the two men finally reached neatly captured political reality. William crossed the river, dismounted, and approached Raoul on foot, thereby deferring to the king. But in turn Raoul kissed William; and though the initiative in giving the embrace belonged to the superior, yet the kiss still signified that the two men were bound by friendship and pact more than by lordship and service. Besides, Raoul never was allowed to cross the river and be received as king in William's domains; and even this hollow victory had required an entire day of negotiation, which Flodoard treats as a political rite every bit as important as the final submission.[9]

Often kings did not even receive this much honor. The political intrigues of the princes produced such cynicism toward the ideals of Carolingian rule that the kings were ultimately treated with open disrespect. Louis d'Outremer was actually seized by his enemies and held in close confinement.[10] Even more unfortunate was Louis's father, Charles the Simple. Charles had tried hard to maintain his authority against princes ever more jealous of their autonomy. He advanced his own men to positions of prominence in the kingdom. He sought access to a military force independent of the magnates by cultivating an alliance with the Norse settled on the Seine.[11] And like his greater ancestors, he promoted his reputation within churches by requiring those that benefited from his patronage to celebrate royal anniversaries with prayers, masses, and commemorative meals.[12] It was all to no avail. The princes forced him to disown his Lotharingian familiars. The Normans proved unreliable allies. Not even the monastic cult remained within his mastery. In prayers and celebratory meals Charles the Bald had been commemorated alone, as befitted a serenely majestic king, or had been honored with such commemoration by loyal *fideles* in thanks for his benefactions and in recognition of his lordship.[13] But Charles the Simple, ruling by the sufferance of powerful magnates like Robert of Neustria, had little choice but to associate them in his ceremonial. He therefore granted Robert the right to be commemorated in anniversary meals and in masses alongside him in Robert's client monasteries. When the monks of Saint-Denis or Saint-Martin celebrated their masses and feasts, it was therefore Robert's lordship and benefaction they were recognizing as much as the king's.[14]

At least the meals and masses perpetuated the fiction of Charles's kingship. Soon not even this much remained. Robert deposed Charles and consigned him to the prisons of Herbert II of Vermandois for safekeeping. After Robert's death the throne passed to his brother-in-law, Raoul of Burgundy, and Charles now became a pawn in Herbert's rivalry with Raoul, appearing publicly only when it suited his jailer's interests.[15] It was hardly the climate to foster respect for the royal office. On one occasion recalled by Flodoard, Raoul visited Charles and "made peace with him, humiliating himself in his presence, while restoring the fisc of Attigny to him and honoring him with royal gifts."[16] The rite recalls the supplications offered to the greatest Carolingian kings, with one important difference: all the while Raoul remained king, and Charles remained Herbert's prisoner.

This is ritual, but ritual as parody, ritual that intentionally and cruelly exposes the fiction of monarchical authority, shredded by decades of war punctuated by periodic self-serving treaties. In this context, supplicating kings must have seemed a travesty. For an ecclesiastic such as Flodoard, who knew the sacred meaning of the act, it would have been a profane travesty at that, an act of disrespect to God himself. Better to ignore the ritual entirely than to dignify its blasphemy with publicity. This is the reason that although Flodoard records suppliant prostrations, he mentions them only to God and bishops and never to the Frankish kings, save in this one painful instance.[17]

Rites of Political Renewal

In the later tenth century the ceremonial portrayal of royal authority seems to have returned to the forefront of men's consciousness. Indeed, the renewed emphasis on political ceremony appears to have been part of a conscious propaganda effort, spearheaded by the kings and their archbishops of Reims. Their intentions were not always the same; far from it, they were often antagonistic. Yet the interests of both were served by the renewal of royal ceremonial, and one suspects that the success of their program resulted partly from the fact that it satisfied the needs of those who were otherwise antagonists.

The background to this development is well known, thanks to Bernd Schneidmüller and Yves Sassier.[18] During the middle of the tenth century the Saxon emperors exercised a real hegemony over the western kingdom. As leaders of the north Frankish church whose dioceses straddled Frankish and imperial lands, the archbishops of Reims were central to the maintenance of that protectorate, and Otto I and his legate, Bruno of Cologne, made certain that the archbishops were their men. Yet until 963 there was too much confusion and factionalism, both within the archdiocese and within the kingdom as a whole, for the archbishops to make much of a positive impact on political affairs. That situation changed in 969 with the election of Adalbero, a man whose capacities equaled his vision.[19] To be sure, Adalbero has often been seen as an agent of the Saxons. Raised in the cathedral of Metz, scion of an important Lotharingian family, he was devoted to the ideal of imperial unity, meaning the subordination of the western subking to the eastern king of kings, who would exercise a generous protectorate for the sake of universal political harmony. But Adalbero's belief in this ideal did not detract from his commitment to building up Lothar's authority. His guiding principle was order; and true order required a Frankish king strong in his own right, though respectful of and subordinate to the emperor: a kind of homunculus king, then, perfect in every respect only smaller.

As for Lothar, during the first years of his reign he had no choice but to tolerate the sometimes stifling patronage of the Saxon emperor. Without Otto I's power he had no chance to rule his magnates at all. But within four years of Adalbero's

election the great Otto had died, leaving a troubled succession;
and Lothar took the opportunity to break free of Saxon tutelage
and inaugurate his own policies. Yet he had learned from his
guardians how important it was to cultivate the image of a king,
for it was the image that separated him from the princes who
obstructed him. Important during his subordination to Otto, the
image was just as important to Lothar during the period of their
rivalry, only the goal was no longer to meekly echo the Ottonians. The goal was to compete with them on their own emblematic ground.

This is the background to the remarkable series of innovations sponsored by Lothar and Adalbero in the late 960s and
970s. In 966, for example, Lothar borrowed the Ottonian seal for
his own use, a seal showing the king full-face, holding the royal
insignia. The setting, with its obvious derivation from Byzantine models and its allusion to the singularity of royal authority, reflected Lothar's increasing self-confidence, not so much
with respect to Otto I (since Lothar was still under the Saxon
protectorate) as with respect to his own magnates.[20] Somewhat
later, Adalbero began to borrow from the Ottonians. In recon-
structing his cathedral the archbishop hung crowns over the altar, a symbolic expression, visible to all visitors, that earthly
kingship derived from and was modeled on the imperial lordship of Christ.[21] The very reconstruction of the cathedral enunciated Adalbero's expectation that Lothar's reign would bring a
return to peace and order, since it required the ramparts built to
protect the city from the Viking invasions to be at long last
destroyed.[22] The same message was conveyed in 976, when Adalbero translated the relics of Saint Theoderic from the cathedral, where they had been taken for safekeeping during the invasions, to their former home outside the walls of the city.[23] Peace
had come to stay—or at least, that was the hope.

The hope rested with the king, for a return to order meant a
return of the dignity of kingship. And so Adalbero not only invited Lothar to preside over Theoderic's translation; he also
awarded him a prominent place in the ceremony. He timed the
king's *adventus* into Reims to coincide with Advent, the time
of Jesus's appearance on earth to claim his Kingdom of Peace.
The meaning was clear: the restoration of harmony between
heaven and earth required the restoration of symmetry between

heavenly and earthly kingship. And in case any doubt remained, the archbishop staged a little miracle. When the moment came to raise the saint's body from the ground, it would not budge. Adalbero claimed to know the reason: legend had it that Theoderic had been placed in his tomb by King Dagobert himself. Buried by the hand of a great Frankish king, the saint would let himself be raised only by the hand of another great Frankish king. Adalbero asked Lothar's aid; and no sooner had the king set his hand on the body than it came up easily. With this drama, Adalbero tried to restore a sense of providential election to the Carolingian, now made an heir not just to Charlemagne but to Dagobert and, through him, to Clovis, all of them chosen by God to lead his people to peace.

Richer's Rites of Consensual Polity

Rituals such as the translation of Theoderic are often intended to make a point; but the intended recipient of the message is not always the audience. It may also be the participants. So in 976 Adalbero may not have been trying to impress the people who witnessed the translation as much as Lothar himself. That very year Lothar's brother had attacked Hainaut, at the time ruled in behalf of Otto II by Adalbero's brother, Godfrey. No one has ever proved the king's complicity in the attack; yet it has always been suspected, since the campaign involved not only Lothar's brother but also enemies of Otto II whom Lothar had given refuge, as well as Otto of Vermandois, Lothar's nephew and ally. In fact, Adalbero had probably been forced to postpone the translation from Easter to Advent because Lothar was too preoccupied with his intrigues to attend to his archbishop's business.[24]

At Reims, then, Adalbero was attempting to recall Lothar to the fold, to restore not just the image of sacral kingship but the royal and episcopal alliance on which it was founded. The effort failed. In the following years Lothar came to regard the archbishop as something of an imperial mole, planted to undermine his quest for autonomy. Relations between the two men deteriorated, until in 985 Lothar seized Verdun and imprisoned Adalbero's brother and nephew. Nor were tensions eased by Lothar's death a year later, for in the first months of his short reign, Louis V showed every intention of renewing his father's hostility. There were occasional passing reconciliations. Indeed, when Louis died in 987, he and the archbishop were at an uneasy peace. But the trend had clearly been against cooperation, and would be as long as the Frankish kings had any interests in Lotharingia.

This awareness led Adalbero and the province's other imperialist bishops to think more deeply about the qualities they desired in a king. To begin with, he had to be someone who would limit his horizons to his proper West Frankish interests and renounce the Carolingians' Lotharingian intrigues. Equally important, he had to be able to present himself as the leader of the West Frankish magnates—but a leader who would remain attuned to their interests, not a tyrant who would ride roughshod over them. In other words, he had to be a king who would govern through consensus rather than mandate.

In this way the church of Reims had renewed contact with an old political ideal, an ideal in which king and magnates would share authority, magnates respecting their leader, but their leader respecting them.[25] In other words, what the ecclesiastics of Reims sought was a greater respect on all sides for political authority—that of the princes as well as that of the king. And respect for political authority required a greater respect for rites of political order, because these were a suitable vehicle for projecting the ideal.

Adalbero was the architect of this movement, seconded by his secretary and ultimate successor, Gerbert.[26] However, we know about their policies mostly through another figure from the church of Reims: Richer, the monk of Saint-Remi who in the 990s wrote a work known as the *History of France*.[27] Richer probably grew up at Saint-Remi during Adalbero's pontificate. Certainly he respected the man greatly. He respected Gerbert even more, and appears to have been quite close to him, since he began his history at Gerbert's request. Whatever the relations between Richer and the two archbishops, the fact remains that Richer's *History* is informed by their desire for a political order founded on consensus.

The means for expressing and inculcating this ideal was ritual, for Richer loved nothing so much as a good political ceremony (save perhaps a good gruesome death scene). The fact is all the more striking in that much of his *History* closely follows Flodoard's *Annals;* yet where Flodoard ignored ceremonies, Richer lavished attention on them. This is apparent in one of the critical moments in the *History*, when Louis d'Outremer is welcomed to France by a gathering of magnates. Flodoard says little about the event: only that Louis was met at Boulogne by Hugh the Great and other *proceres*, who are left unnamed; that as soon as Louis stepped off the boat, these magnates commended themselves to him; and that they then led the king to Laon, where he was anointed and crowned.[28] Richer keeps to the same outline but adds telling details. He underscores the promise of loyalty inherent in the magnates' commendation to their new king by writing that they "bound themselves to him by swearing an oath." He also shows Hugh presenting Louis with a horse all bedecked with royal insignia. As Louis was about to mount the horse it began to buck; but like a consummate horseman the king bounded into the saddle, not even bothering to use the stirrups, to the appreciative applause of the magnates. Then the duke received Louis's arms and acted as his squire for part of the journey to Laon, until Louis ordered him to give the arms to Herbert of Vermandois. Then Herbert acted as squire, until Louis ordered him to surrender the task to Arnulf of Flanders; and so on, until they had arrived at Laon. Finally, Richer treats the entire procession as a formal *adventus*, mentioning that at every city they passed through the new king was solemnly and joyously received, as "all applauded him, all celebrated, so much was everyone of one mind."[29]

Robert Latouche, Richer's editor, believed that none of this really happened; but that hardly matters.[30] What matters is that this is how Richer wanted the event to be remembered. This is how it should have happened. He wanted kings to be leaders, and the ritual Richer described established the contours of that leadership. The magnates served the king loyally; but Louis deserved this honor by virtue of the prowess he demonstrated in taming his horse. Furthermore, the people had to participate in this display of unity, because they too had a role in celebrating this vision of perfect political harmony. Their joy in receiving their new king was to reflect their hope that the condominium of king and magnates would finally succeed in restoring peace and justice to the kingdom.

For Richer, it was not enough to perform rituals. One had to perform them sincerely, or, in his own vocabulary, faithfully.[31] Indeed, one of his reasons for putting Louis's *adventus* in such high relief was that it underscored the king's faithlessness when he later broke with Hugh the Great, who had sponsored his election and served him with honor at Boulogne. Significantly, the occasion for the break occurred when Louis began to make policy without taking the duke's counsel. "This was the cause of the great fall," as Richer put it, a king too proud (*elatus*) to realize that he had to rule with the advice of his magnates.[32]

Necessary in public ceremonies, faithfulness was even more essential to those private rites acted out by individuals, because faith was at its heart a bond between individuals. The keystone of political order was the good faith of Christians, who pledged their sincerity with their souls. If they did not enter into the rites of loyalty with sincerity, then good order was impossible. This is how we must understand Richer's horror at Bishop Adalbero of Laon's faithless oath to Lothar's brother, Charles of Lorraine. In prosecuting his claim to the throne after Louis V's death, Charles had taken control of Adalbero's see. When Hugh Capet's siege failed to evict him, the bishop hatched a treacherous plan to regain control of the city. He ingratiated himself with Charles. To gain his confidence, he even had the temerity to place his hand on relics and swear an oath of loyalty. The real treachery, however, occurred the evening of Palm Sunday (or so says Richer), a day that called to mind a much more famous betrayal. During the morning mass Adalbero had blessed the palms. That night, as he and Charles were dining, Charles offered the bishop his own cup of wine and a piece of bread. Recalling the solemnity of the day's events, Charles asked Adalbero to dispel the slander of those who said he should not be trusted by drinking the wine and eating the bread. "Drink this," he said, "as a sign that you will hold and keep faith. But if you do not intend to keep faith, do not drink, lest you repeat the horrible image of Judas, the traitor." Of course Adalbero did drink, did betray Charles, and did go down in history as a new Judas.[33]

To a certain extent, Richer's christomimetic treatment of his protagonists reflects the special standing of Charles and Adalbero. Adalbero was a bishop, a type or figure of Christ; and Charles was a Carolingian, and may even have been crowned during an earlier bid for the throne. Still, like many of his contemporaries, Richer had no great love for either one. Adalbero was linked with far too many scandals to be fully trustworthy; and Charles was widely regarded as an ambitious opportunist who would commend himself to any lord who promised to advance his fortunes.[34] Given the two men's unsavoriness, it is more likely that Richer's treatment of the oath reflects his attitude toward all oaths, all rites of loyalty. The swearing in this case has been made archetypal by the stature of the two men; but its essence was the same for all men, an act in which religion and politics met.[35]

The same was true of all the rituals recorded (or invented) by Richer, and there are many of them. From Gerbert he borrowed his account of the council of Saint-Basle of Verzy, the council where Arnulf of Reims did penance for his treason; but even more than Gerbert's narrative, Richer's culminates in Arnulf's solemn prostration to the kings, for he says not a word about the unseemly dispute between Burchard of Vendôme and the bishops that marred the trial. Nothing is allowed to detract from the image of political harmony.[36] There is also his description of Lothar's funeral, in his own words a "magnificent" event that would have made even an Otto III envious. A special bed had been made for the occasion, decorated with royal insignia. Lothar's body was dressed in silk and covered with a purple cloth studded with gems and woven with gold thread. The magnates personally carried the bier. In front of them walked the bishops and clergy, bearing crosses and the Gospels. One of them, positioned in the middle of the group, carried a crown glinting with gold and jewels. Behind the bier came the king's knights, each in his proper rank but all walking with downcast heads. The rest of the cortege followed in tears.[37]

The solemn pomp of this funeral, so unlike anything we know of from this period in the western kingdom, is striking enough confirmation of Richer's desire to show rituals affirming the dignity of monarchy and the unity of the polity. But of special interest here is the literally central place Richer gives to the king's crown, carried in the middle of crosses and Gospels. It is well known that the Ottonians had already made the crown a focal point of royal ceremonial: hence their *Festkrönungen*, occasions intended to dramatize the sacredness of royal status, as

on a high feast day the ruler appeared garbed in his finest ceremonial robes and decked out with all the regalia of his office,
the moment culminating in his solemn recrowning by an archbishop.[38] Most historians believe that the French kings had no
equivalent during this period. At least there is generally believed to be no certain evidence of festal coronations in France
until the later eleventh century—to be precise, not until 1071,
when Philip I issued a charter at Laon during a coronation assembly.[39] But the description of Lothar's funeral shows that by
Richer's time the crown had already become a focal insignia of
Frankish rulership. The exaltation of the crown and the eliciting of its christological allusions under Lothar is also visible in
Archbishop Adalbero's decision to hang crowns over the altar of
his cathedral—again a fact that we know from Richer.[40]

There is in any case one piece of evidence—perhaps so obvious that it has been overlooked—showing that festal coronations had in fact been introduced into Francia during this very
same period. As Richer tells it, shortly after his coronation
Hugh Capet decided to associate his son on the throne. He over-
came the objections of Archbishop Adalbero, and then Adalbero
himself crowned Robert in the church of Sainte-Croix at Orléans. What has been overlooked is the syntax of the sentence
that explains why the coronation took place where and when it
did: "And because the magnates had gathered on Christmas to
celebrate the honor of the royal coronation, [the archbishop] solemnly crowned and anointed [the king's] son, Robert, in the
church of Sainte-Croix."[41] The crucial word here is "because"
(*quia*): it was decided to crown Robert at Sainte-Croix because
the magnates were already planning to gather there to celebrate
Hugh's Christmas coronation. In other words, within six
months of his election, the first Capetian was already gathering
his magnates around him to celebrate a festal coronation. Since
neither Hugh nor Louis IV nor Louis V was in any position to
have introduced such a custom, it can only have been introduced under Lothar, at the suggestion of Adalbero of Reims,
who would have known of the Saxon rite.

It is well known that Richer could be wildly inventive, and so
some of the incidents he describes may have existed only in his
imagination. Louis d'Outremer's arrival at Laon may not have

been celebrated as a dominical *adventus*, and Adalbero of Laon may not have sworn his oath over a chalice of wine. But Richer cannot have invented all of his rituals—though he may have embroidered their details to suit his theme. Lothar's funeral, for example, seems quite plausible. Not only does its lavishness echo Ottonian practices; Gerbert, at the time Adalbero's private secretary, personally supervised the ceremonial, as he himself tells us in a letter complaining that the arrangements were taking all of his time.[42] Richer also did not invent the crowns Adalbero hung over the altar of his cathedral—this was another borrowing from imperial practice—nor did he invent Hugh Capet's crown-wearing, since he alludes to it so matter-of-factly.

From the introduction of a new seal to the translation of Theoderic to Lothar's funeral and Hugh's festal coronation, the fact is that beginning in the late 960s and continuing well into the Capetian era, emphasis on royal rituals did increase in Francia. Nor was this simply the unthinking echo of an Ottonian model; for Richer shows that along with the greater use of rituals went a greater desire that they be taken seriously. They may have been only propaganda; yet even that is new and significant. There had been no royal propaganda in the first half of the tenth century, not in the western kingdom. By the 980s there is. Somebody cares that kings present themselves in full regalia; that magnates participate in ceremonies where they at least pretend to serve their ruler; that the burial of a king be a moment of solemnity, when the leaders of the political community can come together and declare their common adhesion to a symbol of unity.

This last is the truly important point. The new rituals did not declare the unilateral authority of kings over magnates. The ideal was not power but unity and consensus, condensing around the figure of the king. There would be loyalty. But the magnates' loyalty to the king was predicated on the kings' respect for the magnates. What these rituals proclaimed, then, was the need for all sides to join together; and the king himself, whether alive or dead, together with those emblems, like crowns, that symbolized his authority, was treated as the focus that could gather the princes together.

Hugh Capet's Sense of Dignity

By the time Louis V died without direct heirs in 987, the leaders of the provincial church had become, quite simply, fed up with the wars and intrigues of the past decades—the more so as they had been their targets. Nor was it only the prelates of the province of Reims that felt this way. The writings of Abbo of Fleury reveal a desire for a government by consensus every bit as strong as Richer's, while in Burgundy the years between 975 and 990 witnessed the first stirrings of the movement that became known as the Peace of God.[43] The mood of frustration even seems to have touched the princes; for according to Sassier, at least some of Louis's allies among the magnates had been put out by Louis's renewal of armed hostilities against Adalbero, and at the moment of his death were actively trying to arrange a peace. Intrigue was one thing; but a return to policies that invited Ottonian intervention and destabilized their own dealings with the empire was quite another. The church's desire for government by consensus must also have appealed to one of the most deeply rooted assumptions of the medieval aristocracy in all countries and all centuries: the belief that kings should govern with the advice and consent of their magnates.[44]

In all likelihood it was this fatigue, coupled with a corresponding hope for a new beginning, that helped Hugh Capet and Robert the Pious over the difficult first years of their accession. No one wanted to plunge Francia into a prolonged war over the kingship. This at least might explain why Charles of Lorraine's legitimate claim to the throne was passed over with such jejune, even contradictory arguments, and why after Charles's defeat Hugh never faced any concerted or extensive resistance to the principle of his rule. It may also explain why he was allowed to crown his son so soon after his accession. Historians have occasionally found the magnates' acquiescence surprising, but only because they have assumed that Robert's co-regency was interpreted as an undesirable extension of Capetian power to be resisted. Perhaps instead it was accepted because it satisfied the hope for stability.

Hugh himself seems to have been aware of this hope. He met Archbishop Adalbero's initial objections to Robert's association by arguing that in such a troubled time the kingdom needed a guarantee of political continuity.[45] The same desire for stability is suggested by the fact that Hugh continued his predecessors' crown-wearings and diplomatic traditions.[46] But there is also a more eloquent and explicit statement of the desire. Like any savvy leader of a new regime, Hugh acted quickly to reassure everyone that nothing would change, that the laws of the old kings would be enforced, that he would not allow his accession to become an excuse for anyone's licentious usurpation of property. As he wrote in a diploma issued for Corbie (but petitioned and subscribed, as it happened, by Adalbero of Reims), "We are not unaware that the highness of our piety cannot otherwise stand in right order [*recto ordine*] except by doing justice to all and in all things, by adhering to the decrees of former kings, and by exalting the Church of God."[47] Even if this statement expresses not Hugh's beliefs but the clergy's demands, it remains a valuable indicator of contemporary expectations. From this perspective, Hugh's appropriation of Carolingian diplomatics was a way to project the legitimacy of his authority; but it was also a way to reassure his subjects that there would be order, not just as good as before, but even better.

Such sentiments represent more than platitudes. They suggest a harmony between Hugh's personality and the expectations of bishops and magnates that goes far toward explaining his and his successors' success in maintaining their position in the face of their material weakness. True, when Hugh was elected in 987 he had been the only serious candidate for the throne, since Charles of Lorraine was too thoroughly disliked for consideration. That left Hugh as the only leader powerful enough to be king but not so powerful as to threaten the magnates. Besides, his grandfather and great-grandfather had been kings. He also had no particular interest in pursuing the Carolingians' expansionist policies in Lotharingia—a quality that must have particularly endeared him to Adalbero. But quite apart from these considerations, Hugh happened to embody just those virtues that the past decades had taught men to prize. Himself nothing but a glorified magnate, he knew from experience the limits of royal and princely power, while recognizing the dignity that magnates deserved. In fact, Hugh had been enraged more than once by the kings' tendency to make secret policy, especially as the policies had often been directed against him.[48]

Here, then, would be a king who appreciated both the limits of royal power and the corresponding need for consensus.

At the same time, Hugh appreciated the need for kings to keep a sense of dignity about them. The awareness went beyond his royal ancestry. It had been burned into his personality by a series of humiliations he had suffered in 981, when he traveled to Otto II's court at Rome in an attempt to break up an alliance between Lothar and the Saxon emperor.[49] He succeeded at least partly in his quest; but in the process he was repeatedly reminded of the inferiority and fragility of his position. First, during his audience with Otto, the emperor insisted on addressing him in Latin. Of course, it was convenient for Otto to speak Latin in Rome; but he could just as easily have spoken German. Speaking in his own vernacular would at least have been friendlier, since it would have placed the two men on a more nearly equal footing and required interpreters for both. But even if uncalculating, Otto's choice called attention to his moral superiority over the duke; because Latin was the language of pontiffs and pontifical kings, and Hugh could not understand it. He could only listen in uncomprehending silence while his bishop of Orléans translated for him.

The second humiliation came at the end of the audience. Otto had offered the duke a kiss and received him into his friendship. But after leaving the hall he suddenly returned, pretending to have forgotten his sword, and asked Hugh to bring it to him. It was a trap, designed to force the duke into performing the kind of service that clients and *fideles* did for their lords. Perhaps Hugh did not immediately realize what his acquiescence would have meant; more likely he realized it, but knew that he could not refuse the request without making a public scene that would undo all his negotiations. Whatever the truth, Hugh went to the seat where the sword lay and bent over to grasp it. Once more he was rescued by the bishop of Orléans, who quickly reached out and picked up the sword and took it to the emperor.

Finally, one last insult: as Hugh prepared to return to France he learned that Lothar had sent word that he was to be arrested and imprisoned. To escape, Hugh was forced to pass through the kingdom of Burgundy disguised as a menial, leading the horses himself and personally loading and unloading them. For a man whose ancestors had been anointed, it must have been degrading, the stuff of farce, not epic.

Given the prominence Richer gives to these anecdotes, given the fact that Hugh often spoke afterward of the bishop of Orléans's cleverness (*prudentiam simul et astutiam*),[50] it is not hard to believe that these incidents infuriated Hugh, and changed him. His resentment would partly explain why he became so determined that his son, Robert, would have an education equal to that of the Saxon monarchs. They would also explain what has otherwise seemed somewhat ludicrous: why, when king, Hugh tried so hard to marry Robert to a Byzantine princess. Robert would never be humiliated by not knowing how to speak Latin. He would speak it like a bishop. And he would marry a woman worthy of the Saxon emperors—if not an imperial princess, then at least the daughter of a king.[51] Hugh had learned by personal experience what Adalbero of Reims was trying to teach: a king could lack power, but without dignity he was nothing.

A Generation in Crisis

The lessons were not forgotten by Hugh's descendants, not even by those who were otherwise rather inglorious figures. Henry I may have been hounded by repeated insurrections; yet it was he who introduced a new seal type, one that depicted the king enthroned "in majesty," a christomimetic pose.[52] And no early Capetian was more adept than Henry at using public trials to assert his authority over upstart castellans and pose as defender of the church and leader of the magnates.[53] Similarly, it is in the time of the fat and uxorious Philip I that we find the first glimmerings of the healing royal touch, as well as indisputable evidence of regularly held festal coronations.[54]

It was the generation of Robert the Pious, however, that seems to have been most interested in giving special honor to royal authority. The most widely known example comes from shortly after the reign, when Helgald of Fleury wrote a life of Robert portraying him as a king of such powerful saintliness that of all princes he alone could heal the sick.[55] But Helgald only made explicit what had been implicit throughout Robert's reign: the desire to present the king as the protector of the church and the Christian people; and this image was too useful politically to be hidden away in hagiographic works accessible only to the literate clergy. It had to be brought to the public. It had to be enacted as ritual. So it was that in 1028 at Sens, in front of a large crowd of nobles, prelates, clerics, and commoners, Robert and his son bore the new reliquary of Saint Savinian on their shoulders and laid it where it could be venerated by the people.[56] He performed the same ritual the next year at the dedication of Saint-Aignan of Orléans. Again our source emphasizes the event's publicity, but to this is added another characteristic incident: at the end of the translation Robert removed his regalia, knelt before the altar, and offered this prayer to God: "Therefore, O Lord, through these your saints, give forgiveness of sins to the living, and to all the dead everlasting life and peace. Look down on our world and care for your kingdom, which has been granted us by your piety, mercy, and goodness."[57] The scene was a powerful dramatization of the humility that kings owed to God. But alongside this rather conventional meaning, Robert's prayer expressed a program more in keeping with his personal attitudes toward his office. As an anointed and pious king, Robert enjoyed a special relationship with heaven that gave him the right to intercede before God like a priest. And the object of his intercession was not limited to the people of Orléans, or members of his family, or his *fideles*. He prayed for the kingdom as a whole and all its people, living and dead. Although he could not presume to rule effectively everywhere in that kingdom, he could still assume a liturgical role as its spiritual protector, the emblem of its unity, transcending class, transcending region.

That this was Robert's intention is suggested by another ritual, one of his most interesting and unexpected. At some point during the latter part of his reign, in a time when West Frankish kings rarely traveled far beyond the Ile-de-France, Robert took to the road on a year-long pilgrimage that took him not to the Holy Land, away from his people, but to the great urban churches and cult centers of Aquitaine and Provence, where they had never seen a king from the north and were beginning to forget that they had one. He traveled to Bourges, Brioude, Le Puy, Nîmes, Toulouse, Conques, and Aurillac, where the saints of the churches received him (*suscipere*) with honor, as they would a lord. Honoring them in turn, Robert "addressed their ears with most humble and worthy prayers." But in remembering the saints he did not forget his people; on the contrary, wherever he went he gave them money, and it was for them that he worked the miracles that made him the first Capetian thaumaturge. Indeed, he actively sought out the poor, entering the hovels of the sick and leprous, giving them coins with his own hands, and with his own mouth kissing the diseased hands that received them.[58]

The belief that kings should protect the church and their people was old; but the success with which the ideal was now passionately reasserted must constitute one of Robert's greatest and most enduring accomplishments. It was not Robert's accomplishment alone, however. He built on the goodwill that had been established between his father and the northern French episcopate at the time of Hugh's accession. But that episcopate, its most prominent leaders half imperial and more Lotharingian than Frankish, was too proud of its autonomy to grant a free hand to a leader whose entire generation had been tainted by the civil wars. They would support him completely; but they would not let him rule them. Hence Hugh's exclusion from Arnulf's trial in 991, and the bishops' distress when the kings and their retinue broke in upon the proceedings.[59] This was an episcopal affair, they thought, and interference by the kings would only make matters worse.

It was different with Robert. He was a student of Gerbert, a Latin-speaking king, a friend of bishops, and, as Helgald's *Vita* shows, a lover of liturgy. His was also a different generation, one from which better things were hoped. The bishops therefore granted Robert the role in their counsels that they had refused Hugh—or at least they granted him its image. When two or three years after Verzy Robert presided over an assembly of bishops at Chelles, it was the first time in a century that a Frankish king had appeared in unambiguous and unchallenged command of his church.[60] The alliance continued thereafter, despite the repeated scandals caused by Robert's irregular marital relations.[61] Between 1019 and 1024, having gained definitive control of Burgundy, Robert set the seal on his victories by authorizing Bishop Hugh of Auxerre to hold assemblies in the province "to reestablish and confirm the peace," meaning the

Peace of God. Robert himself attended the Peace council at Héry; and the chronicler of Auxerre who described the council placed the king alongside the bishops, abbots, and relics of the province: God's rulers, together leading his people and making dispositions, as another source says, "for the benefit of the churches."[62] Just one year before Héry, Robert and his queen had another occasion to display their responsibility for the faithful when they presided over the trial of some heretics from Orléans. The sources for this event are mostly late and its background is exceedingly complex; but this fact stands out in all the evidence: the king took charge of the affair. It was he who had been informed of the existence of heretics in the city; his sergeants who had arrested them; he who presided over the assembly of bishops that condemned them; and he who ordered them burned. Since the heretics were royalists and the charges perhaps trumped up by Robert's enemies, historians have had difficulty explaining why Robert took such harsh action. It is possible, however, that Robert's reputation for sanctity, his strongest asset, the secret of his image as God's king, was endangered by the merest hint of heterodoxy; and the taint could be purged only by fire.[63] If only to this minimal extent Adalbero's effort to rehabilitate the dignity of monarchy had succeeded.

An accomplishment this durable can only have satisfied equally durable needs. In fact, there was a host of reasons for the prolonged interest in the ceremonial display of royal authority in the early eleventh century, the distinctive intensity of the period resulting from the convergence of many vectors. One factor was the continuing desire of the Capetians, like their immediate predecessors, to measure up to the ritual standards set by the German monarchs, masters of liturgical kingship. This desire is particularly obvious in Henry I's borrowing of his seal type from an imperial model, and in Helgald of Fleury's quite evident concern with the christomimetic attributes of kingship. Imitation alone, however, cannot explain what is most noteworthy about the generation of clerical writers who served Robert the Pious: its craving for order, so profound and widespread that it is discernible even in otherwise antagonistic circles. There was, for example, the somewhat cantankerous conservatism of bishops such as Gerard of Cambrai and Adalbero of

Laon, who reiterated the old ideas about peace and justice with renewed intensity.[64] Diametrically opposed to their beliefs but stemming from similar hopes was the energy unleashed by the Peace of God, as men and women joined together under the aegis of their bishops and counts and in the presence of relics swore an end to the evils of unrestrained feuding.[65] Something similar was at work in the crowds that flocked to Ivois in 1023 "to gaze in awe at the imperial dignity," when Henry II met with Robert the Pious. They wanted to see what a real king was like.[66]

However different these responses, all testify to a similar desire to see order restored to society. And though this had also been the desire in Richer's generation, it was given new urgency by a new sense of crisis. For all its chaos, no one in the tenth century had ever doubted that there was anything wrong with the old ideal of order per se. What was lacking was simply the will to effectuate the ideal. In the early eleventh century, however, the validity of the Carolingian world view was itself under attack. Heretics at Orléans, Liège, and Arras challenged the authority of the ecclesiastical hierarchy, while within that hierarchy monks asserted their independence from their diocesans.[67] The Peace of God also troubled some; for though a king like Robert might have regarded it as an instrument of his authority, others, such as Gerard of Cambrai, believed that it undermined respect for the royal office and played into the hands of the crowd.[68]

The most troublesome challenge, however, came from the type of lordship known to historians as the *seigneurie banale*. Robert Fossier has called its appearance "the major social fact of the eleventh century,"[69] and his judgment is fully borne out by the surviving evidence, nearly all of it imprinted with the insistent demands of the new lords. Records of disputes are especially revealing, since conflict can provide a window into a community's distinctive "trouble spots"—areas of social interaction that are structurally prone to conflict.[70] What disputes from eleventh-century northern France show is that the most persistent trouble spots were relations between the new lords and the churches. Thus, out of eighty-three extant disputes between churches and laymen of all statuses, over two-thirds (fifty-eight) involved castellans, advocates, knights, or those ministers of kings and counts who were just as ruthless in exploiting the domains of their lords. Of these fifty-eight disputes, just over 40 percent concerned rights of banal jurisdiction alleged by lords and their minions. Over 60 percent involved "customs" (that is, requisitions and exactions) associated with rights of banal lordship. (This information is detailed in Appendix 1.)

Always difficult to settle, these disputes were often made still more intractable by the venomous insults monks and canons hurled at the lords and their knights, and by the latter's violence against the churches. This is not the place to discuss the reasons for the violence; but the reasons for the churches' intransigent rhetoric are relevant to our investigation. The simplest explanation is that the lords' successes often came at the churches' expense; for the lords built their castles on lands that had originally been reserved for chapters and monasteries; and it was the churches' peasants whom the lords forced to work building and maintaining the castles.[71] A still more profound reason for these institutions' antagonism was cultural. As later chapters will show, the established church's ideal of political order had no room for the lords. The castellans had no Carolingian blood and occupied no Carolingian office. They were (or were regarded as) new men, their powers illegitimate, their claims without precedent. Thus, many of the disputes stress the novelty of the rights claimed by the lords, a reflection of the novel form of lordship based on those rights. Special exactions and claims to jurisdiction were called "usurpations" or were said to be "against customary law."[72] The claim of one such lord, Alberic of Coucy, to jurisdiction over merchants was "unheard of for his predecessors," while of the knight Garin it was said that "no *vicarius* before our time had ever made any such exaction or requisition."[73] Where no fortifications had existed they were erected.[74] Inquests were conducted to show that the rights claimed had never been known.[75] Afraid that the old order was collapsing around them, the churches did everything they could to shore it up. In particular, they insisted that people respect, at least in principle, the fundamental cleavage that cut across the political world: on the one side, those few rulers who held *ministeria* ordained by God; on the other, the castellans and knights who exercised de facto military and judicial power.

The latter could not be eradicated. They were too thoroughly entrenched, too necessary to the rulers themselves, for that thought even to be contemplated. But they had to be kept in their place, and the princes and prelates in theirs. If that were not done, if some kind of political authority were not singled out as special—indeed, as holy—then all rule would become a matter of sheer power, immoral because cut off from the theological principles that raised Christian kingdoms above the "great robberies" disparaged by Augustine.[76]

The king was the linchpin of this ideal political order, since kingship was the earthly embodiment of the heavenly monarchy whose principles informed the world. Hence the conservative clergy's continuing emphasis on those rituals and emblems that epitomized the king's unique, God-given authority. Royal crown-wearings, ceremonial distributions to lepers, church councils presided over by the king (those of the Peace of God specifically targeting the feuds and extortions of the lords and their knights), all showed the king as the agent of God, anointed to protect the church and the poor from the *potentes*. But the king was not the only ruler so exalted. The crisis of order was more general, affecting bishops, counts, and abbots just as much as kings. All such authority needed to be exalted. Thus the church tried to reconfigure the political community so that counts, bishops, and abbots, gathering together in God's name, could protect their people against the depredations of the usurpers.

And what of the counts? What did they believe? The question is a difficult one to answer, and not only because of the absence of sources in which they speak directly, with their own voices, unmediated by clerical amanuenses. The real difficulty is that there is no single answer. Different counts had different expectations.[77] Indeed, the same counts had different expectations at different moments. The very counts of Flanders who surrounded themselves with relics could also joke with their vassals; and Baldwin of Guines, who in good Carolingian fashion claimed to protect widows and orphans, also considered himself the equal of his knights.[78] And though these examples do come from somewhat later in the eleventh century, at a time when lords were tending to identify themselves with their knights more than they had done earlier, yet early medieval lordship had always had something of a protean aspect, as lords found that they had to be both rulers in a Christian tradition and warriors in a Germanic one. Thus Clovis bashed in the heads of his rivals with as much relish as he received consular honors.[79] And if the Carolingians were more subtle, still they also had to show both camaraderie and dignity.[80] Even Louis d'Outremer—at least in Richer's portrait—was applauded for his horsemanship even as he rode to his sacring; and both he and his grandson and namesake died, like true warriors, in hunts.[81]

There were therefore many roles for great lords to play; but minister of God was one of those roles, and it was becoming increasingly important to the princes in the later tenth century. Lothar and Adalbero were partly responsible for this development, for their cultivation of royal insignia and ceremonial required rival magnates to compete with the king on his own terms. For example, in 980, at a time when his coronation was as yet inconceivable, Hugh Capet matched Lothar's translation of Theoderic four years earlier by reforming the monasteries of Saint-Valéry and Saint-Riquer and then personally presiding over the translations of their patrons' relics from Flanders. An eyewitness later recalled the impressive scene as the duke dismounted from his horse, removed his shoes to receive the casket containing the relics of Richarius, and then, lifting the reliquary onto his shoulders, began the barefoot journey back to the monastery.[82] It was an act of piety, to be sure, but piety with an obvious political intent; for Hugh had beaten the king at his own game, and decisively. Lothar, after all, had only set his hand on Theoderic's coffin, and he had not been responsible for reforming the saint's monastery. But Hugh did reform Saint-Valéry and Saint-Riquier; and in a display of the humility true princes were supposed to show, he removed the insignia of his office and received the saint as a simple Christian. Hugh's translation even had its own miracle, though it was probably added later: the horses of Hugh's knights had so trampled the fields where the ceremony took place that the crops were feared lost, but within only a few days the harvest came in even more bountiful than before. The message was clear: Lothar was not the only ruler whose reign could bring order and prosperity to his dominions.

The effort of clerical writers to sanctify princely authority might therefore coincide with the princes' own desires. This continued to be the case in the early eleventh century; for just as interest in the ceremonies and emblems of royal authority born in the late tenth century was reinforced by the new challenges of the early eleventh, so was the princes' interest in imitating them. As usual, the reasons depended on region and period; but beneath them all lay a single trend: the incipient, halting, but nonetheless relentless progress toward the concentration of authority in the hands of a few great princes. Not everywhere was such concentration achieved. The ambitions of Blois failed by reason of their very excess, those of Valois and Poitiers by a combination of bad luck and the spoiling policies of their neighbors.[83] But other counts did begin to forge coherent territorial principalities; and even those who ultimately failed tried. Successful or not, these rulers wanted to project an aura of special authority within their dominions just as much as their clerical apologists wanted them to.[84]

The convergence of interests was all the more complete where princely authority was also challenged by seigneurial power; for though the castellans' assumption of power was not always without the consent of their counts or to their disadvantage, it nonetheless required counts to rethink the nature of their own authority and to put lesser lords in their place. In these regions, the counts' requirements wholly dovetailed with the clergy's. Both found the contrast between sacred ministries and profane power useful. And both found ritual useful as a means to project the distinction.

One of the most common of these rites occurred upon a count's entry into a town, as he was greeted outside the gates by a crowd of townspeople and led into the town by a procession of monks and clerics bearing tapers and singing hymns of praise. Human nature being what it is, we can assume that many people turned out for no other reason than the excitement. But these entries also had a well-established typology more in keeping with the spirit of the age; for in greeting their lord with such ceremony, his people were said to welcome him as Christ had been welcomed to Jerusalem. The *adventus*, then, was yet another ritual designed to celebrate a lordship uniquely sanctioned by God; and if it was not more common than it had been in the early tenth century, it does appear to have been more frequently noted, one more sign of a time that took unusual interest in such matters. When the duke of Aquitaine came to Limoges in 1021, he was welcomed by the entire city and preceded by Gospel books and clouds of incense. The count of Angoulême entered his capital in much the same way in 1027, having been met a mile outside the gates. In both cases, the ceremony was said to be customary, as it was also in Flanders and probably many other parts of France.[85] Nor should we think that counts were merely the passive, disinterested recipients of such honors: Theobald of Blois ordered the monks of Saint-Père to grant him such a welcome as a test of their loyalty. He knew what the ceremony was supposed to mean; and he cared.[86]

Of all the celebrations of political renewal, the most important were those associated with the Peace of God. These assemblies were positively saturated with ritual. Relics were paraded. Kisses of peace were exchanged. Lords and knights took solemn oaths to observe the articles of the Peace, while curses were enjoined against those who would violate the oaths, and those who had violated them came forward to do public penance for their sins. The meetings were veritable carnivals of the pure; and like carnivals, the Peace assemblies were occasions for abolishing ordinary social divisions, as men and women, clergy and laity, lords and commoners joined to declare a common adherence to peace and order.[87] But presiding over it all were the impressive figures of bishops and counts, gathering together the relics of their monasteries, uniting to protect their people from the ravages of knights and castellans. For that was the ostensible purpose of the movement: to restrain the private wars through which the castellans built up their power; to shelter the poor from the abuses of the powerful.[88]

It has been too easy to exaggerate the bishops' leadership of this movement.[89] Certainly they were instrumental in its beginnings: no magnates are mentioned as leaders of some of the more important early councils, such as those of Charroux in 989 and Le Puy in 994.[90] But as E. I. Strubbe saw (and as Gerard of Cambrai did not), the bishops were not trying to use the Peace movement to usurp the responsibilities of kings and counts; rather they were trying (in Strubbe's words) to "supplement" their power.[91] Their ideal is once more best described as a "condominium"; but unlike the condominium of kings and magnates that informed Richer's writings, the partnership in the bishops' new order included all those rulers who held authority from God. Kings, bishops, counts, and, not least, abbots whose monasteries guarded the saints: bound together by a common source of authority, made conscious of their common identity by a common threat, these servants of God would unite to protect the weak and unarmed from the godless.

Whatever their role in the earliest councils, kings and counts were not slow to recognize its benefits. Robert the Pious's interest in the movement has already been mentioned. Duke William V was even more closely involved in the Aquitainian councils.[92] But it is in the principalities north of Paris that the essential conservatism of the movement is most obvious. Here the Peace clearly represented an effort to restore the old Carolingian ideal of political order, as counts and bishops together, aided by the prayers and relics of the monasteries, were seen to provide for their people. At Amiens in the early 1030s, the people gathered under the bishop and count and in the presence of relics from the cathedral swore a pact of peace. There can be no question here of any ecclesiastical usurpation of comital prerogatives: the county and the diocese had long been held within the same family, and counts and bishops consistently supported each other in a common effort to erode the privileges of the nearby monastery of Corbie, whose exemption from episcopal authority and immunity to comital jurisdiction annoyed both bishop and count. This partnership and policy were still active at the time of the Peace, for the bishop of Amiens was actually the count's uncle (and would be succeeded by the count's son).[93] And the purpose of the Peace they initiated was not only to end the feuds and famine that then plagued the region but, more important, to reassert the two rulers' joint supremacy over the territory ruled by Corbie. For instance, one article of this Peace—indeed, the only stipulation thought important enough to be specifically mentioned by our source—required all disputants, whether from Amiens or Corbie, to bring their grievances before the count and bishop together before initiating a feud. Thus count and bishop, sheltering behind an ideology of popular justice, sought to undermine Corbie's privileges.[94]

The counts of Flanders were equally clever in using the Peace. At Douai in 1023 or 1024, as part of his continuing effort to take control of the region, Baldwin IV consciously manipulated popular demands for a Peace by posturing as the people's protector who would fight for their interests against the obstructionism of the bishop of Cambrai.[95] The Peace Baldwin sponsored a few years later at Audenaarde was even more forthrightly a comital initiative. The count himself called the assembly, his purpose being to project an image of stability after a rebellion by his son. He also summoned the relics on which the nobles swore their oaths. Since these relics were taken from the principal comital foundations of his dominions, the assembly of saints must have looked not a little like a gathering of the count's supernatural patrons, called out like oathhelpers to show his favor in heaven.[96] Baldwin's son continued his father's interest in the movement by acting jointly with the bishop of Thérouanne to reaffirm the Peace.[97] Thereafter the Peace was periodically reaffirmed for the rest of the century, usually at the counts' initiative, and always in their or their ministers' vigilant presence.[98]

Significantly, these pacts, like most of those in northern France, assumed a clear distinction between comital authority and seigneurial power, since they tried to curb the abuses only of castellans and knights. When the pacts of Douai and Thérouanne prohibited assaults on men and women and the seizure of towns and villages, they were addressing the crimes of *potentes*, not those of peasants and counts. Only *potentes* made the kind of raids on horseback condemned by both pacts; and only they were regularly denounced in legal sources for using their power to extort wealth from merchants and clerics by threatening them with arrest.[99] It was the same with the royal peace declared at Verdun between 1019 and 1021 and with that sworn in 1023 under the aegis of the bishop of Beauvais. The oaths targeted those who violated the sanctuary of churches or seized the livestock of other lords' peasants or burned houses or destroyed mills—the same crimes of which churchmen accused lords in court cases.[100] The Peace of God aimed at restraining the newfound power of lords and knights, not the authority of rulers. In fact, kings and counts were the only individuals exempted from the stipulations of the Peace, since they alone were allowed to gather armies during the period covered by its special truce.[101] Marked with a special status as protectors of the church and the Christian people, king and count were also protectors of the Peace and therefore exempt from its most stringent requirements.

Translations of saints, joyous entries, proclamations of peace, solemn trials of heretics: in our past obsession with "feudal anarchy" it has been easy to overlook the princes' use of such ceremonies to highlight the singularity of their authority. But in fact they did use them, and all the more emphatically as that authority was newly challenged by a kind of untrammeled power. Of course, ceremonial alone could not create a strong authority where there was no independent basis for it. No eleventh-century prince, for example, staked more on ceremonial than William V of Aquitaine; yet his power over his castellans steadily disintegrated in the face of Angevin intrigues.[102] But if ceremonies could not create authority, they could still represent an ideal political order, one in which princes and prelates together ruled in God's name, protected by the saints so that they might protect the churches and the faithful.

5 Toward an Iconic Kingship

Beginning in the late 960s, the West Frankish king and his archbishop of Reims undertook to rehabilitate the dignity of the throne. For Lothar, little more was sought than to increase his authority; but Adalbero's goal was a complete transformation of the polity in which the rivalry between king and magnates would be replaced by a partnership. Though their aims thus differed and though these differences ultimately destroyed their alliance, yet both men understood that the rehabilitation of royal dignity required a greater emphasis on rituals and emblems—either rituals and emblems of authority, as for Lothar, or rituals and emblems of consensus, as for Adalbero.

Almost immediately the princes responded in kind by accentuating their own quasi-regal authority. Sometimes they acted out of rivalry with the king, as when Hugh Capet translated Richarius and Valerius in 981; sometimes they sought to further the consolidation of their authority within their own territories, as in the counts of Poitou's rites of *adventus*. But what allowed this impulse to endure was the need to redefine comital authority in relation to the power of castellans. This need was just as strong among the leaders of the church. Indeed it was stronger, because their lands and rights were most exposed to the incursions of the *seigneurs banaux*. As a result, they once more placed their considerable talent for ritual at the disposal of the counts, leading to a significant increase in princely ceremonial between the 990s and the early 1030s.

Formal entries and Peace assemblies were among the most important of these rituals; but equally important was supplication, especially in the counties of northern France. The prominence and conscious articulation of its formulas has already been made clear in the case of the Vermandois. Already present in the first comital charters in the late tenth century, their use continued well into the twelfth.[1] Such conservatism did not result from unthinking adherence to tradition. It was really a matter of regenerating a tradition, as the formulas became more important in projecting a correct image of comital authority than ever before. They were especially important to new rulers. In Ponthieu, for example, when the castellans of Abbéville became counts in the 1020s, their new status was signaled by the use of petitionary formulas in their charters. The more secure their title, the more lavish their formulas.[2]

Normandy provides an even clearer example. Though the counts had long exercised power around Rouen, it was only in the late tenth century, under Richard I (942–996) and Richard II (996–1026), that they managed to extend their authority over the entire Seine basin. With greater power and prestige came a greater attention to emblems of authority, like the title *dux Normannorum*, first attested in 1006 under Richard II.[3] An even more crucial emblem of authority was the princely charter. Its symbolic meaning is often overlooked because we tend to regard it as only a utilitarian record. Requesting such a solemn act, however, required not so much literacy or a need for records as a willingness and desire to exalt a prince according to the model of Carolingian rulership. Hence there are no charters from Rollo or William Longsword, but two from Richard I (one of them highly suspect) and twenty-three from Richard II. A difference this great is unlikely to represent the random survival of sources. It makes much more sense to see it as the sign of a profound shift in the idea of authority, particularly because with the very first charters come the traditional liturgical formulas of supplication, the emblem of God-given ministry.[4]

Eleanor Searle believes that one should not exaggerate the importance of such Frankish usages to the Normans themselves. Given the life she has restored to Norman history, her interpretation must be taken seriously. A leader like Richard I was still a Scandinavian chieftain, sent away in his youth to learn

Norse and at his death buried in a mound overlooking the sea.[5]
Yet against this we must also set the fact that his son, Richard
II, while fully maintaining his ties with the Viking world, also
cultivated the image of a great Frankish prince, and did so with
a skill and consistency that speak of conscious intent. He undertook the reform of numerous Norman monasteries according
to the latest fashion by giving them to William of Dijon and his
disciples.[6] He also liked to pose as something of an international
grand homme, devoting himself to making peace between king
and magnates, initiating action against heretics in the king's
own domains, and making donations to great Frankish monasteries such as Saint-Bénigne and Marmoutier—even to monasteries as far afield as Mount Zion in the Holy Land.[7] Yet nowhere is Richard's concern with image more unmistakable than
in his and his father's commission to a Frank for a history of
their ancestors—a history, we shall see, which is nothing but a
celebration of the family's divinely predestined lordship. By the
time of Richard's death, the dynasty was well on the way toward achieving that special status attained in the reign of William the Conqueror, who alone of all princes was feted with his
own *laudes*, the litany that proclaimed a ruler the figure of
Christ the Lord.[8]

One clue to explaining this janus-faced rule comes from
Searle, herself, who argues that the Normans' continuing commitment to Nordic values reflected their need to present a
united front against an enveloping, often hostile Frankish
world. From this perspective, the usefulness of the counts of
Rouen, both to their Norman followers and to the Frankish peoples on their borders, derived from their power and standing in
both societies. To fulfill that role they had to be bilingual, in
culture as in language. To the Normans paramount chieftains
who could rival the great Frankish princes; to the Franks rulers
who knew the Scandinavian world and who could tame the excesses of a people still largely raiders: the counts of Rouen had
to be both chieftain and prince. They even married in both
worlds, taking Frankish wives for external political alliances,
Norman wives for internal.[9] Richard II's cultivation of Frankish
expressions of authority did therefore mean something, both for
Normans and for Franks. His diplomas, reforms, and donations
and his interference in Frankish political affairs—all challenged

the Franks to take him seriously, and by extension his people also. It is therefore all the more significant that so many of his early charters with their sonorous liturgical language were issued for Frankish monasteries, which means written by Frankish monasteries.[10] It was the Franks' recognition that Richard wanted even more than that of his own people. But this came as well. In a highly unusual charter (one for which the original still exists) a woman named Enna recorded her efforts to gain Richard's approval for a donation to Saint-Ouen: "I came to the presence of my lord Richard, illustrious count, . . . whom I long entreated in supplication to fulfill my desire." There is nothing formulaic about the phrasing. It describes the way Enna actually approached Richard. Another Norman charter, this one for Mont-Saint-Michel and again of undoubted validity, also incorporated petitionary formulas. In fact, its petition is so quaintly archaic (addressing the count as *almitas*, for instance) that it suggests the novelty of the formulas in Normandy, as if the scribe were not familiar with contemporary usages and took his model from an old formulary. What he was certain of was the unique authority of his ruler. Richard was *princeps et marchio totius Neustrie provinciae*, and as *princeps* responsible "for the observance of holy religion and the *stabilitas* of the people entrusted to us by God."[11] It is as succinct an expression as one could desire of the emblematic position of those who, ruling with God, were beseeched like God.

Equally instructive is the case of Flanders. No tenth-century count was more powerful than Arnulf of Flanders (918–65). Aggressive and ruthless, he transformed the lands he had inherited from his father into one of the largest and wealthiest principalities in Francia; and he ruled them with an iron hand.[12] More than most tenth-century counts, Arnulf took his success as the sign of a special relationship with God, and he took great care both to protect that relationship and to publicize it. He surrounded himself with relics, led in their translations, and reformed the monasteries of his territories, in essence purifying and fortifying them that they might strengthen his own power.[13] It was he who compared himself to Judas Maccabeus, because he had rebuilt the monastery of Sint-Pieters of Ghent as Judas had rebuilt the Temple of Jerusalem.[14] Clearly Arnulf had been graced by God, and his charters proclaim the fact. Yet oddly, these same charters never use formulas of petition. Instead, they present fiats, as if to present an image of a count who acts entirely by his own authority, the prime mover, as it were, of the political and religious world.[15]

Arnulf left no son, and the succession to Flanders quickly degenerated into a free-for-all. Only with his grandson and great-grandson, Baldwin IV (988–1035) and Baldwin V (1035–67), did the civil wars end and the reconstruction of comital authority commence.[16] But much had changed in the intervening decades. In particular, the advocates of churches had become much more powerful. Baldwin V spent the better part of his reign bringing them under control. He could not abolish their powers; but whenever a church brought a dispute with an advocate before him, he seized the occasion to limit the advocate's powers by regulating his rights over the church.[17] When there was no advocate, he assumed such responsibilities himself.[18] Baldwin and his son also distracted their nobility by leading them in frequent campaigns into imperial territory, a time-honored ploy of government that also strengthened the bonds between the counts and their *fideles*.[19]

Finally, both counts paid a great deal of attention to ceremonial. It was, for example, Baldwin IV who summoned the first great Peace councils in Flanders and the territories he was trying to annex—at Douai in 1024 and at Audenaarde in 1030. Here, as we have already described, the count appeared both as protector of his people and as God's protected, surrounded as he was at Audenaarde by an army of saints.[20] His son's Peace councils were even more striking, since the sources that describe them explicitly represent the count as the legitimate defender of townspeople and churches and the enemy of his nobility's feuds.[21]

These counts used the Peace movement to project the uniqueness of their authority. It was a kind of monarchical authority, insofar as the counts, like the kings, had a special calling to protect the people and churches and to suppress the injustices of the powerful. Indeed, in the time of the two Baldwins Flanders came to be referred to as a *monarchia*.[22] The reason was not any rivalry with the king, since in this period king and counts were for the most part allied with each other. Rather, the word called attention to the singular status of the count within Flanders, and in particular to the qualitative difference between an authority legitimated by God and the raw power of castellans and advocates.[23]

For exactly the same reason, Baldwin V began to use petitionary formulas in his charters. Thereafter all Flemish counts did so. Whereas Arnulf had not used them at all, Baldwin and his successors used them consistently.[24] Like their entries, their Peace councils, their public association with relics, and the description of their county as a "monarchy," the formulas defined comital authority as a sacred ministry. The count was beseeched as God was beseeched, because only the count was God's ruler, protected by His saints in order to protect His people and His churches.

Supplication and the New History

What we are trying to document is a change of perception among the ruling elite of early eleventh-century northern France so profound that it can be considered a basic "cause" of historical events, like political strategy, economic necessity, and demographic growth: the renewed conviction that the traditional distribution of political authority was God-given, and therefore to be preserved at all costs. The petitionary language of comital charters was especially well suited to convey this program, since supplication was essentially the recognition of a ruler's divine office. Yet interpreting the use of this language in charters and diplomas still requires a good deal of conjecture. Even though the pattern seems plausible, and even though it is entirely consonant with the cultivation of other princely rites, one would still like corroboration. One needs what ethnographers call an "informant," a guide to a culture's discourse who can say, "Yes, this language is meaningful."

Although we do not have informants, we do have sources that provide a measure of contemporary perspective. Narrative sources are especially helpful, because they fix the events they describe in a particular context and allow us to discern the motivations of both actors and authors. The memorandum in which Gerbert recounted the events of the council of Saint-Basle, for example, clearly demonstrates the importance he attributed to supplication as a demonstration of political authority, since his description of the event culminates in three prostrate entreaties: Arnulf's confession to the bishops; his later confession to the kings; and the bishop of Orléans's intercession with the kings on his behalf. Coming as they did at the end of the resistance to Hugh's and Robert's coronations, aimed as they were against Otto III's pope and bishops, these prostrations signaled the kings' final victory and proclaimed the bishops' resolve to stand by their kings.[25]

But as we have seen repeatedly, kings and bishops were not the only ones who knew the value of the ceremony. So did counts. In 996, in the course of his campaign to wrest Tours from the counts of Blois, Fulk Nerra of Anjou violated the sanctuary of Saint-Martin by leading his army into the cloister in pursuit of his enemies and ordering some of the canons' fortified houses torn down. In retaliation for the atrocity, the canons set their relics and crucifix on the ground and surrounded them with thorns, then locked the doors of the church so that no one but pilgrims might enter (pilgrims being excepted in part because they could carry news of their grievances abroad). It did not take long for Fulk to make amends. "Penitent for his deed and seeking mercy," he entered the cloister and removed his shoes. Upon entering the church he and his men prostrated themselves, and Fulk gave a pledge to Saint Martin by the hand of the bishop of Angers that he would never commit such an act again. Then he prostrated himself twice more, first before the bodies of the saints and finally before the crucifix.

It is an impressive enough admission of wrong on the face of it; but it is also an impressive demonstration of the multifaceted nature of ritual. The count had acknowledged his wrong; but he had still accomplished his purpose, arresting his enemies and destroying the strongholds where they might hold out in the future. He had also made his peace with Martin and the canons, assuring their support in his continuing struggle with Blois for control of the city. Nor was Fulk's humiliation utterly abject; far from it, his penance seems uncannily like the archetypal penance of Theodosius, also imposed for an act of violence within a sanctuary. This was the kind of imperial humiliation that exalted.[26]

Even more illuminating than the brief memoranda and notices that contain these stories are the many histories written
during the period. Indeed, the writing of history can be taken as
yet another sign of the passion for order that informed the reign
of Robert the Pious. This was the time of Richer and Dudo of
Saint-Quentin, of the *Gesta episcoporum Cameracensium* and
Aimo of Fleury's *History of the Franks*, of Ademar of Chabannes and Raoul Glaber,[27] to mention only a few of the more
prominent examples. These histories were nothing like the
works of earlier writers, such as Flodoard and Prudentius of
Troyes. Whatever their merits, Flodoard and Prudentius were
largely annalists who chronicled their ages without explaining
them. The new historians, in contrast, forthrightly set out to
make sense of the world and of the actions of individuals. Their
points of departure differed, of course; but all shared the belief
that there was a pattern and a purpose to things—in short, that
there was (or should be) an order to events.[28]

Thus Richer's history celebrates the virtues of fidelity and
consensus, demonstrating that unless both kings and princes
are faithful to and respectful of each other, there can be no hope
for peace. The *Gesta episcoporum Cameracensium* is also a
paean to peace, or rather a defense of the idea that maintaining
peace is the special responsibility of kings and bishops, God's
chosen agents on earth. As for Raoul Glaber's chronicle, it
is squarely anchored, so to speak, in a world of quaternities
that harmonizes cosmic diversity through an elegant ordering
of typologically interrelated emblems hierarchically arranged
in groupings of four.[29] The writers take different paths to the
same goal: to understand history as a revelation of a consistent
theme, to see it as inherently ordered.

Supplication was the natural expression of this order. Flodoard had denied it a prominent place among the political rituals he described, because in his world political relations were
structured as bilateral pacts. But in the late tenth and early eleventh centuries, supplication returned to histories as a means of
expressing the symmetry between heaven and earth. Thus
Richer's account of the council of Saint-Basle, like that of Gerbert which was his source, culminates in the three prostrations,
with one substantial revision. Gerbert had discussed at length

the kings' intrusion into the council and made quite clear the bishops' consternation at their interference. Richer omits the entire episode. In his account, the kings thank the bishops for their efforts, ask to hear an accounting of the trial, and declare (*asseverant*: they do not request) that the time has come to pronounce judgment. The bishops immediately tell Arnulf to prostrate himself before the kings and confess to them, and Arnulf does so without hesitation. In other words, Richer removed all the politics that showed the weakness of the polity and replaced them with an image of smooth cooperation between kings and bishops.[30]

Other historians of the period also emphasized the ritual whenever they wanted to depict a stable polity, harmonious when lords and followers recognized their respective places. Raoul Glaber, for example, recounted the prostrate supplication of Crescentius to Otto III, and told of Henry I's vow to resist the rebellion of Odo II of Blois until the count "submitted to him on bended knee and appeared obedient to his command."[31] We have already noted the importance Gerard of Cambrai attached to ritual supplication, portraying God as a lord in whose hall petitioners beg for grace and accepting the prostrate supplication of his humbled castellan in the presence of imperial legates.[32] In narrating the story of Queen Constance's rebellion against her husband, Andrew of Fleury imagined her prostrate and tearful before receiving her husband's "kind assent to her petitions."[33]

Of all the histories from this period, two merit special consideration: Dudo of Saint-Quentin's history of the dukes of Normandy and Helgald of Fleury's *Life of Robert the Pious*. Their importance for the themes discussed here cannot be overemphasized. In both we see the search for order that typified the reign of Robert the Pious; and both exalt one particular kind of political authority, that graced by God, as the key to achieving this order. Most important of all, both authors saw supplication as a crucial expression of the order. Indeed, in their hands supplication not only became an expression of order. It became its single most important ritual, an emblem of the unity of heavenly and earthly lordship and of the moral code that maintained justice.

Dudo of Saint-Quentin and the Ethos
of Good Lordship

Dudo of Saint-Quentin's *De moribus et actis primorum Normanniae ducum* has long been recognized as one of the more remarkable works of the eleventh century, but more for its vices than its virtues.[34] As Eleanor Searle remarked, Dudo has "a small reputation, all of it evil."[35] According to one recent historian, for example (and he is only stating the consensus), the *De moribus* is a wretched work, "thoroughly untrustworthy," "bombastic and rhetorical," "tedious," "little more than a curiosity."[36] It is certainly some of these things: untrustworthy as to facts and highly rhetorical. But it is not tedious, and it is much more than a curiosity. It is, in fact, a coherent political tract which presents an ideal of good lordship in order to attack the failings of the rulers of northern France, Carolingians and Capetians alike.

Dudo was dean of the chapter of Saint-Quentin in the Vermandois. In 987, while he was still only a canon, the count of Vermandois had sent him to Normandy to request the duke's mediation with Hugh Capet, whose recent coronation the count had refused to recognize. Dudo was so well received by Duke Richard I that he stayed for some time and returned to Richard's court for a longer stay some years later. During this second visit (994) Richard asked him to write a history of his family. Dudo undertook the project, although he did not complete it until around 1015, some nineteen years after Richard's death (996).[37]

The meaning of Dudo's history has long been a subject of debate. The best interpretation to date has been Searle's, who has seen the *De moribus* as the Normans' "victory song." From this perspective it appears rather like a clerical "dressing-up" of the stories Dudo heard from the well-placed members of the ducal family who were his sources for much of what he wrote; and certainly many of the *De moribus*'s fine anecdotes, fictitious or not, have the character of saga tales, well honed from long telling. But Searle has also argued that Dudo's history is more than a collection of good stories. It is, in her view, an epic tale of the way one family of chieftains, through perseverance, virtue, and good marriages, forged a single *gens Normannorum* out of competing Norman chieftaincies. It is a celebration especially of

Dudo's second patron, Richard II, in whose time political and religious unity was finally achieved.[38]

It does not detract from the the value of Searle's thesis to say that there must be still more to Dudo's vision. In particular, her interpretation fits the last part of the work better than the first. It has long been recognized that this early section of the history—up to the death of Richard I—constitutes a kind of narrative paean to ducal rule, a demonstration that those who had once been pagans had quickly become not only Christians but also the epitome of Christian lords.[39] At the same time Dudo was concerned to explain the Carolingian kings' steady decline. Perhaps the finality of that decline was not entirely understood at the time of Hugh Capet's accession. This is still a matter debated by historians. Nevertheless, by the time Dudo began to write his history Hugh and his son had long since rid themselves of the last major rival from the old dynasty and ruled securely, if not gloriously. If in 987 no one had intended to inaugurate a new dynasty, by 1015, when Dudo had completed his work, the possibility that Hugh's descendants would hold the throne was very real indeed. Not surprisingly, then, Hugh the Great, Hugh Capet's father, looms large in Dudo's history.

Yet Dudo is strangely ambivalent about his kings and their ancestor. He does emphasize the important role played by Hugh Capet's grandfather in converting the Normans to Christianity; yet he says little about Hugh's own accession, recording only that Lothar (sic) died and that Hugh was enthroned. It is hardly a celebratory remark. About Hugh's subsequent reign he says next to nothing. Nor does he portray Hugh's father, Hugh the Great, in a very positive light. Indeed, Dudo presents him on one notable occasion as a conniver who thought nothing of breaking his word when it suited his interests.[40] From Dudo's treatment of Hugh we might learn much about the qualities that impelled his family to the kingship; but those qualities would not include excellence, piety, or any other royal virtue.

This studied aloofness from the Capetians may simply represent a sop to his Norman patrons' pride; yet Dudo's attitude is puzzling when one remembers that when he wrote, and indeed throughout most of the tenth and early eleventh centuries, the Norman counts were consistent supporters of the Robertians. Perhaps the best explanation for his ambivalence is that Dudo and his circle had been staunch supporters of the last Carolingians. His count, Albert of Vermandois, was married to Lothar's half sister, and Lothar had named Albert's elder brother count of the palace.[41] When Albert at first refused to acknowledge Hugh Capet's coronation, Hugh immediately prepared to attack Albert's lands. It was at this time that Albert sent Dudo to Richard I of Normandy, to request him to use his influence with the king to make peace. The legation evidently succeeded, for we hear no more about a revolt of the Vermandois, neither under Albert, who soon died, nor under his son and successor, Herbert. Yet that does not mean that the counts had come around to supporting the new kings; far from it. After Charles of Lorraine, asserting his right to the throne, had taken Laon from Hugh, he received food from the Vermandois. The Vermandois was therefore one of the principal regions that Hugh ravaged in an attempt to weaken Charles's resistance.[42] Furthermore, Albert of Vermandois's nephews, Herbert of Troyes and Odo of Blois, had consistently supported Lothar in his campaigns against the Ottonians. They just as consistently supported Charles's claims to the succession and aided Charles in his family's plots against the kings. Even after Charles had been captured and imprisoned, the pair continued to make trouble for the new dynasty.[43]

As for Dudo, his counts' politics surely dictated his Carolingian leanings; but Carolingian associations ran strong in his family in any case. Another Dudo (doubtless a close relative, since he also served as one of the count of Vermandois's vassals) is mentioned as a *fidelis* of Lothar. Later, during the struggle between Hugh and Charles, this Dudo entered Charles's household. It was in fact he who arranged the piece of treason that gave Charles possession of Reims.[44]

This tradition of support for the Carolingians coupled with his efforts to please his Norman patrons, makes Dudo's equivocal attitude toward the Capetians more understandable. Unfortunately, it also makes his constant disparagement of the last Carolingians even more puzzling. Perhaps this characteristic, too, is a reflection of his patrons' politics. Given their support of the Capetians, Dudo could not have voiced too much love for the old kings. It would have been impolitic, to say nothing of being dangerous for his career. It would also have been pointless. By the time Dudo wrote, the old dynasty's demise must have seemed quite final. Nothing would have been gained by an attempt to rehabilitate its memory. Dudo could not remain loyal to the Carolingians. All he could do was to make a sincere effort to come to terms with their failure—in other words, to explain it and, if possible, justify it, as a meet sentence of God.[45]

As for the nominal subjects of his history, the dukes of Normandy, it is impossible to penetrate Dudo's real feelings about them. He certainly presented them in the best of lights; but one suspects that he regarded the Normans a little like Tacitus regarded the Germans: he glorified his subjects primarily to shame the true Frankish families who had lost their virtues. And here, perhaps, is another clue to his mind. Dudo clearly saw the Franks as an exhausted race. "Consumed by war, a defeated people," the Franks were "almost effeminate."[46] The fault was in their leadership, since the Frankish princes were motivated solely by "envy and hatred."[47] Yet despising what the Franks had become only caused Dudo to love all the more what they had once represented. This is what shaped his vision in the *De moribus.* A Carolingian exile in a land of pirates, Dudo would perform a *mission civilisatrice.* Unable to be loyal to the Carolingians, Dudo could still remain loyal to the ideals he associated with their rule. From the old culture he could try to preserve what he thought commanded respect. He would salvage what was best in Frankish culture and pass it on to a young and still vibrant people, that they might succeed where his own had failed.

For Dudo, what most deserved preservation were the virtues of good lordship. The Carolingians, and Louis d'Outremer especially, do not show them. Duke Richard does. And with his usual florid excess (the translation is an improvement on the original), Dudo outdoes even his Carolingian models in his litany of Richard's royal virtues.

> He was . . . the strength of the weak, a defender of orphans, a solace to the wretched, a support to the bereaved, a restorer of churches, a pure light to the blind, the crown of clerics, a refuge for the needy, the splendor of prelates, a refuge for widows, the epitome of priests, a lover of peace, a promoter of virtues, the greatest hope of all: to the bereaved, duty itself, a sure pledge in friendship, a support for the desperate, a protector of priests, the seat of laws, the rector of peo-

ples, a pastor of the poor, an epitome of honesty, the arms of the soldiers, a judge between accusers and accused, even-handed in disputes, a soother of quarrels, a father to exiles, a haven to fugitives, a distributor of largesse . . . an example for all, a scourge of thieves, the ruin of robbers, a corrector of those who confess their faults, a worker of pious works . . . , the light of all, a figure of sanctity, gentle chief of consuls, aid of the king, protector of all peoples.[48]

Richard exhibited all the qualities of the good lord, and all France recognized his excellence. After Hugh the Great's death, says Dudo with a medieval canon's typical disregard of facts, Richard took first place in the kingdom:

> And all willingly subjected themselves to his service, and served him freely as their lord. . . . They loved him with all their heart and served him with the highest cult of reverence. Humbly they obeyed his orders and edicts, and obediently they followed his commands. And he ruled them with consideration, as a paterfamilias would his servants, and he cared for them most kindly, as a father would his sons.[49]

This is the proper relationship between a lord and his followers: the lord rules with paternal authority, but also with kindness and consideration; and so he is served with humility and love. It is of course nothing other than a description of the ideal of lordship expressed in supplication. Dudo was fairly obsessed by the ritual, as we can see first of all in a charter he wrote in behalf of Richard II of Normandy in 1015, probably shortly after he had presented the duke with the first text of his history.[50]

> Dudo, canon of the precious martyr of Christ, Quentin, and our beloved and deserving *fidelis*, came to me, who am called Richard, son of the most happy Count Richard, by the grace of the highest and indivisible Triune God duke and *patritius* of the Normans, although unworthy, beseeching in varied and frequent supplications, both through himself and through Count Rodulf, my uncle, that I might concede to the precious martyr of Christ, Quentin, for the release of my soul and that of my father, the churches which my aforesaid father gave to him in benefice. To these most humble petitions and most devout requests I offer and confer my consent, and so I concede the same churches to the aforesaid martyr Quentin.[51]

This is one of the most mannered instances of petitionary formulas applied to a lord other than a king. Knowing that, we
might be tempted to accuse Dudo of shameless flattery; but
much more is involved here than the incontinent use of a hallowed formula. For Dudo, supplication was a concentrated symbol of good lordship, an emblem of the "good faith" that maintained peace.[52] That is why he dwelt on the formula in this
diploma; and that is why he used supplication as the ritual leit-
motif of his *moralia*. It is introduced early in the history, in an
incident which has rightly become the most famous of all the
work's anecdotes. The Normans, as Dudo first presents them to
us, are pagans and pirates. They have no conception of proper
etiquette before a king, though—again like Tacitus's Germans—they do possess a certain brutal charm; and their rude
naiveté gives them the ability to reduce appearances to their
true significance. Their first duke, for example, refused all gestures of subjection to the Carolingian king. The armies of the
Norman Rollo and King Charles met to formalize the treaty by
which Rollo would be ceded extensive lands in return for his
recognition of Charles's suzerainty. As a demonstration of his
submission Charles demanded that Rollo kiss his foot. Rollo
indignantly refused, saying that he would never bend his knee
before any man. A compromise was finally worked out: Rollo
would perform the *proskynesis* by proxy, permitting one of his
men to kiss the king's foot. A follower duly stepped forward,
bent down, and lifted Charles's foot into the air, sending the
king onto his back. *Then* he kissed the foot, as the Normans
(and Dudo) reveled in the king's indignity.[53]

It is not too farfetched to believe that Dudo begins with the
Normans in an eleventh-century version of the state of nature.
The topos had been common among ninth-century authors
whose ideas Dudo frequently echoes.[54] In the 1020s it was reca-
pitulated by the author of the *Gesta episcoporum Cameracensium*, written in an area near where Dudo's family had lands
and, later, a great deal of political power.[55] Moreover, what is
distinctive about all these treatments of the state of nature is
their argument that before entering into social bonds, all men
were equal, without lords and without subjection. This is exactly the way Dudo described the early Normans. When Rollo's
men were asked the name of their lord, for example, they replied that they had no lord "because we are all equal."[56]

The story about Rollo and Charles is therefore more than a good tale. Because for Dudo prostration was the correct way to manifest subjection to a lord, it is also Dudo's way of describing the egalitarian virtues of the pagan Normans. But the Normans left the state of nature when, as part of their settlement with Charles, they ceased to be pagans; and along with Christianity they accepted the supplicatory rituals and prayers of Christian lordship, with which Rollo had previously refused to honor Charles. When Rollo grew "old and worn out," his counts and princes gathered to decide what to do. They determined to ask Rollo to name a successor to govern them. They went to the duke, "and with mild words and submissive faces" begged him to care for the health of the kingdom (*regnum*) by naming a successor. The duke responded in kind: "Then Rollo, constrained by their most humble words," accepted their request and named his son, William, to succeed him. Significantly, Rollo's petitioners had addressed him by his baptismal name, Robert—a Christian name for a Christian ceremony appropriate to a Christian conception of lordship.[57]

Even more than his father, William ruled according to the accepted model of Carolingian authority; and again Dudo expressed that authority in terms of the humble petition. When the Bretons refused to acknowledge William's overlordship, for example, William crushed their rebellion and forced them to send legates to beg his forgiveness. They implored William's mercy in the same language one would have used to implore a king—or God.

> We served your father obediently, and we desire to serve you eagerly. Do not turn away from us, we implore you, do not abominate our service. . . . Blinded by depraved counsel, we have neglected the mandates of your authority [*imperii tui*]. Turn aside your wrath from your servants, and concede to us the happiness of peace. Bend down the merciful ear of your piety to us, slaves of scandal and offense. . . . We are sorry [*poenitet nos*] to have trespassed against you and to have deserted your service.

As a good lord, William was impressed by this "legation of obedience and visible humility," and offered mercy to the duke of the Bretons.[58]

The rebellion of the Bretons was understandable, since they had been subjected to a foreign chief. Far worse was the rebellion of a group of Normans led by one Riulf, who opposed both the increasing power of the dukes over the Normans and their conversion to Christianity. To Dudo this was treason, an inversion of right order; and to make the point absolutely clear, he made the rebels manifest their treason in an abuse of supplication and a perversion of supplicatory values. Riulf sent a legate to William to present their case and demand an extension of their lands—demanding, in other words, a separate state for those Normans who rejected William's suzerainty and his Christian ways. William was "amazed" at the "incredible presumption" of the legate's demands; yet he had only recently come to power, and there was little precedent in Norman custom for an inheritable primacy of the chieftaincy. William was forced to offer a compromise: he could not give the rebels the land they requested because the land did not pertain to him; but what he could properly give—usufruct of the land and of all that was on the land—he would give.

Although such a concession was already bad enough, William went further and offered Riulf a share in his power. For Dudo this weakening of the ducal "monarchy" was a violation of a fundamental principle of political authority. And just as legitimate authority was manifested through petitionary values, so its undermining was expressed as an inversion of those values. Those who should have been humble now lorded it over their ruler. The duke no longer ruled by his pleasure but only by the pleasure of his subjects. "I will place the counsel of my precepts in your mouth, and whatever you want I will fulfill by your order. Whomsoever you want me to crush, I will ruthlessly crush; whomsoever you want me to put aside, I will put aside completely. Him whom you will order me to exalt I will exalt; whom humiliate, I will humble utterly. This land will be ruled and dominated by your counsel. My very life shall be in your power."[59]

Riulf should have been content with this compromise, which gave him effective rule over his followers' lands. Even so much was an unjustifiable diminution of ducal authority. But Riulf was not satisfied. He continued his "presumption" and, indeed, only increased his "arrogance" and demanded still more, until he forced the young William to battle for his rights. Riulf's army was entirely destroyed (inevitably, *prostrati*) in that battle.[60]

The obvious moral: whoever tries to exalt himself beyond his station shall be humbled. Riulf's presumptuous claims represented an inversion of right order. For Dudo, his defeat reestablished that order.

Thereafter William was the undisputed master in Normandy and one of the great princes of the realm. Dudo even refers to him as one who "ruled the monarchy which he held," meaning that he was supreme in Normandy, but also implying that though he held Normandy of the king, he was no ordinary royal vassal.[61] After all, though Rollo may have commended himself to Charles, he had never actually performed a *proskynesis* to him. In fact, the Norman dukes usually did not even perform a real homage to the kings of France, but only an *hommage de paix*, which symbolized a pact of alliance between de facto equals.[62] It is not only by using the term "monarchy" that Dudo conveys his sense of William's special status, but also by recounting ritual moments in which William dealt with other kings almost as an equal. For example, according to Dudo, Otto I would negotiate with Louis d'Outremer only through William's mediation. At their first meeting Otto kissed William, a sign of special favor, then permitted the duke to sit in his presence. William deserved such favor because he exhibited all the qualities of a good lord. He was trusting—so trusting that he refused to accept the hostage that Otto I sent him as a pledge. And he ruled his "monarchy" according to the standards of a true Carolingian king. In William "sanctity and prudence shone. He ceaselessly sought equity and justice. He crushed the proud and malevolent rigorously, but exalted the humble and benevolent reverently."[63]

Reverence is crucial to Dudo's vision of the world, since it is the essence of the proper relationship between a good lord and a good follower, and therefore the essence of social harmony, a guarantee that vassals will be loyal to their lords because their lords have deserved their loyalty. Thus a lord should be served with "the cult of reverence"; but in turn, he must behave reverently toward his dependents. William clearly does so, accepting even treasonous petitions to him if they were made in the proper manner. The Carolingians, in contrast, do not reverence their subjects; and in fact Dudo reveals the dynasty's degeneracy precisely by showing their deceitful attitude toward supplicants. Nor is it the Frankish kings alone who have abandoned virtue. Corruption has infected the entire Frankish aristocracy, until not one knows how to act like a lord.

Dudo's most concentrated treatment of this theme comes in the aftermath of William Longsword's assassination, an event which itself reveals the extent of the moral decay among the rulers of the Frankish people; for the count of Flanders had dissembled his evil intent by proposing peace to William, and the duke, being "of such probity and gentleness," accepted the offer against the advice of others. He should have listened. Arnulf of Flanders met William on an island in the Somme with only a handful of retainers, "and he began to call to him, dissimulating and deceiving him with most humble words," going so far as to profess himself a supplicant of William: "To you," said the count, "I come suppliant." But when William was off guard, Arnulf drew the knife he had hidden in his shirt and killed the duke.[64]

It was Frankish treachery, and all the worse because Arnulf had manipulated the rituals of order and peace in order to deceive and murder; for not only had Arnulf presented himself to William as a suppliant; he had even kissed him as a sign of friendship. For Dudo, the violation of such rituals was a condensed symbol of moral depravity, as well as an explanation of the Franks' political degeneracy; for these rituals were nothing but statements of order. If one performed them with the intention to deceive, then the rituals were travestied, faith could no longer be counted on, and one could no longer depend on lords to protect or followers to serve. The result would be anarchy, just the sort of anarchy that Dudo felt had existed in the tenth century, when kings had ruled by expedients and princes had sought nothing but to extend their lands and power. Even Hugh the Great, father of Dudo's king, had broken a promise he had made to a suppliant vassal in order to gain control of Normandy, thinking nothing of violating the oath he had taken on relics.[65]

But it was far worse that not even the king kept faith. After William Longsword's assassination, Louis d'Outremer went to Rouen to impose his authority; but having received William's son, the young Duke Richard, Louis kept him in close confinement. The king who was supposed to protect his young ward instead turned into his captor. Only when the people of Rouen threatened to riot and kill him did Louis release Richard, his royal indignity accentuated by the fact that he had to act as a suppliant before the people, "beseeching their mercy with a voice of supplication" and begging for his life. "Behold me, your lord. Whatever you would have me do I will do. In supplication I implore you not to kill me."[66]

The king's abject petition echoes William's earlier speech to the Norman rebels, with one important difference. William's humiliation had been unjust, because Riulf and his followers were proud rebels against a good duke. They had therefore been duly "prostrated" in battle, and William exalted. Louis, in contrast, had been an unjust king who did not behave reverently toward his young ward. His humiliation had therefore been just—a true sign of his inner worth, Fulbert of Chartres might have said.[67] And even after the people of Rouen accepted the king's petition, not only sparing his life but even returning their duke into his care, Louis continued to show himself unworthy of his kingship by accepting a bribe from the count of Flanders to keep Richard in captivity once more. Significantly, the count's legates sought this favor from the king through a formal petition—one which the king did not grant "freely" but only, as it were, simoniacally, in return for ten pounds of the purest gold.[68]

As a minister of God the king possessed a holy office; and Louis's betrayal of that office was therefore a betrayal of God. For that reason, Dudo likened Louis's action to a "blasphemy."[69] As for the people of Rouen, they were "shocked" (*stupentes*) by the king's breach of faith, but in Dudo's history they showed no hesitation. Although their own lord was in captivity and the king had betrayed his ministry, they knew they could turn to the supreme Lord, the King of kings. And so they supplicated God's merciful intervention, their true supplication of the true Lord juxtaposed with the false and blasphemous supplications offered by Louis to them and by the count of Flanders to Louis.

> The people of Rouen, shocked by the changed attitude of the evil king [*malefici regis*], sought the aid of counsel from God in supplication. They therefore sent word to every church in the region of Normandy and Brittany so that priests might celebrate together in devo-

tion for him [Richard]; so that clerics might send up psalms; and so
that the people, barefoot and dressed only in sackcloth, might fast.
The prelates of the Normans and Bretons, hearing the news of this
sad legation, decreed to the people three days of fasting in one
month; and joining prayers and giving alms to the poor in supplication, they beseeched the Lord God that he might return to them
Richard, the boy so desired. Monks and canons sang psalms for him
in supplication; and the people, showing their devotion, sent up imploring sighs and groans.[70]

Addressed by his devoted and reverent people, both directly
and through his bishops, priests, and monks, God worked to
obtain Richard's freedom. Louis tried to maintain some control
over affairs; but his efforts only accentuated his lack of faith, as
he went so far as to offer Hugh the Great control over Normandy itself (an offer, incidentally, which the Frankish duke
duplicitously accepted in violation of earlier promises). The
king was finally brought to battle before a combined army of
Normans and Danes; and when his army was defeated ("prostrated," yet again), Louis was forced to flee, wandering alone
until seized by a simple knight, who led him back to Rouen.[71]
Yet so unlordly had Louis become that he could not even accept
his disgrace with dignity. Fitting end for an unfit king, he groveled before the knight in a final effort to regain his freedom,
even going so far as to attribute the lordly virtues of "mercy"
and "piety" to his captor.

> "Have mercy, I beseech you, have mercy on me, and through your
> piety release me from the hands of those who seek my soul and who
> would betray me. . . . All faculty and honor which would be mine
> will be yours also. I will make you king over me if you so desire. . . ."
> And beseeching the knight in this fashion, the anxious king, implor-
> ing him with tears, fell from his horse to the feet of the one who led
> him.

The role inversion is complete when Dudo ascribes a lordly response to the knight: "moved by the doleful spirit and groans of
the king and constrained [*coactus*] by so many petitions," he
consented to take him to his haven at Laon.[72]

"I will make you king over me if you so desire." Jonas of
Orléans had been right: a king who does not behave humbly, as
a minister of God, shall be humbled in turn. Writing in the
early eleventh century, Dudo knew that Louis's dynasty had

indeed been cast down, replaced on the throne by Hugh the Great's sons. As for young Richard, although momentarily humbled by an unholy king, he finally achieved the exalted status merited by a good lord. He rose to achieve the first place in the kingdom, served by all "in the highest cult of reverence" and "obeyed humbly" by them. In turn, "he ruled them mildly, as the head of a household does his servants, and nourished them sweetly with the food of kindness, as does a father his sons."[73] The right order was ultimately vindicated, an order whose essence was captured in the act of supplication, an act which required humility not only from those who served but also from those who ruled.

Royal Supplication as an Imitation of Christ

If Dudo's application of supplication to history was more thoroughgoing than other historians' of the period, it was perhaps because his sense of crisis was unusually strong. He was one of those individuals who by chance find themselves placed at the crossroads of major cultural transitions. Carolingian by upbringing and alliance, he found himself governed by his kings' enemies. A man whose Lotharingian affinities made him receptive to imperial attitudes toward authority, he found his ambitions tied to a people whom Franks had long regarded as pirates.[74] Like many writers of great vision, he was driven to understand the world, and the source of that drive was his sense of being "betwixt and between." He could stand back from his society and see it as a whole because he was not really part of it.

In all these respects Dudo was remarkably like two other writers of the same period: his friend and mentor, Adalbero, bishop of Laon, and Gerard, bishop of Cambrai.[75] Lotharingians by birth and imperial men by appointment and personal sympathy, both men held episcopacies in Francia and served Frankish kings. Like Dudo, Adalbero had been loyal to the last Carolingians but died under the Capetians, whom he even conspired to overthrow.[76] As for Gerard, he had been appointed to the see of Cambrai by Henry II and felt secure there as long as he had that emperor's support; but Henry's successor began to distance himself from the bishop, leaving Gerard to fend for

himself when the count of Flanders began to undermine episcopal authority in the city.[77] Neither man, then, ever felt entirely
at home in his new environment; nor was there much sympathy between them and their Frankish colleagues. And both reacted, as had Dudo, by writing or commissioning major tracts notable for the passion with which the values of the old order
were upheld.[78]

Dudo's conservatism was therefore much more than a personal idiosyncrasy. It represented one of the strongest currents
in the intellectual life of early eleventh-century Francia, the last
contribution of an essentially Ottonian clergy to the political
life of the western kingdom. At the core of this Lotharingian
conservatism was the belief in the homogeneity of heaven and
earth, the former ruled by God, the latter by princes and bishops
in God's image. For Dudo (and, as we have seen, for Gerard
also), supplication was the quintessential expression of this homogeneity. Yet we have also seen that homogeneity did not dictate a rigidly authoritarian ritual. On the contrary, supplication
encapsulated the political virtues that made good order possible,
and those virtues, though asymmetrical, were as incumbent on
rulers as they were on subjects. Indeed, for writers such as Dudo
they were more incumbent on rulers, for rulers set the moral
standards by which the community would be judged. Their justice, their sense of sacred duty, their willingness to honor God
and the saints and to show grace to their subjects were emblematic of the moral health of the polity.

In the paradigm of supplication, the humility and reverence
that supplicants owed their lords were therefore matched by the
grace and beneficence with which lords received their entreaties. Moreover, lords themselves were supposed to be humble and devout, since they had received their authority as an
unmerited gift from God. This idea was also expressed by a
complex of interrelated rites and emblems associated with supplication, only in these the ruler became the humble petitioner,
God his beneficent Lord.

Like other elements of supplication, this image of the ruler as
a suppliant before God had been common under the ninth-century Carolingians: hence Louis the Pious's public devotions and
penances, and the portrait of a prostrate Charles the Bald reach-
ing out to the feet of a crucified Christ.[79] Along with other *Herr-*

schaftszeichen, however, such acts and representations appear to have declined with the disintegration of the empire. Then in late tenth- and eleventh-century Germany they reappeared with a new degree of sophistication and a still greater currency. The most familiar examples are the many ivories and illuminations which show an emperor, with or without his consort, kneeling in devotion at Christ's feet, but there were many variations on the theme.[80] Several have already been mentioned: for example, the iconographic representation of the Adoration of the Magi as an *aurum coronarium*, in which the Magi became kings, kneeling before Christ and presenting their gifts to him as if to an emperor, a king of kings.[81] When Henry II gave Cluny his imperial crown, or when his mother gave Saint-Martin of Tours an imperial chlamys, they were essentially reenacting this primal offering.[82] The crowns hung over church altars were used in the same way: when an emperor entered a church he would remove his regalia and deposit them on or at the foot of the altar as if yielding them to Christ, in whose behalf he exercised the authority the regalia symbolized.[83]

The fact that such rites and emblems were most consistently developed and articulated in the empire does not mean that they were not also cultivated in France. We have already noted that Adalbero and Lothar introduced or promoted several Ottonian customs into the western kingdom and that Hugh Capet maintained them.[84] During the reign of Robert the Pious a new flurry of borrowing occurred. The fact is not surprising, for the Meuse and the Saône were no more frontiers in his time than they had been in Adalbero's. Instead they were membranes, filtering the flow of information rather than obstructing it. Dioceses such as Reims and Cambrai straddled French and imperial territory. So did principalities: the counties of Baldwin of Flanders, Odo II of Blois, and Otto-William of Macon all included imperial lands, and in Robert's time each of these counts was actively campaigning within the empire.[85] Heretics did not respect borders: they were as much a problem in Liège as they were in Arras.[86] Neither did monastic reformers. Odilo of Cluny wrote an epitaph for Henry II's mother, and during his tenure as abbot Cluny began to extend its range into Alsace, just as in the north Richard of Saint-Vanne and Poppo of Stavelot reformed and ruled monasteries on both sides of the Meuse. Richard in particular was well known to both Robert and Henry, each of whom committed monasteries to his care and used him to pass information between them.[87] Nor should we forget Robert's own knowledge of and interest in German ideas. A student of Gerbert, he promoted the careers of Gerbert's other students. Indeed, contemporaries recognized them as a sort of cohort, insofar as many of those implicated in the scandal of 1022 were not only protégés of Robert and his wife but also students of Gerbert or disciples of his spirit of intellectual inquiry.[88] Perhaps most important of all, Robert and Henry not only kept in direct contact with each other; as Robert-Henri Bautier pointed out, they also pursued strikingly convergent policies. Both faced a common enemy in Odo II of Blois and appear to have coordinated their efforts against him. Each promoted monastic reform (and in the case of Richard of Saint-Vanne the same reformer). They also met at least twice, at Ivois on the Meuse, the second meeting being especially noteworthy for the two rulers' attention to ceremonial and for their unusually substantive discussions.[89]

In calling attention to these convergences, Bautier intended to suggest that certain lost pieces of art associated with Robert might have been similar to contemporary imperial works. In the absence of definitive proof, he left the idea as no more than a suggestion; but in fact there were a great many parallels, in ceremony as well as in art, many of them centered precisely on the image of a king's devotional prostration. For example, the context in which Bautier made his suggestions concerned the reliquary of Saint Savinian made by Odorannus of Sens at the command of Robert and his queen. Wishing to honor the saint to whom she credited her reconciliation with the king, Constance persuaded Robert to have Savinian honorably translated into a splendid new reliquary. Though the reliefs that covered the sides of the casket have been lost, Bautier was able to reconstruct their subject matter from inscriptions. One side included portraits of both Robert and Constance, and Constance, at least, was shown kneeling, like an empress in an imperial diptych. Symmetry (and the imperial model) would have required the same posture for Robert.[90]

Other parallels do not require even this much conjecture. Robert, his wife, and his mother were clearly imitating imperial practices. Illuminations from Trier depicted the Adoration of the Magi as an *aurum coronarium*. In Robert's time an illuminator at Autun illustrated an Adoration on just the same pattern: crowned and kneeling, the Magi knelt before Christ and offered their gifts (figures 3 and 8). Did Henry II's mother give an imperial chlamys to Saint-Martin of Tours? Then Robert's mother, Adelaide, would give the same abbey four royal vestments: one *cappa* woven of gold thread, two woven of silver thread, and a *casula* decorated with figures from the Apocalypse. The Apocalypse images on the *casula* are particularly striking, since they also occurred on a mantle given by Otto III to San Alessio in Rome. The Ottonians also possessed a mantle known as an *orbis terrarum*, its imagery modeled on the high priest's mantle described in Wisdom 18:24. But the Capetians had it as well, for Adelaide wove one to give to Saint-Denis.[91]

It is worth pausing a moment over these mantles. Historians have sometimes conflated the *orbis terrarum* patterned on Wisdom with the vestments depicting the symbols of the Apocalypse. They were certainly sometimes combined, as on Henry II's Bamberg mantle.[92] Yet in describing Adelaide's gift to Saint-Denis Helgald of Fleury clearly distinguishes them, and carefully sketches the images of the Apocalypse mantle: on the back between the shoulders cherubim and seraphim bent their necks before Christ enthroned in majesty; on the front, the Lamb of God received adoration from the four evangelical symbols. The reason for Helgald's interest was that such mantles were among the most highly condensed symbols of christomimetic kingship ever devised in the early Middle Ages. Enveloped in the image of Christ, king or emperor was at once wearing the mantle of Christ and mantled by him. He was the judge before whom the proud knelt in fear and the humble in need, as he himself knelt in church to remove the robe, return it to Christ, and render account for his ministry. But on the other side of the mantle, Christ the King became Christ the sacrificial Lamb. This, too, was part of the ruler's own persona, because only if he had ministered well, like Christ humbly sacrificing himself for his people, would he fulfill the prayer made at his anointing: that he might be worthy to join Christ and reign eternally with him in heaven.

This was the program concentrated in the mantle woven by

8. Adoration of the Magi, from the Tropiary of Autun (996–1024). Paris, Bibliothèque de l'Arsenal, ms. 1169, f. 13v.

Robert's mother. At the church of Saint-Pierre at Fleury, the same imagery was projected onto the walls, in frescoes of the Apocalypse commissioned by Abbot Gauzlin. The paintings covered the entire front wall of the church; and though they have long since been destroyed, their content is fully indicated by a series of descriptive titles transmitted by Gauzlin's biographer. Here one could see the messenger descending "from the heavenly court" (*ab eterna aula*), there the martyred witnesses who died "for the name of the high King" (*pro celsi nomine Regis*). The center, above the doors, was dominated by a great majestic Christ, "powerful in majesty, who judged the world," while in other panels the "heavenly ministers" sang the royal *laudes* and all the just bent their knees before him.[93]

It is tempting to imagine the king kneeling in his Apocalypse robe offering a donation, his breast with its image of the Lamb toward the altar of sacrifice, his shoulders with their image of Christ the Judge bent beneath the great painting of Christ in majesty at his back. In fact, something of the sort did happen. In 1027, as soon as the church's remodeling had been completed, Robert came to Saint-Pierre to see his abbot's work and make a donation. There in Peter's church, the king gave the eternal bishop of Rome a silk pallium, the insignia of an archbishop. We do not know if he wore a special robe. But to make the donation Robert would have had to kneel in humility before the altar of Christ's sacrifice, while the newly painted image of Christ in majesty rose behind him, dwarfing him, but at the same time exalting him because it was his image also. In the plasma of images words failed to parse. Robert's joy was "indescribable." The only conceivable response was a gesture as iconic as the tableau, a gesture that became part of the tableau. The king wept.[94]

Helgald of Fleury's Iconic Kingship

Robert died within four years of his visit to Fleury. Almost immediately one of Gauzlin's most devoted disciples, Helgald, began to write the king's life: the *Epitome vitae Rotberti regis*. The work's idiosyncrasies are well known, if not yet fully understood. Helgald was one of the leading apologists of the eleventh-century monastic reform movement, which taught that men might prepare themselves for the coming of God's kingdom to earth by cultivating in themselves the qualities of monks, even as they pursued their worldly functions. In conformity to these ideals, Helgald passed over his king's capacities as a temporal lord who was leader of warriors in order to concentrate on Robert's piety. Throughout the *Vita* Robert appears as one who became increasingly conscious of his sinfulness and who took on a life of monastic purity in atonement.[95]

Yet dwelling on Robert's purity did not at all detract from Helgald's sense of his dignity. On the contrary, the thrust of the work is to exalt the king beyond the reach of all other princes. Alone of all lords Robert had been consecrated, and therefore made to conform to Christ's image. Robert was a christomimetic king, Christlike in the miracles that, alone of all laymen, Robert was privileged to perform; Christlike too in his life of atonement, as much a sign of special status as Christ's crucifixion.[96]

In all this one can again detect a strong Ottonian influence. However, since some would deny it and counterproofs are complex, the issue is better left to one side.[97] What one can say is that like the Ottonians, Helgald's Robert intentionally cultivated a christomimetic image, and the vehicle for projecting the image was ritual. He always kept twelve paupers in his train, in imitation of the twelve apostles, and on Maundy Thursday he imitated Christ's actions, even to the point of washing the feet of more than 160 poor clerics and drying them with his hair.[98] Because the Eucharist reenacted Christ's humiliation and exaltation, Robert held that sacrament in special veneration. He was "the most vigorous guardian of the Lord's body and blood," who personally carried the wine to the altar for consecration and did not shrink from criticizing a bishop who tried to plumb the depths of the real presence. Most important of all, on the eves of Christmas, Easter, and Pentecost Robert kept vigil, going without sleep until he could receive the Eucharist in the morning. Taken in sequence, these three feasts represented the cycle of Christ's humility and glory. Because they were the eves of festal coronations, the vigils simultaneously dramatized Robert's humility, the prelude to his own glory.[99]

To give force to this ideal of kingship, Helgald manipulated the virtues associated with supplication, but inverted them, so that the king became the humble suppliant before his gracious Lord. Thus Robert's constant epithet was "the humble king."[100] Even his body and eyes were "humble," and in humility he cast off the "ostentation of a proud spirit." Humility was the keeper of his royal virtue. Humility provided the key to the kingdom of heaven, and the kingdom of heaven, not that of earth, was King Robert's goal. Only God was "all-powerful." Robert was mindful of his glory and expressed his consciousness of his humility and of God's grace in terms of supplication. After the consecration of the new church of Saint-Aignan at Orléans, Robert came before the altar and prostrated himself. "In the sight of all the people he removed his purple robe . . . and with both knees on the ground poured forth a prayer of supplication to God." In the same way, when he had finally become convinced that he had sinned by contracting an illicit marriage, the *rex humilis* "petitioned" and "beseeched" God's forgiveness, "supplicated" his correction, and finally did that "which kings do not do," "crying and lamenting" in proof of his repentance.[101]

This time the imperial exemplar is unmistakable. What Robert performed at Saint-Aignan in removing his mantle and supplicating God was the kind of *depositio regalium* performed by Ottonian emperors. In fact, Helgald's account establishes the ceremony in France even before it is attested in Germany.[102] Helgald's statement notwithstanding, the Ottonians also undertook the same kind of public penances with which Robert atoned for his adultery.[103] Like the Ottonians, Robert had mantles decorated with figures of the Apocalypse. Like them he was portrayed kneeling with his consort beneath the saints. Even more than theirs his Christic sanctity was celebrated in works verging on the hagiographic. Given these similarities, can we say that Robert and his apologists were purposely imitating the emperors, competing with them through emblems and rituals in order to establish their parity? Of that there is little doubt. In the very beginning of the reign, when Robert still ruled with his father, Abbo of Fleury had formally erased the distinction between royal and imperial authority. Precepts that protected church property, he wrote, were confirmed by the authority of royal commands, which had the same status as imperial decrees: *regalis, id est imperialis jussionis*.[104] When he met with

Henry on the Meuse in 1023, forty years later, the challenge was more direct: Robert refused to cross the river to greet the emperor. He waited until Henry crossed to meet him, to the latter's considerable chagrin.[105]

Still, the matter cannot be quite so straightforward. Had the Capetians' tactic simply been to imitate the emperors, they would inevitably have lost. Emulation would only have invited comparison, and by every visible measure Otto III and Henry II were unquestionably greater rulers than Hugh and Robert. The Frankish rulers had to establish their kingship as an entity entirely independent of the empire, with its own traditions and sources of legitimacy. This task they accomplished by ignoring the Ottonians entirely. The self-avowed model for early Capetian ritual was not the empire. It was the ninth-century Carolingians.[106]

When Abbo wrote that royal decrees have the same standing as imperial decrees, he was not comparing Hugh's and Robert's authority with Otto III's, though the comparison was of course implied. His point was that the Capetians' decrees had the same status as those of the great Carolingian emperors whose place they had taken. The same reference point is implied in Helgald's description of the *orbis terrarum* given by Robert's mother to Saint-Denis. He did not liken it to those of Otto III or Henry II. Instead, he said it was "entirely different from Charles the Bald's." This passing reference to Charles in fact gives us a clue to Helgald's intentions. Charles was not only the last great West Frankish king. As a West Frankish king who had been crowned emperor, Charles also became a kind of totemic figure, emblematic of Francia's legitimate autonomy from the Empire. For that very reason scribes in this period tended to name him as the author of their forged royal diplomas even more often than they chose Charlemagne or Louis the Pious. For the same reason Robert took care to associate himself with Compiègne, holding Easter court there, anointing his son there, and burying him there upon his premature death; for Compiègne had been Charles the Bald's capital, built to rival Aachen, and was therefore known by Robert's contemporaries (including Helgald) as Charles's city, Carlopolis. Against this background, it can be no coincidence that Charles was also the Carolingian ruler most associated with depictions of the ruler as a *servus Christi* who in imitating Christ's humility shared in Christ's glory. His prayerbook shows him prostrate on the ground, arms outstretched toward the feet of a crucified Christ. And in one of his letters Charles compared himself to David in accepting the penance imposed on him by Hincmar of Reims, playing the role of Nathan (II Kings 12).[107]

David and Nathan: the Hebrew king's acceptance of the prophet's admonition was a topos of Carolingian political theory. Hincmar referred to it repeatedly to adjure kings to heed their bishops. Sedulius Scottus used it to illustrate their need for humility.[108] And Helgald placed it at the center of his work, in the pivotal scene describing Robert's penitential supplication, only here Abbo of Fleury took the place of Nathan and Hincmar.

> Just as the holy David, against the law, against morality, lusted for and seized Bathsheba, so this man, acting against the prescriptions of holy faith, wickedly joined the said woman to himself as his wife. ... But by a mild sentence, the true doctor of the human race healed the wound of each man's sin, the former through his prophet Nathan ..., when admitting his guilt David confessed that he had sinned; the latter, in the same way, through the venerable Lord Abbo, who persisted in chastisement until the most gentle king recognized his guilt and, setting aside the woman he had wrongly joined to himself, washed away the stain of sin through a satisfaction pleasing to God.[109]

From all the vast iconography of Carolingian rulership, Helgald reached back across 150 years and picked out the image of a humble king begging God's grace to deliver his partisan message. Monks like Abbo had succeeded to the Carolingian episcopate as guardians of political morality. Christomimetic sacrifice made Robert the Pious the legitimate successor of the Carolingian emperors and the Ottonians' equal, indeed their superior in humility and therefore also in future glory. But behind these stated themes lay an unstated assumption whose importance can be gauged only by its complete absence in the tenth century and its steady progress from Richer to Dudo to Helgald. Political order was not just a matter of a king's superior military might, nor was ritual just a poor substitute for failing power. A true polity was a moral community, and the virtues espoused by its kings and the nature of their rituals defined its ideals.

Of course, much of this had been a Carolingian topos, preached by ninth-century writers to the point of tedium. But the lesson had become irrelevant after the death of Charles the Bald, when kings might count themselves successful if they simply kept their thrones. It took a century of civil wars and the antinomianism of the *seigneurie banale* to make people understand it again. And this time the lesson stuck, because in the course of these two successive crises the power structure of Francia had been transformed in a way that made some such principle of legitimacy a political necessity.

To understand how this transformation came about, one must reinvert Helgald's treatment of supplication, turning from the humility Robert showed when he petitioned God to the humility of Robert's *fideles* when they petitioned him. "Rainald, bishop of Angers, entered the presence of our serenity and humbly beseeched our highness." "Coming before the knees of our serenity, one of our knights named Ansold . . . petitioned with submissive prayer."[110] Taken by themselves, these formulaic protestations of devotion so common in Robert's acts would not mean too much. Not only do they repeat, with scarcely any changes, the petitionary formulas found in the chancery of tenth-century kings; their exalted image of royal authority contrasts strangely with what historians know of Robert's true power, for he was not one of the more powerful Capetian kings, and his reign was marred by rebellion by his son and queen and disobedience by such powerful feudatories as Odo II of Blois.[111] But to dismiss the formulas because of their repetitiveness is to miss the point of ritual and image. Jonathan Smith has said that much ritual describes the world not the way it is but only the way it should be.[112] This prescription certainly applies to supplication and the grandiloquent phrases of petition. They did not pay tribute to the reality of a king's power. They paid homage to what a king's power should be, and the ideal was undoubtedly shared not only by the kings but also, we may readily believe, by the princes. Their authority, too, was sanctioned by divine grace. Their charters also incorporated formulas of supplication as an emblem of transcendent authority. Like Robert, they took the part of the defenseless by summoning their knights and castellans to Peace assemblies. And like him, they prostrated themselves in the presence of God, the saints, and the poor in order to give alms or beg forgiveness for their sins. For them as for the king, exaltation required humility.

In another setting—where princes felt that they did not need kings, for instance—the princes' appropriation of regalian emblems might compete with the king's. But in early eleventh-century France the princes needed the king badly, or more precisely, they needed the idea of him, as badly as they needed the idea of the Lord God. The reason was that only two things made them better than their robber-castellans: the belief that God stood behind their rule and their willingness to accept the moral code of rulership which that belief implied. In this conjuncture, then, if a count held Peace councils, translated relics, or prayed to God or was prayed to by *fideles*, he was not diminishing royal authority. He was appropriating royal authority as the justification of and model for his own rule, just as the king's authority was justified by and modeled on God's.

Royal and princely ritual therefore became symbiotic. When the head of John the Baptist was found in the monastery of Saint-Jean at Angély, Count William of Poitou, duke of Aquitaine, "was filled with joy and decreed that the sacred head be displayed to the people." Not to the *divites* or the *principes* or his private gang of *milites*, but to the people, the *populi*. It was the same ideal of authority transcending class that informed the duke's numerous Peace councils. It was the king's own ideal, one that led him to hold Peace councils, touch the poor, and intercede before God on behalf of his subjects. Far from undermining the king's authority by displaying his own, William actually invited him to see the marvel. When Robert arrived, William received him royally, while the king honored the duke in turn by giving gifts to Saint-Jean, including a gold vessel weighing thirty pounds. There were other guests, and good machiavellian reasons for the invitation. But the king's presence is what Ademar of Chabannes's narrative insists on, because it was the king's participation that brought honor to the duke and legitimacy to his policies.[113]

One might make a similar point with respect to the counts of Flanders. We have already noted their interest in political liturgies during the early eleventh century. In this they were not unusual. What is unusual is that these liturgies are especially well documented in Flemish sources, and that they continued in Flanders well into the next century—much longer than in other parts of the kingdom. The counts sponsored tours of relics across their county and surrounded themselves with those relics when they presided over Peace councils.[114] They were welcomed by their monasteries with formal processions, complete with hymns, incense, and *laudes*.[115] They observed Lent with ritual distributions to the poor (which they made, incidentally, kneeling before an altar as the needy took coins from their outstretched hand).[116] And longer than any other counts they continued to issue charters at the humble petition of *fideles*.[117] What are we to think, then, when we find that among all Philip I's diplomas, the most varied and consistently elegant formulas of petition occur in acts issued for these same counts of Flanders? Baldwin V and his son "petitioned the magnificence of our piety with all humility and reverence." Accompanied by his wife (the king's aunt), the count "approached the serenity of our majesty, fervently beseeching with the greatest humility." "With reverence for the royal highness," Robert of Flanders "came into our presence petitioning and praying with a spirit of pious devotion."[118] These are not the formulas of the royal chancery, which at the time preferred a shorter, less pretentious model. These formulas are the creations of Flemish scribes, trying to impart a tone of sincerity to the record. To them, the sacred authority of their counts did not detract from the king's. On the contrary, it required the king to be treated with still greater honor.

We may therefore speak of Robert's kingship, or that of his immediate successors, as an iconic kingship. Whatever the real power exercised by a king, it was important that the image of authority remain intact, since all those who held authority by the grace of God, whether king or prince, justified their authority by that measure. This is why even counts who were not formally the king's *fideles* (that is, those who did not perform homage and swear fealty to him) still respected the principle of monarchical rule.[119] It is also why beneficiaries of royal acts refused to abandon the old Carolingian formulas of supplication, even as the royal chancery was making its formulas more standardized and less ornate. To come before a king and kneel was in some sense to step into an iconic setting, and thereby to accept the image as the standard by which authority was distributed in the world. Counts and castellans might league against a king in the pursuit of limited interests, and in private even otherwise high-minded ecclesiastics might joke about the king's *imbecillitas*;[120] but to conform one's actions to the traditional iconography of ritual and one's words to the traditional formulas was to proclaim the continuing validity of the ideal. And the ideal was proclaimed all the more loudly by early eleventh-century writers because it was under attack from so many quarters.

From this point of view, the claim of some historians that the king was really only the ruler of one principality among many ignores the importance of an ideal of deferential order rooted in cosmological truth for all princes.[121] And paradoxically, the more princes took over royal attributes in an effort to consolidate their authority over their territories, the more they must have become ideologically dependent on the idea of some common and unassailable source of all authority that set them apart from their castellans. It is therefore at least arguable that the great moral authority of the later French monarchy developed not in spite of the independence of the princes but because of it, since the justification of princely authority justified that of the kings as well. They could not undermine the one without undermining the other.

PART THREE

Begging Pardon

You have a sentence you can speak from beginning to
end and from end to beginning. You have a sentence to
say yes and say nay with. You have a sentence to deny
with. You have a sentence with which you can make
yourself tired or awake. You have a sentence to blindfold
yourself with. You have a sentence to bring order into
every disorder; with which you can designate every disorder in comparison to another disorder as a comparative
order: with which you can declare every disorder an order: can bring yourself into order: can deny every disorder. You have a sentence of which you can make a model
for yourself. You have a sentence you can place between
yourself and everything else. You are the lucky owner of
a sentence which will make every impossible order possible for you and make every possible and real disorder impossible for you: which will exorcise every disorder from
you.

Peter Handke, *Kaspar*

Judicabit pauperes populi,
et salvos faciet filios pauperum,
et humiliabit calumpniatorem.

Psalm 71

Thus far we have concentrated on supplication as an act of begging favor, because that was the most common kind of supplication and the simplest to interpret. Another kind, however, was arguably even more important in dramatizing the typology. This was the act of penance in which a wrongdoer begged for pardon. For the penitent was a supplicant; but as the grace he sought from his lord was greater, so his humility was deeper. Penitential rituals therefore revealed the meanings of ordinary supplications in a particularly intense form, and contemporaries worked out their implications with unusual clarity and subtlety. The integrity of this typology is one reason to have deferred its analysis to a separate discussion; but a more important reason is that penitential rites and the rhetoric associated with them were central to the rehabilitation of political order described in the preceding two chapters.

Once again the council of Verzy is emblematic, for its final scene culminated in just this kind of supplication, as Arnulf prostrated himself before the kings he had betrayed and begged them for mercy. Such acts had once been quite common, especially in the early ninth century, when Louis the Pious and his Aquitanian circle were searching for ways to express the essential identity of church and state as a single community of *fideles*. Public penance became the chief ritual expression of this program. To that end, Louis's bishops restored the use of public

penances in the church while Benedict of Aniane promoted
their use in the monasteries he reformed under Louis's aegis.[1]
And the emperor demanded that as the price of submission, rebels should come before him in a public assembly and beg his
forgiveness. Prostrate entreaties for mercy therefore sealed all
the great events of Louis's reign, from the submission of his
father's courtiers which allowed him to take charge of affairs
after Charlemagne's death to that of his eldest son in 839, less
than a year before Louis's own death.[2]

Thereafter the practice declined with the Carolingians, being
mentioned only twice in the sections of the *Annales sancti
Bertiniani* devoted to the decades after Louis's death.[3] In part
the reason was that Louis's sons and grandsons, regarding each
other as equals, refused each other such a clear sign of subjection. The rituals that ended their wars therefore spoke of brotherhood and peace, not submission and penance.[4] Soon enough,
however, they had difficulty exacting submissions even from
their own sons. When in 871 Carloman promised to do penance
to his father, Charles the Bald, the act was so hedged with negotiations and deception that Hincmar of Reims recalled it with
open disgust. Carloman had had no intention of reforming, he
wrote. He had approached his father with "counterfeit" humility.[5] Charles had no better luck with insolent magnates. His war
against Salomon of Brittany, for example, ended not with a prostrate supplication but with the two sides exchanging mediators
and arranging a "peace."[6] By the mid–tenth century, when
Flodoard was writing, such pacts had become the norm. The
practice of begging pardon was entirely ignored.[7]

Against this background, Arnulf's confession at the council of
Verzy becomes even more special—the first political penance to
a West Frankish king in more than 100 years of extant written
memory which did not have to be qualified as counterfeit,
treated ironically, or contradicted by subsequent political up-
heavals. Nor was this an isolated victory. In subsequent decades
ritual humiliations of the vanquished became customary, performed not only to kings but also to great counts, and always
aping the language and gestures of penance.

The role of political penances was not limited to the humiliation of vanquished rebels, however. As we have seen, in the
early eleventh century the most serious challenge to the estab-

lished order came less from open rebellion and civil war than from the increasing power of the *seigneurie banale*; and the threat was gravest to chapters and monasteries. It was their lands that were usurped by the castellans and their knights; their peasants whose labor was diverted to maintain these lords' castles; and their privileges of judicial immunity that were undermined by the demands of advocates. In response to the challenge, the churches fell back on their traditional texts and rituals and culled from them a wide range of supplicatory behavior and rhetoric associated with the protection of the poor and oppressed.

Because the fundamental principles of this symbolic complex were part of a Carolingian discourse common to all Francia, my discussion occasionally draws on sources that range widely over region and period. But the Carolingian legacy was broad. It could accommodate many different visions of political order, not only the authoritarian ideal expressed in theophanic supplication but also the brotherhood of pacts and the unity of consensus sought from assemblies.[8] Different regions therefore borrowed selectively, according to their distinctive needs. In western and southwestern France, for example, disputes between churches and laymen often ended in bilateral pacts, while in Burgundy and the Ile-de-France local assemblies hammered out a consensus tolerable to the parties and the regional elite.[9] Conversely, none of these regions made much use of the kind of penitential rites described here. The region where these rites did apply was the one where theophanic supplication was strongest: the ecclesiastical province of Reims. The churches here clung to a conservative ideal of political order, and never more tenaciously than when their ideal was threatened by upstart lords and knights. The way they demanded justice against a castellan or knight, the language they used to describe the causes of their disputes, the rites with which trials began and ended—all were subordinated to the dictates of a paradigm of supplication. The result was an ideal of justice so absolute and so biased against change that it rendered the clergy incapable of compromise. For them there could be neither peace nor consensus, because justice was not simply a matter of rights. It was a matter of righteousness.

6 Supplication as Penance

In ancient Rome, those who begged the forgiveness of a patron or protector commonly threw themselves at his knees.[1] This connection between admission of wrong and gestures of humiliation subsequently became one of the most durable aspects of the Christian rite of supplication. Certainly kneeling was already common in the earliest days of the liturgy, more so than was once realized; but even then prostration and kneeling had been associated primarily with entreaties for the forgiveness of sins. In fact, Christians were originally forbidden to kneel on Sundays, which were regarded as days of joy celebrating the risen Christ. The prohibition was gradually extended to feast days and saints' days, until kneeling was appropriate only for days of marked penitential character, as during Quadragesima. The association is still quite visible in the early sacramentaries, which usually reserve prostration for prayers of penance.[2]

In this way the normal pose for the public penitential rituals of the early church became that of the suppliant petition, as sinners, barefoot and dressed in the plainest of cloth, prostrated themselves before the altar to beseech the Lord's forgiveness of their sins—a forgiveness they could not deserve but could receive only as an act of the Lord's grace and mercy.[3] As always, the attributes of supplication were fitted into a larger framework, the meaning of penitential supplication gaining expressive and emotive power by taking over cosmological referents; for the supplication of a sinner, as Anselm of Laon later recognized, restored the proper relationship between God and man that had been broken by the Fall: "As man fell through pride and disobedience, so through humility and obedience he shall return."[4] Seen in this light, penance was a means of restoring men and women to their proper place within the cosmic order, as through penance they showed the humility that corrected the pride of the Fall. Penitential supplication also played on the holiest of Christian inversions, the Resurrection: for even Christ had allowed himself to be humbled only to rise in triumph to his rightful position on heaven's throne. Since in the early church acts of public penance occurred at the end of Lent, which commemorated Christ's humiliation, these ramifications could not but be obvious to the penitents.

As private confession began to replace public penance in the fifth and sixth centuries, the institutional context of penance changed. No longer was penance granted only on Holy Thursday; nor was there now any formally instituted *ordo penitentium*, its rites of initiation controlled entirely by the bishop. Ordinary priests could now absolve men and women of their sins as well as bishops, and confession and absolution had become repeatable.[5] Yet private penance had assumed the supplicatory nature of the old public rite. And even if there was no institution of "public penance," acts of penitential humiliation were still often performed publicly, particularly after the Carolingian period, when it was reserved for those sins whose gravity or publicity scandalized the community.[6]

Thus from the ninth through the eleventh centuries all penance, whether public or private, required the gestures and language of supplication, and through them exposed the laity to a universe structured around the act of entreating a beneficent lord. Significantly, this structure even included intercession; for the sinner did not beg God's forgiveness directly. Rather, the act of penance required the sinner to "humiliate himself in the sight of God" by prostrating himself on the ground and "humbly" beseeching the priest "to intercede" for him and his sins with God. Having accepted this entreaty, the priest sang those psalms that revealed God as a lord who was merciful to his suppliants. Then he prostrated himself in turn to present his own prayer on behalf of the sinner: "O God, whose indulgence no one lacks, we beseech you to give pardon to your faithful servant [*famulus*], N., who, naked on the ground, is confessing. Spare the suppliant, so that he who is accused by his actions can be saved by your compassion. . . . Suppliant we beseech you and petition you, that you might deign to incline the ear of your piety to our prayers."[7]

Since monks were professional penitents, it is not surprising to find these associations most consistently applied in monastic writings, such as the customary compiled by Ulrich of Cluny in the late 1070s. According to Ulrich, penitential supplication was so important to the life of a Cluniac monk that the first thing a novice learned upon entering the monastery was "how to make his petition; and first they are to know how to beg pardon [*veniam petere*] according to our custom." This custom required the novice to "beg pardon" upon his hands and knees three times before the abbot, always turning in a circle upon his haunches, and finally prostrating himself in prayer.[8]

The reason that "begging pardon" was so essential to the Cluniac novice is that it was the centerpiece of the monastic liturgy. The purpose of monks' lives was to seek forgiveness for their own sins and for those on whose behalf they prayed. But such forgiveness could be obtained only as a free gift of God's mercy. It could be beseeched in humility; but it could not be demanded as a right. Thus at the Christmas chapter, when the Nativity was formally announced, the monks met the theophany of Christ's birth by falling to the ground in prayer.[9] In masses and offices throughout Quadragesima, monks prostrated themselves in reverence for the Lord who had humiliated himself by being born and dying a man.[10] "Lord, hear my prayer," they said as they would to bishop or prince. "With your ears take my entreaty in your truth; hear me in your justice. . . . I stretch forth my hands unto you."[11] So crucial were these supplications that few circumstances or inconveniences could excuse a monk of Cluniac observance from performing them. Even when the abbey's deans were riding on the road while seeing to provisions, they still had to observe those hours "when pardon is begged" by dismounting, removing their cowls and gloves, and prostrating themselves on the ground to beg pardon.[12]

A monastery was an *asylum penitentiae* that recreated humanity's proper relationship with God; for by their constant acts of penance monks cultivated the humility which restored the fallen to glory.[13] But a monastery was also a paradise on earth, or more accurately, a figure of heavenly paradise. As such it had to be, so far as possible, a community ruled in perfect order, meaning that deference had to be observed within the monastic community itself. This perfect social order was also signified by supplication, an act through which a monk showed his humility to his superiors—a humility specifically demanded by the Benedictine rule. The most important superior was, of course, the abbot, whom the rule called "the vicar of Christ."[14] Contemporary parlance styled him the "lord abbot," a usage that Benedict had also approved, since it was given to the abbot "out of honor and love of Christ," in whose place he stood.[15] The abbot was, in other words, a lord by the grace of God, and to his monks he was in fact a lord, standing to them as a father to his children, and "ruling" his monastery (*regere*) just as kings were said to rule their kingdoms. The monks were even called his "subjects" (*subditi, subjecti*), and he shared his rites of honor only with kings and bishops.[16]

Liturgical supplication was one of those honors; indeed, it so marked his authority that were the lord abbot merely to criticize a monk in private conversation, the monk had to "immediately prostrate his entire body and beg pardon without cease."[17] In cases of serious offense the supplication was so extreme as to make any prostration performed in the outside world seem mild. A monk who had violated the rule in some grievous way was required to enter the chapter, partially disrobe, and lie prostrate before the abbot while being beaten. He was then permitted to dress; but he still had to remain prostrate throughout the subsequent offices. Only when the elders of the monastery agreed that he had suffered enough did they enter the chapter to "beg pardon" on the offender's behalf—thereby acting as intercessors before the lord abbot as the monastery's saints acted as intercessors before God, as the monks, themselves, acted as intercessors for the laity. As part of their petition, the intercessors argued that the offender's heart was now "contrite" and, of course, "humbled." At last the sinner was summoned before the chapter and permitted to put on his cowl. But once more he had to fall at the abbot's feet—and then crawl before the feet of every member of the chapter, "from the greatest to the very least," "begging pardon" of each.[18]

Public Penance for Political Sins

A monastery was a microcosm of the perfect community, and supplication was the ritual which expressed the perfection of its order. When that order had been violated, penitential supplication was the act that signified its restoration, just as it was through acts of penance that Christians were restored to God. The situation was no different outside the monastery. For the political community was also part of the divine order, although a less perfect part than a monastery; and here, too, the language and gestures of entreaty expressed that subjection to divinely established authority which guaranteed political harmony. As in monasteries, as in the church as a whole, they were especially appropriate as a vindication of authority after acts that had scandalized the community by violating the fundamental rules of political order.

Those rules were essentially the same in kingdom, church, and monastery, for each society was conceived as a community of *fideles* whose stability rested on its members' humility, where humility was the willingness to accept one's role in the society. Conversely, to reject one's role was to reject the very basis of political order. That was the opposite of humility—pride; and pride was thought to be the deadliest of the seven sins simply because it was the greatest threat to social and political stability. Suger, who in so many ways was the heir of late Carolingian political theorists, later recognized this in narrating the rebellion of Haimo of Germigny.[19] Haimo had refused to obey the summons of Louis VI to present himself at court, and Louis retaliated by besieging his castle. The siege was successful, and Haimo soon realized that he would not be able to resist much longer. He realized, too, that there was "only this one way of saving himself. The said Haimo . . . fell prostrate at the feet of the lord king, and groveling constantly to the wonder of many begged fervently that he might act mercifully toward him. He returned to his castle, placing everything in the will of the royal majesty. Thus with as much pride as he had rebelled [*se subduxerat*] did he now with humility return [*se reduxit*], instructed in the ways of justice."[20]

One hundred years earlier Raoul Glaber and Andrew of Fleury had described similar acts of submission to mark the end of rebellions against kings. Robert the Pious's son, the young King Hugh, frustrated by his father's refusal to grant him the wealth and power that befitted a coregent, pillaged his father's property until, "restored to his senses by the will of God, he returned to his parents and in humble satisfaction restored himself to their benevolence." When the powerful Odo II of Blois sought to undermine the king's presence in Sens, Henry "assailed him relentlessly, fighting with bitter ferocity, until, bending his knee, he subjected himself to the king and acknowledged himself obedient to his authority."[21] Most instructive of all is Andrew of Fleury's description of Queen Constance's submission to the same King Henry, her son. Constance's role had not been negligible in the rebellions that plagued Robert and Henry. According to Andrew of Fleury, it was in fact she who had instigated Hugh to assert his interests against his father. It was also she who in 1033 had instigated the barons of France to rebel against Henry, even going so far as to promise Odo of Blois the rights he sought over Sens. Hers was therefore a triple sin, a triple violation of order. She was a rebel against the king. She had violated her responsibilities as queen. And she had stepped above her place as a woman. This last was the fault that stuck in the craw of ·contemporaries such as Andrew, who could think of no worse epithet for her than "amazon"—in other words, one of those women who dared act like a man. But like all those who pridefully seek power beyond measure, Constance came to a just end when Henry's victories over his barons forced her to "do penance" by prostrating herself at Henry's feet and tearfully petitioning his forgiveness.[22]

It was not only rebellion against kings that called for supplicatory gestures of submission. Rebellion against any of God's vicars might require them as well. After rising against the duke of Normandy, William of Bellême was forced to end his "insolence," his "presumption," by going barefoot before the duke, bearing his saddle on his shoulder "in satisfaction" in order to "beg his clemency." The count of Hiémois ended his rebellion against another Norman duke with self-abasement no less extravagant than Haimo of Germigny's: "groaning and rolling on the ground at his feet, he begged pardon from the duke for what he had done."[23]

"He begged pardon" (*veniam expetebat*): the phrase is the same as that used in monastic customaries. Indeed, the language of political submission was nothing but the language of penance. Constance the amazon "did penance" to her son. The barefoot William of Bellême carried his saddle before the duke "for satisfaction." And Haimo of Germigny acted the role of suppliant in order to "save himself." Nor was it merely the language that was the same. The ritual was also the same, for rebellion against God's rulers was a sin against God. It was the sin of pride, of all Catholic sins the most political. Regino of Prüm's penitential had stated the fact clearly, and his interpretation was passed down to the eleventh century by no less an authority than Burchard of Worms: "Pride is the beginning of every sin, the queen of all evils. From it is born every act of disobedience, every presumption, all pertinacity, contention, heresy, and arrogance."[24] It did not matter whether one spoke of the pride of a disobedient monk, a disobedient cleric, or a disobedient subject. The sin was in all cases the same—a violation of order, a desire to set oneself above one's natural superiors. The damage that resulted from such a sin was extensive, because pride attacked the foundation of order itself. For that reason Regino, like Carolingian writers before him, reserved for sins of pride the most public and humiliating of penances, a public humiliation for a sin against the public good.[25]

The Monastic Culture of Deference

Although political penances became more frequent in eleventh-century France than they had been in several generations, their essential meaning had not changed from the time of Louis the Pious. Nor was there a great deal new in the application of penitential rites and language to ordinary disputes.[26] What was new in the north was the fear that the old principles of order were being wholly and lastingly subverted by uncontrollable forces. This fear caused the old paradigm to be marshaled more systematically, and with renewed intensity.

At the heart of the crisis were new social groups that could not be fitted into the traditional categories of power and authority: peasants who resisted the fiscal demands and legal restraints of their ecclesiastical lords, and townsmen who demanded rights of self-government from bishops and churches, including the right to arm themselves in self-protection. But most troubling of all were castellans and knights. The *seigneurs banaux* and their satellites were not part of the traditional order, their offices not instituted by divine Providence. They gained their power by taking advantage of the political turmoil created by struggles between the princes. They gained wealth by demanding labor and payments from the peasants of monasteries and chapters. Or so said the monks and canons of the province of Reims who denounced these men to kings, counts, and bishops and demanded justice against them.

In reading these denunciations, we must remember that the great ecclesiastical houses of the north were also part of the traditional order of things. The greatest monasteries might seek autonomy from their bishops, who in turn railed against their insubordination and demanded suppliant subjection, believing that their claims were simply another sign that the right order of things was being undermined.[27] In reality, bishops and monks only represented different sides of the Carolingian ecclesiastical establishment. The rivalry between the two was therefore latent in the Carolingian legacy; and their arguments were less about the legitimacy of order than about the place of each side within it. Of course, monks accorded themselves an important place, and with some justification. They had grown wealthy under the patronage of those lords who had inherited the Carolingian offices of public authority, and their lands and rights were protected from the interference of temporal rulers by inviolable immunities. Just as those rulers had a role in the divine order, so did the great monasteries. They were intercessors before God on behalf of the princes and their vassals; and their relics protected the prosperity of rulers and peasants alike. They could even justifiably claim that their role was greater than that of temporal rulers, for if counts held their offices by the grace of God, monasteries were "the sanctuary of God" and had been "founded and exalted by him."[28] So strong was the monasteries' identity with the divine realm that donations to them were made as much to their patron saint as to the *monasterium*.[29]

This conviction of their collective righteousness was coupled with a profound deference to rank and tradition. As a result, monks viewed those whom they believed to be undeferential and unrespectful of tradition with the kind of uncomprehending, bigoted fantasies that people reserve for those whose values they imagine as subverting their own hard-won virtues.[30] To monks, those virtues were discipline and subservience. They were imprinted into every liturgical event and every nonliturgical gathering, as when monks processed through the church by rank, priests preceding deacons, deacons subdeacons, and so on, down to the oblates and *conversi*, each rank further graded by date of profession.[31] When a monk was accused of a fault in chapter, he immediately had to admit his sinfulness and beg forgiveness, even if he were blameless. Justifying or explaining his actions came later.[32]

This culture of deference was epitomized in the subordination of monks to abbot. One sign of their subordination comes from the formulas of petition, and not just their protestations of humility. It is even more clearly demonstrated by the fact that in the province of Reims (and in contrast to some other regions of France), monks did not generally present petitions to kings and counts. Rather, abbots presented them in behalf of their monks, who were not usually mentioned as participating in the petition at all.[33] If they were included, they were mentioned in a phrase that accentuated their dependent status, as when the abbot of Homblières "and his brothers" beseeched the count of Vermandois to intervene against one of his vassals. And even if abbot and monks did come before the count together, it was the abbot alone who presented the petition to the count, as is clear from the singular ending of the participle (*postulans*) indicating the request.[34]

Whatever his legal standing, in practice an abbot was more than the *Rechtsvertreter* of his monastery. He was a lord who ruled, and the monks were his subjects.[35] According to the language of charters, the local courts administered by a monastery were "the pleas of the abbot," while its domains were supervised by "the abbot and his ministers" and were exempt from any judicial authority save theirs.[36] Just how unchecked his administration could be was discovered by the regular canons of Saint-Martin of Tournai in the first years of its restoration un-

der Saint Odo of Tournai; for the brothers learned one day that
during a recent famine their abbot had given away all the monastery's stores, leaving the monks with nothing.[37]

The situation was not unusual, for eleventh-century sources
from northern France frequently single out the rule of a poor
abbot as the primary cause of a monastery's decline. The *Vita
Burchardi* claimed that the impoverishment of Saint-Maur-des-
Fossés had been caused by the negligence of its abbots, while
Hariulf appears to have blamed Ingelard of Saint-Riquier for not
doing more to halt the loss of lands to kings, nobles, and his
own relatives.[38] According to the chronicle of Saint-Bertin, the
mere absence of Abbot Heribert from the monastery brought all
sorts of evils and permitted both lands and cells to be lost. In
this particular case the absence had been due to his joint appointment as abbot of Saint-Germain of Auxerre. Significantly,
Heribert resigned the second post when he realized that he
could not adequately meet his responsibilities toward both his
charges—in itself a commentary on the burdens of the abbatial
office during this period.[39]

Conversely, a strong abbot, well connected and full of energy
and will, was the secret of a monastery's success. The monks of
Saint-Bertin had chosen Heribert mostly because of his worldly
expertise, which they hoped would enable him to recoup the
monastery's fortunes. Guimann's chronicle of Saint-Vaast and
Hariulf's chronicle of Saint-Riquier both portray the enrichment
of their monasteries as due solely to the hard work of two abbots, Leduin of Saint-Vaast and Angelran of Saint-Riquier.[40] Nor
should such statements be dismissed as mere rhetorical conceits, since other evidence corroborates the predominance of the
abbot in the administration of his monastery: for instance, the
donation by two individuals of a place they owned to Homblières. In return, their charter records, "Lord Walerann, abbot,
gave to us from the same property as much as pleased him."[41]
The record makes no mention of any counsel, let alone consent,
given by the monks to their abbot's action. Indeed, the fullest
monastic sources from the region rarely record an active role for
monks. It is the abbot alone who receives donations from benefactors, issues charters for his monastery, negotiates legal transactions—and petitions favors from lords.[42]

The chapter of a monastery did have certain rights vis-à-vis its head, at least in principle. The Benedictine rule declared that an abbot was to consult the brothers in administering the affairs of his monastery; it did not, however, require him to follow their counsel. Indeed, contemporaries assumed that the abbot did not require his chapter's consent to administer a monastery's property but only to decide those matters that pertained to the cult—the acceptance of novices, for example, and the ordination and correction of monks.[43] In practice, then, the independence of monastic chapters was limited.

A story from the *Historia monasterii Mosomensis* illustrates the point by providing a rare glimpse into a chapter's deliberations.[44] In the county of Porcien there was a cell called Thin, so small that it supported only eight monks and an abbot. Its patrons, having no children, gave the cell to the monastery of Saint-Remi at Reims. But because of chronic warfare in the region between the houses of Vermandois and Ardennes, its lands were subject to such frequent raids that Thin soon became unviable. Eventually Archbishop Adalbero of Reims decided to fold it into his own church at Mouzon, replacing the latter's canons with monks from Thin, "so that from two small things one large and better thing might be made."

To implement this plan, Adalbero had to obtain Thin from the monks of Saint-Remi. He went to the monastery and explained his proposition to the abbot, waving aside all his objections and promising that he would compensate Saint-Remi for any loss it might incur. The abbot asked leave to take counsel of his monks; but when the chapter convened a split developed, "as is the nature with weak minds," for some of the *seniores* argued that public opinion would be scandalized if they violated the terms of the original donation. Faced with a division of opinion, the abbot simply stopped the debate:

> The abbot commanded silence, and raising his voice in a tone of authority and speaking clearly to quell the sound of murmuring, he began with these words of pious exhortation: "Dearest brothers and beloved of God, these are the words of the Apostle: 'Nothing through contention, nothing through vainglory; but in humility shall superiors bend themselves to each other, considering not what they want, but what others want . . .' (Phil. 2:3). And so, my brothers, if the bishop advises us [*moneat*] in these matters that pertain to God, no one should dare resist, for as the Lord says in the Gospel, 'Who hears

you, hears me; who rejects you, rejects me . . .' (Luke 10:16). We cannot justly object, nor do we dare show the temerity to overturn [*pervertere*] what pertains to the divine cult."

With that pronouncement discussion was closed, but not the show. The abbot asked his monks to "bend toward and accept wiser counsel, so that according to the Apostle all may be done in charity." The monks gave their assent, and the abbot happily returned to the archbishop to inform him that the monks would be "obedient" [*quae fratrum fuerit obauditio*]. Though first resistant, at last, upon reflection, they had been persuaded "by reason."

The incident speaks worlds about the place of monks in the administration of their institutions.[45] Whether the monks of Saint-Remi really were confused or simply cowed, in the final analysis they had no choice. The archbishop was going to get his way. The only question was how much power their abbot would have to apply.

There were generally good reasons for monks to rely on their abbot. He was frequently a member of the old comital nobility—a great lord among great lords; and quite apart from his stature as a prelate of the church, he was often appointed by the king or count and therefore an ally of those lords.[46] There were also psychological reasons for abbatial primacy. As the incidents just cited show, the ethos of the monastic vocation worked to place excessive responsibility in the hands of the abbot by emphasizing the importance of monks' humility and obedience to him. The abbot's vocation was to rule his flock, the monks' to obey and to pray. An abbot was to be venerated as "abbot and father," "father and lord," the "vicar of Christ"; and he was to be obeyed "as if he were God."[47] We have already seen that at Cluny, a monk who merely sensed that his abbot was displeased with him immediately had to fall prostrate to the ground and beg his lord's pardon.[48]

These values perhaps instilled a greater than ordinary passivity in monks, a sense that, like the saints of the early Reformation, they were supposed to suffer and be silent under the reign of an incompetent, or even that of a tyrant. This expectation explains the lament of the monks of Saint-Médard of Soissons, faced with their abbot's resignation: "O Father who

abandons us, why do you so abruptly desert the flock committed to you, leaving the sheep of Christ given to you exposed to
the wolves, again handing over this holy house, which you have
honorably represented, to its wasters . . . ? Have mercy on us,
we, your children, beseech you. Have mercy on your suppliants.
Do not cast us away, we who are joyfully subject to your commands."[49] It also explains the passivity of the monks of Saint-
Riquier, confronted with an abbot who was universally disliked.
Not even the monastery's *seniores* took action against him. Instead they simply waited and prayed for his conversion. And
when their prayers were not granted, their final solution was
fully in keeping with the humility demanded by the petitionary
order: they went to each of their lords and patrons in turn—to
the count of Ponthieu, to the *optimates* of the king's court, to
the archbishop of Reims—to complain of their own lord's
abuses. Even after all this they meekly accepted the abbot's
mere promise to reform. At last the cathedral chapter of Reims
counseled them to bring their grievances before the forthcoming
council to be held at Reims by Urban II. Yet the monks did not
dare go themselves. Instead they sent others to the pope as
legates who could "implore the clemency of his majesty."[50]

Throughout this entire affair the monks of Saint-Riquier never
acted assertively. Always they acted through others; if not their
abbot, then the count; if not him, then the king's favorites; if
not them, then the archbishop; if not him, then members of the
provincial cathedral chapter. In the end, Urban did depose the
abbot; yet so thoroughly did the abbot control the monks' access to the outside world that, according to Hariulf, he somehow prevented them from learning of his deposition for an entire year! Only then did they confront him in chapter and
demand that he resign at once, threatening to inform the pope
of his contumacy.[51]

Supplication and intercession were therefore perfectly natural
vehicles for monks and canons to express their deference to
their protectors, and not only their ecclesiastical protectors. As
the monks of Saint-Riquier recognized, lay lords were also
guardians of churches which they had founded or endowed and
on whose behalf they petitioned favors from the great. The lords
of Péronne petitioned Kings Robert and Henry on behalf of
Mont-Saint-Quentin, over which they exercised advocacy and of

which they were the greatest benefactors. It was also at their petition, not that of the abbot or monks, that King Henry was led to seek papal confirmation of the abbey's privileges—lords petitioning a lord to petition a lord on behalf of their dependents.[52] Until the late eleventh century it was in fact customary for churches of the province of Reims to request privileges and confirmations from the pope, as from the king, only through their natural patrons.[53] Nor was patronage instrumental only in obtaining favors from kings and popes, since the lords of Péronne also petitioned the bishop of Noyon and the countess of Vermandois on behalf of their client abbey.[54] From their liturgy within the cloister to their activity in the world without, monks (and to a lesser extent canons) were habituated to having decisions made for them. They wanted the same to be true of knights and ministers as well. They needed it to be true; otherwise what was the point of their own absence of will?

The Rhetoric of Sin

It is in light of this righteous humility that we must read accounts of disputes written by the churchmen of eleventh-century northern France. While monasteries and secular chapters were part of a divine order requiring deference to tradition and authority, the demands of the *seigneurs banaux* and their satellites were "extra-ordinary" and breached the old values. By claiming "unheard-of" jurisdictions and imposing uncustomary taxes on the churches' peasants, the new lords set themselves against their natural superiors. They upset the equilibrium between heaven and earth by violating the purity of monasteries and their rights of lordship. They were, in other words, every bit as much insurgents against a divine order as were rebels against kings and princes. And in their accounts of disputes, monks and canons described them as such.

The nature of justice in the province of Reims during this period can be understood only when it is realized that all disputes were conceived of in absolute terms, not only political battles between rulers but also—and more especially—those that brought established ecclesiastical institutions face to face with the claims of new social groups. The antagonism voiced by abbots and canons when they railed against their adversaries was justified, in their eyes, by the fact that the accused had acted against the established order. The *perversi homines* who built a tower in Compiègne in violation of Saint-Corneille's immunity were derided as "most obstinate" because they "stood against" an immunity that had existed under the protection of kings and popes since Carolingian times.[55] Similarly, some sergeants of Saint-Vaast who built a tower within the sanctuary of the monastery were derided for their "treason" and "insolence."[56]

When lowly peasants asserted themselves against their ecclesiastical betters and refused to pay customary taxes, their actions of course were construed as "insurrection."[57] But ecclesiastics treated *seigneurs* with the same disdain. The monks of Mont-Saint-Quentin, for instance, claimed that one Oylard Corbeis "rose against us"—his great offense being that he dared claim viscomital rights over a public road.[58] And when the bishop of Noyon founded a new college of canons in a parish where his castellan had existing rights, he received the castellan's claims to compensatory privileges within the new foundation as a personal affront, saying that "in this affair Hugo, the castellan, resisted me."[59] Such attitudes implicitly rejected the possibility that the defendant had advanced a responsible, reasonable claim. Indeed, the very fact that a viscount or castellan had claimed jurisdiction against an ecclesiastical dignitary or institution made him the enemy of the established political order.

To monasteries and chapters, their antagonists had violated not mere temporal norms but, more important, a world order established by God. Because these ecclesiastical institutions were part of the divine order, attacks against their rights were automatically construed as attacks against God himself.[60] Their enemies were guilty not just of injustice but of "impiety" or "sacrilege."[61] They were "violators of the donations of God's holy church" who pillaged "without fear of either man or God."[62] They usurped not the property of an earthly institution but the "allod of the martyr" in whose name and for whose service the donation had originally been made.[63] The enemies of monasteries were, in other words, the enemies of God and his saints, for like the treasonous sergeants of Saint-Vaast, they "re-

belled both against the church and against God."[64] Thus the language of these disputes was the language of political rebellion
and religious apostasy at once. Were not the advocates of Saint-
Valéry-sur-Somme said to be guilty of "sedition" against the
saint?[65]

One can learn a great deal from the slanderous epithets that
eleventh-century scribes applied to their antagonists. Not surprisingly, one of the most common was "proud." We have already seen the sin of pride ascribed to the leaders of political
rebellions, such as Haimo of Germigny; but it was not restricted to them. Those who merely asserted their own limited
interests against monks and canons were also called proud,
since they challenged churches whose inviolability was also
part of the divine order on earth. Godfrid was a "powerful and
strong man, as proud as he was powerful, and he feared neither
man nor God."[66] Abbot Angelran of Saint-Riquier spent much of
his tenure "vanquishing the pride of the powerful." Particularly
troublesome to Angelran was the knight Hubert, who tried to
seize some of the monastery's villages "in a spirit of pride and
rapacity."[67]

Such cascades of slander suggest that the monks never understood the actions of their antagonists and never tried to. Their
way of life imbued them with a profound fear of change and an
exalted sense of their own importance in the world. It also instilled in them a reflexive assumption that the world was riven
by antagonistic forces. On the one hand the proud, on the other
the humble. On the one hand the powerful, on the other the
poor. The corrupt against the pure. The worldly against the
naive. All history was nothing more than the working out of a
ceaseless contest between the Two Cities, and their own contemporary travails were seen as the continuing unfolding of this
providential struggle. But the ending of the story was also familiar to them, through the psalms they sang daily: God would
have mercy on those who suffered for him. He would take vengeance on the proud and raise up the humble.

It was therefore only too easy for monks and canons to fit the
new lords into their foreordained berth in hell. And so they did
not try to understand their motivations, believing that they already did. In the middle of the eleventh century, for example, a
dispute arose between the monks of Homblières and a certain

Fulbert concerning Fulbert's jurisdiction over an allod given to the monastery by his father. Confronted by Fulbert's claims, the monks warned him privately to surrender before they openly denounced him to the count of Hainaut. Doubtless they felt that this act had satisfied Matthew's demand that Christians must give an enemy a private *monitio* before making a dispute public (18:15–18). But in offering this supposedly evangelical warning, the monks confronted Fulbert instead of negotiating with him, "calling on him to make satisfaction" over the donation of his father. Given the technical meaning of *satisfactio*, that was a presumption of sin. Moreover, Fulbert's father had probably given only possession of the allod, not jurisdiction over it; and it was only jurisdiction that Fulbert claimed. Yet the monks were unable to ascribe any reasonable motivation on the part of their adversary, arguing that Fulbert had reneged on his father's donation "because of greed for earthly things."[68]

So it was in most situations in which the Benedictines confronted new lords. The abbot of Corbie alleged that their advocate, Efredo of Encre, was "spiteful and detestable" and responsible for a "calamity of evil."[69] Oylard Corbeis refused to appear before the lord of Péronne when summoned, and so forfeited to Mont-Saint-Quentin his claims to jurisdiction over a public road. Once the lord died, however, he turned to violence to make his claims. The only way the monks could explain Oylard's actions was to point to his "malice," a malice they felt had been restrained only by his miserable fear of the lord of Péronne. "As long as the lord had lived he had not dared bring any force against us. But upon his death . . . he turned to renewed malice by rising up against us."[70] In the same way the monks of Mont-Saint-Quentin believed that they had sufficiently accounted for Dodo of Heudicourt's claims against them by alleging that "his heart was bitter."[71]

The antagonists of ecclesiastical institutions were "presumptuous," "insolent," "rapacious," "malicious," "greedy," "deceitful," "full of hate," "raging," "depraved," and "avaricious," not to mention "proud" and just plain "evil."[72] The clerics' clamors to kings and counts consistently declaimed against the "new" evils of their rivals, their "usurpations," their "unheard-of" exactions that were "against customary laws."[73] Always they emphasized the world that was passing, never the one that was coming to be. The psychology of the *seigneurs banaux* (or that of the new communes, or that of peasants striving to resist the churches' own exactions) was simply one of prideful opposition to a social order which had been established by God and had no room for change.

The *Ordo Rationis*

Of all the vices with which monks and canons defamed their enemies, the only one that equalled pride in frequency and significance was madness. When, for example, the *perversi homines* of Compiègne built a tower in that city in violation of Saint-Corneille's immunity, their insane affront received its fit punishment when they were driven literally insane.

> Their violence reached this point of madness [*vesanie*], that they rose against the said holy church and seized its farms by violence; and at last, their insanity [*insania*] becoming naked fact, they built fortifications and a tower before the church itself. Nor was their madness quieted until the divine piety of God, under whose protection the foundation of the church stood immovable, exercised strict and manifest vengeance on them; for some of those most obstinate men [*obstinatissimis*] were tormented by insanity or madness [*insania aut furore agitati*], while others suffocated in a far worse death, all condemned by the secret examination of God.[74]

The canons of Saint-Corneille themselves drew up this account, and their outrage still echoes. Three different words (*vesania, furor, insania*) were necessary to underscore the madness of the *perversi homines*. Of course, even by eleventh-century standards the canons of Saint-Corneille were somewhat reactionary, as they held on to Carolingian values and formulas long after other monasteries and chapters had begun to discard them. Even so, these other institutions shared the conviction that their antagonists were spiritually "disordered"—insane. The epithet was not simply a random slur. It went to the heart of the conservative vision of society. Henry I had called the political order an "order of reason" (*ordo rationis*) and in a common utterance had granted a petition "because it appeared reasonable."[75] As always, this idea became imbued with cosmological overtones. For Raoul Glaber, the "gift of reason" is what placed

men above beasts; and it was in his reason that man most especially assumed the image of God. Conversely, to act unreasona-
bly was to descend to the level of the raging beasts of the wild.
"Just as moderation and love of its author—in other words, true
humility and perfect charity—maintains the good of man's reason, so concupiscence and madness destroy its usefulness and
render it worthless. By not repelling these evils man is made
like the beasts, whereas by serving them he is made conform-
able to the image of the Saviour."[76] The author of the *Gesta
episcoporum Cameracensium* reached back to an ancient tradition to make the same point: in the early days of the human
race men had wandered about like wild beasts, without the benefit of reason and knowing neither human nor divine laws. Only
when they gathered together in cities "did they learn to cultivate faith and hold to justice and grow accustomed to obey
others willingly."[77]

Reason was therefore bound up with devotion to God, because reason was the faculty that made us like God. But as usually happened with religious attributes in the early Middle
Ages, reason was also a social virtue, since it taught men to
subordinate their own desires to the wills of their lords. As
Raoul had said, reason was maintained by humility. Conversely, to live according to one's own desires (this, after all, is
what Raoul meant by *concupiscentia*) was to abandon the rules
of society, therby clouding one's reason and returning to the
level of the beasts. Although Gerbert does not refer to reason
per se, it is this kind of argument that underlies his refusal to
give a blessing to the traitorous Adalbero of Laon. For Adalbero
had betrayed his king; and so "by your conduct you have ceased
to be a man; for if fidelity renders the mortal like God, treachery brings him down to the level of a beast."[78]

Rationality maintained social order. Insanity destroyed it; or
rather, to seek to undermine social order was to act as if insane,
because selfish, undisciplined actions were what one would expect from a beast without reason. This is why rebels against
political authority were frequently derided as mad, insane, savage, and wild. William of Jumièges spoke of the "madness" (*vesania*) of those who opposed the authority of the Norman duke,
or derided them as "rabid" (*rabie*)—just as one would refer to a
mad dog.[79] Indeed, the canons of Notre-Dame of Noyon said

that a knight who had repudiated a previous settlement with them had "returned to his vomit," like the dog of Proverbs 26:11.[80] Raoul Glaber condemned Queen Constance's hostility toward her sons as "bestial madness." He used similar terms to describe a heretic like Leutard, the rustic who, dreaming, felt bees enter his body "through the secret places of nature" and mistook their buzzing for a revelation.[81]

Of course anyone who hears bees in his bowels might well be insane. But Raoul also applied the word to those who were less whimsical in their heresy. For example, two canons of Orléans who rejected the Church's sacraments were guilty of a "most insane heresy." Raoul also claimed that their doctrine was "insolent," and he made the political overtones of that word explicit when he called heretics in general "rebels against the truth."[82] As for Leutard, even without the bees his teachings were sufficient proof of his madness, which seems to have had a good deal of method in it in any case. Quite apart from his rejection of tithes, Leutard believed that he had received a revelation directly from God, thus violating the intercessory authority of the church. He had put away his wife "according to the Gospel precept," ignoring the fact that the *ordo* of the laity had its own, quite special role in the church. Worst of all, Leutard had entered a church and broken the cross and the image of the Saviour—and what more fitting symbol could there be that to lose one's reason was to lose the image of God?[83] Leutard's madness was more graphic than that of more learned heretics, but at root it was the same madness: a rejection of the intercessory authority of the church's leaders, which of course could only lead to disorder, both within the individual and within the community.

One did not need to rebel against God, kings, or dukes to be likened to a mad beast. Rebellion against any of God's vicars was a repudiation of reason and therefore madness. The author of the *Gesta* of the bishops of Cambrai, having detailed the castellan of Cambrai's acts of defiance against his bishop, said that after his death "his wife . . . did not depart from the insanity of her husband." The same writer dismissed the abbot of Saint-Vaast's insubordination to his bishop as "raging" (*furor*).[84] The bishop of Noyon warned the guardian of the city's fortress against his unfounded claims to public jurisdiction and revenues: "but none of the exhortations of the religious would make him return to reason [*resipiscere*]; and not wanting to bear his madness [*vecordiam*] any longer, the bishop, together with the clergy and the people . . . , proposed to resist him utterly."[85]

In fact, as the earlier example from Compiègne shows, any resistance to any element of the divinely ordained order could be construed by those injured as an indication that the so-called rebel had lost the image of God. Walter Tirel "seized" a village of Saint-Riquier—an act which the abbey's chronicler explained by referring to Walter's "malice of insane avarice."[86] Albert of Creil's usurpation of land claimed by Jumièges was also called "insanity" by the royal charter that recorded his condemnation.[87] Hubert, a knight who claimed land of Saint-Riquier by hereditary right, turned to violence to enforce his claim. Hariulf regarded that act as evidence of his "insanity."[88] Both in chronicles and in charters, charges of madness are so numerous that they might well be mistaken for clichés, mere habits of speech, were it not for their prominence and, still more significant, were it not for the fact that they were part of such a well-worked-out paradigmatic system—a system that monks and canons continued to elaborate quite consciously. The cartulary of Saint-Bertin, for example, tells the story of one Bodora, a lowly "subminister" who oppressed Saint-Bertin's peasants at Chaumont. He was warned to desist. He did not. Far from it, he extended his abuses by seizing the peasants' cattle as they grazed in the fields and using them for his own lord's work. He had been warned once by the abbot's representative. Now he was told that he was about to suffer "the rod of heavenly wrath." Immediately Bodora began to undergo a metamorphosis. His head was turned around so that his face was where his hair should have been and his hair was where his face should have been. His neck swelled, and so did his lips. "What greater wonder could be seen or written about?" marveled the chronicler. "There was nothing human in him to be looked upon." And to complete Bodora's descent into bestiality, the wretch began to bellow like a bull.[89] Just as the political disorder of the *perversi homines* at Compiègne was punished by mental disorder, so Bodora was punished by being transformed into what he really was: a beast without language, without reason, without the image of his Creator.

Begging Pardon

By this time it should be apparent that the conservative ideal of justice was inherently "sympathetic." In other words, it was "proportionate," as William of Poitiers said of the duke of Normandy's justice.[90] Bodora, who seized peasants' cattle and behaved like a beast, was himself transmogrified into a bull, and the figurative madness of the *perversi homines* of Compiègne was punished by their being driven literally insane. Proud knights fell from their horses, emblems of the martial power that literally raised them above lowly peasants, and broke their necks.[91] A monk who refused to respect the silence of the cloister was struck dumb.[92] Some serfs at Viry belonging to Notre-Dame of Paris who had the presumption to claim freedom from servile exactions found that when it was time to testify to their assertions they could not utter a coherent sentence.[93] A count of Vermandois who had a blaspheming tongue was struck with a disease that made his tongue feel as if it had caught fire; and in fact, when his mouth was pried open after his death, it was found to have been burned black.[94]

Of course, these examples are instances of divine punishment. They say nothing about how frequently talion guided the penalties levied by courts or the compositions paid in feuds. A few instances suggest that here, too, proportionate justice could sometimes be quite consciously exacted.[95] It is, however, the general principle of talion in ecclesiastical sources that is most important to retain. The proud were humbled. Those who behaved like beasts were shown to have no reason. Those who spoke ill were struck dumb. True justice required such perfect symmetry as a reflection of the symmetry between heaven and earth. And even if such symmetry did not dictate specific punishments, there is no doubt that it informed the language and structure of litigation, at least as it was described by monks and canons.

If, for example, social disorder demonstrated a loss of reason, then logically, restoring order meant restoring reason. Litigation could therefore be seen as the triumph of the *ordo rationis*. From this point of view the entire judicial process was nothing more than a forum through which reason could be manifested.[96] What was expected from witnesses was that they make "reasonable contradiction" of the opposing party's assertions, while to prove one's case was to *dirationare*.[97] Bishop Harduin of Noyon accepted a claim made against him by one of his clerics because "he had reason against us."[98] Conversely, a lord might reject a suitor's claim because it was "void of all just reason."[99] Finally, a party was expected to "show reason" (*redderet rationem*) in support of his claims. As always, the divine archetype hovered over these habits of speech, since in the final judgment every Christian would "stand before the tribunal of Christ and show reason [*rationem reddat*] for what he has done."[100]

Those who could not show reason for their claims and actions were naturally condemned; but what is relevant in the present context is that their condemnation was made to fit a talion whose terms were dictated by the paradigm of supplication, in ways that illustrate just how dense the ritual could be. Because those who made unjust claims against churches were sinners against God, they had to confess before they could be restored to the church. Because their sin had been a prideful rebellion and a mad opposition to the principles of deference, they had to show that they had returned to reason; in other words, they had to display the humility that maintained reason. Like disobedient monks and disloyal rebels they had to beg pardon, showing by their prostrate supplication that they had renounced their pride, that the *ordo rationis* had been restored.

As one would expect, this pattern was especially prominent in private settlements involving churches and prelates. In these cases a formal confession was often necessary to absolve a party who had been excommunicated in the course of the dispute. Thus Baldwin Caldruns, excommunicated by the abbot of Saint-Vaast for actions left unstated, "instilled with penance humbly called us to him, and tearfully prayed indulgence for what he had done to us."[101] Similarly, in renouncing his unjust entry onto property of Sainte-Croix of Orléans, Lancelin of Bulles came before the bishop of Beauvais, "begged pardon," and thereby "merited absolution."[102] Some texts, however, mention no excommunication at all. Here it may be that churchmen were simply demanding the performance of a ritual that was meaningful to them, and that followed naturally from their understanding of unjust claims as sinful. So the knight Gislebert, having "unjustly and violently" imposed his jurisdiction on property of Saint-Valéry-sur-Somme, at last summoned the monks "so that he might humbly beseech their mercy for him and his."[103]

There can be little doubt that such confessions entailed the customary gestures of penance. The formulas describing Lancelin's and Gislebert's requests for forgiveness are those that denote kneeling or prostration in monastic sources.[104] Other texts clearly describe the condemned's prostration. Some knights who had resisted Saint-Valéry's efforts to take possession of land donated to the monastery finally recognized their fault by coming barefoot before the monks and their relics, bearing sticks as symbols of their pledges, and prostrating themselves on the ground to "beg pardon."[105] Walter Tirel, excommunicated because he had "maliciously seized" a village belonging to Saint-Riquier, finally surrendered his claim; and lying "prostrate on the ground" he received absolution.[106] A young man who had repudiated his father's donation to Saint-Martin of Pontoise remitted his claim by falling at the feet of the abbot, where "with many tears he begged to be absolved by him."[107]

Although these actions are described as confessions, our interpretation of them cannot be restricted to this literal meaning. As we saw with the prostration of kings before their sacrings, ritual gestures are polysemic. Alluding to similar rites performed in different circumstances, they echo them and draw additional meanings from them. So here confession was not simply confession. It was an act that restored a deferential order. It was an act that allowed the penitent to show he had renounced his pride and returned to humility. It was an act that symbolized his return from madness to reason.

In analyzing the symbology of these confessions, however, one should not forget their most obvious meaning: the accused had been publicly humiliated. A confession performed in the privacy of a cloister might not have meant much to a man forced to yield against his will but still convinced of his right; but these were not private events. They were public renunciations before lords, peers, and inferiors. The losing party may still not have agreed that his cause was unjust, and he may not have felt sorry. But the fact remained that he had been beaten and had acknowledged the fact in a public prostration. He had been forced to admit that he did not have the support necessary to win his case. He had, in other words, lost face.

Even in the early church this had been one of the intended effects of public penance. Though in subsequent ages public penance had lost its institutional coherence, yet these penitential acts were still performed publicly, and they were still meant to shame.[108] The case of a ninth-century Breton named Uurbudic illustrates the point convincingly. He had made a formal complaint against Abbot Conwoion of Redon for part of an *exclusa*—meaning, perhaps, access to or control over a mill stream. The men of the nearby *plebes* gathered on the banks of the stream and argued among themselves until Uurbudic, "full of rage," stated his claims more passionately: that the charter recording the donation of the *exclusa* to Redon was false, because the man who had made it was not free. Alarmed by the outburst, the old men of one of the *plebes* openly called him a liar. Upon this open show of dissent, Uurbudic realized he had effectively lost his case. "Confounded and suppliant, he prostrated himself at the feet of the said Conwoion, confessing that he had spoken a falsehood, and that he had no right to that part of the *exclusa*."[109]

In some sense this was a penitential act; certainly Uurbudic's prostration and "confession" were informed by the paradigm of penance. But if the language and gestures of penance informed his action, its matter was something far simpler. As the writer himself realized, Uurbudic became suppliant because he had been confounded. Like those said to have been "prostrated" in battle, the prostration of a loser in court was a sign of defeat.

The fact that Conwoion was an abbot undoubtedly made the penitential aspects of Uurbudic's supplication more apparent; but one did not need to hold a spiritual office to receive a prostration. A fourteenth-century illustration of the *Sachsenspiegel* depicts parties kneeling before a judge; and though this evidence is of course much later than our period, yet prostration was also common among the laity of eleventh-century Flanders, where killers prostrated themselves in front of their victims' relatives to beg for mercy and forgiveness.[110] Such actions were also typical in the courts of lay lords. In fact, they were noted with special frequency in cases that involved castellans, because a public judgment against a banal lord in the court of a prince was nothing less than a public shaming. Alberic of Coucy, who had claimed the right to tax conveyancers of Saint-Médard of Soissons, did not simply lose his case in the court of

Philip I; he also suffered the "censure" (*censura*) of the bishops and counts who judged him.[111] His predecessor at Coucy, Robert, tried before Henry I, was said to have been "vanquished" (*victus*) in his suit, the defeat coming at the hands of the bishops, abbots, "and many nobles" who judged him. Here, too, the language and gestures of penance drove home his failure, as Robert was required to do penance for his "tyranny" against Saint-Médard.[112] Similarly, in condemning Fulbert for his claims against Homblières the count of Hainaut demanded that Fulbert "make satisfaction, first to God and his holy mother Mary through the hand of his abbot, and then over the unjust invasion committed within the bounds of my dominion." The count accepted Fulbert's promise to desist only after he had rendered this formal appeasement.[113]

Most instructive of all is a story told in the *Gesta episcoporum Cameracensium*. Bishop Gerard of Cambrai had long had trouble with the city's unruly castellan, Walter. Unable to restrain Walter's violence against him, Gerard finally sought the aid of the emperor, doing so in a way that contrasted his own respect for authority with his castellan's arrogance. The bishop "hurried to meet the emperor, and showing due subservience [*debitum obsequium exhibens*], he cried out [*exclamavit*] over Walter's injury and disobedience." The emperor sent legates to investigate the crimes of the castellan, who ignored their summons. Frustrated by his recalcitrance, the legates finally threatened to bring Walter before the emperor himself to suffer judgment if he persisted in his contumacy. Before this threat Walter submitted, directing his penitential gestures as much to the legates and public as to the bishop. "Having rendered hostages, and even an oath, and adding prayer upon prayer, he cast himself down in all humility [*tota se humilitate deiecit*] to the satisfaction of all."[114]

Certainly litigation did not always end in prostration. Prostration had no role, for example, when courts confirmed pacts and conventions, for the gestures of these bilateral agreements belonged to another repertoire.[115] Handing over symbolic pledges or breaking *festucae* were still different court rituals in which prostration had no necessary part. (As the case involving Saint-Valéry indicates, however, the giving of pledges could be combined with prostration.) Litigation in the early Middle Ages was accompanied by a range of gestures, each set appropriate to certain circumstances. Suppliant prostration was the gesture appropriate for those whose acts were judged to have violated a fundamental rule of social order.

The Public Persona of Legitimate Authority

If reflexive antagonism marked the attitude of the churches toward their supposed inferiors, what was their attitude toward kings and princes? We may assume that ecclesiastics, and monks especially, respected authority. That was part of their culture, instilled in them through the daily round of psalms and lessons. But their respect was more hopeful than trusting; and it was directed more toward the ideal of authority in general than to any individual lay incarnation, who was often far too near for comfort. Guimann of Saint-Vaast said it openly of the counts of Flanders: "The closer they were to us, the more burdensome the counts became."[116]

Indeed, the closer God's rulers, the more obvious that they could be little better than the advocates they were supposed to protect churches from. The house chronicles of monasteries and chapters betray this ambivalence quite unmistakably. One abbot of Saint-Riquier berated the count of Ponthieu for holding onto the church's property "with invective of such authority that you would have thought a serf was being chastised by a lord, and not a count by a man."[117] In this particular case the abbot's presumption may have been permitted by the fact that the count's title was so recent; the abbot could surely remember a time when the count had been no more than an advocate. But even the oldest comital lineages were often deprecated by monastic and clerical writers—especially when they were writing about counts in another territory, or when they were writing only for each other and not to flatter their lords. The *Gesta* of the bishops of Cambrai described the count of Vermandois as having such an evil, blaspheming tongue that God burned his mouth, and its author's dislike of the count of Flanders is well known.[118] The abbot and monks of Corbie were even more disrespectful toward the counts of Amiens. Walter was remembered as being especially odious. It was he, recalled Abbot Fulk, who had "disturbed" the church and "seized" its viscomital powers, his evil actions motivated in Fulk's view only by his hatred of the preceding abbot.[119] Later in the century the monks of Corbie were no less hostile to the count of Flanders, who had seized the monastery's estates in Flanders.[120]

Yet such expressions of antagonism toward counts are relatively rare. They cannot compare in frequency with the monastic invectives against advocates and knights, not to mention men of lesser status. Moreover, expressions of hostility toward counts were almost invariably reserved for the privacy of the cloister. Fulk of Corbie's condemnation of Walter of Amiens was recorded in a memorandum destined for the monastery's archives. The injustices of the count of Flanders toward Corbie were similarly recorded in a work intended for internal consumption, the twelfth-century *Miracula sancti Adalhardi*. The same is of course true of the *Gesta episcoporum Cameracensium*.[121] For the benefit of their fellows, monks and canons could write what they would never have dared express to a count's face. Not only would it have been impolitic to do so; the iconography of legitimate authority demanded that in public counts be depicted as protectors of churches.

Nowhere is this difference between private opinion and public image more apparent than in Hariulf's description of Saint-Riquier's disputes with the counts of Ponthieu and the king of France. Much of Hariulf's work is actually a commentary on select charters, so that we can look both at the image of authority presented by a charter and at the way Hariulf's informants remembered the event. In two cases we find a considerable discrepancy. In the one just mentioned, the abbot of Saint-Riquier harangued the count for holding lands that had belonged to the monastery during its golden age, before the invasions. The abbot addressed the count like a serf, calling him "unfaithful" and a "thief," and promised that he would excommunicate him "unless he promised to make amends." Even Hariulf was surprised at his abbot's presumption.[122]

The second case is even more surprising, because here Hariulf criticized the king himself.[123] Saint-Riquier had long had problems with a local knight named Hubert, who had claimed to possess the village of Noyelles-en-Chaussée by hereditary right. When the abbot denied his claim, Hubert responded "insanely," imprisoning at least one of the abbey's *fideles*, pillaging its villages, and in spite of his excommunication, acting like a "savage" and a "tyrant." Eventually Henry I prosecuted him; evidently Hubert was executed and his family disinherited.[124] But instead of returning Noyelles to Saint-Riquier, Henry held onto it himself for five years. It was this act that earned him Hariulf's opprobrium, and the monk did not hesitate to apply to the king some of the same invective that he had formerly reserved for Hubert. The king, Hariulf implied, was a man, and "rapacity moves the hearts of mortal men." Henry, like Hubert, was simply "filled with greed."

None of this invective, however, appeared in the charters through which count and king subsequently redressed their wrongs. Henry did eventually return the village to Saint-Riquier; but he did so without a word about his usurpation. From the point of view of his diploma, written by the monks themselves, the king had simply acted the part of a magnanimous lord responding to the wishes of the monks. "For five years I held [the village] entirely and peacefully. After this I remembered my soul, and thinking, though too little, of its redemption, and inclining also to the abbot and the college of monks, I handed it over to Saint Richarius. Count Angelran, advocate of the said place, also added a petition of his own, which I approved, such that henceforth no one shall receive any custom there." The count's charter in favor of the abbey veiled the background given by Hariulf even more opaquely: "I, Angelran, desire it to be made known . . . that while staying in the palace of the most excellent King Robert at Compiègne, I presented a certain charter of donation which I had made to Saint Richarius to be corroborated in his presence. Which concession I presented in the presence of the king and nobles of the kingdom." Were it not for Hariulf's commentary, which of course was never intended for public view, we would never know that there had been any contention. But that is the point of public documents in the eleventh century. They presented an ideal of order, one so strong that even a second-rank count such as Angelran required gingerly treatment.

In these two examples we are a little closer to seeing, albeit indirectly as always, how the great lords conceived of their own authority. If the monks of Saint-Riquier wanted a testament of

auctoritas, they had to use language that the lords would accept. They had to describe not their greed and pursuit of power
but their spirit of largesse, motivated by love of the saints, desire for the health of their souls, and, in the king's case, the
virtues of gracious lords who yielded to the entreaties of their
faithful. Perhaps a certain tension does underlie both charters.
The count was noticeably silent about the reasons for his donation; and the king said more than he usually did about the
needs of his soul. But the public idealization of legitimate authority was still maintained. Neither king nor count was required to admit any wrongdoing.

One might object that it is only natural to flatter the powerful, but that is the point. Throughout most of the province of
Reims, castellans, advocates, and knights did not enjoy such legitimate power that monks and clerics thought it fitting to treat
them with honor. In contrast, charters from monasteries of the
Loire valley regularly describe these laymen as the "friends" of
monks. Lords and knights held benefices from monks and made
donations to them. In return, monks gave them *societas et fraternitas*, acted as mediators in their feuds, and settled their
own, not infrequent disputes with them by means of pacts. Flat-
tering the powerful may have been natural, but it was also cultural, insofar as it required a discriminatory judgment of who
was legitimately powerful and worthy of honor.[125]

This act of discrimination shaped the entire range of the disputing process in the north, excommunication providing the
most obvious indicator. Northern counts simply were not excommunicated in the eleventh century, at least not before the
Gregorian Reform; and even after the Reform there was something jarring about the idea, so that the archbishop of Reims
could describe the count of Rethel's excommunication in 1127
as bringing "the shame of dishonor."[126] An abbot might warn a
count that his actions were endangering his soul. He might
even threaten a curse, as Angelran of Saint-Riquier did to the
count of Ponthieu. But he would not take the final step—or if
he did, mention of it was omitted from the charter.[127]

Thus excommunication was left as a shaming reserved for advocates, knights, and a church's lowly ministers.[128] Mentions of
divine retribution were also limited to lesser men—even in
such private sources as *vitae* and memoranda. It is disputes in-

volving castellans, advocates, ministers, burghers, and peasants that furnish the most numerous and most colorful instances of divine intervention: Bodora, the subminister of Saint-Bertin left bellowing like a bull; the rapacious knight whom Saint Arnulf caused to lose his sons; the *perversi homines* of Compiègne who were driven mad or suffocated within the tower they had built; the peasants who spoke gibberish at court when they were called on to justify their refusal to pay dues; the knight who spilled all his bowels into a latrine and (what no one would doubt) perished horribly.[129] God exacted no corresponding vengeance from his legitimate ministers, save perhaps in the case of the count of Vermandois's blaspheming tongue; and even that sin was a relatively minor one by a somewhat distant count, and as usual one discussed only privately, in the pages devoted to the deeds of the bishops of Cambrai.[130] It was not part of the count's public persona within the Vermandois.

Similarly, though counts might have to acknowledge the injustice of their claims against churches, either privately or in a formal trial, they did not have to suffer the indignity of a public humiliation. Such sensitivity to counts' status was not shown everywhere in France. We will see that several Angevins did penance for violating monastic rights.[131] But in the more conservative north every effort was made to mitigate the shame of their defeats. When toward the end of the century the count of Vermandois was condemned by a formal judgment of Philip I's court, he was allowed to turn the court's judgment into his own gracious concession, as he himself requested its execution and conceded the rights sought.[132] A fictional prostration by the count of Flanders after a dispute was described by the monks of Corbie not as a penitential humiliation but as an act of "devotion" to the relics of their saint.[133] In a charter for Jumièges, Count Galeran of Meulan admitted that he had acted unjustly in seizing land of Jumièges; but far from being portrayed as mad or rapacious, the count was allowed to justify his actions, so that they appeared eminently reasonable. Neither did the count suffer any judgment in this case; nor did the language of the charter slander him in any way.[134] Formal proceedings and judgment were also rejected in a dispute between Count Drogo of Amiens and Saint-Père of Chartres. The count simply remitted his claims, with not a word about his sinfulness.[135]

Such differences in disputes involving the greater and lesser were quite consistent. (The source of the following information may be found in appendix 2.) Disputants identified as viscounts, castellans, advocates, knights, and ministers suffered disproportionately at the hands of earthly judges. In 34 percent of their legal processes with churches (19 of 56) either their claims were condemned by formal judgments or their lords—usually kings or counts—imposed a settlement on them. In another 35 percent of the disputes (20 of the 56) they were pressured to "quit" their claims (*dimittere, guerpire, abrenuntiare*) or to beg absolution for their wrongs. Thus nearly 70 percent of ecclesiastical disputes with such laymen ended in ways that connoted subjection or defeat.

Kings, in contrast, are never shown succumbing to judgments, and counts only rarely. Of the counts involved in fourteen recorded disputes, only two suffered completely adverse judgments in formal court settings, and neither of these judgments was announced in a way that conveyed moral censure. Nor were great lords habitually forced to quit their claims or beg absolution. Instead, they were allowed to "concede" rights they had unsuccessfully claimed as if there had been no dispute at all. We have already seen the euphemism applied to the counts of Flanders and Vermandois and Angelran of Ponthieu. It was also applied to Count Guido of Ponthieu, who "conceded" that the exactions of his agents on the town of Saint-Riquier would be lightened at the "fervent beseeching" of the abbot—admittedly after receiving 100 *solidi* in compensation.[136] Similarly, Herbert of Vermandois "lauded and confirmed" Homblières's claim to liberty from his authority, requiring no more than the testimony of three of the abbey's serfs in support of its claims.[137] The same count "granted the petition" of the abbot and monks of Saint-Prix when they complained to him about the exactions of one of his provosts on their estates.[138]

As the acts of Guido and Herbert suggest, the churches even devised a fiction to save the honor of these great men: their usurpations were not really their fault, but that of their ministers or evil advisers.[139] Occasionally the excuse may have been justified. Kings and counts could not always know what their local agents were doing.[140] But it was doubtless often a lie; and Hariulf's catty remarks about the count of Ponthieu proves that it was recognized as such. So does the slander against the count of Flanders in the *Miracula sancti Adalhardi*, so completely at odds with the portraits given in the counts' public charters. Yet throughout most of the eleventh century it was important to defend the fiction, because to dethrone a count from his place as divinely appointed protector of a divinely authorized polity would have placed all earthly authority at the level of a castellan's. Political authority would have become indistinguishable from military might; and though in private ecclesiastics may have acknowledged that this was true, the secret could not be admitted in public.

7 The Ideal of Discretionary Justice

The most famous definition of justice in the Middle Ages was Ulpian's, according to whom justice was "a constant, permanent will to attribute to each what pertains to them."[1] Yet this elegant proposition gained currency only in the twelfth century; and even then it was most suited for Italian society, where it first developed. Italy had the papal curia and established urban governments, both developing fixed rules of law together with the administrative apparatus to apply them. Italy had also retained a memory of Roman law, whose legitimacy was reinforced by a strong imperial presence. Finally, Italy had cities whose citizens were willing to assert their independence of their natural superiors—whether emperors, bishops, or local nobles. A notion of justice that upheld constancy and the fair distribution of rights was relevant to this type of society.

The definition was also taken up by the lawyers of France in the twelfth century; but as it was less relevant to France's more vertically structured society, there it competed with another definition of justice, one which, though new, was more faithful to traditional values. According to this alternative definition, justice was that capacity "which does most for those who can do least." This justice was a *virtus*, a moral authority exercised in defense of society's *humiliores*—its widows, its orphans, and of course its churches.[2]

Because justice issued from moral authority, it could never be identified with a fixed body of rules. This was just as well; for in the eleventh century the rules of law, such as they were, formed an inchoate collection of contradictory *exempla* and injunctions authorized by successive papal, imperial, and episcopal councils and, most important, by Scripture. In the twelfth century Gratian regarded this mass with the horror of the systematizer. He and his disciples tried to solve the problem by articulating clear and certain principles that could help to establish priorities among the various sources of law. The most important of these guiding principles was natural law. By subordinating all laws to natural law, which he identified with divine law, Gratian could argue that diverse canons are not necessarily contradictory. Human laws may change; indeed, they must change if they are to remain appropriate to the needs of different times and places. But the flux of human laws does not diminish our certitude in the existence of fixed principles of justice; for above the changing laws of societies stands the law of nature, which remains constant because anchored in God's own constant nature. This is the meaning of Gratian's dictum laid down at the beginning of his fifth distinction: "Natural law has primacy in all things, both in time and in dignity. For it began with the beginning of the rational creature and does not vary with time. It stands immutable."[3]

In the early twelfth century Ivo of Chartres also compiled a collection of canons. Like Gratian, he was troubled by their inconsistencies, and he apologized to his readers for the many contradictions that they would inevitably find within his work. But Ivo did not appeal to natural law to harmonize their discord. Instead he had another excuse readily at hand in an older conception of justice—and ultimately in its image of God as a judicial lord. Readers, he said, should not take the authority of the *decreta* absolutely. Rather they should interpret each individually, knowing when to apply a rule rigorously, when in moderation, and when with mercy. After all, he concluded, there can be no contradiction in the Word of God, whose psalms praised both mercy and judgment.[4]

In this way, the very characteristic of law which was seen as an obstacle to justice in the middle of the twelfth century had only a few decades earlier been an expression of its essential nature. Instead of residing in the uniform application of laws, justice was held to reflect that invisible grace beyond all laws. It required a discretionary authority to apply judgment and mercy. Given this interpretation, one is not surprised to learn that Ivo was bishop of that see whose cathedral school would later popularize the idea of justice as moral authority exercised to protect the humble.[5]

God, then, was the archetypal judge, and the final judge. As Christ, he would return in judgment at the end of time to separate the damned from the saved—or as Helgald of Fleury thought, the "proud" from the "humble."[6] The arbitrariness of justice was not a deficiency but an expression of a most profound and true mystery, the mystery of salvation—the mystery, that is, of "justification." There was no way for men to understand God's reasons in damning whom he damned and saving whom he saved. God kept his own counsel. As a Carolingian commentary on Job put it, to plumb his depths was to try to reach the bottom of an abyss, for God acted according to his own good will.[7] Gerard of Cambrai made the point even more forcefully: "The beginning of free salvation resides not in the virtues of nature, or in legal precepts, but in the illumination of the heart and in the willing of the divine will [*voluntario divinae voluntatis*]." Men and women could claim nothing as their own right in that final judgment, since all the good of which they were capable originated in the mercy of God.[8] Besides, said Anselm of Laon, according to the "rigor of justice" Adam's descendants deserved eternal damnation. If God deigned to save any of them, it was only because "God mitigated this strictness with his mercy."[9] Fallen humanity was therefore utterly dependent upon God's good grace; and all sinners who sought forgiveness of their sins gave proof that they recognized their dependence by prostrating themselves before God and begging his mercy. "I beseech, O Lord, the majesty of your clemency and mercy," prayed the kneeling priest, interceding for a kneeling penitent. "Suppliant we ask and beg you to incline the ear of your piety to our prayers. May you deign to offer pardon."[10] Supplication here was the acknowledgment that by strict justice one was lost—and that salvation could be won only by placing oneself in the mercy of the Lord. Before all else, divine justice was an act of the Lord's grace.

As in heaven, so on earth: justice was a manifestation of true lordship and required not the consistent application of rules but the moral authority to decide when to apply judgment and when mercy. "Judgment and mercy" or "justice and mercy": no attributes fell more easily from the pens of early medieval political theorists.[11] Jonas of Orléans marshaled a battery of Old Testament citations to prove "that piety, justice, and mercy were the supports of a kingdom," and that "he who rules piously and justly and mercifully beyond doubt rules through God."[12] Alcuin said the same, and made explicit the connection between a king's mercy and God's: "It pertains to the king to suppress all iniquities through the power of his piety. He should be just in his judgments but ready in his mercy—and accordingly, as he shows compassion to his subjects God will show compassion to him."[13] Indeed, so strong was the pairing of justice and mercy that it caused Gerard of Cambrai's memory some difficulty. For the benefit of the heretics of Arras, Gerard quoted Psalm 83: *Quia misericordiam et judicium diligit Deus.* Psalm 83 should read: *Quia misericordiam et veritatem diligit Deus.*[14]

Simply because it was unwitting, this simple mistake reveals the reflexive assumption that mercy was the obverse of justice. Because great lords held their power by the mercy of God, no lord could be truly just if he did not also know how to act mercifully. This was not merely an abstract principle. Ivo of Chartres applied it to decide specific cases.

> If any person has a land held at *census* which his ancestors gave to one of our churches or villages, in no way can he hold it according to law save by the will of him to whose power that church or village pertains. However, if he be the son or nephew of the one who conveyed the land, then the land may be adjudicated [*placitata sit*] to him to be held in tenure. But in considering this matter, one must consider also whether he who will hold this be rich or poor, and whether he have any other benefice or property. And he who has neither of these things shall be accorded mercy in this matter, lest despoiled of everything he fall into poverty. That man either shall pay such *census* as will be ordained for him or shall receive in benefice such a portion that he shall be able to sustain himself.[15]

In this way Ivo gave approval to those lords who judged not according to the rigors of law but according to the moral demands of mercy. Historians are fond of citing disputes that were resolved by the compromise of ecclesiastical claims as evidence of the failure of medieval law. It would be interesting to know how many of these compromises were not rather implementations of a different kind of law than ours—one which stressed the compassionate distribution of wealth over proprietary right.[16]

But more than compassion toward the poor was at issue here, for the early medieval concept of poverty was notoriously formalistic. The "poor" were, of course, simply the poor. But poverty was also a political and religious concept, since by definition the poor included all those who were defenseless and therefore dependent on the protection of God's vicars. These included widows and orphans. They also included the *pauperes Christi*—the monks who served God without possessing any individual wealth (regardless of the opulence of their institutions) and who, like widows and orphans, lacked means of self-defense and depended on kings and counts for their protection. In this way, poverty came to be a synonym for willing dependence on legitimate authority. To be poor was to be one of the *humiliores*—one of "those who can do least" (in the Chartrean formulation) for whom those in political authority were to do most.[17]

It was therefore the poor and humble who especially merited the mercy of lords, the powerful and proud who merited the rigor of their judgment. According to Suger, Louis VI began his war against Haimo of Germigny "moved by both love of justice and pity [*miseratione*] for the poor."[18] And William of Poitiers extolled the justice of William of Normandy, "a defender full of mercy, a judge who was perfectly just." Merciful, he accepted the complaints of widows, orphans, and the poor. Vengeful, "he knew how to repress unjust greed" so that "no one dared to take advantage of a weaker neighbor."[19]

As William's statement shows, vengeance was also part of the panoply of lordly justice in the early Middle Ages. No one then would have doubted what Fulbert of Chartres assumed: that the punishment of proven criminals, whether guilty of crimes against the *res publica* or against God and his saints, was an act of vengeance.[20] The punishment of both kinds of criminals pertained to the great lords. This aspect of justice was symbolized by the staff a king received at his coronation, which he was warned to use in imitation of the Lord: "Receive the rod of authority and equity [*virgam virtutis atque equitatis*], by which you may learn to comfort the pious and strike the reprobate with terror, teach the right path to the straying, and extend a hand to those who have fallen back; and with it you shall scatter the proud and raise up the humble. . . . And imitate Him who said, 'You shall love justice and hate iniquity.'"[21] The scepter was therefore a symbol of lordship—"a sign of ruling," said one of the West Frankish coronation *ordines*, "by which is signified the rule of divine equity, which crushes the evil and rules the good."[22] This equity had little of the connotation of "beneficence" later found in English Chancery.[23] Early medieval equity was instead that quality which William of Poitiers praised in Duke William of Normandy, a "proportionate justice" by which William gave each his "measure"—his "deserts"—according to "strict equity" (*aequitate districta*).[24] This equity knew how to take vengeance (*ultio, vindicatio*) as well as show mercy.

Since it was a "divine equity," as the coronation prayer said, it was also a judicial quality that earthly rulers shared with God. Where kings struck the reprobate with a "rod of authority," God punished Bodora with "the rod of heavenly wrath."[25] And when those who violated Saint-Corneille's immunity were struck with insanity, the canons interpreted their madness as the judgment of God, who had "exercised strict and manifest vengeance" (*ultio*) upon his enemies.[26] In the same way Suger praised Louis VI for having exercised vengeance (*ultio*) upon those who attacked the poor of the realm, those poor including not only widows and orphans but also monks.[27]

The early medieval ideal of justice presented by ecclesiastical writers was therefore simply the ideal of a lord's authority. That authority was limited morally (not constitutionally) by conformity to the image of God, for a prince could not act out of conformity to his divine model.[28] On the other hand, the very fact that God was conceived as acting with both the rigor of justice and the mildness of mercy justified at least an equal latitude for those who ruled in his name. Earthly lords could be by turns, as God was by turns, wrathful, vengeful, merciful, and rigorous. They were simply to rule, where to rule meant doing whatever was necessary to maintain order in their domains.

This recognition that maintaining order required flexibility and discretion explains why early medieval writers so often defined royal justice by rehearsing a litany of virtues; for royal (or princely) justice could not be subsumed under a single, constant

quality. Justice required lordship, and lordship could be manifested in a host of activities, depending on circumstances. A few
years after the Capetian accession, Abbo of Fleury could think
of no better advice to give his new kings than to quote verbatim
Jonas of Orléans's advice to Louis the Pious a century and a half
earlier:

> The justice of a king is to oppress no one unjustly through the exer-
> cise of power; to judge between a man and his neighbor without
> regard for persons; to be the defender of foreigners and widows and
> orphans; to prevent theft; to punish adultery; to make sure that the
> evil are not exalted; to give no support to the shameless or to enter-
> tainers; to banish the impious from the land; to permit no parricides
> or perjurers to live; to defend the churches; to support the poor with
> alms; to establish just men over the affairs of the kingdom; to have
> old, wise, and sober counselors; to support no sorcerers or sooth-
> sayers or seers; to set aside wrath; to defend the fatherland against
> enemies bravely and with justice; to live in all things through God.[29]

In other words, a king ruled with discretion. As Abbo put it
elsewhere: a king had to have "the gentleness of a dove and the
slyness of a snake."[30]

What gave coherence to this vision of justice was the belief
that law consisted not of rules but of order. Adalbero of Laon, in
a famous passage, gave succinct and eloquent expression to this
idea. The heavenly kingdom, he wrote, is ruled according to a
"special order" so that "a provident power sets some over
others." As subjection was the rule in heaven, it was also to be
the rule on earth. "The house of God, though believed to be
one, is actually triune; for here some pray, while others fight,
and still others work. These three are one and cannot be divided; for the one office supports the work of the other two."
Maintaining this "law," said Adalbero, is the condition of harmony on earth.[31]

In the eleventh century, law was order—an order of subjection. Inferior men are subject to superior men, as body is subject
to soul, as lust is subject to reason, as woman is subject to man,
as man is subject to God. To acquiesce in one's dependence was
an act of humility, deserving of mercy. But to reject one's role
in this deferential society was an act of pride, which merited
the full rigor of judgment. In either case, justice was an act of
lordship that maintained the law of each by maintaining each

according to his law. Articulated by Adalbero at the beginning of the century, the same idea was neatly resumed by Ivo of Chartres at the beginning of the next century. To the established authorities, he wrote, "it pertains to apply justice and mercy as they see fit for the salvation of souls, according to the status of persons and the specifics of time and place."[32]

Ivo was writing of bishops; but no one expected kings to behave any differently—or, in the province of Reims, counts. There was only one legitimate lordship, that established by God, and all exercised judgment and mercy, vengeance and compassion, in the image of God. Neither democratic nor universal, the ideal of early medieval justice was an act of lordship, gracious to the humble, terrifying to the proud.

Clamors and *Querimoniae*

The ideal of discretionary justice had its appeal at many moments in the early Middle Ages, but most of all at those moments when, for whatever reasons, political theorists found it desirable to exalt the special status of kings and lords. Thus it was important to Hincmar of Reims, troubled by the disintegration of Carolingian power late in the reign of Charles the Bald.[33] It was important to Suger, eager to exalt his king above other French princes.[34] And it was important in the generation of the Capetian accession, as the contributions of Abbo of Fleury and Adalbero of Laon to the discussion testify.[35] But between these moments of generalized crisis, the ideal remained vital whenever monks and canons were threatened by the powerful.

Accordingly, the fullest expression of these values is found in monastic liturgies, specifically in the rite known as the "clamor to God," an elaborate ritual supplication through which a monastic community appealed to God for vengeance against those who had seized its lands or otherwise threatened the sanctity of its property and privileges. The clamor was associated with a second ritual called (we should expect the name by now) the "humiliation of relics." There can be no doubt that these two related rituals were used in our region. A complete text of the clamor to God survives in a thirteenth-century manuscript from Saint-Corneille of Compiègne; and the humiliation of relics is

known to have been practiced at Saint-Médard of Soissons and
Saint-Eloi of Noyon in the middle of the eleventh century, as
well as at Flemish monasteries a little later.[36]

The rituals of clamor and humiliation are well known, thanks
to extant sources and historians' recent interest in the less pa-
cific side of monastic piety. The two rituals were not necessarily performed together, since monks and canons could make
a clamor without humiliating their relics. Humiliation, however, was always used in conjunction with clamor. In the combined ritual, the relics of a monastery were unceremoniously
set on the ground before the altar, after which the prayers of
clamor were sung. In this way, the relics that had failed to protect their ministers were punished, forced to share in the humiliation the monks had suffered. At the same time the prostration
of the relics, together with other changes in the ritual of the
mass, signified that the equilibrium between heaven and earth
had been overturned by the actions of the monks' enemies.
Above all, their humiliation gave the relics the pose of supplicants, humble before the Lord and therefore deserving of his
mercy.

Although often performed behind locked doors, the clamor
could also be a public ritual, as the faithful attending mass witnessed the effects of the monks' sufferings: candles on the altar
were extinguished, the monks chanted without removing their
cowls, the holy relics that interceded for the community before
God lay on the ground, humbled by their enemies, humble before their Lord. And the monks themselves, prostrate like their
relics before the newly consecrated Host, petitioned God in
terms which have become familiar to us. The clamor began
with the singing of psalms, including one that prayed, "O Lord,
show us your mercy." Then the prostrate monks made their
entreaty:

> In the spirit of humility and with contrite soul we come before your
> sacred altar [*accedimus*], before your most holy body and blood, Lord
> Jesus, Saviour of the world, and we admit ourselves guilty against
> you because of our sins, for which we are justly afflicted. To you,
> Lord Jesus, we come. To you, prostrate, we clamor because proud
> and iniquitous men, made audacious by others, have risen against us
> on all sides. They seize the lands of this your sanctuary, and of other
> churches subject to it, plundering them and laying waste to them.

They force your poor cultivators of these lands to live in grief and hunger and nakedness. They kill with swords and instruments of terror; and even our property, which blessed souls have bequeathed to this place for their salvation and by which we are supposed to live in your holy service—even this they have seized and taken away from us with violence. O Lord, this your holy church, which you founded in ancient times and raised to the honor of the always blessed Virgin Mary, resides in sadness; and there is no one who can console it and free it if not you, our God. Rise up, then, Lord Jesus, in our aid. Comfort us and aid us. Battle those who battle against us and break the pride of those who afflict us and your place. O Lord, you know who they are and what their names, and their bodies and hearts were known to you before they were born. Therefore, God, by your strength teach them justice. As it pleases you, make them know their misdeeds. Free us by your mercy. Do not turn away from us, O Lord, who clamor unto you in affliction; but because of the glory of your name and the mercy by which you founded this place and raised it in honor of your mother, come to us in peace and deliver us from our present danger. Amen.[37]

The monastic clamor voiced the essential values of the conservative ideal of justice, projected onto God's archetypal judgeship. The aggrieved first of all showed their humility by prostrating themselves before God, thereby proving that they deserved the Lord's mercy because they recognized their dependence. They then railed against those "proud men" who, forsaking humility, had "risen up" against them—and also against God; for it was not only the monastery's wealth that had been endangered but also the salvation of all those Christians for whose souls the monks prayed. The monks therefore phrased their plaint not merely in terms of their own material loss but also in terms of the more fundamental loss of harmony between earthly society and the divine. The violence of their enemies had despoiled the wealth of God's church so that the monks could no longer fulfill their office of serving the Lord. Lands had been stolen which were given to the monastery to support the singing of masses for the donors' salvation. And so God's poor sought talion. Let the Lord comfort the humble with his mercy. Let him break the spirit of the proud. Those who rise up against God shall find that God has risen against them. Like a king, he will "spare those who are subject in spirit and crush the proud." The monks sought a justice which was vengeance and whose execution pertained to a lord who possessed a moral authority that encompassed both judgment and mercy: "Therefore, God, by your strength teach them justice." *Justifica in virtute tua.*

As might be expected, clamors were also addressed to earthly lords. Indeed, the association of special clamors with the need of the poor for equitable justice had already emerged in the Roman empire: since the poor could not be expected to know the arcane procedural rules of Roman law, their appeals to magistrates did not require them. From the beginning, then, the clamor was associated with an act of mercy toward the poor. This specialized *clamor pauperum* was subsequently taken over by episcopal and royal courts and applied by liturgists to the appeals made by poor monks to God.[38]

Although the liturgical clamor of the tenth and eleventh centuries had clearly built upon these associations, it is difficult to know to what extent they were still present in appeals to lay rulers, since the phrase *facere clamorem* (or a related and analogous phrase such as *exclamare, proclamare,* or *querimoniam deponere*) often appears to have denoted no more than a simple public announcement of a grievance, without liturgical echoes.[39] On the other hand, it is also true that such phrases were usually reserved for cases brought before great lords—kings, bishops, counts, and cardinal legates—those figures, in other words, who were otherwise given liturgical honors.[40] One might also assume that the scriptoria that used such phrases knew their liturgical connotations and took them for granted. The liturgical allusions of the clamors must also have been unmistakable to the laity, since kings and counts often received clamors and issued judgments in the churches of their principalities. Thus the countess of Vermandois heard disputes before the altar of Saint-Quentin; the count of Flanders in the church of Saint-Vaast; that of Amiens in the city's cathedral; and the king of France in the cathedral of Laon, the church of Saint-Médard, and the abbey of Saint-Etienne of Choisy: sacred places where men who ruled by God's grace did justice in God's name.[41]

Given these considerations, it is likely that, as with formulas of petition, we are faced with phrases that had a range of possible meanings, depending on context. At root, to "clamor" meant to raise a public outcry, and in many texts this remained its primary meaning.[42] But the fact that clamoring was also common in the liturgy meant that some clamors resonated with special meanings derived from clamors to God.

There is in any case no doubt that on some occasions the parallels between clamors to God and clamors to God's vicars were intentionally drawn. In 1049, for example, the abbot and monks of Saint-Eloi in Noyon humiliated their relics against one Gerard of Roye, who exercised advocacy over one of Saint-Eloi's villages. Doubtless the relics would have included the abbey's prize—the relics of Saint Eligius himself, an early bishop of Noyon. And so, when the abbot simultaneously "made clamor" to the current bishop of Noyon, he was implicitly recognizing that the bishop was the executor of divine justice on earth, and demanding that he avenge the humiliation of his holy predecessor. The bishop accepted the role. "Wishing to succor them in their calamity," he obtained Gerard's excommunication and forced a settlement.[43]

A more elaborate instance comes from the monastery of Saint-Amand in Flanders. Around 1097 its monks made a complaint (*proclamationem fecimus*) to the count of Flanders concerning their advocate, Anselm of Ribemont. The count's court gave judgment against Anselm, who appears to have obeyed the letter of the settlement but not its spirit: he soon found new ways to harass the monks. Having once tried comital justice and found it wanting, the monks now appealed directly to God. They excommunicated Anselm, prostrated their relics and crucifix on the ground, and placed their complaint (*proclamatio*) in the hand of the crucified Christ. Having done that, they later wrote, "we did not cease to make our complaint [*proclamationem facere*] before the body and blood of the Lord every day." At last the barefoot Anselm came to the monastery and "prostrated himself before the body of Saint Amand, making satisfaction in the hand of the crucifix, and tearfully petitioning mercy and absolution."[44]

These two texts enunciate the analogy between the two kinds of clamor more clearly than others; but some of the more extravagant diplomas also leave little doubt that the lord acted in the place of God, while the aggrieved played the role of his prostrate poor. One went to the lord as one would go to God—complaining, grieving, clamoring, beseeching. Robert the Pious received "the tearful complaints and most bitter clamors" of the abbot and monks of Saint-Germain; while the monks of Corbie, angry at the claims of a local lord, came into the presence of the king and "poured forth a tearful complaint and implored his aid and counsel."[45] The phrases were simply borrowed from the monastic liturgies of clamor and curse. The same language could be applied to the pope: when in 1064 the abbot of Corbie appealed to Alexander II against his bishop, he did so as "the most humble Fulk," writing as a suppliant beseeching his lord for aid. And Fulk ended his plaint by drawing attention to the pope's divine mandate to defend the church and begging his mercy in language that would have been equally appropriate for God or king: "Behold, great father, outstanding pastor, such is the weight of our calamity. In you we find our hope, in you our defense. . . . God has set you at the head of the church. Having received her, it is only just that you come to her defense."[46] Most revealing of all is the clamor by the clergy of Flanders against their count in 1093. Addressing the archbishop of Reims by letter rather than in person, the clergy described the gestures with which plaintiffs made their complaints:

> We are compelled to rise up to our holy mother, the church of Reims, whom we beseech in supplication so that moved in the bowels of her piety she may deign to look down on the tears of our wretchedness. Now, though absent in body, we still throw ourselves at your feet, and with sobbing tears importune you and this holy council . . . concerning the count, who like a lion ravishes and devours us, and like a dragon ensnares us with serpent-like cunning.[47]

Whether they addressed kings, counts, bishops, or popes, what the aggrieved sought from their lords was what clamoring monks and clerics sought of God: an act of redress—justice conceived of as protection or vengeance. In a word, they sought an act of lordship like that offered in the late eleventh century by Guido and Ivo, "by the gift of God counts of Amiens."[48] They have heard, said the counts, "how miserably the people of God . . . have been afflicted by viscounts with new and unheard-of calamities," and they were "moved by the heavy groans of the churches and faithful." Here the counts alluded to the iconic pose that testified to their suppliants' humility, the virtue that merited a lord's grace. And Guido and Ivo willingly assumed their own place in the tableau, presenting themselves as compassionate lords who knew that they must "act to free the poor of God"—in other words, God's humble. They also knew that they had to act forcefully, not according to law but according to what they called their "discretion," for as God's rulers they claimed to hold "the rod of equity." It was this discretion that allowed them to "cut short the superfluous running on of words in accusations and replies" in trials heard before viscounts by issuing a "decree by edict" which simplified the rules of procedure and limited the viscounts' right to issue judgments in the absence of witnesses.[49] It is a perfect illustration of how rulers might appeal to a model of divine equity in order to correct the rigors of judgment by an act of free mercy.

If Guido and Ivo's decree was unusually explicit about the nature of their authority, the reason was that in their time comital authority in the Amienois was unusually weak, viscomital authority unusually strong.[50] Moreover, the old comital dynasty had died out nearly twenty years earlier, leaving possession of the county confused. Guido and Ivo had probably only recently been viscounts themselves, perhaps only castellans; yet here they were correcting their former peers, perhaps as a means of augmenting their fragile authority. As a result, the two counts had to be especially clear about the grounds for their action. For the same reason they also were careful to involve the other political powers of the city in their decision by taking counsel from them.[51]

To avoid misunderstanding, it must be reemphasized that the model of discretionary justice was not always applied in settling disputes. Even in the province of Reims and in the royal domains on its edges there were trials and negotiations in which lords played no role whatsoever.[52] When lords did take an active role in settling disputes, they were often careful to adhere to procedural norms and to defer to the judgment of their *fideles*.[53] On the other hand, decisive action—or more accurately, the image of decisive action—was more common than the old picture of weak feudal justice would allow. This was especially true in cases like the one from Amiens, where the counts' decision was backed by powerful groups. It was also true when lords settled disputes involving those who were clearly dependent on them. Thus Elinand, bishop of Laon, "faithfully and religiously" petitioned Philip I to take action against his abusive sergeants and revenue collectors. The petition was made at one of the king's coronation assemblies, a formal setting whose ceremonial openly invoked the analogy between heavenly and earthly kingship. And Philip responded according to the proper protocol, accepting Elinand's petition by issuing a "decree" against his servants.[54] In another case Richard, abbot of Homblières, "postulated" the count of Vermandois to quash the evil customs exacted by one Ivo, *fidelis* of the count. And the count accepted Richard's petition, issuing the settlement "by our grace" as his own concession.[55] Significantly, neither of these texts mentions any formal legal process. Instead they portray the lords as acting on their own initiative with respect to dependents: for Philip, his own ministers; for Otto, a vassal. It was the same in other complaints addressed to a lord by the language of entreaty.[56] In such cases the supplication not only dramatized an ideal relationship of lordship and dependence; it also invoked the model of discretionary justice as the standard by which the plaintiffs wanted the lord to act.

Of course, it is likely that the forceful language of these texts conceals a complex process of negotiation and proofmaking that must have occurred in settling these disputes. The language also says nothing about the difficulty lords may have had securing obedience to their decrees. But that is the point. The language of clamor and edict projected an image of divinely ordained lordship to preserve an ideal that distinguished between the legitimate authority of kings and counts and the illegitimate power of castellans and vicars. Narratives of disputes were therefore structured to conform to the ideal. Consider the trial of Albert of Creil, an important castellan of the Ile-de-France and one of Robert the Pious's vassals. The very terms in which the abbot and monks of Jumièges supplicated the king in the first place proclaimed their humility and their enemy's audacity and announced that Robert was personally responsible for their protection. "Approaching the mildness of our excellency, they requested that I do justice to them concerning that reckless usurper." And although the king mentions that he did receive Albert in a formal court hearing (*coram nostris fidelibus ad placitum ascivi*), he himself is pictured dominating the proceedings: "As I learned of his evil actions, I ordered him by royal warning to cease this insanity; and all that land, cultivated and uncultivated, with the church and its tithe, with vineyards and fields, free and dissolved from all injury of secular laws, I rendered to Saint Peter and the monks of Jumièges."[57] "I learned,"

"I ordered," "I rendered": the abbot and monks had asked that Robert do justice; and that is just what he did.

Showing Mercy

Medieval historians have spoken of the prominence of "liturgical kingship" during the early Middle Ages and have even described medieval culture as a whole as "a civilization of the liturgy."[58] One might with equal justification speak of a "liturgical justice." Certainly one cannot speak of justice in this period without reference to its liturgical associations, not without warping our understanding of cultural attitudes toward litigation. Clamors and *querimoniae* were not merely the formal accusations that announced grievances and began litigation.[59] Through their liturgical allusions and accompanying gestures, they also announced the moral code according to which plaintiffs wanted their grievances heard. In other words, they established a kind of iconographic setting for litigation in which accusers and lord stepped into well-defined roles. The lord who received the clamor was cast in the role of one of God's earthly ministers. Those who made the clamor identified themselves as the poor and humble whom it was the lord's duty to protect, while assimilating their enemies to the proud and rapacious who, fearing neither God nor man, deserved vengeance.[60]

This iconography of justice permits another insight into the prostration of the condemned which sometimes ended disputes. Earlier we examined this phenomenon as a rite of penance and humiliation that restored the order of reason. We can now add another interpretation: by taking on a penitential pose, the condemned assumed the role of the formerly proud sinner who, by his show of humility, now merited the lord's mercy.

As always, the legal domain was defined by heavenly archetypes, as illustrated by the early twelfth-century case of a woman of Laon convicted of having her adulterous husband strangled. A judge sentenced her to be burned; but first she begged permission to go into the church of Notre-Dame to pray. "When she arrived there, in the sight of all the clergy and people she humbly and with pure confession recounted the tale of her iniquity in its entirety, driving several of those present to compassion and tears. Then, prostrating herself on the ground, with much weeping she committed her body and soul to holy Mary." Afterward the woman was tied to a stake within the house that was to be burned. The fire was lit and reduced the structure to ashes; but miraculously the flames did her no harm. Twice more a fire was lit, yet still the woman remained safe. In this way an act of humility, the prostrate confession of wrong, overrode the demands of law and merited what all present recognized as the "mercy" of the Queen of heaven.[61]

Supplication that ended acts of political rebellion conveyed a similar meaning. In ending his resistance to Louis VI, for example, Haimo of Germigny realized that by strict judgment he should be condemned because he had ignored the king's summons to court and turned to armed resistance. He could, as Suger said, "save himself" only by supplicating the king, "groveling" at his feet where he "begged fervently that he might show mercy toward him." Similarly Robert the Pious forgave his prostrate son for his acts of rebellion, as Henry I, "kindly assenting to her petitions," forgave his suppliant mother for her treachery. William of Bellême, having failed in his rebellion against Robert of Normandy, came before the duke barefoot and carrying his saddle and "begged his clemency"; and this was "satisfaction" enough, in the words of the chronicler, for Robert forgave him everything.[62] As with the woman of Laon, those who deserved condemnation according to the dictates of strict justice had no hope but in a lord's mercy.

The same pattern obtained in legal proceedings, as shown by a dispute that occurred in 1107. Nicholas, the son of Albuin, claimed two-thirds of the revenues from an altar pertaining to the dominion of Mont-Saint-Quentin. The abbot of Mont-Saint-Quentin recognized Nicholas's right to one-third of the altar's revenues; but he held that the other two-thirds belonged solely to his abbey. The language of litigation was used to record the claims and counterclaims of the two parties: "Nicholas clamans dicebat hos . . . sui juris esse . . . ; huic igitur clamori dominus abbas respondens . . . ; cum ergo causa hec sepissime ventilata esset." Such jargon indicates that at least some part of the debate was held in a formal court, perhaps even including a structured *narratio* and *responsio* to present the parties' claims. Nevertheless, the dispute dragged on, and a final resolution was achieved only through the mediation of the lord of Péronne, mediation which took the extralegal form of the lord's petition to the abbot that because Nicholas had behaved humbly he deserved his patron's mercy.

> Recently having accepted the counsel of Lord R[obert] of Péronne and his wife, Lady A[delaide], as well as that of several clerics and laymen, Nicholas entered the presence of the lord abbot H[enry] and his monks; and all that he had claimed . . . he set aside entirely, without any [right of] revindication; and he relinquished it into their power. After this was accomplished, the aforesaid lords and also the clerics and laymen, taking into consideration the humility of that young man, asked on his behalf that the lord abbot show him some mercy for his lifetime. Receptive to their entreaties, the lord abbot, with the assent of his monks, conceded that he might hold for his lifetime those two parts which . . . he had relinquished.[63]

At first glance the abbot's show of mercy appears to be one of those cases in which a church compromised its claims under political pressure—the kind of case, in other words, that is said to demonstrate the failure of medieval legal procedures to award right where right was due.[64] But given the fact that Nicholas hardly appears to have been one of the local *potentes*, the abbot's action reminds one still more of Ivo of Chartres's prescription: a lord should show mercy to the poor by granting them a life interest in the rights they claim, even if their claims are not fully valid.[65] But since *paupertas* was defined as a social attribute and not an economic condition, to be poor was to be humble or deferential. And for the abbot of Mont-Saint-Quentin, Nicholas's deference was the real issue in this dispute, possession of the altar's revenues only a secondary concern. The abbot's primary intention was to have his lordship, his power over the altar, recognized by Nicholas and publicized before the local laity. In contemporary language, he wanted Nicholas to recognize that the altar was held by his "mercy." Nicholas's show of humility was therefore itself the desired goal. Once that goal had been attained, the abbot could afford to restore Nicholas to the enjoyment of the altar's revenues which he had sought in the first place.

In this context, showing mercy was not an act of weakness. It was a prerogative of lordship which required a demonstrated superiority over the dependent who had placed himself at the lord's mercy. This legal exegesis of mercy was a familiar one throughout the lordships of northern France during this period, as shown by the fact that *ad misericordiam* was the phrase used by the neighboring abbey of Saint-Vaast to describe lands that were technically held at the pleasure of its abbot.[66] Nor was Nicholas's dispute the only one that was settled by such a compromise. In the preceding chapter we left a luckless Breton named Uurbudic lying prostrate at the feet of the abbot of Redon, having failed to convince his neighbors in court of his claim to part of a weir. The gesture was archetypal; but so was the abbot's response: "Then Conwoion, moved by mercy, raised him from the ground, and granted him the part of that weir for as long as he would be his *fidelis* and friend and the monks were willing."[67] Two centuries later, in Ponthieu, the abbot of Saint-Riquer refused a man's claim to a mill until the man, recognizing Saint-Riquier's title, "beseeched that he be allowed something for himself" and his heirs. This the abbot was "pleased" to grant—giving the man the very mill he had earlier demanded, but now begged for, not only for his own lifetime but for that of his son and grandson as well.[68]

The same was done at Saint-Amand and Saint-Aubin—indeed, at nearly every monastery that has left a fair sampling of records; and the circumstances were often identical. A family that had been given rights at *census* by one abbot and passed them down to heirs found itself sued by his successor, who feared their permanent loss through prescription. When a court found for the abbot, the defeated party or an intercessor beseeched mercy. The usual result (so common that in some cases it may have been collusive) was for the property to be returned to the individual for his lifetime enjoyment.[69] As at Saint-Riquier, a life interest might also occasionally be granted to one or more of the defendant's heirs.[70] But even when the *census* was to revert to the church upon the defendant's death, there could still be an understanding that his heirs might repeat the process.[71]

Thus, through acts of supplication the condemned were also required to commit themselves to an iconography of right lordship. From this perspective, it is immaterial whether or not the supplicant really felt humble, for his feeling mattered less than his public profession of loyalty to the ideal before his peers and lords. Furthermore, what mattered as much as the dependent's humility was the final occasion it offered the lord to fulfill his divinely ordained role. For the second component of petition, the corollary of the dependent's humiliation, was the lord's proffering of mercy, an act through which he showed himself to be a true lord, ruling according to the image of God, and therefore worthy of his ministry.

We have already seen a lord play this part at the council of Saint-Basle; for no sooner had Arnulf confessed his sinfulness than the kings spared his life, urged on by "the most humble prayers" of the archbishop of Bourges, who threw himself at their feet to beg the favor.[72] The same iconic reaction is found in the castellan of Cambrai's humble prostration before imperial legates: once the castellan had "cast himself down in all humility, adding prayer upon prayer, to the satisfaction of all," the bishop of Cambrai was free to meet his humility with the reciprocal mercy of a lord. Walter's display of humility was such that "even the lord bishop, moved by compassion [*miseratione pulsatus*], soothed the wrathful counts with his entreaties."[73]

Of course, not all lords respected the conventions; or rather, the conventions also permitted a lord to show righteous anger, to withhold the sought-after mercy, to damn as God damned. Otto III, for example, refused to pardon Crescentius, a rebel who had opposed the emperor's pope with his own antipope. Crescentius came before the emperor, cloaked but bareheaded, and fell at his feet to beg for his life. But Otto had been "fired with wrath" at Crescentius's actions and had already cut off the papal pretender's hands and ears and gouged out his eyes, the traditional punishments for traitors and perjurors. Crescentius's prostration made no difference. He was executed by being thrown from the tower where he had been besieged, his corpse then dragged through the muddy streets behind an ox and publicly hanged.[74] Frederick Barbarossa also refused to pardon an unnamed retainer, despite the latter's groveling and in spite of the fact that the supplication was made at Frederick's coronation at Aachen—a ceremony the man had doubtless counted on to remind Frederick of the divine model of kingship. No matter, for that very model permitted the rigor of justice as well as the mildness of mercy, and it was "out of regard for justice" that Frederick justified his flinty resolve.[75]

Often enough, however, supplication did gain a lord's mercy. Perhaps the lords were constrained by reasons of politics more than by reason of good ritual form. Hugh Capet could never have executed Arnulf; even his punishment would have been problematic enough. Even so, such political constraints only made supplication more important as a paradigm of political order: for if the paradigm allowed a lord to condemn a suppliant, it also justified his forgiveness, offering a convenient way for the lord to save face when he had no other choice. Then the lord could bow to the inevitable only after a convincing game in which his retainers and the friends and kin of the condemned begged him for mercy. In this way supplication was able to justify as a moral imperative what the cynical would have seen only as a confession of weakness.[76] Acts of amnesty were therefore every bit as much acts of lordship as were acts of damnation, for in both kings, counts, and bishops played the part of God.

PART FOUR

Ritual and Reality

I lay there dismally calculating that sixteen entire hours must elapse before I could hope for a resurrection. Sixteen hours in bed! The small of my back ached to think of it. And it was so light too; the sun shining in at the window, and a great rattling of coaches in the streets, and the sound of gay voices all over the house. I felt worse and worse—at last I got up, dressed, and softly going down in my stockinged feet, sought out my stepmother, and suddenly threw myself at her feet, beseeching her as a particular favor to give me a good slippering for my misbehavior; anything indeed but condemning me to lie abed such an unendurable length of time. But she was the best and most conscientious of stepmothers, and back I had to go to my room.

Herman Melville, *Moby Dick*, chap. 4

April 21, 1931

His Most Gracious Majesty Prajadhipok, Descendant of Buddha, King of North and South, Supreme Arbiter of the Ebb and Flow of the Tide, Brother of the Moon, Half-Brother of the Sun, Possessor of the Four-and-Twenty Golden Umbrellas
Ophir Hall
White Plains, New York

Sir:
Welcome to America.

John Barth, "Petition"

One often thinks of rituals as being changeless, and it is true that many rituals accentuate a periodic routine in order to present tradition as eternally true and vital. Hence the Catholic liturgy before Vatican II, and the language and gestures of supplication in preindustrial Europe. But we should not mistake image for reality. We have already seen that the perception of rituals can change even as their language and gestures do not.[1] But even the meanings of rituals can change as the society changes. Indeed, they must change; for individuals confront change in terms of their established discourse, adapting that discourse to transformations in the world around them and transforming their world according to the possibilities and limitations inherent in their discourse.[2] As a result, those rituals that carry the discourse are continually adapted to their environment.

It is because of this interaction between rituals and society that changes in the performance and perception of rituals can be studied as indicators of social change, just as historians study changes in the language of social categorization (*milites* and *nobiles*, for example) to understand changes in social organization. And just as social categories varied not only from period to period but also from community to community within the same period, so a ritual like supplication varied with the social organization and cultural attitudes of the political community. Although the language was the same, it had many dialects.

One can therefore understand that the trends we have described were not equally pronounced everywhere in northern France. The feeling of crisis provoked by the tenth-century wars and the rise of the *seigneurie banale* was strongest among the counts and clerics of the ecclesiastical province of Reims, as was the concomitant desire to reassert the divine basis of traditional authority. In other regions, those changes were not necessarily perceived as a crisis; nor were responses to the appearance of powerful castellans always so reactionary as in the north.

It is not possible to describe and account for these differences everywhere in northern France. But one can compare the use of formulas of petition in a few regions in order to generate a typology applicable to other areas. Within the province of Reims, the Vermandois must of course be examined in some detail, since it was here that the paradigm of theophanic supplication was most consciously and consistently applied. Conversely, the lack of emphasis on the formulas in documents from the county of Amiens provides a test case for our typology. Though outside the province of Reims, Normandy has also been given considerable attention, because the wide variation in the use of the formulas in ducal charters illustrates their close connection with political organization.

But the crux of the comparison is the counties of western France, in particular Anjou, the Chartrain, and the Touraine. Possessing excellent documentation, these counties have been the subjects of numerous monographs; and these monographs describe political structures quite different from those north of the Aisne. To take only the best-known example, one that will figure in the ensuing discussion: although these regions are known for their famous counts, they are not famous for the deference shown to their counts. On the contrary, as in the Midi, political, social, and legal relations here were structured through *convenientiae* and *pactiones*—bilateral agreements negotiated directly between lords and vassals and churches and laymen which assumed the equality of the partners and which promoted reciprocity by binding them in a relationship of *societas et fraternitas*. Although the counts might engage in such pacts with others, their consent was not necessary to the validity of pacts between others unless their rights were directly affected—and even that qualification was lost over time. Instead, the legal validity of the pact derived from the consent of the parties themselves.[3]

One might well wonder what supplication had to offer this kind of society. Certainly its authoritarian associations must have been much less pronounced here than in the Vermandois or Flanders, or in Normandy under Richard II. In fact, supplication had a great deal to offer, but to the castellans and knights, not to the counts. For the hallmark of petitions in this region is the extent to which the language of prayer was taken over by lesser nobles—indeed, became one of the means by which a new idea of nobility was fashioned. And this fact offers one further reason for emphasizing this region. To study petitions in the west is not just to analyze a variant use of the formulas. It is to witness the origins of a new ideal of political order.

8 The Sublimity of Knighthood

The unusually strong hold of theophanic and regalian supplications in the northern counties was partly due to the region's distinctive culture. One might first of all call attention to the ancientness and stability of two of the counties, Flanders and Vermandois. From the late ninth century until sometime in the early 1080s, the county of Vermandois descended directly in the male line from a son of Charlemagne, with no known successional strife whatsoever.[1] The line of the counts of Flanders also dated back to the ninth century, and had received royal blood when Baldwin I (d. 879) abducted and married Charles the Bald's daughter. Though its smooth transmission was occasionally marred by conflict and one nearly disastrous minority, the county remained within the same family throughout our period, always passing through male descent. Royal blood and stable succession quickly became a source of pride both to the counts and to their clerical apologists. Already in the mid-tenth century the abbot of Sint-Pieters at Ghent was celebrating Arnulf the Great's Carolingian ancestry.[2] By the late eleventh century, extolling the counts' ancestry had become a standard technique for praising them.[3]

Dynastic and territorial stability cannot be the whole story, however. The counts of Blois and Poitou boasted equally illustrious ancestries without being able to turn them to their advantage.[4] And not all comital authority in the north was so firmly settled. The royal castellans of Abbéville became counts of Ponthieu only in the 1020s; and no one in the early eleventh century had yet forgotten that Normandy had originated in a royal grant to a Scandinavian pirate in 911. But as we have seen, these more recent political entities quickly became assimilated into the traditional model of lordship. Even the counts of Normandy came to vaunt their descent from pirates and fostered a mythic identity between Normandy and its ducal house so powerful that only recently has it been seen as the fiction that it was.[5]

Thus dynastic stability was but one factor in the ability of the northern counts to maintain an image of authority. Far more important was the character of the provincial church. After all, monks and canons were the ones who normally drew up charters; so it was their attitude toward authority that most directly shaped diplomatic language. In the ecclesiastical province of Reims, that attitude was especially conservative. To begin with, this was a region strongly imbued with Carolingian traditions. It was here that the last Carolingians had their domains, in its churches that they had been crowned and buried, and here that they found their most loyal allies—including, significantly, the counts of Flanders and Vermandois.[6] Imperial influence was also quite marked here, given the prominence of Lotharingian bishops such as Adalbero of Reims, Adalbero of Laon, and Gerard of Cambrai, and the tendency of the region's counts to involve themselves in imperial affairs—again, particularly in Flanders and Vermandois.[7] The royal and imperial model of theophanic supplication was therefore quite familiar to established counts, and new counts naturally turned to it in order to justify and project their own authority.

Even more important for explaining the region's conservative ideology was the political strength of its prelates. Historians have long recognized that the bishops of the province exercised unusual power. In Reims, Châlons, Noyon, Beauvais, and Cambrai the bishops replaced the counts and vested their worldly power in their own hands. Even in dioceses where they failed to do so, they still had more temporal power than bishops elsewhere in France. In Soissons, for example, the count remained, but his power was greatly reduced to the benefit of the bishop, to whom he owed fealty. In Laon the office of count disappeared, its rights, if not the title, passing to the bishop.[8]

The extensive lands and privileges of the older ecclesiastical establishments were also characteristic of the late Carolingian regime; and the political vacuum of the tenth and eleventh centuries, coupled with the Capetians' reliance on monastic support, enabled these houses to retain a major role in regional political affairs. In the absence of any dominant secular authority, a monastery with immunity might provide an element of local stability, and several ecclesiastical foundations increased their power as competing princes extended their privileges in an effort to secure allies in the region. This was the case with Saint-Pierre of Corbie, which came to control the northern part of the old county of Amiens on behalf of the later Carolingians. The chapter of Saint-Corneille similarly dominated Compiègne on behalf of the Capetians. After 1048 the Capetians also protected the rights of Saint-Médard of Soissons, which received so much authority over its sector of the city that it later used its royal privileges to dispute its subordination to the bishop.[9] Monastic exemption from episcopal authority (or the demand for such exemption) was in fact quite common here, as it was claimed not only by Saint-Médard but also by Corbie, Saint-Corneille, and Saint-Vaast of Arras. Indeed, Saint-Vaast was so powerful and owned so much of the land at Arras that in the twelfth century even the count of Flanders rented the site of his residence at Arras from the monastery.[10]

Given the strength of the region's Carolingian heritage, new institutions penetrated only by adapting to traditional structures. The Peace of God in the north, for example, appears to have been much less chiliastic, much more a practical agent of episcopal and comital control, than was the case in the south.[11] Religious reform in the province of Reims also occurred within a traditional framework. Given the political strength of bishops, princes, and anciently endowed abbeys, there was little room for the extensive liberties of reformed monasteries, like those then becoming associated with Cluny. Only late in the eleventh century did the count of Valois and his retainers begin to establish Cluniac priories on their domains.[12] In the diocese of Noyon there was only one such priory—Saint-Médard at Cappy, founded by the lord of Péronne in 1086. Like most Cluniac priories in the province, Cappy was dependent on Saint-Martin-des-Champs, a royal abbey whose restricted privileges were not at all typical of Cluny's exemptions.[13] With such a slender foothold, the Burgundian order could not challenge episcopal authority here.

The need for religious reform was not ignored in the province; but it was made to serve the interests of the traditional elites. Thus when bishops undertook reform, they did so by establishing houses of regular canons whose statutes required their subordination to the bishop.[14] And when the counts of Vermandois and Flanders reformed monasteries in the early part of the eleventh century, they imposed no Cluniac abbot but Richard of Saint-Vanne, a conservative Benedictine from imperial lands whose political and religious attitudes were to the liking even of such traditionalists as Gerard of Cambrai and Adalbero of Laon. Richard was, after all, an occasional legate for the emperor; and the king of France had tried to obtain him as abbot of Saint-Riquier, a monastery that the kings themselves had restored.[15]

The Hegemony of the Northern Counts

Whatever the importance of cultural factors in shaping perceptions and institutions, culture cannot be isolated from social structure. In explaining the image of strong comital authority in the north, one must also look at the material conditions that supported the culture.

In this regard, what is most pronounced about the northern counties is the relative weakness of the *seigneurie banale,* at least during the first half of the century. The success with which the Flemish counts reduced the powers of independent advocates and kept their castellans in strict subordination is well known.[16] So is the cohesiveness of Norman ducal government under Richard II, in whose time the ruling class in Normandy was limited to the duke's closest relatives.[17] It also appears that relatively few individuals held banal rights in Ponthieu. In fact, Hariulf's chronicle of Saint-Riquier and the charters he included in it mention no other banal lords save the counts. And though the counts' own acts mention two families of viscounts, they mention but one castellan—and all are referred to only as witnesses.[18] They do not otherwise appear in the sources and appear to have had little independence. There were other important families in the region: the king's butlers from Senlis, for example, and the Tirels, one of whom tried to assume a comital title in neighboring Hesdin. But the power of the butlers came from their positions as royal ministers, and the largest part of their holdings was located nearer to Paris. Within Ponthieu they had fewer rights, and what they did have was probably limited to land, not lordship.[19] As for the Tirels, they did not succeed in becoming recognized as counts, and they always depended on greater lords for what rights of lordship they had.[20]

Comital hegemony was even more strongly marked in the Vermandois, a region whose institutions Robert Fossier described as positively "archaic." As elsewhere in the north, Carolingian political structures endured here long after they had disappeared or been transformed out of all recognition in other parts of France. *Generalia placita* and tribunals of *scabini* continued to provide acceptable forums for local litigation. And at a time when the courts of the counts of Macon had been deserted by their subordinates, the castellans of the Vermandois continued to accept their dependent status within the counts' entourage. True, by the eleventh century the areas under the counts' direct control had greatly diminished. Though the entire county stretched across some fifty to sixty kilometers, their core domains covered an area in the east of the region only ten kilometers wide. Yet here the counts dominated the social order. They alone held the most important jurisdictional rights; and having concentrated their holdings along trade routes in areas of dense population, they also held the most valuable rights.[21]

We can see the counts' dominance clearly in the case of ecclesiastical institutions, such as the abbey of Homblières. Between 959 and 1050 the counts issued half of the abbey's charters—charters that confirmed donations not only of the counts but also of their vassals and even of allodists.[22] When the abbey required a royal confirmation of its possessions, it was the count who obtained it. When it needed an abbot with political influence, the count found him.[23]

The counts' supremacy over their lay dependents is more difficult to establish, since it began to break down after 1050, if not before, as subalterns received lands that might furnish their families with a permanent basis for their own domination. But

Fossier has shown that this process of emancipation was not well advanced in any region of Picardy, including the Vermandois, during the eleventh century. Feudalism in the strict sense of the term—homage and military services in return for specific lands or rights—made only a belated appearance compared to other regions of France. Sheltered from the disintegrating impact of eleventh-century wars, the counts' domains remained coherent, and their vassals did not dilute their allegiance to them by swearing fealty to other lords, as did castellans of the Ile-de-France. As a result, even well into the twelfth century comital acts emphasized the personal ties that bound their vassals to them over truly feudal, landed obligations. Allods still predominated over fiefs in the patrimonies of the nobility, a fact that may have helped the survival of the notion that a lord's jurisdiction stemmed from his public office rather than from his private lordship. In any case, of all lords only the count was said to be surrounded by *vassalli*, the term retaining its early meaning of personal dependents. If the count's men did distribute their own lands as "fiefs" to their own "vassals," this fact only rarely appears in the documents before the last part of the century.[24]

Whether their territories formed large, influential principalities, such as Normandy and Flanders, or small ones of lesser importance, such as Ponthieu and the Vermandois, these northern counts exercised real hegemony. Their castellans (in the Norman case, viscounts) had little political autonomy, their vassals only limited economic resources. No rivals intruded themselves into the rulers' territories to undermine their influence by dividing loyalties. And they had the support of a church that believed deeply in the God-given rightness of comital authority. When, therefore, castellans first appeared in the Vermandois and advocates in Flanders, or when the castellans of Abbéville became counts of Ponthieu and tried to prevent others from imitating their success, the counts had the wherewithal to keep these lesser lords in their place. And if a monastery wanted a dispute settled, its jurisdiction recognized, or a diploma granted, the monks' course of action was clear: they went to their count and begged his intervention. Seen from this perspective, the churches' continuing respect for a protocol of petition at once regal and theophanic was in no way utopian.

Theophanic supplications accurately reflected a political regime in which power, and not just authority, was concentrated in the hands of a few.

Supplication in Pluralistic Communities

Many of the characteristics typical of the counties of the province of Reims can be found elsewhere in northern France. Ancient and unbroken descent, for example, was hardly unique to the counts of Flanders and Vermandois.[25] The eleventh-century counts of Poitou could trace their ancestry through the male line to Ramnulf, a count of Louis the Pious who in 839 received Poitou from the emperor. The counts were also graced with Carolingian blood, since Ramnulf's successors were born from his marriage with one of Charlemagne's granddaughters.[26] Even more august was the ancestry of the counts of Blois and Chartres, descendants of Herbert II of Vermandois and, through him, of Charlemagne's eldest legitimate son, Pepin.[27]

The case of Poitou is especially interesting, because as dukes of Aquitaine its counts also ruled Limoges and Angoulême, and in these regions we have already noted the same sort of conservative backlash against the *seigneurie banale* that occurred in the province of Reims. Thus the Peace of God, princely entries, trials of heretics, and the count's special association with totemic saints, such as Martial and John the Baptist, all issued from the effort of prince and prelates to remind castellans of their own special authority as God's rulers.[28] The sacred nature of the counts' authority was also made visible in the theophany of supplication, since their acts for Poitevin houses continued to employ its formulas.[29] Nevertheless, the use of these formulas differed in important ways from that current in the province of Reims.

The most important difference is the wide diffusion of the language of petition in charters from eleventh-century Poitou, as viscounts and vassals, husbands and mothers were all spoken of as being "petitioned" or "beseeched" in one form or another.[30] How to interpret this language is a difficult question. Though many individuals were petitioned, only the counts' acts consistently used such language, and occasionally it could be as fulsome as any tenth-century formula. Yet comital formulas in the charters of Saint-Hilaire of Poitiers do tend to be more truncated.[31] Is this brevity a sign that the supplication of counts had become so second nature that even the tersest formulas could evoke the divinity of the ducal office? Or is it perhaps a sign that the formulas no longer meant as much as they had in the years when the counts of Poitou had first attained ducal stature in Aquitaine? If the latter, to whom did the formulas mean less, the count or the monks and canons who wrote his charters?

It is also unclear what to make of the petitioning of other individuals, since to a certain extent this practice only continued earlier ones. In the first half of the eleventh century Viscount Geoffrey of Thouars approved a donation to Saint-Cyprien of Poitiers *per deprecationem Ramnulfi militis;* but because petitions to viscounts had not been uncommon in the tenth century, one cannot conclude that the later petition reflected an increase in the prestige of Geoffrey's house.[32] Similarly, if in 959 Duke William III himself entreated a *fidelis* to end a dispute with Saint-Maixent (*suegissimus, propter noster peticionem*),[33] it is difficult to read any political meaning into the later use of such words as *postulare* and *deprecare* to describe requests made to castellans and knights. In spite of such difficulties, this much seems evident: deferential language was much more widespread in Poitou than in the north.

The situation is clearer in the other counties of western France whose sources have been examined. Not that there are more tenth-century charters from these regions to clarify the trend of eleventh-century usages; in fact, there are many fewer. But the few tenth-century charters that are extant, together with the many eleventh-century acts, reveal an unmistakable pattern of development.

What is most striking about these sources is the frequency with which viscounts, castellans, and knights were spoken of as being petitioned. As in Poitou, the wider usage seems to continue tenth-century practices; yet beginning in the late tenth and early eleventh centuries, the acts of the greater nobles become noticeably more grandiloquent. To be sure, the benefactors do not style themselves "clement"; but they do announce that individuals had approached them and made a formal entreaty; and there is often some special phrase that implies, if not condescension, then at least a noble beneficence.[34] Thus, sometime before 1000 the viscount of Chartres recalled that "the abbot of Saint-Père came into my presence with some of the brothers, begging that I concede to him" some fields held by one of his vassals. "Considering this petition reasonable," he responded, "I offer my assent to their desire."[35] Then there was Marannus, a noble of the Touraine important enough to have married the daughter of the treasurer of Saint-Martin. Sometime after 1015 he issued an act for Marmoutier recording that one of his *fideles* named Heriveus had approached him (*adiid [sic] presentiam meam*), "beseeching" that he give a female serf to Marmoutier. "Receiving this entreaty with kindness, I granted them the said woman."[36] Between 1008 and 1012, one Hubert, calling himself a "knight of the castle of Saumur" but holding a *vicaria* and the *dominatio* of the abbey of Bourgeuil, surrendered his rights to the abbot, who approached him and beseeched him "with humble prayer" (*accessit ad nostram presenciam . . . humili prece deposcens*).[37]

It was not only the viscounts and greater *fideles* of these regions that were entreated. The language was also assumed by ordinary knights. Abbots and monks approached otherwise unknown vassals and *milites* to beseech benefactions "with many prayers" or "with humble prayer." In turn, the benefactors granted the requests "with goodwill" (*benivole*).[38] Interestingly, such language appears as part of the ordinary discourse of the lesser nobility from quite an early date, since knights and lords not only were beseeched by monks and canons; they also beseeched each other. In the early 1030s, for example, when a certain Leudo permitted a vassal to sell some land to Count Geoffrey Martel for the building of La Trinité of Vendôme, he did so *deprecante fidele meo*.[39] A garrison knight from the Chartrain conceded a small parcel to Saint-Père at the prayers of two of his companions (*nostris precibus*). Most revealing of all is a notice from late in the century recording the language contemporaries believed a knight of a castle would have used to address his lords and friends: "I pray you who are here, and especially you, my lords, all you who eat with me, that you will be witnesses to the monks of Saint-Aubin for what I am about to say."[40]

Again, the widespread use of such deferential language was to some extent traditional in these regions, since it echoes the practice found in formularies of the Merovingian period from Angers and Tours. The influence of the formularies on eleventh-century charters is also revealed in common phrases. For example, both sometimes noted a benefactor's acceptance of a petition with a terse *quod et fecimus*, instead of the gracious and authoritative concession common in royal diplomas and in episcopal and comital acts from the north.[41] Yet the eleventh-century protocol for the formulas cannot be explained by these exemplars. The formularies provide no model for statements of accession to *potentes* (*accessit ad nostram praesentiam*) or for humble prayers to them. Still less do they account for the style of discourse knights adopted to address their lords and friends: *precor vos qui astatis, et vos maxime, domini mei*. This is not a stale formula copied from a book, or even from contemporary comital charters. It is the language of daily life, rooted in the social reality of the eleventh-century nobility of western France.

The old formularies cannot have dictated eleventh-century usages. At best they only created a scribal tradition favoring the application of petitionary language to *potentes*. What was crucial in promoting the spread of deferential language in western France was the continuing strength of a local elite that was effectively independent of the counts and whose power and prestige made its members deserving of honor.

A complex of related factors was responsible for this. The first was the large number of disparate political entities ruled by the counts. During the late tenth century the count of Vendôme was also count of Paris, Corbeil, and Melun. The counts of Anjou exercised hegemony in Maine, Brittany, and northern Poitou. Luck and a good marriage had brought them Vendôme by 1020; conquest brought the county of Tours in 1044. The territories controlled by Odo II of Blois were even more extensive, including—besides Blois—the counties centered on Chartres, Tours, Troyes, Meaux, Château-Thierry, and Provins, comital rights in Beauvais and Reims, scattered holdings in Lotharingia, and even a claim to the kingdom of Burgundy.[42] There was no way that any single individual could rule all these territories, not even if he were gifted with all the drive of a Geoffrey Martel. The counts had to depend on their castellans, who in consequence assumed unusual importance.

Of course, the counts of Flanders and Normandy also ruled

large territories; but Flanders and Normandy were relatively coherent principalities. The counts had built up their power over
generations. Facing no competitors within their core dominions, they had molded government around themselves and their
families and had managed to keep control of rich and strategic
resources.[43] In contrast, the western counts ruled agglomerations of territories rather than real principalities. They had been
put together piecemeal by conquest and marriage alliance, and
they remained subject to dismemberment by reconquest or inheritance. The assembled territories had correspondingly little
institutional coherence as a whole, no traditional loyalty to a
single princely family around which a united polity could be
constructed.[44]

Even within the individual counties of their dominions, the
counts' powers were often surprisingly thin—especially in the
most recently acquired territories, where comital authority had
to be built around existing centers of power. When Geoffrey
Martel took over the Touraine in 1044, he found it impossible
to dispossess the castellan families that were already entrenched there. He contented himself with reassigning custody
of the castles to other members of the families that already
ruled them. No one was fooled. The count may have expelled
Guicher from Château-Renault and given it to Guicher's
brother, Rainald; but the monks of Marmoutier continued to
call Guicher the "lord" of the castle. Rainald they described as
merely its "possessor."[45]

The castellans of the Touraine had become entrenched during
the notably loose rule of the counts of Blois. These counts' willingness to allow their castellans a good deal of autonomy resulted partly from the problems inherent in ruling their vast
territories; but it also resulted from the indigenous position
of many of the region's seigneurial families. In contrast to
the counts of Flanders and Vermandois, the counts of Blois/
Chartres came relatively late to their titles, and they ruled regions where a number of noble families had already been long
established. The new counts could bring some of these families
into their vassalage, but not all; and even those that did enter
the orbits of the counts demanded a price for their support. As a
result, far from causing their decline, the advent of the counts
only confirmed them in their position.[46]

The situation is clearest in the county of Chartres, held by the counts of Blois. Because they took over the county only after the death of Hugh the Great in 956, the distribution of resources among the local nobility was already defined. The counts therefore had relatively few lands and comital prerogatives in the county, or even in the city of Chartres. The bishop was the real master of resources here. Whereas the material supremacy of the count of Flanders over Thérouanne made that city's bishop an unquestioned supporter of comital policy, at Chartres the bishop consistently and successfully obstructed the designs of Odo I and II.[47] But it was not only the bishop of Chartres whose resources were independent of the count. So were those of many of the greatest lords of the region, descendants of tenth-century *potentes* already established in the area before Theobald I had taken his new title. The Gouets, for example, controlled two important castles and a vast expanse of territory on the edge of the Chartrain fronting Maine, none of it held from the counts. They clearly prized their autonomy, since William Gouet called himself *princeps*, and his mother proclaimed herself lady of Alluyes *jure hereditario, divino nutu.* Even more powerful were the viscounts of Châteaudun. Descended from a ninth-century count in Maine, the family possessed offices and resources that antedated Theobald I's accession to the comital office, and they remained essentially independent of the counts. During the late tenth and eleventh centuries the clan included the most famous men of the region, counting as members two archbishops of Tours, the first castellans of Saumur, the viscounts of Chartres and Blois, and the lords of Breteuil and Le Puiset.[48]

The power of the seigneurial families in western France was also augmented by the unusual belligerence and expansionism of the counts. Why the counts should have been so embroiled in warfare is difficult to explain. Perhaps the contiguity of many political entities led to friction, particularly on their edges, where castellans were easily pried from their loyalties. Whatever the reasons, from the last decade of the tenth century through the second third of the twelfth century, the border regions of these counties were scenes of intrigue, invasion, and rebellion. The counts of Anjou fought the duke of Aquitaine for hegemony over the northern castellans of Poitou, the counts of Blois for possession of Tours. The counts of Blois retaliated by trying to undermine Angevin designs on Brittany and Maine, while the dukes of Normandy, fearful of Angevin encroachments, later did the same.[49]

These wars did not necessarily diminish comital authority; on the contrary, successful wars increased a ruler's authority by fostering camaraderie between him and his followers and by giving him the wherewithal to reward them. But in the long run the turmoil also reinforced the power of the castellans, especially those whose fortresses guarded or fronted disputed territories. To hold these threatened locations, castellans had to be given wide military and judicial authority. It was therefore in these areas fronting the lands of their enemies that the counts of Anjou permitted their castellans to assume the *dominium* of their castles, allowing them control over the disposition of appurtenant lands and rights.[50]

The strategic location of the marcher castles provided their lords with an avenue to still greater authority. Their loyalty had to be rewarded to be kept, and the cost of that loyalty was bid up by the possibility that they might ally with rival counts. This was the source of the power of the lords of Amboise, for example, who rose to prominence after the seizure of Tours by the counts of Anjou. Vassals of both Anjou and Blois, they controlled the castles that controlled access to Tours and the corridor between the two counties. To retain Tours, the counts of Anjou needed Amboise, and to keep Amboise the counts were willing to overlook repeated affronts from its lords.[51] The pattern was similar elsewhere in western France. The viscounts of Thouars gained de facto independence from the counts of Poitou by siding with the counts of Anjou and maintaining a close relationship with the dukes of Normandy.[52] Similarly, the lords of Bellême used the rivalry of Normandy, Anjou, and Blois to carve out their own independent lordship on the edges of Maine.[53]

It was just this class of men who consistently received formal petitions; indeed, in many cases it was just these lords who received them—the viscounts of Thouars, for example, and the viscounts of Chartres and their relatives at Le Puiset and Blois.[54] The rules of petition had not changed a great deal from Carolingian times: though petitions to counts might be more grandiloquent, *potentes* still deserved to be approached with deference. What is special about the Loire valley, then, is that the ancientness of the noncomital families, coupled with the political autonomy afforded them by the expansionist policies of the local counts, permitted a more liberal protocol of deference to become entrenched and allowed the language of deference applied to *potentes* to become more elaborate. If in the province of Reims theophanic petitions reflected a real gulf between counts and castellans, in western France castellans could be petitioned as well as counts because there was in reality less distance between them.

Thus far we have been concerned with the power of viscounts and castellans; but we have noted that the *milites* of western France were also beseeched.[55] This practice was no late corruption of an originally more restrictive protocol. Although it became more common in the course of the eleventh century, it appears to have been followed even in the late tenth century, when charters from Anjou show vassals of the cathedral granting petitions.[56] Such petitions may be related to another consequence of frequent warfare in the region: the rapid diffusion of benefices among knights of the region.[57] To be able to afford their arms and mounts, knights had to be supported; and in this age support took the form of land. This is not to say that there were not still allods. They continued to exist, even in the Loire counties.[58] But in reading the charters one is even more impressed by the number of times one encounters men holding lands of others and by the depth of the chain of tenure. Even charters of the early eleventh century show us not only vassals, but vassals of vassals.[59] And this diffusion of landholding also served to spread the language of deference; for where real control over property (*seisin* remains a good word for this) was so diffuse, abbots who wanted donations or sales would have gained little by going to the count to authorize the transaction. They needed to address the men who actually disposed of the property.[60] The diffusion of the language of petition in western France was in this sense an accurate reflection of the distribution of economic resources.

Supplication and the Ideal of Political Order in Pluralistic Communities

A sacral and regal interpretation of petition was therefore not feasible in western France. The counts lacked the command of resources that might have made an authoritarian rite of supplication plausible. Nor could supplications treat the counts as iconic figures, emblems of the ordered unity of a principality, since their assorted territories possessed no such unity. An alternative vision of political order had to be created, one which recognized the essential pluralism of these communities.

This is the secret behind the proliferation of pacts in western France (and one might extend the observation to other communities with a similar conjunction of pacts and dispersed political authority, such as the Narbonnais and the Maconnais). Throughout the early Middle Ages the language and gestures of peace had been used to express relationships and transactions freely entered into by autonomous groups or individuals. Equality, autonomy, and reciprocity: these were the the characteristics of "peace" as it was defined in this period.[61] They had defined the meaning of *pacta* in Roman and Vulgar Roman law.[62] They had been the essence of the ninth-century *Verträge* (*conventiones*) by which Charles the Bald and his magnates agreed on their respective rights and obligations. With the decline of Carolingian authority in the tenth century, warring princes of Francia had relied on mediation and treaties (*pacta, foedera, amicitiae, fraternitates*) to structure their interactions.[63] Where a prostrate supplication recognized a lord's dominance, the kisses of peace and exchanges of gifts associated with pacts bound individuals in friendship or brotherhood (*amicitia, fraternitas*) independently of their lords. Pacts were therefore well suited to societies like those of western France, where if there were to be peace it could not be imposed by a count. It would have to be agreed to by the parties and bind them directly in a partnership that was essentially independent of the counts.

Far from resisting this trend, the churches of western France contributed to it. Monasteries such as La Trinité at Vendôme, Marmoutier at Tours, and Saint-Aubin at Angers became part of the regional network of interlocking alliances and interests. From castellans and their knights they received gifts of land. In countergift they granted *societas et fraternitas*, admitting the donors as honorary members of their brotherhood, burying them in their churches, praying for their souls, receiving their children as oblates, mediating their feuds, and, significantly, settling their own quarrels with them by means of *concordiae*. Because so many of the reciprocal rights and obligations linking monasteries to local nobles and knights reached into the afterlife, even the court of the heavenly king had to be reconfigured to match the new reality on earth. In a society in which friendship seemed more useful than authority, it just did not make sense to imagine the saints as the "servants" of God (*famuli*). They came to be thought of instead as God's "friends" (*amici*), interceding with the Lord on behalf of monks who in turn offered prayers of intercession for those with whom they were bound in *amicitia*.[64]

There were other ways in which the distinctive pluralism of western France began to reshape the region's political culture, particularly as it came to reflect the social transformations caused by endemic warfare. The most visible change was the increasing tendency for those who were not counts to identify their status in terms of their martial capacities. Paradoxically, we first notice this trend in charters in which lords vaunt their knighthood—the paradox being that at the time when this practice began, *milites* were still regarded as quite lowly figures, the personal dependents of their lords. The paradox can be resolved only by recalling the polysemy of the word *miles*. Meaning essentially "armed servant," the term could be applied to almost any such service, whether base or noble. Thus a lord's household bodyguard, the garrisons of his castles, and the motley horsemen he brought into battle were all *milites*. But a king or a prince might also be called a *miles* insofar as he exercised a *militia* by enforcing justice. When a young lord married or entered into a public office, like that of count or viscount, he would be girded with the belt of *militia saecularis* and might thenceforth call himself a *miles* as a sign that he had come of age. Finally, a lord could call himself another's *miles* as a synonym for *fidelis*, but with the emphasis on his duty to serve his lord in arms. In this way, a term that usually denoted the armed service of the humble could also be used to describe the honorable humility with which great men served still greater lords.[65]

In certain contexts, then, calling oneself a *miles* could be an act of self-exaltation. This was particularly likely when a man issued his own charter and joined other proud appositives to his knightly title. Corbo, first known lord of Rochecorbon but scion of a venerable family of the Touraine, referred to himself in 999 as "by the grace of God most noble knight."[66] Another example from the same year is offered by Rotrocus, a vassal of the counts of Blois. A man on the rise, he had been entrusted with the protection of Perche by his counts and would soon marry his daughter to the viscount of Châteaudun. Much later his descendants would become counts of the *pagus*. But in 999 he was still only a proud man with great ambitions: "I, Rotrocus, given to worldly knighthood and devoted in fidelity to count Odo."[67]

Significantly, these men's references to their knighthood are immediately followed by another sign of honorable status: they announce that they have been petitioned—Rotrocus by the abbot and monks of Saint-Père, Corbo by the abbot of Saint-Julien of Tours and the monks of Bourgeuil. The language of Corbo's charter is especially grand. "Beseeched" (*deprecatus est*) by the abbot and monks, he granted Bourgeuil a portion of his fief like the most noble knight he was, "receiving their entreaty kindly" and issuing "this testament of my authority" in its memory.[68] Knighthood and petition were therefore both treated as marks of honor. Nor is it only these charters that establish this connection. When the viscount of Chartres granted a petition from the abbot of Saint-Père, he did not mention his office, only that he was "Harduin, given to worldly knighthood and devoted in fidelity to Count Odo."[69]

Grandiloquent phrases of petition and references to the "belt of worldly knighthood" were not signs of these lords' aspirations to autonomy. Not only do many of these early charters record the count's consent; like Harduin of Chartres, the authors of these acts also often call attention to their loyalty to the counts.[70] Indeed, Odo I himself issued a charter which mentioned that Harduin, *vir nobilis* and *fidelis noster*, had been petitioned by the monks of Saint-Père. Similarly, the fact that Rotrocus was entreated by one of his vassals did not prevent him from calling himself "devoted in fidelity to Count Odo," or from demonstrating that fidelity by presenting his charter to Odo for confirmation.[71]

As in the province of Reims, early eleventh-century petitionary protocols represent a reconfiguration of the political community in response to the regime of the castellans; but here the nature of that reconfiguration was different because the political structure was different. In the north, theophanic supplication made visible the difference between the holy authority of counts and the profane power of castellans and knights. In contrast, the widespread use of the language of deference in western France assumed the comparability of these men. It is one of the earliest signs of a phenomenon that would later become a distinctive characteristic of twelfth-century society: the forging of a common nobility, which included all *potentes*, castellans and knights as well as counts.

To be sure, there were differences between counts and castellans and castellans and knights which no one could have ignored.[72] But these men also shared a great deal. In the first place, a close relationship between castellans and knights was inherent in the nature of castle warfare. During the tenth century, *milites* throughout northern Francia had been humble figures, the household warriors of lords and the men of their garrisons. Their status was little better than that of the *ministeriales* and peasants from whose ranks they came. Yet by the eleventh century forces were working to increase the knights' prestige. Though they may not have been much wealthier than peasants, they had a proximity to power that peasants could never claim. And all could boast a skill in mounted combat that set them apart from both peasants and household domestics and drew them closer to their lords. It also drew them closer to each other. Loyal to the same lord, living in the same castle, they shared a common table (*precor vos . . . qui mecum manducatis*),[73] fought side by side, and fostered a sense of caste by marrying into each other's families. They became like brothers, bound by that *amicitia* which soon became such a prominent feature in monastic reforms like the Cistercians' that drew their strength from just this class.[74]

The clearest sign that they had become aware of their special status is their appropriation of the language of prayer. Knights not only beseeched their feudal lords for favors (whether or not these lords were counts, bishops, or abbots); they also beseeched each other, just as they were beseeched in turn by abbots and monks and their own vassals.[75] Like counts and viscounts and castellans, they were worthy of being treated with honor, for their association with lords set them apart.

A New Image of Comital Authority

Inevitably, this new culture affected the perception and projection of comital authority. To be sure, counts could still be thought of as bearers of regal attributes such as *sapientia* and *clementia*, and even in the early twelfth century they could still be granted honors appropriate to God's vicars. When Fulk the Young, count of Anjou, formally made a donation to Saint-Aubin for the care of the poor, the almoner's immediate response was "humbly" to prostrate himself at the count's feet and request a confirmation of the act.[76] Still, one wonders if the almoner would not have done as much for any benefactor who aided the poor. Certainly the notice recounting the incident ascribes to Fulk none of the special attributes that usually denoted comital grace. In fact, such language is generally missing from Angevin charters. Only rarely (in about 20 percent of their charters) are Fulk Nerra (987–1040) and Geoffrey Martel (1040–60) called counts *Dei gratia*. Even rarer are full regalian supplications of the kind that call attention to the liturgical nature of the entreaty. They amount to no more than one or two per reign—in spite of the fact that at least twenty of each count's charters survive.[77] Truncated petitions (entailing a simple reference to a *deprecatio*) are hardly more frequent: only six of Fulk Nerra's twenty charters mention them; two of Geoffrey Martel's twenty-one charters; only three of twenty-five charters examined from Fulk le Réchin (1067–1109).[78] Having been stripped of such honorifics, the counts' charters are left looking remarkably ordinary. Like the private charters of knights and castellans, their acts simply announce that they are giving land to a church for the salvation of themselves and their lineal ancestors. All that distinguishes them from any other noble benefactor is their title, a spartan *comes Andegavorum*.[79]

Periodically, however, the counts would issue a charter that did say something about the nature of their authority. What is remarkable about such charters is that their description of that authority departed radically from the traditional model, even as they used traditional conceits. The pattern goes back to the very foundations of their power in the later tenth century, during the rule of the first great count, Geoffrey Greymantle (960–87), one of whose few surviving acts recounts the story of a pilgrimage to Rome. There is, as always, exaltation in the act, as Geoffrey proudly recalls that the pope received him with great honor and devoted five consecutive days to his reform. But the exaltation is achieved by humiliation, as on the sixth and seventh days the pope lectured him on the need to practice fasts, prayers, vigils,

and almsgiving to erase his sins. Humility was in fact the purpose of the entire trip, since according to Geoffrey he had made
the pilgrimage "to beg pardon" and be "freed from the bondage
of my sins."[80]

The sentiments seem conventional enough: great lords are
known by their great humility. They revere God because they
hold their authority by his grace. That Geoffrey's act was somewhat different is proclaimed at the charter's outset, in the intit-
ulation: "I, Geoffrey, made count by the praiseworthy vigor
[*strenuitas*] of my ancestors" (a variant proudly adding, "and by
mine also").[81] Geoffrey is not a count by the grace of God. He is
a warrior, and he glories in the fact even as he records an act of
devotional humility. When he speaks of receiving *laudes*, he
does not mean the liturgical acclamations that bonded kings to
Christ but the epics that perhaps even then were celebrating his
victories.[82] Geoffrey is also careful to give his knights their due.
If he is powerful, it is because of them: *Andegavorum militum
generositati potenter comes appositus*, he calls himself. In fact,
he and his followers are inseparable. They are his "best men"
(*optimates*), his "comrades" (*socii*). He undertakes the pilgrimage on their advice. They are with him during his audi-
ences with the pope and receive the same counsel he does. They
will give land to the church he will found on his return from
Rome. And it is a *miles* of Lucca whom he charges to oversee
the building of the church.

Geoffrey said that he would found the church not only for his
salvation but also so that God would give his descendants the
opportunity to do penance before their deaths. His descendants
seem to have received that opportunity, for their charters voice
the same humility and concern for penance. Geoffrey's son,
Fulk Nerra, built the church of Saint-Nicolas, even though, as
his charter says, he was "one of the least of men, and one of the
most useless."[83] A charter for Marmoutier issued by Fulk le Réchin begins with the axiom of Christian lordship, "God resists
the proud but gives grace to the humble." Remembering this,
Fulk continues, "I exult in humbling my soul beneath the hand
of God . . . so that I may find grace"; and he expresses the hope
that God will look mercifully down on him, "a wretched penitent," sinful in everything but beseeching forgiveness with
tears.[84]

Here again conventional expressions disguised an unconventional meaning. When a king like Robert the Pious or a count like Robert of Flanders professed his humility and undertook humiliating acts of devotion, he was implicitly reinforcing the traditional meanings of devotional supplication. When a ruler supplicated God because he held his power by God's grace, his humility strengthened his power by sanctifying it. Because such acts were often associated with the poor (almsgiving, for example), the ruler also dramatized his responsibility for all his people. He was not just the leader of a faction of warriors. His ministry was to nurture the poor in times of need, just as in his Peace assemblies he protected them from the tyranny of castellans and knights. Doubtless these same associations informed Angevin expressions of humility; but they were also compatible with a new meaning. Whereas the humility of Robert the Pious underscored the unique sacredness of his office and established his concern for the poor, that of the counts of Anjou diminished the sacredness of their office and thereby erased the distance that separated them from their nobles. Hence the oddly secular, seigneurial aspects of Angevin diplomatics are of a piece with its expressions of pious humility, since both drew the counts closer to their *fideles*.

This convergence of interests and outlook is the most distinctive characteristic of Angevin diplomatics. Geoffrey Martel spoke of his *fideles* as his *amici*, as Greymantle had called them his *socii*, thus raising his men to his level.[85] Conversely, on occasion the counts came down to the level of their men and described themselves as knights. Geoffrey Grisegonelle, vaunting his own *strenuitas*, had set the pattern. His lead was followed by his descendants, particularly in those rare charters whose formulas or settings alluded to the sacredness of their office. It is as if the counts could not accept exaltation without somehow undercutting it. Thus an act from Marmoutier calls Fulk Nerra count of Anjou and Tours "by the grace of God" but immediately qualifies this by adding "dedicated to worldly knighthood."[86] *Militiae secularie deditus*: it is the same formula used by western monasteries—including Marmoutier—for the great seigneurial families of the region, those of viscomital rank or those descended from viscomital families.[87] And though Fulk's charter does style him count *Dei gratia*, yet what could this have meant to a monastery that also called a lesser figure like Marannus *gratia Dei miles*?[88] The parallel is revealing, but not as revealing as another charter written in Fulk's name, this one by the monks of Saint-Florent of Saumur. The abbot petitioned Fulk to grant his monastery a church located in one of his castles. He not only petitioned him (*expetiit*), he begged him in supplication (*suppliciter expostulans*), addressing Fulk as "sublimity." But he did not beg the sublimity of his "majesty" or the sublimity of his "clemency," the phrases one would expect. He was addressing an Angevin count; and so he made up a unique coinage, one that appears in no other charter from northern France. He begged "the sublimity of our knighthood."[89]

Such usages are too consistent, both across time and across the region, to be the accidental results of local scribal traditions. Nor do they speak only to the beliefs of the clergy who wrote the documents, for their elevation of knighthood runs too much against the grain of traditional ecclesiastical values, too much with contemporary social trends. The formulas of Angevin charters reflected a regional consensus about the nature of comital authority and political community shared and shaped by churches, counts, and nobles alike. These rulers could not cultivate the aura of serene distance that seemed natural in the north, where a gulf really did separate counts from their castellans and knights. The persistence of warfare and the power it placed in the hands of castellans required the counts of the Loire valley to become leaders of retinues, managers of coalitions of vassals. They had to rule the nobility by accommodating it.[90] And that meant that if they sometimes received deference, they were never to flaunt it.

This need for accommodation may explain why no Peace councils ever gathered in Anjou (or in Blois or Chartres, for that matter). Standing alongside bishops and abbots, surrounded by relics and condemning the depredations of castellans against the poor: this was not the way Angevins ruled, exalted by God with a sacred authority beyond the reach of their men. The need to accommodate their vassals certainly explains why the counts showed deference at least as often as they received it; for something truly surprising about the Angevins is the frequency of their formal acts of penance. The meaning of these acts was no more conventional than were the professions of humility in Angevin charters. Instead of being willing ritual enactments of the divine basis of their authority, the counts' prostrate penances were by and large imposed on them by the force of circumstances; and implicit in these displays of humility was their recognition of another institution's sacrosanct autonomy. We have already seen a barefoot Fulk Nerra enter the church of Saint-Martin of Tours and offer a prostrate confession of his wrong after he had invaded the canons' cloister and destroyed some of their houses. It is the perfect illustration of that combination of raw power and subtle accommodation that typified the dynasty. Fulk got what he wanted, indeed, more than he had wanted, for not only had he destroyed a possible focus for resistance to his authority, he had also gained an alliance with Saint Martin. But he had achieved all this by humbling himself to the canons and implicitly recognizing the principle of their chapter's inviolability.[91]

Significantly, it was not a weak count like Fulk le Réchin who undertook this penance. It was precisely the strongest, most ruthless Angevin count who did so, because suppleness was a source of his power. To rule such extensive territories, the counts had to share political authority and economic wealth. The result was a fractious polity, whose essential pluralism the counts had to accept in order to govern.

If on occasion even Fulk Nerra had to display humility, his weaker successors had even more occasions to do so. In 1064 Fulk l'Oison, nephew of Geoffrey Martel and count of Vendôme, "begged pardon" of the monks of La Trinité of Vendôme for his depredations against their lands and churches. A decade later, in the course of a dispute with Fulk le Réchin and one of his castellans (note, acting together), the monks of Vendôme set a crucifix on the ground in front of the altar of a church the two lords had seized. At the end of the dispute Fulk and his castellan went to the church and "with great compunction of heart and humble satisfaction of penance, most devoutly raised the standard from the ground with their own hands"—to the great approval of the crowd of men and women who had gathered to watch the event.[92]

Typically, these humiliations occurred with respect to churches in the counts' satellite territories; that is, in regions where their power was least complete. It is also typical that the power of both Fulk l'Oison and Fulk le Réchin was particularly compromised, for the former chaffed under the protectorate exercised by his uncle over Vendôme, and the latter, having seized power from his brother, had been forced to acquiesce in his castellans' growing autonomy as the price of their consent to his usurpation.[93] Finally, it is typical that Fulk le Réchin should have been forced to his penance by his recognition that he needed La Trinité's support (if only its prayers) for an imminent battle against the duke of Aquitaine.[94] In all these ways the penances of the two counts not only conformed generally to the pattern of supplication in a pluralistic society; they issued directly from its exigencies.

Even in Anjou the counts' power was compromised, so that Fulk le Réchin once had to do penance to the monks of Saint-Aubin for his exaction of customs on their lands.[95] Still more revealing in this respect is a document analyzed by Olivier Guillot, because it shows the extent to which the language of entreaty became ingrained in the fabric of government and, no less significant, how much the development of this pattern resulted from the counts' military needs. Toward the middle of the century, Geoffrey Martel reached an agreement with the monastery of Saint-Nicolas of Angers over the latter's military obligations. Actually, the problem was not the monastery's obligations per se but the form in which they would be demanded. In effect, the monks refused to be lumped together with the count's ordinary vassals in fulfilling their service. They demanded that the count treat them with dignity. The compromise, then, was Geoffrey's promise that in the future he would not send an ordinary minister to demand military service. Rather, he would dispatch a friend or familiar who would "beseech the monks with prayers" (*pro orationibus expostulandis*) to send their men. Then the monks would reciprocate by sending their forces "with willing peace and free will." The effect would be the same, of course: the count would get his troops. But to do so he had to recognize the monastery's autonomy. He had to deal with it honorably. Whereas the counts of Vermandois and Flanders were entreated by their monks and clerics, if he wanted to govern the count of Anjou had to entreat them.[96]

Guillot's document permits one other interesting conclusion.

Although the count and his man beseech the monks, their petitions no longer represent a recognition of the monks' sacrality. Even petitions to the great have become a form of etiquette, a display of deference to recognize worldly honor, just like petitions addressed to castellans and knights. Supplication was becoming so thoroughly secularized that in the west one might call a castellan's exactions from his peasants *petitiones*.[97] Nor was there anything odd in the count's or countess's entreaty of a vassal to make a donation or yield a legal claim.[98]

Against this backdrop, one can better understand one final aspect of Angevin supplications: the counts' ambivalence toward displays of deference. That gestures of humility continued to be assumed at least periodically is suggested by the occasional reference to petitions in comital charters. The suggestion is confirmed by two sources that describe the act. One has already been mentioned. It is the early twelfth-century notice that describes the almoner's prostration to Fulk the Young as he requested the count to confirm a donation. And though there is no explicit sign of ambivalence, yet it does seem strange that the prostration should have been mentioned at all. Normally it was not, the formulas of supplication alone sufficing to denote the act.

The second act is undeniably enigmatic. In 1092 Fulk le Réchin issued a charter to record a donation to Saint-Nicolas of Angers, the very monastery his uncle had agreed to entreat when he demanded troops. As in most Angevin charters, the count bears none of the usual marks of divinely sanctioned lordship. There is no reference to him as a *comes Dei gratia*, no mention of any entreaty by the monks. On the contrary, Fulk made every effort to assimilate his gift to the donation of any ordinary noble benefactor, dedicating it to the salvation of his father and grandfather and framing it not as the result of the monks' prayers to him but as a way of obtaining their prayers for him: *ut ipsi semper Deum pro me obsecrent*. All the same, the abbot insisted on prostrating himself at his feet; but he did so, wrote Fulk, "against my will." A conventional expression of lordly humility? Perhaps, for Fulk knew the convention well. He was the count who exulted in humbling his soul. Yet an unconventional feeling breaks through the cliché, when after mentioning his disapproval of the abbot's prostration Fulk adds, with more than a hint of embarrassment, that one of his *optimates* had "even kissed my hand."[99]

Perhaps the kiss represented only a token of thanks; but kisses could also be acts of reverence and subjection, and as such had once been demanded by kings. Which was it, then, thanks or reverence? In eleventh-century Anjou, the ambiguity was intolerable, because insofar as the kiss did imply reverence and subjection, it opened up a distance between count and *fideles* that did not match reality, and so threatened to make the ritual laughable. Fulk's discomfort was therefore real. To escape it, he had to close the distance with a voluntary show of diffidence.

It is always dangerous to read so much into so few words. In this case, however, the interpretation is justified by one of the most entertaining anecdotes about a dynasty rich in them. This particular tale recalls how Geoffrey Greymantle got his name. It was told in the counts' own house chronicle, written in the early twelfth century, although the story probably originated soon after Geoffrey's lifetime. Ever in the pursuit of glory, the count had disguised himself and singlehandedly beaten the Danes who were besieging Paris—all of them. The king marveled at the feat, but could not learn the hero's identity. But the count had been sheltered in his exploit by a miller, and the miller told the king that although he did not know the knight's name (*personam militis*), he would surely recognize him if he saw him. On an appointed day the miller came to an assembly in Paris attended by all the *principes*. As he looked around the hall, his eyes fixed on Geoffrey, cloaked in a grey mantle. "With jovial expression" (*vultu jocundus*) he stepped up to the count (*accessit*), knelt before him (*genu flexu*), seized hold of his grey tunic (*arrepta tunica*), and proclaimed him the hero who "in prostrating the Danes relieved the Franks of their shame."[100]

Like most prostrations or genuflections to counts, this one is an epiphany: Geoffrey's true self is "revealed" by the prostration. Yet what is revealed is not a serene and clement prince but "the face of a knight" who gloried in his prowess. The entire scene becomes a supplication turned on its head. There is nothing reverential in the miller's "accession" to the lord. There is nothing humble about his expression. And far from kneeling to establish distance between the count and himself, the simple miller grabs Geoffrey and rudely takes hold of his cloak. However told, the story is entertaining; but Angevins would have especially appreciated the scene. Their count was a great man, and they might kneel before him. But he was not a sacred figure. He was one of their own; above all, a warrior like themselves.

Test Cases: Amiens

We are therefore left with two analytically distinct types of polity, entirely different in traditions, organization, and culture. In the north—that is, in Ricardian Normandy and the province of Reims—principalities coalesced around single comital dynasties, which maintained control of strategic resources and borrowed royal and imperial models to project the uniqueness of their own authority. Here supplication was theophanic and regalian. In the west, counts had no such long-standing monopoly of authority. Political power was more widely diffused among a number of well-established viscounts and castellans, many of them descendants of families already prominent in the late ninth and early tenth centuries. The counts' frequent wars and their need to govern agglomerations of heterogeneous territories only increased the castellans' autonomy. They concentrated wealth, in the form of benefices, in the hands of vassals. And they permitted the evolution of a distinctive culture, as castellans and even knights began to regard themselves as partners of their lords, set apart from the mass of ordinary subjects by their proximity to power and their martial skills. Here supplication developed into an etiquette which members of a nobility used to honor friends and peers.

Implicit in this analysis is the assumption that the explanation for these differences lies not in regional diplomatic traditions but in social structures; for a tradition lasts only as long as it can be made to conform to reality. If this assumption is correct, then wherever one finds similar structures one should also find similar kinds of supplication. That this is the case is shown by the fact that even within the province of Reims there were areas where theophanic supplication was, if not unknown, then at least underused. The best example is the Amienois.

Amiens had many of the characteristics of other counties in the province of Reims. The dynasty that ruled the county from 985 to 1077 had long been established in the region, having also controlled the county in the early tenth century.[101] The early eleventh-century counts also had the full support of the city's bishops, since they were members of the same family.[102] However, other factors undercut the counts' supremacy. The family lost control of the county in 926 and did not regain it until sometime between 966 and 985. During the interlude the Amienois fell prey to the worst of the tenth-century civil wars. Before the native dynasty managed to recover its position, control over the county passed from the counts of Vermandois to the Carolingians, to the counts of Flanders, back to the Carolingians, and finally to the Robertians.[103] The Amienois began to take on the characteristics of a march, a region not dominated by any single house but divided among princely factions, each trying to protect a core territory outside the area.

In the wake of these wars lordship within the Amienois became hopelessly fragmented. The counts and bishops controlled the *civitas*. But not fifteen kilometers from the city's walls lay the abbey of Corbie, exempt from episcopal oversight and the center of a powerful immunity.[104] Although it was nominally a royal abbey, Corbie's abbots often conducted themselves as independent lords, flouting the kings' wishes just as they obstructed the policies of counts and bishops.[105] Luckily, the kings had other rights in the area, including a castle at Encre.[106] The counts of Flanders also regained a presence in the region when Corbie passed into their control in 1028 as part of a marriage alliance between Robert the Pious and Baldwin IV. It remained under Flemish control until about 1071, when the abbey returned to the royal domain.[107]

Like the counts of Chartres, Blois, and Tours, and unlike those of Flanders, the Vermandois, and early eleventh-century Normandy, the counts of Amiens had competitors who kept them from extending their authority throughout their county. Had it not been for their large holdings outside the Amienois, they would not have had the prestige they did; and this provides another similarity between them and the counts of western France. For the better part of the period, Walter I and his descendants were counts not only of Amiens but also of Valois and the

Vexin. Because the counties were not contiguous, it was difficult to provide them with a single administration. They were,
in fact, temporarily divided between the two eligible heirs of
Walter II, and the territories became, for all practical purposes,
autonomous entities.[108] Thus the Vexin was oriented politically
and economically toward Normandy and Paris, the Amienois
toward Flanders and the Vermandois. The regions' nobilities
also became quite separate. There were exceptions, such as the
Tirels, who held rights in both regions.[109] But for the most part
the families that ruled the Amienois did not have rights in the
Vexin, and those who ruled in the Vexin did not have rights in
the Amienois.[110]

Like the counts of Blois/Chartres, the counts of Amiens also
engaged in a politics of *beaux gestes* that further diverted their
attention from their counties. Drogo died in the Holy Land in
the company of Duke Robert of Normandy.[111] Raoul III led an
insurrection against Henry I in 1041, along with the counts of
Meulan and Troyes, and thereafter was one of the most visible
military campaigners of his age.[112] His son, Simon, heir to what
was potentially one of the largest principalities in France, remained true to his family's tradition of flamboyance even as he
broke with its martial values. Upon seeing his father's decaying
body lying in a tomb, he resigned all his powers and became a
monk at Cluny.[113] With that the dynasty ended.

Given the family's extensive but fragmented dominions and
its preoccupation with political affairs outside those dominions,
the counts had to delegate much of their authority. In fact, after
1030 the counts were not very active within the Amienois at
all.[114] Increasingly it was their relatives the bishops who protected the family's interests, while the counts' military and judicial authority was exercised by their viscounts, the lords of
Boves.[115]

Power in the Amienois was therefore divided among a group
of families and institutions that were at least de facto autonomous. As in western France, political autonomy was the precondition for the spread of *convenientiae*. In the 1030s, for example, Amiens and Corbie swore to a Peace of God which was
really a pact between the rulers of the two communities. One of
its articles required disputes to be brought to a yearly convoca-
tion held partway between the two centers and there "brought

to peace." This meeting on neutral ground institutionalized the equality of partners which was typical of pacts, as did another stipulation: that relics of both churches were to be taken to the convocations, the parity of Amiens and Corbie being symbolized by the parity of their saints.[116]

There can be little doubt that the idea of peace helped the contending powers of the region to conceptualize the problem of political order in the absence of dominant lordship. The proof is that sources from this region refer to peace far more frequently and far earlier than those from neighboring areas. Contemporary with the pact of the 1030s the inscription *pax* appears on episcopal coinage, while after the middle of the century the charters of Bishop Gui began to dwell on the virtues of peace and charity and the expectation of *societas* in the afterlife.[117] At about the same time Gui concluded a pact (*pactum, conventio*) with Abbot Fulk of Corbie, which they confirmed in the presence of the count of Flanders, at that time Corbie's overlord. Indeed, peace terminology seeped into the language of supplication with the specific purpose of underscoring Corbie's equality vis-à-vis its bishop. Bishop Gui approached Abbot Fulk and "beseeched our friendship," while the abbot in turn approached the bishop and "entreated our paternity in fervent charity"—this at a time when the bishop was still begged "most humbly" by his lay and clerical subordinates.[118] Nor was the language of peace restricted to Corbie's dealings with the bishop. The monastery also settled disputes with its powerful lay neighbors by means of *concordiae* in which overlords did not intervene, or intervened only to confirm their engagement.[119]

Against this background, the diplomatic characteristics of comital charters make perfect sense. The counts of Amiens exercised power in a region that customarily reserved humble entreaties for the greatest lords. They were actively supported by the bishops of Amiens. And the churches of the province, who as beneficiaries of the counts' acts presumably drew up their charters, approved of the theophanic meaning of supplication. These factors account for the religious tone of many of the acts, in which the counts call attention to the sacred meaning of prayer.[120] They also account for the fact that these charters were issued "at the entreaty" of abbots.[121] Yet the same charters do not mention any formal accession; nor do they describe the petitioner as humble or devoted, the lord as gracious or clement. Nothing in the charters, in other words, makes explicit the sacred meaning of petition or its royal model. In fact, most comital acts do not use the formulas at all. Instead, the counts of Amiens confirmed donations and settled disputes as feudal lords, and recorded their own donations as *Privaturkunden*.[122] They called attention to the sacrality of the churches that benefited from their largesse, but not to their own. Having parceled out much of their authority to viscounts, castellans, and bishops, and conducting themselves like warriors and courtiers, the counts saw the images of stable rulership, paternalistic responsibility, and supreme authority afforded by the solemn formulas of petition as simply unimportant.

Test Cases: Normandy

Other facets of the relationship between petitionary formulas and political structure are shown by the development of the formulas in Normandy. We have already noted their prominence in the acts of Richard II. As the first count of Rouen to extend his rule beyond the valley of the Seine and the first to be taken seriously by the Franks as something more than a pirate, Richard's status and power were acknowledged by the varied and august titles his beneficiaries awarded him: *princeps et marchio, dux et patritius, dux et princeps*. For the same reasons— often in the same charters—they granted him the honor of liturgical entreaties, their language as grandiloquent and studied as the titles themselves.[123]

Their number is particularly dense in the earliest charters, those issued in the years immediately after the appearance of these new titles: between 1009 and 1020 four of Richard's five extant charters describe his acts as gracious responses to reverent petitions. Thereafter the dukes' use of the formulas declined precipitously. Only one of Richard's fifteen acts over the next six years includes such language (and it may belong to the earlier period). Although the number of petitions rises in the following decades, the trend is still downward. Under Duke Robert (1030–35) only 33 percent of ducal acts (four of twelve) mention formal petitions (with formulas of accession and the attribution of regal virtues to the duke). During William II's minority (1035–47) only 20 percent do so (one of five), in the nineteen years after his majority (1048–66) only 13 percent (three of twenty-one).[124]

If the overall trend is clear, it is difficult to explain its variations and their timing, particularly the sharp decline between 1020 and 1026 and the partial resurgence under Robert. One explanation would correlate the use of the formulas and contemporary political events. Thus the absence of petitionary acts during the last part of Richard's reign may indicate that his numerous donations to churches during this period were not sought by the beneficiaries. Instead, Richard was distributing his lands to the major monasteries of his dominions in order to transfer part of the burden of government onto the church. The policy is well known, and it dates precisely to these years. The reason that no petitions were mentioned in Richard's later acts may therefore be the simplest one possible: Richard was not acting at the instigation of petitioners. Instead, he himself initiated the donations; and his chancery drew up the documents recording them, thus accounting for the marked uniformity of ducal acts of this period noted by Marie Fauroux.[125]

Richard III ruled only briefly after his father's death. He was soon succeeded by his brother, Robert I, in whose time Normandy finally succumbed to the political fragmentation so common elsewhere in France. Robert had none of the moral authority of his father. In fact, he was accused of poisoning his brother and was personally unpopular with churchmen because of his seizures of church property to the benefit of himself and his followers. But Robert was only acting in self-defense, for the ducal demesnes had been depleted by decades of benefactions, and he was losing control over the property and offices that his predecessors had given out. Counts and lords treated delegated lands and powers as family property to be passed on to their heirs. Nor could Robert prevent them from using those powers to extend their lands by encroaching upon church estates and forcing lesser men into dependence on them. When Robert died and the duchy passed to William II, a boy no more than eight years old, all restraints were removed. Normandy entered a twenty-year anarchy in which competing families vied for control of Rouen and the county. Only in 1053, after a set of military victories made possible by royal support, did William and his faction manage to consolidate their authority.[126]

It is against this backdrop that we must interpret changes in the use of petitionary formulas in ducal acts. Their reappearance under Robert and the lavishness of their style immediately suggest that the duke was falling back on an image of authority as the legitimacy of his rule was being questioned and the reality of power was being stripped from him. The same explanation could apply to petitions in William's charters, most of which are concentrated during his minority. Yet even if this interpretation is partly true, it places the impetus for the petitions in the wrong hands. A minor like William could not have initiated such a policy. It would have been initiated for him. Moreover, one of the signs of the collapse of ducal authority in this period is the demise of Richard II's nascent ducal chancery. Under Robert and William, responsibility for drafting acts appears to have reverted to beneficiaries.[127] Extravagant petitions to the dukes in this period must therefore represent a scriptorium's decision to use this language, although that decision may have been made with the connivance of the duke or his entourage. In the final analysis, the choice of style was therefore dictated by the needs and values of those who either wrote the charter or were responsible for having it written.

Because the choice depended on circumstances, the specific reasons for using the formulas in any given situation were highly variable. Unfortunately, lacking adequate contextual information we can only make hypotheses about what those reasons were. One petition may have represented a kind of quid pro quo between the duke and his petitioner—Robert acquiescing in the act of a powerful viscount, the viscount in return recognizing the duke's authority by making a formal entreaty.[128] Another looks like a humiliation: as the price of being secured from attack by William's allies, a man of questionable loyalty endowed a monastery under terms that effectively brought the greater part of his family's lands under the duke's control and ruined its political independence. This despoilment he himself had to petition before the duke would accept him as a *fidelis*.[129] There is less doubt about the most important act. When Robert's uncle, the archbishop of Rouen, issued a joint charter with his nephew, their act spoke of their *serenitas* and recalled the need to give heed to just and reasonable petitions. Such language, in part borrowed from royal and papal diplomatics, marked a momentary return to the days of Richard II, when duke and archbishop had ruled Normandy together and the family's power had been strengthened by the cooperation of its members. The relevance of the message would only have been underscored by the recent war between the two men. The joint charter may in fact have been a sign or a product of their reconciliation.[130]

Still, the trend was toward the decline of the formulas. Even after William II had reasserted his authority, formal petitions remained extremely uncommon. It is not that individuals ceased to fall on their knees before the duke; chronicles make it clear that rebels did just that when begging his mercy.[131] Such gestures leave little trace in the charters, however. Between 1050 and 1066 only two of William's fifteen acts used the formulas in a clearly honorific sense—that is, described the petition as an expression of the suppliant's piety or the duke's serenity. Two others refer tersely to *preces* or *petitiones*.[132]

This discrepancy is due to a significant change in ducal government. To begin with, liturgical entreaties were first and foremost displays of political authority. But to work on this level they had to be made in formal public assemblies, and such assemblies were becoming less and less common in William's reign, at least as a forum for issuing charters. The attestations of the charters themselves prove this, since witnesses of this period less often included the phalanxes of bishops and great counts who had attended Richard II. Instead, ducal charters were now witnessed by household officials and a coterie of loyal *fideles*.[133] No longer part of a celebration of political order, issuing a charter had become a private matter; and so instead of referring to the accession and petition of his *fideles*, William explains his actions by saying that he has acted at the advice (*interpellatio, suggestio*) of individuals or with their consent (*annuente fideli nostro*).[134] Perhaps there were still moments when petitioners made their requests on bended knees. Earlier discussions have taught us to beware of assuming that such gestures did not occur where their language does not appear in the charters.[135] But even if they did occur, the act no longer provided an occasion to declare the sanctity of the ducal office, and no longer needed to be depicted as such.

Test Cases: The Vermandois

Although this process unfolded much more slowly and much later in Flanders and the Vermandois than in Normandy, ultimately it affected comital authority there, too. For instance, in the Vermandois the counts consistently awarded privileges according to the old formulas until 1076, and as late as 1114 the countess of Vermandois could use them in all their former elegance. But at that time the formulas had already become outmoded. By the middle of the twelfth century, petitions have no place in comital charters.[136]

What occasioned this change can be described briefly, since the components will be familiar. The most obvious factor was that the Carolingian dynasty of the counts of Vermandois died out shortly after 1080. It was replaced by a cadet branch of the Capetians, which simultaneously inherited lands in the Valois and Amiens from the counts of Valois, whose own line had become extinct in 1077.[137] The Capetian alliance of the new counts, together with the importance of their holdings in the Valois, tended to draw their interests away from their northern domains and into the intrigues of the royal court, of which Raoul IV, count of Vermandois and Valois, was seneschal. Raoul was far too busy campaigning for himself and his king against the house of Champagne or intriguing against the king's chief counselor, Abbot Suger, to take much interest in the affairs of his northern county. Even his name identified him with the old counts of Valois, not with the counts of Vermandois; and he was buried at the Valois foundation of Saint-Arnoul of Crépy instead of in the chapter of Saint-Quentin, the ancestral resting place of the Carolingian counts of Vermandois.[138]

As in the Amienois and the Loire valley, absentee rulers both allowed and required seigneurial families to play a more active role in local affairs. Yet this process of emancipation had actually begun before the change of dynasty, though it was accelerated by it. In the late tenth and early eleventh centuries, the castellans of the Vermandois are little more than names among lists of witnesses in comital charters, and because the names change, it is impossible to associate a particular family with a particular castle until mid-century.[139] One suspects that castles had not yet become inheritable within families until that time. Instead, they shifted from generation to generation within a close-knit group of families dependent on the counts.[140]

Toward the middle of the century the count's *fideles* began to free themselves from his entourage. Not that the castellans ever became troublesome to the counts. Even the most powerful remained outstanding for their loyalty, in the twelfth century as in the eleventh. But they do increasingly appear on their own, issuing their own charters, settling their own disputes without reference to the count, and pursuing their own political interests outside the Vermandois. In 1055 Ivo, "castellan of Ham," issued a charter recording his donation of a woman to Notre-Dame of Noyon; some thirty years later his son, now called *Hamensis dominus*, issued another charter to quit his claim to the same woman.[141] From the 1040s the lords of Péronne appear in command of judicial proceedings at Péronne. Still, their interests remained parochial until the late 1090s, when the lordship fell to Robert of Boves. Brother of the infamous Ingelran of Coucy, Robert was ipso facto one of the leading nobles of northern France, and his horizons now extended far beyond the Vermandois.[142] Robert's contemporary Anselm (or Ansellus), castellan of Saint-Quentin, was at the same time one of the leading nobles of Flanders, where he was advocate of Saint-Amand and castellan of Bouchain. He also founded the monastery of Saint-Nicolas-des-Prés at Ribemont, and occasionally appears as count in its acts. He died on crusade.[143] Finally, the lords of Nesle, known previously only through occasional appearances in comital acts, are shown after 1115 settling disputes involving their own vassals. By 1141 they had become counts of Soissons.[144]

With the castellans came knights. True, the term *miles* had been used in local charters as early as the 950s and during the next century was regularly applied to a wide range of men. A favored vassal like Dudo, an allodist like Arpadius, a *vir nobilis* like Amolric, or a future castellan like Geoffrey—at one time or another all were called *milites*, right along with the most obscure comital retainers. Yet the common term was not the sign of a common nobility. All it signified was their common military obligation to the count, for these men were *his* knights (*noster miles, miles meus*).[145] In this context, *miles* was simply a synonym for "vassal" that emphasized the military services greater and lesser men alike owed to their lord. Of these services, the most pertinent was the duty to attend the count in his castles and to garrison them. Hence a surprisingly large proportion of eleventh-century charters that mention *milites* also mention castellans (and vice versa), while a posthumous charter confirming the last acts of the castellan of Saint-Quentin brought together a full contingent of his old comrades to attest their lord's donation. One could be a vassal without a castle, for a vassal could live on his benefice and serve his lord in many ways; but a knight without a castle was becoming a contradiction in terms, to the point that a knight who appeared in a charter by himself, without a lord, needed to be identified more fully by the name of his castle: "Ultric, knight of the castle of La Fère" or "Goisbert, knight of Péronne."[146]

Thus knights spread throughout the Vermandois in the wake of the castellans, until by the late eleventh century they had come to form a recognizable caste. That was when they began to employ the term *miles* to identify themselves, and to be identified as, a distinct and privileged order. One sign of this new consciousness is the eventual disappearance of the term's association with dependence, as individuals began to call themselves "knights" as a badge of honor. In 1090 Goisbert, "knight of Péronne," donated land to Mont-Saint-Quentin, and Alelm, "a certain knight" (*quidam miles*), and his wife made another donation to the same monastery. In 1106 "Werric, knight, surnamed the Governor," issued a charter in his own name recording his donation to Homblières.[147] The use of the epithet *miles* as a sign of status, the assumption of a surname (Satrapa) indicative of high office, and the decision to have a document written in his own name, all reveal Werric's pride in his status, a pride not at all evident in the public image of knights' dependence during the preceding century.

Controlling their own lands, intermarrying with other knightly families, finding prestige in the retinues of castellans, these men demanded to be treated with consideration. As in western France, this meant that they could receive entreaties.

Between 1055 and the early 1120s, three consecutive lords of Ham received petitions from the canons of Notre-Dame of Noyon. Early in the twelfth century the abbot of Saint-Crépin took care to approach Raoul of Nesle "in the way that was proper" (*modo quo decuit*), a phrase that makes sense only if it is taken to refer to a formal entreaty. And in 1138 one Thomas of Roye "acquiesced" in the "many repeated prayers" of the abbot of Saint-Prix, who requested the right to cultivate lands held by Thomas's vassals.[148]

Two similar instances in Beauvais suggest that the same process was occurring elsewhere in the province of Reims. One, a passing reference to "prayers," concerns the local castellan of Auteuil. The other, more studied, involves the more prominent Ingelran of Boves.[149] Yet Ingelran's act aside, these petitions are utterly unadorned. And all were addressed to castellans. The language did not filter down to knights, at least not in diplomatic texts. It may also be significant that five of the petitions involved interactions between lords and churches of different areas, as if it were especially appropriate for monks and canons to bear themselves deferentially when dealing with powerful men outside their own territory.[150] In any event, this new protocol, undeveloped to begin with, had little future in the charters. In contrast to western France, the rise of castellans and knights in the Vermandois (and in northern France generally) did not mean that the language of entreaty was extended to them in public documents. Too many factors militated against the practice. The tradition of theophanic supplication was too entrenched. The residual power of bishops, firmly attached to the formulas' traditional meaning, was too strong. And royal formulas of supplication remained a fixed standard in a region where the kings exercised considerable personal power.

Nevertheless, it was impossible for northern counts to keep their old aura of transcendent authority in this new environment. The problem was not just that castellans and knights installed on their own lands now had the means to act as patrons in their own right, though that was part of the equation. The other part, ironically enough, stemmed from the very success with which rulers had earlier tamed the *seigneurie banale*. In the first half of the century monks and canons had sought the aid of kings and counts against advocates, vicars, and unsupervised ministers. In some cases the rulers simply ended the occasion for disputes by granting rights of advocacy and administration to the churches.[151] In others they defined a more precise delimitation of their respective rights, stipulating what an advocate could take, when and from what lands he could take it, when he was to distrain a peasant's goods and when not, how much he should receive in judicial fines if he helped to judge a case, how much if he did not.[152] But both solutions effectively eroded the churches' dependence on their former protectors; for the one gave churches the capacity to resist local lords themselves, while the other unwittingly created the kind of horizontal, interlinking bonds between them that had long existed in the west.

Once the scope of the *seigneurie banale* had become fixed through such accords, the old idea of comital authority became anachronistic. The churches were not slow to recognize the fact. They saw that the dangers to them no longer came as they once had, unpredictably and catastrophically, in the violent usurpation of an estate, the forcible imposition of novel exactions, or the wholesale invention of new jurisdictional rights. In the new regime of intense and unending agrarian exploitation, the primary danger came from the possibility that a church's rights would be whittled away "little by little," as a charter for Saint-Prix put it.[153] The recognition forced ecclesiastical institutions to become more efficient, even ruthless seigneurial lords themselves. Thus in the Vermandois, the years between 1070 and 1120 saw a notable increase in the economic activity of the region's monasteries, as Homblières and Mont-Saint-Quentin each undertook a concerted program to buy up land and gain control of churches in the areas where they already had rights. Homblières, for example, acquired several peasant holdings that had broken up its arable; and when individuals donated parts of fields to the monastery, the monks set out to buy the remaining parts from the donors' relatives.[154] Similarly, when the lords of Péronne donated various lands and altars to Mont-Saint-Quentin, the monks fleshed out the new acquisitions with further donations and sales from the lords' retainers and local peasants. In 1110 the monastery even authorized one of its monks, Oillart, to buy up land in and around Etricourt for the abbey. In executing his commission Oillart acted in over sixty-nine separate transactions, ranging from the acquisition of large fields and woods to that of mills, water rights, fragments of peasant manses, and even *hospites*.[155] In the course of these transactions neither monastery referred to the count or the lord of Péronne (the protector of Mont-Saint-Quentin). Instead, they dealt directly with individual small holders and their lords.

Overdependence on counts could only hinder these initiatives. Indeed, the counts became such hindrances that by the 1070s even the churches, the mainstay of conservative ideology in the Vermandois, actively began to seek restrictions on their authority. The date can be fixed quite precisely; for in 1075 and 1076 Herbert IV, last of the Carolingian counts, awarded a batch of charters to the two principal monasteries of his county by which he recognized the freedom of their lands, peasants, and churches from his own advocacy and his agents' exactions. In each case the count acted at the insistence of the monks, who had formerly petitioned the counts' intervention as eagerly as they now petitioned its cease.[156] Nor did Vermandesian houses only seek freedom from their counts. In 1102 the chapter of Saint-Fursy demanded that the bishop of Noyon cede his jurisdictional and commercial rights in Péronne to the chapter. Though the effort only partly succeeded, it is another sign of these churches' desire to escape the tutelage of those who only a generation earlier had been seen as their natural protectors.[157] Moreover, this urge for emancipation appears to have been widespread, for the same claims were being advanced with greater success by many other chapters in northern France.[158]

At just this moment when the churches of the province found that they no longer needed their counts so much, the Gregorian Reform began to tell them that they should not need their protection, thereby providing an ideological justification for what had been a sociological fact and giving monasteries and chapters a distant, poorly informed, but prestigious ally whose court they could manipulate to escalate a local dispute over comital rights into a principled struggle over ecclesiastical freedom. That was the point at which counts passed from being patrons to enemies, no longer looked to as saviors from knights but lumped along with them in the same category, slandered openly, even excommunicated. As we have seen, nothing of the sort had occurred earlier in the century; even threats were rare.[159] But in 1078 the counts of Saint-Pol were threatened with

excommunication by Gregory VII, not for simony or lay investiture but for appropriating a village claimed by Saint-Omer.[160] In
1093 an ecclesiastical council threatened to excommunicate the
count of Flanders because he had imposed new fiscal burdens on
his churches. He was, wrote the Flemish clergy in their appeal,
"a lion that tramples and devours," "a dragon oppressing us
with serpent-like cunning." In the early twelfth century the
count of Rethel was excommunicated, as were the counts of
Soissons and Roucy and the countess of Hainaut, all but one in
the course of rather ordinary legal disputes.[161] Comital authority
was no longer sacred.

Yet it was impossible for monks and canons to conceive of a
political world without any grounding in a sacred order at all.
The demise of a paradigm of supplication that had emphasized a
count's transcendent authority did not, therefore, leave a moral
vacuum. It simply required a shift to the other traditional paradigm of political order. Charters and letters began to speak of
peace and mediation. Apart from the Amienois, such language
had not been commonly applied to local disputes within the
province of Reims. The exceptions were just where one would
expect them: in negotiations between equals, as when in 1036
the prelates of Arras and the count of Flanders' representatives
in the city negotiated the payment of market taxes "out of mutual love for each other."[162] By the early twelfth century, what
had been exceptional became normal. Terms belonging to the
paradigm of peace invaded the charters.[163]

These developments have something to do with the appearance of Cistercians and Arrouaisians in the area, religious orders
that consciously repudiated litigation (and, significantly, the
clamor against enemies) and sought to negotiate *concordiae*
with local lords.[164] But in light of the preceding analysis, we can
understand that the reformers' emphasis on peace, love, and
mediation was responding to and systematizing a cultural
change rather than creating one. The proof is that the language
of peace appears in charters at a time when Arrouaise-(founded
about 1090) was still little more than a hermitage, and consid-
erably before the foundation of the Cistercian abbey at Ourscamp, near Noyon, in 1133. Moreover, when the language of
peace does appear, it appears in charters from the region's most
conservative monasteries.[165]

The language of peace became more common in the province

of Reims in the late eleventh century because its political structure had become more pluralistic. For the first time, monks and
canons found repeatedly that absentee counts could not or
would not help them settle disputes with knights and castellans
who possessed their own lands, whether fiefs or allods, by hereditary right. They had little choice but to deal with their antagonists directly. Thus a dispute between Mont-Saint-Quentin
and local knights over the siting of a mill dragged on for years,
because whenever the knights felt too much pressure they simply sold the mill to a proxy. At last, in 1116, the monks gave up
their efforts at legal coercion and decided to deal directly with
their antagonists. The dispute was then quickly resolved in the
monks' favor by the mediation of "common friends passing
back and forth" between the parties.[166] Only the year before the
abbot of Saint-Crépin of Soissons had learned a similar lesson.
He had approached Raoul of Nesle to request the restitution of
property that Raoul had given to a *miles* as a fief (*feodum*).
Raoul agreed; but the knight refused to give up his rights, and
his adamance forced Raoul to renounce the settlement and re-
take the land. Raoul did finally surrender the land, but in return
the abbot gave him seven pounds "in charity" (*caritative*).[167]

As in Anjou and the Amienois, the values of peace and friendship also occasionally found their way into petitions, which
then became less acts of deference to a lord than expressions of
honor to a peer. Traditional episcopal formulas had emphasized
a bishop's authority by apostrophizing him with exalted epithets and describing his favors as acts of condescension. In
contrast, around the turn of the century the lord of Péronne
wrote to the bishop of Arras to "beseech your charity most piously," while the bishop of Noyon wrote that it was his duty to
act "reasonably and with charity" by showing clemency to suppliants.[168] Whereas the formulas had once required entreaties to
be made humbly, in the early twelfth century the chapter of
Saint-Quentin described one as being made "in friendship."[169]
Ultimately the new values even penetrated comital acts. The
first signs appear early in the century, when Countess Adele
opened a charter recording a settlement between herself and
Saint-Corneille by wishing her readers "greetings and good
peace."[170] By the middle of the century the transition was complete. In 1146 and 1148, when Raoul IV intervened in two dis-

putes between monasteries and *fideles*, there were no petitions to him for aid, and the count issued no judgment. Instead, he strove "to bring the parties into perpetual peace," even giving one disputant a substantial sum of money "so that peace and love might be firmer between them."[171]

Once social order had required the authority of lords who ruled in the image of God. But that was at a time when those lords had controlled the distribution of rights and resources within their dominions. As their unilateral authority receded, so did the ideal of social order associated with it. Now if there was to be order, it had to be maintained by willing agreements between autonomous knights, castellans, and churches. No longer standing above their subjects, counts had become part of the network of reciprocal exchanges and mutual tokens of honor; and they could settle disputes only by participating in those exchanges. When this happened, an ideal of peace through obedience to God's rulers yielded to a vision of peace created by love between friends.

Honoring the Lords of Amboise

At the beginning of 1153, just two years after his father's death, Henry Plantagenet had overextended even his driving energies. By inheritance duke of Normandy and count of Anjou, Maine, and Tours, he also exercised the customary Angevin protectorate over Brittany, had just become count of Poitou and duke of Aquitaine by his marriage with Eleanor, and at the same time was fighting a full-scale war for possession of the English throne. If other princes were jealous of or threatened by his power, they were also sensitive to Henry's latent weaknesses, and none more so than the new count of Blois, Theobald, who decided that the moment was right to reassert his family's dwindling control over Tours, if only to give Henry something else to worry about. He therefore decided to enforce a dormant claim to suzerainty in the Touraine by demanding that Henry perform homage for his holdings there. Henry refused, acting upon the advice of Supplicius, lord of Amboise and the most powerful castellan of the region. Backing up his words with actions, Supplicius himself refused to do the homage he owed Theobald for the castle of Chaumont, located fewer than twenty kilometers east of Amboise.[172]

There was little Theobald could do about Henry, but Supplicius was another matter. Vassal of both Anjou and Blois, he possessed castles that controlled access to Tours and the corridor between the two counties. If Theobald were to assert himself in the Touraine, he would need Supplicius's support. In 1153 that was not such a distant possibility, for if the castellan had often caused trouble for Theobald's father, he had been no less nettlesome to Henry's—almost as if he took pains to divide his disloyalties between his two lords as evenly as his loyalties.[173] Theobald attempted to bring him over to his side. Once more he approached Supplicius, but this time he proposed not so much the homage as the alliance that came with it. "Humiliating himself, Theobald of Blois petitioned his friendship." Still Supplicius refused, and the two men prepared for war. The lord of Amboise and his sons were captured in an ambush and imprisoned at Châteaudun, along with a large part of their army and some of their closest relatives. Bereft of their protector, defenseless in the face of certain retaliation, the men of Amboise could only write to Supplicius's brother, lord of distant Jaligny, "imploring him in complete supplication and great grief to succor them."[174]

Now the lords of Amboise were certainly great men. Had their castles been located in the northern Ile-de-France, their lord would have been a king and they would surely have been ranked as counts. But in fact their lords were counts, they were their castellans, and it is striking to see castellans treated with such open reverence, formally entreated by their own men and even honored by counts with deferential gestures. Nor are these supplications the only examples of these lords' sense of honor recorded in their house chronicle, the *Gesta Ambaziensium dominorum*. The very fact that their exploits were celebrated in a *gesta* proclaimed their stature, since this was a type of heroic history ordinarily reserved for bishops and counts—including the counts of Anjou, whose *Gesta consulum Andegavorum* provided its model. The lords of Amboise had also founded their own house chapter, Saint-Florentin (one of whose canons wrote the *Gesta*), and they had their own necropolis, the monastery of Pontlevoy. There the heads of the family, men and women alike, were buried with a solemnity known in earlier centuries only for kings and counts.[175]

Though Supplicius's sister was buried at Déols, her husband's castle, rather than at Pontlevoy, her funeral might illustrate the ceremony (while also demonstrating that it had become widespread among castellans). Her knights were of course present, wailing as they bore Dionysia to her tomb. The townspeople and local villagers also had a role, the former singing funeral songs "as though they had lost their parents," the latter crowding around the bier to touch and kiss the body. Then Dionysia was handed over to the clergy to be laid to rest in a place of honor, next to the wall of the church; and here the *Gesta* lists "priests, clerics, abbots, and monks"—in other words, representatives of every ecclesiastical order. It was the theory of orders made visible; and at the apex was a member of a castellan's family, the focus of unity, the guardian of harmony in a world of unequals.[176]

This is the outcome of the preceding century's social developments. Ritual continued to keep pace with the increasing social and political prominence of castellans, their power now regarded as completely legitimate. If the romances are any guide, knights also shared in such honors. In Chrétien's *Yvain*, for example, women try to throw themselves at the hero's feet, grateful for his aid against giants; and if Yvain rejects their gesture, it is not because it is inappropriate to him as a knight but because as a knight he is far too honorable to accept such a show of subjection from his peers. Certainly the gesture seems quite proper on other occasions. Yvain's lion thanks him for saving his life by bowing to the earth and stretching out his hands, and then kneeling before the hero, his face "wet with tears of humility." And in *Lancelot*, Arthur tells Guenevere to do everything she can to prevent Kay from leaving court—if necessary even falling at his feet to beg him. As it happened, it was necessary. The queen, "high though she was," prostrated herself before him.[177]

This kind of supplication was still a peculiarly Christian ritual, informed by the language and gestures of liturgical prayer. But in this period the virtues and emblems of kings and counts had passed to knights, now regarded as *milites Christi* and girded with a belt of knighthood as kings and princes had once been invested with a sword.[178] So far one would think that knights had simply stepped into the place of kings; but in spite of their superficial similarity, the two types of supplication differed in one important respect: the supplication of knights and castellans was not tied to their possession of an office ordained by God. This kind of supplication was not a theophany but an etiquette, a badge of honor which members of an aristocracy, conscious of their status, awarded themselves.

The image of comital authority continued to be affected by these changes. On the one hand, the Norman case became more common; for as rulers increasingly relied on favorites and officials to execute their will, some aspects of rulership became more private and routinized. Here there was little call for the public displays of authority afforded by supplication. On the other hand, relations between the counts and their nobles became even more personal, "familiar" in a modern sense. An authoritarian model of supplication was inappropriate for such relationships. Hence supplication to counts did not so much decline in the twelfth century as it receded from public view, to be replaced by an ethos that saw lords as the friends of their vassals, as knights ruling knights.

These trends were most pronounced where they had also been most precocious: in the domains of the Plantagenets, the lords of the lords of Amboise. It is Angevin chronicles and encomia that first began to celebrate counts as chivalric heros, Angevin princes (most notably the sons of Henry II) who were most renowned for their devotion to chivalric pursuits; and from Anjou comes the earliest complete description of a great prince being dubbed a knight: Geoffrey le Bel, future count of Anjou, in 1128.[179] The same sources also reveal the extent to which Angevin ideas of authority became impregnated with the chivalric ethos. The *Gesta consulum Andegavorum* as rewritten by Breton of Amboise and John of Marmoutier in the second half of the twelfth century makes the point quite clearly. A count does not cease to be a knight for being a count. He is instead, like Breton's Fulk the Good, "a learned count *and* a valiant knight" (*litteratum consulem ac strenuum militem*). Indeed, "among the greater and better and more valiant knights, he was reputed the best."[180] John of Marmoutier made the point even more explicitly. When Geoffrey le Bel discovered four knights in his prisons, he personally ordered their release. He ate with them at his table. He returned their horses and arms. Finally he freed them, showing them such magnanimity, wrote John, simply because they were knights, like him, and as such shared his "profession." "For if we are really knights," said the count, "we should show compassion to knights, especially those who have been defeated."[181]

Whatever the differences among counts, lords, and knights (and they were of course significant), there was a sense of brotherhood between them. It was therefore impossible for supplication to accentuate an unbridgeable difference between counts and their dependents, because no such difference existed. Instead, supplications began to proclaim each side's respect for the other's honor. What the twelfth-century suppliant begged was not an act of beneficent grace bestowed with condescension but a favor bestowed in friendship (*amicitia*), and this etiquette obliged a count like Theobald of Blois every bit as much as it did his vassals. If for Dudo of Saint-Quentin good order had required deference to God's rulers, for the author of the *Gesta Ambaziensium dominorum* good order resided in honorable friendship between good knights.[182]

Of course, the language and gestures of prayer still remained meaningful. In fact, the most thoughtful discussions of prayer gestures come from the late twelfth and thirteenth centuries, first in the *De penitentia* of Peter the Chanter and then in works associated with the Dominicans. But these works are concerned solely with the religious meaning of the gestures. Prayer to God is their subject, not prayer to lords or by lords.[183] They do not describe prayer as a visible expression of the link between the kingdoms of God and men. That this emphasis is not merely a by-product of their devotional themes is shown by the fate of petitions at Rome; for though thirteenth-century suitors still presented petitions to the papal curia, these requests made no significant statement about sacred foundations of papal authority. As one early thirteenth-century notary wrote, a petition to the pope was no more than "a brief and direct statement that touches on the principal issues without omitting the relevant ones."[184]

And what of the king, the ruler who more than any other lord was emblematic of political stability and authority? In royal acts, too, the formulas seem to have lost their relevance. As government became more routinized and more dependent on familiars with expertise, as the rulers came to govern more as "feudal monarchs" than as pontifical kings, then, as in William the Conqueror's Normandy, the old models of liturgical kingship became less relevant.[185] Still normal in acts of Philip I, formulas of supplication decline in the acts of his two successors and almost disappear entirely in those of Philip II.[186]

And yet the kings always retained a special dignity. The work of Adalbero of Reims, Lothar, and Robert the Pious was not forgotten. The kings remained emblematic figures, symbols of order and unity, defenders of the church and the poor, and in the later Middle Ages symbols of the divine election of their people. They healed the scrofulous with the touch of their hands. They were anointed with a chrism perpetually replenished by the Holy Spirit. And they alone did not belong to one of the orders of society; they were protectors of the orders.[187] So even if formulas of supplication almost disappeared from their acts, they never disappeared entirely. They could still be used to express a king's special majesty.[188]

In one set of circumstances in particular, the supplication of kings retained its former resonance, not only in France but also in England and all other European countries that looked to the same political traditions. When innocent subjects had been condemned in a royal court of law; when resident foreigners would suffer an injustice simply because they had no standing at law; when Jews required the king's help to obtain their rights: whenever laws proved too brittle to provide justice, men and women still knelt before the king or those who spoke for him and made a humble prayer for mercy.[189] Well into the early modern period, petitions for equity required the language and gestures of supplication, because only a king's grace was enough like God's to suspend the rigors of the law.

9 How Does a Ritual Mean?

"Lying, the telling of beautiful untrue things, is the proper aim of Art," wrote Oscar Wilde;[1] and many would say the same about ritual, in its economy of symbolism so much like a poetry of gesture. Certainly critics have not lacked arguments against our taking ritual seriously.[2] The problems begin with the term itself, notoriously vague and incapable of precise definition. Define "ritual" narrowly to emphasize its repetiveness or its reference to transcendent values and one excludes the formalized and symbolic behavior of unique events and everyday life. Define it broadly to encompass these and one includes the trivial along with the sublime. The term simply possesses an ineradicable vagueness and ambiguity foreign to the precision of social science.

The problem is not just with the term, however. Vagueness and ambiguity are inherent in rituals themselves, whose meaning can be as puzzling to contemporaries as it is to scholars.[3] Worse, not even the most solemn rituals need mean anything to contemporaries. In fact, the conservative nature of many rituals guarantees that they will eventually lose whatever meaning they once had. In the later Middle Ages, for example, royal anointing formulas copied in French pontificals still referred to the "scepters of the Saxons, Mercians, and Northumbrians," simply because the prayers had originally come from those lands. And though these prayers may never have been recited at a real French coronation, those that were said and the ceremonial that accompanied them in large measure repeated the hallowed models of Carolingian and Capetian anointings. Perhaps they had been meaningful in the age of Hincmar of Reims, when they were first composed; but there is no reason to believe that they remained meaningful two centuries later, let alone six.[4]

One cannot even be certain that they originally had much meaning; for ritual is often highly propagandistic, proclaiming not the values of its actors but the dogma of their rulers. Of course, if rulers and ruled believe in a common political program, the performance of a ritual can serve its intended purpose of acculturating participants in the approved ideology; but if ideology and social beliefs are too far apart, the result will only be mockery, or worse, apathy.[5]

This problem is certainly relevant to the rituals of the early Middle Ages, especially the most striking ones, which seem so packed with profound meaning; for anointings, crown-wearings, and *laudes* were generally orchestrated by ecclesiastics eager to promote their own political ideals, or merely their own factional interests. They themselves may have been susceptible to the message, already inculcated as they were with the necessity of obedience and accustomed to venerating God and Christ as great kings. But as Janet Nelson has remarked, in this case they were simply "preaching to the converted."[6] There is no guarantee that the ceremonies meant much to the attending laity.

Indeed, the magnates had their own separate rituals for electing and acclaiming a king, where they may well have ignored, or even contradicted, the church's teachings.[7] Certainly their actions often enough belied the high moral tone of the liturgies. At one of his crown-wearings, Otto I had to rely on his palace knights to thwart a conspiracy, while at his coronation the carefully cultivated image of divinely sanctioned authority was countermined by the absence of Otto's brother, kept under guard a safe distance away from Aachen lest he disrupt the proceedings to further his own claim to the throne.[8] But the most striking example of this disjunction between ritual and reality is the celebrated crown-wearing of William the Conqueror, when a jester (*scurra*), seeing the king bedecked in his jeweled regalia, shouted, "Behold, I see God! Behold, I see God!" Lanfranc told William that he should not allow such things to be said and advised him to have the man beaten. The reason was not that the jester had blasphemed against Christianity; it was that he had revealed William for what he really was: a bastard count who was assuming too many airs for his own good, who was forgetting that he was king of England not by the grace of God but by the strong arms of his Norman supporters.[9]

So not only is this kind of ritual propaganda; often enough it is not even good propaganda. This observation gives rise to a final criticism. Ritual not only tolerates hypocrisy. It positively invites it by requiring participants to perform actions that they realize are completely out of sync with reality. Did any vassal really feel more loyal to his lord because he had knelt before him and placed his own hands in his? Did receiving a king with honor ever prevent a prince from making war on him when it suited his interests?

Pertinent to all rituals, these criticisms are especially so to supplication. Gestures of deference and entreaty have been common in nearly every preindustrial society possessing any degree of social stratification.[10] Within tenth- and eleventh-century France they were ubiquitous. God and kings were supplicated, but in one form or another so were persons of every other status. Supplications also appeared in countless settings: in penance and masses, during trials and in prayers of clamor, to signal submission after a rebellion but also to signal fidelity when making ordinary requests of a lord. And even more than most rituals the meanings of these actions were varied and ambiguous. In one context, I have argued, supplication served to acknowledge the divine basis of political authority; in another it was no more than a formal way to honor a peer. To be sure, prostration and protestations of humility were well suited to a society that prized deference; but why believe that such pervasive gestures were any more meaningful than handshakes are in our more egalitarian society?

Finally, no matter how often the ritual was performed, the fact remains that the ritual was strongly imprinted with a liturgical meaning; and this calls into question its significance for the laity. Churchmen such as Dudo and Helgald have left the most elaborate treatments of the ritual. Histories, hagiography, and diplomas, all written by monks and canons, produce its fin-

est examples. Though the interpretation of supplication articulated in this study may be correct, it may also only reflect the
attitudes of this literate elite. The laity performed the requisite
gestures and said the necessary words, and kings and counts accepted the use of petitionary formulas in their diplomas; but
without the lay equivalent of a Dudo of Saint-Quentin, one cannot prove conclusively that any of them understood supplication in the same terms as the clergy. Even if we assume their
understanding, we still cannot assume their sincerity, or their
regard for supplication's distinctive values. Peter the Chanter
may have said that humble gestures reflect a humble spirit and
Augustine may have believed that they could even induce that
spirit;[11] but we know better, and it is likely that they did too. A
rebel defeated by a king prostrated himself and begged for mercy
because he had to, not because regret had melted his heart. The
same was in all likelihood true of suppliant litigants. It was certainly true of those sinners who believed, however incorrectly,
that no matter what the state of their souls, the priest would
absolve them if only they knelt and "begged pardon."[12] The
stakes were high—forgiveness of sins, obtaining a *precaria*, amnesty for insurrection. The cost was small—literally no more
than a gesture.

Reifying Ritual

There is an obvious core of common-sense truth to this skepticism. Above all it reminds us that if ritual is like art, art is not
life, so that we can no more accept rituals uncritically than we
can the sources that describe them. Yet skepticism can be carried too far if it leads us to ignore gestures and rhetoric that
pervade the sources. If we should not take them at face value,
neither can we dismiss them as meaningless.

The problem may be that it is so easy to "reify" rituals—that
is, turn them into a prescribed set of actions efficacious in and
of itself, without regard to the minds of the people who create
them or the historical context that gives similar rituals different
meanings at different moments.[13] The fault lies partly with the
rituals themselves; for many do seem to cultivate an aura of
changelessness, while their language and gestures appear to be

regarded, like magical incantations, as inherently powerful. Fault is also perhaps shared by the ethnographers and ethnographically minded historians who study rituals, for too often a ritual is said to be understood when its symbolism has only been described in exhaustive detail or raised to a higher level of abstraction. Without doubt these are essential steps toward understanding rituals. But they provide less explanation than exegesis, since the analysis tends to remain within the cultural system that is being explicated. In other words, they assume the system's meaningfulness rather than explaining how it can be meaningful while also being manipulated, or how apathy, skepticism, and belief can coexist in regard to the same ritual. The skeptics' questions remain unaddressed and unanswered.[14]

As for historians, our tendency to dismiss the historical significance of rituals probably reflects a predisposition to skepticism, deeply rooted in our intellectual heritage. The radical Protestant desacralization of established church sacraments; liberalism's vaunting of the individual at the expense of the community; the Marxian search for the material "base" behind the ideological "superstructure"; the positivist reduction of history to the pure datum—all have biased us against anything so intangibly and vaguely "collective" as ritual.[15]

Our skepticism has only been confirmed by the awkward status of the more obvious rituals we have received from our own preindustrial past. Coronations and religious liturgies, for example, seem curiously divorced from the concerns of everyday life. We go to religious services leaving the world behind, then reenter the world leaving religion behind. And coronations have become matters of tourism more than expressions of community bonding. No wonder that "ritualistic" often seems synonymous with "unthinking routine," and that it has become so difficult to separate ritual—ambiguous, transcendent, and emotionally charged—from the mere pageantry of ceremonial.[16]

This is not, however, the only way to view these rites. The religious services of established churches may be sealed off from the real world; but for many this is the source of their value, since the church represents a haven untouched by the compromises and difficulties of ordinary life. In other words, far from being irrelevant to real life, these rituals may carry an emotional impact because they are so separate from it. As for coronations, they are not so timeless as they first appear. It was after, not before, Britain's industrial revolution that they evolved into their modern form, and only then that they became great public rites of bonding. When the empire was being built up, their elaborate ceremonial provided a means for ordinary citizens to participate in their country's power and glory. As the empire was being challenged by international hostilities and the industrial revolution had completely transformed workplace and home, then the coronations created an oasis of tradition and manifested the spiritual superiority of British conservatism.[17]

Thus a disjunction between ritual behavior and the concerns of daily life does not always indicate the former's devaluation. One should also not assume that such disjunctions are typical. Alternatives do exist, even in our own profane and individualistic society; for we do have rituals, not all of them avatars of our preindustrial past. Indeed, it has been argued that we have a greater need for them, as our society has become more prone to anomie; and their potential reach has broadened with the advent of national and international media coverage. Sporting events, holiday celebrations, May Day parades, strikes, mass political rallies like those of Nazi Germany, evangelical prayer meetings (quite unlike high church liturgies), moments when a nation becomes fused into a community by a televised disaster—these are only a few our modern rituals.[18] Some are quite public, others very private. Their values may be transcendent or utterly secular. Some repeat the actions of past years and generations, and this is why they give pleasure; others seem spectacularly new and unpredictable, and this is why they have power. But all are recognizably rituals, because all represent patterned behavior by which a community, whether as large as a nation or as small as a family, affirms the values that define it as a community.

The Naturalness of Symbolic Behavior

The point of the preceding discussion is two-fold. First, even our secular society has its rituals, and the most revealing are precisely those we are least conscious of as rituals. Second, a corollary: rituals may provide special, even "sacred" moments that heighten our perception of a dichotomy between different sets of values, some reserved for the sacred, others for the profane. But other rituals are not segregated from ordinary values. They are living parts of the culture, and their language and actions pervade our social interactions.

Early medieval rituals were also a natural part of life, vehicles for pursuing competition and agreement, not means of escaping the struggle. They therefore evolved along with social relations and political organization, their overt meaning reflecting these material structures and changing with them. In speaking of these rituals, then, one should present them not so much as fixed by an original act of creation and then rotely repeated as renewed and reaffirmed in repeated acts of re-creation. We have already seen this process at work in rituals of supplication;[19] but it occurred in other rituals also, even coronation *ordines*. Here is ritual at its most static; yet between the eighth and tenth centuries the ceremony had been quite adaptable, with new or revised rites and prayers added continually in lockstep with developing attitudes toward royal and priestly authority.[20]

By the middle of the tenth century the ceremony does appear to have become fixed, at least in Francia. Two points should be noted, however. First, we have little information on how coronations were actually conducted after that time. The liturgies recorded in pontificals are no more than templates. It is quite possible, even probable, that in practice there were still significant variations within an established framework.[21] More important, even if the prayers and acts of the ceremony were static, they were not necessarily stagnant. As with old-style Latin masses, incomprehensible but solemn and magical, lack of change need not be a sign of decrepitude. It can also indicate a ritual's sacredness. An unchanging coronation, for instance, only underscored the stability of monarchy as a divine institution. Indeed, this had already been one of the intentions of those ninth-century bishops who established the contours of the ceremony; for they did not create the orders ex nihilo but rather by adapting existing prayers and the language of Scriptures[22]—because Scripture and prayer were the language of God and the language one used to speak to God. Being sacred language appropriate for the King of Eternity, it could not change. Being sacred and unchanging, it was also appropriate for anointing kings, who on earth would rule under God and after death would rule with him in heaven. Even in the later Middle Ages this remained an important aspect of the coronation: in a time when kings went mad and the very security of the dynasty was at stake, Joan of Arc insisted that Charles VII be crowned at Reims. No other place would do, because only a coronation at Reims in the time-honored fashion would demonstrate the legitimacy of her king.[23]

The core of the ritual was therefore sacred, and its appearance of sempiternity was the emblem of this sacredness. Adaptation remained necessary; but it was achieved by grafting new ceremonies—royal funerals and *lits de justice*, for example—onto this sacred core.[24] In this way, political rituals were able to accommodate both the ideal of stability and the reality of change.

If we do not see this process in early medieval rituals, it is because the most famous are those most accessible to study, and these are the sacred ones whose formulas were fixed in writing by churchmen and which were intended to appear timeless. Others, not perhaps more meaningful but certainly more common, were as evanescent as their gestures. Even these have left passing traces, however, which reveal the interest contemporaries had in generating new rituals by adapting old ones. For example, when a priest gave Thietmar of Merseburg a list of his sins, Thietmar laid it on a reliquary in the priest's church so that the saints would be more certain to aid him. With noticeable pride in his inventiveness Thietmar writes, "I had never heard or seen this done."[25] Perhaps not, but he had probably seen the elements of his new ritual in other settings, for handing a list of sins to a crucifix or laying it on an altar was a relatively common practice; the intercession of saints in obtaining forgiveness for sinners was well established; and intercessors usually handed petitions to lords on behalf of their clients, as the saints were now being asked to submit their priest's sins to God.[26] From three different customs, one new ritual. Like a good teacher, Thietmar had found a striking new way to impart an old truth.

Similarly, when the monks of Lobbes took their relics on a tour through Flanders in 1066 to end a cycle of feuding, they brought pressure to bear on the reluctant by using techniques suggested by familiar ecclesiastical rituals. They tried to establish an expectation of a holy time at odds with feuding by making formal processions into towns, just as they would have done to celebrate a calendrical feast or receive a lord. Circling altars, churches, or battlements with relics and incense was also a standard method for consecrating the structure contained within the circle, for the circle and sacring fortified the holy object within by separating it from the world of demons without. Just so, the monks of Lobbes turned profane space into holy space by processing around the feuders, enclosing them in a circle at whose center they laid their relics. Finally, monastic discipline required the ritual isolation of those who violated the rule, as they were physically separated from the brotherhood and required to prostrate themselves as the others stood. In the same way, the circle within which the monks enclosed a feuder ritually divided the town in two, the community without and the offender, now isolated from his fellows, within. Only when the circle was complete did they unveil their relics, a theophany requiring the offender's immediate prostration and entreaty for absolution, unless he was willing to be known as a blasphemer who cared more for his private vengeance than for the good of the community.[27]

There was nothing routine in rituals like these, no blind enslavement to gestures and formulas made meaningless by repetition. Quite the contrary, even those who are predisposed to see rituals as meaningful may be surprised at the creativity and intelligence with which Thietmar and the monks of Lobbes adapted existing rituals and by their sensitivity to context. Nor are these isolated examples. Suppliants showed the same adaptability, as when knights began to make their supplications by kneeling and folding their hands in imitation of homage, or when the pluralistic distribution of power in Anjou required the count to beg churches for aid that other rulers would have demanded.[28]

Rituals and symbols could be adapted in these ways because contemporaries lived in a world saturated with overlapping symbols and symbolic behavior.[29] They used symbols and gestures to express themselves as naturally and ceaselessly as they spoke words. They gave gifts endlessly: to celebrate marriages and seal alliances, to support entreaties for aid, to reward faithful service, and to show that one served faithfully.[30] When men and women surrendered their worldly freedom to a monastery and its saint, they did so by approaching the altar with four pence on their head or a rope around their necks.[31] When grieving, they fell to the ground and pulled their hair.[32] When sorrowful, they fell to the ground and grasped the knees of the person they had offended, begging for mercy.[33]

Mourners wailed and lamented at funerals, public enemies were forced to ride backward on asses, fraternal societies celebrated their brotherhood by sharing food and drink: these are only a handful of the gestures and rituals of ordinary life documented on the Continent between the tenth and early twelfth centuries.[34] Were we to assume that rituals found earlier and later were also practiced then, the list would quickly become tedious. Nor has anything been said about the great political ceremonies, or homage, or the investiture of lords with arms, or church liturgies—many of which were not hidden away within churches but, like processions, entered the public spaces of towns and villages.[35] Neither have the numerous rituals of law been mentioned: the many varieties of ordeals, the battles, the oaths sworn on relics, the giving of sureties, the conveyance of *festucae*.[36] And then there were the rites of magic, performed in solemn secrecy to beget children, capture lovers, cure ailments, kill enemies. These magical prescriptions constituted a veritable liturgy in themselves, with litanies and implements every bit as holy as the consecrated tools and grave invocations of the ordeal.[37]

A ritual appears to be extraordinary behavior requiring a suspension of ordinary beliefs and activities only if we place it in a vacuum in order to observe it. But the experiment kills the ritual by isolating it from the complex of related symbolic behavior that makes it seem perfectly normal to contemporaries.[38] The mistake is especially serious in the case of the great political liturgies of the early Middle Ages. Anointings, for example, were surely important events; but since they generally occurred only once in a king's lifetime, one may rightly question their impact on ordinary political behavior. Festal coronations were more common, yet even they took place only a few times a year at best.[39]

What may be forgotten, however, is that these rites were only the high points of a continuous political ceremonial. In fact, much formal political activity was ritual activity, nearly all of it issuing from the same matrix of symbols that informed these better-known rituals, or from matrices that were complementary. Coronations and *Festkrönungen* were only the most liturgical of the many formal occasions when a king might appear in his regalia.[40] And quite as splendid as these festal coronations were those moments when kings set their crowns aside, as when entering churches or performing special acts of public penance and thanksgiving.[41] If the Latin sonorities of the *laudes regiae* were largely an affair of the clergy, the *adventus* brought out the laity and clergy of an entire town to receive a king with honor, while a burial like Lothar's brought together the elite of Francia.[42]

In addition to these solemn ceremonies there were also special occasions which, though lacking the conscious institutionalization of ideology characteristic of ceremonial, still possessed the patterned, symbolic behavior typical of ritual. Hunting, for example, celebrated not only aristocratic courage and prowess but also the cooperation between lords and followers that made government work. Given the number of them that died in the chase, kings and magnates may have been expected to play a leading role in the sport as they were in war and government.[43]

We may also assume that order and deference were expressed at the table, although there is little evidence of West Frankish customs during our period, and what evidence there is from other regions seems contradictory. The etiquette appears to have varied greatly according to time, region, and context, and it makes sense that a given political community would have different customs for different occasions, some more festive than others, some more hierarchical than others. The patterns are quite complex and have not received the study they deserve.[44] What one can say is that common meals might provide occasions for cementing a formal brotherhood, as in the *Speisegemeinschaften* of the tenth century.[45] But they could also reveal the hierarchy of the court, as in the elaborate etiquette of Charlemagne's dinners (at least as they were later described by Notker) or that of the meals that followed Ottonian *Festkrönungen*.[46]

We are on firmer ground in respect to other public gatherings, for here we have enough evidence to be absolutely certain that the order of seating and standing reflected political rank and favor. To the king's right and left stood the magnates most in his favor. The other notables gathered beside them, behind them, or beneath them, according to rank, so that the lord was surrounded by his favorites and *fideles*.[47] Something similar appears to have been the rule in princely courts. In Flanders, for example, the count presided over trials flanked by his *circumstantes*, who included the great lords of his territories.[48] Within this setting, small actions made large statements about rank and favor within the court. When a ruler allowed someone to sit on his right or left, that was a political statement, interpreted by contemporaries as a declaration of policy as well as of favor.[49] When the pope rose as an archbishop entered his hall and a king stepped forward to kiss a magnate, or refused to give a kiss, these were also political statements.[50]

Then there were the rules of ordinary social interactions: the kisses with which enemies became "friends" and friends greeted each other (and lords greeted those to whom they had granted their friendship); or the sullen deference with which peasants, at least in the later Middle Ages, spoke to their lords (but only if they had been spoken to).[51] Acts of supplication also occurred constantly within a ruler's entourage. Intercessors knelt before the king to make entreaties on behalf of clients or allies. Lords fell to the ground to confess their fault after being condemned in trials. Rebels prostrated themselves to beg for mercy. Kings knelt to remove their regalia before the altar of the heavenly King. Finally, and most important, the language of entreaty became imprinted on nearly all social interactions. Inferiors beseeched superiors as a sign of their loyalty and in recognition of the lords' high status. Peers honored each other by begging favors. And the great showed their magnanimity and humility by entreating their inferiors as if they were lords.

Great ceremonies and events were thus played out against a backdrop of continuing symbolic behavior, a kind of suspension of symbols of which the great solemnities were crystallizations. We may still doubt the efficacy of any single ritual, but not because the behavior it required and the values it professed were incompatible with normal behavior and values. Ordinary political behavior was ritual behavior, and the values encoded in ritual were also encoded in the interactions of everyday life.

The Regeneration of Rituals

Although it is often useful to speak of symbols as having meanings, like words, and of symbolic actions as being like linguistic propositions, there are significant differences. One of the most important concerns the matter of denotation. Words can denote objects, and propositions refer to the world of denoted objects. Symbols, on the other hand, *are* objects, objects which mean something at that; and if symbolic propositions make statements about the world, they do so about a world of symbols.

To say even this much is to stand at the gates of a puzzle-palace ruled by *rois-philosophes* and their devoted but fractious viziers. I have no intention of entering. But just as rivalries occur on a common ground, so the debate over symbols assumes agreement on these points. Whether part of a cognitive system or a semiological one, whether their deep structure is determined by the structure of the human mind or the structure of society, symbols take on their specific meanings only in association with other symbols. What is true of symbols is also true of symbols in action, or rituals.[52]

For example, to place oneself beneath another person is clearly a sign of inferiority. Indeed, this meaning is so widespread among social mammals generally that one wonders if it does not have some common source, perhaps in their perception of space or in the reinforcement of dependent, infantile behavior.[53] Nevertheless, the kind of inferiority a prostration represents is not inherent in the physical act. Still less does the act convey any information about the world. These meanings are determined entirely by other occurrences of prostration within the culture. Thus, in Francia the meaning of gestures of inferiority made before rulers was defined through their analogies with similar liturgical gestures. As Christians knelt before God and his saints, so they knelt before lords who ruled in the image of God. Projecting this core analogy into different situations produced other meanings. As *fideles* knelt before rulers, rulers knelt before God, indicating that though they ruled subjects, they themselves were subject to God and could use their authority only in the pursuit of justice. The rite could also be inverted, as when abbots prostrated themselves before the poor on Maundy Thursday, or bishops before canons, or kings before holy men. In this way rulers were reminded to conduct themselves with humility, since they had been exalted only to serve their subjects, and the poor wore the image of God as much as the powerful.

A ritual complex can also be condensed in a kind of ritual synecdoche that concentrates the meaning of a symbolic matrix by allowing a single object to stand for the whole. In the case of supplication, this took the form of an unusual concern with people's feet. Petitioners who wanted to make a point of their lowliness might prostrate themselves and grasp or kiss the feet of a lord, while kings sometimes demanded that powerful subjects kiss their feet as a sign of subjection.[54] The act could also be revised with small touches to accentuate one or another of its implicit meanings, just as Thietmar and the monks of Lobbes adapted old rituals to new needs. For example, when Conrad II wanted to reward the abbot of Saint-Gall for his services as choirmaster, he ordered him to "look at the feet of the Empire." The abbot approached, and took several ounces of gold from the emperor's shoes.[55]

If touching or kissing the feet of lords was an act of special veneration, going barefoot was an act of special humiliation commonly associated with acts of penitential supplication. Penitents often entered churches barefoot as a sign of their contrition.[56] Monks who had violated the rule received their lashes barefoot, and defeated rebels sought mercy from their lord by coming into his presence barefoot.[57] The symbol was so important that in negotiating his absolution from excommunication in 1119, the only privilege sought by Emperor Henry V was that he be allowed to wear shoes during his audience with the pope.[58]

Like all rituals, these formal acts only made explicit what was already tacit in ordinary social relations, for here too we find an unusual amount of attention paid to lords' feet. In public assemblies monks were described as sitting at the feet of their abbots, just as students sat at the feet of their masters.[59] Similarly, for a layman to be buried "at the feet" of an abbot was a high honor.[60] And one could always tell a lord by the care his servants lavished on his feet: when in his flight from Italy Hugh Capet disguised himself as a servant, his deception was almost undone when a tavernkeeper entered his room unannounced and discovered the duke's shoes being removed by kneeling servants while others rubbed his feet.[61] As always, the act could be inverted: one of the high points of Holy Week was the Maundy, when monks washed the feet of the poor.[62]

Analogy, projection, inversion, and condensation: this is the language used by ethnographers and ethnologists to describe symbolic systems. There is little doubt of its necessity or virtues. Yet this kind of analysis inevitably tends to reify symbolic action, turning behavior into an abstract paradigm. Symbols may take their meaning through projection and inversion; but people do not project and invert them in order to give them meaning. Rather, symbols have meaning, and therefore can be used in a variety of settings. We have already described this creative process in Thietmar of Merseberg and the monks of Lobbes. But it can now be defined more precisely as essentially the cyclical process of feedback loops: rituals and symbols are part of social discourse. They are therefore used in social interactions, and being used, are seen to be meaningful and are used again.

This is the generative process that extends the use of symbols and rituals into new settings and allows them to be adapted to new social and political relationships. But the generative process is at the same regenerative; for as in feedback cycles, the source is always transformed in the operation.[63] For example, the supplication of the Loire Valley counts in the eleventh and twelfth centuries continued to have theophanic overtones. But the increasing use of supplicatory language and gestures for addressing knights and castellans also gave supplications to counts new significance as a protocol that vaunted the common nobility which set *potentes* apart from ordinary men. At the same time, the tendency of these supplications to become a matter of chivalric etiquette only accentuated the uniqueness of entreaties to kings, until by the thirteenth century they had become a distinctive protocol of those royal courts that corrected the rigors of law with a gracious equity.[64]

The tour of the monks of Lobbes through Flanders provides another illustration of this regenerative process. When the monks used processions and relics to create sacred space in the middle of towns where the laws of the feud were suspended, they did more than project the use of liturgical processions into a new sphere. They also unwittingly strengthened the meaningfulness of ordinary processions during feasts, lordly entries, and relic delations. They strengthened it first by recalling men and women to the primal meaning of these rites as sacred times when a community was made whole and brought to peace. But more important, they strengthened it by redefining wholeness and peace in terms relevant to the concerns of their own age. Thus, in the processions that accompanied relic translations in Flanders during the late ninth and early tenth centuries, wholeness had meant Christian unity and peace had meant primarily relief from external enemies, either safety from invasion or victory in war.[65] In the course of the monks' tour in 1066, however, conducted in a context of divisive feuding, peace came to mean freedom from internal fighting, wholeness an end to internal factionalism. Significantly, it was these new meanings that came to be associated with relic translations and elevations in Flanders during the next three decades.[66] The monks' activities had strengthened the significance of such events not by reimposing old meanings but by allowing people to discover new meanings within them.

In this way, symbols and symbolic behavior are like any currency or set of conventional signs. They can be used because people agree to use them. To be sure, contextual factors tend to imbue certain objects and actions with specific symbolic meanings: in the case of supplication, for example, a Roman heritage, a Christian liturgy, and a highly stratified society. But when people are raised with such exemplars, they learn to use them. And because they are used as if they mean something, they do mean something. Yet with each use the meaning and values of the actions also shift subtly. In this respect rituals are again like currency and language; but even more they are like another institution highly valued in the early Middle Ages: like custom, rituals are always changing and yet always the same.

A Shared Discourse

We cannot ask how rituals are created, since the question almost always leads into an infinite regress. All we can say is that people recreate them by using them; and they use them in countless interactions until the ritual, with its analogies, projections, and inversions, permeates all social behavior. The entire world comes to be defined in terms of a symbolic system. As a result, the system as a whole becomes plausible because it is not only congruent with the world; it is the world. Of course, the paradigm of supplication would not have been plausible had it run only vertically, from God to rulers and back again. In that case its theophanic assertions would have been brittle propaganda. But supplication was not propaganda. It was part of social discourse. Used for all deferential communication, rooted in the nature of the cosmos, sanctioned by its appearance in Scripture and liturgy, concentrated in such homely symbols as feet, the language, gestures, and symbols of supplication, with all their contradictions and ambiguities, became real.

From this perspective, it is only partly correct to say that rituals legitimate political or religious order. More important for understanding how rituals mean, the use of rituals legitimates the use of rituals. The rituals become neutral, a shared discourse. They are not agents of legitimacy so much as indicators of whether or not a political system is legitimate.

The point is an obvious one, but we would do well to keep it in mind when studying the symbolic behavior of an openly combative society like early medieval Francia. If, as we have seen, ritual behavior was normal political behavior, then rites of rulership and symbolic expressions were not an ideal opposed to a chaotic reality. They were a vehicle for competition as well as for consensus. Overtly expressions of deference, they could also be used to express defiance. They could test a man's loyalty or a ruler's control. We may think of them as games, as long as we realize that in these games, victory brought loyalty and respect, defeat shame and insubordination, and the rules of the game were the ways of the world.

An illustration of this is William the Conqueror's failure to impose respect for his crown-wearing; and the ridicule he suffered oddly foreshadowed his ignominious death, when instead of burying him with honor, his attendants ransacked his chamber and left his body nearly naked.[67] His is not the only example. In fact, a clear sign of how much these protocols mattered is the attention chroniclers paid to them. In describing the meetings of Otto I and Louis IV, Flodoard and Richer noted

whether Otto had sat before Louis or whether they had sat simultaneously. Richer remembered that Otto III had tried to
trick Hugh Capet into carrying his sword. When Henry II and
Robert the Pious met on the Meuse in 1023, each monarch
wanted the other to cross the river and "accede" to himself. The
problem was so serious that for a time their advisers considered
holding the conference in boats in the middle of the river.[68]

Nor did these protocols matter only to kings. They mattered
just as much to the magnates. If Otto III wanted Hugh Capet to
carry his sword, Hugh did not want to be seen carrying it; and
so the bishop of Orléans stepped forward to carry it in his place.
Had Hugh's king participated in the translation of a saint? Then
the duke would personally lead the translation of two saints.[69] If
kings understood the symbolism of crossing frontiers, so did
magnates: it took an entire day's haggling to decide whether
King Raoul would be allowed to cross the Loire into William of
Auvergne's territory, or William cross the river and receive the
king's kiss.[70] The final rebellion against Charles the Simple was
sparked by the undue favor the king showed to a Lotharingian
favorite named Hagano; and one of the things that galvanized
the magnates' resistance was a sign of that favor, when Charles
insisted that Hagano sit on his left. It especially infuriated Robert of Neustria, who had the privilege of sitting on his right.[71]

Rituals therefore became a currency for measuring power and
honor. They did not inevitably vaunt royal authority; they
could express the power of the magnates or the strength of the
prelates just as easily. In fact, the more closely one looks at
formal ceremonies such as coronations, burials, and royal entries, the more clearly one sees that they are fundamentally mis-
construed as rites of royalty. They are more accurately described
as dramas for the political community as a whole, which tested
its cohesiveness and measured the standing of its members.[72]

The principalities were also political communities, and as
such had their own vibrant ritual life. Counts made solemn entries into the towns of their territories and presided over Peace
councils and translations of relics.[73] A few of the greatest (or at
least most pretentious) tenth-century princes are known to have
worn diadems, an act that must have figured in a solemn ceremony.[74] William II of Normandy had the *laudes* sung for him.[75]
And of course, all received the humble supplications of their
faithful. Rituals were therefore as important to the magnates as

they were to the kings. Yet the great counts could no more control these rites than could the kings. When the monks of Saint-Père rejected Theobald of Blois's candidate for abbot, the count challenged their loyalty by demanding that they receive him with a formal *occursus*. Instead, the monks greeted him with what must have been perceived as an open insult since it was so clearly a reversal of the rite Theobald had wanted: as the count entered the monastery with his candidate, the monks fled.[76] If William the Great's intention in sponsoring Peace councils in Limoges and Poitiers was to show his superiority to his castellans, that intention was compromised by the fact that he had to swear the oath with them. However much the ceremony exalted ducal authority, the pact was still basically a *convenientia* that placed William and his castellans on the same level.[77]

What was true of the kings and princes was, *mutatis mutandis*, also true of their subalterns. They, too, had places of honor in these ceremonies, for it would have been an honor for *milites* to ride with a powerful lord in his *adventus* or to be asked to intercede with him as someone high in his favor.[78] They could also be paid honor more directly by being entreated in their own right for forgiveness and favor; and as we have seen, the greater their autonomy, the greater the honors attributed to them.[79]

Ritual discourse therefore worked because it was a shared discourse, common to all members of the ruling elite, all of whom were capable of using it to their advantage—if they had the power. The condition is crucial. Ritual could not make a weak ruler strong or create consensus where there was none. On the contrary, if a ruler were weak or a community divided by factionalism, a ritual would only call attention to his weakness or focus dissension. Rituals could amplify currents; they could not create them.[80] And this is one more reason why they remained meaningful. Ritual was not propaganda out of touch with political reality or a static tableau depicting an ideal. It was part of political reality—a currency of power, a measure of perceptions, a test of strength.

The Problem of Ambiguity

Critics claim that rituals are incorrigibly ambiguous, and therefore about as meaningful as oracles. Those who study rit-

uals prefer to say that they are "polysemic."[81] That is, every ritual action is capable of conveying several possible meanings,
many of them contradictory. A kiss, for example, was usually a
sign of friendship (*amicitia*) or brotherhood (*fraternitas*), and
therefore an acknowledgment of a rough parity between two
parties. But kissing a reliquary was a sign of reverence, as was
kissing a king's foot; and when a lord embraced and kissed a
fidelis, that was a sign of friendship, but friendship at the discretion of the lord.[82]

Some scholars discuss this polysemy as if the ambiguity pertains only, or primarily, to their "potential" meanings. In performance the ritual is supposed to become, as it were, "ki-
netic," fixed to a meaning clearly apprehensible by actors and
audience. Thus Heinrich Fichtenau believes that the difficulty
historians encounter in deciphering the meanings of ambiguous
rituals could not have been shared by contemporaries. "The significance of a medieval symbol had to be clear at least to the
members of the concerned group," he writes, "since a gesture
fails in its purpose when it is either misunderstood or not understood at all." The example he cites is Stephen II's *proskynesis* to Pepin at Ponthion, which may have been intended as
either a kind of "commendation" or an appeal for help. Which it
was contemporaries must have known; but we cannot.[83]

But ethnographers know this is not so. Members of a culture
are often less knowledgeable about the meanings of their rites
and symbols than the scholars who visit them.[84] Though this
lack of understanding may indicate how little they care about
these activities, it may just as well indicate that the rituals are
perfectly "meaningful" (that is, beautiful, important, and capable of eliciting emotional responses) without their "meaning"
being precise. One might go further and say that rituals are all
the more meaningful for having no precise meaning. Here again
the differences between words and symbols can be instructive.
Both may be spoken of as having meanings. But words denote,
and sentences fail to communicate information accurately if
their words have too many possible referents. In contrast, symbols are inherently ambiguous because multivalent; and the
more possible referents a symbol has, the more evocative it becomes—in other words, the more "meaningful."[85]

An illustration is provided by pictorial art. Whereas language can produce only one proposition at a time, which must be modified sequentially, visual depictions can present several images at once. They may be complementary or contradictory, but they are simultaneous, and the viewer must "read" the images simultaneously in order to understand their message. Artists of the Middle Ages took great advantage of this potential. With its constituent scenes organized in ranks, a tympanum or illumination could convey both diachronic and synchronic information, remaining true to both the narrative unfolding of biblical history and its timeless anagogy. Where one level of an imperial portrait represented earth and another heaven, the emperor's figure might be spread out across both, signifying (in Ernst Kantorowicz's words) his Christlike "twin-natured being."[86] Medieval artists might even use the technique to cultivate ambiguity intentionally. The twelfth-century tympanum at Autun, for example, includes a Christ frozen halfway between sitting and standing. As Jean-Claude Bonne has discerned, this pose was no accident. It was an iconographic solution to the problem of conveying an eternal truth when that truth was not only revealed historically (that is, sequentially) but also described by different scriptural passages in contradictory terms. The bent-kneed Christ at Autun, then, was simultaneously ascending to his Father (who might be enthroned on a level above him) and himself enthroned in majesty. At the same time he was also *seated* in heaven on God's right (as required by Mark 16:19) while *standing* on his right (as witnessed by Stephen in Acts 7:55–56). Most important, Bonne has located a contemporary discussion of this iconographic pose whose author was fully aware of the intentional multivalence of this representation. For him, the meaning of the pose was at once clear and ambiguous.[87]

Rituals, an iconography of gestures, were equally capable of multiple readings. There is no reason why contemporaries needed to reduce them to a single meaning on any given occasion. Indeed, part of the beauty of a ritual such as supplication, what made it so perfect as a tool of diplomacy, was its indelible ambiguity. In the case of Pope Stephen's prostrate entreaty to Pepin, for example, the king could have read it either as a sign of subjection or as a mark of unusual honor, since this was the kind of prostration expected by Byzantine emperors and high officials. But the pope's retinue could have read it as an appeal to a lord made great by God, or as the kind of honorific demonstration of humility so common among prelates. In either case, it would have implied no subjection at all.

The ambiguity here need not have been purposeful; but in other cases it clearly was. When Conrad commanded the abbot of Saint-Gall to approach "the feet of the Empire" and take a reward from the emperor's shoes, the act conveyed at one and the same time familiarity and distance, favor and abasement, gravity and humor. Even Fichtenau saw that its power derived from its "polysemy."[88] As with the Autun Christ, the meaning was clear, but clearly and intentionally ambiguous. Another example: Fulk Nerra's prostrate atonement before the altar of Saint-Martin of Tours—was it a capitulation to the canons or an imperial act of exaltation through humiliation of the type performed by Theodosius and Louis the Pious? The act permitted canons and magnates to draw the conclusion most favorable to them. It did not widen their quarrel by forcing them to choose.[89]

Such ambiguity was not only occasionally helpful; it was absolutely essential to the success of rituals. It kept them from becoming just what critics say they were: gestures whose repetition emptied them of meaning. On the contrary, their ambiguity assured their continued meaningfulness by allowing them to mean whatever their participants and audience thought they should mean. In the heyday of Carolingian authority, the gestures and language of supplication could honor a king as God's anointed. With the disintegration of that authority, the same gestures and language could venerate princes as lords who ruled by God's grace while maintaining the fictive structure of divinely sanctioned monarchy. Then in the early eleventh century they were used to honor knights, because these were important men who deserved to be treated with consideration.

It was the ambiguity of rituals like supplication that allowed them to shift their meaning and remain relevant to social reality. Here, the audience played a crucial role, for spectators were essential to a ritual—not because they were the target of its propaganda but because their attitude determined the ritual's meaning. This has been well established in the case of ordeals, but it was true in many other rituals as well.[90] Would William the Conqueror's crown-wearing be considered a celebration appropriate to his renown, or would its declaration of divine approval be regarded as a dangerous precedent? The audience decided, just as it decided whether a king's refusal to grant mercy to a suppliant rebel was justice, tyranny, or an astute exercise of power, his offering of that mercy weakness, cunning, or prudence.[91] The bishops and magnates who overthrew Louis the Pious in 833 had intended the emperor's penance at Saint-Médard to be a public humiliation; instead, its manifest injustice shamed his supporters into rallying behind him.[92]

Once again we see that rituals could not create emotions out of nothing. At best they could only galvanize responses that were already brewing. And by no means were these responses necessarily consensual or deferential. That might be the case, particularly if the audience's members were homogeneous, their loyalties clear and undivided. But if that was not the case, if a community was divided against itself, then the ritual amplified the division. When in *Ljósvestninga Saga* a woman's hand was unwrapped after an ordeal by hot iron, her accusers and her defenders both ran for their weapons, the former convinced that her festering wounds had clearly demonstrated her guilt, the latter equally convinced that the wounds were healing normally and proclaimed her innocence.[93] As with Louis's penance and William's crown-wearing, rituals cannot create harmony where a basis for it does not exist. They will only reveal what is already present. Put more crassly, ritual will justify actions that people must already take, deepen feelings they already have.[94]

The Sources of Emotion

If we regard rituals simply as formal, repetitive actions that transmit ideologies, it is difficult to see how they could ever elicit emotional responses from their participants. Yet once again, this difficulty arises only when we divorce a ritual from its immediate context. Restoring that context allows us to recapture the source of its power. For example, the kinds of supplications that most impressed contemporary chroniclers did not occur against a neutral backdrop. They occurred at the end of disputes that involved open acts of armed hostility on the part of laymen and, on the part of monks and canons, humiliations of relics, excommunications, and venomous insults.[95] Performed in this setting, the prostration of the condemned was not an empty gesture. It was the mark of his defeat.

Context is equally important to understanding the success of the monks of Lobbes in using ritual to settle feuds; for when the monks made their processions into the towns of Flanders, they entered communities already tense from years of war and invasion, disasters immediately followed by an outburst of feuding; and they often entered these towns during feast days, such as Pentecost and Ascension, when people would have been even more excited and expectant than usual. At such moments, the response of the crowd to the monks' rites of peacemaking was especially emotional. Townsmen and knights, "silent except for their sobs," hovered around the young men who lay prostrate before the saint's relics, eating dirt in grief. And when these youths finally rose to accept peace, the members of the crowd embraced and moved en masse to the church, singing the Te Deum.[96]

When their symbolism is part of real life and when they occur in moments of social stress, then, like good drama, rituals can be cathartic. But one might suggest a more specific way in which rituals create emotional fervor: by the juxtaposition of symbols and values that do not belong together—more, whose joining violates current definitions of what is proper.[97] A useful, if unusual, analogy comes from the later medieval and early modern periods, a time when we first have evidence about what men found sexually alluring or, what is often the same thing, sexually threatening. It was not a woman's open flaunting of feminine charms. It was instead the bisexual: the woman who dressed in masculine clothing, whose hair was short-cropped and whose breasts were small.[98] Sexual excitement was created by joining what was not supposed to be joined.

Similarly, the excitement aroused by rituals may have been a combination of confusion, threat, and pleasure at seeing opposing social and moral categories juxtaposed or fused. Certainly such opposition is a common feature of many of the liveliest early European rituals—the saturnalian inversions of carnival and the "woman on top" studied by Natalie Zemon Davis are two famous examples.[99] There are also the rites of fourteenth-century Florentine confraternities, whose defining characteristic as described by Ronald Weissman was their consistent inversion of or opposition to their members' ordinary values and practices.[100]

We find similar patterns in early medieval rituals, including supplication. This society's ambivalence toward authority has already been emphasized. Kings and counts were supposed to be honored; and peace required that they possess a "long iron hand" that could strike down the proud as well as raise the humble.[101] Hence the praise, common to all generations in the early Middle Ages, given to those kings who knew how to impose harsh judgments as well as to show mercy. Yet kings and princes could rule successfully only if they had the support of their magnates, and throughout the Middle Ages, the lord who forgot that he was bound to his men by reciprocal ties of honor stood in danger of losing his power, if not his life. As for the church, if it granted lords the power of *correctio*, it also taught that this power had to be used in the pursuit of justice, not gain. Above all, rulers had to remember that in God's sight they were the equals of those whom they ruled, and therefore sinners themselves.

Hence the inversions of supplication, when lords knelt before their inferiors or did penance, and the expectation that lords would grant the requests of those who approached them with humility. These acts were reminders, to lords and *fideles* alike, that rulership did not confer a license for tyranny but a responsibility to "do justice to each according to his law."[102] If lords ruled by the grace of God, they had to rule not only with God's power but also with his justice. Seen in this light, the contradictory uses of supplication were not signs that the ritual had become so commonplace as to be empty of meaning. Instead they should demonstrate to us, as they surely demonstrated to contemporaries, that this ritual was true because it captured the contradictions inherent in their own ideas of lordship.

The Peace of God, which always raised strong passions in contemporaries, was also a bundle of contradictions. This was especially true when its assemblies gathered in fields outside the walls of cities, rather than within urban churches. To declare a reign of peace its crowds gathered where men and women were not normally safe, or in no-man's-land between two contested jurisdictions.[103] Monks abandoned their cloisters and brought their relics into the fields; and liturgies were conducted outside, in the open air, not within a closed sanctuary where the hermetic gestures of priests were ordinarily hidden behind an opaque screen.[104] Emblemizing all these contradictions was the central rite of the Peace assemblies; for the kiss of peace joined the liturgical (hence sacred) kiss of the mass with the lay (hence profane) kiss of *amicitia*.[105]

Yet the oppositions that give rituals their emotional force need not be purely symbolic or ideational. They can be quite real. In the Peace councils, for example, the most tangible oppositions were those between various social groups within the crowd itself. They are not often mentioned in the canons issued by the councils. They are, however, implicit in the distinctions the canons draw between armed and unarmed, poor and powerful.[106] And they come to the surface in narrative accounts of the councils, as in Andrew of Fleury's contrast between the *milites* and the *multitudo inermis vulgi*, and Raoul Glaber's frequent reference to the *universa plebs* that included *maximi, mediocres ac minimi*.[107] The contrasts are even more apparent in accounts of other public gatherings akin to the Peace assemblies. The crowds that witnessed princely entries and relic delations, for example, were often described as the sum of opposed categories: rich and poor, old and young, men and women, people from the town and people from the countryside, townsmen and knights, knights and commoners. To be sure, this was a rhetorical convention for expressing the achievement of Christian unity. But since the categories of opposition found in descriptions of such celebrations changed in conformity with known changes in social organization, there is no reason to doubt that the descriptions also reflected reality.[108]

To a certain extent the release experienced in these celebrations stemmed from the momentary suspension of habitual social oppositions. But the situation was actually far more complex. In fact, the gatherings did not really suspend social divisions at all. Instead, they confronted ideal and reality, liminal and structural; for beneath the patina of unity one could still see the groupings of power and dependence that divided these communities. Thus in the crowds that attended a translation of saints at Ghent in 944 and a peacemaking at Lissewege in 1066, the warriors (*regalis militia, milites*) still formed a distinct group alongside the townpeople, just as they did alongside the *inermis vulgus* in the Peace assembly at Bourges in 1038.[109]

One final set of oppositions appears within these gatherings, the most obvious and intractable of all: the feuds and quarrels that divided the attending nobility and that pitted the clergy and *mediocres* against the castellans and knights. After all, the purpose of the Peace oaths was largely to restrict the *potentes'* excesses by designating certain places and categories of persons as off limits to attacks.[110] Even so, the memory of recent violence and the threat of renewed violence were always present: witness the need of the archbishop of Bourges to arm the local peasantry to enforce the Peace oaths in 1038, or (much earlier, in 975, before pacts of peace had become the Peace of God) the decision of the bishop of Le Puy to call out his nephews' armies in the middle of the night to surround the field where the oaths would be sworn the next morning.[111] At least once the monks of Lobbes had to make peace in the presence of an armed retinue ready to seize the killer they were trying to protect.[112]

It is hard not to see the tension inherent in such settings. If one does not see it, then many of these assemblies' most distinctive characteristics are incomprehensible. It was the precondition for the sometimes bloody miracles that occurred around the relics during the Peace assemblies and validated the proceedings as truly inspired by God. And the tension mounted until the crowd, "burning with zeal," responded to the bishops' appeals by raising their hands to God and crying out, "Peace! Peace! Peace!"[113] Nor is this somewhat general account of a Peace assembly from Raoul Glaber's chronicle the only example of the dynamic. We see the same crescendo of excitement in more specific accounts of other public gatherings, where miracles and the pacification of feuds were not obstructed by surrounding tensions, but facilitated by them.[114]

Thus the threat of armed conflict and the visibility of social cleavages did not vitiate these rituals. Far from it, they only heightened their emotiveness. A declaration of equality in the face of the powerful; public space accorded women and the young within an event controlled by older men; an effort by counts, bishops, and monks to restrain increasingly independent knights and castellans (at Le Puy, even as these warriors held their weapons): not for a moment did an ideal of unity supplant the reality. Rather, these public rituals thrived on making latent conflict visible. From this point of view, it hardly matters whether the laity who witnessed a monastic procession understood the christological typology of the act, or whether the crowds who swore the oaths of Peace cared about Christ's injunctions to love God and neighbor; for the excitement and tension made these events memorable—"meaningful" without anyone having to understand their "meaning"—eleventh-century versions of carnival, and not much easier to control.

It was the same in other rituals. Troubled crown-wearings like William the Conqueror's and Otto I's, meetings between rulers along the rivers separating their territories, peacemakings like the one where Arnulf of Flanders assassinated William Longsword, ordeals that caused fighting instead of ending it— the fact that these rituals ended in violence or were steeped in tension is not an indication of their failure. It is rather a sign of the unpredictability of events that occurred against a backdrop of barely restrained violence. Far from overcoming or excising social contradictions, these rituals concentrated them; and that was the source of their power.

Where others have seen rituals as agents of political or ideological control, I see instead battles for power, either between competing social and political groupings or between competing cultural values. Rituals may end with a victory of order over disorder that momentarily ends tension. But before it can do so it must draw out the emotions of audience and participants by dramatizing a struggle between opposing categories, groups, and values that amplifies tension and brings social and cultural contradictions into the open. Ambiguity and contradiction, then, are the very soul of ritual, the secret of its flexibility, the sources of its emotional power. Where there is neither ambiguity nor contradiction, no spiritual or social conflict either within the event or on its edges, there is no longer ritual. There is only ceremony.[115]

The Problem of Hypocrisy

We are still left with the problem of hypocrisy. In addressing it, we might begin this time not with the differences between language and ritual but with a similarity so obvious that it is easily overlooked. Some people tell the truth; some people lie. That this is so is not a problem with language but with human nature. So, too, with ritual in general, and supplication in particular. Not history but common sense tells us this. There were doubtless cynics who perceived that the rituals were not parts of Creation but creations of the culture. These were the jesters and hypocrites who mocked the customary actions or performed them only for their own gain. But there were also those who sincerely believed in the ideals they expressed—Burchard, count of Vendôme, for example, Hugh Capet's loyalest supporter. It was he who exploded at the council of Verzy when Arnulf of Reims tergiversated in his confession. And at the end of his life, when he took the habit at Saint-Maur-des-Fossés, he is supposed to have answered the ridicule of his entourage by holding up to them the ideal of loyalty that had governed his life, reminding them that his decision was really the logical fulfillment of the royal processions in which he had participated. "With my own hand," he said, "I carried the taper before the mortal king to light his way. Should I not now serve the immortal Emperor and with my hands reverently bring before him the burning candelabrum with manifest humility?"[116]

The majority probably fell somewhere between William the Conqueror's jester and the count of Vendôme. Some may have seen through the rituals but tolerated them because their image of order gave hope in a time of turmoil. Richer seems to have been this kind of person, juxtaposing the most extravagant royal ceremonies with the basest treacheries.[117] Others (we can easily imagine the northern princes among them) accepted the value of royal ceremonies because they were advancing similar ceremonies in their own principalities. They could not undermine one without undermining the other.[118]

In any case, contemporaries were well aware that rituals of loyalty could be faked. The biographer of Bishop Gerard of Cambrai, for example, knew that Gerard's castellan could never be trusted. He made pacts only to gain momentary advantages, and broke them as soon as he had the chance. Accordingly, when imperial legates came to Cambrai and the castellan prostrated himself before them to beg forgiveness, the author knew that his humility counted for little. In fact, he described his groveling as "putting on an unbelievable show of penance" (*incredibilis poenitentiae speciem induit*), using a word (*induere*) which implied that what the castellan put on he would take off as soon as the legates left the city—as in fact he did.[119]

Significantly, even though Gerard did not believe in his cas-

tellan's sincerity, he nevertheless responded to his prostration
by interceding with the legates to absolve him. If some people
are habitually disposed to manipulate rituals for their own ends,
others are morally bound to honor the code. As a priest, Gerard
was one of the latter, for priests were obligated to intercede
with God on behalf of any penitent who made a proper confession of his sin, and the castellan's confession had been formally
proper. Gerard had no choice. Nor was he the only bishop
whose commitment to sacramental form was taken advantage
of by another's opportunism: Henry IV did much the same to
Gregory VII at Canossa.[120] High-minded priests, then, were people whose profession required them to take ritual forms seriously; cynical castellans and desperate kings were not.

As these two incidents show, the problem of hypocritical supplications was most visible to the literate clergy in cases of false
penance; and so it is their writings about penance that come
closest to addressing this issue. The problem was quite straightforward. All writers taught that penitents had to confess "with
all humility and contrition of heart," for acts of satisfaction
were worthless without true compunction.[121] But how could a
priest know that a penitent's humility and contrition were sincere? There was only one answer: through his or her exterior
signs of humility. Raban Maur, for example, emphasized the
tears of true penitents, Hincmar of Reims their tears and sighs.[122]
For Regino of Prüm "their very garb and countenance" gave witness to their guilt, as public penitents approached the doors of
the church at the beginning of Lent "clad in sackcloth, with
bare feet and faces downcast toward the earth."[123] The problem,
of course, was that these signs had long ago become customary.
They were easily "put on."

The very prevalence of this problem is one of the reasons that
private penance became increasingly attractive to the church;
for private confession was essentially a means for the church to
educate the laity and examine the conscience of a sinner.[124] And
manuals were written to alert priests to the signs of a true confession. True penitents would manifest their sorrow by extreme
acts of satisfaction, such as fasting on bread, salt, and water.[125]
Indeed, true penitents would do more than had been required of
them, not only avoiding what had been expressly forbidden but
also abstaining from pleasures that had not been forbidden.[126]

And they would give proof of their humility by signs that priests were taught to recognize, such as their refusal to defend themselves against the priest's criticisms.[127]

Yet the underlying problem remained, for all these things were still external signs of an internal state, and as such, they could mislead. A penitent might feel true compunction for the wrong reasons—out of fear of God's punishment, for example, or the social stigma attached to excommunication. Over time, his penance would be proven false: in the absence of a true conversion the sinner would return to his evil ways once he had been absolved.[128] But the priest could not see into the future any more than he could see into the penitent's heart. How then to judge if "the gesture of the body" really did reveal "the devotion of the mind"? Two answers suggested themselves. The first had already been offered by Augustine: acts of devotion could themselves render individuals susceptible to devotion.[129] The more common variant of this argument in the early Middle Ages was to see penitential acts as so inherently humiliating that they induced shame in the penitent. Thus the very act of confessing, even in private, was supposed to cause embarrassment and blushing.[130] According to Raban Maur, the humiliation could be so intense that it alone could win absolution.[131] What was true of private confession was a fortiori true of the extravagant humiliations of public penance, which were indisputably a public shaming.[132]

The difficulty with these arguments is that they had it backward. To feel shame in confessing one had to be already predisposed to feel shame.[133] Augustine himself recognized the problem; for he did not argue that gestures of devotion could create devotion out of nothing, only that they could reinforce an already existing devotion, imparted by grace, which induced the gesture in the first place.[134] The hardhearted and the cynical were beyond embarrassment. The gesture would mean little to them, and so would do little for them.

This left only one possible answer, whose frequent declaration by many authors attests to its fundamental importance in the doctrine of penance. A priest could not know the truth in a sinner's heart. Only God could know; and God would withhold absolution from a hypocritical penitent, even if a priest mistakenly accepted his confession.[135] The problem with the argu-

ment, of course, was its implication that the church did not
absolve a sinner at all. Technically it did not. A priest's penitential role was essentially that of an intercessor who begged God's
mercy on a sinner's behalf.[136] But this means that the church
found no way to solve the problem of hypocrisy, for a priest
could know God's mind even less than the sinner's. Ultimately,
the priest was left with "garb and countenance" as the basis for
his decision.[137]

There was no solution to the problem in the earthly church;
nor was there any in a churchly society that relied on the same
gestures and formulas to express faithfulness to its rulers. There
was no way to guarantee that a prostrate supplication was sincere. Yet the problem may have been largely theoretical, of only
incidental importance in ordinary life. Certainly there were
liars and hypocrites. To monks, clerics, and the historians who
read their writings, the words have seemed almost synonymous
with faithless lords like the castellan of Cambrai, who thought
nothing of violating oaths, pacts, and judgments.

But seeing a ritualistic society as inherently prone to hypocrisy is surely misleading. It ignores the possibility that members
of an authoritarian society who are raised with rituals of deference to authority may be more likely to take them seriously
than a society of individualists.[138] Far more important, such
skepticism ignores the social significance of rituals, by taking
their overt meaning too seriously, their practical use not seriously enough. Precisely to be rid of the kinds of difficulties discussed here, Augustine had taught that in its earthly sojourn
the City of God was a polity much like any other, required to
believe in brotherhood but enforce obedience.[139] The early medieval church enthusiastically accepted his argument. The question
of excommunication's ontological efficacy was simply sidestepped. For all practical purposes it was the political conse-
quences of the sentence that counted, the excommunicant's exclusion from the church as a social body.[140] Similarly with
penance: whether it took place in private or public, what mattered
in practice was that it enforced the law of the church.[141] Even
though there was no effective sanction to ensure continued good
behavior, and even though priests could not, in theory, be absolutely certain of God's forgiveness of those they restored to the
church, yet the ritual purity of the community was enforced.

Those who were thought to be sinners were punished; those who were thought to be contrite were absolved.

The system was therefore visibly consistent. Judging forms of behavior, the church demanded forms of behavior in atonement. Sincerity was desirable but not entirely relevant. The appearance of obedience, on the other hand, was essential. Maintaining the image of authority is what mattered most, and that is what ritual did best.

The role of ritual in lay society was no different. As we have seen, many early medieval rituals can be interpreted as tests of power and social cohesiveness; and so can ritual supplications for mercy. Criticizing the ritual's importance to contemporaries simply because its professions of humility were insincere therefore misconstrues its role within the political community—its use, that is, as a test of strength and of the balance of forces. It did not matter whether the castellan of Cambrai were truly contrite, or the lord of Bellême when after a rebellion he approached the duke of Normandy, barefoot and carrying his saddle, and prostrated himself, or Haimo of Germigny as he groveled to "save himself" at the feet of Louis VI.[142] What mattered was that the contumacy of these men had been punished, their rebellions suppressed. In other words, it was not the gesture that mattered. It was the fact that they had been forced to make the gesture.

The Problem of Evidence

Throughout this book we have remarked the congruence between the discourse of supplication and the society's cultural assumptions, a congruence so complete that it reiterated inconsistencies in the culture along with consistencies. Such perfect correspondence may seem artificial to some readers, an indication that supplication has been made to seem more consistent than it in fact was. Quite the contrary, every effort has been made to show that supplication was not consistent, but as flexible and contradictory as the society itself. Yet it cannot be denied that there was harmony among the various facets of the ritual, and congruence between the ritual as a whole and cultural beliefs. This symmetry need not indicate artifice, however. As argued in this and preceding chapters, in many cases it may only reflect the extent to which the patterns of supplication and intercession had woven themselves into the culture's fabric of thought, so that different situations and new challenges were comprehended with familiar assumptions.

At the same time, one must admit that the symmetry is in part a conscious construction; but in this case the artifice is not the historian's but contemporaries'. Those who articulated the rituals were clerics; and clerics were trained to seek out the order in the universe, to show the workings of Providence in the *événementielle*.[143] Given this predisposition, there had to be a link between the supplication of God and that of God's lords, between prostrate entreaties in penance and those in litigation, between the intercession of the saints and the intercession of patrons for clients. More than a link, there had to be analogy, for clerical exegesis was founded on the search for types or figures—that is, divinely instituted archetypes that informed historical characters and events, historical patterns that pointed to archetypes of Creation.[144] In the case of supplication, the prostration of a king to God, the prostration of a count to a king, the prostration of all lords to the holy were the many tropes of a single truth: Christ had allowed himself to be humbled that he might be exalted and restore humanity to grace.

The question that remains is whether this interpretive elegance reflected only clerical attitudes. At least in its less transcendental aspects, it surely did not. Indeed, one of the most important aspects of the discourse of supplication is that here the teachings of the church and the beliefs of the laity converged and were made compatible, if not identical. Preaching to the laity and the reception of sacraments by them may have been infrequent or, when they did occur, misunderstood; but supplication they could understand and make their own. It was not a ritual hidden within the cloister or performed only rarely. It was a mode of behavior used by laymen and laywomen to express their desires, and the expression was much the same whether these desires were announced to God and saints, kings and counts, bishops and abbots, or peers and the alms-taking poor. Supplication was the one ritual, the one system of values, that the laity and clergy shared. And though neither group could have seen it in exactly the same way, the ambiguity of the discourse made it possible for both to overlook possible discrepancies and see instead a common culture, in which church, government, and society were one.

Such a thesis can never be proved directly, in part because of the intrinsic limits of historical evidence. As David Herlihy has said, historians, unlike ethnographers, cannot ask their sources what a ritual means.[145] Yet such a statement exaggerates the value of the informants used by ethnographers, since even they produce partial, biased, or remarkably unforthcoming responses to direct questions. Ethnographers are therefore left to the same processes of deduction and induction that historians apply to their sources.[146] When trying to interpret supplication, for example, we note how thoroughly the ritual and its discourse pervade the sources. We see how often they were called upon, in all sectors of the society, in many regions and decades, to bring conceptual order to social change. And we show that variations in the use of the ritual can be explained according to variations in the distribution of power and resources. These are clear signs that the ritual was meaningful to contemporaries, including the laity.

The best indicator of the historical significance of this and other ritual complexes, however, is how much would remain puzzling if we knew nothing about them. Without understanding the values of supplication, we cannot understand the language of disputing in northern France, its harshness and vindictiveness and its liturgical tone. If we do not assume the importance contemporaries ascribed to those values, we cannot understand the recurrence of gestures of humility when they announced disputes and surrendered claims. Unless we believe that some people took the gestures seriously, it is difficult to understand why a bishop like Gerard of Cambrai so willingly pardoned his castellan. If we do not assume the importance contemporaries placed on the language of peace and deference, then we must assume that the people we study did not care about what they wrote, and that there was no reason at all for using one kind of language or the other. Finally, unless we assume the power of a discourse that only knew a world structured by deference and reciprocity in all things great and small, it is difficult to understand why strong counts tolerated weak kings, or why every castellan capable of doing so did not simply usurp the title of count. The belief in order and deference, peace and brotherhood may not always have corresponded with political and social reality; but without that belief to fall back on, authority and honor would have had no grounding at all. And that was as unthinkable to knights and castellans as it was to counts and kings.

Disputes involving churches and laity in northern France, 1000–1100, by region

This table includes disputes culled from the primary sources listed in the bibliography. It encompasses a region bounded roughly and inclusively by Paris, Arras, the French Vexin, and Reims, a region I know well and whose source material I could control. Normandy, the diocese of Cambrai, and Flanders (save Artois, whose institutions are quite similar to those of Francia) have therefore been excluded. I have also included a few disputes over rights located outside the area if both parties were from the area (e.g., *Homblières*, no. 34). Disputes are grouped primarily by the location of the rights disputed. One bracketed item has not been included in the totals given in the text because the nature of the dispute is so uncertain.

Historians of other regions in France may be surprised at how few disputes have been recorded, despite every effort at thoroughness. This is another sign of the poverty of the region's source material before the twelfth century. But the rarity of recorded disputes is also, I believe, a result of relatively stable and coherent political communities, whose courts had little need of writing, just as they had little need of *convenientiae*.

Region, date	Source	Status of lay party[a]	Juris-diction[b]	Customs[c]	Other
Artois					
Early 11th c.	Guimann, 45–46	count/*miles*		x	
1008–12	MGH SS, 8:377	min. (eccl.)	x	x	
1036	[Guimann, 170][d]			x	
1089	[Guimann, 381]	uncertain			x
n.d.	[Guimann, 277]	uncertain			x
Ponthieu					
1027	*Pontieu*, 1	count			x
1031	[Hariulf, 4.7/9]	*miles*			x
1036	Hariulf, 4.7	king			x
1043	Hariulf, 4.7	uncertain			x
1053	Hariulf, 4.21	*miles*			x
1062–63	Hariulf, 4.22	*miles*			x
1053–75	*Pontieu*, 5	count		x	
n.d.	*Mir. s. Richarii*, 463	lord		x	
n.d.	*Mir. s. Walarici*, 29	*miles*	x		
Amienois					
1004–9	Ramackers, *PUF*, 3[e]	*miles* = visc.	x		
Early 11th c.	*Philippe Ier*, 75	count			
1016	Langlois, *Textes*, 1	*miles*/adv.	x	x	
1042	Newman, *Domaine*, doc. 2	adv. = cast.		x	
1055–56	Fossier, *Chartes*, 2	adv. = cast.	x	x	
1071–79	*Philippe Ier*, 75	visc.	x		
1091–94	*Amiens*, 9	visc.	x		
Vermandois					
1021–27	*Homblières*, 23	cast.		x	
1040–45	[BN, Moreau 23:190]	uncertain			x
1045	[ND Noyon, 51–52]	*miles*			x
Mid-11th c.	*Homblières*, 34[f]	adv	x		
1056	St-Eloi, 109v	adv.	x	x	
1059–81	*Homblières*, p. 100	cast.			x
1075	*Homblières*, 31	count	x		
1076–77	Fossier, *Chartes*, 3	min. (com.)	x	x	
c. 1089	ND Noyon, 29v	cast.			x
1090	BN, Moreau 36:52	cast.		x	
1094–98	BN, Moreau 37:198	vassal	x		

Region, date	Source	Status of lay party[a]	Jurisdiction[b]	Customs[c]	Other
1060–1101	*Philippe Ier*, 143[g]	count		x	
n.d.	ND Noyon, 60	*miles*			x
Noyonnais					
1027	*RHF* 10: 236	cast.	x		
1058	ND Noyon, 52–53	cast./adv.	x		
1044–60	ND Noyon, 20v[h]	min. (royal)			x
1064	Lefranc, *Noyon*, doc. 3	cast.		x	
1067	*ND Paris*, 3:354	peasants		x	
1067	*ND Paris*, 1:308	cast.	x	x	
Laonnais/Remois					
1018	Bur, *Chron. Mouzon*, doc. 3	min. (epis.)	x	x	
1046	AD Aisne, G 1850, 250	*miles* = adv.		x	
1049	*RHF* 11:586	cast. = adv.	x	x	
1031–60	Soehnée, 34	adv.		x	
1071	*Philippe Ier*, 61	min. (royal)		x	
1096	Gousset, *Actes*, 2:131	min. (epis.)/count		x	
1052–98	AD Aisne, H 325, 124	cast./*miles*			x
Beauvaisis					
1030–59	Guyotjeannin, "Recherches," doc. 2	min. (epis.)	x	x	
1075–79	Lohrmann, *PUF*, 11	cast.			?
1080	BN, Baluze 141, 52v	uncertain			x
1089–92	BN, Baluze 71, 19	uncertain			x
1089–92	PL 151:378	cast.			?
1092	Thillier/Jarry, *Ste-Croix*, 3	lord	x	x	
1092–95	Thillier/Jarry, *Ste-Croix*, 3	lord	x	x	
1092	Louvet, *Beauvais*, 2:208	lord	x	x	
1089–95	[Guyotjeannin, "Recherches," 1:161–64]	uncertain			x
1100	Guyotjeannin, "Recherches," doc. 6	min. (epis.)	x		
Compiègne/Soissonais					
1048	Fauroux, 114	count	x		
1049	*RHF* 11:580	cast.	x	x	

Region, date	Source	Status of lay party[a]	Juris-diction[b]	Customs[c]	Other
1031–60	*St-Corneille*, 15[i]	min. (royal)		x	
1031–60	Tardif, *Monu-ments*, 280	adv.		x	
–1066	*Philippe Ier*, 27	cast.	x	x	
1066	*Philippe Ier*, 28	count		x	
1085	Bourgin, *Soissons*, doc. 8	cast.		x	
–1092	*Philippe Ier*, 125	burghers	x		
Vexin/Pontoise					
1030	Fauroux, 63	count		x	
c. 1030	*St-Germain*, 52	count		x	
–1031	*Jumièges*, 16	count	x		
1031?	*St-Père*, 1:173	count		x	
1031–35	*St-Père*, 1:175	visc.		x	
–1068	*Pontoise*, 1	*miles*			x
c. 1075	*ND Paris*, 1:292	count		x	
c. 1086	[*Pontoise*, 22]	uncertain			x
n.d.	*Jumièges*, 46	uncertain			x
Senlis/Paris					
1005–6	Tardif, *Monu-ments*, 243	min. (royal)		x	
1027	Fauroux, 59	cast.	x	x	x
1025–30	*St-Germain*, 49	min./*miles*		x	
1030	*St-Germain*, 51	*miles*		x	
1031–60	BN, Moreau 21, 193	*miles*		x	
1057–67	*Jumièges*, 28	*miles*/min.		x	
c. 1091	Müller, *St-Leu*, 3	*miles*			x
c. 1093	*ND Paris*, 1:288	count		x	
Unknown locations					
n.d.	*Vita Arnulfi*, 234	cast.		x	
n.d.	*Vita Arnulfi*, 241	*miles* = lord		x	

/: More than one party holding the indicated statuses are involved in the dispute.

=: The individual or individuals are described as having both of the statuses indicated.

[a]adv. = advocate; cast. = castellan; lord = banal lord of unstated office but exercising power over others; *miles* = knight; min. = minister: comital (com.), episcopal (epis.), ecclesiastical (eccl.), or royal; visc. = viscount. So far as possible, statuses have been determined according to the ascriptions of the texts. If a text gives an inadequate ascription, one has been supplied from other sources when they exist.

[b]A dispute over rights of justice exercised by a lord or his agents.

[c]Demands for revenues or labor associated with the *seigneurie banale*.

[d]A regulation concerning St-Vaast's right to take tolls within Arras, issued by the abbot of St-Vaast with the advice of the bishop and archdeacon of Arras, the advocates of the monastery, and the castellan of Arras. The regulation was probably occasioned by a dispute (although it may also have been issued to head one off); but it is impossible to know whether the trouble involved one or more of these figures or the burghers of the town, who later created great difficulty over the *teloneum*.

[e]It is said only that one Drogo seized a *villa* of Corbie, but given the later claims of Drogo's family to viscomital rights in the region, and given the contemporaneous claims of the counts of

Amiens to viscomital rights in Corbie's villages, it is likely that something similar was at issue here. Certainly more was involved than the mere possession of an estate.

ᶠThe dispute dates to the mid–eleventh century, but the record was not written until later.

ᵍIt is alleged only that the count of Vermandois "usurped" ecclesiastical property, but the charge probably refers to the exaction of customs on the chapter's lands. Given the king's assumption of jurisdiction over this case, the count mentioned here (identified only as "H.") was probably Philip's brother Hugh, and not Herbert. If so, then the act would date to after c. 1080.

ʰThe canons and bishop complained of the *violentia* committed by *seruientes* against the property of the chapter. When more information is given, such a claim generally refers to the exaction of illicit customs.

ⁱA provost of St-Corneille abused his position to "usurp" the chapter's property. Although it is possible that he actually took over the property, it is more likely that the usurpation consisted of his exaction of customs on the property as if it were his own.

APPENDIX 2

Procedural patterns in disputes between churches and laity in northern France, 1000–1100

This table enables the reader to visualize at a glance the broad correlations between disputing strategies and political status as described in chapter 7. A few disputes noted in appendix 1 have been omitted, either because the source gives too little information or because the course of the dispute is difficult to categorize.

In categorizing the disputes I have stayed quite close to the language of the sources, having found that generalization usually leads to misleading anachronism. In the eleventh century, for example, there was a great deal of difference between "quitting" a claim and "conceding" one, between a "judgment" issued by a lord in a private audience and a public "judgment" announced by a court of peers after a formal trial. Procedures are ranged from left to right roughly in terms of greater and lesser voluntarism, graciousness, and privacy: that is, divine chastisements and public censures on the left, private accords and "spontaneous" concessions on the right.

Date and disputants	Source	Status of lay party[a]	Curse[b]	Divine judgt.[c]	Trial[d]	Judgt.[e]	Impos.[f]	Press.[g]	Beg[h]	Quit[i]	Lord med.[j]	Amic. med.[k]	Conc.[l]	Accd.[m]
Kings and counts														
1005–6	Tardiff, *Monuments*, 243	min. [royal]											■	
1018	Bur, *Chron. Mouzon*, doc. 5	min. [epis.]											■	
Early 11th c.	Guimann, 45–46	count/ miles												■
1027	Pontieu, 1	count											■	
1030	Fauroux, 63	count												■
c. 1030	St-Germain, 52	count									■			■
–1031	Jumièges, 16	count												■
1031?	St-Père, 1:173	count								■				
1036	Hariulf, 4.7	king											■	
1030–59	Guyotjeannin, "Recherches," doc. 2	min. [epis.]											■	
1044–60	ND Noyon, 20v	min. [royal]											■	
1066	Philippe Ier, 28[n]	count			■	▨								■
1071	Philippe Ier, 61	min. [royal]											■	■
1053–75	Pontieu, 5	count											■	■

1075	*Homblières*, 30°	count
c. 1075	*ND Paris*, 1:292	count
1076–77	Fossier, *Chartes*, 3	min (com.)
c. 1093	*ND Paris*, 1:288	count
1096	Gousset, *Actes*, 2:131	min. (epis.)/count
1100	Guyotjeannin, "Recherches," doc. 6	min (epis.)
1060–1101	*Philippe Ier*, 143	count
Other lay disputants		
1004–9	Ramackers, *PUF*, 3	*miles* = visc.
1016	Langlois, *Textes*, 1	*miles* = adv.
1021–27	*Homblières*, 23	cast.
1027	Fauroux, 59	cast.
1025–30	*St-Germain*, 49	min./*miles*
1030	*St-Germain*, 51	*miles*
1031	Hariulf, 4.7/9	*miles*
1031–35	*St-Père*, 1:175	visc.

Date and disputants	Source	Status of lay party[a]	Curse[b]	Divine judgt.[c]	Trial[d]	Judgt.[e]	Impos.[f]	Press.[g]	Beg[h]	Quit[i]	Lord med.[j]	Amic. med.[k]	Conc.[l]	Accd.[m]
1036	Guimann, 170													■
1042	Newman, *Domaine*, doc. 2	adv. = cast.						■		■				
1043	Hariulf, 4.7[p]	unc.°						■	▨					■
1040–45	BN, Moreau 23:190	unc.°									■			■
1045	ND Noyon, 51–52	*miles*									■			■
1046	AD Aisne, G 1850	*miles* = *adv.*												
1049	*RHF* 11:586	cast. = adv.					■				■			
1049	*RHF* 11:580	cast.	■		■	■	■		■	■				
1053	Hariulf, 4.21	*miles*	■						■	■				
1055–56	Fossier, *Chartes*, 2	adv. = cast.	■					■			■			■
1056	*St-Eloi*, 109v	adv.								■	■			
1058	ND Noyon, 52–53	cast./ adv.												
Mid-11th c.	*Homblières*, 34	adv.			■	■		■	■					
1031–60	*St-Corneille*, 15	min. (royal)					■							

Date	Source	Category
1031–60	BN, Moreau 21:193	*miles*
1031–60	Tardif, *Monuments*, 280	adv.
1062–63	Hariulf, 4.22	*miles*
1064	Lefranc, *Noyon*, doc. 3	cast.
–1066	*Philippe Ier*, 27	cast.
1057–67	*Jumièges*, 28	*miles*/min.
1067	*ND Paris*, 3:354	peasants
1067	*ND Paris*, 1:308	cast.
–1068	*Pontoise*, 1	*miles*
1059–81	*Homblières*, p. 100	cast.
1071–79	*Philippe Ier*, 75	visc.
1075–79	Lohrmann, *PUF*, 11	cast.
1080	BN, Baluze 141: 52v	unc.*
1085	Bourgin, *Soissons*, doc. 8	cast.
c. 1086	*Pontoise*, 22	unc.*
1089	Guimann, 381	unc.*

Date and disputants	Source	Status of lay party[a]	Curse[b]	Divine judgt.[c]	Trial[d]	Judgt.[e]	Impos.[f]	Press.[g]	Beg[h]	Quit[i]	Lord med.[j]	Amic. med.[k]	Conc.[l]	Accd.[m]
c. 1089	ND Noyon, 29v	cast.												
1090	BN, Moreau 36:52	cast.											█	
c. 1091	Müller, *St-Leu*, 3[g]	*miles*			▨									█
1089–92	BN, Baluze, 71:19	unc.*			█				█					
–1092	*Philippe Ier*, 125	burghers		█										
1092	Thillier/Jarry, *Ste-Croix*, 3	lord							█	█				
1092	Louvet, *Beauvais* 2:208	lord	█						█	█				
1091–94	*Amiens*, 9	visc.					█							
1092–95	Thillier/Jarry, *Ste-Croix*, 3	lord	█		█				█	█				
1053–98	AD Aisne, H 325, 124[q]	cast./*miles*							▨					
1094–98	BN, Moreau 37:198	*miles*	█						█					
n.d.	ND Noyon, 60	*miles*												
n.d.	*Mir. s. Walarici*, 29	*miles*							█	█				

n.d.	Vita Arnulfi, 241	miles = lord
n.d.	Vita Arnulfi, 234	cast.
n.d.	Mir. s. Richarii, 463	lord
n.d.	Guimann, 277	unc.*
n.d.	Jumièges, 46	unc.*

* unc. = uncertain.

a "adv. = advocate; cast. = castellan; lord = banal lord of unstated office but exercising power over others; miles = knight; min. = minister: comital (com.), episcopal (epis.), ecclesiastical (eccl.) or royal; visc. = viscount. So far as possible, statuses have been determined according to the ascriptions of the texts. If a text gives an inadequate ascription, one has been supplied from other sources when they exist."

b "The layman was cursed and/or excommunicated."

c "Divine intervention forced the layman to capitulate or avenged his misdeeds."

d "The dispute was heard in a formal trial in the court of a lord. Most of these trials resulted in judgments against the layman."

e "A judgment was issued by the court or the lord. In all but a few cases these judgments were issued against the layman. In itself this outcome cannot be taken as a sign of structurally biased proceedings. Rather the bias is inherent in source transmission: there was no reason for churches to maintain records of cases they had lost."

f "A lord imposed a settlement on one or both of the parties by virtue of his personal authority or took unilateral action to end the dispute."

g "A lord brought pressure to bear on a layman to force his capitulation."

h "The record specifies that termination of the dispute required the condemned to beg pardon."

i "The layman quit his claim, the language used (dimittere, abrenuntiare) connoting loss or surrender."

j "A lord mediated the dispute. Though he may have pressured the parties, the terms used by the record to describe his intervention are neutral."

k "Amicable mediation of a dispute, either through friends or through lords who did not exercise any personal or institutional authority over the layman."

l "The layman surrendered his claim, the language used (donare, concedere) connoting a free, uncoerced gift. In the case of disputes involving a lord's ministeriales, the outcome may have involved a lord's administrative decree granting a church direct exercise of the right previously exercised by the ministers. Although the language is not that of concession, it has still been counted as such because the award involved a gracious, voluntary act of a lord."

m "The dispute was settled by a bilateral accord."

n "An inquest was held into the rights of the count of Soissons over St-Médard. The language used to report the findings (ostensum est, adjudicatum est) was neutral and did not imply the censures found in most other judgements (e.g., Philippe Ier, no. 27, against the castellan of Coucy)."

o "In a dispute with the monastery, the count of Vermandois accepted the testimony of three of the abbey's serfs. A trial is therefore only hinted at. It is quite possible that the serfs presented their information in a private audience (a hypothesis supported by the number of domestics included in the witness list). Even if there was a trial, the count himself heard the grievance and accepted the testimony."

p "Claimants "prayed" or "petitioned" unsuccessfully for a precarial interest for themselves or their families. In other circumstances these terms denote a formal, prostrate supplication."

q "The monks' threat to bring a claim to trial drove the claimant to accept a settlement."

Notes

Introduction

1. On Arnulf's trial, *Acta concilii Remensis*, summarized and analyzed in detail by Ferdinand Lot, *Etudes sur le règne de Hugues Capet et la fin du Xe siècle* (Paris, 1903), 31–79, and discussed most recently by Claude Carozzi, "Gerbert et le concile de St-Basle," in *Gerberto*, 661–76; Riché, *Gerbert d'Aurillac*, 126–36.

2. On their objections see J.-F. Lemarignier, "L'exemption monastique et les origines de la réforme grégorienne," in *A Cluny: Congrès scientifique* (Dijon: Société des Amis de Cluny, 1950), 288–340 at 301–15; Mostert, *Political Theology*, 46–51.

3. *Acta concilii Remensis*, 681: "Addebant praeterea confessores episcopi, eum suis pedibus provolutum, cum lacrimis et gemitu sua crimina sub nomine confessionis declarasse, seque a sacerdotali officio, quo hactenus indigne usus fuerat, removeri velle."

4. Ibid., 685: "'Prosternere ergo,' inquit pater Arnulfus, 'coram tuis dominis, coramque tuis regibus, quos inexpiabiliter offendisti, propriamque confitens culpam, pro tui vita supplica.' Qui cum in modum crucis prostratus, pro vita et membris eiulatu quo poterat supplicaret, in lacrimas et suspiria synodum totam convertit."

5. Ibid.: "Moxque Daibertus, Bituricensium archiepiscopus, ad genua principum obvolutus, humillimas preces omnium pro salute viri offert. Qui pietate flexi: 'Vivat,' inquiunt, 'vestro beneficio, nostraque degat sub custodia, nec ferrum nec vincula metuens, nisi forte in fuga spem posuerit.'"

6. Throughout this book, "Francia" usually refers to the territory between the Loire and the Meuse (as in contemporary usage), "France" to the larger kingdom that recognized some sort of allegiance to the kings of the Franks.

7. Janos Bak, "Medieval Symbology of the State: Percy E. Schramm's Contribution," *Viator* 4 (1973): 33–63 at 60.

8. See, e.g., Kertzer, *Ritual, Politics, and Power*; Cannadine and Price, *Rituals of Royalty*; Wilentz, *Rites of Power*; Hobsbawm and Ranger, *Invention of Tradition*.

9. Nelson, "Lord's Anointed"; Reuter, "Plunder and Tribute"; Brühl, "Kronen- und Krönungsbrauch," 15–17; also Jäschke, "Frühmittelalterliche Festkrönungen?" 556–88.

10. Kantorowicz, *King's Two Bodies*, 78.

11. McCormick, *Eternal Victory*, chap. 9; P. E. Schramm, *Kaiser, Rom und Renovatio: Studien zur Geschichte des Römischen Erneuerungsgedankens vom Ende des Karolingischen Reiches bis zum Investiturstreit*, 2 vols. (1929; rpt. Darmstadt, 1962).

12. Lauer, *Règne de Louis IV*, 76.

13. *Chronique . . . de Mouzon*, 152, 1.7.

14. Hallam, "Kings and Princes," 156. Hallam's *Capetian France*, chaps. 1–3, summarizes this tradition of French scholarship, which was in some way canonized by Jean-François Lemarignier and the early work of Georges Duby. See also Yvonne Bongert, *Recherches sur les cours laïques du Xᵉ au XIIIᵉ siècles* (Paris, 1949), bk. 1, chap. 1.

15. Lemarignier, *Recherches sur l'hommage en marche*, 79–85.

16. See below, 110, 255.

17. Guillot, "Administration et gouvernement" and "Concept d'autorité." See also Werner, "Westfranken-Frankreich," 759–67, 776–79; Poly and Bournazel, *Mutation féodale*, 136–45.

18. Cf. Duby, "L'image du prince"; Werner, "Westfranken-Frankreich," 765–67.

19. Sassier, *Hugues Capet*; Schneidmüller, *Karolingische Tradition*.

20. Below, chap. 1.

21. As with Charles the Simple's honoring of the Lotharingian Hagano, which the Frankish magnates rightly interpreted as a sign that the king was trying to free himself from their oversight; and Hugh the Great's reception of the newly anointed Lothar at Paris, which signaled the duke's acceptance of Lothar's rule: Flodoard, *Annales*, 140–41; Richer, *Histoire de France*, 1:38–40, 2:10. See Sassier, *Hugues Capet*, 80–84, and Fichtenau, *Lebensordnungen*, 1:46.

22. Below, chap. 4.

23. Lemarignier, "L'exemption monastique" (above, n. 2).

24. For what follows see Bourdieu, *Outline of a Theory of Practice*, and below, chap. 9.

25. This criticism has been made of Victor Turner, for example; see the review of his *Dramas, Fields, and Metaphors* by James W. Fernandez in *Journal for the Scientific Study of Religion* 14 (1975): 191–97, and esp. Fernandez's "Dark at the Bottom of the Stairs." Ivo Strecker, *Social Practice of Symbolization*, 22–26, correctly identifies the essential problem as Turner's concern with symbols as objects rather than as products of human creation—a criticism similar to the one Bourdieu, *Theory of Practice*, levels at much social anthropology.

26. Below, chap. 9.

27. Alföldi, *Monarchische Repräsentation*, 49–54; Koskenniemi, *Studien*, 140–43; Taylor, "Proskynesis."

28. Rordorf, "Gestes accompagnant la prière"; Cazelles, "Gestes et paroles"; and esp. Neunheuser, "Gestes de la prière à genoux," all in *Gestes et paroles*. On the application of royal attributes to God in early Christian liturgy and thought see Per Beskow, *Rex Gloriae: The Kingship of Christ in the Early Church* (Stockholm, 1962), pt. 2.

29. Klauser, *Short History*, 33–37, 113–14, and *Ursprung der bischöflichen Insignien*, esp. 18 and 36 n. 33, corrected in part by H. U. Instinsky, *Bischofsstuhl und Kaiserthron* (Munich, 1955), 83–102. Also Suntrup, *Bedeutung der liturgischen Gebärden*, 154, 166–69; Cutler, *Transfigurations*, 61–63; Alföldi, *Monarchische Repräsentation*, 77–79; Neunheuser, "Gestes de la prière à genoux," 153; Lechner, *Liturgik des römischen Ritus*, 72–73; and Koskenniemi, *Studien*, 143. Given the number of Old Testament depictions of prostration; the early church's immediate

and instinctive borrowing of political terminology for addressing God; the early date at which Antiochene bishops were regarded as figures of Christ; the importance of prostration in acts of public penance that were controlled by bishops in the early church; and the currency of gestures of humility before the great (and not only before people with official rank), I find it difficult to believe that men and women did not at least occasionally and spontaneously kneel or prostrate themselves before bishops to seek their intercession. To argue that such honors were paid to bishops only late in the history of the church (they are first attested only in the sixth century) is to argue from silence and against common sense.

30. Below, 288.

31. Natalie Zemon Davis, *Fiction in the Archives: Pardon Tales and Their Tellers in Sixteenth-Century France* (Stanford, 1987), 1, 10–11, 53–77, and app. A.

32. Berbig, "Zur rechtlichen Relevanz von Ritus und Zeremoniell."

33. Overviews and orientation can be gained from the articles by Mulders, Snijders, Leclercq, Lesètre, and Fink, listed in the bibliography, as well as from the works cited in the following notes.

34. Above, n. 27; Treitinger, *Oströmische Kaiser- und Reichsidee*, 84–90; also Cutler, *Transfigurations*, 58–73, 81–88, 91–93, 101. Both works contain references to the essential earlier studies on ancient, late Roman, and Byzantine practices.

35. Bornscheuer, *Miseriae regum*.

36. P. E. Schramm, "Das Herrscherbild in der Kunst der Mittelalters," *Vorträge der Bibliothek Warburg, 1922–23* (Leipzig, 1924), pt. 1, pp. 174–77; Schramm et al., *Deutschen Kaiser und Könige*, 53; Kantorowicz, *Laudes Regiae*, 13–14, 36 and n. 89, 198; Nelson, "Ritual and Reality," 46.

37. Schmidt-Wiegand, "Gebärdensprach im mittelalterlichen Recht" and "Gebärden." Fichtenau, *Lebensordnungen*, 1:55–57, devotes not much more than a page to prostration and genuflection and appears to confuse homage and theophanic prostration. The same problem appears in Dietmar Peil's discussion of *Kommendationsgebärde* in *Gebärde bei Chrétien, Hartmann und Wolfram*, 200–203. In contrast, the brief discussion by Van Winter, "Uxorem de militari ordine sibi imparem," 122–24, correctly distinguishes between homage and "le geste du suppliant qui reçoit une faveur"; but he, too, is unaware of the frequency of the gesture and its regalian and theophanic implications. See, however, the brief but insightful discussion of "foot-falls" in Leyser, *Rule and Conflict*, 79, 95, with notes.

38. Lauer, *Règne de Louis IV*, xxix.

39. Bresslau, *Handbuch der Urkundenlehre*, 1:1–3, 2:193–200, regarded the use of petitionary and intercessory formulas in the diplomas of the Salians as a sign of increasing royal weakness, since the king's authority was now mediated by that of the princes who presented petitions on behalf of their clients—though in fact both formulas went back to the Merovingians and Carolingians, and, beyond them, to imperial rescripts. Similar arguments have been advanced by Gawlik, "Zur Bedeutung von Intervention und Petition," 73–74, and by Goetz, "Letzte 'Karolinger'?" 90–97. Gawlik further uses the formulas to substantiate his belief that some of the king's property was regarded as inalienable, for which reason distributions from it had to be specially solicited. He may be right, but the theory explains a subsidiary aspect of the ritual at the expense of its primary meaning. Hülle, "Supplikenwesen in Rechtssachen," 194–212, also interprets supplication in a narrowly legalistic fashion, without reference to the distinctive equitable justice that supplication invoked. Other studies provide information on the mechanics of presenting written and oral petitions in the Merovingian and Carolingian chanceries but say little about the liturgical models of the formulas: Classen, *Kaiserreskript und Königsurkunde*, 156–57; Sickel, *Lehre von den Urkunden*, 1:64, 67, 69–70; Lo-

thaire, xvii–xviii. Similarly *Charles II,* 2:95–97, 103–5, 154, offers an especially good guide to the use of petitions in Carolingian chanceries; but far from interpreting their meaning, the editor says that the formulas reveal "l'ossature d'une remarquable constance" (162–63). Finally, Guillot, "Actes de Henri Ier," makes several important points about the formulas' use in eleventh-century royal acts; but he says little about the meanings of the formulas, and follows tradition in seeking the diplomas' ideological content in their preambles.

40. See bibliography.

41. Treitinger, *Kaiser- und Reichsidee,* 84; Willmes, *Herrscher-"Adventus,"* 28–29, 32–33, 48, 63, 67–68, 74.

42. Willmes, *Herrscher-"Adventus,"* 11–14.

43. See Sahlins, *Islands of History.*

44. On the distinctive political structure and ideological conservatism of the province see in general Kaiser, *Bischofsherrschaft,* 535–612; Duby, *Three Orders,* 21–60; Schneidmüller, *Karolingische Tradition,* 49–60, 147–85.

45. Among numerous excellent works, see Schneider, *Brüdergemeine,* modified by Anton, "Zum politischen Konzept karolingischer Synoden"; also Magnou-Nortier, *Foi et fidélité,* 12, 16–19, 29, and chap. 4; White, "*Pactum Legem Vincit*"; Paul Ourliac, "La *convenientia,*" in *Etudes d'histoire du droit privé offertes à P. Petot* (Paris, 1959), 413–22; Pierre Bonnassie, "Les conventions féodales dans la Catalogne du XIe siècle," *Annales du Midi* 80 (1968): 529–61.

46. Magnou-Nortier, *Foi et fidélité;* Bonnassie, "Conventions féodales"; and Ourliac, "La *convenientia*"; also Martindale, "Conventum," with discussion and bibliography in Poly and Bournazel, *Mutation féodale,* 137–42.

47. Below, 110.

48. Sassier, *Hugues Capet,* 150–98; Schneidmüller, *Karolingische Tradition,* 49–60, 147–85; below, chap. 4.

49. Below, 70.

Part One. Begging Favor

1. Duby, *Trois ordres,* 79 (my translation). See also Fichtenau, *Lebensordnungen,* 1:13–49.

2. Johannes Chydenius, *Medieval Institutions and the Old Testament,* Societas Scientiarum Fennica, Commentationes Humanarum Litterarum 37/2 (Helsinki, 1965), 46–54; and Michael J. Enright, *Iona, Tara and Soissons: The Origins of the Royal Anointing Ritual* (Berlin, 1985), 5–24.

1. The Language of Petition

The citations for this chapter are not intended to be complete. I intend them only to provide some indication of the formulas' temporal and geographical range and the variety of usages, in order to demonstrate that the formulas were not rote copies of traditional models.

1. Brief discussions of petitions are provided by Sickel, *Lehre von den Urkunden,* 64–70; Bresslau, *Handbuch der Urkundenlehre,* 1:1–3, 2:193–200; Gawlik, "Zur Bedeutung von Intervention und Petition," 73–75. Neither of the two standard works on medieval French diplomatics discusses petitionary formulas: Giry, *Manuel de diplomatique*; Tessier, *Diplomatique royale française.* The editors

of French royal diplomas published by the Académie des Inscriptions et Belles-Lettres discuss them only in passing and without reference to their liturgical allusions or their corresponding political import: above, 12, with notes. The same is true of A. de Boüard, *Manuel de diplomatique* (Paris, 1929), 1:66–71, who in any case concentrates on practice at the papal curia.

2. *Lothaire*, no. 6 (955): "Nostram regiam celsitudinem adiit et ut nostra authoritate votum suum confirmaremus humiliter expetivit. Quod et nos libenter audientes et summa alacritate collaudantes, nostrae regiae praeceptionis stabili decreto constituimus atque confirmamus . . . "

3. Fichtenau, *Arenga*, 85–86; Michaud, *Grande chancellerie*, 211.

4. The phrase is taken from the coronation order of Stavelot.

5. See, e.g., *CLA* 13:22, no. 554 (629–39), 28, no. 555 (639–42), 36, no. 558 (654); 14:4, no. 573 (691–92), and 20, no. 578 (694–95); 15:3, no. 595 (751), 34, no. 602 (768), 52, no. 605 (769); 16:12, no. 621 (774–76), and 38, no. 625 (779); 17:3, no. 651 (779), and 82, no. 658 (769); 19:12, no. 672 (772), 22 no. 675 (769), 28, no. 679 (777). On the Roman and sub-Roman use of *suggere* see Classen, *Kaiserreskript und Königsurkunde*, 156–57. The limited use of petitionary phrases in authentic diplomas of the seventh and eighth centuries is corroborated by contemporary chronicles and annals but contradicted by their liberal use in contemporary letters. Resolution of this paradox will require a more extended treatment at another time.

6. There are scattered uses of *preces* and *deprecationes*, the latter becoming moderately more common in the second half of the eighth century (*CLA* 13:28, no. 556 (639–42); 15:22, no. 599 (755); 16:92, no. 637 (797)). References to *supplicationes*, more common in the eighth century, may also represent a transitional form toward the application of prayer language to a monarch, made palatable because it was consonant with late Roman usage: *CLA* 14:58, no. 588 (716); 15:46, no. 604 (768), 56, no. 606 (769), 94, no. 616 (775). The lavish formula found in MGH Dipl. Karol. 1:20–21, no. 15 (762), is clearly interpolated, as the editor shows. Only with no. 207 (808) does *deprecatio* come to be an ordinary term for the petition, regularly supplemented by *obsecratio* and *prex*.

7. *St-Maur*, 369, no. 26 (Guillot, Cat., C 129 [1040–52]), an act of Geoffrey Martel: "Si peticionibus servorum Dei . . . benigno favore annuimus, regiam consuetudinem frequentamus."

8. *St-Père*, 1:75–76 (– 996): "quaedam a nostra mansuetudine exposcens"; Fleury, nos. 74 (1035): "postulavit nostre serenitatis humilitatem," 94 (1088): "nostram humiliter clementiam deprecantes"; Gousset, *Actes*, 2:87–88 (1076): "praesentiam serenitatis nostra humiliter adiit, obnixe postulando deprecans et precando postulans"; Lasteyrie, *Cartulaire général*, vol. 1, nos. 70 (995), 74 (c. 1005): "nostram serenitatem adierunt, humiliter deprecantes"; *Montierender*, nos. 15 (971): "venerunt ad nos obsecrantes similiter mansuetudinem nostram," 34 (1050): "ad nos venit, supplicans mansuetudine nostre"; *Autun*, vol. 1, nos. 36 (972): "advenerunt ante celsitudinem nostram," 38 (954): "adierunt conspectum nostrum . . . precantes serenitatem nostram"; *St-Etienne*, no. 36 (934): "Qui nostram adiens maiestatem, humiliter deprecatus est," and similarly nos. 44 (mid–tenth century), 55 (1006), etc.; *Cluny*, vol. 1, no. 274 (926): "adiit nostram serenitatem Adso, . . . qui innotuit nostre clementie quod . . ."; vol. 2, no. 1537 (980): "adiit nostre munificentie serenitatem . . . deprecans"; vol. 3, no. 1991 (c. 1025–31): "adierunt . . . ejus magnificentiam . . . humiliter ejus intimantes celsitudini"; vol. 4, no. 2962 (1046): "imploravit nostram clemenciam." See also *St-Vincent*, nos. 27 (968–71), 40 (885–927), 265 (971–77), 395 (968–71), 396 (952), 397 (907), 401 (937–54), 415 (c. 939), 478 (968–71); *St-Aubin*, 1:372–75 (c. 1100); Quantin, *Cartulaire général*, 73–74 (938, 968).

9. BN, Coll. Baluze 75, ff. 54–55 (1067): "postulauerat . . . nostrae paternitatis . . . diligenti precum instantia"; *Redon*, no. 285 (1062): "abbas postulavit benivolentiam nostre parvitatis"; *ND Chartres*, no. 22 (1095): "parvitatem nostram humiliter adierunt, petentes"; *Nouaillé*, no. 56 (943–52): "accedens venit ad nostram pietatem; precatus est nos"; *Dipl. Belg.*, vol. 1, no. 157 (1064): "nostram adierunt mediocritatem," "at nos hanc petitionem iusta ratione uigere considerantes"; *Autun*, vol. 1, nos. 31 (938): "viscera pietatis nostra pulsaverit," 47 (906): "adierunt praesentiam nostram . . . innotescentes paternitati nostrae"; *St-Etienne*, 33–34, no. 18 (904): "Si iustis et rationabilibus nostre indignitati comissorum petitionibus aures mediocritatis nostre libenter accomodamus"; *Cluny*, vol. 2, no. 1553 (981): "aggressus est genua pietatis ejus . . . deprecans" (and similiarly vol. 3, no. 2721 [1019?]); *St-Vincent*, nos. 9 [c. 949], 22 [c. 948]); *St-Aubin*, vol. 1, nos. 35–37 (972): "adierunt humilitatis nostre presentiam . . . satis suppliciter postulantes"; Gousset, *Actes*, 2:204 (1018): "adiit humilitatem et praesentiam nostram . . . obsecransque humiliter ut . . ." For *paternitas* see also *St-Vincent*, nos. 254 (968–71), 296 (937–54), 403 (864–72), 407 (864–73); *St-Aubin*, vol. 1, nos. 32–33 (966); Poupardin, *Recueil des chartes . . . de Saint-Vincent de Laon*, 20. For *humilitas* or *parvitas*, *St-Père*, 1:244–45 (1084); *Angers*, no. 47 (1047–55); Gousset, *Actes*, 2:58–59, 98–99 (1039, 1089); *Chronique . . . de Mouzon*, 192–96, docs. 5–6 (1018, 1024–25); AN, LL 158, p. 261 (St-Denis); Kurth, *Chartes de . . . Saint-Hubert-en-Ardennes*, 53.

10. *St-Cyprien*, no. 251 (c. 936–54): "ad nostram accedens mansuetudinem, deprecatus est nos"; *Nouaillé*, no. 68 (970–73): "accessit ad nostram sublimitatem . . . deprecat nos," and similarly no. 96 (1004–7); *St-Maixent*, no. 85 (1011–26): "accessit ad nostram magnificentiam . . . , deprecati sunt," and similarly no. 89 (997–1031); BN, ms. lat. 17761, f. 52 (Corbie, 1061–63): "quod quidam homo . . . nostram mansuetudinem adiit, deprecans nos." The canons of Macon once styled themselves *serenitas*: *St-Vincent*, no. 280 (928–36). Epithets of humility: *St-Amand*, vol. 1, no. clii, f. 160 (1134): "nostram sincere intentione rogaueret humilitatem quatinus pro dei amore et pro sua sana petitione . . . benigne concederemus"; BN, Coll. Moreau 21, f. 251r-v (Fécamp, 1028–79): "ad humilitatem nostram homo quidam cum uxore sua . . . venit petentes ut concederemus eis terram. . . . Quorum preces suscipientes . . . concedimus eis . . ."; *St-Père*, 1:169–70 (986) (with canons): "nostrae devotionis unanimem consensum suppliciter deprecans"; *Nouaillé*, no. 58 (953–56): "ad nostram accedens paternitatem, deprecatus est nos"; *Cluny*, vol. 3, no. 2014 (1030–40): "adiit presentiam nostre humilitatis, suppliciter deprecans." The canons of St-Etienne of Dijon were especially fond of such formulas; e.g., *St-Etienne*, 44, no. 26 (early tenth century): "veniens . . . ante nostros obtus, humiliter deprecatus est nostram serenitatem ac benignissimam fraternitatem," 67–68, no. 45 (972): "pervenit ad aures nostre pietatis, humillima precatio," 73–74, no. 50 (990): "humiliter explorans nostram piissimam benevolentiam," and similarly nos. 40 (944), 49 (977), 50 (990), 51 (998), etc.

11. See Hallam, *Capetian France*, 13–17, 30–34.

12. Kienast, *Herzogstitel*, 355–57; Wolfram, *Intitulatio I*, 213–17; Brunner, "Fränkische Fürstentitel," 203–6.

13. Dukes of Brittany: *Redon*, nos. 240 (860): "adiit . . . abbas . . . clementiam nostram postulans," 241 (869): "nostram adierit presenciam . . . petiit." See also the charter, no less interesting for being highly suspect, by Alan and Egius, "Brittanorum monarchi," in *St-Florent*, ff. 66–61 (n.d. 1014–22?): "aurem libenter accomodamus eorumque iustas et rationabiles petitiones ac postulationes," "nostram deprecatus est magnificentiam."

Dukes of Normandy: Fauroux, nos. 12 (1009): "quia accerssierit [sic] nostram almitatem contio . . . exposcens," 20 (1010–17): "clementiam nostram expetierit," 23

(1013–20): "adiit sublimitatis nostram dignitatem, supliciter [sic] deprecans." These and other examples are discussed in detail in chaps. 6 and 8.

Dukes of Aquitaine (houses of both Auvergne and Poitou): Doniol, *Cartulaire de Brioude*, nos. 51 (909): "justis fidelium virorum petitionibus aurem saerenitatis nostrae accomodaverimus," "quia veniens quidam sacerdos fidelis noster . . . humiliter expetiit," 66 (918): "si justis petitionibus fidelium nostrorum aurem accomodamus," "adiit serenitatem nostram . . . proclamans"; St-Florent, f. 26r–v (994): "adiit nos fidelis noster Aymericus toarcensium uice comes cum multa deprecatione et humili supplicatione"; St-Hilaire, nos. 18 (941–42): "accessit . . . peciit a nobis scilicet nostram magnificentiam," 20 (942): "ad nostram accedens mansuetudinem, deprecati sunt," 25 (957): "accessit ad nostram presentiam et magnificentiam, deprecatus est," 26 (c. 957): "accessit ad nostram sublimitatem . . . subtiliter obsecrans ut . . . ," 92 (1078–86): "nostram deprecati sunt clementiam." After 957, ducal acts for St-Hilaire usually omit the attributes of exaltation and humility and simply write of the accession and entreaty; e.g., "accedens ante nostram presentiam N., deprecatus est nos ut . . ." For similar petitions apostrophizing the duke as *sublimitas, magnificentia,* or *celsitudinis,* see St-Maixent, nos. 14 (939), 17 (948), 27 (951–63), 37 (968); Nouaillé, no. 40 (917–22).

Dukes of Burgundy: *Autun,* 1:85–86 (887–96): "cujus munificentiam humili prece precantes [nos, episcopus], obtinuimus"; 2:5–7 (1079–86): "nostram adierunt presentiam . . . obnixe postulantes ut . . . Placuit itaque sublimitati nostrae eorum saluberrimis adquiescere postulationibus"; St-Bénigne, 2:87, no. 310 (1031–46), 95, no. 315 (1034–39), 117, no. 338 (1054), 126, no. 347 (1076–77); St-Etienne, 18, no. 15 (c. 1103).

Dukes of Francia: see below, nn. 62–63; and also *RHF* 9:722–23 (942): "accessit . . . ad nostri culminis magnitudinem, humiliter postulans, ac omnimodis deprecans."

14. *Robert Ier,* nos. 41 (899), 43 (900).

15. Examples from the Vermandois and Ponthieu are discussed later in this chapter. For examples from Flanders and Valois, see chaps. 5 and 8. Other instances are so numerous that only a few of the fuller formulas can be listed.

For Anjou: Fulk Nerra: *St-Jouin,* 19 (Guillot, Cat., C 64 [1006–39]): "quia accedens quidam abbas . . . ad nostram mansuetudinem peciit ut . . ." Geoffrey Martel: *GC* 7:Instr. 222 (Guillot, Cat., C 206 [1046–60]): "quod accedentes ad praesentiam meam canonici . . . humiliter deprecanti sunt. . . . Quorum postulationem humiliter et libenter suscipiens. . . ." Fulk le Réchin: *St-Maur,* no. 23 (Guillot, Cat., C 363 [1090]), speaking of *nostre dignitatis celsitudinem* in the preamble: "Ubi dum in claustris monasterii cum nobilibus viris . . . residerem, pars monachorum ejusdem loci nos circumstetit, obnixe deprecancium. . . . Eorum igitur piis peticionibus adquiescens . . . "; Angers, no. 57 (Guillot, Cat., C 382 [1093]): "adierunt serenitatem meam canonici . . . postulantes." These acts are discussed in chap. 8.

Blois/Chartres: *Montierender,* 135, no. 15 (Herbert the Old [968]): "ante presentiam nostram venerunt, et causas sue necessitatis humiliter intimaverunt, reclamationem facientes. . . . Petitione eorum libenter adsensum dedimus," 166, no. 39 (– 1057): "Abbas . . . obnixis precibus me accersivit," "petierunt . . . atque supplici voto coegerunt me ut . . . "; Ronceray, 113–14, no. 170 (Theobald I [1037–46]; see Guillot, *Comte d'Anjou,* 1:204 n. 34): "[praesentiam meam] adiit . . . comitissa, humiliter deprecans uti . . . "; ND Chartres, nos. 18 (Theobald [1084]): "venit ad me . . . humiliter postulans ut . . . Precibus . . . dissentire indignum duxi," 24 (Stephen [1100–1101]): "presentiam nostram adiit, et a nobis obnixe postulavit. Nos igitur tanti viri peticionem dignam frustrari indignum esse judicantes . . . liberam reddimus"; St-Père, 1:74 (Odo I [986]): "adiit praesentiam nostram vir nobilis . . . manifestans nobis. . . . Quorum [viri ac monachi] petitionem rationabilem considerans . . .

assensum dedi," 295 (Stephen and Adele [1089–1101]): "adiit presentiam nostram Eustachius, abbas . . . , benignissime nos interpellans. . . . Quod, quia petitio ejus justa et idonea apud nos videbatur esse, libenti acquievimus"; Lex, doc. 1 (983), in which Odo I speaks of his need to *clementer augere* the property of the churches of God whose servants *Dei exposcunt clementiam*; also doc. 6 (996): "accedens Deo amabilis Pictavorum comitissa Emma, ante presentiam venerabilis comitissae Berthae, humiliter deprecata est. . . . Cujus petitionem . . . congrua devocione suscipiens . . . assensu praebuit"; and doc. 26 (1034–37): "Qui [monachus, missus abbatis Majoris Monasterii] cum apud ipsum gloriosissimum comitem [Odonem] precem . . . fudisset, sine mora quod petebat, benignissime indulsit."

Burgundy: *St-Vincent*, nos. 71 (937–62): "domnus Maimbodus antistes cum collegio . . . serenitatem domni Leutaldi, imperatorii comitis, ut . . . justitiam faceret humillime expetiit," 103 (958): "unde alloquens domnum Hugonem marchionem insignem ac domnum Leotaldum piissimum comitem . . . deprecatus est [episcopus] serenitatem eorum," 157 (c. 955): "serenitatem domni Leotaldi adiit [episcopus] . . . justitiam faceret humillime expetiit"; *Cluny*, vol. 1, nos. 729 (948–49): "abbas Maiolus humiliter expetiit comitem Leotbaldum et Richildem, conjugem ejus. . . . Hanc igitur petitionem considerans Leotbaldus comes justem esse, verpivit . . . omnem servitium," 738 (949): "Precatus est autem prefatus monachus . . . magnitudinem principum [i.e., comitum Ugonis et Gisleberti], ut . . . confirmarent." See also *Cluny*, vol. 2, nos. 1094, 1662; vol. 3, nos. 2277, 2719; vol. 4, nos. 2852, 3388, 3391.

Miscellaneous examples: *St-Etienne*, 58, no. 38 (count of Autun [934]); Quantin, *Cartulaire général*, 159–60, no. 83 (count of Auxerre [1002], though the formula is truncated to a simple mention of supplication), and 178–79, no. 93 (count of Joigny [1042]); *St-Bénigne*, 2:78, no. 295 (count of Bolenois? [1030]); *Jumièges*, 60–63, no. 19 (count of Evreux [1038–39]); *Ronceray*, 257–59, nos. 421–22 (count of Nantes [c. 1040]); Métais, *Saint-Denis de Nogent*, 238, no. 118 (count of Perche [c. 1078]); Fauroux, no. 92 (count of Evreux [1038]); Wauters, "Exploration des chartes et des cartulaires belges," 182–84, no. 4 (count of Hainaut [1092–96]); St-Florent, f. 82 (count of Brittany [1136]); Müller, *Cartulaire . . . de Saint-Leu d'Esserent*, no. 21 (count of Clermont [c. 1119]); St-Thierry, ff. 80–81v (count of Roucy [1147]).

16. Teudo, viscount of Paris: Lasteyrie, *Cartulaire général*, vol. 1, no. 62 (925). Viscounts of Chartres: *St-Père*, 1:90 (–996), 159 (–1070): "adierant meam presentiam . . . monachi, deprecantes ut. . . ." Also *St-Cyprien*, no. 583 (Geoffrey, viscount of Thouars [1015–58]): "per deprecationem Ramnulfi militis et Aienoris uxoris sue, concessit"; and *GC* 2:Instr. 334 (Hubert, viscount of Thouars [1098]): "adhortans me multis et rationabilibus supplicationibus." St-Florent, f. 130r–v (Rodulf, viscount of Le Mans, with his wife and sons [c. 1020]): "pro deprecationem cujusdam militis nostri . . . condonamus." Lex, doc. 7 (996–1001), provides a formal petition to Hugh, viscount of Châteaudun; but he also styles himself "Sancti Mauricii decanus, favente Dei gratia," and the liturgical supplication may have reflected that office. On the other hand, this is yet another sign of the high status of this family and of the tendency to mingle spiritual and temporal attributes, as discussed below. See also *St-Père*, 1:240 (1096) and *St-Maixent*, no. 87 (1029), where petitions to viscounts are mentioned in an act of the abbot and in a notice.

17. *St-Père*, 1:87 (–996); Boussard, "Droit de *vicaria*" ("Hubert, miles, de castro Salmuro" [1008–12]): "quoniam accessit ad nostram presenciam venerabilis abba . . . humili prece deposcens"; *Cluny*, vol. 2, no. 1297 ("Hugo, miles" [971]): "nostre adiit presenciam humanitatis, humiliter exorans nobis, ut . . ."; *Angers*, nos. 18 (Robert, who holds a benefice from the chapter [970]): "quia postulavit me quidam vassallus . . . ut concederem," and 21 (Griferius, vassal of St-Maurice [969]): "quia postulavit me quidam levita, ut . . . concederem"; *Livre des serfs*, no. 122 (980–

1022): "Marannus, gratia Dei miles . . . quoniam adiid [sic] presentiam meam quidam fidelis meus . . . deprecans ut concederem. . . . Cujus deprecatione benigne suscipiens, concessi."

18. K. F. Werner, "Quelques observations au sujet des débuts du 'duché' de Normandie," in *Droit privé et institutions régionales: Etudes historiques offertes à Jean Yver* (Paris, 1976), 691–709, and *"Missus—Marchio—Comes*: Entre l'administration centrale et l'administration locale de l'Empire carolingien," in *Histoire comparée de l'administration*, 191–239. See also Brunner, "Fränkische Fürstentitel," 179–340.

19. Thomas Bisson, *Conservation of the Coinage* (Oxford, 1979), 3–4.

20. Bedos, "Signes et insignes du pouvoir," 55–56; Guillot, *Comte d'Anjou*, 2:10–12, with pls. XX and XXI.

21. Werner, *"Missus—Marchio—Comes"* (above, n. 18); Nelson, "Dispute Settlement in Carolingian West Francia," in *The Settlement of Disputes in Early Medieval Europe*, ed. Wendy Davies and Paul Fouracre, 45–64 (Cambridge, 1986), and "Lord's Anointed."

22. MGH Formulae, *Formulae Salzburgenses*, 454, no. 64: "et in gratia vestra fideliter permanere valeant."

23. Ibid., *Formulae Salicae merkelianae*, 259, no. 51: "Taliter exinde certamen age, qualiter gratia nostra vellis habere." These last two examples were already noted by Ganshof, "La *gratia* des monarques francs," *Annuario de Estudios Medievales* 3 (1966): 7–28 at 16 n. 38.

24. MGH Formulae, 116, nos. 4 and 5, noted by Tessier, "A propos de quelques actes toulousains," 568 and n. 3.

25. The epithets are consistent with the tone of the letters as a whole and with the tone of letters actually sent in the early ninth century, as discussed shortly.

26. MGH Formulae, *Formulae Andecavenses*, nos. 1a and b, 48, 52 (administrators), 32 (counts). On the urban administration of the period as it appears in this formulary see Werner Bergmann, "Die *Formulae Andecavenses*, eine Formelsammlung auf der Grenze zwischen Antike und Mittelalter," *Archiv für Diplomatik* 245 (1978): 1–53.

27. Gregory of Tours, *Decem Libri Historiarum*, 1.1. Supplications of kings and/or queens (which include supplications offered by beggars, bishops, royal princes, dukes, and criminals): 119, 122, 303, 391–92, 433; of bishops (including a prostrate entreaty by Chilperic himself): 122, 259; of an abbot by a warrior (though the supplication is made more to the abbot as a holy man than as minister of the church): 87; of a count by a criminal condemned to death: 278; of a *minor* by a bishop: 110.

28. MGH Epist. 1:476–79, no. 2 (740). See also 476–77, no. 1, and esp. 296–97, no. 48, addressed by Boniface to Charles's son Gripo: "Obsecro et adiuro pietatem vestram . . . ut . . . adiuvare studeas servos Dei."

29. MGH Formulae, *Marculfi formulae*, 2.39, 40, 47; *Formulae marculfinae*, nos. 1, 3, 6, 10; *Formulae Salzburgenses*, nos. 6, 9, 16, 21.

30. Ibid., *Formulae Salzburgenses*, 454, no. 64: "Rogamus humiliter prudentiam vestram, ut . . . indulgentiam mereantur apud vestram suscipere clementiam. . . . Obnixa prece deposcimus, ut nostro rogatui annuere atque consentire faciatis." For other petitions to counts: *Marculfi formulae*, 2.41, 50; *Formulae marculfinae*, nos. 4, 21; *Formulae Salburgenses*, nos. 37, 38; *Formulae Pataviensis*, no. 2.

31. *Capitularia Aquisgranensia* (825), MGH Capit. 2:243, c. 3: "ut unusquisque vestrum in suo loco et ordine partem nostri ministerii habere cognoscatur." Also 244, c. 8: "ut memores sitis fidei nobis promissae, et in parte ministerii nostri vobis commissi."

32. E.g., MGH Epist. 5:113, no. 10 (830?), 118, no. 15 (830), 122, no. 25 (833), 126–27, nos. 33–34 (c. 834, 833–34), 182, no. 7 (826–27), 300–302, no. 2 (c. 815), 309–10, no. 7 (823), 324–25, no. 18 (834), 503–4, no. 49 (854–55); 6:52–53, no. 45 (845), 179–80, no. 25/ii (860–70).

33. Ibid., 5:125–26, no. 32 (c. 833), 127–28, no. 34 (833–34), 129, no. 39 (816–36), 131, no. 42 (822–40), 132, no. 44 (826–40).

34. Ibid., 109, no. 1 (c. 823): "Obsecro dilectionem tuam, ut non graviter, sed potius misericorditer et amicabiliter accipere digneris, quod apud te pro necessitate N., quondam hominis nostri . . . intercedo, ut eum beneficium . . . sub qualicumque censu tibi placuit, habere permittas." See also 118, no. 16 (830), addressed to a bishop: "tamen interim parvitatem meam tue karitati ac per te illius pietati commendo, ac deprecor, ut . . ."

35. Ibid., 6:285, no. 13 (828–29). Though long, the letter deserves to be quoted extensively, since it demonstrates that far from applying received formulas, petitioners used considerable ingenuity in finding striking new phrases of adulation: "Excellentissime veneracionis honore dignissimo Hilduino domino vere sanctissimo senonicae plebis humillima devotio . . . salutem. Quia divina inspirante misericordia fastidiose inportunitatis nostrae clamoribus, mi domine, saepe compati dignati estis, idcirco etiam nunc nimia compulsi necessitate vestra celsitudinis aures inquietare praesumpsimus. Novimus etenim, reverentisime [sic] domine, quomodo prioribus peticionibus nostris benigne et misericorditer adsistere dignati estis. . . . Sed quoniam peccatis nostris . . . exigentibus vota et desideria, quibus sanctitatem vestram totiaes pulsare ausi sumus, plurimum impedita ad effectum pervenire non meruerunt, idcirco . . . ad vos causas miseriae nostrae referre compulsi sumus. . . . Propterea vestra pietatis vestigiis animo provoluti flebiliter postulamus, ut tamdiu rem suspendere dignemini, quousque cum scripto homine ad vestram celsitudinem properantes, ipsi vobis melius nostram pandamus miseriam. . . . His ita claemenciae vestrae suggestis . . . oramus supernam misericordiam, ut multimodo vos prosperitate valere concedat. . . ." This letter may be compared with the only marginally less florid petitions that the same writers addressed to Einhard and Empress Judith (ibid., 286–89).

36. Ibid., 5:112, nos. 6–7 (–830?, 828–30?), 119, no. 18 (830), 124, no. 29 (c. 833), 133, nos. 46–47 (828–40).

37. Ibid., 201, no. 109 (c. 818–28), 337, no. 22 (c. 836), 144, no. 70 (n.d.).

38. Tessier, "A propos de quelques actes toulousains." Good examples are Fleury, no. 27 (876), and Coussemaker, *Cartulaire de . . . Cysoing*, 1, no. 1 (867).

39. See the donations of the bishops of Cambrai to St-Sépulcre (Cambrai, Bm, ms. 1222, ff. 8v–9) and Notre-Dame of Cambrai (BN, ms. lat. 10968, ff. 32–33); also the discussion of Angevin diplomatics below, chap. 8. The formulas are similarly missing from royal acts, such as RHF 10:621, in which Robert and Constance give, "humbly and with devotion," rights to St-Corneille for the good of their souls and in memory of their recently deceased son. For foundations and reforms, *Dipl. Belg.*, vol. 1, no. 53; *Vendôme*, vol. 1, no. 35; *RHF* 10:605; Cambrai, Bm, ms. 1222, ff. 1–2v; *Chronique . . . de Mouzon*, doc. 2, pp. 180–85. Purely administrative acts were also often nonpetitionary: St-Remi, A, ff. 911r–v, 309r–v.

40. Robert Fossier, "Sur les principautés médiévales particulièrement en France," in *Principautés au Moyen Age*, 9–17 at 11–12. Most diplomatists reserve the term "diploma" for royal acts, an overly narrow usage that slights the regalian nature of princely acts in this period. There are obviously differences between a true diploma with monogram, chancery subscription, and seal; a princely act without these signs of validation, perhaps with witnesses, but with all the other regalian formulas; and a charter issued by a prince recording a private act of devotion and

using few if any regalian formulas. The fact that these differences were respected is what makes us know that contemporaries took protocol seriously. But it is equally obvious that the form of these acts lies on a continuum, and that the princely *auctoritas* is no mere *Privaturkunde*.

41. E.g., MGH Formulae, *Marculfi formulae*, 2:31; *Formulae Turonenses*, nos. 2, 13, 43; *Cartae Senonicae*, nos. 3, 4, 13, 24, 48, 50.

42. MGH Epist. 5:133–34, no. 48 (828–40). Cf. 111, no. 5 (–830): "notum sit, quia volumus, ut homines aliquos mittas ad Aquis," "sicut te facere praecipimus"; 113, no. 9 (828–30?), a chastizing letter ending "si tibi de gratia nostra ulla cura sit, rogamus, ut negligentiam tuam emendare studeas et nos cito certos efficias, quid de te sperare debemus"; 122–23, no. 26 (833), a letter to a priest and a *vicedominus*: "Notum sit vobis, quia volumus, ut eulogias preparari faciatis."

43. Lasteyrie, *Cartulaire général*, vol. 1, no. 62 (925). Note, however, that it was also about this time that the viscount of Angers took the title of count, a fact that Sassier, *Hugues Capet*, 90–91, sees as a sign of an incipient diffusion of power in the Robertian principality.

44. *St-Père*, 1:74 (986), 90 (–996), 240 (1096), all relating to the family of the viscounts of Chartres.

45. E.g., Lex, doc. 20 (1023–37); *St-Père*, 1:122–23 (–1070), 458–59 (c. 1090); *Angers*, nos. 18 (970), 21 (969); Marchegay, *Chartes mancelles de . . . Saint-Florent*, no. 4 (c. 1040–50).

46. *Angély*, no. 126 (c. 1080). Similarly *Vendôme*, vol. 1, no. 197; Chevalier, *Cartulaire . . . de Noyers*, 39–40, no. 34 (c. 1064); MGH Formulae, *Formulae Turonenses*, app. 165; *Ronceray*, 221, no. 362 (a brother acting "precibus suarum sororum" [c. 1075]).

47. *Redon*, no. 116 (834).

48. *Angers*, no. 18 (970); *St-Aubin*, 1:363 (c. 1090); *Livre des serfs*, no. 122 (980–1032). Also *Cluny*, vol. 2, no. 1297 (971); vol. 4, nos. 3246 (1049–1109), 3472 (1074, the petition of a castellan); Marchegay, *Chartes mancelles de . . . Saint-Florent*, no. 4 (c. 1040–50).

49. Beseeching wives: *St-Père*, 1:165–66 (–1080); *Angély*, no. 126 (c. 1080). Beseeching in-laws: *St-Père*, 1:152–53 (1060). Beseeching brothers and cousins: *St-Père*, 1:166–67 (1061); *Redon*, no. 192 (826–40); *Angély*, no. 87 (1095–1103); *St-Cyprien*, no. 195 (c. 1080); *St-Aubin*, 1:375 (1060–67). See Chevalier, *Cartulaire . . . de Noyers*, 24–26, no. 20 (1061?), a notice in which a lord consents to a donation at the "prayers" of his father and his father's wife.

50. Fleury, no. 51 (956), discussed below, chap. 3; Lex, doc. 6 (996), in which the countess of Poitiers beseeches the countess of Blois: "accedens . . . comitissa Emma, ante presentiam venerabilis comitissae Berthae, humiliter deprecata est quatinus. . . ."

51. *St-Père*, 1:148–51 (–1070), 152–53 (1060).

52. *Jumièges*, no. 28 (1056–67): "ad meam humilitatem dirigere, poscens." On Peter's family see *Pontoise*, 270–71.

53. *St.-Père*, 1:74 (986), 90 (1096), 159 (–1070), 240 (1096). On the family see Chédeville, *Chartres*, 258–59; Boussard, "L'origine des familles seigneuriales," 311–14.

54. Wendy Davies, *Small Worlds: The Village Community in Early Medieval Brittany* (Berkeley, 1988), 63–67, 91–104, 138–42, and chap. 7, and "On the Distribution of Political Power in Brittany in the Mid-ninth Century," in *Charles the Bald: Court and Kingdom*, ed. Margaret Gibson and Janet Nelson, British Archaeological Reports, International Series 101 (1981): 87–107; J. G. T. Sheringham, "Les machtierns," *Mémoires de la Société d'histoire et d'archéologie de Bretagne* 58 (1981):61–71. On the relatively high status of priests in ninth-century Brittany

which accounts for their being petitioned as *viri magnifici*, see Wendy Davies, "Rural Priests in East Brittany in the Ninth Century," *Etudes Celtiques* 20 (1983):177–97. Davies has increasingly emphasized the derivative nature of the Redon charters, whose language is clearly modeled on formularies from Angers or Tours (Davies, *Small Worlds*, 137–38, and "Forgery in the *Cartulaire de Redon*," in *Fälschungen im Mittelalter*, 265–74). But Redon's cartulary also reveals a more active community life, a more active peasantry, and a less rigidly hierarchized elite than do sources from Francia. The question here is not whether the words of East Breton charters derive from West Frankish formularies but whether the protocol for applying the formulas does so.

55. *Redon*, no. 192 (826–40).

56. Ibid., nos. 116 (834), 162 (854), 133 (826).

57. Duke, counts, bishops: ibid., nos. 23 (859), 72 (859), 240 (868), 241 (869), 274 (913), 285 (1062), 296 (1026), 302 (–1052), 309 (1081–82), 323 (c. 1019), 341 (1108), 356 (1021), 373 (1037). Machtierns, castellans, nobles: ibid., nos. 1 (832: an entreaty of a machtiern by the future abbot of Redon to give the land on which the abbey would be sited), 190 (863: an entreaty by the abbot of a woman highly placed enough to have later been adopted by Duke Salomon [82]), 314 (1100: a request humbly offered to a *dominus terrae* by the abbot), 373 (1037, on which see below). Abbot, monks: ibid., nos. 284 (1051–60), 373 (1037), 385 (–1050).

58. Ibid., no. 314 (1100): "ipse enim Fredorius monachis nichil horum antea concesserat," "militem sedavit [abbas] et cum humilitate ab ipso requisivit."

59. Ibid., no. 373 (1037).

60. See the insightful comment of Timothy Reuter on the use of *topoi* in chronicles of this period: "The majority of these writers had probably never heard of a *topos*; what they used were clichés and formulae, and these, unlike *topoi*, which have a literary function, are used to make the description of reality easier" ("Plunder and Tribute," 76).

61. Richard Trexler remarked on a similar phenomenon in Renaissance Florence: when two nobles of roughly equal status greeted each other, each proclaimed his inferiority to the other, in contrast to the openly patronizing air they would have assumed in greeting a member of a lower order (*Public Life in Renaissance Florence*, 108–10).

62. *Robert Ier*, 174, no. 45 (904): "Quapropter nos, in Dei nomine, Rotbertus, gregis incliti confessoris Christi beati Martini necnon et rerum abba . . . quoniam accessit ad nostri regiminis familiaritatem quidam venerabilis vassallus . . . et uxor ejus . . . postulantes suppliciter charitatem nostram ut . . . Quorum petitionem . . . concessimus." Similarly no. 43 (900): "Nos igitur . . . Rotbertus, rerum basilicae incliti confessoris Christi beati Martini ejusque etiam cleri abbas sed et comes . . . quoniam accessit ad nostrae paternitatis consilium quidam nobilis vassallus fidelis noster . . . , simulque deprecabantur quatinus . . . concederemus . . ."

63. Ibid., no. 43; also nos. 41 (899): "Nos siquidem Rotbertus, gratia ejusdem omnipotentis Dei, gregis sancti Martini abbas sed et comes . . . quoniam accessit ad nostrae paternitatis ac pietatis mercedem idem grex . . . humiliter ac lacrimabiliter reclamans et dicens . . ."; 39 (895): "Ego Rotbertus, gratia Dei, inclitae congregationis egregii patris beati Martini abbas. Notum . . . qualiter quidam humilis diaconus ejusdem congregationis . . . petiit mercedis nostrae benivolentiam, ut beneficiolum quoddam ei concedere dignaremur"; 40 (897): "Ego, in nomine summi Salvatoris Dei, Rotbertus, misericordia Dei comes et abbas inclitae congregationis Beati Martini . . . rei veritatem cognoscentes et saepissima eorumdem clericorum deprecatione tacti, jussimus praeceptum saepius ante nos recitare, et . . . nostra mercede studuimus tractare."

64. Brunner, "Fränkische Fürstentitel," 198–203, 278–79.

65. *Dipl. Belg.*, 1:144, no. 53, discussed by Dunbabin, *France in the Making*, 49–50, and "Maccabees as Exemplars," 36–38.

66. For William the Pious, Doniol, *Cartulaire de Brioude*, nos. 51, 228; for William Towhead, *St-Hilaire*, nos. 18, 23, 25, 26; for Robert, above, nn. 62-63. On the use of the title see Kienast, *Herzogstitel*, passim.

67. Kienast, *Herzogstitel*, 196–98.

68. Brunner, "Fränkische Fürstentitel," 249, 265, 268; Jacques Brejon de Lavergnée, "Le royaume de Bretagne," and Hubert Guillotel, "Le premier siècle du pouvoir ducal breton (936–1040)," both in *Principautés au Moyen Age*, 58–59, 79.

69. Brunner, "Fränkische Fürstentitel," 197–98; also 182–83, 187–88, 278–79.

70. See below, chap. 8.

71. Clamors and liturgical *querimoniae* (see below, chap. 7) have been included as petitions. Citations for Fleury, Homblières, Montierender, St-Amand, St-Florent, and St-Etienne are given in the list of abbreviations under these names. For Fécamp see BN, Coll. Moreau 21, ff. 20v–31v; 28, f. 192r–v; 30, ff. 190r–91; 40, f. 220r–v; 341, ff. 171r–v, 281; and Emily Zack Tabuteau, *Transfers of Property in Eleventh-Century Norman Law* (Chapel Hill, N.C., 1988), 266–67; also Fauroux, nos. 31, 34, 35, 70, 71, 85, 87, 94. Few originals or even medieval cartulary copies from St-Quentin and St-Quentin-en-l'Ile survive; but most charters have been transmitted by antiquarians and published in one place or another, the principal collections being Colliette, *Mémoires*, vols. 1 and 2, and Hémeré, *Augusta Viromanduorum*, "Regestum." The acts of Sint-Pieters, found in Van Lokeren, *Chartes . . . de Saint-Pierre*, and in *Dipl. Belg.*, vol. 1, pose particular problems because of the number of forgeries and interpolations. But the outright forgeries have been excluded, and the interpolations do not affect the diplomatic form of the charters, as argued below, chap. 5, n. 15.

72. The following figures give royal, comital, papal, episcopal, and capitular petitions as a ratio of all petitions found in the charters. From *St-Maixent*, 900–949: 3/3 (including 2 comital); 950–99: 8/9 (including 4 comital); 1000–1049: 8/10 (including 1 comital); 1050–99: 14/15 (including 7 comital). From *Redon*, ninth century: 11/17; 900–949: 2/2; 950–99: 1/1; 1000–1049: 11/12; 1050–99: 8/9.

73. Above, n. 16.

74. E.g., *Dipl. Belg.*, vol. 1, no. 70 (982–83), by one Bernard, confirming the desire of one of his serfs to be given to Sint-Pieters, Ghent, "secundum petitionem et uoluntatem ipsius." Also Delaville le Roulx, *Notices sur les chartes originales*, no. 15 (999); *Livre des serfs*, no. 122 (1015–32); *Vendôme*, vol. 1, nos. 8 (1032–34), 82 (1044–49); *St-Aubin*, 2:304 (998–1001); *St-Maur*, no. 40 (c. 1090); *St-Père*, 1:87 (–996), 144 (–1070), 144–45 (–1080), 238–39 (–1091), 458–59 (c. 1090); Lex, doc. 10 (1009–12); *Cluny*, vol. 1, no. 854 (953); vol. 2, no. 1297 (971); vol. 4, no. 3246 (1049–1109).

75. Above, nn. 58–59. The petition to Gurk is also contrasted with the subsequent formal, liturgical supplication of Gurk and the abbot to the duke: "Qui cum ante comitem venissent, illumque salutassent, comes honorifice eos resalutavit et accuratissime suscepit. Deinde venerabilis abbas et sepefatus vir, erigentes se cum magna mansuetudine, peticionem quam querebant comiti suisque baronibus notificaverunt; petierunt namque quatinus comes . . . prefatam insulam . . . tribueret et concederet." See also St-Remi, B, 45–46 (1089), in which the vidame of Reims finally yields to a request from the abbot of St-Remi on the insistence of his uncle the archbishop, whose prayer contained a threat: "prece et imperio auunculi sui . . . ad ultimum consensit."

76. Above, n. 52.

77. Formal clamors and *querimoniae* have been included as petitions (see below, chap. 7), as have charters that refer to any sort of postulation. However, the most abbreviated petitions (referring simply to a *petitio* or *postulatio* without another element of the complete formula) make up only about 16% of the total number of petitions. On the relative decline under Philip see below, 52 and 172.

78. *Philippe Ier*, no. 119 (1089).

79. Hémeré, *Augusta Viromanduorum*, "Regestum," 32–37; *Homblières*, nos. 3, 9, 16–19, 21, 23–25, 27, 29; Fossier, *Chartes de coutumes*, no. 3. The exceptions involve some of the counts' own donations to their monasteries: Colliette, *Mémoires*, 1:692–94; *Homblières*, nos. 20, 30–31; Hémeré, *Augusta Viromanduorum*, "Regestum," 32–33, 35–36.

80. Counts of Flanders: *Dipl. Belg.*, vol. 1, no. 96; *St-Bertin*, 24–25, 28, 184–85, 205–6; Lille, AD Nord, 10 H 323, 104–5, 107–8, nos. 61, 63 = Courtois, "Chartes originales," 62–65; Van Lokeren, *Chartes . . . de Saint-Pierre*, no. 127; Vercauteren *Actes*, nos. 2, 5, 12, 14, 18 (to 1100). Counts of Amiens-Valois: *Amiens*, no. 5; *St-Père*, 1:170–71, 2:625–26; *Jumièges*, no. 14; Lot, *Etudes sur . . . Saint-Wandrille*, no. 7; BN, Coll. Picardie 233, ff. 215–16.

81. Bishops: Maurice Prou, *Une charte de Garin, évêque de Beauvais* (Paris, 1904), 397; Guimann, 61–67, 389–91 (with the wrong date); *St-Bertin*, 192ff.; Haigneré, *Chartes de Saint-Bertin*, vol. 1, no. 70; *St-Corneille*, no. 56; *Dipl. Belg.*, vol. 1, no. 157 (1064); *Chronique . . . de Mouzon*, 190–96, docs. 4–6 (acts of 1015, 1018, 1024–25); Gousset, *Actes*, 2:58–59 (1039), 87–88 (1076), etc.; Hariulf, 184–85, 236–40; *Amiens*, nos. 2, 4, 7, 10; Aubert Le Mire, *Opera diplomatica et historica* (Louvain, 1723), 1:53–54; Depoin, *Recueil des chartes . . . de Saint-Martin-des-Champs*, vol. 1, no. 30; Cartulary of St-Jean-des-Vignes, BN, ms. lat. 11004, f. 24; ND Noyon, ff. 51–52, 54r-v, 68–69; BN, Coll. Baluze 75, ff. 54–55; AN, R 135, f. 2 (charters of Picquigny); Cartulary of St-Acheul, London, British Museum, addit. 15604, ff. 6r-v, 10v–11. Abbots: Hariulf, 174, 193, 232–33; Guimann, 288–89; *St-Bertin*, 194ff.; *Homblières*, no. 19, and from the early twelfth century 39 and BN, ms. lat. 5473, f. 100. Chapters: *St-Corneille*, nos. 35, 48; Colliette, *Mémoires*, 2:261, 272–73.

82. De Vogüé, "L'abbé, vicaire du Christ."

83. See above, n. 79, for the counts. Neither act issued by the lords of Péronne (ND Noyon, f. 33, and MSQ, no. 9 [= BN, Coll. Moreau 38, ff. 39–41v]) uses the formulas. The latter act (from 1095) is especially significant, for though the lord did not issue it in response to a petition, he noted at the end that he and his wife had requested confirmation from the bishop of Noyon. Moreover, acts and notices drawn up by others mentioning the lords' interventions do not recall any petition, even though the same scribal houses record petitions to kings, counts, and bishops: *St-Corneille*, no. 18, and the series of charters and notices from Mont-St-Quentin (MSQ, nos. 2–5, 8–9, 11, 13, 15, 17, 18, 22: Newman, *Cat.*, no. 76; Soehnée, no. 41; *GC* 10:Instr. 363–64; BN, Coll. Moreau 23, f. 190r-v; 36, ff. 52–53v; 37, f. 198; 38, ff. 39–41v; 41, ff. 99–100, 127r-v; 42, f. 215; ND Noyon, ff. 56–57; *Amiens*, AD Somme, H XVI, 56–58, no. 1).

84. Not in notices, their own charters, or charters issued by other lords at their request or involving their activities: Newman, *Cat.*, no. 76 (1028); Soehnée, no. 41 (1034); MSQ, nos. 4, 8, 9, 11, 15, 17, 22 [= BN, Coll. Moreau 23, f. 190r-v [1040–45]; 36, ff. 52–53v [1090]; 37, f. 198 [1094–98]; 38, ff. 39–41v [1095]; 41, ff. 99–100 [1103]; 42, f. 215 [1107]; *Amiens*, AD Somme, H XVI, 56–58, no. 1 [1102]).

85. Hariulf, 174, 184–85, 192, 230–40.

86. *Pontieu*, Introduction; Hariulf, 230.

87. *Pontieu*, no. 1.

88. Ibid., no. 3.

89. Ibid., no. 5 (1053–75). See also no. 4, issued in 1067; that is, after Angelran II had set the precedent: "Guido, comes Pontivae patriae, exoratus a domno Gervino abbate, annuentibus proceribus meae provinciae."

90. Fulbert of Chartres, *Letters and Poems*, no. 14: "ut sano consilio praebeatis assensum, ad subiectionem episcopi uestri suppliciter redeatis." Also no. 8, in which Fulbert admonishes the abbot of Fleury to reread Benedict's third step of humility and "episcopo uestro subiciamini sicut decet"; and no. 7, identifying humility's opposite, pride, with a refusal of "subjection." Also Génestal, *Rôle des monastères*, doc. 7: "Urgente siquidem prenimia necessitate supradictum Rannulfum adiit multimodis precibus et summissis venerabilem Bernardum abbatem." Cf. *Vita Hludowici pii*, 64, c. 21: "humillime subiectione se eius nutui secundum consuetudinem Francorum commendans subdidit"; and, again describing entry into vassalage, *Vie de Bouchard*, 19: "suis manibus ac ejus potestati humiliter se submisit." On the importance of humility in this age see Little, "Pride Goes before Avarice"; Morton W. Bloomfield, *The Seven Deadly Sins* (East Lansing, Mich., 1952), 74–75, 95–96.

91. E.g., *Philippe Ier*, nos. 98, 136; *GC* 10:Instr. 363–64; MSQ, no. 22 (1107 = BN, Coll. Moreau 42, f. 215); *Homblières*, nos. 27, 39, 40; Poupardin, *Recueil des chartes . . . de Saint-Vincent de Laon*, 26–27, no. 10.

92. *Homblières*, no. 40; *Jumièges*, 51, no. 15 (Newman, *Cat.*, no. 97 [996–1031]); *Vie de Bouchard*, 8.

93. *Philippe Ier*, no. 43: "mei presentiam supplici devotione adiit, materno affectu obnixe deprecans et postulans quatinus . . ."; no. 61: "decrevimus et quod fideliter ac religiose expeciit pia devotione concessimus."

94. *Annales regni Francorum*, 47, s.a. 776: "immensam illius perfidi populi multitudinem velut devotam ac supplicem . . . veniam poscentem [Karolus] invenit." (This wording, however, comes from the early ninth-century revision of the *Annales*. It represents ninth-century ideology, not eighth-century reality.) Also *Charles II*, vol. 1, no. 12; *Annales de Saint-Bertin*, 19.

95. Fulbert of Chartres, *Letters and Poems*, no. 65. Similarly Duchet and Giry, *Cartulaires de l'église de Térouanne*, 3, no. 3 (the bishop of Thérouanne supplicating the canons: "decani ceterorumque fratrum istius adii presentiam, devote expetens"); *Chronique . . . de Mouzon*, doc. 6 (archbishop of Reims: "adiit nostrae parvitatis praesentiam, humili devotione rogans"); Gousset, *Actes*, 2:93–94 (bishop of Thérouanne, "devotioni ac precibus cujusdam militis . . . condescendens"; also *St-Bénigne*, vol. 2, no. 227; Colliette, *Mémoires*, 2:107 (bishop of Cambrai); *Mir. s. Vulfranni*, 155B (archbishop of Rouen); ND Noyon, ff. 43v, 51–53 (bishop of Noyon); Serrure, *Cartulaire de Saint-Bavon*, no. 17 (bishop of Cambrai [1108]).

96. William of Jumièges, *Gesta Normannorum ducum*, 70: "Arnulfus petiit Ricardum supplex et devotus."

97. MSQ, no. 17 (= BN, Coll. Moreau 41, ff. 99–100 [1103]): the countess of Vermandois grants the "just and pious petition" of the lord and lady of Péronne, by which they "devoutly requested" that the countess approve their donation to Mont-St-Quentin. Also, for Flanders, Vercauteren, *Actes*, nos. 18 ("pie postulavit"), 32 ("religiosa petitione"); for Normandy, Fauroux, nos. 35 (1025, Richard II): "nostram pie expostulans unanimitatem ut . . . faverem; quia vero hujusmodi supplicationibus semper libenter annui . . . assensum prebui"), 110 (Robert I [1037–46]): "devotissime postulavit," 92 (count of Evreux [1038]): "adientes me . . . monachi, supplici devotione petierunt"). Count of Clermont: Müller, *Cartulaire de . . . Saint-Leu*, 26, no. 21 (c. 1119): "ejus humili et simplici devotione poposcerunt; qui pre-

cibus eorum benigne assentiens"); count of Bolenois: *St-Bénigne*, vol. 2, no. 295 (1030); countess of Blois: *Lex*, doc. 6 (996); duke of Burgundy: *St-Etienne*, no. 78 (mid–eleventh century).

98. Kaiser, *Bischofsherrschaft*, 547–51, 577, 585–88, 593–98, 603–7; Vercauteren, *Etude sur les "civitates,"* 128, 339–41, 421; Guyotjeannin, "Recherches," 1:87–104, 111–35; Michel Parisse, "L'évêque d'Empire au XIe siècle: L'exemple lorrain," *Cahiers de civilisation médiévale* 27 (1984): 95–105.

99. *Homblières*, nos. 23, 25, 27, 32. See below, chap. 8, on the disappearance of the formulas.

100. *Homblières*, no. 25. For the relevant papal models see Lohrmann, *PUF*, no. 4 (956, bull of John XII for Homblières; *GC* 10:Instr. 363–64); and Dietrich Lohrmann, *Kirchengut im nordlichen Frankreich* (Bonn, 1983), 70–71.

101. *Philippe Ier*, nos. 119, 126; cf. Bloch, *Rois thaumaturges*, 64–76.

102. Schramm, *KKP*, 3:90–93, 100–101, nos. 21, 22, 25 (from the Stavelot order, apparently used in France for the anointings of the last Carolingians and perhaps also the first Capetians. See Bouman, *Sacring and Crowning*, 21–22, 112–18; Schneidmüller, *Karolingische Tradition*, 149–50.)

103. Schramm, *KKP*, 3:92, no. 1, 96, no. 11; 2:246, no. 7, quoting the West Frankish *ordines* of Fulrad and Stavelot, echoed in *Philippe Ier*, nos. 11, 39, 43, 61, 94. See also Frederick Behrends, "Kingship and Feudalism according to Fulbert of Chartres," *Medieval Studies* 25 (1963): 93–99 at 95 and n. 10, on the king's commands being termed "sacred."

104. For the Carolingians see Hännig, *Consensus fidelium*, 198–99, and the particularly good examples in the *Royal Frankish Annals*, MGH SS 1:172 ("Carolus . . . contenuit ab ipsis Dei ac suis fidelibus"), and MGH Capit. 2:312, no. 273 (Pîtres, 864): "Notum esse volumus omnibus Dei et nostris fidelibus." For the later period see Behrends, "Kingship and Feudalism" (n. 103), 96 n. 13. Also relevant is Wido of Ferrara's explicit linking of Catholic *fides* with the *fides* given to a lord: "When we swear, we make public a pledge of our faith and commend it as a security. But what is that pledge but our faith, by which we believe in God?" (cited by I. S. Robinson, *Authority and Resistance in the Investiture Contest* [Manchester, 1978], 97).

105. Dudo of St-Quentin, *De moribus*, 263: "summo reverentiae cultu recolebant [ducem]." Cf. MGH Capit. 2:281, no. 262, c. 10 (Quierzy [856]): "nos omni sui [regis] fideles . . . ut . . . illum honeste et cum reverentia, sicut seniorem decet, ammonemus . . ."; also Bernard of Clairvaux, quoted by Bur, *Formation . . . de Champagne*, 397, speaking of the homage owed to a bishop: "hominium quod debetis, reverenter et humiliter offeratis."

106. *Philippe Ier*, no. 21; see also nos. 5, 16; *Recueil des actes de Charles III*, 198; Fauroux, no. 221.

107. *GC* 10:Instr. 364; Haigneré, *Chartes de Saint-Bertin*, vol. 1, no. 70; BN, Coll. Baluze 75, ff. 54–55; *Amiens*, nos. 4, 11; Guimann, 61, 63. See also *St-Etienne*, 77–78, no. 54 (1005), an act of the dignitaries and chapter of St-Etienne addressed "omnibus sancte Dei Ecclesie nostre fidelibus, de quodam fidele nostro nomine Rotberti"; and Guimann, 171, an act of the abbot of St-Vaast addressed "successuris ecclesie mee filiis fideliter prospiciens."

108. *Homblières*, no. 29: "Si fidelium nostrorum petitionibus acquieverimus, promptiores eos in nostro servitio invenimus. Quapropter ego Otto . . . scire volo sanctae ecclesiae fideles futuros et praesentes." See also nos. 16, 18, 19, 21, 30; and, for other counts, Van Lokeren, *Chartes . . . de Saint-Pierre*, 92, no. 127; *Amiens*, no. 2; *St-Corneille*, no. 23. Two acts of castellans addressed to *fideles* recording donations to religious institutions appear to limit fidelity to the Christian faithful: *St-Corneille*, no. 44 (Odo of Péronne "omnibus ecclesie fidelibus notum"); *Pontieu*, no.

1 (Angelran of Abbéville, not yet count of Ponthieu, "cunctorum sanctae Dei ecclesiae fidelium").

109. Cf. the citations in n. 108 with *Homblières, nos.* 14, 22, 26, 28, 32, 33.

110. *Philippe Ier, nos.* 136 ("celsitudinem nostram per quosdam optimates nostros humiliter deprecatus est"), 26 ("nostram regiam serenitatem sedulo postulare").

111. *RHF* 10:625 (Newman, *Cat.,* no. 88 [1031]): "ad majestatis nostrae mansuetudinem supplex accessit noster a secretis Manasses comes, postulans . . ."; ibid., 602 (Newman, *Cat.,* no. 49 [1019]): "celsitudinis nostrae magnificentiam humiliter adiit, et auribus nostrae serenitatis devote intimavit. . . ." Other examples from Robert's acts as catalogued by Newman: 583 (no. 23), 584 (no. 15), 585 (no. 10), 586 (no. 18), etc.

112. On the history of these imperial virtues see Fichtenau, *Arenga,* 30–52, a study of value for many of the formulas discussed in this section.

113. See Fichtenau, *Lebensordnungen,* 1:57, on the sense of space ("Freiraum in verstärktem Mass") that surrounded a king and that was violated only by his consent.

114. *Lothaire,* no. 24 (966): "nostras devenit ad aures petitio"; Fauroux, no. 22 (1017): "nostram adiens excellentiam regiis intimavit auribus"; *RHF* 10:602 (above, n. 111). Of similar effect is the phrase "intulerunt obtutibus nostris" or "nostris aspectibus": *Lothaire, nos.* 29, 33; *RHF* 10:553, 620.

115. *Lothaire,* no. 24 (966): "eorum voluntati aurem accomodantes . . . , unde regale auctoritate et indulgentia per hoc preceptum nostrae confirmationis stabili jure eundem locum permanere concedimus"; similarly no. 44 (980): "horum principum nostrorum precibus aurem benigne accomodantes." Similarly in Robert's acts: *RHF* 10:589, 594–96, 613, 616, 625; and for Henry, *St-Père,* 1:127.

116. *Lothaire,* no. 24; also nos. 5 (955): "cujus petitioni benignum praebentes assensum" (the phrase taken from a diploma of King Raoul), 31 (968): "placuit itaque celsitudini nostrae . . . petitioni annuere," 36 (974): "quorum denique preces . . . clementer audivimus"; *RHF* 10:624 (Newman, *Cat.,* no. 83): "per nostri regium numinis praeceptum, ac nostrae celsitudinis gratiam, ac excellentiam benevolentiam," and 595 (Newman, *Cat.,* no. 39): "placuit nostrae excellentiae his annuere precibus."

117. *Lothaire, nos.* 5, 6, 12, 18, 21, etc. From acts of Robert: *RHF* 10:588–89 (Newman, *Cat.,* no. 28): "petens . . . regali auctoritate firmari"; 589 (Newman, *Cat.,* no. 30): "summa prece deposcens, uti auctoritate nostrae praeceptionis ediceremus praeceptum"; 617 (Newman, *Cat.,* no. 72): "humilius postulavit ut . . . auctoritate nostri precepti roborare dignaremur"; 620 (Newman, *Cat.,* no. 73): "imploraverunt . . . auctoritatis nostrae praecepto concedere et corroborare dignaremur"; etc.

118. *RHF* 10:616 (Newman, *Cat.,* no. 95): "nostra auctoritate stabilendis"; 586 (Newman, *Cat.,* no. 18): "postulavit quatinus . . . perpetua lege habendas nostra praeceptione confirmare dignaremur"; 595 (Newman, *Cat.,* no. 39): "petiit quatienus . . . sub authoritate praecepti perpetualiter concederemus."

119. *RHF* 10:612–13 (Newman, *Cat.,* no. 67 [1027]): "adeuntes genua serenitatis nostrae . . . humiliter petierunt, ut . . . sempiternum regalis praecepti stabilimentum secundum statuta regalia concederemus."

120. *Angers, nos.* 15 (886–88) and 19 (966–73).

121. *Cluny,* vol. 4, no. 2816 (1029): "Pio affectu, humili vultu, deprecati sunt per nostre auctoritatis scriptum. . . . Quod ego audiens, nulla cupiditate coactus, sed factus humili illorum deprecatione placatus, consensi . . ."; *St-Etienne,* no. 44 (midtenth century): "humili efflagitatione nostram exposcens serenitatem, quatinus . . . per auctoritatem nostrorum apicum, pie et misericorditer non dedignaremus. Cuius vocem iuste implorationis benigniter suscipientes et eius obsecrationem in aures

nostre dignitatis inclinantes . . ."; St-Eloi, f. 111r–v (1049): "Videns ergo memorati viri devotionem erga loca sanctorum . . . non audeo ejus petitioni surdae auris dare tractamentum"; ND Paris, no. 314 (1005): "Quorum orata cordis sereno susci-pientes" (and similarly no. 320 [1041]); Piette, Cartulaire de Saint-Michel-en-Thiérache, 17–18 (1049–52): "attenta nostre fauoralitatis gratia postulauit"; BN, Coll. Baluze 75, ff. 54–55 (n.d.): "per nostra largitionis manum . . . quod fideliter petiit gratanter concessimus"; Herbomez, Chartes de . . . Saint-Martin de Tournai, 1–3, no. 1 (1094): "benivole condescendentes"; Dipl. Belg., vol. 1, no. 159 (1085): "paterna benignitate." Also Gousset, Actes, 2:59–60, 74–75, 93–94, 132–33, 144, etc.; Dipl. Belg., vol. 1, nos. 143 (1096), 157 (1064); St-Bénigne, vol. 2, nos. 358 (1082–95), 366 (1087–92); Charters of Saint-Amé de Douai, Lille, AD Nord, 1 G 13, ff. 12v (1097), 131–v (1116), 15v–16 (1123); Hautcoeur, Cartulaire de . . . Saint-Pierre de Lille, nos. 6 and 7 (1088, 1090); Nicaise, Cartulaire de . . . Saint-Martin d'Epernay, no. 2 (1074); Serrure, Cartulaire de Saint-Bavon, nos. 16 and 17 (1104, 1108); Bétencourt, Cartulaire . . . d'Auchy, 24–25 (1099); etc.

122. Quantin, Cartulaire général, no. 74 (act of the bishop of Langres, 968): "hu-militer nostram efflagitantes dignitatem, et flexis poplitibus nostram exposcentes mansuetudinem, ut . . . per testamentum nostre largitionis pie et misericorditer conferre, et . . . condonare non dedignaremur. Nos vero . . . aures nostre celsitudinis illorum obsecrationi adclinantes . . ."; St-Vincent, no. 36 (919): "aurem inclinans petitionibus illorum jussit fieri quod petebat" (similarly no. 225 [928–36]). See also ND Paris, no. 318 (act of bishop of Chartres, c. 1055): "indignum est necessaria petentibus abundantes petita negare atque eorum precibus aurem misericordie non prebere"; similarly Jumièges, 20–23, no. 8 (act of the bishop of Bayeux together with the count of Ivry, 1020–30); Gousset, Actes, 2:169–70 (1108); Piot, Cartulaire . . . d'Eename, no. 7 (1096); St-Bénigne, vol. 2, nos. 260 (1016), 270 (1019–26); St-Etienne, nos. 10 (883), 17 (903), 18 (904), etc.; Quantin, Cartulaire général, no. 77 (980).

123. Vendôme, vol. 1, no. 40 (1040): "petierunt a nobis . . . quatinus . . . pro amore Dei et supplici prece ipsorum . . . concederemus, et nostra firmaremus auc-toritate. . . . Concedimus itaque et nostra auctoritate firmamus. . . ." Also St-Vin-cent, nos. 36 (quoted in n. 122) and 327 (996–1018): "cujus aut audivimus peti-tionem non denegavimus facere quod voluit, sed jussimus . . ."; Fauroux, no. 116 (c. 1042–49): "quam largitionem litteris . . . mandare decrevimus et nostre auctoritatis signo . . . roborare statuimus"; Autun, no. 36 (972): "jussimus ei tales gram-matoforas nostrae auctoritatis in membranam adscribi"; also nos. 38 (954), 42 (968–75: "praecepimus ei tale scriptum nostrae auctoritatis fieri"). Similarly Grand-maison, "Fragments de chartes," 248–51 (archbishop of Tours [983]): "per hujus nostrae auctoritatis testamentum concederemus"); Chronique . . . de Mouzon, 5–6, doc. 6 (archbishop of Reims [1024]): "pontificali decreto nostrae auctoritatis inter-dicens"); Dipl. Belg., vol. 1, 157 (bishop of Cambrai [1064]): "nostram adierunt me-diocritatem, quatinus suum inceptum nostra adiuuaret hinc indulgentia, hinc auc-toritas"; St-Etienne, no. 10 (synodal notice [887]) "cum quantis precibus potuit, humiliter deprecatus est, quatinus . . . privilegio sue auctoritatis corroborare dig-narentur," and no. 22 (synodal notice [912]): "huius decreti auctoritatem eis fieri jussit."

124. Acts of archbishop Harduin of Tours, St-Florent, ff. 9–12: "Ut autem haec auctoritas firmior sit." Needless to say, royal diplomas were also called auctori-tates; e.g., Lothaire, no. 5.

125. The chapter of St-Etienne of Dijon was especially fond of such statements, e.g., St-Etienne, no. 26 (early tenth century): "humiliter deprecatus est nostram se-renitatem ac benignissimam fraternitatem, ut ei quasdam vineolas . . . con-

cederemus. Ad cuius humilimam deprecationem aures nostras communiter accomodavimus atque non honerosam sed potius facillimam eius postulationem devote suscepimus." See also, e.g., nos. 45 (972), 49 (977), 50 (990). The abbots of Fécamp and Corbie also used conservative diplomatic formulas vaunting abbatial grace and authority until quite late: for Corbie, BN, ms. lat. 17761, f. 52 (1061–63): "quidam homo . . . nostram mansuetudinem adiit, deprecans nos. . . . Et placuit ergo devotioni nostre ut . . . ejus precibus assensum preberemus"; for Fécamp, BN, Coll. Moreau 21, ff. 22r–v, 25r–v, 30r–v (1028–79). See also *St-Cyprien*, no. 251 (c. 936–54): "ad nostram accedens mansuetudinem, deprecatus est nos . . . eis sub censo per nostre auctoritatis scriptum concedere dignaremur: quod et omni modo nobis placuit fecisse"; and for other examples, *St-Hilaire*, no. 84 (1068); *St-Maixent*, no. 85 (1011–26); *Cluny*, vol. 1, no. 372 (928–29), and vol. 2, no. 1423 (976); *St-Jouin*, 15–16 (c. 990); *St-Bertin*, 161 (857); St-Amand, 12 H 1, no. clii, f. 160 (1134).

126. *Redon*, no. 385 (– 1050): "humili supplicatione postulatione abbatem . . . et monachos ut filium meum . . . in monachum suscipere dignarentur. Quo gratanter ab omnibus concesso . . .", *Cluny*, vol. 4, no. 3021; *St-Aubin*, 1:65–67 (– 1095), 69 (1082–1106), 338 (c. 1070). Requests for *societas*: *Redon*, no. 357 (990–92); Fleury, no. 37 (923–30); *Cluny*, vol. 4, no. 3312; *Angers*, no. 58 (1095); St-Remi, C, f. 26r–v (1083–95); St-Florent, f. 33 (n.d.).

127. *St-Maixent*, nos. 55 (988), 89 (997–1031: "quod accesserunt quidem nostri fideles . . . qui etiam nostram magnificentiam deprecati sunt ut aliquid . . . concedere dignemur; quod et omnimodo nobis placuit hoc fecisse). Also *Nouaillé*, nos. 58, 68, 96, 116 (953–1078); *Cluny*, vol. 2, nos. 920, 942 (954–94), 1073 (959–69), and vol. 3, no. 2014 (993–1048); *St-Aubin*, 1:69–70 (1082–1106), 88–89 (1060–67), 237 (1039–55); *St-Vincent*, nos. 37 (1060–1108), 39 (882); BN, Coll. Moreau 21, ff. 22r–v, 25r–v, 30r–v (Fécamp, 1028–79); St-Florent, ff. 26v–27v (n.d.), 38v, 40v. For examples from the formularies, MGH Formulae, *Marculfi Formulae*, 77–78, 2.5, the language ("nostra fuit petitio, et vestra benevolentia") similar to that still used much later by the scriptoria of St-Aubin, Cluny, and some other institutions.

128. Above, 28.

129. For dukes of Aquitaine: *St-Hilaire*, no. 20: "deprecati sunt nos . . . ei per nostrae auctoritatis scriptum . . . hanc . . . concedere dignaremur: quod et omnimodo nobis placuit fecisse"; *St-Maixent*, no. 27 (951–63): "Has res prescriptas . . . concedere dignaremur, quod omnimodo nobis placuit hoc fecisse, non abnuentes illius peticionem," and no. 14 (939): "quod et nobis omnimodo placuit fecisse"; similarly nos. 56 (988) and 61 (992). Dukes of Francia: *Robert Ier*, nos. 39 (895): "Quorum sanam admonitionem et non inconvenientem Odalrici petitionem cognoscentes, placuit nobis illi concedere . . ."; 43 (900): "Quorum petitionem non superfluam nec importunam . . . , alta mentis nostrae consideratione perpendentes, concessimus eis . . ."; Emile Mabille, Introduction to Marchegay and Salmon, *Chroniques des comtes d'Anjou*, no. 9 (941): "Quorum legitimis petitionibus misericorditer annuens . . ."

130. Mabille, "Invasions normandes," 446, no. 10 ("postulantes suppliciter charitatem nostram ut . . . nostra auctoritate concederemus"). Also *RHF* 9:707–8 ("deprecatione tacti, jussimus praeceptum saepius ante nos recitare"); Jusselin, "Acte d'Hugues," 146 ("deprecatus est nos . . . per hujus nostrae auctoritatis testamentum, concederemus"); Fauroux, nos. 20 ("decrevimus"), 23 ("supliciter deprecans uti . . . per hujus nostre auctoritatis testamentum concederemus"), 61 ("a nostre majestatis edicto roboramus"), etc.; Doniol, *Cartulaire de Brioude*, 87, no. 66 ("decrevimus"); *St-Maixent*, nos. 20 ("decrevimus"), 37 ("deprecatus est nos ut ob nostre auctoritatis . . . tribueret").

131. Cf. *Robert Ier*, nos. 39, 40, 41, 43, 45, with Jusselin, "Acte d'Hugues," 145–

49 (969): "deprecatus est nos quidam vasallus. . . . Cujus . . . deprecationem benigne recipientes, concessimus"; and *RHF* 9:733 (Hugh Capet [975]): "adiit nostram praesentiam quidam episcopus . . . reclamans. . . ." Hugh's acts before mid-century are also quite lavish; e.g., Mabille, Introduction to Marchegay and Salmon, *Chroniques des comtes d'Anjou,* no. 9 (941), a notice: "ante presentiam domni Hugonis dulcissimi . . . abbatis . . . intimantes piissimae familiaritati ipsius flebiliter lamentabiliter flebilem . . . necessitatem et querimoniam . . . submissa prece rogantes"; *RHF* 9:722–23 (942): "accessit quidam venerabilis fidelis noster . . . ad nostri culminis magnitudinem, humiliter postulans, ac omnimodis deprecans. . . ." After 957, ducal acts for St-Hilaire rarely ascribe any regal epithets to the dukes, and the standard acceptance formula becomes "quod ita et fecimus" (a formula, however, frequently found in older formularies from the region): *St-Hilaire,* nos. 26, 32, etc.

132. Below, chap. 8.

133. On letters, above, 32. For tenth-century charters and notices, *St-Etienne,* no. 38 (934), act of Gislebert, count of Autun: "qualiter pervenit ad aures nostre pietatis, humiliter deprecatio Rotberti Divionensis, nostrique per omnia fidelissimi. . . . Ad cuius humillimam postulationem aures nostras inclinantes et devote suscipientes, hoc quod petebat gaudenter studuimus agiliter adimplere"; *St-Vincent,* nos. 71 (937–62): "Noticia . . . qualiter . . . serenitatem domni Leutaldi, imperatorii comitis, ut . . . justitiam faceret humilime expetiit"; similarly nos. 103 (950–58),156 (941–60): "Domnus quoque comes aurem suam inclinans"; Lalore, *Cartulaire . . . de Montiéramey,* no. 1 (837), recounts the foundation of Montiéramey, speaking of *religiosus comes.* (See also Giry, "Etudes Carolingiennes, V.," 2, no. 2.) Note also an unidentified Count Bernard's address to Count Lambert of Chalon as *vestra celsitudo* in Fleury, no. 51, a notice from 956 recounting earlier events. The grandiloquent titles taken by such counts as Gerard of Roussillon in his foundation charter for Vézelay (858–59: "divinae pietatis munere apud gloriosam regalem mansuetudinem comitis honore sublimatus") also demonstrate the legitimacy of such early epithets and, in this case, their consistency with fidelity to the principle of monarchical rule (Huygens, *Monumenta Vizeliacensia,* 244–45).

134. Such truncated petitions were especially common in Anjou (as discussed below, chap. 8) and were not uncommon in acts of the counts of Blois: Arbois de Jubainville, *Histoire des ducs,* vol. 1, doc. 34 (1028–32): "favente meo fideli . . . ac deprecante . . . suo fideli"; Lex, doc. 15 (1016): "favente ac deprecante fideli meo . . . facio liberum."

135. *St-Père,* 1:100–101 (Odo II of Blois): "quia quidam clericus . . . nostram ante praesentiam postulavit, ut . . . concambiassem . . . . Quod quidem et feci"; *ND Chartres,* no. 17 (Thibaud of Blois [1084]): "Facio quod . . . petierunt." See also *Livre des serfs,* no. 1; Odile Gantier, "Recherches sur les possessions et les prieurés de l'abbaye de Marmoutier du Xe au XIIIe siècle," *Revue Mabillon* 53 (1963): 60–61; *Angers,* no. 22; Arbois de Jubainville, *Histoire des ducs,* vol. 1, doc. 34; Lex, doc. 15.

136. Below, chap. 8.

137. Boussard, "Diplôme de Hugues Capet, de 988"; Lemarignier, *Gouvernement royal,* 42. Under Henry, as Lemarignier shows (136–39), subscribers became witnesses.

138. Giry, *Manuel de diplomatique,* 751–52, also 735–38 (a good example being reproduced in Tessier, *Diplomatique royale,* pl. VI); Guillot, "Actes de Henri Ier," 90–91, 93–94. See *Philippe Ier,* nos. 5 and 21, both documents identified by Prou as having been drawn up within the chancery. Although these changes are usually put down to declining royal authority and loss of control over the redaction of documents, I find this explanation unconvincing, since the same process occurred in Normandy under William II, who was hardly a weak ruler. I prefer to believe that as

in Normandy, these trends in royal diplomatics reflect an increasing privatization of government, entailing a decline in the frequency of ceremonial settings within which solemn diplomas had been issued (below, chap. 8).

139. Guillot, "Actes de Henri Ier," 90–91, 93–94.

140. St-Père, 1:126, containing not only Baldwin's formula but also other signs of his hand identified by Guillot, yet then adding, "ut, regali pietate nostrae munificentiae aurem assentando, suis precibus inclinare dignaremur." Similarly RHF 11:597, for St-Germain, contains all those elements distinctive to Baldwin, but specifically describes the act as a supplication: "suppliciter rogans et obnixe postulans." In RHF 11:572, a chancery official appears to have built on Baldwin's formulas to create a more distinctive result: "nostrae tranquillae serenitatis praesentiam humiliter et fideliter convenisse, obnixe atque exanimo postulantem, ut. . . ." For Philip see Phillippe Ier, nos. 4 (probably redacted by Baldwin), 20, 24, 41, 115. These documents have been taken from charters identified by Prou (lxxiii–lxxix) as written within the chancery. Because it is possible that Prou's list includes documents in which the chancery added initial and final protocols to a text redacted by the beneficiaries, only those diplomas in which the texts themselves indicate chancery writing have been included.

141. Examples are Philippe Ier, nos. 24 and 115.

142. Guillot, "Actes de Henri Ier," 94. See Philippe Ier, nos. 26, 31, 126, 141, for acts regarded by Prou as drawn up outside the chancery. Among other likely examples are nos. 11, 23, 39, 43, 94; see also below, 172.

143. Fauroux, 321–23, no. 142 (1059); St-Aubin, 1:99 (1119), in which the almoner of St-Aubin of Angers prostrated himself before Count Fulk the Younger and grasped his feet when he requested confirmation of his gift to the abbey.

144. Lex, doc. 26 (a notice concerning an act of Odo II, referred to as comes illustrissimus [1034–37]): "Qui cum apud ipsum gloriosissimum comitem precem pro eisdem pratis . . . fudisset, sine mora quod petebat, benignissme indulsit." See also Arbois de Jubainville, Histoire des ducs, vol. 1, doc. 47 (1008–37, dated by Bur, Formation . . . de Champagne, 183 and n. 106): "culminis nostri adiens sublimitatem . . . humiliter peciit [episcopus] ut . . . Cujus . . . benignam petitionem clementer audientes . . ."

145. St-Maur, no. 23 (Guillot, Cat., C 363 [1090]). See also GC 7:Instr. 222 (Guillot, Cat., C 206; Geoffrey Martel [1046–60]); St-Jouin, 19 (Guillot, Cat., C 64; Fulk Nerra [1006–39]); Angers, no. 57 (Guillot, Cat., C 382; Fulk le Réchin [1093]).

146. Above, 43.

147. Vercauteren, Actes, nos. 5 (1080): "nostram adiere praesentiam, obnixe postulantes ut . . . corroborarem. Quorum justis petitionibus condescendens . . ."; 19 (1096): "me . . . suppliciter adisse et quae pie postulavit a me Dei gratia facillime impetrasse." This, however, is one of the last full petitions found in comital acts from Flanders. For earlier examples and the absence of the formulas in the acts of Arnulf of Flanders, see below, chap. 5.

148. On the cut-off date see below, chap. 8.

149. Homblières, nos. 24–25.

150. Ibid., no. 23: "Notum scire volo . . . quod accessit ad nostram praesentiam laudabilis Ricardus, abbas . . . postulans ut . . . Quam petitionem non abnuentes et saepius adclamantes . . . ex beneficio nostro ei concessimus ut . . ."; no. 27: "sed quia id facere nequiebat absque permissu nostro nos expetiit humiliter ut ei faveremus in hoc negotio."

151. St-Corneille, no. 35: "Illius igitur petitioni, quia nobis multum bene placuit, benigne condescendentes."

152. Adquiescens: Haigneré, Chartes de Saint-Bertin, no. 94; Serrure, Cartulaire

de Saint-Bavon, nos. 16–17; Hautcoeur, Cartulaire de . . . Saint-Pierre de Lille, nos.
6–7; Hariulf, 183, 4.3; Philippe Ier, no. 4; Gousset, Actes, 2:59–60, 144; St-Bénigne,
vol. 2, no. 366; Montierender, no. 48; etc. Condescendens: Vercauteren, Actes, nos.
5, 18; Philippe Ier, nos. 24, 65; BN, ms. lat. 12895, ff. 7–10; Amiens, no. 4; Herbomez, Chartes . . . de Saint-Martin de Tournai, 1–3, no. 1; St-Corneille, no. 48;
Gousset, Actes, 2:94–95, 132–33; Duvivier, Actes et documents anciens, 54–55
(1107); St-Bénigne, vol. 2, no. 358. See also Lille, AD Nord, 10 H 323, 107–8, no. 63
(= Courtois, "Chartes originales," 64; act of Baldwin V of Flanders for
Marchiennes): "mihi . . . ad humilem . . . petitionem . . . placuit confirmare";
Fauroux, no. 20: "clementiam nostram expetierit, quatenus ipsi sancto largitione
nostrae eleemosynae conferremus aliquid"; BN, Coll. Baluze 75, ff. 54–55: "quod
fideliter petiit gratanter concessimus"; Montierender, 155, no. 26: "gratanter quod
petivit . . . ei indulsimus."

153. Homblières, no. 25: "Si vicem potestatis nostrae a Deo nobis temporaliter
concessae gerere volumus utinam juxta salutem animae, oportet indefesse justis
petitionibus assensum praebere, maxime cum de rebus ecclesiasticis est negotium."

154. Vie de Bouchard, 9–10: "Cumque ab eo [Maiolo abbate Cluniacensis] reverenter, ut dignum erat susceptus fuisset humo prostratus [comes Burchardus], tam
admirabilem humilitatis exhibitionem adventusque ejus ad eum causam a tam
longinqua patria inquirere studuit. Cui comes: 'Supplex namque requiro ut peti-
tionis meae verba suscipias.'"

155. Dudo of St. Quentin, De moribus, 254: "Extemplo rex Otho, humillimis
regalium petitionum monitis coactus"; 236–37: "venit Bernardus ante conspectum
regis Luthdovici, et coepit in dolo compellare eum verbis humillimis"; 181: "Tunc
Rollo, humillimis suorum verbis coactus. . . ." Montierender, no. 39 (– 1057?):
"supplici voto coegerunt me"; Fauroux, no. 94 (1035–c. 1040): "deprecatione compulsus"; St-Aubin, 1:374 (c. 1100): "tandem victi tum pro necessitate, tum precibus
Waldini"; Autun, no. 31 (938): "quorum precibus evicti"; Cluny, vol. 4, no. 3391
(1063): "devictus petitionibus"; Platelle, Justice seigneuriale, 418–19, doc. 2 (1062–
76): "victus fidelium nostrorum precibus."

156. Angers, no. 47 (1047–55): "arctissimo familiaritatis et amoris ligamine
tantis fratribus debitor et astrictus, flagitata negare non potui."

157. Dudo of St-Quentin, De moribus, 263: "Ipsi [subjecti] autem toto mentis
affectu diligebant eum [Ricardum ducum], summoque reverentiae cultu recolebant
eum. Parebant humiliter ejus jussionibus et dictis, et obtemperabant obedientes ejus
praeceptis. Ipse regebat eos blande, ut paterfamilias servos, et alebat eos dulciter
fomite benignissimo, ut pater filios."

158. Anton, Fürstenspiegel, 369–72, 404–7.

159. St-Aubin, 1:372–75 (Guillot, Cat., C 155, [1040–55, though the notice was
written much later]). Also p. 363 (c. 1090): a knight addresses his companions and
lords: "Precor vos qui astatis, et vos maxime, domini mei, qui mecum manducatis,
ut . . . testes sitis."

160. Deloche, Cartulaire . . . de Beaulieu, no. 1 (860).

161. RHF 10:602 (Newman, Cat., no. 49 [1019]).

162. For a coronation assembly, Philippe Ier, no. 61 (1071), and probably also GC
10:Instr. 203. Examples of petitions announced in local synods are St-Etienne, nos.
10 (887), 16 (899), 22 (912); Autun, vol. 1, no. 36 (972); Quantin, Cartulaire général,
nos. 45 (864), 73 (938); Cluny, vol. 1, no. 642 (943), and vol. 2, no. 1000 (956); St-
Vincent, nos. 2 (1018–30), 8 (c. 930), 9 (c. 949). For petitions delivered in chapters
presided over by lay abbots (or held in the presence of a powerful lay patron), see, for
e.g., St-Hilaire, nos. 18 (941–42), 23 (954–55); Mabille, "Invasions normandes," no.
10 (904); St-Maur, no. 23 (Guillot, Cat., C 363 [1090]). Petitions and the special

judicial entreaties known as "clamors" were also often made before unusually large assemblies: e.g., *Chronique . . . de Mouzon,* 192–94, doc. 5 (1018); Gousset, *Actes,* 2:58–59 (1039).

163. Elinor Keenan, "A Sliding Sense of Obligatoriness," in Bloch, *Political Language,* chap. 5, with Bloch's Introduction, 9–10. Late antique rhetoric displays similar qualities: MacCormack, *Art and Ceremony,* 7–14.

164. White, *Custom, Kinship, and Gifts to Saints,* 36–37; Tabuteau, *Transfers of Property,* 119–23 (above, n. 71).

165. Fulbert of Chartres, *Letters and Poems,* no. 127.

166. *Autun,* vol. 2, no. 3 (1079–86): "Si petitionibus fidelium nostorum aurem serenitatis nostre accomodamus. . . . Nostram adierunt presentiam . . . obnixe postulantes ut . . . Placuit itaque sublimitati nostrae eorum saluberrimis adquiescere postulationibus."

2. The Act of Supplication

1. Fichtenau, *Lebensordnungen,* 1:16–17, 47–49, 75. Also Schmidt-Wiegand, "Gebärden" and "Gebärdensprache," the latter with copious references.

2. For examples of kisses, Laurent, *Cartulaires de . . . Molesme,* 2:177 (1076–85); Dudo of St-Quentin, *De moribus,* 158, 224; *Mir. s. Ursmari, AASS* Apr. 2:572–74 passim. See Suntrup, *Bedeutung der liturgischen Gebärden,* 362–79; Fichtenau, *Lebensordnungen,* 1:57–59. Oaths: *Annales de Saint-Bertin,* 42, 52, 83, 168–69, 170, 186, etc.

3. Acting as grooms: Sylvia Thrupp, *The Merchant Class of Medieval London (1300–1500)* (Ann Arbor, Mich., 1962), 23; *Le "Liber pontificalis,"* ed. L. Duchesne, 3 vols. (Paris, 1955–57), 1:447; Richer, *Histoire de France,* 1:132 and n. 2, on which see below, chap. 4. On table protocol see below, p. 299.

4. Fulbert of Chartres, *Letters and Poems,* 6–7, no. 1. On the ceremony as a whole during this period see below, chap. 4.

5. The phrase is used of monastic observance: Hugh of Flavigny, *Chronicon Virdunense,* 371, 2.5; *MSB,* 101.

6. E.g., *RHF* 10:615 (Newman, *Cat.,* no. 97): "supplex voce humili . . . postulans." Also *Vie de Bouchard,* 8; *Vita beati Simonis,* 1217; *MSB,* 254. Cf. also Dudo of St-Quentin, *De moribus,* 205: "submissaque voce suppliciter compellare verbis pacificis coeperunt," and 225: "supplici voce poscens misericordiam illorum." Also Galbert of Bruges, *Histoire du meurtre de Charles le Bon,* 62 (c. 38) and 98 (c. 60), the latter especially interesting because the supplication is made from a window.

7. *Vie de Bouchard,* Dudo of St-Quentin, *De moribus, MSB,* as above; Galbert of Bruges, *Histoire du meurtre,* 62 (c. 38) and 98 (c. 60).

8. *Mir. s. Vulfranni,* 151A ("voce flebili clamare coepit"), 151E ("lacrymabiliter implorant"); *MSB,* 243 ("Qui prostratae matris flexus lacrymis, benigne petitionibus ejus assensum praebuit"), 264 ("implorare coepit voce tremulis"); *Mir. s. Richarii,* 462F ("lacrymis humectus misit legatos duci Hugoni, orans"); Dudo of St-Quentin, *De moribus,* 245 ("exorans cum lacrymis").

9. Below, chap. 7.

10. William of Jumièges, *Gesta Normannorum ducum,* 43–44. See also Dudo's account of Hastings' funeral, with "clamor ululantium" and "tumultus lugentium" (*De moribus,* 132–33). Also *MSB,* 335, again describing the reaction of warriors to their lord's sudden death: "Videntes vero satellites ejus dominum suum exan-

imatum, ululatibus aerem, lacrymis genas opplentes, humeris corpus imponentes abire maturant." Cf. Fichtenau, *Lebensordnungen*, 1:63–64.

11. *MSB*, 184. Also *Mir. s. Ursmari, AASS* Apr. 2:574, about a young lord pressured to end a feud by the intervention of the saint: "prouens cum fletibus in facie, miserum se clamans, mordebat terram prae dolore."

12. Bloch, *Political Language*, 6–7, notes that traditional societies often associate special gestures and intonations with formal speech.

13. Peter the Chanter, *De penitentia*, 208: "Gestus vero corporis est argumentum et probatio mentalis devotionis. Status autem exterioris hominis instruit nos de humilitate et affectu interioris." Similar sentiments were expressed during the Carolingian period, by Alcuin, for example ("per hunc habitum corporis mentis humilitatem attendamus," cited by Fink, "Knien") and by Amalarius of Metz ("unde prosternimur ante crucem, ut fixa humilitas mentis per habitum corporis demonstretur," cited by Suntrup, *Bedeutung der liturgische Gebärde*, 168).

14. Neunheuser, "Gestes de la prière," 153, 159; Rordorf, "Gestes accompagnant la prière à genoux," 195; Peter the Chanter, *De penitentia*, 182–85, with illustrations for modes 1 and 3; also De Wald, *Illustrations of the Utrecht Psalter*, illustration for Ps. 71. It is probably this *orans* position that is denoted in Gousset, *Actes*, 2:98–99 (1089): "dilectus noster abbas, universaque loci ejusdem congregatio surgentes, ante faciem nostram adstiterunt, et . . . humillimis obsecrationibus implorarunt."

15. Gougaud, "Attitudes of Prayer." Garnier, *Langage de l'image*, provides abundant iconographic evidence, with insightful commentary, of the varied postures associated with humble beseeching; he also emphasizes that the gestures accompanying prayer have no inherent fixed signification but are indicative of and subordinate to the actor's internal state: 50, 113–14, 120. Cutler, *Transfigurations*, 58–59, emphasizes that not even Byzantine *proskynesis* denoted a fixed, unvarying gesture.

16. Garnier, *Langage de l'image*, 112–13 and plates cited; Schmidt-Wiegand, "Gebärdensprache," 366. Cf. also *Annales de Saint-Bertin*, 205: "stante illa iuxta imperatorem, surrexerunt omnes, stantes quique in gradu suo." A contemporary illustration discussed below shows the bishop of Paris kneeling before a sitting King Henry I of France while others stand. In the *Acta concilii Remensis* the priest Adalger, testifying against Arnulf of Reims, is shown a place to stand before the sitting episcopal judges (662, c. 9), while Arnulf himself, accused but not yet condemned, is allowed to sit among the bishops as their equal while answering their charges (677, c. 30). See also Fichtenau, *Lebensordnungen*, 1:43–44, for sitting on a bench as a sign of equality. Christopher Walter, *L'iconographie des conciles dans la tradition byzantine* (Paris, 1970), 15 and 35–38, gives examples of condemned parties arrogantly standing in the presence of sitting judges.

17. *Vita beati Lanfranci*, 48–49.

18. MGH SS 8:372.

19. Walter, "Iconographie des conciles," 35–38 (and relevant illustrations), 146; also 14–16; Fichtenau, *Lebensordnungen*, 1:32–34.

20. Delisle, "Notices sur les manuscrits," 266, 270. Richer recorded a similar situation, when a provincial council held under Adalbero of Reims allowed the abbot of St-Remi to preside while the archbishop sat across from him, other dignitaries placed in a circle around them: *Histoire de France*, 2:40.

21. Richer, *Histoire de France*, 1:172, on which see Lauer, *Règne de Louis IV*, 83–85 and app. 2, and Fichtenau, *Lebensordnungen*, 1:43–44; Flodoard, *Annales*, s.a. 948 ("simul residentibus"). See also *Histoire de France*, 1:38–40, where Richer recounts another slight to a magnate's pride arising over seating arrangements.

Again, though the story is perhaps apocryphal, it is still significant as an indicator of late tenth-century *mentalité*.

22. Mommsen and Morrison, eds., *Imperial Lives and Letters of the Eleventh Century* (New York, 1967), 98. On the custom see Bornscheuer, *Miseriae regum*, 4–5, 130–31.

23. Adolf Katzenellenbogen, *Allegories of the Virtues and Vices in Medieval Art*, trans. Alan J. P. Crick (1939; rpt. New York, 1964), 11–12 and pl. IV, fig. 9. Also indispensable is Garnier, *Langage de l'image*, 113–14, where he identifies the "request for a favor" and respect owed to a superior as two reasons for a gestural demonstration of humility.

24. Fauroux, 321–23, no. 142 (1059): "Robertus abba [sic] . . . donum . . . confirmavit et in manu comitis, genu ejus osculato, cum baculo custodiendum tradidit." Also Merlet, *Cartulaire de Saint-Jean-en-Vallée de Chartres*, 2–3, no. 2 (1083): "Pro qua nimirum concessione tam Girogius quam ejus uxor gratias agens, ad pedes ilico episcoi uterque cecidit."

25. Gousset, *Actes*, 2:98–99 (1089), quoted above, n. 14.

26. *Recueil des actes de Louis II*, no. 78: "quod adiens genua serenitatis nostre, illuster fidelis noster ugo venerabilis abba . . . humiliter petiit ut . . . " Also nos. 79, 81, 88, 93 bis.

27. Font-Réaulx, "Propos sur les diplômes," 426.

28. Doniol, *Cartulaire de Brioude*, 63, no. 231: "postravit [sic] se quidam homo . . . petens ut . . . concederemus."

29. Deloche, *Cartulaire . . . de Beaulieu*, no. 1 (860).

30. The long history of epistolary formulas of prostration has been discussed by Lanham, "Prostrate at Your Feet." Lanham does not, however, realize that her epistolary references to prostration built on a current ritual, though one of her primary authorities does; see Koskenniemi, *Studien*, 151.

31. MGH Formulae, 441–46, nos. 6, 9, 16, 21, 29, giving such phrases as "quasi pronus prostratus in presentia vestra," "quasi prostratrus pedibus vestris," and "prono in terram vultu."

32. MGH Epist. 5:285, no. 13 (828–29): "Propterea vestra pietatis vestigiis animo provoluti flebiliter postulamus"; 324–25, no. 18 (834): "Quapropter, clementissime domine, precamur omnes, precamur singuli, quasi corporaliter dulcissimis pedibus vestris provoluti, ut pastorem, quem iam pridem vestra largissima concedente gratia suscepimus, eundem iterum . . . suscepturi gaudeamus."

33. *Redon*, no. 89 (871): "Domino ac beatissimo apostolici ordinis aecclesiae Sedis Romane Adriano, Salomon Brittonum dux, flexis genibus clinoque capite. . . . Precor Almipotentiam vestrae dignitatis ut . . ." See also MGH Epist. 5:142, no. 67: "intimantes devotionem . . . pronam," in a letter to a bishop; and in letters to monarchs, 309–10, no. 7 (823): "provoluti vestigiis iterum petimus"; 314–15, no. 11 (826–27); "tanquam presentialiter coram vestris vestigiis terre provolutus"; 135–36, no. 4 (842–53): "prostratis imploro precibus."

34. Richer, *Histoire de France*, 2:160–63: "Quomodo capiti suo praeponet cujus pares et etiam majores sibi genua flectunt, pedibusque manus supponunt?" Fichtenau, *Lebensordnungen*, 1:41, translates this last phrase as "who place their hands under his feet," and interprets it as referring to grooms or other inferiors helping their lord to mount a horse. Though this meaning is possible, one would expect a writer to be more explicit if this were his intention; and to place their hands "at his feet" is well within the standard meanings of *supponere* and strains the sense of the sentence less. Certainly J. M. van Winter, in his discussion of this passage, interpreted it as indicating a *proskynesis*, basing his opinion on the frequent mention of such prostrations in chronicles: "Uxorem de militari ordine sibi imparem," 122–23.

35. *St-Vincent*, no. 9 (c. 949): "adiit genua pietatis ejus quidam vir fidelis . . . omni supplicatione poposcens conferri sibi aliquid ab eo ex rebus prescripti martiris"; Quantin, *Cartulaire général*, 143, no. 74 (968): "humiliter nostram efflagitantes dignitatem, et flexis poplitibus nostram exposcentes mansuetudinem, ut altare . . . per testamentum nostre largitionis pie et misericorditer conferre, et justo moderamine condonare non dedignaremur." Other references to kneeling or prostration: *St-Vincent*, nos. 22 (c. 948) and 27 (968–71); *Cluny*, vol. 2, no. 1553 (981), and vol. 3, no. 2721 (1019?).

36. *St-Vincent*, no. 497 (c. 939): "prono capite aggressus est clementiam serenitatis ejus quidam illustris vir Willebertus." Another formulation whose irregularity argues for verisimilitude is *Cluny*, vol. 1, no. 734 (949), "humili deposcentes affectu."

37. Deloche, *Cartulaire . . . de Beaulieu*, no. 154 (1005–28): "sed jam provolutus tuis pedibus, domine meus episcope, tota animi et corporis devotione deprecor tuam benignitatem ut . . ." Note how closely this formulation corresponds to the ideas of Peter the Chanter, above, n. 13.

38. *RHF* 10:595, 612–13 (Newman, *Cat.*, nos. 39, 67).

39. *RHF* 15:169–70. On the date of this letter see John F. Benton, *Self and Society in Medieval France* (Toronto, 1984), 95 n. 6 and references.

40. Fulbert of Chartres, *Letters and Poems*, nos. 100, 65. Two other eleventh-century letters mentioning prostration can be found in Gousset, *Actes*, 2:111, 116–17, the former addressed to the archbishop of Reims by the clergy of Flanders, the latter to the church of Reims by the bishop of Arras.

41. Above, n. 31.

42. Richer, *Histoire de France*, 3.5 ("Hugo . . . regem suppliciter adiit, petitque pontificalem dignitatem ei restitui"), 3.19 ("sese eis [regibus] supplicem monstrans"), 87 ("peto supplex filia matrem"); William of Poitiers, *Histoire de Guillaume*, 1:38 ("supplex adiit, manibus ei sese dedit"), 2.35 ("jussit multotiens misericordiam, cum supplices conspiceret aut egenos, matres animadverteret voce et gestibus precari cum liberis"). Also William of Jumièges, *Gesta Normannorum ducum*, 70 ("Arnulfus petiit Ricardum supplex et devotus"); Hariulf, 198–99, 4.9; *Vie de Bouchard*, 9–10; *Mir. s. Vulfranni*, 152A and E; Galbert of Bruges, *Histoire du meurtre*, cc. 65, 73. For the classical and ecclesiastical definition of *supplicatio* as a beseeching prayer with gestures, see Charlton T. Lewis and Charles Short, *A Latin Dictionary* (Oxford, 1969), s.v. *supplex*; Du Cange, *Glossarium*, 6:454.

43. Dudo of St. Quentin, *De moribus*, 232, 203, 197, 244, respectively. Cono and Bernard are fictitious, however. See also 181 ("lenique sermone submissoque vultu ad eum dixerunt. . . . Tunc Rollo, humillimis suorum verbis coactus . . ."), 205 ("proclivo vultu, submissaque voce suppliciter compellare verbis pacificis coeperunt eum"). Dudo's use of supplication is discussed in chap. 5.

44. *Lothaire*, no. 68 (= *St-Père*, 1:81): "quia fideles regni nostri, Odo scilicet, Carnotensium presul, atque illustrissimus comes, fidelis noster ac inter alios magis dilectus Odo cum sua eque conjuge Berta, nepte utique nostra dulcissima, magnificentie nostre genua suppliciter adierunt, accedent quoque etiam in hoc incliti ducis, fidelis nostri Hugonis, favorabili obsecratione, ut . . ."

45. *Recueil des actes d'Eudes*, no. 57, on which see also *Robert Ier*, no. 47, and Guyotjeannin, "Interpolation." Given the frequency of references to prostration, Guyotjeannin overreaches in attributing Marmoutier's formula to Livy.

46. Chronicle of Saint-Martin-des-Champs, London, British Museum, addit. 11662, f. 4; Depoin, *Recueil des chartes . . . de Saint-Martin-des-Champs*, 1:14–18, no. 6. On this sketch see Maurice Prou, "Dessins du XIe siècle et peintures du XIIIe siècle," *Revue de l'art chrétien* 33 (1890): 122–28; G. R. C. Davis, "A Norman Charter," *British Museum Quarterly* 25 (1962): 75–84.

47. Newman, *Seigneurs de Nesle*, vol. 2, no. 1 (−1115): "Domnus abbas Odo . . .

predictum Radulfum Nigelle dominum adiit, modo quo decuit ab eo terram repoposcit." The land in question was held by one of Raoul's vassals, yet the abbot sought out not the vassal but his lord.

48. *Redon*, no. 341.

49. *Autun*, vol. 1, no. 31 (938). See also nos. 36 (972), 42 (968–75), and 49 (935–68), where dignitaries of the chapter of Autun approach the bishop to introduce petitioners.

50. *Charles II*, vol. 1, nos. 40 (requests), 4, 22, 56, 61, 62 (confirmations).

51. Ibid., nos. 172, 213, 223 (queen, cantor), 65, 84 (*fideles*).

52. Ibid., nos. 1, 3, 30, 36–39.

53. Ibid., nos. 2, 12, 14, 23 (diplomas), 42, 78, 79, 134 (donations).

54. Ibid., nos. 63, 81, 113, 114 (churches), 164, 208–10 (vassals).

55. Ibid., nos. 157 and esp. 171.

56. *Lothaire*, nos. 12, 29, 31, 32, 41.

57. Ibid., nos. 18, 22, 24, 35, 36.

58. Sassier, *Hugues Capet*, 75; also 69–70, where the author traces the beginnings of this development to the reign of Odo. German historians have interpreted the practice of intercession at the court of Henry I in a similar fashion: see Gawlik, "Zur Bedeutung von Intervention und Petition," and Goetz, "Letzte 'Karolinger'?"

59. *Lothaire*, nos. 5, 44.

60. Boussard, "Diplôme de Hugues Capet," 63.

61. The trend is parallel to that of attestations of royal charters: Lemarignier, *Gouvernement royal*, 68.

62. *Philippe Ier*, nos. 65, 126.

63. Ibid., no. 120.

64. Lohrmann, *PUF*, nos. 12, 17, 21, 27, 30, 44–46, 48–50; Ramackers, *PUF*, nos. 6, 10, 28. The exceptions to this rule are privileges for secular and regular canons, presumably because secular canons had no abbots and both types of institution placed great emphasis on their collegiality. See also the list in Hilpisch, "Rat der Brüder," 230–31. Note that in Hilpisch's list of papal addresses (which the author admits is random and fragmentary), the earliest examples, dating from the first half of the eleventh century, invoke abbatial supremacy (e.g., "abbati cum omnibus sibi commissis," "abbati et eius fratribus").

65. Lohrmann, *PUF*, nos. 57–58, 62; Ramackers, *PUF*, nos. 30, 42–43, 50; Hilpisch, "Rat der Brüder."

66. Odo: *Philippe Ier*, no. 39; Elinand: ibid., no. 61; Gebouin: Soehnée, no. 16; Baldwin: *Philippe Ier*, no. 136; Baldwin's predecessor: Fauroux, no. 22 (Newman, *Cat.*, no. 46).

67. Lemarignier, *Gouvernement royal*, 148–57.

68. *Philippe Ier*, no. 9. On Waleran's position as chamberlain see Prou's introduction to ibid., cxliv–cxlvi; on the importance of his family within Philip's entourage see Lemarignier, *Gouvernement royal*, 156.

69. *Philippe Ier*, no. 134; Lemarignier, *Gouvernement royal*, "Tableaux des souscripteurs, (d) Philippe Ier," s.v. "Châtelains, Aubry (Renaud) de Coucy," noting that Ingelran's name does not appear on Lemarignier's list. Barthélemy, *Deux âges de la seigneurie banale*, 58, explains this oddity by suggesting that Renald was the one who really wanted the royal diploma, Ingelran being indifferent. Though this explanation is possible, the one offered here is more consistent with other evidence about the criteria for choosing intercessors.

70. *Philippe Ier*, no. 136; Lemarignier, *Gouvernement royal*, "Tableaux des souscripteurs," s.v. "Radbod"; Newman, *Domaine royal*, 123 and notes s.v. "Laigue," "St-Léger-aux-Bois," 216 and note.

71. *Philippe Ier*, no. 98; Newman, *Domaine royal*, 123 (s.v. "Soissons," "Crépy,"

"Bois de Crépy," "Bus," "Wary") and notes, 116 and 139 (s.v. "Laon," "Bruyères," "Crépy") and notes, 216 and notes; Lemarignier, *Gouvernement royal*, for Theobald of Soissons and Elinand of Laon.

72. *Philippe Ier*, nos. 98, 42, 82.

73. *Corbie*, no. 40. See also *St-Aubin*, 1:233 (1082–1107), where the abbot of St-Aubin takes over a dispute begun by one of his *famuli*.

74. ND Noyon, ff. 55v–56.

75. St-Eloi, ff. 109v–10. See also *RHF* 11:650 (Soehnée, no. 42), in which the bishop of Angers beseeches Henry at the prayer of the abbot and monks of Marmoutier. Also *Ronceray*, no. 125 (c. 1028–29) (cf. Guillot, *Comte d'Anjou*, 298), in which a disgraced vassal seeks the intercession of the countess of Anjou for reinstatement in the count's favor.

3. The Court of the Heavenly King

1. Wallace-Hadrill, "*Via Regia*," 23.

2. One expects language of this sort in such liturgies as coronation *ordines*, as in the supplicatory prayer "Omnipotens sempiterne Deus," with its apostrophes to the "rex regum et dominus dominorum" (Schramm, *KKP*, 2:218, no. 5; 3:92, no. 1, 96, no. 11; Bouman, *Sacring and Crowning*, 112–15). But such usages also penetrated more quotidian literature, often with the authors' explicit mirroring of divine and earthly kingship; e.g., *Vie de Bouchard*, 29 ("mortali regi . . . immortali imperatori"); Dudo of St-Quentin, *De moribus*, 230 (a supplication of the "Dominum Deum" to rectify the malfeasance of the earthly king); William of Poitiers, *Histoire de Guillaume*, 222 ("ad servitium tamen regis omnium regum cor propensius habebat"), 232 ("Esse jugiter in oculis habendum, cujus vicerint praesidio, aeternum imperatorem); *Philippe Ier*, 50 ("ego Philippus, gratia Regis aeterni, rex"). See also Fulbert of Chartres, *Letters and Poems*, 180, no. 100; *Mir. s. Adalhardi*, 1.4; *MSB*, 178–79. Such phrases call attention to the archetypal majesty of divine kingship; at the same time they more specifically denote God's imperial status, as an emperor was by definition a "king of kings." See Deshman, "*Christus rex*," 387–88, 399–401, with references.

3. The literature on this subject is immense. Among the more notable works are Wallace-Hadrill, "*Via Regia*" and *Early Germanic Kingship*; Carlyle and Carlyle, *History of Mediaeval Political Theory*, vols. 1–3; Kantorowicz, *Laudes Regiae*, 56–75; Ewig, "Zum christlichen Königsgedanken"; also J. Chydenius, *Medieval Institutions and the Old Testament*, Societas Scientiarum Fennica, Commentationes Humanarum Litterarum, 37/2 (Helsinki, 1965), and Walter Ullmann, *Principles of Government and Politics in the Middle Ages* (Methuen, 1961).

4. For liturgical archetypes see esp. Manz, *Ausdrucksformen*, 80–82, 108–13, 287, etc. For their application in hagiographical texts, usually within a supplication: divine *clementia*: *MSB*, 105, 321, 354; *Vita s. Honorati*, 611D–E; *Mir. s. Ursmari*, MGH SS 15/2:839, c. 6, l. 30; *Vie de Bouchard*, 25. Divine "majesty": *Vita s. Arnulfi*, 234. Divine "highness": Peter the Chanter, *De penitentia*, 188 (specifying a contrast between the prostrate petitioner and God's *altitudo*).

5. E.g., *Vie de Bouchard*, 20: "Deo fidelis comes."

6. *MSB*, 337.

7. As in the prayer "Omnipotens aeterne Deus" in the Stavelot recension: Bouman, *Sacring and Crowning*, 114.

8. Among many possible examples, see the prayers quoted from early sacramentaries by Tellenbach, "Römische und christliche Reichsgedanke": "Deus, cuius

regnum est omnium saeculorum, supplicationes nostras clementer exaudi et Romanorum regnum tibi subditum protege principatum" (57, no. 9); "Deus, qui regnis omnibus aeternis dominaris imperio, inclina ad preces humilitatis nostrae aures misericordiae tuae, et Romani regni adesto principibus, ut tua tranquillitatem clementer tua sint semper virtute victores" (61, no. 18). Other examples of supplications to a God conceived of in royal or imperial terms are quoted by Biehl, *Liturgische Gebet*, 149–50; Manz, *Ausdrucksformen*, 192 (s.v. *flebilis oratio, flebilis vox*), 203 (s.v. *gemitus lacrimarum*), 299–307, 437, 455, 512, 571, 584–85, 603, 603A, 664–66, 738, 740–41, 782–90.

9. *Acta synodi Atrebatensis*, 1286: "Unde licet nullum locum vacare a praesentia majestatis ejus sciamus, in hac tamen praesertius atque uberius suae gratiae beneficia petentibus tribuit." On this council see Van Mingroot, *"Acta synodi Attrebatensis"*; Moore, *Origins of European Dissent*, 9–15; Duby, *Trois ordres*, 45–53; Stock, *Implications of Literacy*, 120–38.

10. *PL* 142:1306: "Prosternimur corpore ante crucem, mente [ante] Deum; veneramur crucem per quam redempti sumus, sed illum deprecamur qui nos redemit."

11. Peter the Chanter, *De penitentia*, 179–80, citing in part Cassiodorus.

12. *MSB*, 264, 176.

13. *Vita s. Arnulfi*, 241, 246F.

14. Ulrich of Cluny, *Consuetudines Cluniacenses*, 730, 2.37; cf. Schäfer, *Fusswaschung*, 20–21, 26–27.

15. Among many examples, two of the most important are found in the Gospel Book of Poussay, Paris, BN, lat. ms. 10514, f. 18v, reproduced in A. Haseloff and H. V. Sauerland, *Der Psalter Erzbischof Egberts von Trier* (Trier, 1901), pl. 54/4; and the Codex Egberti, reproduced in Franz J. Rorig, *Codex Egberti: Das Perikopenbuch des Erzbischofs Egbert von Trier (977–993)* (Trier, 1977), 39. On the origins of the Poussay text see C. R. Dodwell and D. H. Turner, *Reichenau Reconsidered*, Warburg Institute Surveys, no. 2 (London, 1965), 13–16. A late tenth- or early eleventh-century French example of kneeling but uncrowned Magi is in the Tropiary of Autun, Paris, Bibliothèque de l'Arsenal, ms. 1169, f. 6v (reproduced in fig. 6). On the crowned Magi see Deshman, "Christus rex," 377–81. It should also be pointed out that like all gestures of supplication, the Magis' homage could be expressed by their outstretched hands—a gesture that goes back to the classical *aurum coronarium*. See esp. Deshman, "Christus rex"; Hugo Kehrer, *Heiligen drei Könige in Literatur und Kunst*, 2 vols. (Leipzig, 1908, 1909), 2:1–8, 50, 102–14; Gilbert Vezin, *L'Adoration et le cycle des Mages dans l'art chrétien primitif* (Paris, 1950).

16. Garnier, *Langage de l'image*, 115C and pl. 7.

17. Fauroux, no. 63 (1030). Similarly, St. Odo came to reform Fleury mounted, like Christ, on an ass. Though the monks had previously resisted the reform, when they finally recognized him, they went out to meet him and embraced his feet (Rosenwein, *Rhinocerous Bound*, 88).

18. *Mir. s. Richarii*, 462B: "Quod si haec imples, promitto tibi ex Dei jussu, per Sancti pia merita Richarii et meas preces, te prolemque tuam fore Regem Francigenarum, stirpemque tuam regnum tenere usque ad septem successiones." This later version of the story derives from the *Mir. s. Walarici*, 25, which speaks similarly (though less dramatically) of Valerius's intercession for Hugh: "accelera petitionem nostram: per nostras enim orationes rex efficieris Galliae." On the prophecy see Werner, "Legitimität der Kapetinger," 214–15; Andrew Lewis, *Royal Succession in Capetian France* (Cambridge, Mass., 1981), 36, 50.

19. E.g., *Jumièges*, no. 6.

20. *MSB*, 174–75.

21. Celestial court: *ND Paris*, 1:314–15 (1005), where the archbishop of Sens accepts the petition of the canons of Paris, "celestis curia palacia nobis . . . mercari curantes"; similarly 320 (c. 1041), 337 (c. 1030), and *St-Père*, 1:222 (– 1080), where a man lays down his sword, trading his place as an earthly knight for a place as a monk at St-Père so that "ad etheris aulam anhelat tendere"; *Dipl. Belg.*, 1:145 (941), where Arnulf of Flanders compares the poverty of the saints' honor on earth with their brilliance "in celesti curia." Mary as queen: *MSB*, 189–90: "Dei mater solito laetior, tantorum principum media throno splendidiore resedit." The antecedent of this vision is also worth quoting for its equally explicit depiction of heaven as a royal court. When Christians were besieged by an overwhelmingly superior Moorish force, they sought Mary's help: "Mariam totis precibus praeoptantes, primatem superni palatii magnis vocibus implorantes, excubitorem regni coelorum iterata oratione reclamantes."

22. *Autun*, vol. 1, no. 27 (1077): "cumque apud mundanos principes saepe fieri videamus, ut quoties aliquis a qualibet potenti persona quidpiam magnum impetrare desiderat, illum pro se faciat interventorem quem potenti esse cognoverit familiarem; ita et nos si apud regem regum perpetuam salutem obtinere cupimus, sanctos ejus martyres caeterosque ipsius fideles quos in coelorum curia praevalere credimus, pro nobis necesse est intercessores acquirere studeamus."

23. Hincmar of Reims, *De cavendis vitiis et virtutibus*, 901–2, c. 6: "Hoc ergo in causa nostri examinis, quam cum districto judice habebimus, patronos nobis facere debemus, hos in die tanti terroris illius defensores nobis adhibere satagere debemus. Certe si apud magnum judicem causa quaelibet nostra esset die crastina ventilanda, totus hodiernus dies in cogitatione duceretur: patronum quaereremus, magnisque precibus ageremus, ut apud tantum judicem nobis defensor veniret. Ecce districtus judex Jesus venturus est, tanti illius angelorum archangelorumque concilii terror adhibetur, in illo conventu causa nostra discutitur. . . . Qui igitur de nullo nostro opere confidimus, ad sanctorum protectionem currere, atque ad sacra eorum corpora fletibus insistere, et ut veniam promereamur eis intercedentibus necesse est nobis deprecari."

24. BN, Coll. Picardie 233, ff. 214–15 (– 1069): "quatinus pro anima illius intercedat atque in die judicii ductor ei et advocatus ante Deum existat."

25. *Amiens*, no. 5 (1069).

26. *St-Bertin*, 176–77 (c. 1026).

27. The leap of faith is greatest in Wolfram, *Intitulatio I* (see, e.g., pp. 9–10), least in Léopold Genicot, *Les actes publics*, Typologie des sources du Moyen Age occidentale 3 (Turnhout, 1972), 19, and Font-Réaulx, "Propos sur les diplômes."

28. These comments are based primarily on originals from Cluny in BN, Coll. Bourgogne, vols. 76 and 77; those from Sint-Baafs and Sint-Pieters of Ghent in the Rijksarchief, Ghent (facsimiles in *Dipl. Belg.*, vol. 2); and Dudo of St-Quentin's charter for Richard II of Normandy, BN, Coll. Picardie 352, f. 1 (= Fauroux, no. 18). Although only the first nineteen lines of Dudo's original survive, the manuscript is 575 mm high. One can conservatively estimate its original length as at least 843 mm, and more likely 943 mm—just over a yard!

29. Royal and comital originals in the Ghent Rijksarchief allow 15–23 mm between lines (counting from the base of sample minims on one line to the base of those on the line immediately above), although one suspect diploma of Lothar (*Dipl. Belg.*, vol. 1, no. 134 = *Lothaire*, no. 1 [Dec. 11, 954]) has 28 mm between lines. An authentic act of Bishop Radbod of Noyon (*Dipl. Belg.*, vol. 1, no. 76 [Mar. 18, 994]) leaves 20–23 mm interlinear spacing. Line spacing in ordinary charters, by contrast, averages 6–7 mm. On the difficulties of discerning authentic and forged royal acts in these archives see Verhulst, "Note sur deux chartes." Good facsimiles of elabo-

rate chrismons and trellises in royal acts are published in *Recueil des actes de Louis IV.*

30. Brigitte Bedos Rezak's work on royal seals has led her to similar conclusions, provisionally enunciated in two unpublished papers: "Ritual in the Royal Chancery: Diplomatics of the Early Medieval West (7th–11th Centuries)," 23d International Congress of Medieval Studies, Kalamazoo, Mich. (1988), and "Text, images et stratégies de la représentation royale dans les diplômes français du Moyen Age (VIIIe–XIIIe siècles)," Maiestas II, Paris, June 21–24, 1990.

31. Above, 38–39.

32. Fleury, 110–14, no. 44; Hodüm, "Réform monastique," and the articles by A. C. F. Koch, Henri Platelle, and Jean Laporte in the collection devoted to the reforms of Gerard of Brogne in *Revue Bénédictine* 70 (1960): 119–26, 127–66.

33. Besides the reforms cited here, see also Gerard of Roussillon's foundation charter for Vézelay (858–59), where this connection between the two types of prayer is articulated quite clearly: Huygens, *Monumenta Vizeliacensia,* 244–45.

34. *Dipl. Belg.,* 1:144, no. 53 (941), on which see Dunbabin, "Maccabees as Exemplars," 36–38, and *France in the Making,* 49–50.

35. Fleury, no. 44.

36. Willmes, *Herrscher-"Adventus,"* 108 and n. 413.

37. Huyghebaert, *Translation de reliques,* 26–27, 37–51.

38. *Dipl. Belg.,* 1:145, no. 53 (941).

39. Fleury, 127–30, no. 51. On the event, of which almost nothing is known, see Maurice Chaume, *Les origines du duché de Bourgogne* (Dijon, 1925), 1:446 n. 1. I have been unable to identify Bernard in spite of a thorough search through the standard regional studies (Chaume, Bouchard, Duby, Rosenwein, Lauranson-Rozas).

40. Bouchard, *Sword, Miter, and Cloister,* 307.

41. See Sahlins, *Islands of History,* 81, for a position close to my own. Sophisticated Marxian interpretations of ideology are of course not so narrowly materialistic, just as Marx's own statements in *The German Ideology* were not. The term has been so debased in common parlance, however, that it seems pointless to fight it.

42. Above, 36–37.

43. Michel Foucault, *The Archaeology of Knowledge,* trans. A. M. Sheridan Smith (New York, 1972).

44. Stephen Pepper, cited by Turner, *Dramas, Fields, and Metaphors,* 26; also 63–67.

45. Crick, *Explorations in Language and Meaning,* 131–32, 141.

46. E.g., Flodoard, *Annales,* 28; Dudo of St-Quentin, *De moribus,* 189, 191, 242.

47. Notker the Stammerer, *Gesta Karoli,* 92, trans. in Lewis Thorpe, *Two Lives of Charlemagne* (Harmondsworth, Suff., 1969), 171.

48. McCormick, *Eternal Victory,* 97, 144–46, 162, 165–66, 313, 316–17. A two-paneled ivory tablet from c. 800 shows two royal figures, each spearing an enemy supine beneath his feet. Nothing is known about the meaning of the iconography, which in any case was copied from a fifth-century Byzantine model (Schramm et. al., *Deutschen Kaiser und Könige,* 155–56 [pl. 11]). One should also note the twelfth-century story in William of Malmesbury (*De gestis regum Anglorum,* ed. William Stubbs, Rolls Ser. 90/2 [London, 1887–89], 292) about the young Geoffrey Martel, who is said to have placed his neck under his father's feet after his rebellion as his father cried out, "You are beaten! You are beaten at last!" The story could be true, given the Angevin temper. But William knew his Suetonius very well and probably embellished a simple supplication. For the rest, Einhard commissioned an arch on which two emperors were depicted trampling serpents, not men (Deshman,

"Exalted Servant," 401). Just before the imperial coronation Theodulf of Orléans, in a poetic set piece thoroughly saturated with Byzantine conceits, described Christ (not the emperor) as trampling the necks of the pagans Charlemagne had subjected to Christianity (MGH Poetae, 1:484, ll. 45–46). There are also iconographic depictions of a triumphant God or Christ trampling his enemies (Deshman, "Exalted Servant," 401; Garnier, *Langage de l'image*, 60A, 114E; De Wald, *Illustrations of the Utrecht Psalter*, pl. LXVI). These examples only leave one more impressed by the care with which contemporaries avoided showing rulers themselves trampling the necks of those they had defeated, for these people were their *fideles*, not simply Christians but nobles.

49. Nelson, "Lord's Anointed"; D. H. Green, *The Carolingian Lord* (Cambridge, 1965).

50. Töpfer, *Volk und Kirche*.

51. Magnou-Nortier, *Foi et fidélité*, chap. 4; Sassier, *Hugues Capet*, 73–87.

52. Hugh of Flavigny, *Chronicon Virdunense*, 394, 2.20.

53. *Vita Herluini*, 206, trans. in Vaughn, *Abbey of Bec*, 82.

54. Fleury, 128, no. 51: "Eorum ergo petitionibus Lanbertus laetus assentiens sic fatus Bernardum exorat. . . . 'Unde, quia tua nobilitas saepe in talibus est Dei dono experta, petimus nostrorum te ducem fieri succurrendumque tantae necessitati.'"

55. Alföldi, *Monarchische Repräsentation*, 46–47.

56. Le Goff, "Symbolic Ritual of Vassalage," 262.

57. Ulrich of Cluny, *Consuetidines Cluniacenses*, 730.

58. Galbert of Bruges, *Histoire du meurtre*, 20–21, c. 12.

59. Helgald of Fleury, *Vie de Robert*, 114, c. 23.

60. MGH SS 14:291, on which see Albert d'Haenens, "Moines et clercs à Tournai au début du XIIᵉ siècle," in *La vita comune del clero nei secoli XI e XII*, Miscellanea del Centro di studi medioevali 3 (Milan, 1962), 2:95 n. 97.

61. *Mir. s. Walarici*, 25E.

62. Alcuin, *De virtutibus et vitiis*, 64–67, c. 10; *Vita Herluini*, 206, trans. in Vaughn, *Abbey of Bec*, 82 (from Eccl., 3:20).

63. Anselm of Laon, *Sententie*, 78.

64. Jonas of Orléans, *De institutione regia*, 142–43 (quoting Isidore). See also Bornscheuer, *Miseriae regum*, 76–93, 111, 131–36, 197–201.

65. Respectively, "Chronicle of St.-Martin-des-Champs," f. 4r (pl. 2); Galbert of Bruges, *Histoire du meutre*, 106, 117, cc. 65, 73; Dudo of St-Quentin, *De moribus*, 203–4, 232–34.

66. Schramm et al., *Deutschen Kaiser und Könige*, pls. 37, 93; Deshman, "Exalted Servant," fig. 9a, both with commentaries.

67. As in the Early German and Mainz *ordines* (Schramm, *KKP* 2:89, 95. See below, n. 71.

68. On Attigny, *Vita Hludowici pii*, 108–9, c. 35; for Otto, Bornscheuer, *Miseriae regum*, 113–14. The intent of Henry III's penance at his mother's funeral is even more unclear. See Karl Schnith, "Recht und Friede: Zum Königsgedanken im Umkreis Heinrichs III.," *Historisches Jahrbuch* 81 (1962): 22–57 at 39; Bornscheuer, *Miseriae regum*, 206.

69. Turner, *Forest of Symbols*, 27–30.

70. Nelson, "Ritual and Reality," 46.

71. Deshman, "*Christus Rex*," 387–90; Bornscheuer, *Miseriae regum*, 195–96, 200–201. Bornscheuer rightly points out that few coronation liturgies explicitly mention the king's prostration. But as he acknowledges, it does appear in the Mainz *ordo* and the Edgar *ordo*; the Fulrad *ordo* mentions a queen's prostration at her coronation (Schramm, *KKP*, 2:247, no. 24); and at the Council of St-Basle Arnulf

prostrated himself *in modum crucis* (MGH SS 3:685). Moreover, the early *ordines* are notoriously short on stage directions. The absence of an explicit mention of prostration in early texts is no grounds for believing that no prostration occurred if other indicators suggest that it did.

72. Notker the Stammerer, *Gesta Karoli*, 68–69, trans. in Thorpe, *Two Lives of Charlemagne*, 152 (above, n. 47).

73. Thegan, *Vita Hludowici imperatoris*, 594.

74. *Vita Hludowici pii*, 108–9: "palam se errasse confessus est, et imitatus Theodosii imperatoris exemplum, poenitentiam spontaneam suscepit, tam de his, quam quae adversus Bernhardum nepotem gesserat proprium"; Helgald, *Vie de Robert*, 112, c. 22, discussed below, chap. 5.

75. While Otto I fasted: Jäschke, "Frühmittelalterliche Festkrönungen?" 560–61. See also Bornscheuer's account of Otto I's preparations for the battle at the Lech, fasting and, in a later account by Thietmar of Merseberg, prostrating himself and declaring his sinfulness: *Miseriae regum*, 113–14. Similarly, before his battle against the Huns, Henry III set aside his mantle and regalia and, dressed in penitential clothing, prostrated himself in the form of a cross: Schnith, "Recht und Friede," 39–40 (above, n. 68).

76. *Mir. s. Adalhardi*, 863, 2.1, commented on by Zoller-Devroey, "Domaine de l'abbaye . . . de Corbie," 434–38.

77. Halphen, *Comté d'Anjou*, 348–49, for Fulk; also *St-Aubin*, 17–18; *Vendôme*, vol. 1, nos. 175 and 245; *Angers*, no. 27, all discussed in chap. 8.

78. Albert Hauck, *Kirchengeschichte Deutschlands* (1906; rpt. Berlin, 1954), 3:574.

79. *Relatio corporis et miracula s. Walarici*, 25: "Cernens Dux venientem Arnulfum cum sanctorum corporibus, profusis lacrymis, poplitibus flexis, cum omnibus militibus suis gratias Domino egit, quod Sanctorum corpora recipere meruit." Though this account was written at least thirty-five years after the event, it is important for its conceptualization of ducal ritual. In describing a somewhat different ritual (or perhaps only a different phase of the same ritual), the metrical *Historia relationis s. Richarii*, written by an informed contemporary about the same event, also portrays Hugh as exalted through a self-imposed humiliation (464): "Dux jam praefatus, equino / Descendens dorso, nudis incedere plantis / Incipit, et propriis scapulis portare feretrum, / Et secum plebis qui visi nobiliores: / Illud tamque diu portat, lacrymis madefactus, / Altari donec gaudens proprio imposuisset."

Part Two. Constructing a Political Community

4. The Rehabilitation of Royal Dignity

1. Schramm, *KKP*, 3:92, no. 3; 100, no. 22.

2. Flodoard, *Annales*, 101.

3. See in general Nelson, "Lord's Anointed"; Reuter, "Plunder and Tribute"; Brühl, "Fränkischer Krönungsbrauch." Although references to great public rituals continue throughout the *Annales de Saint-Bertin*, one can already discern a greater use of peace terminology, at first referring primarily to agreements between kings but after c. 860 referring increasingly to agreements between kings and magnates (e.g., 60–63, 136, 218). On this trend see Magnou-Nortier, *Foi et fidélité*, chap. 4.

4. E.g., *Annales regni Francorum*, 47; Thegan, *Vita Hludowici imperatoris*, 593–94, 600, 602; *Vita Hludowici pii*, 65, c. 21; 91, c. 29; 108, c. 35; 187, c. 53; Nithard, *Histoire des fils de Louis le Pieux*, 30, 1.7; Notker the Stammerer, *Gesta*

Karoli, 24, 61, 68–69, 72, 79–80 (1.18; 2.8, 11–12, 15); *Annales de Saint-Bertin*, 31, 92, 182.

5. Flodoard, *Historia*, 564, 573–74, 590; *Annales*, 68–69, 118–19. For diplomas see, e.g., *Historia*, 536, 556–58, 567–71.

6. In the *Historia* they are especially common in describing events after 927: e.g., 579–82. They are even more common in the *Annales*, as on 5–6, 12, 17, 19, 24, 32, 34–35, 37, 38–45.

7. *Historia*, 579; *Annales*, 12, 17, 24, 34–35, etc.

8. Below, 255.

9. *Annales*, 19–20: "Rodulfus . . . ei obviam super Ligerim venit et, intercurrentibus alternatim legatis, tandem ad colloquium super ipsum flumen Ligerim infra pagum Augustodunensem convenere. Ubi tota die immorati, Rodulfus ex hac, Willelmus ex illa fluminis ora, nunciis utrimque progredientibus, sicque, die consumpta, flumen tandem Willelmus transiens ad Rodulfum jam noctu pervenit et, equo desiliens, ad regem equo insidentem pedibus accessit; quem postquam rex osculatus est utrimque discessum." See Fichtenau, *Lebensordnungen*, 1:75–76.

10. Lauer, *Règne de Louis IV*, 130–43.

11. Searle, *Predatory Kinship*, 42–47.

12. Discussion and handlists are given in Michel Rouche, "Les repas de fête à l'époque carolingienne," in *Manger et boire au moyen âge*, Actes du colloque de Nice (Oct. 15–17, 1982) (Nice, 1984), 1:265–96 at 267–69, 285–90.

13. E.g., *Charles II*, vol. 1, nos. 147, 153, 162, with other citations given in Rouche, "Repas de fête," 287–89 nn. 23–26; for prayers offered for the king at the request of a *fidelis*, see Huygens, *Monumenta Vizeliacensia*, 244–45.

14. *Recueil des actes de Charles III*, 106–10, no. 49 (904), and 200–202, no. 89 (917). Charles also regularly confirmed the prayers and commemorative meals established by Robert's father during the period when he had ruled in Charles's place: ibid., 102, no. 46 (903); 106–10, no. 49 (904); 168, no. 74 (913–22). When Charles was promoting Hagano's career against the Frankish magnates, he also allowed prayers for his soul: 220, no. 95 (918).

15. See Philippe Lauer, *Robert Ier et Raoul de Bourgogne, rois de France (923–936)* (Paris, 1910), 20–23.

16. Flodoard, *Historia*, 579.

17. Ibid., 573–74, 586, 590; *Annales*, 188–90.

18. Sassier, *Hugues Capet*, 150–98; Schneidmüller, *Karolingische Tradition*, 49–60, 147–85.

19. Besides Sassier and Schneidmüller, see Bur, "A propos de la *Chronique de Mouzon*"; *Chronique . . . de Mouzon*, 111–20.

20. Schneidmüller, *Karolingische Tradition*, 99–100, 158–59. Also R.-H. Bautier, "Echanges d'influences dans les chancelleries souveraines du Moyen Age, d'après les types des sceaux de majesté," *Comptes-rendus de l'Académie des Inscriptions et Belles-Lettres*, 1968, 192–220 at 197–98; and Bedos, "Signes et insignes," 50. It was about this time that Lothar entered into an alliance with the Vermandois and perhaps with Anjou, a sign of his greater independence from the Robertians: Sassier, *Hugues Capet*, 153–55, 159.

21. Richer, *Histoire de France*, 2:30. References to discussions of this custom can be found in Deshman, "*Christus rex*."

22. Bur, "A propos de la *Chronique de Mouzon*," 302.

23. Mabillon, *De elevatione corporis s. Theoderici*. On the abbey and its reform see the articles by Jacques Hourlier and Michel Bur in *Saint-Thierry, une abbaye du VIe au XXe siècle*, ed. Bur, Actes du colloque international d'histoire monastique, Reims/St-Thierry, Oct. 11–14, 1976 (St-Thierry, 1979).

24. Mabillon, *De elevatione corporis s. Theoderici;* Lot, *Derniers carolingiens,* 65–87; Sassier, *Hugues Capet,* 161; *Chronique . . . de Mouzon,* 120–23.

25. Nelson, "Lord's Anointed."

26. On Gerbert see Riché, *Gerbert d'Aurillac,* and the papers in *Gerberto.*

27. On Richer and his work see H. H. Kortüm, *Richer von Saint-Remi: Studien zu einem Geschichtsschreiber des 10. Jahrhunderts* (Stuttgart, 1985); Sassier, *Hugues Capet,* 280–81; and Schneidmüller, *Karolingische Tradition,* 52–60.

28. Flodoard, *Annales,* 63.

29. Richer, *Histoire de France,* 1:130–32, with note d: "Inde quoque deductus, in vicinis urbibus gratulanter excipitur. Universi ei applaudunt, omnes letantur, tanta omnium fuit et eadem mens."

30. Lauer, *Règne de Louis IV,* 13, expressed the same doubts. I am tempted to credit Richer's account, at least in its broad outline. True, Richer is a poor source by the standards of positivist history, and he did later revise this particular story, leaving Herbert and Arnulf out of the rite, something Robert Latouche believes he would not have done had the story been true. But even the revision retains the gist of the earlier account; and Richer may have revised it not because Herbert and Arnulf had never participated in the ceremony but in order to give greater prominence to Hugh the Great, Hugh Capet's father, at the expense of the Vermandois faction. As for Flodoard's silence on the subject, this is just the sort of ceremonial incident he consistently omitted; and even he alludes to a commendation at Boulogne and a journey to Laon. This is also the kind of tale that might have been current within Louis's entourage, embittered as these men were over Hugh's and Herbert's purported betrayals. Since Richer's father was one of the king's counselors (*Histoire de France,* 1:274), he may well have known of the incident and told his son about it.

31. In this Richer echoed Gerbert: H. Feld, "Die europäische Politik Gerberts von Aurillac: Freundschaft und Treue als politische Tugenden," in *Gerberto,* 695–731.

32. *Histoire de France,* 1:136.

33. *Histoire de France,* 2:214–19; see Claude Carozzi, "Le dernier des Carolingiens: De l'histoire au mythe," *Le Moyen Age* 82 (1976): 453–76.

34. On Adalbero, Sassier, *Hugues Capet,* 188–89, and on Charles, 196–97. Also note the allusion to Adalbero's continued scurrilous dealings twenty years later hinted at in the *Gesta episcoporum Cameracensium,* 7:473–74.

35. This is also suggested by Richer's treatment of the affair of Melun (2:272), where a traitorous castellan is hung but his men freed, because "faithful" to their lord.

36. *Histoire de France,* 2:258–61. Nor does Richer mention that the Archbishop of Bourges interceded for Arnulf and won his liberty; cf. *Acta concilii Remensis,* 3:685.

37. *Histoire de France,* 2:142.

38. See most recently Brühl, "Kronen- und Krönungsbrauch," with references to Jäschke, Klewitz, and Brühl (1962).

39. *Philippe Ier,* no. 61. See Schramm, *König von Frankreich,* 122, and Jäschke, "Frühmittelalterliche Festkrönungen?" 556–57.

40. Richer, *Histoire de France,* 2:30. Note also the prominence given to the crown in the accession of Lothar's son as king of Aquitaine in 982: Brühl, "Fränkischer Krönungsbrauch," 286.

41. Richer, *Histoire de France,* 2:166: "Et quia tunc in nativitate Domini regnorum principes convenerant ad celebrandum regiae coronationis honorem, in basilica Sanctae crucis ejus filium Rotbertum . . . sollempniter coronavit [metro-

politanus] . . . et ordinavit." This passage is mentioned by Brühl, "Fränkischer Krönungsbrauch," 290; but he misinterprets it as a "joint coronation," Hugh being crowned only because Robert was crowned.

42. See Bornscheuer, *Miseriae regum*, 130–31; Gerbert, *Lettres*, 67–68, no. 71; also Alain Erlande-Brandenbourg, *Le Roi est mort: Etudes sur les funérailles, les sépultures et les tombeaux des rois de France jusqu'à la fin du XIIIe siècle* (Geneva, 1975), 9–12. Elizabeth Hallam ("Royal Burial and the Cult of Kingship") ignores the significance of Lothar's funeral, not knowing Bornscheuer's or Erlande-Brandenbourg's work. She also exaggerates the significance of the chaos that followed the death of William the Conqueror, since William was a notoriously unpopular king and, as Nelson shows ("Rites of the Conqueror," 130–31), had considerable difficulty imposing respect for his rituals of sacral kingship. Note also that German sources emphasize that a ruler's successor carried his body. Richer's contrasting emphasis on the magnates' role is another sign that these rituals were rites of consensus specifically tailored to the Frankish polity.

43. Abbo: Sassier, *Hugues Capet*, 268–76; Mostert, *Political Theology*; Peace of God: Bachrach, "Northern Origins of the Peace Movement"; Lauranson-Rosaz, *Auvergne et ses marges*, chap. 5.

44. Sassier, *Hugues Capet*, 191–92, 278–82. Hännig, *Consensus fidelium*, discusses the historiography.

45. Richer, *Histoire de France*, 2:164–66.

46. Lemarignier, *Gouvernement royal*, 44–45.

47. Boussard, "Diplôme de Hugues Capet," 62. Note that this phrase occurs in the part of the act Boussard regards as likely to be authentic.

48. Sassier, *Hugues Capet*, 166–68, 170–71, 180, 188–93.

49. Richer, *Histoire de France*, 2:106–12. Two of the anecdotes are discussed by Sassier, *Hugues Capet*, 168–69, without comment on their possible impact on Hugh.

50. Richer, *Histoire de France*, 2:108.

51. Pfister, *Etudes sur . . . Robert le Pieux*, 36–38; Joel Rosenthal, "The Education of the Early Capetians," *Traditio* 25 (1969): 366–76 at 370–71; Lewis, *Royal Succession*, 20–21.

52. Bautier, "Echanges d'influences," 200 (above, n. 20); Bedos, "Signes et insignes," 51.

53. *RHF* 11:580–82 (Soehnée, no. 88 [1049]); Tardif, *Monuments historiques*, no. 268 (Soehnée, no. 65 [1043]); Fauroux, no. 114 (Soehnée, no. 80 [1048]).

54. Bloch, *Rois thaumaturges*, 29–41; *Philippe Ier*, no. 61. See also his central role in the very public relic translation at Compiègne in 1072 (*Philippe Ier*, no. 126).

55. Below, chap. 5.

56. Odorannus of Sens, *Chronique*, in *Opera omnia*, 16–25.

57. Helgald of Fleury, *Vie de Robert*, 110–12.

58. Ibid., 124–27, discussed by Lauranson-Rosaz, *Auvergne et ses marges*, 442–53. The date of 1019–20 proposed there for the pilgrimage, while possible, rests on so many assumptions (not the least of which is that it really did begin in Lent and end at Easter) that it cannot be regarded as firm.

59. Above, 3.

60. Richer, *Histoire de France*, 2:290–91. The last ecclesiastical council in which a king had played a role anywhere near so dominant was that of Meung-sur-Loire in 891, convened by Odo *regia jussione*. See I. Schröder, *Die Westfränkischen Synoden von 888 bis 987 und ihre Überlieferung* (Munich, 1980), 105–9. Excluded are such councils as Ingelheim, a testimony more to Otto I's power than to Louis IV's.

61. Robert's marital problems appear to have caused little sensation within the kingdom anyway: Duby, *Knight, Lady, and Priest*, 75–85; Pfister, *Etudes sur . . . Robert le Pieux*, 50–59.

62. *Gesta pontificum Autissiodorensium*, 1:388: "concilium . . . in quo rex Robertus cum episcopis et abbatibus adfuit, simul et innumerabilia sanctorum pignera totius pene provincie." Also *Chronique de Saint-Pierre-le-Vif*, 116: "Ibi vero presentes fuerunt Rotbertus rex et Goslinus Bituricensis archiepiscopus cum aliis episcopis et abbatibus et populo innumerabili. Ibi etiam multa disposita sunt ad utilitatem ecclesiarum." For the dates of these councils see Hoffmann, *Gottesfriede*, 51–53; for their interpretation, Yves Sassier, *Recherches sur le pouvoir comtal en Auxerrois du Xᵉ au début du XIIIᵉ siècle* (Auxerre, 1980), 37 with citations.

63. Andrew of Fleury, *Vie de Gauzlin*, 98–99, 182–83; *St-Père*, 1:108–15; Bautier, "L'hérésie d'Orléans."

64. Duby, *Three Orders*, 21–55.

65. Goetz, "Kirchenschutz"; also Head and Landes, *Peace of God*.

66. *Gesta episcoporum Cameracensium*, 480, 3.37: "Ad hoc autem plurimi convenerunt, ut dignitatem imperatoriam mirarentur, quam tantopere fama laudabat." See Fichtenau, *Lebensordnungen*, 1:78. Also relevant is Raoul Glaber's interest in the symbology of Emperor Henry II's *Reichsapfel*: *Histoires*, 21–22; Edmond Ortigues and Dominique Iogna-Prat, "Raoul Glaber et l'historiographie clunisienne," *Studi medievali* 26 (1985): 537–72 at 558–62.

67. Duby, *Three Orders*, 130–34; E. Van Mingroot, "*Acta synodi Attrebatensis* (1025): Problèmes de critiques de provenance," *Studia Gratiana* 20 (1976): 201–29; Moore, *Origins of European Dissent*, 9–30; Stock, *Implications of Literacy*, 106–39.

68. Duby, *Three Orders*, 21–43.

69. Fossier, *Terre et hommes*, 2:560. For an overview see Poly and Bournazel, *Mutation féodale*, 81–103.

70. K. N. Llewellyn and E. Adamson Hoebel, *The Cheyenne Way* (Norman, Okla., 1941), 21, 25–29; Lloyd A. Fallers, *Law without Precedent: Legal Ideas in Action in the Courts of Colonial Busoga* (Chicago, 1969), esp. 84–86; Laura Nader and Harry F. Todd, Jr., *The Disputing Process: Law in Ten Societies* (New York, 1978), 3–8.

71. Langlois, *Textes*, no. I; *RHF* 10:236–37; *Philippe Iᵉʳ*, no. 75; Newman, *Domaine royal*, doc. 2; MGH SS 8:377; Hariulf, 161–62, 229.

72. "Against customary law": Fossier, *Chartes de coutume*, no. 3. "Usurpation": ibid.; *St-Corneille*, no. 15; Guimann, 277–28; Paris, BN, Coll. Moreau 23, f. 190r–v; Amiens, AD Somme, H XVI, 56–58, no. 1; *St-Germain*, nos. 49, 51, 52; *Mir. s. Walarici*, 290; *Philippe Iᵉʳ*, no. 143. An accord between Roger, count of St-Pol, and St-Bertin expressly states that Roger had established the customs denied by the abbey: Haigneré, *Chartes de Saint-Bertin*, no. 3.

73. *Philippe Iᵉʳ*, no. 27; *St-Germain*, no. 49.

74. *Philippe Iᵉʳ*, no. 125; MGH SS 8:377.

75. *Philippe Iᵉʳ*, no. 28; *Homblières*, no. 34.

76. *The Political Writings of St. Augustine*, ed. Henry Paolucci (Chicago: Regnery Gateway, 1962), 29.

77. See below, chap. 8.

78. *Vita s. Arnulfi*, 248, c. 85; Henri Platelle, "La violence et ses remèdes en Flandre au XIᵉ siècle," *Sacris erudiri* 20 (1971): 101–73 at 141. Dunbabin, *France in the Making*, 241–43, provides an excellent discussion of the topic and well-chosen examples.

79. Gregory of Tours, *Decem libri historiarum*, 88–90 (2.38, 40).

80. Nelson, "Lord's Anointed."

81. Richer, *Histoire de France*, 1:130–32, 292–94, 2:150. On hunting see Nelson, "Lord's Anointed," 168–69.

82. Angelran of St-Riquier, *Historia relationis s. Richarii*, 464, on which see Werner, "Legitimität der Kapetinger," 214–15.

83. Bur, *Formation . . . de Champagne*, 157–73; Feuchère, "Tentative manquée"; Bachrach, "Toward a Reappraisal of William the Great" and "A Study in Feudal Politics: Relations between Fulk Nerra and William the Great, 995–1030," *Viator* 7 (1976): 111–22.

84. See Duby, "L'image du prince."

85. Fichtenau, *Lebensordnungen*, 1:77–78, with references; also Willmes, *Herrscher-"Adventus*," esp. 109 and n. 413. Princely *adventus* and the related ceremony of *occursus* are documented for Flanders in the mid–tenth century and in the late eleventh century, a fact that implies, but does not prove, their use in between: Huyghebaert, *Translation de reliques*, 45–46, 49–51; St-Thierry, ff. 214–15 (1090); and Vercauteren, *Actes*, 65–67, no. 22 (1096).

86. Fulbert of Chartres, *Letters and Poems*, 6–7, no. 1. Also Lex, doc. 21 (1034), an *occursus* for Odo II of Blois and the archbishop of Tours by St-Julien; and Vercauteren, *Actes*, 65–67, no. 22 (1096), in which a dispute between St-Thierry and Robert II of Flanders ends with the monks welcoming the count to the monastery *cum processione ecclesiastica*.

87. Raoul Glaber, *Histoires*, 103–5; Delisle, "Notices sur les manuscrits," 266–68, 271.

88. Goetz, "Kirchenschutz."

89. Hoffmann, *Gottesfriede*, 11–13, is representative. For a corrective see Goetz, "Kirchenschutz."

90. Mansi, 19:89–90; Elisabeth Magnou-Nortier, "La place du Concile du Puy (v. 994) dans l'évolution de l'idée de paix," in *Mélanges offertes à Jean Dauviller* (Toulouse, 1979), 489–506 at 499–500. Hoffmann, however, suspected that the duke of Aquitaine was involved at Charroux. He also noted that the Peace assembly at Narbonne (c. 990), although presided over by the metropolitan, included the major lords of the region: *Gottesfriede*, 24–26.

91. Strubbe, "Paix de Dieu," 490; Duby, *Three Orders*, 21–43.

92. Daniel Callahan, "Adémar de Chabannes et la Paix de Dieu," *Annales du Midi* 89 (1977): 21–43," and "William the Great and the Monasteries of Aquitaine," *Studia Monastica* 19 (1977): 321–42.

93. *Philippe Ier*, no. 75; *GC* 10:Instr. 286–89; Ramackers, *PUF*, no. 3; Fossier, *Terre et hommes*, 2:486–87, 501; Feuchère, "Tentative manquée," 35–36.

94. *Mir. s. Adalhardi*, 861: "Fuit autem haec repromissio, ut, si qui disceptarent inter se aliquo discidio, non se vindicarent preda aut incendio, donec statuta die ante aecclesiam coram pontifice et comite fieret pacificalis declamatio." Also Bonnaud-Delamare, "Paix d'Amiens," supplemented by Hoffmann, *Gottesfriede*, 64–65.

95. Bonnaud-Delamare, "Institutions de paix," 184 bis, gives the text; *Gesta episcoporum Cameracensium*, 476–77, gives the context; Duby gives the critical commentary and bibliography in *Three Orders*, 25–27, and "Gérard de Cambrai."

96. *Annales Elmarenses*, in *Annales de Saint-Pierre de Gand*, 89.

97. Bonnaud-Delamare, "Institutions de paix," 184 bis; H. Wasserschleben, "Zur Geschichte der Gottesfrieden," *ZSSRG*, Rom. Abt. 12 (1891): 112–17.

98. Koziol, "Monks, Feuds, and the Making of Peace."

99. Bonnaud-Delamare, "Institutions de paix," 148–53. Representative disputes involving similar accusations: *PL* 162:653; Hariulf, 198–200; *Philippe Ier*, no. 27; Lefranc, *Histoire . . . de Noyon*, doc. 4.

100. Bonnaud-Delamare, "Institutions de paix," 84 bis. Cf. *ND Paris*, 1:308; St-

Eloi, ff. 109v–10; *Homblières,* 100, c. 21; Bourgin, *Commune de Soissons,* doc. 8; Langlois, *Textes,* no. 1; Fossier, *Chartes de coutume,* no. 1; Newman, *Domaine royal,* doc. 2; MSQ, nos. 4 and 11 (= BN, Coll. Moreau 23, f. 190r–v and 37, f. 198).

101. Bonnaud-Delamare, "Institutions de paix."

102. Bachrach, "Toward a Reappraisal" and "A Study in Feudal Politics" (above, n. 83); Callahan, "Adémar de Chabannes" and "William the Great" (above, n. 92).

5. Toward an Iconic Kingship

1. Above, 54.

2. Above, 43–44.

3. Fauroux, no. 9; Bates, *Normandy before 1066,* 24–38, 56–58, 65–67, 148–49, 156, 193–96; Searle, "Frankish Rivalries" and *Predatory Kinship,* esp. chaps. 5, 9–11.

4. For Richard I, Fauroux, no. 3 (for St-Denis [968]), a copy known from a late thirteenth-century cartulary and singular in every way. For Richard II see Fauroux, nos. 12 (for Mont-St-Michel [1009]), 18 (for St-Quentin [1015]), 20 (for St-Riquier [1010–17]), 23 (for Marmoutier [1013–20]), and 50 (for St-Père [1016–26]). I have excluded subscriptions and notices. As for copies, I have not found that their use of petitionary formulas differs in either style, frequency, or chronology from that of originals.

5. Searle, *Predatory Kinship,* 75, 88–89, 123–26, 286 n. 2.

6. Cassandra W. Potts, "Les ducs normands et leurs nobles: Le patronage monastique avant la conquête de l'Angleterre," *Etudes Normandes* 3 (1986): 29–37 at 30.

7. Bates, *Normandy before 1066,* 66–67, 191–96; Lemarignier, "Paix et réforme monastique," 454–57; Fauroux, 25 and no. 23. Also relevant here are his daughter's marriage to the count of Burgundy, his son's to a daughter of Robert the Pious: Searle, *Predatory Kinship,* 138, 141.

8. Cowdrey, "Anglo-Norman *Laudes Regiae.*"

9. Support for this view comes from Richard's role in obtaining the release of the wife of the viscount of Limoges from Viking raiders, and by the role of Rouen and Caen as entrepôts for Norse plunder, some of which would eventually have found its way into Francia. See Searle, *Predatory Kinship,* 94–95, 124–25, 129, 141–42; also Beech, "Participation of Aquitanians," 11.

10. Above, n. 4.

11. Fauroux, nos. 43 (1015–26) and 12 (1009): "quia accerssierit [sic] nostram almitatem contio sancti agminis coenobii magni ierarchi caelorum Michaelis bene provida sua salutis, exposcens sibi patrem institui de suis."

12. Dhondt, *Origines de la Flandre,* 39–45; also Ganshof, *Flandre sous les premiers comtes,* 20–22.

13. Hodüm, "Réforme monastique," supplemented by the the articles by A. C. F. Koch, Henri Platelle, and Jean Laporte on Arnulf's relationship with Gerard of Brogne in *Revue Bénédictine* 70 (1960); also Huyghebaert, *Translation de reliques,* 26–27, 37–51.

14. *Dipl. Belg.,* 1:144, no. 53.

15. *Dipl. Belg.,* vol. 1, nos. 53 (941), 57 (960), 59 (962), and Van Lokeren, *Chartes . . . de Saint-Pierre,* no. 22 (with *Dipl. Belg.,* 1:106–8, 113). For other tenth-century counts see *Dipl. Belg.,* vol. 1, nos. 56 (Countess Adele [955]) and 67 (Count Godfrey of Verdun [975–80]), which are also not petitionary. (Nor is no. 62, by Count Theoderic of West Frisia [964–65]; but this charter executes Arnulf's testament, and

such acts never employ our formulas; similarly *GC* 5:Instr. 351, a foundation charter for St-Donatien). Otto Oppermann, *Die älteren Urkunden des Klosters Blandinium und die Anfänge der Stadt Gent*, 2 vols. (Utrecht, 1928), argued that many of the tenth- and early eleventh-century charters from Sint-Pieters, Ghent, were forgeries; but his utter dismissal of their worth was excessive and was criticized as such by Koch (*Dipl. Belg.*, 1:85–122). The charters received numerous interpolations (as with *Dipl. Belg.*, vol. 1, nos. 57 and 59, which Koch holds to have been forged or reworked); but the basic diplomatic form of the original acts appears to have been retained. Indeed, it is only on this assumption that we can explain the great differences between tenth- and eleventh-century comital acts described here. For an example of the problems posed by the Ghentish archives see Verhulst, "Note sur deux chartes."

16. On the successional crisis, Dhondt, *Origines de la Flandre*, 49–54, and Ganshof, *Flandre sous les premiers comtes*, 27–30. On Baldwin IV and V, Dhondt, 55–79, and Ganshof, 30–43.

17. Dhondt, *Origines de la Flandre*, 66–67, 71–73; for examples, Haigneré, *Chartes de Saint-Bertin*, nos. 71 (1042) and 73 (1051); Van Lokeren, *Chartes . . . de Saint-Pierre*, 81, no. 116 (1034–60), and 95–96, no. 113 (1056); *St-Bertin*, 184–86, no. 14 (1056).

18. As with Marchiennes: Courtois, "Chartes originales," 62–63 (= Lille, AD Nord, 10 H 323, 105, no. 61 [1038]); Piot, *Cartulaire . . . d'Eename*, no. 3 (1064), creating, however, a subadvocacy.

19. On the history of these wars, see Ganshof, "Origines de la Flandre impériale"; Dhondt, *Origines de la Flandre*, 57–71, 73–77.

20. Above, 136.

21. *Mir. s. Ursmari*, MGH SS 15/2:839–40, cc. 8–9, on which see Koziol, "Monks, Feuds, and the Making of Peace." See also the Peace of Thérouanne, above, 136.

22. Kienast, *Herzogstitel*, 197 and n. 156.

23. These concerns are brought together in Lille, AD Nord, 10 H 323, 107–8, no. 63 (1046) (= Courtois, "Chartes originales," 64–65), where Baldwin V confirms the property of Marchiennes, speaking particularly of the need to protect that property against oppression and injustice, and in so doing compares himself with *predecessores principes*, Charlemagne and Lothar.

24. Lille, AD Nord, 10 H 323, 104–5, no. 61 (1038) and 107–8, no. 63 (1046) (= Courtois, "Chartes originales," 62–65); Van Lokeren, *Chartes . . . de Saint-Pierre*, no. 133 (1056); *Dipl. Belg.*, vol. 1, no. 96 (1047); *St-Bertin*, 184 (1056); Vercauteren, *Actes*, nos. 2, 5, 12, 14, 18, etc. See also Serrure, *Cartulaire de Saint-Bavon*, 16–19, a letter from Abbot Othelbold to Countess Otgive offering "debita seruitutis et orationis obsequia."

25. Above, 2–4.

26. Halphen, *Comté d'Anjou*, 348–49, doc. 3; Guillot, *Comte d'Anjou*, 2:27, *Cat.*, C 12. My thanks to Bernard Bachrach for calling my attention to this source and suggesting this interpretation.

27. Though Raoul continued to work on his *Historiae* until his death in 1047, he had completed the distinctive first two books by 1035 (Ortigues and Iogna-Prat, "Raoul Glaber," 545).

28. P. Rousset, "La conception d'histoire à l'époque féodale," in *Mélanges Louis Halphen* (Paris, 1951), 623–33; also R.-H. Bautier, "L'historiographie en France aux Xᵉ et XIᵉ siècles," in *La storiografia altomedievale*, Settimane di studio del centro italiano di studi sull'alto medioevo 17/2 (Spoleto, 1970), 793–850, esp. 848.

29. Sassier, *Hugues Capet*, 280–81; Duby, "Gérard de Cambrai" and *Three Orders*, 21–43; J. France, "The Divine Quaternity of Rodulfus Glaber," *Studia Monastica* 17 (1975): 283–94; Ortigues and Iogna-Prat, "Raoul Glaber." I have been unable to use the new edition of Raoul's *Histories* by John France (*The Five Books of the Histories* [Oxford, 1989]).

30. *Acta concilii Remensis*, 683–85; Richer, *Histoire de France*, 2:260.

31. Raoul Glaber, *Histoires*, 13–15: "veniens inprovisus corruit ad imperatoris pedes, oransque se ab imperatoris pietate vitae servari"; 85–86: "acra animi ferocitate tamdiu illum insecutus est debellando, quousque genu flectens ei se subderet ejusque ditioni oboediens pareret."

32. Above, 78; also *Gesta episcoporum Cameracensium*, 466.

33. *MSB*, 243: "Qui prostratae matris flexus lacrymis, benigne petitionibus ejus assensum praebuit."

34. In addition to the works cited below, see Henri Prentout, *Etudes critiques sur Dudon de Saint-Quentin et son "Histoire des premiers ducs normands"* (Paris, 1916); R. H. C. Davis, *The Normans and Their Myth* (London, 1976), 50–63; Elizabeth M. C. Van Houts, "Gesta Normannorum ducum," *Anglo-Norman Studies* 3 (1980): 106–18; Gerda C. Huisman, "Notes on the Manuscript Tradition of Dudo of St. Quentin's *Gesta Normannorum*," *Anglo-Norman Studies* 6 (1983): 122–35; Leah Schopkow, "The Carolingian World of Dudo of Saint-Quentin," *Journal of Medieval History* 15 (1989): 19–37. Useful perspectives may also be found in Olivier Guillot, "La conversion des Normands peu après 911," *Cahiers de civilisation médiévale* 24 (1981): 101–16, 181–219. I have not consulted the thesis by Barbara Vopelius-Holtzendorff, "Studien zu Dudo von Saint-Quentin, dem ersten Geschichtsschreiber der Normandie, 987–1015" (University of Göttingen, 1967). Nor have I followed the suggestion made by Huisman and Van Houts to call the work *Gesta Normannorum*, among other reasons simply to avoid confusion with William of Jumièges's work of that title.

35. Eleanor Searle, "Fact and Pattern in Heroic History: Dudo of St. Quentin," *Viator* 15 (1984): 119–37 at 119.

36. Bates, *Normandy before 1066*, xii–xiii. Even William of Jumièges discounted Dudo's stories about the first Normans as simple flattery, neither useful nor honest: Van Houts, "Gesta Normannorum ducum," 108 (above, n. 34).

37. Huisman, "Notes on the Manuscript Tradition," 122 (above, n. 34). On the date of Dudo's completion of his history, see below, n. 50.

38. Searle, "Fact and Pattern" (above, n. 34) and *Predatory Kinship*, 132–37.

39. Davis, *Normans and Their Myth*, 52 (above, n. 34).

40. Dudo of St-Quentin, *De moribus*, 294–95 ("Lothario rege defuncto, Hugo dux filius magni ducis intronizatus in regno"), 232–35.

41. Bur, *Formation . . . de Champagne*, 101–2, 112–13.

42. Richer, *Histoire de France*, 2:172; also Bur, *Formation . . . de Champagne*, 121.

43. Bur, *Formation . . . de Champagne*, 114–202.

44. Lot, *Derniers carolingiens*, 235 and n. 3; Bur, *Formation . . . de Champagne*, 119–20, 267–68; *Acta concilii Remensis*, 662.

45. Dudo was willing to appeal to God's predestination in his efforts to understand Duke William's assassination (*De moribus*, 202). His discussion of the failure of Louis d'Outremer and, by extension, of the last Carolingians, as discussed below, also indicates a tendency to fall back on providential explanations of troubling events.

46. *De moribus*, 160: "Franci imbelles armisque frigidi, quasi effeminati." Also see the sardonically bitter poem addressed to Louis IV on 229, and the portrait of

Charles the Simple's haplessness on 160–61. Guillot, "Conversion des Normands," 204 (above, n. 34), recognizes the importance of these statements, pointing out that they are coupled with Dudo's profession of high expectations for Rollo.

47. *De moribus*, 103: "Franciae autem principes invidiae pondus et odii ferebant adversus Willelmum." On 282 the Normans and Daci, repulsed by the constant treachery of the Frankish leaders, go so far as to say that there will be no peace until they are all killed.

48. Ibid., 262: "Erat . . . fortitudo debilium, defensor orphanorum, solator miserorum, baculus orborum, reparator ecclesiarum, lux sincera caecorum, apex clericorum, salus egentium, culmen generum, decus praesulum, salus viduarum, cacumen sacerdotum, amator foederum, cultor virtutum, maxima spes omnium: pietas moestorum, memorabile pignus amicitiarum, palma desperantium, tutela presbyterorum, sedes legum, rector populorum, pastor pauperum, forma proborum, arma militum, judicium accusantium et accusatorum, libra quaestionum, mitigator rixarum, pater exsulum, receptor profugorum, distributor bonorum . . . , exemplum cunctorum, poena furum, detrimentum latronum, emendator confessorum, opus pietatum . . . , lumen cunctorum, specimen sanctitatum, dulce caput consulum, auxiliator regum, protector omnium populorum."

49. Ibid., 263, quoted above, chap. 1, n. 157.

50. Huisman, "Notes on the Manuscript Tradition," 122 (above, n. 34), gives the termini for Dudo's basic text as 996 and 1015. The latter year is the date Dudo became dean of St-Quentin, and during his tenure in that office he added an interlacing of poems. The donation to St-Quentin recorded in the diploma under consideration may well have enabled Dudo to gain election as dean, as Prentout suggested; but it may simultaneously have been the reward for his having completed the work of which Dudo himself spoke (Prentout, *Etudes critiques*, 19–20 [above, n. 34]).

51. Fauroux, no. 18: "quod accessit Dudo preciosi martyris Christi Quintini canonicus, nosterque fidelis idoneus, ad me qui noncupor Ricardus, felicissimi comitis Ricardi filius, dicorque gratia summe individueque Deifice Trinitatis Northmannorum licet indignus dux et patritius, deprecans per comitem Rotdulfum meum avunculum, multimodisque et crebris supplicationibus per se ipsum, ut ecclesias quas dedit pater meus suprascriptus ei in benefitio, concederem precioso martyri Christi Quintino pro anime patris mei et meae remedio. Cujus petitionibus humillimis postulationibusque devotissimis assensum prebens et annuens, concedo prescripto martyri Quintino easdem acclesias [sic]." Note that Dudo used several of these idiosyncratic phrases to describe his reception by Richard I in 987: *De moribus*, 295.

52. *De moribus*, 242: "Servantes stabili tenore pacem, / Et sacrae fidei petitionem."

53. Ibid., 169.

54. Carlyle and Carlyle, *History of Mediaeval Political Theory*, 1:199–209.

55. *Gesta episcoporum Cameracensium*, 402, 1.1. On the viscomital family that appears to have been related to Dudo, see Bur, *Formation . . . de Champagne*, 267–68.

56. *De moribus*, 155.

57. Ibid., 181. Dudo described non-Normans supplicating Rollo even before this event (e.g., 141–42, 167–68); but these incidents should be taken as signs of Rollo's election by God, as discussed by Guillot, "Conversion des Normands," 203 (above, n. 34).

58. *De moribus*, 185.

59. Ibid., 187–88.

60. Ibid., 189 ("multosque incoepto praelio prostravimus"), 191 ("prosternit quos gladio reperit").

61. Ibid., 193.

62. Lemarignier, *Recherches sur l'hommage en marche*, 75–84; also *De moribus*, 169 ("statim Francorum coactus [Rollo] verbis, manus suas misit inter manus regis").

63. *De moribus*, 196, 193.

64. Ibid., 206–7.

65. Ibid., 232–35. Hugh, however, found himself deceived in turn by the Normans. Thus Dudo's justice remains proportional: one who had unjustly deceived was himself justly deceived.

66. Ibid., 224–25.

67. Fulbert of Chartres, *Letters and Poems*, no. 80. Of course what Dudo intended was to exemplify the early medieval conceit that a king who behaved as a tyrant lost the name of king.

68. *De moribus*, 228–29. The comparison is not anachronistic, since other contemporaries were also concerned with simony; e.g., Abbo of Fleury (Mostert, *Political Theology*, 96–97).

69. *De moribus*, 230. There is a similar usage on 235.

70. Ibid., 230.

71. Ibid., 233–35, 242.

72. Ibid., 243.

73. Ibid., 263, quoted above, chap. 1, n. 157.

74. Searle, "Frankish Rivalries" and *Predatory Kinship*, 21–22, 57–58, 61–62.

75. Dudo's friendship with Adalbero is known from the fact that he dedicated *De moribus* to him (115–20). Though there is no evidence of friendship between Dudo and Gerard, it is quite likely, given the similarities between Dudo's treatment of the state of nature and that of the *Gesta episcoporum Cameracensium* (above, 152), as well as the similarities in their ideas of peace (Bonnaud-Delamare, "Institutions de paix," 157–88).

76. Robert T. Coolidge, "Adalbero, Bishop of Laon," *Studies in Medieval and Renaissance History* 2 (1965): 1–114; Duby, *Three Orders*, 44–55.

77. H. Sproemberg, "Gerhardt I, Bischof von Cambrai (1012–1051)," in *Mittelalter und demokratische Geschichtsschreibung* (Berlin, 1971), 103–18, esp. 106–10, 112, 116–17.

78. For the Frankish episcopacy's dislike of Adalbero, see Sassier, *Hugues Capet*, 188–89 (though cf. Coolidge, "Adalbero," 4 and 113–14 [above, n. 76]). See *Gesta episcoporum Cameracensium*, 474, 485–86, for the lack of sympathy between Gerard and his cosuffragans, and 477–79 for Gerard's frequent, often meddlesome and sanctimonious letters to his colleagues. On their works: Duby, *Three Orders*, 21–55, and "Gérard de Cambrai"; Adalbero of Laon, *Poème au roi Robert*.

79. Deshman, "Exalted Servant."

80. E.g., the Milan ivory from the Castello Sforzesco; the Pommersfelden prayerbook of Otto III; and the Basel Antependium, depicting Henry II and Kunegunde: ibid., 397, 415–16; Schramm et al., *Deutschen Kaiser und Könige*, pl. 93, 105, 128. Essential for the context of the renewal of this program is Bornscheuer, *Miseriae regum*.

81. Above, 79.

82. Karl Josef Benz, "Heinrich II. und Cluny," *Revue Bénédictine* 84 (1974): 313–37 at 331–32; Odilo of Cluny, *Epitaphium domne Adalheide auguste*, 41, c. 17.

83. Above, 121.

84. Above, chap. 4.

85. Ganshof, "Flandre sous les premiers comtes," 32–34; Dhondt, *Origines de la Flandre*, 55–61; Bur, *Formation . . . de Champagne*, 165–73; Georges Duby, *La société au XIe et XIIe siècles dans la région maconnaise* (Paris, 1953), 155–57.

86. Russell, *Dissent and Reform*, 21, 39–40, 179, 183; cf. Moore, *Origins of European Dissent*, 15–16, 293 n. 15.

87. Bornscheuer, *Miseriae regum*, 41–59; Corbet, *Saints ottoniens*, 81–110; Dauphin, *Bienheureux Richard*, chaps. 7–8; Benz, "Heinrich II. und Cluny," 313–15 (above, n. 82). On Richard's legation, Lemarignier, "Paix et réforme monastique," 445–46.

88. Bautier, "Hérésie d'Orléans," and Odorannus of Sens, *Opera omnia*, 9–10, 11–16. Also Pierre Riché, "L'enseignement de Gerbert à Reims dans le contexte européen," in *Gerberto*, 51–69 at 64–68; Pfister, *Etudes sur . . . Robert le Pieux*, 34–38.

89. Odorannus of Sens, *Opera omnia*, 21–22; also Lemarignier, "Paix et réforme monastique," 448–49; Bur, *Formation . . . de Champagne*, 163–65; *Gesta episcoporum Cameracensium*, 480, 3.37; Raoul Glaber, *Histoires*, 38–39, 3.2.8. I have not, however, been able to document the special concern with peace that Henry is sometimes alleged to have shown, apart from the fact that the subject was discussed at Ivois.

90. Odorannus of Sens, *Opera omnia*, 20–21: "Galliarum et primati / Saviniano nobili / Vota solvit Constancia / Francorum supl[ex] regina, / Ejus ut prece maxima / Sibi donentur debita." For Ottonian examples see esp. the Milan ivory of Otto III and the Basel Antependium, in Schramm et al., *Deutschen Kaiser und Könige*, pl. 105 and 128.

91. Odilo of Cluny, *Epitaphium*, 41, c. 17; Helgald of Fleury, *Vie de Robert*, 80–85, c. 14; Hansmartin Decker-Hauff, "Die 'Reichskrone' angefertigt für Kaiser Otto I.," in *Herrschaftszeichen und Staatssymbolik*, ed. P. E. Schramm, vol. 2 (Stuttgart, 1955), 560–637 at 578–79.

92. See Reinhart Staats, *Theologie der Reichskrone: Ottonische "Renovatio Imperii" im Spiegel einer Insignie* (Stuttgart, 1976), 71 and n. 171; Schneidmüller, *Karolingische Tradition*, 178 and n. 53, both following indirectly, via Decker-Hauff, the old interpretation by Robert Eisler, *Weltenmantel und Himmelszeit* (Munich, 1910), 1:22–24, 37–38.

93. Andrew of Fleury, *Vie de Gauzlin*, 120–25, esp. nos. 1, 2, 5, 6, 7, 16, 18; R.-H. Bautier, "Le monastère et les églises de Fleury-sur-Loire sous les abbatiats d'Abbon, de Gauzlin, et d'Arnaud (988–1032)," in *Mémoires de la Société nationale des antiquaires de France* 4, 9th ser. (1969), 71–154 at 115–31.

94. Andrew of Fleury, *Vie de Gauzlin*, 136, no. 66.

95. On the *Vita Rotberti* see the introduction to the edition by Bautier and Labory; also Carozzi, "Vie du roi Robert" and "Roi et liturgie"; Duby, *Three Orders*, 181–85; Joel Rosenthal, "Edward the Confessor and Robert the Pious: Eleventh-Century Kingship and Biography," *Medieval Studies* 33 (1971): 7–20.

96. Carozzi, "Vie du roi Robert" and "Roi et liturgie."

97. Corbet, *Saints ottoniens*, 78–79, 100 n. 72 (which is wrong on both Helgald and Carozzi), 105, 211 n. 12, 247 n. 21. I expect to deal with this issue in a forthcoming article.

98. Helgald of Fleury, *Vie de Robert*, 104, c. 21; Carozzi, "Roi et liturgie," 418, 420–21, and "Vie du roi Robert," 104–5.

99. Helgald of Fleury, *Vie de Robert*, 66, c. 7; 90, c. 16; 64–66, c. 6; 102, c. 20. On this theme in analogous Ottonian writings see Bornscheuer, *Miseriae regum*, 48–51, 76–77. Corbet, *Saints ottoniens*, believes that this theme was traditional.

Although he is correct, there also appears to have been a significant gap in its development between the late ninth and late tenth centuries. See Deshman, "*Christus rex*" and "Exalted Servant."

100. Helgald of Fleury, *Vie de Robert*, 74, 78, etc. Elisabeth Carpentier has found that Helgald uses the adjective *humilis* more frequently (22 times) than any other save the somewhat anodyne *sanctus* (213) and *bonus* (39): "Histoire et informatique: Recherches sur le vocabulaire des biographies royales françaises," *Cahiers de civilisation médiévale* 25 (1982): 4–30.

101. Helgald of Fleury, *Vie de Robert*, 58, 70–72, 80, 78 (citing Gregory the Great), 56–58, 94–97, 78 (in which God's omnipotence is juxtaposed to the king's humility: "Oremus omnipotentem Deum ut hic Dei electus qui, deposito omni tumore superbie, conjunctus est Christo Deo sancte humilitatis virtute"; see also 56), 112 ("In conspectu omnium populorum et exuens se vestimento purpureo . . . utroque genu fixo in terram, toto de corde ad Deum supplicem fudit precem in his verbis"; on the meaning of such acts see Schramm et al., *Deutschen Kaiser und Könige*, 203; Deshman, "Exalted Servant"), 94–97 ("Uterque [reges] peccavit, quod solent reges; sed a Deo visitati, penituerunt, fleverunt, ingemuerunt, quod non solent reges. Siquidem exemplo beati David, domnus iste noster Rotbertus confessus est culpam, obsecravit indulgentiam, deploravit erumnam, jejunavit, oravit et confessionis sue testimonium in perpetua secula vulgato dolore transmisit").

102. Schramm et al., *Deutschen Kaiser und Könige*, 203.

103. Bornscheuer, *Miseriae regum*, 112–19, 205–6, noting how similar Helgald's description of Robert's penance is to Bern of Reichenau's description of Henry III's penance at his mother's burial.

104. *Collectio canonum*, PL 139:480, c. 7; "praecepta regalis, id est imperialis, jussionis auctoritate roborata." Cf. Schneidmüller, *Karolingische Tradition*, 71–72.

105. Raoul Glaber, *Histoires*, 58–59.

106. Schneidmüller, *Karolingische Tradition*, 69–76, 175–83.

107. Helgald of Fleury, *Vie de Robert*, 62, 82, 92; Schneidmüller, *Karolingische Tradition*, 30, 64, 101–5; Jean Dufour, "Etat et comparaison des actes faux ou falsifiés intitulés au nom des Carolingiens français (840–987)," in *Fälschungen im Mittelalter*, 4:167–210 at 208–9; Pfister, *Etudes sur . . . Robert le Pieux*, 71, 75, 121; Deshman, "Exalted Servant"; PL 124:884.

108. Deshman, "Exalted Servant," 406–12; Anton, *Fürstenspiegel*, 276, 347.

109. Helgald of Fleury, *Vie de Robert*, 92–96. On the centrality of this passage see Carozzi, "Vie du roi Robert," 221.

110. RHF 10:583, 595 (Newman, *Cat.*, nos. 23, 39).

111. Bur, *Formation . . . de Champagne*, 153–73.

112. Jonathan Z. Smith, *Imagining Religion: From Babylon to Jonestown* (Chicago, 1982), 57–65.

113. Ademar of Chabannes, *Chronique*, 179–80; on the context, Pfister, *Etudes sur . . . Robert le Pieux*, 286–87. Since Ademar studiously avoids giving the name of Robert's queen; since around this time Robert had repudiated Constance, seal of his Angevin alliance, and gone back to Bertha, mother of Odo II and an ally of Odo and William against Anjou (Pfister, 66–70); and since Robert was accompanied at William's ceremony by Odo of Blois—for these reasons it is likely that Bertha was the queen who accompanied Robert in 1010 and that the ceremony was meant to celebrate the anti-Angevin alliance and/or to provide an occasion to discuss Robert's predicament.

114. Koziol, "Monks, Feuds, and the Making of Peace."

115. Vercauteren, *Actes*, no. 221; St-Thierry, ff. 214–15; Galbert of Bruges, *Histoire du meurtre*, 106, c. 66.

116. Galbert, *Histoire du meurtre,* 20–21, c. 12.

117. Above, chap. 1, n. 80.

118. *Philippe Ier,* nos. 23, 24, 115; cf. Guillot, "Actes de Henri Ier."

119. Cf. J.-F. Lemarignier, "Les fidèles du roi de France (936–987)," in *Recueil des travaux offert à M. Clovis Brunel* (Paris 1955), 2:138–62; K. F. Werner, "Kingdom and Principality in Twelfth-Century France," in *The Medieval Nobility,* ed. Timothy Reuter (Amsterdam, 1979).

120. *Gesta episcoporum Cameracensium,* 474, 3.27.

121. The claim is stated most forcefully by Hallam, "Kings and Princes" and *Capetian France,* chaps. 1–3. Cf. Schramm's astute perception about the Capetians' ability to maintain the integrity of their domains: if the princes wanted to pass on their own estates intact, they had to allow the kings to do the same: *König von Frankreich,* 107–8.

Part Three. Begging Pardon

1. Amann, "Pénitence," 862–94; Benedict of Aniane, *Modus penitentiarum,* ed. J. Semmler, in *Corpus Consuetudinum Monasticarum,* 1 (Siegburg, 1963), 563–82, esp. 573, 578.

2. *Vita Hludowici pii,* 65, c. 21 ("supplices veniam inter iter agendum poposcissent"), noting that this ritual, explicitly linked to the crime of *lèse majesté,* is contrasted with Wala's earlier homage "according to the custom of the Franks" (64, c. 21; "humillima subiectione se eius nutui secundum consuetudinem Francorum commendans subdidit"); Nithard, *Histoire des fils de Louis le Pieux,* 30, 1.7. Many of the references to supplications cited in chap. 4, n. 4, are of this sort.

3. *Annales de Saint-Bertin,* 92 (s.a. 862), 177, 182 (s.a. 870–71).

4. Ibid., 37 ("pariter coniuncti, sicut fraterna caritate," "ad pacis fraternitatisque concordiam"); similarly 41, 48, 56, 57, etc. On the pattern see Schneider, *Brüdergemeine,* and Anton, "Zum politischen Konzept karolingischer Synoden."

5. *Annales de Saint-Bertin,* 177, 182.

6. Ibid., 136–37; Magnou-Nortier, *Foi et fidélité,* chap. 4.

7. Above, 110.

8. Schneider, *Brüdergemeine;* Anton, "Zum politischen Konzept karolingischer Synoden"; Hännig, *Consensus fidelium.*

9. Duby, "The Evolution of Judicial Institutions," in his *Chivalrous Society,* 26–35, 44–45, 50–51, 54; *Pontoise,* nos. 20 (noting the prominence of the witnesses who attended the *placitum*), 40 ("multis vicibus . . . placitaverunt"); and the works on *convenientiae* cited above, Introduction, n. 45.

6. Supplication as Penance

1. Alföldi, *Monarchische Repräsentation,* 49.

2. Jungmann, *Mass of the Roman Rite,* 1:239, 240, 298–99, 303; 2:292; Lechner, *Liturgik,* 72; Rordorf, "Gestes accompagnant la prière," 199–200; Neunheuser, "Gestes de la prière à genoux," 154.

3. Amann, "Pénitence," 801–6, and Van de Paverd, "Disciplinary Procedures."

4. Anselm of Laon, *Sententie,* 78: "Et sicut homo per superbiam et inobedientiam ceciderat, ita per humilitatem et obedientiam redeat."

5. Amann, "Pénitence," and Frantzen, *Literature of Penance*, with bibliography.

6. Vogel, "Rites de la pénitence publique"; see also the related complex of penitential acts described by Henri Platelle, "La violence et ses remèdes en Flandre au XIe siècle," *Sacris erudiri* 20 (1971): 101–73 at 144–60.

7. Burchard of Worms, *Decretum*, 977–78, 19.7 (part taken verbatim from Regino of Prüm, *De ecclesiasticis disciplinis*, 251–52): "Ergo si superbus usque modo fuisti, humilia seipsum in conspectu Dei. . . . Tunc prosternat se poenitens in terram, et cum lacrymis dicat: '. . . Humiliter etiam te sacerdos Dei exposco, ut intercedas pro me, et pro peccatis meis ad Dominum et creatorem nostrum. . . .' Deinde sacerdos cum poenitente prosternat se in terram. . . . Tunc dicat . . .: 'Deus cujus indulgentia nemo non indiget, memento famuli tui N. qui lubrica terreni corporis fragilitate nudatus est, quaesumus, da veniam confitenti, parce supplici, ut qui suis meritis accusatur, tua miseratione salvetur. . . . Te supplices rogamus, et petimus, ut precibus nostris aurem tuae pietatis inclinare digneris. . . . Precor, Domine, clementiae et misericordiae tuae majestatem . . . et veniam praestare digneris.'"

8. Ulrich of Cluny, *Consuetudines Cluniacenses*, 701, 2.1.

9. *Liber tramitis*, 17.

10. Ibid., 55, 57, 67, for the recitation of the prostrate psalms during Lent; also 72, 81, 167–68, 243–44, 276, for other prostrate supplications, apart from the ordinary genuflections and inclinations that would have occurred during the mass.

11. Ps. 142 (143):1, 6 (*Domine exaudi*), one of the prostrate psalms required during Lenten vespers (*Liber tramitis*, 57).

12. Ulrich of Cluny, *Consuetudines Cluniacenses*, 739, 3.5.

13. Cowdrey, *Cluniacs*, 128.

14. De Vogüé and Neufville, *La Règle de Saint Benoît*, 1:440–43, c. 6, 2:646–47, c. 63, on which see De Vogüé, "L'abbé, vicaire du Christ" and *La communauté et l'abbé dans la règle de Saint Benoît* (Paris, 1961), 139. Giles Constable, "The Authority of Superiors in the Religious Communities," in Makdisi et al., *Notion d'autorité*, 191–94.

15. De Vogüé and Neufville, *Règle de Saint-Benoît*, c. 63; also BN, Coll. Moreau 23, f. 190 r–v; 36, ff. 52–53v; 42, f. 215 (= MSQ, nos. 4, 8, 22); Fossier, *Chartes de coutume*, no. 3; Hariulf, 193; *Pontoise*, nos. 8, 20, 21, 23, 40; St-Eloi, ff. 109v–10.

16. *St-Bertin*, 178, 187–88; *Dipl. Belg.*, vol. 1, no. 69; Knowles, *Monastic Constitutions of Lanfranc*, 2–3, 74; Willmes, *Herrscher-"Adventus,"* 108–9.

17. Ulrich of Cluny, *Consuetudines Cluniacenses*, 736, 3.3: "Ubicunque autem contigerit ut colloquantur domnus abbas et aliquis fratrum, et si frater senserit contra se iram et indignationem domini abbatis, continuo veniam petere toto corpore prostrato non moratur." Also Knowles, *Constitutions of Lanfranc*, 73.

18. Ulrich of Cluny, *Consuetudines Cluniacenses*, 734–75, 3.3. See also *Liber tramitis*, 218; Knowles, *Constitutions of Lanfranc*, 100–102.

19. On Suger's conservatism see Spiegel, "Defense of the Realm," 117–19.

20. Suger, *Vie de Louis VI*, 180–82, c. 25: "Videns autem prefatus Haimo nullo modo se posse resistere, jam et persone et castri spe sublata, hanc solam salutis sue repperiens viam, pedibus domini regis prostratus et multorum admiratione sepius revolutus, ut in eum misericorditer ageret efflagitans, castrum reddit, seipsum regie majestatis arbitrio totum exponit et, quanto superbius se subduxerat, tanto humilius his edoctus justicie se reduxit." Note that Suger described the original complaint against Haimo, brought by one Alard, as a humble petition: "Querelam deponens, domino regi humillime supplicat, rogans quatinus nobilem baronem Haimonem nomine . . . justiciam recusantem imperialiter in jus traheret." Thus

those who supplicate a lord's grace show by this demonstration of true humility that they merit his mercy.

21. Raoul Glaber, *Histoires*, 82: "Tamen paulo post Dei nutu in se reversus, ad genitores rediens, humili eos satisfactione benivolos erga se reddidit"; 85–86: "Quod cernens Heinricus, acra animi ferocitate tamdiu illum [comitem] insecutus est debellando, quousque genu flectens ei se subderet ejusque ditioni oboediens pareret."

22. *MSB*, 243: "Et nisi amazonidis Constantia, poenitens facti, satisfaciens filii voluntati, quaeque pervasa cum sese subjiciendo illi, succurrisset obsessis, vitae dispendium protulissent universi. Qui prostratae matris flexus lacrymis, benigne petitionibus ejus assensum praebuit, illatarumque immemor injuriarum, eam deinceps, quo vixit tempore, decenti veneratus est honore." On the figure of the amazon in patriarchal societies see Joan Bamberger, "The Myth of Matriarchy: Why Men Rule in Primitive Society," in *Woman, Culture, and Society*, ed. Michelle Zimbalist Rosaldo and Louise Lamphere (Stanford, 1974), 263–80.

23. William of Jumièges, *Gesta Normannorum ducum*, 101: "Ad cujus atrocem insolentiam propere conterendam, adveniens dux cum militaribus turmis, tamdiu eum intra munitionem tantae presumptionis adjutricem conclusit, donec ejus clementiam expeteret nudis vestigiis, equestrem sellam pro satisfactione ferens humeris"; 74–75: "Novissime deliberavit apud se equius illi fore cum vitae discrimine fratris [i.e., ducis] clementiam attentare. . . . Cujus vestigiis illico solo tenus provolutus, veniam commissi ab eo expetebat lugubris."

24. Burchard of Worms, *Decretum*, 977, 19.6 (= Regino of Prüm, *De ecclesiasticis disciplinis*, 251): "De superbia, quae initium omnis peccati est, et regina omnium malorum, nascitur omnis inobedientia, omnis praesumptio, et omnis pertinacia, contentiones, haereses, arrogantia."

25. For this use of public penance, developed during the ninth century, see Amann, "Pénitence," 862–86; Vancandard, "Confession," 890–91; Frantzen, *Literature of Penance*, chap. 2.

26. See, e.g., *Redon*, no. 195 (c. 840); MGH Epist. 5:133 (828–40), 309–10 (823), 339–40 (814–40); Elisabeth Magnou-Nortier, "Enemies of the Peace: Reflections on a Vocabulary (6th-11th centuries)," in Head and Landes, *Peace of God*.

27. See esp. the conflict between Fulrad of St-Vaast and the bishops of Cambrai/Arras: *Gesta episcoporum Cameracensium*, 446–47, 1.107, 116.

28. As declared in the clamor to God: below, chap. 7.

29. E.g., *Homblières*, nos. 27–29, 34. See Hermann Krause, "Königtum und Rechtsordnung in der Zeit der sächsischer und salier Herrscher," *ZSSRG*, Germ. Abt. 82 (1965): 1–98 at 40.

30. Gavin I. Langmuir, "Prolegomena to Any Present Analysis of Hostility against Jews," *Social Science Information* 15 (1976): 689–727 at 707–9.

31. Fichtenau, *Lebensordnungen*, 1:36–38.

32. Ulrich of Cluny, *Consuetudines Cluniacenses*, 708, 2.17.

33. Above, 73.

34. Fossier, *Chartes de coutume*, no. 1.

35. Above, 184.

36. Hémeré, *Augusta Viromanduorum*, "Regestum," 32–33, 35–36; Fossier, *Chartes de coutume*, no. 3; Soehnée, no. 88; Newman, *Cat.*, no. 45. See also the decree on minting issued by the abbot of Corbie in 1085: Paul Doubliez, "Le monnayage de l'abbaye Saint-Pierre de Corbie," in *Corbie, Abbaye royale: Volume du XIIIe Centenaire* (Lille, 1963), 283–310 at 298.

37. Charles Dereine, "Odon de Tournai et la crise du cénobitisme au XIe siècle," *Revue du Moyen Age Latin* 4 (1948): 365–406 at 146.

38. *Vita Burchardi*, 849; Hariulf, 161–62, 175, 193–94 (though cf. 155–56, 160, where it appears that Ingelard had done much to recoup several lost possessions from local lords). Note also the comments of the *Gesta episcoporum Cameracensium*, 470, on Engebrand, abbot of Lobbes, who had nothing of religion in him and so "bona aecclesia turpiter dissipabat." Also Pfister, *Etudes sur . . . Robert le Pieux*, 311: one abbot of St-Germain was responsible for dispersing its property, his successor for its restoration.

39. *St-Bertin*, 197. In this case the writer was not just complaining generally but referring to specific incidents.

40. Ibid., for Heribert; see also the account of John of Ypres's rule at St-Bertin, 200–201. For Leduin, see Guimann, 115–16; for Angelran, Hariulf, 178–207, noting esp. his leadership in reconstituting the domain (passim), his ability to face down the count of Ponthieu (189), his free distributions to the poor (194–96), and the rapidity with which matters grew worse at the monastery as Angelran slipped into senectitude (204–7).

41. *Homblières*, no. 28.

42. At Homblières, for example, the abbot alone represented the monastery in 70% of its eleventh-century transactions—even more before 1075. Hariulf recorded charters issued in the name of the abbot alone on 174–75, 193–94, 232–33, 233–34. See esp. 174–75, where the abbot, in response to a petition addressed to him alone, sells a property in Lotharingia, without mention of his monks' counsel or consent; and 193–94, where he rejects out of hand a claim made against the monastery and on his own authority, without mention of counsel or consent, lets out the disputed *res*.

43. Hilpisch, "Rat der Brüder," 224–31; also Karl Blume, *Abbatia: Ein Beitrag zur Geschichte der kirchlichen Rechtssprache*, Kirchenrechtliche Abhandlungen 83 (Stuttgart, 1914), 60–62; Constable, "Authority of Superiors" (above, n. 14).

44. *Chronique . . . de Mouzon*, 161–64.

45. Also relevant is the reluctance of Abbot Guibert of Nogent to speak out publicly against a superior: Guibert of Nogent, *Histoire de sa vie*, 141–42, 3.4.

46. At St-Riquier, Ingelard, "virum nobilitate valde insignem," was appointed by Hugh Capet (Hariulf, 154). Angelran, though not of noble birth, was well known to the king, having accompanied him to Rome, where he had impressed everyone with his learning, eloquence, and upright manners. Upon his election to the abbacy he fled the monastery to avoid promotion. The king had to send out a posse to hunt for him, but not, says Hariulf, before giving a homily on the virtues of such humility as Angelran had shown (180–83). Gervin appears to have come from a noble family; he was in any case well placed within reforming circles, having served as Richard of St-Vanne's chaplain. He was appointed abbot by Henry I, who personally asked Richard to free Gervin for the office (207–11). He was succeeded by his nephew, also named Gervin (274), whose own successor, Anscherus, was also "nobili genere ortus," the son of a castellan (*GC* 10:1252–53). Other prominent examples: Leduin, "magnum inter primores Flandrie, et fame et potentie" (Guimann, 115), appointed by the count of Flanders to head not only St-Vaast but also Marchiennes and Hamages (Adolphe de Cardevacque, *L'abbaye de Saint-Vaast* [Arras, 1865], 104). The counts were, in fact, instrumental in nominating or appointing outright nearly all of St-Vaast's abbots, most of them from powerful lordly families: Cardevacque, 106 (John), 109 (Poppo), 112 (Adelelm), and 113 (Erchembauld). The counts also appointed Roderic to the abbacies of St-Bertin and Bergues-St-Winnoc (*St-Bertin*, 178). Franz J. Felten, *Äbte und Laienäbte in Frankenreich* (Stuttgart, 1980), 51–53, has argued the importance of well-connected lay abbots to the prosperity of their monasteries during the Carolingian period. The same can be said

about reforming abbots of the eleventh century, given the support counts gave to their hand-picked abbots in forcing reform on unwilling monasteries, such as Fossés (*Vita Burchardi*, 851) and Bergues-St-Winnoc (*St-Bertin*, 187). One might also call attention to the success of the noble Maingaud of Corbie in resisting Robert the Pious's efforts to depose him (*Philippe I*er, no. 75), and to the ability of Fulrad of St-Vaast to turn the count of Flanders against the bishops of Cambrai (*Gesta episcoporum Cameracensium*, 446, 452, 1.107, 116).

47. *St-Bertin*, 179, 199; Hugh of Flavigny, *Chronicon Virdunense*, 372; *Vita Herluini*, 201, trans. in Vaughn, *Abbey of Bec*, 78.

48. Above, 184.

49. *Vita s. Arnulfi*, 236: "O amande pater, quid voluisti facere, gregem commissum tam inconsulte deserere, oves Christi tibi creditas lupis exponere, et domum sanctam, quam sic honorifice tractabas, vastatoribus iterum tradere . . . ? Miserere, quaesumus, filiis tuis, miserere supplicibus tuis, et non abjicias nos subesse gaudentes dictis tuis." The monks' fears were fully justified, since Arnulf's resignation came at a time when the monastery had earned the king's ire.

50. Hariulf, 274–75, 278–80.

51. Ibid., 280–81.

52. Newman, *Cat.*, no. 76; Soehnée, no. 41; *PL* 142:575 (= *GC* 10:Instr. 363).

53. Lohrmann, *PUF*, nos. 4 (Lothar for Homblières), 6 (Harduin of Noyon for his chapter), 9 (Gilduin, "in partibus Galliarum prepotens et diues," for Notre-Dame de Breteuil), 12, 14, 15, 22 (the bishops of Beauvais for local houses); Ramackers, *PUF*, nos. 7 (the bishop of Noyon and archbishop of Reims for Mont-St-Quentin), 8 (the bishop of Amiens for Notre-Dame de Berteaucourt), 10 (the bishop of Noyon for St-Quentin-en-l'Île); Guimann, 70–73 (Count Robert of Flanders for St-Vaast).

54. BN, Coll. Moreau 38, ff. 39–41v; 41, ff. 99–102 (= MSQ, nos. 9, 17).

55. *Philippe I*er, no. 125, quoted below, n. 74.

56. Hugh of Flavigny, *Chronicon Virdunense*, 377, 2.11: "Quidam servientium sancti Vedasti in tantam eruperat proterviam, in tantam excreverat insolentiam . . . ut infra atrium monasterii domum sibi constitueret magnae altitudinis et fortitudinis quasi pro tuitione loci." That the issue here was essentially insubordination is shown by the fact that bishops also described as "insolent" abbots who sought exemption: *Gesta episcoporum Cameracensium*, 452, 1.116; Gousset, *Actes*, 2:136.

57. *ND Paris*, 3:354–55 (1067).

58. MSQ, nos. 11 (1094–98 = BN, Coll. Moreau 37, f. 198): "ad redivivam malitiam recurrit insurgendo in nos."

59. Lefranc, *Histoire de la ville de Noyon*, doc. 3: "Qua in re Hugo castellanus mihi resistit."

60. See the perceptive comments by Krause, "Königtum und Rechtsordnung," 40–41 (above, n. 29); also Devisse, *Hincmar*, 1:500–502.

61. Hariulf, 239–40: "cujus injustitiae et impietati pius pater occurrens"; BN, Coll. Baluze 141, ff. 52v-53: "penitentia compunctus . . . nudis pedibus procidens ante altare . . . petiit de . . . sacrilegio veniam."

62. *St-Corneille*, 39–40, no. 15; *Vita s. Arnulfi*, 234–35.

63. MSQ, no. 4 (= BN, Coll. Moreau 23, f. 190r-v (1040–45)); see also *Mir. s. Walarici*, 29: "quidam miles . . . quadam praedicti Patris nostri Gualarici possessionem . . . injuste et violenter suae adscivit ditioni." On the idea that a monastery's property was actually held by the patron saint, see Krause, "Königtum und Rechtsordnung," 40–41 (above, n. 29).

64. Hugh of Flavigny, *Chronicon Virdunense*, 377, 2.11.

65. *Mir. s. Walarici*, 29–30.

66. *Vita s. Arnulfi*, 234–35.

67. Hariulf, 189, 199.

68. *Homblières*, no. 34: "Fulbertus . . . instigante inimico, saecularem ob cupiditatem invasit idem alodium, dicens loci ejusdem advocationem jure hereditario
sibi debere; quod cum audissemus provocavimus eum ad satisfactionem." Note also
that according to the customs of the lay nobility, Fulbert appears to have had perfectly good reason to take control of the allod when the monks denied him his right.
On "satisfaction" as penitential atonement for sin see Galtier, "Satisfaction."

69. Langlois, *Textes*, no. I (Newman, *Cat.*, no. 45 [1016]): "pro qua re
saepenumero dum interpellatus essem a venerabili abbate . . . qui hanc perniciem
mali soepe [sic] experitur a nefando et maligno Efredo." A more realistic interpretation would see Efredo as acting as an agent of the king and the count of Amiens,
who were trying to undermine Corbie's immunity and faced resistance from its
abbot: see *Philippe Ier*, no. 75.

70. MSQ, no. 11 (= BN, Coll. Moreau 37, f. 198 [1094–98]): "Mortuo autem illo
patreque ejus Roberto Perone dominium recipiente, Oylardus omnium timore sub-
lato, eo enim vivente vim nobis inferre ausus non fuerat, ad redivivam malitiam
recurrit insurgendo in nos."

71. MSQ, no. 4 (= BN, Coll. Moreau 23, f. 190r–v [1040–45]): "et quia erat acer
animo per vim conabatur aecclesie nostre predium subtrahere."

72. Hariulf, 156: "pravis operibus"; 189: "fraude subducta," "multam poten-
tium superbiam," "infidelem," "raptorem"; 192–93: "illo insaniente," "multa iniq-
uorum insidia," "tyrannorum atrocitas," "eorum cupiditas," "eorum saevitia,"
"rapacitas"; 199–200: "superbo et rapaci spiritu," "nequitia sui cordis," "pro odio et
injuria abbatis," "pestifer Hucbertus"; 232–33: "malitiose invasit," "insanae cupiditatis malitia," "perfidus Hucbertus," "sua avaritia"; 239–40: "rapacitatis studio
sauciam." ND Noyon, ff. 20v-22: "irruentes malefactores." *Homblières*, no. 34:
"saecularem ob cupiditatem invasit idem alodium," "in sua malitia perseverante."
Vita s. Arnulfi, 234–35: "sua superbia," "ferox cervicositas." Bourgin, *Commune de
Soissons*, doc. 8: "dictante malitia." Tardif, *Monuments historiques*, 152, no. 243:
"malitiose pravorum hominum calliditas." *St-Germain*, 80: "rapaciter et injuriose."
Herman of Tournai, *Liber de restauratione* (Continuatio), MGH SS 14:319–20, c. 7:
"ferocis animi existebat." *Jumièges*, no. 11: "hac insania." *Philippe Ier*, nos. 75:
"odio Galterii"; 125: "vesania," "insania eorum," "quorum furor"; 117: "presump-
sit causare." Langlois, *Textes*, no. 1: "perniciem mali," "nefandus et malignus."
Hugh of Flavigny, *Chronicon Virdunense*, 377: "insolentia," "protervia," "contra
superbiam disseruisset," "tumidus superbiebat." BN, Coll. Moreau 23, f. 190r–v:
"acer animo," and 37, f. 198: "rediviva malitia." Even this ample list is far from
complete.

73. *Homblières*, no. 23; *Philippe Ier*, no. 27. Similar slurs are found in *St-Germain*, 82; Fossier, *Chartes de coutume*, no. 3; *Philippe Ier*, no. 28; *Pontieu*, no. 5; St-
Eloi, ff. 109v–10; ND Noyon, ff. 52–53; *Historia relatione s. Richarii*, 463. Usurpation: *St-Germain*, 78, 80, 82; Fossier, *Chartes de coutume*, no. 3; *St-Corneille*, 39–
40; *Mir. s. Walarici*, 29; MSQ, nos. 4 (= BN, Coll. Moreau 23, f. 190r–v) and 15 (=
Amiens, AD Somme, H XVI, 56–58, no. 1).

74. *Philippe Ier*, no. 125 (–1092): "Sed ante tempora nostra fuere perversi homines, quorum violentia ad id vesanie prorupit ut in sanctam predictam ecclesiam
insurgerent, predia ipsius diriperent, ad ultimum vero, incrudescente eorum insania,
etiam munitiones et turrim quamdam ante ipsam ecclesiam construerent, quorum
furor non ante quievit donec divina Dei pietas, cujus protectione fundamentum ecclesie stat immobile, districtam et manifestam in illos exereret [sic] ultionem; nam
ex illis obstinatissimis hominibus alii insania aut furore agitati, alii morte pessima
suffocati, omnes interiere divino examine condempnati."

75. *Ordo rationis*, in *GC* 10:Instr. 96 (Soehnée, no. 75 [1047]): "cujus petitioni quoniam rationabilis uisa est libentissime assensum prebuimus"; similarly ND Noyon, ff. 20v–22 (1044–60); *Montierender*, no. 20 (1027); *St-Etienne*, 1, no. 18; etc. Reference to "reasonable" petitions was common in both royal and papal diplomatics: Dietrich Lohrmann, *Kirchengut im nordlichen Frankreich* (Bonn, 1983), 70–71. See also the act of Bishop Drogo of Thérouanne (Haigneré, *Chartes de Saint-Bertin*, 23, no. 70): "a me rationabili et humili petitione adquirere potuit [abbas]," and similar acts by the bishops of Amiens, Laon, and Noyon (BN, Coll. Picardie 197, f. 177; Charters of Picquigny, AN, R (1) 35, f. 2; Reims, Bm, 1602, ff. 178r–v, 219–20), by the bishop and count of Chartres (*St-Père*, 1:74–78 [–986]), by the dukes of Brittany and Normandy (St-Florent, ff. 60–61; Fauroux, no. 67), etc. The phrase *ordo rationis* was also well known. See Valenziano and Valenziano, "Supplique des chanoines," 7; *Cluny*, vol. 4, no. 2890 (1032).

76. Raoul Glaber, *Histoires*, 78, 3.8.29.

77. *Gesta episcoporum Cameracensium*, 402, 1.1, noting that the author writes "homines." Peter Damian's interpretation of Isa. 43:20 made the same point: "What does the savage beast signify if not the Gentiles totally unacquainted with reason?" (cited by A. Cantin, "*Ratio* et *Auctoritas* de Pierre Damien à Anselme," *Revue des études augustiniennes* 18/1–2 [1972], 152–79 at 156–57). Note also the abbot of St-Remi's association of obedience with reason, above, 191.

78. Gerbert, *Lettres*, 241: "Si fides mortalem Deo sotiat, perfidia nichilominus rationabilem brutis animalibus aequat."

79. *Gesta Normannorum ducum*, 116, 117, 119 (7.1, 2, 4), all denouncing rebellions during William the Bastard's minority.

80. ND Noyon, ff. 60–62.

81. Raoul Glaber, *Histoires*, 85, 3.9.36: "Diu multumque vastando res proprias debacatum est donec Fulco Andegavorum comes . . . matrem [i.e., Constanciam reginam] redarguens cur bestialem vesaniam erga filios exerceret"; 49–50, 2.11.22: "cujus etiam vesanie pervicatia"; "[episcopus] ostendens hominem insanientem hereticum factum, revocavit ab insania populum ex parte deceptum."

82. Ibid., 74, 3.8.26: "Fertur namque a muliere quadam ex Italia procedente hec insanissima heresis in Galliis habuisse exordium"; 80, 3.8.30: "extiterunt veritatis rebelles." Also 80, 3.8.31, where the heretics welcomed being put to the stake, believing that they would not be burned: "At illi in sua male confisi vesania nil pertimescere se jactantes"; "cernens quoque rex, et universi qui aderant, minus posse illos revocari ab insania."

83. On Leutard see Stock, *Implications of Literacy*, 101–6, with references.

84. MGH SS 7:489–90, 452.

85. Herman of Tournai, *Liber de restauratione* (Continuatio), 319–20, c. 7. Earlier the castellan had been characterized as being "of savage spirit" (*ferocis animi*)— in other words, like a wild animal.

86. Hariulf, 232–33, 4.21: "insanae cupiditatis malitiam."

87. *Jumièges*, no. 11.

88. Hariulf, 192–93.

89. *St-Bertin*, 190ff., no. 18.

90. Below, 219.

91. Little, "Pride Goes before Avarice," 31–37.

92. *Vita Odonis*, PL 133:74, 2.23, cited by A. Davril, "Le langage par signes chez les moines," in *Sous la règle de Saint Benoît: Structures monastiques et sociétés en France du Moyen Age à l'époque moderne*, Abbaye bénédictine Sainte-Marie de Paris, Oct. 23–25, 1980 (Geneva, 1982), 51–74 at 51.

93. *ND Paris*, 3:354–55 (1067).

94. *Gesta episcoporum Cameracensium*, 473, 3.23.

95. E.g., the trial narrated by Guibert of Nogent, *Histoire de sa vie*, 212–15, 3.17; see also Ivo of Chartres, *Correspondance*, 208–9, no. 51.

96. Cf. Boussard, "Droit de *vicaria*," 51–52: "Diffinitio rationis quae facta est Turonis." Kaufmann, *Aequitatis iudicium*, 28, has noted the frequent reference to *ratio* and *rationabilis* in early medieval judicial texts, but he considers them nothing but synonyms for "just" (*gerecht*) or "legitimate" (*rechtmässig*). Certainly procedural expressions derived from *ratio* were habits of speech, and one may of course translate them as Kaufmann has done. Yet such translations are insensitive to the political and theological paradigm to which these terms alluded. *Ratio* may have been a synonym for "justice"; the question is, however, what kind of justice?

97. *St-Germain*, 78: "Ille vero ad judicium veniens nullo modo resistere valuit, propter rationabilem contradictionem servorum sancti Vincentii et sancti Germani." *Dirationare*: Hariulf, 192–93; *Homblières*, 100, no. 44, c. 21; Guimann, 188–90; *Pontoise*, no. 22; *Jumièges*, no. 46. See also *St-Cyprien*, 103 (1086): "Hec contra ratiocinatus est abbas."

98. ND Noyon, ff. 55v–56 (1016): "Rationem igitur quam contra nos habuit Gerardus noster canonicus omnibus palam facere rectum esse decreuimus." See *Ronceray*, no. 170 (1075–93): "ab ipsis calumpnie sue ratione prolata"; *Montierender*, no. 13 (968): "hoc rationabiliter demonstrarunt."

99. Hariulf, 193–94: "Nos ergo ejus reclamatione justa ratione vacuata." Also *RHF* 11:580–82 (Soehnée, no. 88 [1049]): "tandem tam jussu potentissimi principis, quam praesentium ratione firmissima nobilium victus . . . de praeteritis poenitens compulsus annuit"; *Marmoutier, Dunois*, no. 98 (1032–64): "Tunc iniquitatis miles ille convictus ratione deficiens, praecibus innititur." Note also the related usage that describes a demandant renouncing an unjust claim as being "persuaded by reason" or returning to "saner counsel": *Marmoutier, Dunois*, no. 74 (1092–1101) and p. 53 (1096–1101).

100. ND Noyon, ff. 60–62; *RHF* 14:624. For the divine archetype, Fauroux, nos. 75 and 132; St-Florent, f. 115v; Anton, *Fürstenspiegel*, 368, citing Louis the Pious's "Programmatic Capitulary" of 818–19; and Herbert Kolb, "Himmlisches und irdisches Gericht in karolingischer Theologie und althochdeutscher Dichtung," *Frühmittelalterliche Studien* 5 (1971): 284–303 at 284–89.

101. Guimann, 381–82 (1089): "penitentia ductus nos humiliter revocavit, nec sine lacrymis eorum que in nos commiserat indulgentiam oravit."

102. Thillier and Jarry, *Cartulaire de Sainte-Croix d'Orléans*, 4–5, no. 3 (1092): "paenitentia ductus, venit Aurelianis ante altare Sanctae Crucis . . . pro isto malefacto veniam postulavit, absolutionem promeruit." On the event see Guyotjeannin, *"Episcopus" et "comes,"* 73–75, 102–5.

103. *Mir. s. Walarici*, 29: "ut sui suorumque misereantur humiliter postulat."

104. See also SQB, ff. 68–69 (1124): an individual is described in passing as "confessing his guilt." Later, when he renounced his quitclaim, a priest was produced as a witness to the fact that he had at that time made a formal confession. The brief formula therefore denoted a concrete ritual action.

105. *Mir. s. Walarici*, 29–30: "nudis pedibus virgas ferentes in manibus, humi prostrati veniam postulant."

106. Hariulf, 232, 4.21 (1053): "insanae cupiditatis malitiam deserens, a sancto Richario atque a fratribus veniam expetivit. Redditaque villa . . . absolutionem excommunicationis cum praesente uxore sua Ermina, terrae prostratus accepit . . . et causam componens."

107. *Pontoise*, no. 21 (1099–1104): "ad monasterium eorumdem, illis volens satisfacere, venit. Tunc convocatis fratribus . . . ante altare sanctorum . . . procedens ad

pedes Domini Theobaldi abbatis cum multis lachrymis ab eo absolvi petiit." Similarly BN, Coll. Baluze 141, ff. 52v–53, for St-Pierre of Beauvais (quoted above, n. 61); St-Thierry, ff. 105v–6v (1129, without excommunication), 106v–7v (1125, with excommunication); Platelle, *Justice seigneuriale*, doc. 4 (c. 1097).

108. Amann, "Pénitence," 804; Frantzen, *Literature of Penance*, 52; Teetaert, "Confession aux laïques," 41–42.

109. *Redon*, no. 195 (c. 840): "Tunc Uurbudic, confusus et supplex, prostratus ad pedes supradicti Conuuoion, confessus mendacium dixisse, et porcionem de exclusa non deberet habere."

110. Eike von Repgow, "Sachsenspiegel," Görlitz, Ratsarchiv, varia 1, f. 131, and the brief comments by Schmidt-Wiegand, "Gebärdensprache," 372; *Mir. s. Ursmari*, MGH SS 15/2:840–41, c. 16.

111. *Philippe Ier*, no. 27 (–1066): "omnni submota ratione communi, censura totius conventus episcoporum atque laicorum . . . legaliter convictus"; *St-Germain*, no. 51 (1030): "secundum curie nostre sententiam et totius conventus censuram."

112. *RHF* 11:580–82 (Soehnée, no. 88), quoted above, n. 99.

113. *Homblières*, no. 34: "'Accede ergo, inquit, Fulberte, et satisfac Deo inprimis et ejus Matri Sanctae Mariae per manus abbatis sui, atque insuper hac injusta pervasione in procinctu potestatis meae facta'; datque vadimonio et satisfactione peracta, promisit coram omnibus qui aderant ex illo die se advocationem non quaesiturum super alodium illud."

114. *Gesta episcoporum Cameracensium*, 467, 3.2: "Ad haec ille perterritus, mox incredibilis poenitentiae speciem induit et . . . obsidibus quidem cum sacramento oblatis, congestis etiam precibus, ad totius generis satisfactionem tota se humilitate deiecit; adeo sane, ut etiam ipsius domnus episcopus miseratione pulsatus, irratos comites precibus mitigaret."

115. Above, 59.

116. Guimann, 45–46.

117. Hariulf, 189.

118. Above, n. 92; Duby, *Three Orders*, 22–23, and "Gérard de Cambrai."

119. *Philippe Ier*, no. 75.

120. *Mir. s. Adalhardi*, 863. On the context see Zoller-Devroey, "Domaine de . . . Saint-Pierre de Corbie," 434–36.

121. Zoller-Devroey, "Domaine de . . . Saint-Pierre de Corbie," 434–36; Duby, *Three Orders* and "Gérard de Cambrai."

122. Hariulf, 189; *Pontieu*, no. 1.

123. Hariulf, 192–93, 199; also 232–33 and Soehnée, no. 47. These passages suggest that St-Riquier's title to Noyelles was severely flawed, since at various times in the eleventh century Hubert, Henry, and Walter Tirel all claimed rightful possession of it.

124. Hariulf, 200: "Sed et pestifer Hucbertus . . . judicio regis postmodum cum omni sua stirpe interiit, quia revera boni viri persequuntur, quieta non debuerat morte perfungi."

125. See Crick, *Explorations in Language and Meaning*, 91–92.

126. Gousset, *Actes*, 2:198–200: "Comes hujus ignominae opprobrium fere non praevalens praesentiam nostram adiit et satis lacrymosis precibus, ut concordiam . . . componeremus nos exoravit."

127. Fossier, *Chartes de coutume*, no. 3 (1076–77); Hariulf, 189. The only clear instance of a count's excommunication (from the context, actually a series of curses—*prolixe excommunicationis frequentatione importuna*) that I have found is Fauroux, no. 95 (c. 1040), concerning that of the young (*puer*) William II of Normandy by the abbot of St-Wandrille; and even here the context and wording make it

possible that only William's familiars were excommunicated. In 988 Adalbero of Reims speaks of the excommunication of one "Bal.," a person powerful enough to have gone to Rome to argue his case. Wauters, *Table chronologique des chartes*, 1:415, identifies "Bal." as Count Baldwin IV. However, none of the editors of Gerbert's letters makes this identification (Gerbert, *Lettres*, 103; Fritz Weigle, ed, *Die Briefsammlung Gerberts von Reims* [Berlin, 1966], 141; H. P. Lattin, ed., *The Letters of Gerbert* [New York, 1961], 154). It is unlikely in any event since in 988, the year of his father's death, Baldwin was still a minor (Léon Vanderkindere, *La formation territoriale des principautés belges au Moyen Âge*, 2 vols., [1903], rpt. Brussels, 1981], 1:296).

128. Hariulf, 232–33; Guimann, 381–82; Bourgin, *Commune de Soissons*, doc. 8; ND Noyon, ff. 60–62, 67v–68; St-Eloi, ff. 109v–10; Louvet, *Histoire et antiquitez*, 2:208; Gousset, *Actes*, 2:133–34; also the curse in MGH SS 8:377, and the excommunication of Hugh of Inchy (*PL* 162:648–49), though neither is recorded in a charter and the latter occurred in the context of reform councils. See also Chronicle/Cartulary of Nogent, AD Aisne, H 325, f. 124r–v, an early twelfth-century act recounting the mid-eleventh-century excommunication of Alberic of Coucy's *milites* which probably took its information from a contemporary charter.

129. Respectively, *St-Bertin*, 190ff.; *Vita s. Arnulfi*, 241; *Philippe Ier*, no. 125; ND Paris, 3:354–55; *Historia relationis s. Richarii*, 463.

130. *Gesta episcoporum Cameracensium*, 473, 3.23.

131. Below, chap. 8.

132. *Philippe Ier*, no. 143 (1060–1101): "tandem recitato ecclesie precepto, judicium ab episcopis qui aderant illatum est. . . . Facto autem judicio, postulavit prefatus comes ut canonici ad ipsum pergentes ablata reciperent et deinceps . . . secundum precepti institutionem, cetera possiderent, qui profectis ad se canonicis et ablata restituit et reliqua secundum precepti normam quieta habenda concessit." The count concerned is probably Hugh rather than Herbert, since no sources show the king acting so directly in the Vermandois under Herbert, while as Hugh's brother Philip would have had reason for just this type of delicate intervention.

133. MGH SS 15/2:863: "Cum tanta devotione, suis gestatorio, militibus onus eius leve certatim alleviantibus, in aecclesiam haut longe positam tulit. . . . Fratres vero vice Domini, qui cor contritum et humiliatum non despicit, sanctique Petri . . . eum absolverunt et eum gaudentem suisque orationibus commendatum ad obsidionem oppidi remiserunt."

134. *Jumièges*, no. 16.

135. *St-Père*, 1:173–74.

136. *Pontieu*, no. 5; Hariulf, 239–40.

137. *Homblières*, no. 31 (1075).

138. Fossier, *Chartes de coutume*, no. 3.

139. Claims against royal or comital ministers closely associated with their lords, from this and other regions: ibid.; *Pontieu*, no. 5; Tardif, *Monuments historiques*, no. 243; RHF 11:600; *Philippe Ier*, no. 61; Marmoutier, Dunois, no. 4; Thillier and Jarry, *Cartulaire de Sainte-Croix*, 96; BN, Coll. Baluze 41, f. 187. Blame on evil advisers: Vercauteren, *Actes*, nos. 22 (p. 67) and 75; Fauroux, no. 74; Lot, *Etudes critiques*, no. 18 bis; Bièvre Poulalier, ed., *Chartes . . . de St-Etienne*, no. 15. Bishops received the same gentle treatment: *Chronique . . . de Mouzon*, 192–94, doc. 5 (1018); Guyotjeannin, "Recherches," docs. 2 and 6; Reims, Bm, 85, f. 3. See also Odo II's letter to Robert the Pious: "si maligno consilio non tollatur, ut iam tandem a persecucione mea desistas" (Fulbert of Chartres, *Letters and Poems*, 154).

140. Vercauteren, *Actes*, no. 22.

7. *The Ideal of Discretionary Justice*

1. "Iustitia est constans et perpetua uoluntas ius suum cuique tribuendi." On this definition see Kuttner, "Forgotten Definition of Justice," 75–77. Also Fichtenau, *Arenga*, 53, 119, noting that after the late empire the phrase disappeared from preambles until the later eleventh century, reappearing first, apparently, in acts of Henry IV. Fichtenau believes that Suger's later reference to *ius suum unicuique custodire* in the *Vita Ludowici* alludes to this definition; but it was more likely taken from analagous statements in ninth-century Carolingian *Verträge*.

2. Kuttner, "Forgotten Definition," 96, citing Placentinus, *Summa inst.*, 1.1: "Iustitia est secundum Platonem uirtus que plurimum prodest his qui minimum possunt, nempe in personis miserabilibus euidentius clarescit iustitia." Gabriel Le Bras, *Histoire du droit et des institutions de l'église en Occident*, vol. 7, *L'âge classique* (Paris, 1965), 352–55, also emphasizes that justice in the early period of legal reform (eleventh and early twelfth centuries) was a matter of *virtus*, for it pertained to justice to act rather than to divide and distribute. So in the eleventh century, the monks of Cluny prayed God that he might "fiat pax in virtute tua" (Ulrich of Cluny, *Consuetudines Cluniacenses*, 648–49), and their clamor, cited below, asked of God, "Justifica in virtute tua." See also Ivo of Chartres's prologue to the *Decretum*, 47.

3. Gratian, *Decretum*, distinction 5, dictum ante c. 1. The superiority of natural law to custom and constitution is laid down in Distinctions 8–9. On Gratian's use of natural law see esp. Michel Villey, "Sources et portée du droit naturel chez Gratien," in *Leçons d'histoire de la philosophie du droit* (Paris, 1957), 221–36. For a broader treatment of the issues discussed here see Geoffrey Koziol, "Lord's Law and Natural Law," in *The Medieval Tradition of Natural Law*, ed. Harold Johnson (Kalamazoo, Mich., 1987), 103–17.

4. Ivo of Chartres, *Decretum*, 47, alluding to Ps. 100. On Ivo's rules for interpreting contradictory canons see J.-M. Salgado, "La méthode d'interpretation du droit en usage chez les canonistes," *Revue de l'Université d'Ottawa*, 22, special issue (1952): 25–35; F. Chiovaro, "*Discretio pastoralis* et *scientia canonica* au XIe siècle," *Studia moralia* 15 (1977): 445–68 at 461–62; and Rolf Sprandel, *Yvo von Chartres und seine Stellung in der Kirchengeschichte* (Stuttgart, 1962), 28–31.

5. Kuttner, "Forgotten Definition."

6. Helgald of Fleury, *Vie de Robert*, 78, c. 13. Imagining the Last Judgment in terms of an earthly court, and conversely modeling earthly courts on Christ's court at the Last Judgment, was a topos throughout the Middle Ages. See Kuttner, "Forgotten Definition," 77–78; Samuel Y. Edgerton, Jr., "The Last Judgment as Pageant Setting for Communal Law and Order in Late Medieval Italy," in Trexler, *Persons in Groups*, 79–100.

7. *Epitome Moralium s. Gregorii in Job*, 503, on Job 41:23. Having been shown to have circulated in the ninth century, the *Epitome* can no longer be attributed to Odo of Cluny: Gabriella Braga, "Problemi di autenticita per Oddone di Cluny: L'Epitome dei *Moralia* di Gregorio Magno," *Studi Medievali* 18, ser. 3 (1977): 43–145.

8. *Acta synodi Atrebatensis*, 1310: "Proinde nosse debet unusquisque Christianus, neque in viribus naturae, neque in legalibus praeceptis, sed in illuminatione cordis et voluntario divinae voluntatis munere constare gratiae salutaris exordium." "Proinde bona opera quae Deus misericorditer donat, juste coronat, opera vero quae non ipse tribuit, juste punit. In istis ergo coronatur divina largitio, in illis transgressio humana damnatur. Nihil igitur iste habet, quod propriis meritis ascribere, nec ille, quod divino judicio jure possit derogare."

9. Anselm of Laon, *Sententie*, 35: "Dicit autem Augustinus in enchridion, quod rigor iustitie hoc exigeret, sed deus misericordia sua hunc rigorem temperauit."

10. Burchard of Worms, *Decretum*, 978, 19.7: "Te supplices rogamus, et petimus, ut precibus nostris aurem tuae pietatis inclinare digneris. . . . Precor, Domine, clementiae et misericordiae tuae majestatem . . . et veniam praestare digneris."

11. Carlyle and Carlyle, *History of Mediaeval Political Theory*, 1:224–25.

12. Jonas of Orléans, *De institutione regia*, 154 ("quod pietas, iustitia et misericordia stabiliant regnum"), 156 ("qui pie et iuste, et misericorditer regnant, sine dubio per Deum regnant"). On the history of these royal virtues see Fichtenau, *Arenga*, 38–58.

13. MGH Epist. 4:51–52.

14. *Acta synodi Atrebatensis*, 1310. He had probably conflated Ps. 83:12 with Ps. 32:5 ("diligit misericordiam et judicium") and 100:1 ("misericordiam et iudicium cantabo tibi Domine").

15. Ivo of Chartres, *Decretum*, 956 (16.280): "Si quis terram censualem habuerit, quam antecessores sui, vel aliquam ecclesiam, vel ad villam nostram dederunt, nullatenus eam secundum legem tenere potest, nisi ille voluerit ad cujus potestatem vel illa ecclesia, vel illa villa pertinet, nisi forte filius aut ejus nepos sit qui eam tradiderit, et ei eadem terra ad tenendum placitata sit. Sed in hac re considerandum est utrum ille qui hanc tenet dives an pauper sit, et utrum aliud beneficium habeat vel etiam proprium. Et qui horum neutrum habet, circa hunc misericorditer agendum est, ne ex toto dispoliatus in egestatem incidat, aut talem ille censum inde persolvat, qualis ei fuerit constitutus, vel portionem aliquam inde in beneficium accipiat, unde se sustentare valeat."

16. Some examples are given below, 231; also suggestive is Fleury, no. 76 (1066).

17. Karl Bösl, "*Potens* und *Pauper*: Begriffsgeschichtliche Studien zur gesellschaftlichen Differenzierung im frühen Mittelalter und zum 'Pauperismus' des Hochmittelalters," in his *Frühformen der Gesellschaft im mittelalterlichen Europa* (Munich/Vienna, 1964), 117, 121–23; also Lester Little and Barbara Rosenwein, "Social Meaning in the Monastic and Mendicant Spiritualities," *Past and Present* 63 (1974): 6, 10–16; Rosenwein, *Rhinocerous Bound*, 66–70; Aboucaya, "Politique et répression criminelle," 13–16, 21; Spiegel, "Defense of the Realm," 117–19.

18. Suger, *Vie de Louis VI*, 180, c. 25; Spiegel, "Defense of the Realm," 117–19.

19. Raymonde Foreville, "Aux origines de la renaissance juridique: Concepts juridiques et influences romanisantes chez Guillaume de Poitiers, biographe du conquérant," *Moyen Age* 58 (1952): 43–83 at 57–58.

20. Fulbert of Chartres, *Letters and Poems*, 54, no. 29: "Nunc ergo tanta causa, quia iudicacio eius obscura non est, solam . . . ulcionem expostulat. Sed cum iuris sit ad utilitatem rei publicae cunctos punire maleficos, illos tamen uehemencius exturbare necesse est qui in Deum et sanctos eius tam impie tamque crudeliter audent."

21. Schramm, *KKP*, 2:237–38, no. 18, 247, no. 18 (from the tenth-century "Fulrad" *ordo* associated with Corbie and Arras): "Accipe virgam virtutis atque equitatis, qua intellegas mulcere pios et terrere reprobos; errantes viam doce, lapsisque manum porrige, disperdasque superbos et releves humiles. . . . Et imitare ipsum, qui dicit: 'Diligas iustitiam et odio habeas iniquitatem.'"

22. Ibid., 222, no. 4 (from the tenth-century pontifical from Sens): "Accipe sceptrum, insigne regnantis, quo significatur regula divinae aequitatis, que bonos regit et malos conterit; in hac virga regni disce amare iustitiam et odisse iniquitatem."

23. Cf. Kaufmann, *Aequitatis iudicium.* Kaufmann does say (22) that Carolingian judges were supposed to adhere to written laws in handing down their judgments; but he also acknowledges (95–100) that kings assumed much greater freedom in both procedural matters and the application of laws. It is this royal discretion that post-Carolingian counts assumed as one of their attributes.

24. Foreville, "Aux origines de la renaissance juridique," 57–58 (above, n. 19).

25. *St-Bertin*, 190ff., no. 18.

26. *Philippe Ier*, no. 125.

27. Aboucaya, "Politique et répression," 13–16, 21; Spiegel, "Defense of the Realm," 117–19.

28. Wallace-Hadrill, "*Via regia.*"

29. Abbo of Fleury, *Collectio canonum*, 477. See also the catalogues of royal virtues given by Alcuin in MGH Epist. 4:51; by Sedulius Scottus in *Liber de rectoribus Christianis*, 49; and by Dudo of St-Quentin in *De moribus*, 262.

30. Abbo of Fleury, *Collectio canonum*, 480: "Propterea denique jubemur habere simplicitatem columbinam ac serpentinam astutiam."

31. Adalbero of Laon, *Poème au roi Robert*, 14, 22: "Triplex ergo Dei domus est, quae creditur una. / Nunc orant, alii pugnant aliique laborant. / Quae tria sunt simul et scissuram non patiuntur: / Vnius offitio sic stant operata duorum, / Alternis uicibus cunctis solamina prebent. / Est igitur simplex talis conexio triplex. / Dum lex preualuit tunc mundus pace quieuit. / Tabescunt leges, et iam pax defluit omnis. / Mutantur mores hominum, mutatur et ordo." See Duby, *Three Orders*, 44–55.

32. Ivo of Chartres, *Correspondance*, 67–68.

33. Wallace-Hadrill, *Early Germanic Kingship*, 134–35, 138–40.

34. Spiegel, "Defense of the Realm," 117–19; Aboucaya, "Politique et répression criminelle," 13–16.

35. Duby, *Three Orders*, 44–55; Sassier, *Hugues Capet*, 268–76; Mostert, *Political Theology*, 52–54, though Mostert's constitutional perspective is quite different from my own (see esp. his chaps. 8–9, 11–12).

36. Geary, "Humiliation of Saints," esp. 132–33, 136, and nn. 8, 14–16; Canal, "De clamoribus liturgicis," 199–212; Little, "Morphologie des malédictions." A letter from Radbod, bishop of Noyon, to Lambert, bishop of Arras, written in the last decade of the eleventh century, mentions that a clamor and humiliation might be used against one of Lambert's parishioners (PL 162:656–57); and the rite is quite well documented at St-Amand (Platelle, *Justice seigneuriale*, 79, 99).

37. "In spiritu humilitatis et animo contrito ante sanctum altare tuum et sacratissimum corpus et sanguinem tuum, domine Ihesu redemptor mundi, accedimus et de peccatis nostris pro quibus juste affligimur culpabiles contra te nos reddimus. Ad te, domine Ihesu uenimus, ad te prostrati clamamus, quia uiri iniqui et superbi suisque uiribus confisi, undique super nos insurgunt, terras huius sanctuarii tui caeterarumque sibi subiectarum aecclesiarum inuadunt, depraedantur et uastant; pauperes tuos cultores earum in dolore et fame, atque nuditate uiuere faciunt, tormentis etiam et gladiis occidunt. Nostras etiam res, unde uiuere debemus in tuo sancto seruitio, et quas beatae animae huic loco pro salute sua reliquerunt, diripiunt, nobis etiam uiolenter auferunt. Aecclesia tua haec domine quam priscis temporibus fundasti et sublimasti in honorem beatae et gloriosae semper uirginis Mariae sedet in tristitia. Non est qui consoletur et liberet eam nisi tu deus noster. Exurge igitur, domine Ihesu in adiutorium nostrum, conforta nos et auxiliare nobis, expugna impugnantes nos, frange etiam superbiam illorum qui tuum locum et nos affligunt. Tu scis domine qui sunt illi et nomina illorum, corpora quoque eorum et corda antequam nascerentur tibi soli sunt cognita. Quapropter eos domine sicut scis

justifica in uirtute tua. Fac eos recognoscere prout tibi placet sua malefacta et libera nos in misericordia tua. Ne despicias nos domine clamantes ad te in afflictione, sed propter gloriam nominis tui et misericordiam qua locum istum fundasti et in honorem genetricis tuae sublimasti uisita nos in pace et erue nos a praesenti angustia. Amen": *Liber tramitis*, 244–47. On the use of this prayer see Geary, "Humiliation of Saints," n. 8.

38. Canal, "De clamoribus liturgicis," 202–5.

39. Some examples: *Philippe Ier*, nos. 27 (− 1066), 75 (1071–79); Newman, *Domaine royal*, doc. 2 (Soehnée, no. 62); Guimann, 179–81 (1101), 182–85 (1101), 332–34 (1115); ND Noyon, ff. 60–62 (n.d.); *Homblières*, 100, c. 21. *Clamorem facere* also commonly described the public announcement of grievances within communal jurisdictions in the twelfth century; e.g., *Recueil des actes de Philippe Auguste*, 1:48, 71–73, 237, 270–71, 285, 334. Although these usages probably had no liturgical overtones, this does not mean that these clamors were without their own special gesticulations or rhetoric suitable to communal justice.

40. Clamors to kings: *St-Germain*, 82, no. 52 (Newman, *Cat.*, no. 85); *St-Corneille*, no. 15 (Soehnée, no. 22); *Philippe Ier*, no. 27, etc. Clamors to counts: Fauroux, no. 115; *Pontieu*, no. 5; *Amiens*, no. 9; *Homblières*, 100, c. 21; Guimann, 45–46, 179–81, 182–85, 332–34; Guesnon, *Cartulaire de . . . Saint-Vaast*, 32–34. Clamors to bishops: St-Eloi, ff. 109v–10; ND Noyon, ff. 60–62, etc. Clamors to Cono of Praeneste: Newman, *Seigneurs de Nesle*, vol. 2, no. 1; Gordière, *Prieuré de Saint-Amand*, 152–53, doc. 2. Frequently the grievances of lay lords were also referred to as clamors (e.g., *Philippe Ier*, nos. 75: "crebris clamoribus apud regem courgere"; 159: "immo super hoc de clericis clamorem faceret"). Whether such usages also denoted a formal, liturgical language, as I believe the clamors of churches did, cannot be verified, since "clamor" could also refer simply to a grievance (e.g., *Corbie*, no. 40: "clamorem quem de foratico habebant").

41. Guimann, 171–81, 182–88, 332–34; *Amiens*, no. 9; *ND Paris*, 1:308; *Philippe Ier*, nos. 28, 61; *RHF* 11:580–82.

42. See Pissard, *Clameur de haro*, 11–16, 28–30, 34–38; Besnier, "Actualité de la clameur de haro," 63–68; Canal, "De clamoribus liturgicis," 202–3; Little, "Morphologie des malédictions," 56. "Clamor" was often used in the same sense in hagiographical texts; e.g., *Vita beati Simonis comitis Crispeiensis*, in *RHF* 14:40 ("vox populi et turbae laetantis clamor attollitur"); Andrew of Fleury, *Vie de Gauzlin*, 50–52, c. 18 ("burgensium clamor exoritur"). Cf. also Cassiodoris, "Iubilatio est enim gaudium cum feruore animi et clamore indistinctae uocis expressum," cited by Jean Leclercq, "L'interdit et l'excommunication d'après les lettres de Fulbert de Chartres," *Revue d'histoire du droit français et étranger* 23 (1944): 71. There are numerous other examples.

43. St-Eloi, ff. 109v–10. On the relics see Erika J. Laquer, "Ritual, Literacy, and Documentary Evidence: Archbishop Eudes Rigaud and the Relics of St. Eloi," *Francia* 13 (1985): 625–37.

44. Platelle, *Justice seigneuriale*, 79 and doc. 4: "Quam citius potuit ad monasterium nostrum venit, ante corpus sancti Amandi nudis pedibus se prostravit, emendationem in manu crucifixi faciens, misericordiam et absolutionem lacrimabiliter petiit." Note also that the monks respond to this entreaty with the same phrases found in authoritative diplomas: "Nos vero lacrimis et petitionibus ejus condescendentes, hac conditione eum absolvimus."

45. *St-Germain*, 1:82: "nostram adiit presentiam Adraldus abbas . . . cum monachis secum Deo servientibus, lacrymosas deponens querimonias et clamores accerrimos super tantarum molestiarum injuriis, petens ut censura nostri judicii . . . cessare facerem quidquid injuste in prenominatis terris . . . agebatur." *Mir. s. Ad-*

alhardi, 863, 2.1: "Unde Fulco abbas . . . et fratres non modice perturbati, quaerimoniam lacrimabilem coram regis praesentia fuderunt et super hoc eius consilium et auxilium imploraverunt."

46. *GC* 10:Instr. 286–87: "Ecce, pater praecipue, pastor egregie, tantus est cumulus calamitatis nostrae, ad te spes nostra, in te defensio nostra, patiente membro compati debet et caput; te Deus praefecit ecclesiae, quam acceptam justum est deffensare; desolatus locus S. Petri, cui dignum est adstipulari, quia specialiter es defensor sancti Petri." Among many possible models see the clamor of Esther cited by Canal, "De clamoribus liturgicis," 201: "Exaudi vocem eorum qui nullam aliam spem habent."

47. Gousset, *Actes*, 2:111–12. See 132–33 (1096), the response of the archbishop of Reims to a clamor of the clergy of Cambrai: "credimus Cameracensis ecclesiae miseriam et afflictionem vos . . . respexisse," and referring to the "need and nakedness" of the church; also *RHF* 10:613–14, an act of Robert II (Newman, *Cat.*, no. 67 [c. 1027?]): "ante praesentiam nostram venerunt et causas suae necessitatis humiliter intimaverunt, reclamationem facientes"; Cartulary of Notre-Dame of Laon, Laon, AD Aisne, G 1850, f. 250 (1046, to the bishop of Laon); *RHF* 11:586 (Soehnée, no. 84 [1049], to Henry I); *Chronique . . . de Mouzon*, doc. 5 (to the archbishop of Reims [1018]); Métais, *Saint-Denis de Nogent*, no. 85 (to the bishop of Chartres [c. 1100]); Vercauteren, *Actes*, nos. 75 and 119 (to the count of Flanders [1111–15, 1125]). Also the interesting clamor in *Actus pontificum Cenomannis in urbe degentium*, ed. G. Busson and A. Ledru, Archives historiques du Maine 2 (Le Mans, 1901), 341–47 (by the bishop of Le Mans [890–913]).

48. *Amiens*, no. 9 (1091–94).

49. "Clamore igitur ecclesiarum et gemitu fidelium ingravescente compuncti."

50. See below, chap. 8.

51. "Consilio accepto a domno episcopo G. et archidiaconis Ansello et Fulcone, et a primoribus urbis et ab aliis juris autenticis in clero et plebe habentibus pondus testimonii, ex edicto decrevimus . . ."

52. This practice was especially common around Pontoise, in spite of the king's proximity; e.g., *Pontoise*, nos. 1, 8, 20–23, 24, 40.

53. E.g., *Philippe Ier*, nos. 27, 28, 143; *St-Germain*, no. 84; Guimann, 179–81, 332–34; Lefranc, *Histoire de la ville de Noyon*, doc. 3; *Homblières*, no. 34.

54. *Philippe Ier*, no. 61 (1071): "Petitionibus adquiescere decrevimus."

55. *Homblières*, no. 23: "Quam petitionem non abnuentes et saepius adclamantes . . . ex beneficio nostro ei concessimus ut . . ."

56. E.g., Labande, *Histoire de Beauvais*, doc. 2 (1069); *ND Paris*, 1:2 278–79 (two disputes); *St-Corneille*, no. 15; *ND Noyon*, ff. 20v–22.

57. *Jumièges*, no. 11 (Newman, *Cat.*, no. 74; Soehnée, no. 8 [1027–28]): "Cujus prejudicium ut agnovi, regali animadversione illum ut ab hac insania resipisceret jussi, terramque cultam et incultam cum ecclesia et decima . . . reddidi."

58. Kantorowicz, *King's Two Bodies*, 78; J.-F. Lemarignier, "Structures monastiques et structures politiques dans la France de la fin du Xe et des debuts du XIe siecles," in *Il monachismo nell'alto Medioevo e la formazione della cività occidentale*, Centro italiano di studi sull'alto Medioevo 4 (Spoleto, 1957), 357–400 at 357, quoting Etienne Delaruelle.

59. For a standard discussion of accusations (*Klage*), see Köbler, "Klage."

60. See *Chronique . . . de Mouzon*, doc. 5 (Arnulf of Reims [1018]): "per deprecationem Bosons abbatis, quaedam bonae . . . misericorditer indulsi. . . . Adiit humilitatem et praesentiam nostram . . . insinuans suam necessitudinem, et pauperum oppressionem, obsecransque humiliter ut . . ." Also the discussion of precarial grants above, 49 with notes.

61. Herman of Laon, *De miraculis s. Mariae Laudunensis*, 1008–10.

62. For these examples see above, 185–87.

63. MSQ, no. 22 (= BN, Coll. Moreau 42, f. 215, and Coll. Picardie 209, f. 176).

64. E.g., Stephen Weinberger, "Cours judiciaires, justice et responsabilité sociale dans la Provence médiévale: IXe–XIe siècles," *Revue historique* 542 (1982): 273–88 at 284.

65. Above, 217.

66. Guimann, 374, 380–81, 383, 388, etc. The phrase meant the same thing elsewhere: *St-Aubin*, 1:101; *St-Cyprien*, 33.

67. *Redon*, no. 195 (and above, 232): "Deinceps Conuuoion, misericordia motus, elevavit eum de terra, beneficiavit illi portionem de exclusa, dum fidelis et amicus illi fuisset, et monachi voluissent."

68. Hariulf, 193–94 (and see 174–75): "Ille vero, videns quod contendendo non proficeret, precatus est ut sibi permitteretur, et post se filio suo, postque filium suum, filio filii sui, sicque tandem reciperet ecclesia quod suum erat. Placuit abbati id facere."

69. Platelle, *Justice seigneuriale*, 75 and docs. 1 (1071), and 2 (1062–76); Ramackers, *PUF*, no. 3 (1004–9); *St-Aubin*, 1:237 (1039–55); *Philippe Ier*, no. 37 (1067–68); BN, Coll. Baluze 141, ff. 52v–53 (1080); MSQ, no. 15 (= Amiens, AD Somme, H XVI, 56–58, no. 1 [1102]); Guyotjeannin, "Recherches," doc. 5 (1123–42); *Jumièges*, no. 46 (n.d.); Cartulary/Chronicle of Nogent, AD Aisne, H 325, f. 124r–v (1052–98). See also Fauroux, no. 74 (1027–35), concerning the unsuccessful effort of Roger II of Montgommery to establish a market that would compete with Jumièges's own market: "sciens me nullo pacto illud posse recuperare, nisi per monachorum consensum, eos supplex adii et multis precibus vix obtinere valui ut . . . michi liceret in meo supradicto vico aliud extruere." Note also that as churches began to accept feudal relations, homage often replaced supplications at the end of disputes; e.g., SQB, f. 39 (1113).

70. MSQ 4 (= BN, Coll. Moreau 23, f. 190r–v, for a daughter).

71. See *St-Cyprien*, 33 (1073–1100), where the original grant envisions that the beneficiary may name one of his relatives to succeed him, if he "accedet ad misericordiam abbatis et monachorum."

72. Above, 4.

73. *Gesta episcoporum Cameracensium*, 467, 3.2.

74. Raoul Glaber, *Histoires*, 13–15.

75. Otto of Freising, *Gesta Friderici I. imperatoris*, 2.3, ed. G. Waitz and B. de Simpson, 3d ed., MGH SRG (Hanover, 1912), 104–5.

76. See Koziol, "Monks, Feuds, and the Making of Peace," and the excellent discussion of these points by Leyser, *Rule and Conflict*, 36, 95.

Part Four. Ritual and Reality

1. A more complete discussion of this problem is presented in chap. 9.

2. Sahlins, *Islands of History*, 125, 138.

3. For *convenientiae* in general see the works cited above, Introduction, n. 45. For bilateral agreements in the west see White, "*Pactum Legem Vincit*," and Martindale, "Conventum."

8. The Sublimity of Knighthood

1. Still the only overview of the dynasty as a whole is Colliette, *Mémoires*, vol. 1, passim. For the rest, their history must be reconstructed from incidental references in monographs, among them Werner, "Untersuchungen" (1960); Bur, *Forma-*

tion . . . *de Champagne,* 97–99, 114–16; *Chronique . . . de Mouzon,* 120–26; *Hom-blières,* 3–8.

2. MGH SS 9:303; Otto Oexle, "Die Karolinger und die Stadt des heiligen Ar-nulf," *Frühmittelalterliche Studien* 1 (1967): 250–364 at 263 n. 61; L. Genicot, "Princes territoriaux et sang carolingien: La *Geneologia comitum Buloniensium,*" in his *Etudes sur les principautés Lotharingiennes* (Louvain, 1975), 220.

3. *Vita s. Bertulfi,* 635, on which see Huyghebaert, *Translation de reliques,* lxxiii, and Genicot, "Princes territoriaux," 218 and n. 4 (above, n. 2). An even more extravagant genealogy, tracing the counts' ancestry back through Wandregisilus's and Charlemagne's ancestors, appears in the *Sermo de adventu Wandregisili,* in Huyghebaert, *Translation de reliques,* 23–24. Although this work was written in the early twelfth century, it revised an earlier work written shortly after the transla-tion of Wandregisilus in 944 (Huyghebaert, lxxv–lxxxviii). It is therefore quite possi-ble that this ancestry had appeared in the original, especially since it was already known in Flanders at that time (Oexle, "Karolinger und die Stadt," 262–63; above, n. 2).

4. Above, 133.

5. *Pontieu,* iii–iv; Searle, "Frankish Rivalries."

6. Lot, *Derniers carolingiens,* 9, 46–48, 58–59, 108–9, 165, 173, 181–85, 196; Lauer, *Règne de Louis IV,* 13–14, 74, 106–7, 124–28, 156, 159–60, 231–32; Bur, *Formation . . . de Champagne,* 101–2, 112–19.

7. Ganshof, "Origines de la Flandre impériale"; *Chronique . . . de Mouzon,* 120–26, 152–53, on which see also Bur, "Salut et libération dans la pensée reli-gieuse vers l'an mil," *Francia* 14 (1986): 45–56, and esp. "A propos de la *Chronique de Mouzon.*"

8. Kaiser, *Bischofsherrschaft,* chap. 3 and 584–88, 593–96.

9. Corbie: A. d'Haenens, "Corbie et les Vikings," in *Corbie, Abbaye Royale: Volume du XIIIe Centenaire* (Lille, 1963), 182–83 and 189 n. 19; Fossier, *Terre et hommes,* 2:486; Vercauteren, *Etude,* 309 and 314; and Grierson, "L'origine des comtes d'Amiens," 82 n. 1. St-Corneille: Newman, *Domaine royal,* 70, 213 n. 62; Lemarignier, *Gouvernement royal,* 106. St-Médard: Vercauteren, *Etude,* 118–23; Newman, *Domaine royal,* 78 n. 4, 79–80, 213 n. 63; Lemarignier, *Gouvernement royal,* 52 n. 43, 98, 149 n. 31, 164; Bourgin, *Commune de Soissons,* 63–64; A. Fliche, *Le règne de Philippe Ier* (Paris, 1912), 491–92; Lohrmann, *PUF,* 169ff.; Bur, *Formation . . . de Champagne,* 195–96, 200 and n. 24. A letter of Fulbert of Chartres reveals that St-Médard had made claims to independence from its bishop from an early date: *Letters and Poems,* no. 14 (1008).

10. Corbie: GC 10:Instr. 286–87. St-Corneille: *Philippe Ier,* no. 117, and *St-Cor-neille,* no. 41. St-Vaast: *Gesta episcoporum Cameracensium,* 446, 452, 1.107, 116; A. Koch, "Continuité ou rupture? De la justice domaniale et abbatiale à la justice urbaine et comtale à Arras," *Revue du Nord* 40 (1958): 289–96 at 291.

11. Bonnaud-Delamare, "Institutions de paix" and "La paix en Flandre pendant la première croisade," *Revue du Nord* 39 (1957): 147–52; Strubbe, "Paix de Dieu," 489–501.

12. See G. Charvin, *Statuts, chapitres généraux et visites de l'ordre de Cluny,* 9 vols. (Paris, 1965–80), 6:326, for a listing of priories by diocese; and Cowdrey, *Cluniacs,* 81, 104. In 1077 Philip I subscribed a charter issued by Simon of Valois recording Simon's donation of St-Arnoul of Crépy to Cluny (*Philippe Ier,* 268, no. 105). Around the year 1092 Hugh of Coudun presented his foundation at Elincourt to Cluny (*St-Corneille,* 96–97, and E.-E. Morel, *L'origine du prieuré d'Elincourt-Sainte-Marguerite* [Compiègne, n.d.]). Other Cluniac priories were founded by lords who had probably been important vassals of Raoul and Simon of Valois—at Cappy

and Cressonsacq, for example; but by the time these foundations had been established their lords owed primary allegiance to the kings of France, which perhaps explains why these and most other priories in the region depended on St-Martin-des-Champs, the royal foundation at Paris, rather than directly on Cluny.

13. Lohrmann, *PUF*, 129.

14. As with the bishop of Noyon's foundation of St-Barthélemy in 1064 (Lefranc, *Histoire de la ville de Noyon*, doc. 3) and the bishop of Beauvais's foundation of St-Lucien in 1067 (Lohrmann, *PUF*, 42; *Philippe Ier*, no. 94). See also Charles Dereine, "Vie commune, règle de saint Augustin et chanoines réguliers au XIe siècle," *Revue d'histoire ecclésiastique* 41 (1946): 365–406 at 386–88, 392–93; and Georges Duby, "Les chanoines réguliers et la vie économique des XIe et XIIe siècles," in *La vita commune del clero nei secoli XI e XII*, Miscellanea del Centro di studi medioevali 3 (Milan, 1962), 72–78, reprinted in Duby, *Chivalrous Society*.

15. Dauphin, *Bienheureux Richard*, 176–97, 219–225; Lemarignier, "Paix et réforme," 458–60.

16. Above, 142.

17. Searle, *Predatory Kinship*, chap. 11; Bates, *Normandy before 1066*, 99, 156–59.

18. Hariulf, 193 (Geoffrey, viscount [1036]); *Pontieu*, nos. 6 (Ivo, castellan [1053–90]), 8 (Geoffrey, viscount of Abbéville [1100]), 11 (Geoffrey, viscount, and Waszelin, "at that time viscount of Montreuil and the town of Rue" [1100]), 14 (Geoffrey, viscount [1053–1100]).

19. Bournazel, *Gouvernement capétien*, 54; *Pontoise*, 298–300.

20. Fossier, *Terre et hommes*, 2:484, 502–5; *Pontoise*, 451–52. Theodore Evergates, studying the same sources, has come to a similar conclusion about the restricted diffusion of banal jurisdiction in Ponthieu: "Historiography and Sociology in Early Feudal Society: The Case of Hariulf and the *Milites* of Saint-Riquier," *Viator* 6 (1975): 35–49 at 44–45. The example he cites of "usurpation" in n. 49 concerns Walter Tirel, who is hardly a *miles* in the sense in which Evergates uses the term in his text. Walter also probably had a valid claim to the land he seized (above, chap. 6, n. 123).

21. Fossier, *Terre et hommes*, 2:439–45, 484–85, 503–4, 506–7.

22. Or nine of eighteen acts (five of eight acts between 1000 and 1050): *Homblières*, nos. 9 (959), 12 (963), 20 (982–88), 21 (987–88), 24 (1021–43), 25 (1021–43), 27 (1036–43), 29 (1043), 23 (1021–27 or 1043: see Fossier, *Chartes de coutume*, no. 1). Two other transactions occurred in the count's presence (*Homblières*, nos. 13 [968] and 28 [1043]), and two (nos. 13 [968] and 19 [988]) involved Eilbert, *nobilis et prudens vir* (60, no. 16), reformer of Homblières, founder of St-Michel-en-Thiérache and Waulsort, and one of the last of the great international aristocrats of the old Carolingian mold. See Daniel Misonne, *Eilbert de Florennes: Histoire et légende, la Geste de Raoul de Cambrai*, Université de Louvain, Recueil de travaux d'histoire et de philologie 35, ser. 4 (Louvain, 1967).

23. *Homblières*, no. 27 (1036–43); Dauphin, *Bienheureux Richard*, 219–20.

24. For benefices held immediately of the count mentioned in the charters of Hombilières, see *Homblières*, nos. 2, 9, 12, 16, 27, 29 (949–1043). Dudo held a benefice of Raoul, who probably held it of the count (no. 18 [982]); but Dudo held other rights directly of the counts, with whom his family was in any case closely linked (no. 9 [959]). For fiefs in the region see Fossier, *Terre et hommes*, 2:439–45, 546–47; Chédeville, *Chartres*, 286; Poly and Bournazel, *Mutation féodale*, 136–42.

25. See, in general, Constance Bouchard, "The Origins of the French Nobility," *American Historical Review* 86 (1981): 501–32.

26. Kienast, *Herzogstitel*, 175–78 and n. 69.

27. Bur, *Formation . . . de Champagne*, 87; Werner, "Untersuchungen" (1960), 87 and n. 1.

28. Above, 134–35, 171.

29. Above, chap. 1, nn. 13, 131.

30. Desiring to become a monk at St-Jean, William donated land at Tiers; "qui postulans a Stephano Grenola, a Batilde, uxore ejus, filia Fucaldi de Poterna, de cujus parte foedium illud pendebat, fideliter impetravit ut totum illud foedium . . . dimisisset" (*Angély*, no. 260 [c. 1001]). Hugh, son of Emeltrude, the former wife of Katalo, *miles*, petitioned by the abbot of St-Maixent: "supravenit abbas supradictus illi suplicans [sic] ut votum sue genitricis ne impedire presumeret poscens. Animum vero suum ad hoc donum flectens, hujus rei causa rogatus adquievit" (*St-Maixent*, no. 107 [1044]). Viscount Geoffrey of Thouars, "per deprecationem Ramnulfi militis et Aienoris uxoris sue," granted a church to St-Cyprien (*St-Cyprien*, no. 583 [1015–58]). Constantine Petit, with his wife and his lords, the sons of Ebulo of Niort, confirms a donation "Achardi [clerici] consilio et preci" (*St-Maixent*, no. 175 [1075–91]). Aldenode became a nun "filii sui admonitione ac precibus pulsata" (*Angély*, no. 298 [1092]). See also *St-Jouin*, 1–3 (1038), an act issued by Dodelinus, "miles unus ex primoribus castri Toarcensis": "accessit ad me abbas Simon et ejus monachi, poscentes ut . . . Quod ego audiens libentissime concessi." One also notes a tendency to apply lordly attributes to such men as Dodelinus, as in *St-Cyprien*, no. 440 (998–1031), in which Hugh of "Liziniacensis" granted a house to the monastery "benigne et clementer." Equally common are references to *rogationes* made to the same wide range of persons. I have not cited them, however, since it is not clear that their meaning is deferential.

31. Above, chap. 1, n. 13.

32. *St-Cyprien*, no. 583 (1015–58, quoted in n. 30 above), and above, 34.

33. *St-Maixent*, no. 20 (959).

34. Besides the examples given below, see the following: *St-Père*, 1:159 (–1070), an act of Ebrard, viscount of Chartres ("quod adierunt meam praesentiam Sancti Petri Carnotensis monachi, deprecantes ut . . . dimitterem calumpniam meam"), and 240 (1096), an act of the abbot and monks of St-Père recalling their entreaty to Hugh, viscount of Chartres, lord of Le Puiset ("precibus ad hoc vicecomitem fleximus, ut . . . concederet"); *GC* 14:Instr. 66, no. 44 (dated to 1020 by Guillot, *Comte d'Anjou*, 1:464), an act of Burchard, *miles seniorque* of L'Île-Bouchard, granting the petition of the abbot and monks of St-Martin of Tours: "adiit presentiam meam . . . deprecantes"; Marchegay, "Chartes mancelles . . . de Saint-Florent," no. 3 (c. 1020), a donation by Raoul, viscount of Le Mans, "per deprecationem cujusdam militis nostri"; St-Florent, f. 55r–v, referring to a request to a local *dominus* as a *supplicatio*, and f. 77r–v, "domnus Haimericus deprecatus a domno Eudone de Curron."

35. *St-Père*, 1:90 (–996); on Harduin see Chédeville, *Chartres*, 258–59, 311 n. 396. An even earlier charter involving Harduin, this one issued by Count Odo I, speaks of him as being petitioned, while Harduin in turn petitioned Odo (*St-Père*, 1:74 [986]).

36. *Livre des serfs*, no. 122 (1015–32); on Marannus see *Marmoutier, Dunois*, xxxi, and Chédeville, *Chartres*, 256; on the treasurers of St-Martin, Boussard, "L'origine des familles seigneuriales," 317–19.

37. Boussard, "Droit de *vicaria*," 48–51, doc. 3.

38. *St-Père*, 1:247–48 (1086), an act by Hanric and his younger brother, both *militari balteo accincti*, surrendering customs to St-Père "humili prece Eustachii, abbatis"; and 126–27 (–1070), an act of Abbot Landric recording the surrender to St-Père of vicarial rights in a village by one Roscelin, the son of a *miles*, "precibus

multis exoratus." A few other examples out of many: *Angers*, no. 21 (969), an act by one Griferius, vassal of the cathedral, "quia postulavit me quidam levita . . . ut ei terram . . . concederem"; *St-Aubin*, 1:86 (+ 1000), an act by Teto, vassal of one Fulk: "Ego Teto petitionem abbatis . . . voluntati annuens, cum consensu senioris mei Folchoni . . . et consilium fidelium meorum, collibertam . . . trado"; 215–16, a notice from 1000–1027 recalling a *deprecatio* by the abbot to a woman who held a *benefitium* of the abbey; 2:3–4 (Guillot, Cat., C 18 [996–1001]), an act of Fridricus (unidentified by Guillot, but see Werner, "Untersuchungen" [1960], 172, no. 6): "quoniam adiit me quidam abbas . . . uti ei ex rebus . . . quas ex beneficio senioris mei Fulchonis comitis tenere video, eis ad censum concederem. . . . Qui peticioni eorum annuens, cum voluntate senioris mei Fulchoni, concedo"; *Livre des serfs*, no. 6 (1064–84), a notice recalling the donation of a serf by Teduin of Roches at the petition of the prior ("precatus est eum," "cujus precibus adquiescens Teduinus, promisit se facere quod petebatur"); *St-Père*, 1:144 (– 1070), an act by Gualerius, father-in-law of one Ansgot and vassal of one Hubert: "sepissime meam praesentiam adivit, deprecans"; 232–34 (1084), an act by William "de Sumbone" (unidentified by Chédeville, *Chartres*, 312 n. 410), recording his consent to a donation by one of his *fideles*: "Eustachii abbatis et monachorum prece ductus"; 458–59 (c. 1090), an act by William, castellan of "Molendinis" (Moulins-la-Marche?): "quia adierunt meam presentiam Carnotensis monachi . . . ut ei concederem . . . quasdam res. Libentissime quoque quod petierunt annui."

39. *Vendôme*, vol. 1, no. 8 (1032–34). For other petitions among the lesser lay nobility (again exclusive of *rogationes*), see also ibid., no. 13 (c. 1037); *Angers*, no. 18 (970); *Livre des serfs*, no. 122 (1015–32); *St-Aubin*, 1:100 (987–1040); Marchegay, "Chartes mancelles . . . de Saint-Florent," no. 4 (c. 1040–50); *St-Père*, 1:148–51 (– 1070), 152–53 (1060); *Marmoutier, Dunois*, no. 85 (c. 1096; Ursio, son of Nivelo of Fréteval, confirms a donation *prece patris*).

40. *St-Aubin*, 1:363 (c. 1090): "Precor vos qui astatis, et vos maxime, domini mei, que mecum manducatis, ut hujus rei quam dicturus sum, monachis Sancti Albini testes sitis." After the donor's death, his brother disputed the alms. The monks sought help from the lord of the fief: "monachi vero . . . auxilium Hucberti de Campani contra eum petierunt atque ejus precibus et voluntate ad concedendum supradictum elemosinum eum inflexerunt."

41. MGH Formulae, 24 (no. 56), 158 (no. 43). Cf. *Angers*, nos. 18, 21, 29 (from episcopal acts).

42. *Vie de Bouchard*, ix–xiii; Halphen, *Comté d'Anjou*, 1–12, 45–48; Guillot, *Comte d'Anjou*, 1:1–56, 63; Bur, *Formation . . . de Champagne*, 97–99, 106–7, 114–16, 124–25, 154, 158–59, 165, 171–72.

43. E. Warlop has tried to fit Flanders into the pattern developed by Werner and Boussard for the Loire, arguing that the eleventh-century Flemish nobility derived from powerful families already entrenched in the later ninth century. Although I do not doubt such continuity, many of his examples are unconvincing. Indeed, he can provide only one irrefutable instance of continuity between ninth- and eleventh-century families—that of the Wenemars, a family that does indeed seem to appear as early as 896, and even the first Wenemar appears at that time as the count's *satelles*. None of Warlop's other families can be traced before the 960s, and most appear some decades later. Save for one brief statement, Warlop also ignores the common practice by which a new family, promoted by a count, married into an older one and took the name of the more prestigious, indigenous line. Whatever the truth of Warlop's hypothesis, even he admits that the Flemish nobility quickly and completely came to orient itself around the counts; that the regime of castellans was entirely the work of the early eleventh-century counts; and that in the core of

Flanders the counts were exceptionally wealthy and powerful, and no indigenous, autonomous nobility existed. See Warlop, *The Flemish Nobility before 1300*, 2 vols. (Courtrai, 1975), vol. 1, chaps. 1–3, esp. 29–30, 45–46, 52, 74, 86–88, 106–8 (with relevant notes in vol. 2).

44. Jacques Boussard, "Aspects particuliers de la féodalité dans l'empire plantegenêt," *Bulletin de la Société des antiquaires de l'Ouest* 7, 4th ser. (1963): 29–47. Though aimed at the twelfth century, Boussard's analysis is equally pertinent to the eleventh. Cf. Guillot, *Comte d'Anjou*, 1:366–70.

45. Guillot, *Comte d'Anjou*, 1:325–33.

46. Werner, "Untersuchungen" (1960), 146–93, esp. 169–90; Boussard, "L'origine des familles."

47. Chédeville, *Chartres*, 261–66; Kaiser, *Bischofsherrschaft*, 408–14, 611–12.

48. Chédeville, *Chartres*, 256–58, 260–61; Boussard, "L'origine des familles," 311–14.

49. Halphen, *Comté d'Anjou*, 17–53, 56–62, 72–80; Guillot, *Comte d'Anjou*, 1:5–8, 39–41, 45–46, 51–55, 63–75, 78–87; Bernard S. Bachrach, "A Study in Feudal Politics: Relations between Fulk Nerra and William the Great (995–1030)," *Viator* 7 (1976): 111–22, and "Toward a Reappraisal of William the Great."

50. Guillot, *Comte d'Anjou*, 1:301–12.

51. *Gesta Ambaziensium dominorum*, in *Chroniques des comtes d'Anjou*, 119–24; J. Boussard, *Le comté d'Anjou sous Henri Plantagenêt et ses fils (1151–1204)* (Paris, 1938), 40–45; Joseph Chartrou, *L'Anjou de 1109 à 1151* (Paris, 1928), chap. 2.

52. Bachrach, "Study in Feudal Politics" (above, n. 49), 112–13, 119; Halphen, *Comté d'Anjou*, 23–24, 61 n. 7 (noting the viscounts' change in alliance); similarly Guillot, *Comte d'Anjou*, 1:6–7, 43. On relations between Thouars and Normandy, Beech, "Participation of Aquitainians."

53. J. Boussard, "La seigneurie de Bellême aux Xe et XIe siècles," in *Mélanges Louis Halphen* (Paris, 1951), 43–54.

54. *St-Père*, 1:74 (986), 90 (–996), 159 (–1070), 240 (1096), and *Marmoutier, Dunois*, no. 117 (1050–60), all petitions to the viscounts of Chartres; Marchegay, "Chartes angevines," 388 (c. 1045), a narrative recording the abbot of Marmoutier's entreaty of Geoffrey, castellan of Chaumont, son of the former castellan of Saumur, related to the family of Châteaudun; Marchegay, "Chartes mancelles . . . de Saint-Florent," no. 3 (c. 1020), a petition to the viscount of Le Mans. Note also two charters in which petitions are associated with self-proclaimed nobility: *St-Maur*, no. 40 ("Burchardus Pilosus de Vierio castro, vir illustris illustrique progenie procreatus . . . ad deprecacionem videlicet predicti monachi, propinquitate parentele michi conjuncti . . . contuli" [c. 1090]); *St-Père*, 1:165–66 ("Adelina, parentibus orta secundum seculi dignitatem natalibus, clarissimo cuidam viro, nomine Rodberto . . . nobiliter copulata . . . ejus quidem deprecatione . . . concedo" [–1080]).

55. Above, 249.

56. *Angers*, no. 18 (970), an act by one Robert at the petition of *quidam vassallus* that he and his wife be given a church at a rent. Also ibid., no. 21 (969); *St-Aubin*, 1:86, 2:3–4, both quoted above, n. 38.

57. See the abundant examples in Bachrach, "Geoffrey Greymantle, Count of the Angevins, 960–987: A Study in French Politics," *Studies in Medieval and Renaissance History* 7 (1985):3–65 at 5–7 and passim; Poly and Bournazel, *Mutation féodale*, 129–36.

58. Chédeville, *Chartres*, 289–90.

59. E.g., St-Florent, ff. 17–18 (974), in which Archbishop Harduin of Tours confirms a donation by his *vassalus ac nepos*, Wandalbert; but already the act required

the consent of Wandalbert's brother, who also held the land *in beneficium*; *Marmoutier, Dunois*, nos. 29 (1051–60), 115 (1050–55), 123 (1060–66), 124 (1060–75), 138 (c. 1080); Bachrach, "Geoffrey Greymantle" (above, n. 57).

60. Some examples demonstrating the connection between control of property and petitions from before 1050: *Angers*, nos. 18 (970), 21 (969); *St-Aubin*, 2:3–4 (Guillot, Cat., C 18 [996–1001]), and 1:86 (+ 1000), 215–16 (1000–1027); Lex, doc. 10 (1009–12); *Livre des serfs*, no. 122 (1015–32); *Vendôme*, vol. 1, nos. 8 (1032–34), 82 (1044–49); Marchegay, "Chartes angevines," 388 (c. 1045), and "Chartes mancelles . . . de Saint-Florent," no. 4 (c. 1040–50). A good later example is *Marmoutier, Dunois*, no. 46 (1079).

61. See the works cited above, Introduction, n. 45.

62. *Digest*, 2.14, *De pactis*, c. 1: "Huius edicti aequitas naturalis est. quid enim tam congruum fidei humanae, quam ea quae inter eos placuerunt servare? Pactum autem a pactione dicitur . . . et est pactio duorum pluriumve in idem placitum et consensus." Also Isidore of Seville, *Interrogationes*, 670: "Pactum dicitur inter partes ex pace conveniens scriptura legibus ac moribus comprobata, et dictum pactum quasi ex pace factum ab eo quod est pango, id est statuo vel definio; unde et pepigit, id est, spopondit, foedus, hoc est pactus quod est amicitia optima."

63. See esp. Magnou-Nortier, *Foi et fidelité*, chaps. 3 and 4; Schneider, *Brüdergemeine*, 49–54 and chaps. 9–11; Anton, "Zum politischen Konzept karolingischer Synoden," 96–97. Above, 110–11.

64. White, *Custom, Kinship, and Gifts to Saints*, 29–30, 157–58.

65. Jean Flori, *L'idéologie du glaive: Préhistoire de la chevalerie* (Geneva, 1983), 24–28, and *L'essor de la chevalerie*, chaps. 2, 3, and pp. 122–40.

66. Delaville le Roulx, *Notices sur les chartes*, no. 15; Boussard, "L'origine des familles," 317–18; Guillot, *Comte d'Anjou*, 1:464, no. 44; Werner, "Untersuchungen" (1960), 169–71.

67. *St-Père*, 1:87; Chédeville, *Chartres*, 39–40, 312.

68. *St-Père*, 1:87; "Rotrocus seculari miliciae deditus et Odonis comitis fidelitati devotus," "quia petiit michi Gisbertus abbas . . . et cuncta congregatio sibi commissa, ut eidem loco concederem terram. . . . Itaque amnui [sic] petitioni eorum." Delaville le Roulx, *Notices sur les chartes*, no. 15: "quoniam deprecatus est quidam venerabilis abba Gauzbertus . . . una cum caterva sibi commissa . . . ; quorum deprecationem benigne suscipiens, concessi. . . . "

69. *St-Père*, 1:90 (−996): "Arduinus, seculari miliciae deditus, et Odoni comiti fidelitati devotus"; "quia adiit praesentiam meam abbas Sancti Petri . . . cum quibusdam fratribus, expostulans concedi sibi. . . . Cujus petitionem rationabilem considerans, voluntati eorum assensum praebui." See also Boussard, "Droit de vicaria," doc. 3 (1008–12), an act of Hubert, *miles, de castro Salmuro*: "quoniam accessit ad nostram presenciam venerabilis abba Berno, humili prece deposcens quatinus . . . condonassem, nostrae auctoritatis roboratione . . . confirmarem." *GC* 14:Instr. 66, no. 45 (1020: see Guillot, *Comte d'Anjou*, 1:464): "ego Burchardus, miles, seniorque castri quem vocant Ad Insulam. . . . [A]diit praesentiam meam venerabilis abbas . . . et . . . decanus . . . quoque . . . monachus, frater meus, caeterique utriusque ordinis homines, deprecantes ut . . . Quorum petitionem audiens . . . delegavimus." *Livre des serfs*, no. 122 (1015–32), *Marannus, gratia Dei miles*: "quoniam adiid [sic] presentiam meam quidam fidelis meus . . . deprecans ut concederem monachis . . . quandam mulierem . . . quam ex benefitio meo idem Heriveus tenebat. . . . Cujus deprecatione benigne suscipiens, concessi. . . . " *St-Père*, 1:247–48 (1086), Hanricus and his brother: "militari utrique accincti . . . et humili prece Eustachii, abbatis."

70. *St-Père*, 1:90; Lex, doc. 10; *St-Aubin*, 2:3–4 (Guillot, Cat., C 18 [996–1001]); *Angers*, no. 18 (970).

71. *St-Père*, 1:74 (986), 87.

72. The pithiest formulation of this complex problem is Bur's (*Formation . . . de Champagne*, 417): "Si donc tous les princes sont chevaliers, rares sont les chevaliers qui peuvent prétendre à un titre princier." Also Flori, *L'essor de la chevalerie*, 134–35.

73. *St-Aubin*, 1:363 (above, 249).

74. Flori, *L'essor de la chevalerie*, chap. 6, esp. 119–20; Bournazel, *Gouvernement capétien*, 49–51; Jean Leclercq, *Monks and Love in Twelfth-Century France* (Oxford, 1979); Bouchard, *Sword, Miter, and Cloister*, 131–38.

75. Men identified as *milites* petition lords who are not counts: *Vendôme*, vol. 1, no. 13 (c. 1037). *Milites* petition each other: *St-Aubin*, 1:363 (c. 1090); *St-Père*, 1:148–51 (−1070), 152–53 (1060). *Milites* are petitioned by abbots and/or monks: *St-Père*, 1:87 (−996), 126–27 (−1070), 232–34 (1081), 247–48 (1086), 458–59 (c. 1090); Lex, doc. 10 (1009–12). Men identified as *milites* are petitioned by their own vassals: *Livre des serfs*, no. 122 (1015–32). It must be pointed out that any such listing is inevitably flawed, since it throws together castellans and members of castle garrisons, all of whom might be called *milites*. It also excludes petitions to lesser vassals who were not, for whatever reasons, assigned the title *miles*. Inclusion of these groups would expand the above list. Petitions within this vassalic group (and therefore exclusive of petitions made by or to churchmen, counts, and viscounts) include *Vendôme*, vol. 1, no. 8 (1032–34); Marchegay, "Chartes mancelles . . . de Saint-Florent," no. 4 (c. 1040–50); *St-Aubin*, 1:100 (987–1040).

76. *St-Aubin*, 1:99.

77. This information is taken from charters in Guillot's catalogue. Full supplications have been considered those that mention at least a liturgical term for an entreaty and an epithet connoting grace. For Fulk Nerra see St-Florent, f. 76r–v (Guillot, Cat., no. 62); *St-Jouin*, 19 (no. 64). For Geoffrey Martel, *GC* 7:Instr. 222 (Guillot, Cat., no. 206). For Fulk le Réchin, *St-Maur*, no. 23 (Guillot, Cat., no. 363); *Angers*, no. 57 (Guillot, Cat., no. 57). I was unable to examine three of Fulk le Réchin's charters held in departmental archives: Guillot, Cat., nos. 314, 321a, and 334.

78. For Fulk Nerra, Guillot, Cat., nos. 8, 14, 27, 29 (a *reclamatio* with an accession), 35, 46. For Geoffrey Martel, nos. 105, 129. For Fulk le Réchin, nos. 307 (a *conquestio* with an accession), 317 (a mere *rogatio*, but made *humiliter*), 347. Excluded are references to *suggestiones* (nos. 30, 72, 99), since this is not a liturgical term, and references to exhortations or warnings (*adhortationes, admonitiones*; nos. 89, 96, 425). The rare charters that do employ lavish formulas tend to come from houses whose diplomatic formulas as a whole were unusually conservative (e.g., St-Florent) and shaped by royal models (St-Maur and Ste-Geneviève, on which see Guillot, *Comte d'Anjou*, 2:99). It may also be significant that these monasteries tended to be somewhat eccentric to the centers of Angevin power: Ste-Geneviève in Paris, St-Jouin near Thouars, St-Florent near Saumur.

79. BN, Coll. Housseau 2/2, f. 18, no. 770 (Guillot, Cat., C 304): "Ego Fulco Andegavorum comes dedi Deo et Christi martiribus . . . pro redemptionem avunculi mei Goffredi comitis et patri mei et matris, et antecessorum meorum." Sainte-Marthe and Sainte-Marthe, *Gallia Christiana*, 4:822 (Guillot, Cat., C 285 [1060–68]): "Ego Gaufridus Andegavorum comes, pro remissione peccatorum meorum, et pro remedio animae patris mei, et matris meae, auunculi quoque mei . . . confero . . . Condono etiam . . ." *St-Aubin*, vol. 1, no. 179 (Guillot, Cat., C 260 [1060–67]): "Ego, Gaufridus Junior, comes Andecavi, dono . . ."

80. Boussard, "Charte de fondation" (Guillot, Cat., C 4), dating the act to 979–85, the pilgrimage to 969.

81. Ibid.: "Ego Goffridus, ob meorum antecessorum strenuitatem meique simili-

ter, laudibus nonnullis, extollendam, Andegauorum militum generositati potenter comes appositus." Sainte-Marthe and Sainte-Marthe, *Gallia Christiana*, 1:753–55, gives the variant, which Boussard does not note, although he collated this text. I discovered it too late to verify the reading in the manuscript copies of the charter.

82. Ferdinand Lot believed that the epics about Geoffrey's exploits must have originated shortly after his death: "Geoffroi Grisegonelle dans l'épopée," *Romania* 19 (1890): 377–93.

83. *PL* 155:481 (Guillot, Cat., C 77 [1039]): "ego Fulco comes Andegavorum, licet de ultimis et desidiosis hominibus unus."

84. BN, Coll. Housseau 3, no. 881, f. 83 (Guillot, Cat., C 347 [1085]): "animam meam humiliare sub potenti manu dei gaudeo . . . ut gratiam inveniam . . . ; sed me miserata penitentem et per omnia peccasse ferentem atque petentem cum lacrimis locum penitentiae pietas divina respexit."

85. *St-Maur*, 369–70, no. 26 (Guillot, Cat., C 129 [1040–52]): "quoniam deprecati sunt nobis quidam fideles et amici nostri."

86. BN, Coll. Housseau 3, no. 881, f. 83 (Guillot, Cat., C 347 [1085]): "ego Fulco Dei gratia comes Andegavorum atque Turonorum militiae secularie deditus."

87. Above, 256; on the meaning of this phrase see Flori, *L'essor de la chevalerie*, 46–49, 56–58, 68–69, 134.

88. *Livre des serfs*, no. 122 (1015–32).

89. St-Florent, f. 76 r–v (Guillot, Cat., C 62 [1006–39]): "expetiit sublimitatem nostram miliciae nostre quidam uir strenuus nomine Sigebrannus suppliciter expostulans."

90. Guillot, "Administration et gouvernement" and "Concept d'autorité." See also Chédeville, *Chartres*, 284–88.

91. Halphen, *Comté d'Anjou*, 348–49, doc. 3.

92. *Vendôme*, vol. 1, nos. 175, 245 (1074); see Johnson, *Prayer, Patronage, and Power*, 72, 76–77. Geoffrey the Bearded was remembered as having done penance to the monks of St-Florent, probably in 1062: St-Florent, ff. 99–100v ("suam penitendo culpam suppliciter clamauit"), and Guillot, Cat., C 241, 252.

93. Johnson, *Prayer, Patronage, and Power*, 5, 76–77; Guillot, *Comte d'Anjou*, 1:112–15.

94. *Vendôme*, vol. 1, no. 245.

95. *St-Aubin*, 1:17–18 (1087).

96. Guillot, "Administration et gouvernement," 322–24 and doc. 1, dating the act to 1049–60.

97. *Nouaillé*, 281 (1091–1115); *Vendôme*, vol. 1, no. 77 (1047–49); *Marmoutier, Dunois*, 2–3, no. 1 (1038–40).

98. *Vendôme*, vol. 1, no. 82 (1044–49), an act by Guarin the Ill-Tonsured, vassal of Geoffrey Martel: "quoniam deprecata est me Agnes, nobilis comitissa . . . cujus petitioni adquiescens, concessi." Cf. ibid., no. 74 (1047), in which the same countess "asks" (*rogavit*) two castellans to quit a claim against La Trinité, and no. 86 (1045–49), in which a convention is agreed to by Geoffrey Focalis "per deprecationem comitisse."

99. Le Peletier, *Epitome*, 49 (Guillot, Cat., C 370 [1092]): "Baculum itaque iustitiae et misericordiae, qui crocia dicitur, in manu Natalis sancti Nicolai abbatis pro confirmatione doni pono. Vnde et ipse me inuito ad pedes meos se prosternit. Robertus etiam Burgundus vnus ex optimatibus manum meam propter hoc osculatus est."

100. *Chronica de gestis consulum Andegavorum*, in *Chroniques des comtes d'Anjou*, 38–40. On the background to the story see Lot, "Geoffroi Grisegonelle" (above, n. 82).

101. Grierson, "L'origine des comtes d'Amiens," 93–123.

102. Feuchère, "Tentative manquée," 9 n. 18.

103. Grierson, "L'origine des comtes d'Amiens," 107–19.

104. Fossier, *Terre et hommes*, 486–87; J. Massiet du Biest, *Etudes sur les fiefs et censives et sur la condition des tenures urbaines à Amiens (XIe–XVIIe siècles)* (Tours, 1954), with map 2; Kaiser, *Bischofsherrschaft*, 600–605.

105. *Philippe Ier*, no. 75; Bonnaud-Delamare, "Paix d'Amiens."

106. Hariulf, 299. The kings' continued possession of Encre is suggested by their intervention in disputes between Corbie and the castellan of Encre, even during the time when the counts of Flanders held the *abbatia* of Corbie: Langlois, *Textes*, no. 1 (1016); Newman, *Domaine royal*, 226–28, doc. 2 (1042).

107. Newman, *Domaine royal*, 109 n. 18; J. Verlinden, *Robert Ier le Frison, comte de Flandre* (Antwerp, 1935), 73–75.

108. Feuchère, "Tentative manquée," 35–36.

109. For the Tirels, castellans of Poix and Pontoise, see *Pontoise*, 451–52; Fossier, *Terre et hommes*, 2:502–3.

110. Thus the laymen who witness *Amiens*, no. 5 (1069), are all important figures in the Amienois (the lords of Boves and Picquigny, the castellans of Encre, the guardian of the comital tower in Amiens) or have names that identify them as local men (Hugh of Abbéville, Oilard, *miles* in the retinue of Drogo of Boves, whose name is common in the Vermandois). A comital act for the Vexin, in contrast, was witnessed by the castellans and knights of the Vexin, who come from different families (*St-Père*, 1:199–200 [1055]).

111. Feuchère, "Tentative manquée," 10.

112. *MSB*, 249–52; Jan Dhondt, "Quelques apsects du règne d'Henri Ier, roi de France," in *Mélanges Louis Halphen* (Paris, 1951), 199–208 at 204–5.

113. Guibert of Nogent, *Histoire de sa vie*, 28–29, 1.10.

114. Between 987 and 1069 the counts issued no acts for the Amienois. Nor is this lacuna the result of the chance survival of sources. When the counts of Blois and Troyes granted Cressy to the chapter of Amiens in 1034 (*Amiens*, no. 2), their act was subscribed by the viscounts of Boves and their relatives, but not by the count himself, who at the time was probably with Robert of Normandy on a pilgrimage to the Holy Land, where he died. In the early 1030s the counts were involved in the Peace of God, one of whose articles required disputes to be brought to Amiens to be heard in the presence of bishop and count (*Mir. s. Adalhardi*, 861); and in 1057 Henry I did confirm the privileges of the church of Amiens "Gualtero comite ad quem Ambianice civitatis ammistratio [sic] pertinebat concedente" (*Amiens*, no. 3). But title to the administration of the county did not require the counts actually to administer it in person. Assuming that the Peace did not become a dead letter, disputants could have met its stipulation by bringing their quarrels before the count's agent (the viscount) or before his relative the bishop. And though Walter III assented to the king's confirmation, he did not actively petition for it; that task was left to his cousin Bishop Fulk II. See also n. 115.

115. Bishops: see Kaiser, *Bischofsherrschaft*, 604–6. After the death of Walter II, the bishops increasingly took control of the coinage. Bishop Wido (1058–1075/76) claimed to be both "presul et procurator rei publice Ambianensis." Viscounts: see *Amiens*, no. 2 (1034), noting the subscriptions only of Drogo and Nivelo of Boves; also *Philippe Ier*, no. 75.

116. *Mir. s. Adalhardi*, 862, on which see Bonnaud-Delamare, "Paix d'Amiens," 172–73; Guy Oury, "Gérard de Corbie avant son arrivée à la Sauve-Majeure," *Revue Bénédictine* 90 (1980): 306–14; Hoffmann, *Gottesfriede*, 64–67, who concentrates, however, on an earlier Peace. For meetings on neutral ground, see Lemarignier, *Recherches sur l' hommage en marche*, 85–91; above, 111.

117. Kaiser, *Bischofsherrschaft*, 604, noting that at the same time coinage was issued, probably to commemorate this Peace, carrying the bishop's name on one side and Corbie's on the other; *Amiens*, no. 4 (1058–76); *GC* 10:Instr. 290 (1066).

118. *GC* 10:Instr. 286–87 (c. 1061), 288–90, nos. 7–8. This protocol can also be found in an act of Gui's predecessor, Fulk, in a charter issued at the request of the abbot of Corbie's legate, who "meam suppliciter et caritative mediocritatem adierit" (BN, Coll. Picardie 197, f. 177, dated to 1037–49 by Morelle, "Chartes de l'abbaye de Corbie"). For traditional formulas in episcopal acts see *Amiens*, nos. 4 (1058–76), 7 (1073); *GC* 10:Instr. 290, no. 9 (1066); Bétencourt, *Cartulaire . . . d'Auchy*, 24–25 (1099). For a traditional abbatial act, BN, ms. lat. 17761, f. 52.

119. Fossier, *Chartes de coutume*, no. 2 (1055–56); BN, ms. lat. 17142, f. 295v; *Philippe Ier*, no. 75 (1071–79).

120. Thus the petition of the bishop of Amiens to Count Walter I with relics (*Corbie*, no. 40 [985]); Count Drogo's unusual admission of the sacredness of the abbatial office (Fauroux, no. 63 [1030]); Count Raoul's evident grief at the death of his son and the preamble recalling the intercessory functions of saints at the heavenly court in BN, Coll. Picardie 233, ff. 214–15 (– 1069); and another act recalling the intercessory functions of saints (*Amiens*, no. 5 [1069]). The counts were also styled *gratia Dei comites*: e.g., *Corbie*, nos. 40, 44; AD Aisne, H 455, ff. 70v–72 (Newman, *Cat.*, no. 8 [992–96]); *St-Père*, 1:170–71 (c. 1006); Lot, *Etudes critiques sur . . . Saint-Wandrille*, nos. 7 and 8 (c. 1024); *Philippe Ier*, no. 163 (c. 1023–26); Fauroux, no. 63 (1030).

121. *St-Père*, 1:170–71 ("per deprecationem Mainardi abbatis et ceterorum fratrum" [c. 1006]), 199–200 ("per deprecationem Landrici abbatis" [1055]); Lot, *Etudes critiques sur . . . Saint-Wandrille*, no. 7 ("petente itaque concione" [1024]); Fauroux, no. 63 ("[abbas] studuit a me obtinere, meritis et precibus" [1030]); *Amiens*, no. 5 ("ipsius [episcopi] deprecatione et gratia" [1069]). I have excluded *St-Père*, 2:625–26 (1060) as a suspicious act, in part because it largely repeats *St-Père*, 1:199–200 (1055), inserting only an extravagant judicial immunity, and comes from a scriptorium known for its forgeries.

122. *Corbie*, nos. 40 (985) and 44 (987); AD Aisne, H 455 ff. 70v–72 (Newman, *Cat.*, no. 8 [992–96]; *Jumièges*, no. 6 (1006–7); *St-Père*, 1:173–74 (1031–36); Lot, *Etudes critiques sur . . . Saint-Wandrille*, no. 8 (c. 1024); BN, Coll. Picardie 233, ff. 214–15 (for St-Remi [– 1069]). It should be pointed out that petitionary and nonpetitionary formulas appear in acts written for the same beneficiaries (and therefore written by the same scriptoria). Nor is there any discernible evolution over time. An indifference to petition is part of the basic culture of the territories ruled by the counts.

123. Above, 139–41.

124. Fauroux, nos. 12, 18, 20, 23 (1009–20); 50 (1016–26; the possible dates of acts 24, 29, 30, and 31 overlap this chronological division, but because the limiting dates tend toward the 1020s and their diplomatic form is quite similar to that of chancery acts known to have been issued around 1025, I have assigned them to the later period); 61, 67, 69, 71 (ranging in date from 1030 to 1034), 102 (1037–c. 1045), 122 (1050), 140 (1049–58), 146 (c. 1050–60, with mention of an accession and petition but no ascription of regal virtues).

125. Fauroux, 41–43; Bates, *Normandy before 1066*, 154–55, 193–96.

126. Bates, *Normandy before 1066*, 100–107, 157–60; Searle, *Predatory Kinship*, chap. 15.

127. Bates, *Normany before 1066*, 154–55.

128. Fauroux, no. 61 (1030), a petition by Gozelin, viscount of Arques, on whom see Bates, *Normany before 1066*, 100–102, 104, 117, 159, and esp. 171.

129. Fauroux, no. 122 (1050). The man was Robert II of Grandmesnil, the monas-

tery St-Evroul; and though this is not the usual interpretation of the event, it explains why Robert spent the next several years trying to take over the monastery and why, having gained control of it, he immediately set about using the monastery and its lands to rebuild his family's power and attack its enemies. See Searle, *Predatory Kinship*, chap. 15, esp. 312 n. 31; Orderic Vitalis, *Ecclesiastical History*, 2:12–68, 75–114; William of Jumièges, *Gesta Normannorum ducum*, 174–78, 183–86.

130. Fauroux, no. 67 (1028–33); on the context, William of Jumièges, *Gesta Normannorum ducum*, 100–101, 6.3; Bates, *Normandy before 1066*, 100, 197. A similar explanation may lie behind Bishop Hugh of Bayeux's supplication of Robert in 1034 (Fauroux, no. 71), since Hugh was also involved in armed conflict with the duke. Bates dates this dispute to the beginning of Robert's reign, but this supposition does not necessarily follow from William of Jumièges's account (102–3, 6.5).

131. E.g., William of Jumièges, *Gesta Normannorum ducum*, 74–75, 101; Orderic Vitalis, *Ecclesiastical History*, 6:30–31, 278–79.

132. Fauroux, nos. 122 (1050), 140 (1049–58), 146 (c. 1050–60), 219 (c. 1060–66).

133. Bates, *Normandy before 1066*, 158–59.

134. *Interpellatio*: Fauroux, no. 126 (1051). *Suggestio*: ibid., no. 146 (c. 1050–60), though this word still often has a notion of authority. *Annuente fideli nostro*: ibid., no. 128 (c. 1040–53); cf. no. 156 (1063). Similarly, no. 122 (1050): "intercedente Roberto fideli meo, hoc totum concedo." Note also nos. 146 and 148, in which William acts at the *rogatio* of individuals. The term is quite neutral in this context and has no liturgical connotations.

135. Above, 68–70, 265–66.

136. Fossier, *Chartes de coutume*, no. 3 (1076–77); *St-Corneille*, 71–72, no. 35; Colliette, *Mémoires*, 1:691–92 (1076); 2:257–58 (1123), 264–65 (1144); Hémeré, *Augusta Viromanduorum*, "Regestum," 39–40 (1120), 40 (1130); BN, Coll. Picardie 17, ff. 22 (1112–34), 25 (c. 1143), 26 (1148), 27 (c. 1156); Newman, *Charters of St. Fursy*, no. 7 (1110).

137. Fliche, *Philippe Ier*, 19, 98 (above, n. 9); L.-L. Borelli de Serres, *La réunion des provinces septentrionales à la couronne par Philippe Auguste* (Paris, 1899), v–xiii.

138. Marcel Pacaut, *Louis VII et son royaume* (Paris, 1964), chap. 2 passim, esp. 39–45. Also Luchaire, *Louis VI*, index, s.v. "Raoul de Péronne," noting Raoul's frequent sojourns in Paris and his almost continuous involvement in Louis's major wars. Less rigorous but providing a decent overview of Raoul's career is A. Moreau-Neret, "Le comte de Vermandois Raoul IV de Crépy et Péronelle d'Aquitaine, soeur de la reine Aliénor," *Mémoires de la Fédération des sociétés d'histoire et d'archéologie de l'Aisne* 18 (1972): 82–116.

139. E.g., the castellans of St-Quentin include Hildrad (*Homblières*, no. 3 [954]); Gilbert (Hémeré, *Augusta Viromanduorum*, "Regestum," 32–33 [986]); one or two Lamberts (ibid., 34 [1015]; *Homblières*, nos. 17 [982], 18 [982], 20, [982–88], 21 [987–88], 23 [1021–27]); Rodulph, Lambert's son (*Homblières*, no. 24 [1027–43]); Godofred (Hémeré, 36–37 [1047]); Baidobo or Bardelo, castellan or subcastellan (*Homblières*, nos. 20–21 [982–88]); and Ansellus (BN, Coll. Picardie 352, f. 2 [1084–90]; *Homblières*, no. 31 [1075]; Fossier, *Chartes de coutume*, no. 3 [1076]). Because Ansellus's (i.e., Anselm of Ribemont's) son was also named Godofred (Colliette, *Mémoires*, 2:109 [1104]), the earlier Godofred was most likely his father, perhaps an uncle. As for other castellans, only toward mid-century are toponymics associated with particular individuals; thus "Yvo de Nigella," "Walzelinus Calniacensis," "Robertus magni Peronensis principis" (*Homblières*, nos. 25, 27, 30). See also n. 140.

140. Thus the Ivo who appears in *Homblières*, no. 23 (1021–27) (= Fossier, *Chartes de coutume*, no. 1 [1043]), may be identified with the later lords of Nesle,

who used the names Ivo and Raoul (or Ralph). He could also be identified with the contemporary castellans of Ham, since an Ivo appears in that position in 1055 (ND Noyon, ff. 29v–30) and in 1076–77 (Fossier, *Chartes de coutume*, no. 3). But the lords of Ham also included Odos (ND Noyon, ff. 29v–30 [1089], 67v–68 [1106–21]; *St-Corneille*, no. 26 [1101]), a name that does not occur in the family of Nesle; while the lords of Péronne included both Ivos and Odos (BN, Coll. Moreau 23, f. 190r–v; 36, ff. 52–53v; 37, f. 198 [charters for Mont-St-Quentin, 1040–98; MSQ, nos. 4, 8, 11]). Finally, that the lords of Nesle and Ham used the name Ivo independently is suggested by *Homblières*, no. 23, which lists two different Ivos as vassals of the count. Perhaps there was a relationship among all these families; but simply because of the frequency of these names we cannot discern which families were in control of Nesle, Ham, and Péronne at any given moment before the middle of the century. Certainly one cannot claim, with Fossier, that the lords of Nesle possessed the lordship of Ham. See Fossier, *Terre et hommes*, 467, 508, and *Chartes de coutume*, no. 1; *Homblières*, commentary to no. 23.

141. ND Noyon, ff. 29v–30.

142. MSQ, nos. 4, 8, 11, 15, 22 (= BN, Coll. Moreau 23, f. 190r–v; 36, ff. 52–53v; 37, f. 198; 42, f. 215; Amiens, AD Somme, H XVI, 56–58, no. 1); St-Corneille, no. 18 (1040–1107); PL 162:653; Fossier, *Terre et hommes*, 467–68; Barthélemy, *Deux âges de la seigneurie banale*, 66, 74; Luchaire, *Louis VI*, 15, no. 26.

143. Above, n. 139; Warlop, *Flemish Nobility* (above, n. 43), 1:169, 170; 3:781, no. 64/3 (although the article by Dhondt which he there cites says nothing about the lords of Ribemont); Henri Platelle, *Le temporel de l'abbaye de Saint-Amand des origines à 1340* (Paris, 1962), 131–33, 137; Fossier, *Terre et hommes*, 2:474; Stein, *Cartulaire de . . . Ribemont*, docs. 15 (= *Philippe Ier*, no. 110), 19–21.

144. Newman, *Seigneurs de Nesle*, 1:25 and vol. 2, nos. 1 (1115), 4 (1135). Cf. *Homblières*, nos. 23 (1021–27), 25 (1021–43); Fossier, *Chartes de coutume*, no. 3 (1076–77); BN, Coll. Moreau 41, ff. 99–100 (1103) for the family's appearance in comital charters.

145. *Homblières*, nos. 20 (982–88, for Dudo), 21 (987–88, for Arpadius), 24 and 29 (1021–43, for Geoffrey [or Godofred], *nostrum militem*), 27 (1036, for Amolric, *vir nobilis tamen miles meus*). Geoffrey's name occurs among the castellans of St-Quentin (above, n. 139). On Amolric see F. Vercauteren, "Note sur un texte du cartulaire d'Homblières et sur un passage de la *Vita altera sanctae Hunegundis*," in *Recueil de travaux offerts à M. Clovis Brunel* (Paris, 1955), 2:651–59.

146. *Homblières*, no. 26; BN, Coll. Picardie 111, f. 125r–v; Fossier, *Terre et hommes*, 2:537–39, 548–49; Poly and Bournazel, *Mutation féodale*, 85–87, 175.

147. MSQ, no. 6 (= BN, Coll. Picardie 111, f. 125r–v); *Homblières*, no. 35. See also Newman, *Seigneurs de Nesle*, vol. 2, no. 1 (1115), where two witnesses to a charter were called "knights," as was a vassal of the lord of Nesle; and MSQ, no. 37 (= BN, Coll. Moreau 48, f. 50r–v [1116]), in which Herbert, "a knight, surnamed Pisel," disputed water rights with Mont-St-Quentin. Thereafter the epithet *miles* appears frequently, if not invariably, in documents.

148. ND Noyon, ff. 29v–30, 67v–68 (1055, 1089, early twelfth century; *Philippe Ier*, cxcix, n. 2, transcribes the 1089 act); Newman, *Seigneurs de Nesle*, vol. 2, no. 1 (1115); Colliette, *Mémoires*, 2:263–64.

149. SQB, f. 115 (1078): Hugh of Auteuil makes a donation to St-Quentin "precibus domini mei Guidonis episcopi." Ibid., ff. 80–81 (1106–12): Ingelran of Boves confirms a donation at the request (*rogatio*) of Walter Tirel: "cuius petitioni cum pro gloriosi martyris christianissimi Quintini reuerentia tum pro nobilis militis id obnixe postulantis amicitia libenter assensum prebui."

150. Above, 36–37.

151. *St-Germain*, no. 51; Cartulary of N.-D. of Laon, Laon, AD Aisne, G1850, f. 250; *RHF* 11:586 (Soehnée, no. 84, for St-Thierry); BN, Coll. Moreau 21, f. 193 (Soehnée, no. 19, for Fécamp); *Chronique . . . de Mouzon*, 192–94, doc. 5; Tardif, *Monuments historiques*, no. 243 (Newman, *Cat.*, no. 27); *Homblières*, no. 34; Fossier, *Chartes de coutume*, no. 3; Guyotjeannin, "Recherches," docs. 2 and 6; *Jumièges*, nos. 11 and 28; *Philippe Ier*, nos. 27 and 61; *St-Corneille*, no. 15; *St-Père*, 1:175; Soehnée, no. 34.

152. *ND Paris*, 1:308; Fossier, *Chartes de coutume*, no. 1; St-Eloi, ff. 109v–10; ND Noyon, ff. 52–53; Tardif, *Monuments historiques*, no. 280 (Soehnée, no. 26); *RHF* 11:580–82 (Soehnée, no. 88); Bourgin, *Commune de Soissons*, doc. 8; Langlois, *Textes*, no. 1.

153. Fossier, *Chartes de coutume*, no. 3.

154. *Homblières*, no. 44 with n. 1; Fossier, *Terre et hommes*, 2:458–76.

155. MSQ, nos. 8, 15 (= BN, Coll. Moreau 36, ff. 52–53v [1090]; Amiens, AD Somme, H XVI, 78–80, no. 1).

156. *Homblières*, no. 31 (1075); Fossier, *Chartes de coutume*, no. 3 (1075–76), and Colliette, *Mémoires*, 1:691–92 (for St-Prix [1075–76]).

157. Newman, *Charters of St. Fursy*, no. 4 (= Lohrmann, *PUF*, no. 18).

158. See esp. Paul Hinschius, *System des katholischen Kirchenrechts* (1893; rpt. Graz, 1959), 2:144–45, 5:293–94; P. Torquebiau, "Chapitres de chanoines," in *Dictionnaire du droit canonique* 3:539–42; J.-F. Lemarignier, *Etude sur les privilèges d'exemption et de juridiction ecclésiastique des abbayes normandes depuis les origines jusqu'en 1140* (Paris, 1939), 74–77, 82–109; G. Le Bras, *Institutions ecclésiastiques de la Chrétienté médiévale*, vol. 12 of *Histoire de l'église depuis les origines jusqu'à nos jours*, ed. A. Fliche et V. Martin (Paris, 1959), 378–87; Georg Schreiber, *Kurie und Kloster im 12. Jahrhundert* (Stuttgart, 1910), 1:58–70.

159. Above, 210.

160. Leo Santifaller, *Quellen und Forschungen zum Urkunden- und Kanzleiwesen Papst Gregors VII*, pt. 1, *Quellen*, Studi e testi 190 (Vatican City, 1957), 183–85, no. 159; Pierre Feuchère, "Regeste des comtes de Saint-Pol (1023–1205)," pt. 1, *Revue du Nord* 39 (1957): 43–48 at 44.

161. Gousset, *Actes*, 2:111–12, 198–200, 217–19; *PL* 162:669–70; St-Thierry, ff. 78v–80.

162. Guimann, 170–75.

163. A few of many examples: BN, Coll. Picardie 17, f. 22 (1112–34), a *conventio* and *pactus* between the monks of Corbie and the countess of Vermandois; ND Noyon, ff. 50–51 (1116), a *conventio* between the cathedral chapter of Noyon and one of its mayors; Gordière, *Prieuré de Saint-Amand*, 152–53, doc. 2, a *concordia* between the lord of Thourotte and the chapter of Noyon; and numerous examples in SQB, ff. 19–20, 77v, 83v, 90, etc. Similarly Guimann, 313–16; *St-Corneille*, 56–57, no. 25 (1101), and 97–98, no. 49 (c. 1128); Cartulary of Saint-Jean-des-Vignes, BN, ms. lat. 11004, f. 211r–v (1127); Colliette, *Mémoires*, 2:257–58 (1123).

164. J.-B. Mahn, *L'ordre cistercien et son gouvernement des origines au milieu du XIIIe siècle (1098–1265)* (Paris, 1951), 99, 136–37; Charles Dereine, "La spiritualité 'apostolique' des premier fondateurs d'Affligem (1083–1100)," *Revue d'histoire ecclésiastique* 54 (1959): 41–65; Leclercq, *Monks and Love* (above, n. 74); Little, "Morphologie des malédictions," 55.

165. As in the acts of St-Corneille cited above, n. 163.

166. MSQ, no. 37 (= BN, Coll. Moreau 48, f. 50r–v): "communibus intercurrentibus amicis."

167. Newman, *Seigneurs de Nesle*, vol. 2, no. 1.

168. *PL* 162:653; BN, Coll. Picardie 352, f. 2 (1084–90).

169. Colliette, *Mémoires*, 2:261: "praesentiam nostram amicabiliter adisse . . . expetisse."

170. *St-Corneille*, 70–71, no. 34 (1114).

171. *Homblières*, no. 54 (1146): "in pacem misimus perpetuam"; BN, Coll. Picardie 17, f. 26 (1148): "ut firmior pax et dilectio inter eos fieret dedi eidem Radulfo 1 marcam argenti."

172. *Gesta Ambaziensium dominorum*, 124–25. For the context, see W. L. Warren, *Henry II* (Berkeley, 1973), 42–52. Boussard, *Comté d'Anjou*, 67–71 (above, n. 51), states that Henry repudiated his homage to Theobald because of Supplicius's troubles with Theobald; but this explanation accords neither with the sequence of events as recorded in the *Gesta* (whose chronology cannot always be trusted, however) nor, more important, with Henry's current strategy, since at this moment Henry had nothing to gain by adding a new front to his many wars. In contrast, Theobald not only had much to gain by forcing the issue; he would also have been continuing his father's confrontational policies, but applying them to a new area.

173. *Gesta Ambaziensium dominorum*, 119–24; Boussard, *Comté d'Anjou*, 40–45, and Chartrou, *L'Anjou*, chap. 2 (both above, n. 51).

174. *Gesta Ambaziensium dominorum*, 125: "cum Theobaudus Blesis humiliando ejus amicitias peteret"; 128: "cum omni supplicatione lamentabiliter implorant ut . . . eis succurrat."

175. Ibid., lxi–lxv, 96, 98, 100, 109, 123, 131.

176. Ibid., 123.

177. Chrétien de Troyes, *Yvain*, ed. T. B. W. Reid (Manchester, 1984), ll. 3976–85, 3392–3401; *Lancelot*, ed. William Kibler (New York, 1981), ll. 123–25, 145–53.

178. Flori, *L'essor de la chevalerie*, 46–49, 72–75.

179. Ibid., 305–6; Georges Duby, *William Marshal*, trans. Richard Howard (New York, 1985).

180. Flori, *L'essor de la chevalerie*, 305–6.

181. *Chroniques des comtes d'Anjou*, 195–96; cf. Flori, *L'essor de la chevalerie*, 307.

182. Duby, *Knight, Lady, and Priest*, 230–31, 236.

183. Trexler, *Christian at Prayer*; Schmitt, "Between Text and Image," in *Gestures*, 127–62; Neunheuser, "Gestes de la prière à genoux," 159–61.

184. From Buoncompagno of Florence's *Rhetorica antiqua*, 445: "Petitio est brevis et expressus dicendi modus, qui principalia tangit et accessoria non omittit; vel petitio est quedam verborum congeries, que affectum breviter exprimit petitoris; vel petitio est quedam cedula memorialis, que breviter propositum petitoris declarat."

185. Bournazel, *Gouvernement capétien*, 19–26, 133–43; John Baldwin, *The Government of Philip Augustus* (Berkeley, 1986), 104–13, 115–25, 259–303.

186. See *Recueil des actes de Philippe Auguste*, passim. A perusal of Louis VII's acts published in Tardif, *Monuments historiques*, shows that the formulas were already becoming rarer in his reign and were often truncated or displaced toward the middle of the charter. For examples see nos. 432, 433, 445, 457, 465, 466, 507, 508, 510, 518, 524, 529, 542, 552.

187. Bloch, *Royal Touch*; Baldwin, *Government of Philip Augustus*, 365–66, 374–80, 386–92 (above, n. 185); Joseph Strayer, "France: the Holy Land, the Chosen People, the Most Christian King," in *Action and Conviction in Early Modern Europe*, ed. T. K. Rabb and J. M. Siegel (Princeton, 1968), 3–16; Duby, *Three Orders*, 345–53. A similar desire to preserve the king's uniqueness can be seen in the doctrine that he cannot hold fiefs of others: R. Barroux, "Suger et la vassalité du Vexin," *Moyen Age* 64 (1958): 1–26.

188. *Recueil des actes de Philippe Auguste*, vol. 1, nos. 9, 20, 22, 29, 74, all in the first years of the reign. Thereafter the relatively rare mentions of petitions refer simply to the king's acting *ad petitionem cuiusdam*, or occasionally *ad preces*. But see vol. 3, no. 1729 (1221): "Accesserunt ad nos nuntii . . . eligendi . . . licentiam a nobis humiliter requirentes."

189. *Rotuli parliamentorum*, ed. Richardson and Sayles, 17–18, 21–24, etc.; Meyers, "Parliamentary Petitions," 386–87, 590; Baildon, *Select Cases in the Court of Chancery*, 3–5, 8–14, etc. Also Beugnot, *Les Olim*, 2:668: a man suspected of murder who did not respect a summons, "asserenti se esse de morte predicta penitus innocentem, supplicanti nobis humiliter ut super hoc ageremus misericorditer"; similarly Langlois, "Rouleaux d'arrêts" (1887), 193, 197, 199, 201–2.

9. How Does a Ritual Mean?

1. Oscar Wilde, "The Decay of Lying," in his *Intentions* (New York, 1907), 55.

2. The criticisms discussed in this chapter are argued forcefully and entertainingly by Jack Goody, "Against 'Ritual': Loosely Structured Thoughts on a Loosely Defined Topic," in Moore and Meyerhoff, *Secular Ritual*, 23–35. See also David Herlihy's comments in his foreword to Christiane Klapisch-Zuber, *Women, Family, and Ritual in Renaissance Italy* (Chicago, 1985), x; and Felix Gilbert's review of Trexler, *Public Life in Renaissance Florence*, in *New York Review of Books*, Jan. 21, 1982, 62–66.

3. Christiane Klapisch-Zuber, "An Ethnology of Marriage in the Age of Humanism," in her *Women, Family, and Ritual*, 247–60 (above, n. 2); Sperber, *Rethinking Symbolism*, 17–19.

4. Nelson, "Ritual and Reality," 44–45.

5. Christel Lane, *The Rites of Rulers: Ritual in Industrial Society—The Soviet Case* (Cambridge, 1981), 11–16.

6. Nelson, "Rites of the Conqueror," 128–30.

7. In general see Nelson, "Ritual and Reality."

8. Leyser, *Rule and Conflict*, 141.

9. Nelson, "Rites of the Conqueror," 131–32.

10. Goody, "'Greeting,' 'Begging,' and the Presentation of Respect"; Firth, "Postures and Gestures of Respect."

11. Peter the Chanter, *De penitentia*, 208; Augustine, *De cura gerenda pro mortuis*, 632, 5.7 (quoted in full below, n. 129).

12. See, e.g., Raban Maur, *De videndo deum*, 1304, 1326 (3.1, 3.20). Especially interesting is an anonymous eleventh-century letter criticizing the popular belief that "se nec confessione postea indigere, sed omnia crimina sua tamquam denuo baptizatis, dimissa sibi esse": Edmond Martène and Ursin Durand, *Veterum scriptorum . . . amplissima collectio* (Paris, 1724), 1:357–59 at 357, discussed by Russell, *Dissent and Reform*, 18–19.

13. Bourdieu, *Outline of a Theory of Practice*, chap. 1, sec. 1; Melford E. Spiro, "Collective Representations and Mental Representations in Religious Symbol Systems," *Other Realities* 3 (1982): 45–72, though I do not subscribe to Spiro's Freudian solution to the problems he discusses; David Cannadine, "The Context, Performance and Meaning of Ritual: The British Monarchy and the 'Invention of Tradition,' c. 1820–1977," in Hobsbawm and Ranger, *Invention of Tradition*, 103–8.

14. Sperber, *Rethinking Ritual*, chap. 1, makes this point forcefully; see also Spiro, "Collective Representations" (above, n. 13), and Fernandez, "Dark at the Bottom of the Stairs," esp. 22–24.

15. Christopher Hill, *The World Turned Upside Down* (New York, 1972), esp. 159–63, 200, 234, 296–300; Hobsbawm, "Introduction," in Hobsbawm and Ranger, *Invention of Tradition*, 1–14.

16. For efforts to distinguish them see Mary Gluckman and Max Gluckman, "On Drama, and Games and Athletic Contests," in Moore and Myerhoff, *Secular Ritual*, 227–43; Max Gluckman, *Politics, Law, and Ritual in Tribal Society* (Chicago, 1965), 250–59; and, refining an idea of Victor Turner, Ronald L. Grimes, *Symbol and Conquest: Public Ritual and Drama in Santa Fe, New Mexico* (Ithaca, 1976).

17. Cannadine, "Context, Performance and Meaning" (above, n. 13).

18. Kertzer, *Ritual, Politics, and Power*; also Harry C. Payne, "The Ritual Question and Modernizing Society, 1800–1945—A Schema for a History," *Historical Reflections* 11 (1984): 403–32; D. Chaney, "A Symbolic Mirror of Ourselves: Civic Ritual in a Mass Society," *Media, Culture, and Society* 5 (1983): 119–35; Moore and Myerhoff, *Secular Ritual*; Robert Bocock, *Ritual in Industrial Society* (London, 1974).

19. Above, chaps. 4, 5, 8.

20. Bouman, *Sacring and Crowning*.

21. Ibid., 132; Nelson, "Ritual and Reality."

22. Bouman, *Sacring and Crowning*, 112–14.

23. Marina Warner, *Joan of Arc: The Image of Female Heroism* (New York, 1981), 43–47, 60–62, 70–72.

24. Ralph E. Giesey, "Models of Rulership in French Royal Ceremonial," in Wilentz, *Rites of Power*, 41–64. The *lit de justice* itself then changed—or rather, was perceived in a new way—to accommodate changing political relationships between the kings and *parlementaires*: Sarah Hanley, "Legend, Ritual, and Discourse in the *Lit de Justice* Assembly: French Constitutional Ideology, 1527–1641," in ibid., 65–106.

25. Fichtenau, *Lebensordnungen*, 1:53.

26. E.g., Platelle, *Justice seigneuriale*, 79; *Charles II*, 3:96; *Recueil des actes de Louis IV*, xix; *Lothaire*, xvii–xviii.

27. Koziol, "Monks, Feuds, and the Making of Peace." Ethnographers know that rituals are more changeable than many historians assume. Ivo Strecker discusses a case in which a ritual was considered "better" than usual simply because it contained innovations (*Social Practice of Symbolization*, Epilogue). And Stanley Brandes documents the sudden embracing of a new ritual at the expense of a tradition espoused by authorities (*Power and Persuasion: Fiestas and Social Control in Rural Mexico* [Philadelphia, 1988], 112, also 146).

28. Peil, *Gebärde bei Chrétien*, 200–203; above, 264.

29. Trexler, *Public Life in Renaissance Florence*, Introduction and pt. 1, makes these points quite forcefully.

30. Among recent or lesser-known works on this important topic see White, *Custom, Kinship, and Gifts to Saints*; Barbara Rosenwein, *To Be the Neighbor of Saint Peter: The Social Meaning of Cluny's Property (909–1049)* (Ithaca, 1989); John M. Hill, "Beowulf and the Danish Succession: Gift Giving as an Occasion for Complex Gesture," *Medievalia et Humanistica* 11 (1982): 177–92; Roman Michalowski, "Le don d'amitié dans la société carolingienne et les *Translationes sanctorum*," in *Hagiographie, cultures et sociétés*, 399–416; William Ian Miller, "Gift, Sale, Payment, Raid: Case Studies in the Negotiation and Classification of Exchange in Medieval Iceland," *Speculum* 61 (1986): 18–50.

31. *Livre des serfs*, 26, 29–30, 33–34, 65, etc.

32. Schmidt-Wiegand, "Gebärdensprache," 369.

33. *Mir. s. Donatiani*, 856–58. Cf. *Mir. s. Ursmari*, MGH SS 15/2:840, c. 16, where a manslayer stretches out in the form of a cross at the feet of his victims' brother.

34. Above, 60; Ruth Mellinkoff, "Riding Backwards: Theme of Humiliation and Symbol of Evil," *Viator* 4 (1973): 153–76; McCormick, *Eternal Victory*, 135, 144, 181, 186; Karl Hauck, "Rituelle Speisegemeinschaft im Mittelalter," *Studium Generale* 3 (1950): 611–21, esp. 612–15.

35. Le Goff, "Symbolic Ritual of Vassalage"; Flori, *L'essor de la chevalerie*; Maurice Keen, *Chivalry* (New Haven, 1984), chap. 4; Suntrup, *Bedeutung der liturgischen Gebärden*, 245–55; Knowles, *Monastic Constitutions of Lanfranc*, 22–26, 49–50; *Liber tramitis*, 240–41. In this connection one should also mention *delationes* of relics, since they also were occasions when the ritual lives of laity and clergy crossed: P. Héliot and M.-L. Chastang, "Quêtes et voyages de reliques au profits des églises françaises du Moyen Age," *Revue d'histoire ecclésiastique* 59 (1964): 789–822 and 60 (1965): 5–32; P.-A. Sigal, "Les voyages de reliques aux onzième et douzième siècles," in *Voyages, quête, pèlerinage dans la littérature et la civilisation médiévales* (Paris, 1976), 75–95, 104.

36. Schmidt-Wiegand, "Gebärdensprache" and "Gebärden"; Emily Zack Tabuteau, *Transfers of Property in Eleventh-Century Norman Law* (Chapel Hill, N.C., 1988), 119–22.

37. Karen Louise Jolly, "Anglo-Saxon Charms in the Context of a Christian World View," *Journal of Medieval History* 11 (1985): 279–93; C. Vogel, "Pratiques superstitieuses au début du XIe siècle d'après le *Corrector sive medicus* de Burchard, évêque de Worms (965–1025)," in *Mélanges offertes à Edmond-René Labande* (Poitiers, 1974), 751–61.

38. Trexler, *Public Life in Renaissance Florence*, chap. 3.

39. See Brühl, "Kronen- und Krönungsbrauch," 6–12, with Jäschke, "Frühmittelalterliche Festkrönungen?" on the development of these liturgies.

40. Brühl, "Kronen- und Krönungsbrauch," 6–12.

41. Above, 167, below, 306; Bornscheuer, *Miseriae regum*, 114–16, 205–7; Schramm et al., *Deutschen Kaiser und Könige*, 205.

42. Kantorowicz, *Laudes Regiae*, 76–87, 92–101; above, 119. The *laudes* were also sung as part of episcopal masses; but on these occasions their audience must have been restricted to the local clergy, outside of a few select lay nobles who might be invited to attend.

43. Nelson, "Lord's Anointed," 168–69; C. Warren Hollister, "The Strange Death of William Rufus," *Speculum* 48 (1973): 653.

44. Some indications are offered by Fichtenau, *Lebensordnungen*, 1:44–45, 82–91.

45. Hauck, "Rituelle Speisegemeinschaft" (above, n. 34).

46. Notker the Stammerer, *Gesta Karoli*, 16, 1:11; P. E. Schramm, *A History of the English Coronation*, trans. Leopold G. Wickham Legg (Oxford, 1937), 62–65, and Schramm, *KKP*, 1:31; 2:155–57, 214–16; 3:47–49, 57, 124.

47. Fichtenau, *Lebensordnungen*, 1:45–46; Hugh of Flavigny, *Chronicon Virdunense*, 372.

48. Vercauteren, *Actes*, 247–51, no. 108 (1122): "Atrebati sedens in camera abbatis iterum conventus a monachis, baronibus meis circa me positis, et Ingelberto adstante;" 161–62, no. 69 (1115): "quia me comite Balduino demorante Atrebati, et circumstante curia mea sedente in camera abbatis."

49. Below, 306.

50. Above, 61; Fichtenau, *Lebensordnungen*, 1:53, 57–58; W. L. Warren, *Henry II* (Berkeley, 1973), 500; Dudo of St-Quentin, *De moribus*, 158, 224.

51. Above, 59, on pact-sealing kisses; Hugh of Flavigny, *Chronicon Virdunense*, 394, for kisses between friends; Michael Toch, "Asking the Way and Telling the Law: Speech in Medieval Germany," *Journal of Interdisciplinary History* 16 (1986): 667–82, for peasants' speech.

52. See Sperber, *Rethinking Symbolism*; Crick, *Explorations in Language and Meaning*, 116. The point is made especially clearly in Roy A. Rappaport, *Pigs for the Ancestors: Ritual in the Ecology of a New Guinea People* (New Haven, 1967), all the more so because the symbolic matrices of the Maring's cognitive grid cut across the author's professed functionalism.

53. Current theory holds that such submissive postures reflect a learned reversion to infantile behavior associated with strong physical or emotional needs (e.g., feeding): Rudolf Schenkel, "Submission: Its Features and Function in the Wolf and Dog," *American Zoologist* 7 (1967): 319–29; John B. Oppenheimer, "Communication in New World Monkeys," in *How Animals Communicate*, ed. Thomas A. Sebeok (Bloomington, Ind., 1977), 851–89 at 868–69; Frans de Waal, *Peacemaking among Primates* (Cambridge, Mass., 1989), 44, 52–53, 63, 208. Edmund Leach believes that a propensity toward physical self-abasement within human societies may derive from the proportions of the human body: "The Influence of Cultural Context on Non-Verbal Communication in Man," in *Non-Verbal Communication*, ed. R. A. Hinde (Cambridge, 1972), 315–47.

54. Hugh of Flavigny, *Chronicon Virdunense*, 372; Dudo of St-Quentin, *De moribus*, 169; Fichtenau, *Lebensordnungen*, 1:58 (though he confuses *proskynesis* and *commendatio*).

55. Fichtenau, *Lebensordnungen*, 1:60.

56. Regino of Prüm, *De ecclesiasticis disciplinis*, 245, c. 291; cf. Johnson, *Prayer, Patronage, and Power*, 81.

57. Ulrich of Cluny, *Consuetudines Cluniacenses*, 734–35, 3.3; Leyser, *Rule and Conflict*, 174 n. 15; William of Jumièges, *Gesta Normannorum ducum*, 101; and in general Fichtenau, *Lebensordnungen*, 1:65–66.

58. "Udalrici Babenbergensis codex," in *Monumenta Bambergensia*, ed. Philip Jaffé (Berlin, 1869), 359–60.

59. Hugh of Flavigny, *Chronicon Virdunense*, 372; *Vita beati Lanfranci*, 48–49, c. 11.

60. The "Livre Blanc" of St-Martin de Sées, AD Orne, H 938, f. 8: "Si uero in laicali habitu moreretur in capitulo sancti Martini ad pedes domni abbatis Rotberti sepeliretur."

61. Richer, *Histoire de France*, 2:112; see also 2:162 ("Quomodo capiti suo praeponet, cujus pares et etiam majores sibi genua flectunt, pedibusque manus supponunt?").

62. Schäfer, *Fusswaschung*, 44–50; Suntrup, *Bedeutung der liturgischen Gebärden*, 355–61.

63. Sahlins, *Islands of History*, esp. 77, 125, 138.

64. Above, chap. 8.

65. E.g., *Historia translationis s. Vedasti*, 817–18; Huyghebaert, *Translation de reliques*, 26–27, 49–51, from sections believed by the editor to form part of the Ur-text of the *Adventus*.

66. *Vita s. Arnulfi*, 247–49; *Mir. s. Donatiani*, 856–58; Koziol, "Monks, Feuds, and the Making of Peace."

67. Hallam, "Royal Burial and the Cult of Kingship," 359.

68. Flodoard, *Annales*, s.a. 948; Richer, *Histoire de France*, 2:108, 172; Raoul Glaber, *Histoires*, 38–39. In 921 Charles the Simple and Henry I actually concluded a treaty on a boat in the middle of the Rhine: Fichtenau, *Lebensordnungen*, 1:43.

69. Above, 114–15, 132.
70. Flodoard, *Annales*, 19–20.
71. Richer, *Histoire de France*, 1:38–40; cf. Fichtenau, *Lebensordnungen*, 1:46.
72. See Nelson, "Lord's Anointed."
73. Above, chap. 4.
74. Brunner, "Fränkische Fürstentitel," 212, 249, 265, 267–68.
75. Cowdrey, "Anglo-Norman *Laudes Regiae*."
76. Fulbert of Chartres, *Letters and Poems*, 7, no. 1 (1004).
77. As at the council of Limoges in 994: "pactumque pacis et justicia a duce et principibus vicissim foederata est" (Ademar of Chabannes, *Chronique*, 158; Hoffmann, *Gottesfriede*, 27–31); and that at Poitiers (c. 1010): "Firmaverunt per obsides et excommunicationem dux, et reliqui principes, huiusmodi pacis et justitiae restaurationem" (G. D. Mansi and N. Coleti, eds., *Sacrorum conciliorum nova et amplissima collectio* (Paris, 1901–1927), 19:267; Hoffmann, *Gottesfriede*, 31–32); and again at Poitiers (1031–32), where no sooner was the Peace reaffirmed than the monks of St-Maixent appealed to the duke to stop his own ministers' violations on his lands (Mansi and Coleti, *Sacrorum conciliorum . . . collectio*, 19:495–96; Töpfer, *Volk und Kirche*, 72–73).
78. Huyghebaert, *Translation de reliques*, 45 ("inclytus scilicet marchysus, cum omni exercitu"), 50 ("Omnis patria occurrit, quique pagenses . . . obviam ruunt. Confluit regalis militia et omnis plebs urbana"). The distinction of these warriors is clear (1) from their being singled out from the *pagenses* and *plebs*; (2) from the presence of the count's *exercitus* when he expropriated the relics from Boulogne; and (3) from the absence of this group in the translation of Vedast (above, n. 65).
79. Above, chap. 8.
80. Koziol, "Monks, Feuds, and the Making of Peace."
81. Turner, *Forest of Symbols*, 50–51; Strecker, *Social Practice of Symbolization*, 43–44; Schmitt, "Introduction," in his *Gestures*, 8. Good European examples are provided by Klapisch-Zuber, *Women, Family, and Ritual*, 236 (above, n. 2).
82. Herman of Laon, *De miraculis s. Mariae Laudunensis*, 985. The examples cited above make me doubt Le Goff's statement ("Symbolic Ritual of Vassalage," 243) that it did not matter who initiated the kiss in homage. The overtones of a lord's initiating or receiving a kiss might vary from place to place, but that there were overtones cannot be doubted.
83. Fichtenau, *Lebensordnungen*, 1:49–50.
84. Sperber, *Rethinking Symbolism*, 17–19; Strecker, *Social Practice of Symbolization*, 22–26.
85. Turner, *Forest of Symbols*, 43–44; Lévi-Strauss, "The Structural Study of Myth," in his *Structural Anthropology*, 213–30.
86. Kantorowicz, *King's Two Bodies*, 61–78.
87. Jean-Claude Bonne, "Depicted Gesture, Named Gesture: Postures of the Christ on the Autun Tympanum," in Schmitt, *Gestures*. Similarly Garnier, *Langage de l'image*, 128.
88. Fichtenau, *Lebensordnungen*, 1:60.
89. Above, 144, 263. Similarly, the festive meal that concluded a crown-wearing might be interpreted either as a christomimetic representation of the Last Supper or as a ceremony of sharing and service appropriate to a beneficent lord.
90. Peter Brown, "Society and the Supernatural: A Medieval Change," in *Society and the Holy in Late Antiquity* (Berkeley, 1982), 302–32; Paul Hyams, "Trial by Ordeal: The Key to Proof in the Early Common Law," in *On the Laws and Customs of England: Essays in Honor of Samuel E. Thorne*, ed. Morris S. Arnold et al. (Chapel Hill, N.C., 1981), 90–126. Although Robert Bartlett, *Trial by Fire and Water:*

The *Medieval Judicial Ordeal* (Oxford, 1986), believes that lordly authority was more important in ordeals than audience consensus, I see no reason why both could not play a role—not only in different ordeals but even in the same one. On the role of the audience see also Koziol, "Monks, Feuds, and the Making of Peace"; Lévi-Strauss, "The Sorcerer and His Magic," in his *Structural Anthropology*, 167–85.

91. Leyser, *Rule and Conflict*, 95.

92. *Vita Hludowici pii*, c. 49, esp. 172–73.

93. Bartlett, *Trial by Fire and Water*, 40 (above, n. 90).

94. Koziol, "Monks, Feuds, and the Making of Peace."

95. Above, chap. 7.

96. Koziol, "Monks, Feuds, and the Making of Peace"; *Mir. s. Ursmari*, MGH SS 15/2:839, c. 6, 840, c. 12, 841, c. 16.

97. I dissent here from Victor Turner's explanation for the emotive force of rituals (*Forest of Symbols*, 28, 54), that they join the moral or ideological order with the natural; for though Turner speaks of the relation between these two realms as a "polarization," it is in his handling simply a projection of the natural onto the social, too transparent to be truly moving (save, perhaps, where these categories are perceived as opposites, as in Gnosticism). As discussed below, this analysis would also seem to lead to a better understanding of the difference that anthropologists often perceive between ritual and ceremony.

98. Warner, *Joan of Arc*, 202–3 (above, n. 23); Sandra Clark, "*Hic Mulier, Haec Vir*, and the Controversy over Masculine Women," *Studies in Philology* 82 (1985): 157–83, esp. 160–61.

99. Natalie Zemon Davis, *Society and Culture in Early Modern France* (Stanford, 1975), chaps. 4–6.

100. Ronald Weissman, *Ritual Brotherhood in Renaissance Florence* (New York, 1982). Similarly Brandes's excellent account of *La Danza* in Tzintzuntzan, Mexico: *Power and Persuasion*, chap. 7 (above, n. 27).

101. Fichtenau, *Arenga*, 43–44.

102. MGH Capit. 2, no. 205, c. 6, p. 73 (Meersen II); no. 254, c. 3, p. 255 (Coulaines).

103. E.g., Rodez, 995–1015 (Auguste Bouillet, ed., *Liber miraculorum s. Fidis* [Paris, 1897], 71–72); Limoges, 994 (*Commemoratio abbatum Lemovicensium*, PL 141:82–83); Amiens, c. 1036 (*Mir. s. Adalhardi*, 862); probably also Verdun and Héry, 1019–21 and 1024 (*Gesta pontificum Autissiodorensium*, 388); Bourges, 1038 (*MSB*, 193–94); and the many other occasions where sources indicate semiurban conditions or tremendous crowds.

104. Arnold William Klukas, "The Architectural Implications of the *Decreta Lanfranci*," *Anglo-Norman Studies* 6 (1983): 136–71.

105. For kisses of brotherhood, see above. For the liturgical kiss, Suntrup, *Bedeutung der liturgischen Gebärden*, 371–79; in the context of a Peace assembly, *Mir. s. Ursmari*, MGH SS 15/2:839–40, cc. 9, 12, though the act is inherent in such terms as *pax* and *foedus*, used for the central event of all councils.

106. Duby, "Laity and the Peace of God," in his *Chivalrous Society*.

107. *MSB*, 194 (see Flori, *L'essor de la chevalerie*, 167–68); Raoul Glaber, *Histoires*, 103 (and Flori, 170–71); *Mir. s. Bercharii*, in RHF 10:375 ("innumerae plebis multitudines, diversi utriusque sexus et aetatis concurrerent"); *Gesta pontificum Autissiodorensium*, 388 ("concilium episcoporum ac multorum tam nobilium quam plebeiorum innumere multitudinis").

108. Cf., e.g., *Historia translationis s. Vedasti*, 818 (which does not mention *milites* or any other terms suggestive of later classes or statuses); Huyghebaert, *Translation de reliques*, 50 (mentioning the *regalis militia*); *Mir. s. Ursmari*, MGH SS

15/2:838, 840–41 (cc. 3, 5, 6, 12, 16, 17, 19, referring at various points to *milites, populi, oppidani,* and *rustici*).

109. Huyghebaert, *Translation de reliques,* and *Mir. s. Ursmari,* MGH SS 15/2:838, 840–41.

110. Goetz, "Kirchenschutz," 205–6, 224–25, cites the older literature, though he qualifies the statement more than I would. Many of the actions that were outlawed by the various Peace councils were just those that would have occurred in the prosecution of feuds in the course of pillaging another's property.

111. Albert Vermeesch, *Essai sur les origines et la signification de la commune dans le nord de la France (XIe et XIIe siècles)* (Heule, 1966); Bachrach, "Northern Origins of the Peace Movement."

112. *Mir. s. Ursmari,* MGH SS 15/2:839, c. 6.

113. Raoul Glaber, *Histoires,* 103–5. Also Richard Landes, "Between Aristocracy and Heresy: Popular Participation in the Limousin Peace of God (994–1033)," in *The Peace of God,* Head and Landes, eds.

114. *Mir. s. Ursmari,* MGH SS 15/2:839–41, cc. 6, 12, 16, 20; also cc. 13, 18, 19, in AASS Apr., 2:572–74; *Mir. s. Donatiani,* 856–58.

115. This analysis contradicts Victor Turner's interpretation but is quite close to the various formulations offered by Gluckman, *Politics, Law, and Ritual,* 250–59, and Gluckman and Gluckman, "On Drama," 227–43 (both above, n. 16). See also the criticisms of overly structured analyses of symbolic systems by Fernandez, "Dark at the Bottom of the Stairs."

116. *Vita Burchardi,* 860.

117. Above, chap. 4.

118. Above, chap. 5.

119. *Gesta episcoporum Cameracensium,* 466–67, 3.2.

120. Erich Caspar, ed., *Das Register Gregors VII.* (Berlin, 1967), 312–13, 4.12.

121. Regino of Prüm, *De ecclesiasticis disciplinis,* 245, 1.288, trans. in McNeill and Gamer, *Medieval Handbooks of Penance,* 314. Also Teetaert, "Confession aux laïques," 41–42; Galtier, *L'église et la rémission des péchés,* 126–29, and "Satisfaction," 1129, 1146, 1176; Amann, "Pénitence," 874, 891.

122. Raban Maur, *De ecclesiastica disciplina,* 1257: "Compunctio cordis est humilitas mentis cum lacrymis et recordatione peccatorum, et timore judici. Ex genuino fonte compunctionis solent profluere lacrymae"; Devisse, *Hincmar,* 1:548, with incorrect citation to PL 125:687; similarly Gregory the Great as cited by Galtier, *L'église et la rémission des péchés,* 423–25.

123. Regino of Prüm, *De ecclesiasticis disciplinis,* 245, 1.291.

124. Franzten, *Literature of Penance,* chap. 1.

125. Galtier, "Satisfaction," 1167.

126. *De vera et falsa poenitentia,* 1125, 15.30.

127. Raban Maur, *De videndo deum,* 1325–26, 3.19.

128. *De vera et falsa poenitentia,* 1121, 9.23; Raban Maur, *De videndo deum,* 1326, 3.20; Hincmar of Reims, *De cavendis vitiis,* 899, 891.

129. The passage is interesting enough to be quoted in full: "Nam et orantes de membris sui corporis faciunt quod supplicantibus congruit, cum genua figunt, cum extendunt manus uel etiam prosternuntur solo et si quid aliud faciunt uisibiliter, quamuis eorum inuisibilis uoluntas et cordis intentio deo nota sit nec ille indigeat his indiciis, ut animus ei pandatur humanus. sed hinc magis se ipsum excitat homo ad orandum gemendumque humilius atque feruentius, et nescio quomodo, cum hi motus corporis fieri nisi motu animi praecedente non possint, eisdem rursus exterius uisibiliter factis ille interior inuisibilis qui eos fecit augetur, ac per hoc cordis affectus, qui, ut fierent ista, praecessit, quia facta sunt crescit." The logic of his

argument then requires Augustine to admit that the gestures are not after all necessary for prayers, since it is quite possible for a person imbued with grace to pray as if prostrate within himself. Augustine, *De cura gerenda pro mortuis*, 632, 5.7. See Ohm, *Gebetsgebärden*, 105.

130. E.g., *De vera et falsa poenitentia*, 1122, 10.25; Teetaert, "Confession aux laïques," 41–42, 67–69, 80–81.

131. Teetaert, "Confession aux laïques," 41–42.

132. Amann, "Pénitence," 804; Frantzen, *Literature of Penance*, 52.

133. Cf. *De vera et falsa poenitentia*, 1113–14, 1.2, 3: "Praedicat enim converti. Sed unde se converteret aliquis, cui primus status placeret? Qui itaque convertitur, necessario dolet habere, quod gaudet perdere."

134. Above, n. 129.

135. Galtier, *L'église et la rémission des péchés*, 121–24, 130. The converse is also true: God would not condemn a truly contrite sinner, even in the absence of external works: Vogel, "Discipline pénitentielle," 20–21, 25–26, 157, 163–66; Galtier, "Satisfaction," 1142.

136. E.g., Halitgar, *De vitiis et virtutibus*, 270. See Russo, "Pénitence et excommunication," 438–39; Poschmann, *Ablass*, 9–12, 27; Galtier, *L'église et la rémission des péchés*, 107–11.

137. As shown particularly by the fact that a priest could not withhold absolution from a penitent *in extremis* if his penance was formally correct: Halitgar, *De vitiis et virtutibus*, 277: "In dispensandis itaque Dei donis non debent [sacerdotes] esse difficiles nec se accusantium gemitus lacrimasque negligere cum ipsam penitendi affectionem ex Dei credamus inspiratione conceptam."

138. John M. Roberts, "Oaths, Autonomic Ordeals, and Power," in *The Ethnography of Law*, ed. Laura Nader, 186–212, *American Anthropologist* 67, no. 6, pt. 2 (special issue, 1965).

139. Peter Brown, *Augustine of Hippo* (Berkeley, 1967), chaps. 19 and 21.

140. Russo, "Pénitence et excommunication," esp. 269–70.

141. See Vogel, "Rites de la pénitence publique," 140; Stock, *Implications of Literacy*, 77–79; Vancandard, "Absolution," 162; Galtier, "Satisfaction," 1145–46, 1166–68, 1174–76.

142. Above, 185–86.

143. Jean Leclercq, "Monastic Historiography from Leo IX to Callistus II," *Studia Monastica* 12 (1970): 76–86; R. W. Southern, "Aspects of the European Tradition of Historical Writing: The Classical Tradition from Einhard to Geoffrey of Monmouth," *Transactions of the Royal Historical Society* 20, 5th ser. (1970): 173–96 at 182–84; Jacques Chaurand, "La conception de l'histoire de Guibert de Nogent," *Cahiers de civilisation médiévale* 8 (1965): 381–96 at 382–84.

144. E.g., Willmes, *Herrscher-"Adventus,"* 23–24; Suntrup, *Bedeutung der liturgischen Gebärden*, 46–66.

145. Herlihy, Foreword to Klapisch-Zuber, *Women, Family, and Ritual*, x (above, n. 2).

146. See the citations above, n. 84, and Lévi-Strauss, *Structural Anthropology*, 17. Thus the puzzlement of a sixteenth-century Roman over the meaning of his city's marriage ceremonies, to which Herlihy points as proof of the difference between ethnographic and historical inquiries into the meaning of rituals (above, n. 2), should really be taken as a demonstration of their similarity.

Selected Bibliography

Given the number of disciplines relevant to the themes of this book, it has not been possible to list every work cited, much less every work consulted. This bibliography is therefore necessarily selective. For primary sources I have generally limited myself to items that were systematically and entirely analyzed for material on supplication and dispute processing, whether they are cited in the text or not. I have not listed collections or editions consulted primarily to trace references to specific charters (BN, Collections Picardie, Moreau, Baluze, Housseau, and Duchesne), although I have listed a handful of important charters or copies in these collections. It should be noted that only a few of these manuscript sources contain many tenth- or eleventh-century documents from northern France, and much of what there is has already been edited, if only as supporting documents in monographs. Although I have cited these editions in the notes, I have still listed the manuscripts here in order to give readers a sense of the range of collections consulted. In this way they may better judge the foundation for the findings of this book. As for secondary sources, I have listed only works cited with some frequency in the notes. The exceptions are works on supplication and diplomatic rhetoric; here the bibliography is reasonably complete.

Editions of cartularies and charters are listed under the names of their editors, except the editions of royal *acta* in the Chartes et diplômes series, which for convenience are listed together by title (*Recueils des actes . . .*). Other items are listed by author, title, or editor, as they are cited in the notes. When two or more articles from the same symposium proceedings are cited, the title of the proceedings is abbreviated in each entry and given in full separately.

Finally, it should be noted that microfilms or microfiches of the majority of the manuscripts cited are available through the Institut de Recherches et d'Histoire des Textes at Paris and Orléans, often with detailed analyses of their contents.

MANUSCRIPT SOURCES

Alençon. Archives départementales de l'Orne.
  H 938. "Livre blanc" of Saint-Martin de Sées.
Amiens. Archives départmentales de la Somme.
  G 2966. Cartulary of the cathedral chapter of Amiens.
——. Bibliothèque municipale.
  1077. Cartulary of Arrouaise.
Arras. Archives départementales de Pas-de-Calais.
  H (unnumbered). Cartulary of Auchy-les-Moines.
  H (unnumbered). Cartulary of Saint-Josse-sur-Mer.
Avranches. Bibliothèque municipale.
  210. Cartulary of Mont-Saint-Michel.
Beauvais. Archives départementales de l'Oise.
  G 1984. Cartulary of the cathedral chapter of Notre-Dame of Noyon.
Cambrai. Bibliothèque municipale.
  1041. Cartulary of Saint-Sépulchre of Cambrai.
  1042. Cartulary of Sainte-Croix of Cambrai.
  1222. Cartulary of Saint-Sépulchre of Cambrai.
Cambridge, Mass. Medieval Academy of America.
  William Mendel Newman. "Charters of Mont-Saint-Quentin" (typescript).
Châlons-sur-Marne. Archives départmentales de la Marne.
  G 1130. Cartulary of the chapter of La Trinité of Châlons.
Charleville-Mézières. Archives départmentales des Ardennes.
  H 11. Cartulary of the priory of Novy.
Ghent. Rijksarchief.
  Archief van der Sint-Baafskathedraal (originals). Fonds Sint-Pietersabdij. Fonds Sint-Baafsabdij.
Laon. Archives départementales de l'Aisne.
  G 253. Cartulary of the cathedral chapter of Soissons.
  G 1850. Cartulary of Notre-Dame of Laon.
  H 325. Chronicle/cartulary of Nogent-sous-Coucy.
  H 455. Cartulary of Saint-Crépin of Soissons.
  H 477. Cartulary of Saint-Médard of Soissons.
  H 534. Cartulary of Saint-Quentin-en-l'Ile.
  H 1508. Cartulary of Notre-Dame of Soissons.

Lille. Archives départementales du Nord.
  I G 13. Cartulary of Saint-Amé of Douai.
  3 H 256. Cartulary of Saint-Sépulchre of Cambrai.
  10 H 323. Cartulary of Marchiennes.
  12 H 1 and 2. Cartulary of Saint-Amand.
London. British Museum.
  Addit. ms. 15604. Cartulary of Saint-Acheul.
Orléans. Institut de Recherches et d'Histoire des Textes.
  Commenchon, "Cartulaire de l'abbaye de Saint-Eloi-Fontaine."
Paris. Archives Nationales.
  LL 985B. Cartulary of Saint-Quentin.
  LL 1016–17. Cartularies of Saint-Quentin-en-l'Ile.
  R (1) 35. Cartulary or "Livre rouge" of the lordship of Picquigny.
———. Bibliothèque Nationale.
  Fonds latin
    5650. Cartulary of La Trinité of Caen.
    10968. Cartulary of the cathedral chapter of Cambrai.
    11004. Cartulary of Saint-Jean-des-Vignes of Soissons.
    11070. Cartulary of Saint-Quentin.
    12669. Charters of Saint-Eloi of Noyon, ff. 105–25v.
    12683. Charters of Nogent-sous-Coucy, ff. 98–99, 104–7.
    12695. Cartulary/chronicle of Saint-Saulve of Montreuil, ff. 242–66.
    12701. Charters of Saint-Valéry-sur-Somme, ff. 232–53.
    12704. Charters of Saint-Valéry-sur-Somme, ff. 156–201.
    12895. Cartulary of Saint-Quentin-en-l'Ile.
    17758. "Cartulaire noir" of Corbie.
    17760. The Esdras cartulary of Corbie.
    17764. Charters of Corbie.
    18375. Cartulary of Saint-Michel-en-Thiérache.
  Nouvelles acquisitions latines
    1921. Cartulary of Saint-Quentin of Beauvais.
    1930. "Livre noir" of Saint-Florent of Saumur.
    2574, f. 1. Original charter of Eilbodo for Sint-Pieters, Ghent, Oct. 6, 975
      (= *Dipl. Belg.*, vol. 1, no. 64).
  Collection Baluze
    Vol. 47, ff. 194–205. Charters of Saint-Valéry-sur-Somme.
    Vol. 75, ff. 34–72v. Charters of Saint-Prix.
  Collection Bourgogne
    Vols. 76–77. Original charters from Cluny.
  Collection Moreau
    Vol. 21, ff. 20v-31v; vol. 28, f. 192r–v; vol. 30, ff. 190–91; vol. 40, f. 220r–
      v; vol. 341, ff. 171–v, 28. Charters of Fécamp.
  Collection Picardie, vol. 352, f. 1. Partial autograph charter by Dudo of Saint-
      Quentin for Richard II of Normandy (= Fauroux, no. 18).
Reims. Bibliothèque municipale.
  85. Augustine. "Expositio in Psalmos 119–133."
  1600. Chronicle of Saint-Thierry of Reims.
  1602. Cartulary of Saint-Thierry of Reims.
———. Bibliothèque municipale, fonds départementales.
  H 373. Cartulary of the abbey of Saint-Nicaise of Reims.

H 1411. Cartulary B of Saint-Remi of Reims.
H 1412. Cartulary C of Saint-Remi of Reims.
H 1413. Cartulary A of Saint-Remi of Reims.
H 1414. Cartulary D of Saint-Remi of Reims.
Soissons. Bibliothèque municipale.
    Collection Perrin, ms. 3308. Robert Wiard, "Histoire de l'abbaye de Saint-Prix."
Troyes. Archives départementales de l'Aube.
    G 1252. Cartulary of the cathedral chapter of Troyes.

CHARTERS AND DIPLOMAS

Anquetil, E., ed. *Le "Livre rouge" de l'évêché de Bayeux.* 2 vols. Bayeux, 1908, 1911.
Arbois de Jubainville, H. d', ed. *Histoire des ducs et des comtes de Champagne.* 6 vols. Paris, 1859–66.
Bernard, Auguste, and Alexandre Bruel, eds. *Recueil des chartes de l'abbaye de Cluny.* 6 vols. Paris, 1876–1903.
Bertrand de Broussillon, A., ed. *Cartulaire de l'abbaye de Saint-Aubin d'Angers.* 3 vols. Angers, 1896–1899.
Bétencourt, P.-L. de, ed. *Cartulaire de l'abbaye d'Auchy.* n.p., n.d.
Bièvre Poulalier, Adrien, ed. *Chartes de l'abbaye de Saint-Etienne de Dijon de 1098 à 1140.* Dijon, 1912.
Bled, O, ed. *Regestes des évêques de Thérouanne (500–1553).* 2 vols. Saint-Omer, 1904, 1907.
Bourassé, J.-J., ed. *Cartulaire de Cormery précédé de l'histoire de l'abbaye et de la ville de Cormery.* Mémoires de la Société archéologique de Touraine 12. Tours, 1861.
Bourienne, V., ed. *Antiquus cartularius ecclesiae Baiocensis ("Livre noir").* 2 vols. Paris/Rouen, 1902.
Boussard, Jacques. "Actes royaux et pontificaux des Xe et XIe siècles, du chartrier de Saint-Maur des Fossés." *Journal des Savants,* 1972, pp. 81–113.
——. "La charte de fondation de Notre-Dame de Loches." Actes du colloque médiéval, Loches, 1973. *Mémoires de la Société archéologique de Touraine* 9 (1975): 1–10.
——. "Le diplôme de Hugues Capet, de 988, pour l'abbaye de Corbie." *Journal des Savants,* 1976, pp. 54–64.
Brunel, Clovis, ed. *Recueil des actes des comtes de Pontieu (1026–1279).* Paris, 1930.
Carlier, Claude. *Histoire du duché de Valois . . . depuis le temps des Gaulois jusqu'en l'année 1703.* Paris, 1764.
Cartier, M.-E. "Charte de 908, contenant un accommodement devant Thibaut, vicomte de Tours." *Mémoires de la Société royale des antiquaires de France* 5, ser. 2 (1840): 435–50.
Charmasse, A. de, ed. *Cartulaire de l'église d'Autun.* 2 vols. Paris, 1865, 1900.
Chartae latinae antiquiores. Ed. Hartmut Atsma et al. Vols. 13–17, 19. Zurich, 1981–87.
Chevalier, Casimir, ed. *Cartulaire de l'abbaye de Noyers.* Mémoires de la Société archéologique de Touraine 22. Tours, 1872.

Chevrier, Georges, and Maurice Chaume, eds. *Chartes et documents de Saint-Bénigne de Dijon (900–1124)*. Dijon, 1911.

Colliette, L.-P. *Mémoires pour servir à l'histoire ecclésiastique, civile et militaire de la province du Vermandois*. 3 vols. Cambrai, 1771–73.

Courson, Aurélien de, ed. *Cartulaire de l'abbaye de Redon en Bretagne*. Paris, 1863.

Courtois, J., ed. *Chartes de l'abbaye de Saint-Etienne de Dijon (VIIIe, IXe, X^e et XIe siècles)*. Paris/Dijon, 1908.

Courtois, Michel, ed. "Chartes originales antérieures à *1121* conservées dans le département du Nord." Mémoire de maîtrise. Université de Nancy II, 1981.

Coussemaker, E. de, ed. *Cartulaire de l'abbaye de Cysoing et de ses dépendances*. Lille, 1896.

———. *Documents relatifs à la Flandre Maritime extraits du cartulaire de l'abbaye de Watten*. Lille, 1860.

Delaville le Roulx, J. *Notices sur les chartes originales relatives à la Touraine, antérieures à l'an mil*. Tours, 1879.

Deloche, Maximin, ed. *Cartulaire de l'abbaye de Beaulieu (en Limousin)*. Paris, 1859.

Denis, L.-J., ed. *Cartulaire de l'abbaye de Saint-Sauveur de Villeloin*. Paris/Le Mans, 1911.

Depoin, Joseph, ed. *Cartulaire de l'abbaye de Saint-Martin de Pontoise*. Pontoise, 1895–1909.

———. *Recueil des chartes et documents de Saint-Martin-des-Champs, monastère parisien*. 5 vols. Paris, 1912–21.

Deville, Etienne, ed. *Cartulaire de l'église de la Sainte-Trinité de Beaumont-le-Roger*. Paris, 1912.

Deville, Jean Achille, ed. *Cartulaire de l'abbaye de la Sainte-Trinité du Mont de Rouen*. In *Cartulaire de Saint-Bertin*, ed. B. Guérard, 403–87. Paris, 1840.

Doniol, Henri, ed. *Cartulaire de Brioude*. Clermont-Ferrand, 1861.

Duchet, T., and A. Giry, eds. *Cartulaires de l'église de Térouane*. Saint-Omer, 1881.

Du Monstier, Arthur. *Neustria Pia seu omnibus et singulis abbatiis et prioratibus totius Normanniae . . .* Rouen, 1663.

Duvivier, Charles, ed. *Actes et documents anciens intéressant la Belgique*. 2 vols. Brussels, 1898, 1903.

Evergates, Theodore, ed. *The Cartulary and Charters of Notre-Dame of Homblières*. Cambridge, Mass., 1990.

Fauroux, Marie, ed. *Recueil des actes des ducs de Normandie (911–1066)*. Caen, 1961.

Feuchère, Pierre, ed. "Regeste des comtes de Saint-Pol (1023–1205)." *Revue du Nord* 39 (1957): 43–48.

Fossier, Robert, ed. *Chartes de coutume en Picardie (XIe–XIIIe siècles)*. Paris, 1974.

Garnier, Joseph, ed. *Chartes bourguignonnes inédites des IXe, X^e et XIe siècles*. Paris, 1845.

Gasnault, Pierre, ed. "Les actes privés de l'abbaye de Saint-Martin de Tours du VIIIe au XIIe siècle." *Bibliothèque de l'Ecole des Chartes* 112 (1954): 244–66.

Giry, Arthur. "Etudes Carolingiennes, V. Documents carolingiens de l'abbaye de Montiéramey." In *Etudes d'histoire du moyen âge dédiées à Gabriel Monod*, 122–36. Paris, 1896.

Gordière, Louis-Alfred. *Le prieuré de Saint-Amand, de l'ordre des bénédictins . . . sur le terroir de Machemont (Oise), suivi de son cartulaire . . .* Compiègne, 1886.

Gousset, T., ed. *Les actes de la province ecclésiastique de Reims.* 4 vols. Reims, 1842–44.

Grandmaison, Charles Loiseau de, ed. *Cartulaire de Saint-Jouin-des-Marnes.* Société de statistique du département des Deux-Sèvres 17. Niort, 1854.

———. "Fragments de chartes du Xe siècle provenant de Saint-Julien de Tours." *Bibliothèque de l'Ecole des Chartes* 46 (1885): 373–429; 47 (1886): 226–73.

Grasilier, T., ed. *Cartulaire de l'abbaye royale de Notre-Dame de Saintes.* Cartulaires inédits de la Saintonge 2. Niort, 1871.

Guérard, Benjamin, ed. *Cartulaire de l'abbaye de Saint-Bertin.* Paris, 1841.

———. *Cartulaire de l'abbaye de Saint-Père de Chartres.* 2 vols. Paris, 1840.

———. *Cartulaire de l'église de Notre-Dame de Paris.* 4 vols. Paris, 1850.

Guesnon, A., ed. *Un cartulaire de l'abbaye de Saint-Vaast d'Arras, codex du XIIe siècle.* Paris, 1896.

Guyotjeannin, Olivier. "Noyonnais et Vermandois aux Xe et XIe siècles. La déclaration du trésorier Guy et les premières confirmations royales et pontificales des biens du chapitre cathédral de Noyon." *Bibliothèque de l'Ecole des Chartes* 139 (1981): 143–89.

Gysseling, M., and A. C. F. Koch, eds. *Diplomata belgica ante millesimum centesimum scripta.* 2 vols. Tongres, 1950.

Haigneré, D., ed. *Les chartes de Saint-Bertin d'après le grand cartulaire de Dom Charles-Joseph Dewitte.* Saint-Omer, 1886.

Hautcoeur, Edouard, ed. *Cartulaire de l'église de Saint-Pierre de Lille.* 2 vols. Paris/Lille, 1894.

Hémeré, Claude. *Augusta Viromanduorum vindicata et illustrata duobus libris . . . Regesta veterum chartum.* Paris, 1643.

Herbomez, Armand d', ed. *Les chartes de l'abbaye de Saint-Martin de Tournai.* 2 vols. Brussels, 1898, 1901.

Hoop, F.-H. d', ed. *Recueil des chartes du prieuré de Saint Bertin, à Poperinghe.* Bruges, 1870.

Huygens, R. B. C., ed. *Monumenta Vizeliacensia: Textes relatifs à l'histoire de l'abbaye de Vézelay.* Corpus Christianorum, Continuatio Medieualis 42. Supplement: *Vizeliacensia II.* Turnholt, 1976, 1980.

Jusselin, Maurice. "Un acte d'Hugues, duc des Francs et ses souscriptions en notes tironiennes." *Moyen Age* 33 (1922): 145–49.

Kurth, G., ed. *Chartes de l'abbaye de Saint-Hubert-en-Ardenne.* Brussels, 1903.

La Fortelle, Bernard de. *Histoire et description de Notre-Dame de Melun.* Melun, 1843.

Lalore, Charles, ed. *Cartulaire de l'abbaye de Montiéramey.* Collection des principaux cartulaires du diocèse de Troyes 7. Paris/Troyes, 1890.

———. *Cartulaire de Montier-la-Celle.* Collection des principaux cartulaires du diocèse de Troyes 6. Paris/Troyes, 1882.

———. *Chartes de Montierender.* Collection des principaux cartulaires du diocèse de Troyes 4. Paris/Troyes, 1878.

Lasteyrie, Robert-Charles de, ed. *Cartulaire général de Paris.* Vol. 1, 528–1180. Paris, 1887.

Laurent, Jacques, ed. *Cartulaires de l'abbaye de Molesme (916–1250).* 2 vols. Paris, 1907, 1911.

Le Mire, Aubert. *Opera diplomatica et historica.* 2 vols. Louvain, 1723, 1748.

Le Peletier, Laurent. *Rerum scitu dignissimarum a prima fundatione monasterii s. Nicolai Andegauensis . . . epitome.* Angers, 1635.

Lépinois, Eugène de, and Lucien Merlet, eds. *Cartulaire de Notre-Dame de Chartres.* 3 vols. Chartres, 1862–65.

Levillain, Léon. *Examen critique des chartes mérovingiennes et carolingiennes de l'abbaye de Corbie.* Paris, 1902.

——. "Jugement d'un pape Jean en faveur de Corbie." *Moyen Age* 10 (1906): 27–34.

Lex, Léonce. *Eudes, comte de Blois, de Tours, de Chartres, de Troyes et de Meaux (995–1037), et Thibaud, son frère (995–1004).* Troyes, 1892.

Lohrmann, Dietrich, ed. *Papsturkunden in Frankreich*, n.s. 7, *Nordliche Ile-de-France und Vermandois.* Abhandlungen der Akademie der Wissenschaften in Göttingen, Philologisch-historische Klasse 95, ser. 3. Göttingen, 1976.

Loisne, A. de, ed. *Le cartulaire du chapitre d'Arras.* Arras, 1896.

Lot, Ferdinand. *Etudes critiques sur l'abbaye de Saint-Wandrille.* Paris, 1913.

Louvet, Pierre. *Histoire et antiquitez du païs de Beauvais.* 2 vols. Beauvais, 1631, 1635.

Luchaire, Achille. *Etudes sur les actes de Louis VII.* Paris, 1885.

——. *Louis VI le Gros: Annales de sa vie et de son règne.* Paris, 1890.

Mabille, Emile, ed. *Cartulaire de Marmoutier pour le Dunois.* Châteaudun, 1874.

——. "Les invasions normandes dans la Loire et les pérégrinations du corps de Saint Martin." *Bibliothèque de l'Ecole des Chartes* 30 (1869): 149–94, 425–60.

Marchegay, Paul, ed. *Cartulaire de l'abbaye du Ronceray d'Angers (1028–1184).* Paris/Angers, 1900.

——. "Le cartulaire de Saint-Maur-sur-Loire." *Archives d'Anjou* 1. Angers, 1843.

——. "Chartes angevines des onzième et douzième siècles." *Bibliothèque de l'Ecole des Chartes* 36 (1875): 381–441.

——. *Chartes mancelles de l'abbaye de Saint-Florent près Saumur, 848–1200.* Mamers, 1878.

Merlet, René, ed. *Cartulaire de Saint-Jean-en-Vallée de Chartres.* Chartres, 1906.

Métais, Charles, ed. *Cartulaire de l'abbaye cardinale de la Trinité de Vendôme.* 5 vols. Paris, 1893–1904.

——. *Marmoutier: Cartulaire blésois.* Blois, 1889–91.

——. *Saint-Denis de Nogent-le-Rotrou (1031–1789).* Archives du diocèse de Chartres 1. Vannes, 1895.

Monsabert, P. de, ed. *Chartes de l'abbaye de Nouaillé de 678 à 1200.* Archives historiques de Poitou 49. Poitiers, 1936.

Morel, E.-E., ed. *Cartulaire de l'abbaye de Saint-Corneille de Compiègne.* 2 vols. Paris/Montdidier, 1904, 1909.

Morelle, Laurent. "Les chartes de l'abbaye de Corbie (988–1196)." 2 vols. Thèse présentée pour le Doctorat de IIIᵉ cycle. Université de Paris IV, 1988.

Mühlbacher, E., ed. *Die Urkunden der Karolinger.* MGH Diplomatum karolinorum 1. Berlin, 1956.

Müller, Eugène, ed. *Cartulaire du prieuré de Saint-Leu d'Esserent.* Pontoise, 1901.

Musset, Georges, ed. *Le cartulaire de l'abbaye de Saint-Jean d'Angély.* 2 vols. Archives historiques de la Saintonge et de l'Aunis 30 and 33. Paris, 1901, 1904.

Musset, Lucien, ed. *Les actes de Guillaume le Conquérant et de la reine Mathilde pour les abbayes caennaises.* Mémoires de la Société des antiquaires de Normandie 37. Caen, 1967.

Newman, William Mendel. *Catalogue des actes de Robert II, roi de France.* Paris, 1937.

——. *Charters of St. Fursy of Péronne.* Cambridge, Mass., 1977.

——. *Les seigneurs de Nesle en Picardie (XII*^{e}*–XIII*^{e} *siècles), leurs chartes et leur histoire.* 2 vols. Philadelphia, 1971.

Nicaise, A., ed. *Cartulaire de l'abbaye de Saint-Martin d'Epernay.* Châlons-sur-Marne, 1869.

Paris, Louis. *Histoire de l'abbaye d'Avenay.* 2 vols. Paris, 1879.

Pécheur, L., ed. *Le cartulaire de l'abbaye de Saint-Léger de Soissons (1070–1666).* Soissons, 1870.

Peigné-Delacourt, J., ed. *Cartulaire de l'abbaye de N.-D. d'Ourscamp.* Société des antiquaires de Picardie, Documents inédits 6. Amiens, 1865.

Pélicier, P., ed. *Cartulaire du chapitre de l'église cathédral de Châlons-sur-Marne par le chantre Warin.* Paris, 1897.

Piette, A., ed. *Cartulaire de Saint-Michel-en-Thiérache.* Vervins, 1883.

Piot, Charles, ed. *Cartulaire de l'abbaye d'Eename.* Bruges, 1881.

Planchenault, Adrien, ed. *Cartulaire du chapitre de Saint-Laud d'Angers.* Documents historiques sur l'Anjou, Société d'agriculture, sciences et arts d'Angers 4. Angers, 1903.

Poupardin, René. "Une charte inédite de Bernard Plantevelue." *Annales du Midi* 14 (1902): 350–53.

——, ed. *Recueil des chartes de l'abbaye de Saint-Germain-des-Prés des origines au début du XIII*^{e} *siècle.* Paris, 1909.

——, ed. *Recueil des chartes de l'abbaye de Saint-Vincent de Laon.* Paris, 1902.

Prou, Maurice. "Supplique et bulle du XIIe siècle." In *Mélanges offerts à M. Emile Châtelain,* 614–21. Paris, 1910.

—— and Alexandre Vidier, eds. *Recueil des chartes de l'abbaye de Saint-Benoît-sur-Loire.* Paris, 1907.

Pruvost, Alexandre, ed. *Chronique et cartulaire de l'abbaye de Bergues-Saint-Winoc.* Bruges, 1875.

Quantin, Maximilien, ed. *Cartulaire général de l'Yonne.* 2 vols. Auxerre, 1854, 1860.

Ragut, M.-C., ed. *Cartulaire de Saint-Vincent de Macon.* Macon, 1864.

Ramackers, J., ed. *Papsturkunden in Frankreich,* n.s. 4, *Picardie.* Abhandlungen der Akademie der Wissenschaften in Göttingen, Philologisch-historische Klasse 27, ser. 3. Göttingen, 1942.

Recueil des actes de Charles II le Chauve, roi de France. Ed. Arthur Giry, Maurice Prou, and Georges Tessier. 3 vols. Paris, 1943–55.

Recueil des actes de Charles III le Simple, roi de France (893–923). Ed. Ferdinand Lot and Philippe Lauer. Paris, 1940–49.

Recueil des actes d'Eudes Ier*, roi de France (888–898).* Ed. R.-H. Bautier. Paris, 1967.

Recueil des actes de Lothaire et de Louis V, rois de France (954–987). Ed. Louis Halphen and Ferdinand Lot. Paris, 1908.

Recueil des actes de Louis II le Bègue, Louis III, et Carloman II, rois de France (877–884). Ed. Félix Grat et al. Paris, 1978.

Recueil des actes de Louis IV, roi de France (936–954). Ed. Philippe Lauer. Paris, 1954.

Recueil des actes de Philippe Ier, roi de France (1059–1108). Ed. Maurice Prou. Paris, 1908.

Recueil des actes de Philippe Auguste. Ed. H.-F. Delaborde et al. 4 vols. Paris, 1916–1979.

Recueil des actes de Robert Ier et de Raoul, rois de France (922–936). Ed. Jean Dufour. Paris, 1978.

Redet, Louis, ed. *Cartulaire de l'abbaye de Saint-Cyprien de Poitiers*. Archives historiques de Poitou 3. Poitiers, 1874.

———. *Cartulaire du prieuré de Saint-Nicolas de Poitiers*. Archives historiques de Poitou 1. Poitiers, 1872.

———. *Documents pour servir à l'histoire de l'église de Saint-Hilaire de Poitiers*. Mémoires de la Société des antiquaires de l'Ouest, 1847. Poitiers, 1848.

Richard, Alfred, ed. *Chartes et documents pour servir à l'histoire de l'abbaye de Saint-Maixent*. Archives historiques de Poitou 16. Poitiers, 1886.

Rodière, Roger, ed. *Les chartes de Saint-Martin-des-Champs relatives au Ponthieu et aux pays voisins*. Abbéville, 1916.

Roserot, Alphonse. "Chartes inédites des IXe et Xe siècles appartenant aux archives de la Haute-Marne (851–973)." *Bulletin de la Société des sciences historiques et naturelles de l'Yonne* 51 (1897): 162–207.

Roux, J., and E. Soyez, eds. *Cartulaire du chapitre cathédrale d'Amiens*. 2 vols. Mémoires de la Société des antiquaires de Picardie, Documents inédits 14 and 18. Paris/Amiens, 1905, 1912.

Sainte-Marthe, Scévole, and Louis Sainte-Marthe. *Gallia Christiana qua series omnium archiepiscoporum, episcoporum et abbatum Franciae, vicinarumque ditionum . . .* 4 vols. Paris, 1656.

Salmon, André, ed. *Le "Livre des serfs" de l'abbaye de Marmoutier*. Tours, 1865.

Serrure, P., ed. *Cartulaire de Saint-Bavon*. Ghent, 1836.

Soehnée, Frédéric. *Catalogue des actes d'Henri Ier, roi de France (1031–1060)*. Paris, 1907.

Stein, Henri, ed. *Cartulaire de l'ancienne abbaye de Saint-Nicolas-des-Prés sous Ribemont*. Saint-Quentin, 1884.

Tardif, Jules, ed. *Monuments historiques: Cartons des rois (528–1789)*. Paris, 1866.

Thillier, Joseph, and Eugène Jarry, eds. *Cartulaire de Sainte-Croix d'Orléans (814–1300)*. Mémoires de la Société archéologique et historique de l'Orléannais 30. Paris, 1906.

Urseau, C., ed. *Cartulaire noir de la cathédrale d'Angers*. Angers, 1908.

Van Drival, E., ed. *Cartulaire de l'abbaye de Saint-Vaast d'Arras rédigé au XIIe siècle par Guimann*. Arras, 1875.

Van Lokeren, A., ed. *Chartes et documents de l'abbaye de Saint-Pierre de Mont Blandin à Gand*. Ghent, 1868.

Vercauteren, F., ed. *Actes des comtes de Flandre, 1071–1128*. Brussels, 1938.

Vernier, J.-J., ed. *Chartes de l'abbaye de Jumièges (v. 825 à 1204)*. 2 vols. Paris/Rouen, 1916.

Wauters, Alphonse. "Exploration des chartes et des cartulaires belges existants à la Bibliothèque Nationale, à Paris." *Compte-rendu des séances de la Commission Royale d'Histoire* 2, 4th ser. (1874): 79–198.

——, ed. *Table chronologique des chartes et diplômes imprimés concernant l'histoire de la Belgique.* 11 vols. Académie Royale des Sciences, des Lettres et des Beaux-Arts de Belgique, Commission Royale de l'Histoire. Brussels, 1866–1946.

Zimmermann, Harald, ed. *Papsturkunden, 896–1046.* Vol. 1, *896–996.* Österreichische Akademie der Wissenschaften, Philosophisch-historische Klasse, Denkschriften 174. Vienna, 1984.

NARRATIVE AND LITERARY SOURCES

Abbo of Fleury. *Collectio canonum.* PL 139:471–508.

Acta concilii Remensis ad sanctum Basolum. MGH SS 3:658–86.

Acta synodi Atrebatensis. PL 142:1269–1312.

Actus pontificum Cenomannis in urbe degentium. Ed. G. Busson and A. Ledru. Archives historiques du Maine 2. Le Mans, 1901.

Adalbero of Laon. *Poème au roi Robert.* Ed. Claude Carozzi. Paris, 1979.

Ademar of Chabannes. *Chronique.* Ed. Jules Chavanon. Paris, 1897.

Alcuin. *De virtutibus et vitiis.* Ed. Ole Widding. Copenhagen, 1960.

Andrew of Fleury. *Vie de Gauzlin, abbé de Fleury.* Ed. and trans. R.-H. Bautier and Gillette Labory. Paris, 1969.

Angelran of Saint-Riquier. *Historia relationis s. Richarii metrice descripta.* AASS April, 3:464–66.

Annales de Saint-Bertin. Ed. Félix Grat, J. Vielliard, and S. Clémencet. Paris, 1964.

Les annales de Saint-Pierre de Gand et de Saint-Amand. Ed. Philip Grierson. Brussels, 1937.

Annales regni Francorum. Ed. F. Kurze. MGH SRG. Hanover, 1895.

Anselm of Laon. *Sententie diuine pagine.* Ed. F. P. Bliemetzrieder, "Anselms von Laon Systematische Sentenzen." *Beitrage zur Geschichte der Philosophie des Mittelalters,* Texte und Untersuchungen 17/2–3. Münster, 1919.

Augustine. *De cura gerenda pro mortuis.* Corpus scriptorum ecclesiasticorum latinorum 41, sect. 5.3, pp. 619–60. Vienna, 1900.

Bernerus, abbot of Homblières. *Translatio prima s. Hunegundis virginis.* AASS August, 5:232–37.

Buoncompagno of Florence. *Rhetorica antiqua.* Ed. Geoffrey Barraclough, "Formulare für Suppliken aus der ersten Hälfte des 13. Jahrhunderts." *Archiv für katholisches Kirchenrecht* 115 (1935): 435–56.

Chronique de Saint-Pierre-le-Vif de Sens, dite de Clarius (Chronicon sancti Petri Vivi Senonensis). Ed. and trans. R.-H. Bautier and Monique Gilles. Paris, 1979.

Chronique ou Livre de fondation du monastère de Mouzon. Ed. and trans. Michel Bur. Paris, 1989.

Chroniques des comtes d'Anjou et des seigneurs d'Amboise. Ed. Louis Halphen and René Poupardin. Paris, 1913.

Delisle, Léopold. "Notices sur les manuscrits originaux d'Adémar de Chabannes." *Notices et extraits des manuscrits de la Bibliothèque nationale et des autres bibliothèques* 35 (1896): 241–358.

De vera et falsa poenitentia. PL 40:1113–30.

De Vogüé, A., and Jean Neufville, eds., *La règle de saint Benoît.* 7 vols. Sources chrétiennes 181–186a. Paris, 1972–77.

Dudo of Saint-Quentin. *De moribus et actis primorum Normanniae ducum.* Ed. Jules Lair. Caen, 1865.

Epitome Moralium s. Gregorii in Job. PL 133:105–512.

Flodoard. *Annales.* Ed. Philippe Lauer. Paris, 1905.

——. *Historia ecclesiae Remensis.* MGH SS 13:409–599.

Galbert of Bruges. *Histoire du meurtre de Charles le Bon, comte de Flandre (1127–1128).* Ed. Henri Pirenne. Paris, 1891.

Gesta Ambaziensium dominorum. In *Chroniques des comtes d'Anjou et des seigneurs d'Amboise,* ed. Louis Halphen and René Poupardin. Paris, 1913.

Gesta episcoporum Cameracensium. MGH SS 7:393–525.

Gesta pontificum Autissiodorensium. In L.-M. Duru, *Bibliothèque historique de l'Yonne,* 1:309–509. Auxerre/Paris, 1850–64.

Gregory of Tours. *Decem libri historiarum.* Ed. B. Krusch and W. Levison. MGH SRG 1/1. Hanover, 1951.

Guibert of Nogent. *Histoire de sa vie: De vita sua sive monodiarum suarum libri tres.* Ed. Georges Bourgin. Paris, 1907.

Halitgar of Cambrai. *De vitiis et virtutibus et de ordine paenitentium.* In H. J. Schmitz, *Die Bussbücher und das kanonische Bussverfahren* 2. 1898; rpt. Graz, 1958.

Hariulf. *Chronique de l'abbaye de Saint-Riquier.* Ed. Ferdinand Lot. Paris, 1894.

Heckel, Rudolf von. "Das päpstliche und sicilische Registerwesen: Der *Libellus petitionum* des Kardinals Guala Bichieri." *Archiv für Urkundenforschung* 1 (1908): 371–511.

Helgald of Fleury. *La vie de Robert le Pieux (Epitome vitae regis Rotberti pii).* Ed. and trans. R.-H. Bautier and Gillette Labory. Paris, 1965.

Herman of Laon. *De miraculis sanctae Mariae Laudunensis. PL* 156:961–1018.

Herman of Tournai. *Liber de restauratione sancti Martini Tornacensis (cum continuatione).* Ed. G. Waitz. MGH SS 14:266–327.

Hincmar of Reims. *De cavendis vitiis et virtutibus exercendis ad Carolum Calvum regem. PL* 125:857–930.

——. *De divortio Lotharii regis et Tetbergae reginae. PL* 125:619–772.

Historia relationis s. Richarii. AASS April, 3:461–64.

Historia translationis s. Vedasti. AASS February 1:817–20.

Hugh of Flavigny. *Chronicon Virdunense seu Flavinienses.* MGH SS 8:280–503.

Huyghebaert, N., ed. *Une translation de reliques à Gand en 944: Le "Sermo de Adventu Sanctorum Wandregisili, Ansberti et Vulframni in Blandinium."* Académie Royale de Belgique, Commission royale d'Histoire. Brussels, 1978.

Ivo of Chartres. *Correspondance.* Ed. and trans. Jean Leclercq. Paris, 1949.

Jonas of Orléans. *De institutione regia.* In J. Reviron, *Les idées politico-religieuses d'un évêque du IXe siècle. Jonas d'Orléans et son "De institutione regia."* Paris, 1930.

Knowles, David, ed. *The Monastic Constitutions of Lanfranc.* London, 1951.

Liber tramitis aevi Odilonis abbatis. Ed. Petrus Dinter. Corpus Consuetudinum Monasticarum 10. Siegburg, 1980.

Little, Lester K. "Formules monastiques de malédiction aux IXe et Xe siècles." *Revue Mabillon* 58 (1975): 377–99.

Mabillon, J. *De elevatione corporis s. Theoderici abbatis Remensis*. AASS July, 1:73–75.

McNeill, John T., and Helena M. Gamer. *Medieval Handbooks of Penance.* New York, 1938.

Marchegay, Paul, and André Salmon, eds. *Chroniques des comtes d'Anjou.* 2 vols. Paris, 1856, 1871.

Les miracles de saint Benoît. Ed. Eugène de Certain. Paris, 1858.

Miracula s. Adalhardi. MGH SS 15/2:859–65.

Miracula s. Donatiani. MGH SS 15/2:854–58.

Miracula s. Richarii. AASS April, 3:451–61.

Miracula s. Ursmari in itinere per Flandriam facta. AASS April, 2:570–75. Excerpts in MGH SS 15/2:837–42.

Miracula s. Vulfranni. AASS March, 3:149–60.

Miracula s. Walarici. AASS April, 1:24–30.

Nithard. *Histoire des fils de Louis le Pieux.* Ed. Philippe Lauer. Paris, 1926.

Notker the Stammerer. *Gesta Karoli magni imperatoris.* Ed. Hans Haefele. MGH SRG. Berlin, 1962.

Odilo of Cluny. *Epitaphium domne Adalheide auguste.* Ed. Herbert Paulhart, *Die Lebensbeschreibung der Kaiserin Adelheid von abt Odilo von Cluny.* Mitteilungen des Intitut für österreichische Geschichtsforschung, Erganzungsband 20/2. Graz/Cologne, 1962.

Odo of Cluny. *Vita s. Geraldi comitis Aureliacensis.* PL 133:639–704.

Odorannus of Sens. *Opera omnia.* Ed. R.-H. Bautier and Monique Gilles. Paris, 1972.

Orderic Vitalis. *The Ecclesiastical History of Orderic Vitalis.* Ed. and trans. Marjorie Chibnall. 6 vols. Oxford, 1969–80.

Peter the Chanter. *De penitentia.* Ed. Richard Trexler, *The Christian at Prayer: An Illustrated Prayer Manual Attributed to Peter the Chanter (d. 1197).* Binghamton, N.Y., 1987.

Raban Maur. *De ecclesiastica disciplina libri tres.* PL 112:1191–1262.

———. *De videndo deum, de puritate cordis et modo poenitentiae libri tres.* PL 112:1261–1332.

Raoul Glaber. *Les cinq livres de ses histoires.* Ed. Maurice Prou. Paris, 1886.

Regino of Prüm. *De ecclesiasticis disciplinis.* PL 132:185–370.

Richer. *Histoire de France.* Ed. Robert Latouche. 2 vols. Paris, 1930, 1937.

Sedulius Scottus. *Liber de rectoribus Christianis.* In S. Hellmann, *Sedulius Scottus.* Munich, 1906.

Suger. *Vie de Louis VI le Gros.* Ed. and trans. Henri Waquet. Paris, 1964.

Thegan. *Vita Hludowicî imperatoris.* MGH SS 2:585–604.

Vie de Bouchard le Vénérable, comte de Vendôme, de Corbeil, de Melun et de Paris (Xᵉ et XIᵉ siècles). Ed. Charles Bourel de La Roncière. Paris, 1892.

Vita beati Lanfranci archiepiscopi Cantuariensis. PL 150:19–58.

Vita beati Simonis comitis Crispeiensis. PL 156:211–24.

Vita domini Burchardi venerabilis comitis. PL 143:847–62.

Vita Herluini. In *The Works of Gilbert Crispin, Abbot of Westminster,* ed. Anna Sapin Abulafia and G. R. Evans, 183–212. London, 1986.

Die Vita Hludowici pii auctore Astronomo. Ed. Wolfgang Tenberken. Freiburg im Breisgau, 1982.

Vita Richardi abbatis s. Vitoni Virudunensis. MGH SS 11:281–90.

Vita s. Arnulfi Suessionensis episcopi. AASS August, 3:230–59.

Vita s. Bertulfi. MGH SS 15/2:633–41.
Vita s. Godefridi auctore Nicolao monacho Suessionensi. AASS November, 3:905–44.
Vita s. Honorati. AASS May, 3:609–13.
Vrégille, B. de. "Fragment d'un traité de la prière, dédié par Bernon de Reichenau à Henri III, roi de Germanie." *Revue du Moyen Age Latin* 2 (1946): 261–68.
William of Jumièges. *Gesta Normannorum ducum.* Ed. Jean Marx. Paris, 1914.
William of Poitiers. *Histoire de Guillaume le conquérant.* Ed. Raymonde Foreville. Paris, 1952.

LAWS AND LETTERS

Abbo of Fleury. *Epistolae. PL* 139:417–62.
Baildon, W. P. *Select Cases in the Court of Chancery.* Seldon Society 10. London, 1896.
Beugnot, A.-A. *Les Olim, ou registres des arrêts rendus par la cour du roi.* 4 vols. Paris, 1839–48.
Burchard of Worms. *Decretorum libri viginti. PL* 140:537–1058.
Fulbert of Chartres. *The Letters and Poems of Fulbert of Chartres.* Ed. F. Behrends. Oxford, 1976.
Gerbert. *Lettres de Gerbert (983–997).* Ed. Julien Havet. Paris, 1889.
Gratian. *Decretum. Corpus iuris canonici, editio lipsiensis secunda,* vol. 1. Ed. Emil Friedberg. Graz, 1959.
Isidore of Seville. *Interrogationes seu interpretationes de legibus divinis et humanis.* In Joseph Tardif, "Un abrégé juridique des *Etymologies* d'Isidore de Séville," *Mélanges Julien Havet,* 660–81. Paris, 1895.
Ivo of Chartres. *Decretum. PL* 161:47–1036.
———. *Panormia. PL* 161:1037–1428.
Lambert of Arras. *Epistolae. PL* 162:647–702.
Langlois, C.-V. "Rouleaux d'arrêts de la cour du roi au XIIIe siècle." *Bibliothèque de l'Ecole des Chartes* 48 (1887): 177–208, 535–65; 50 (1889): 41–67.
———. *Textes relatifs à l'histoire du Parlement depuis les origines jusqu'en 1314.* Paris, 1888.
Rotuli parliamentorum Anglie hactenus inediti. Ed. H. G. Richardson and G. O. Sayles. Camden Society 51, 3d ser. London, 1935.
Ulrich of Cluny. *Consuetudines Cluniacenses. PL* 149:633–778.

SECONDARY SOURCES

Aboucaya, Claude. "Politique et répression criminelle dans l'oeuvre de Suger." In *Mélanges Roger Aubenas,* 9–24. Montpellier, 1974.
Alföldi, Andreas. *Die monarchische Repräsentation im römischen Kaiserreiche.* Darmstadt, 1970.
Amann, E. "La pénitence primitive" and "La pénitence privée." *Dictionnaire de Théologie Catholique* 12/1:749–948.
Anton, Hans Hubert. *Fürstenspiegel und Herrscherethos in der Karolingerzeit.* Bonn, 1968.

——. "Zum politischen Konzept karolingischer Synoden und zur karolingischen Brüdergemeinschaft." *Historisches Jahrbuch* 99 (1979): 55–132.

Bachrach, Bernard S. "The Northern Origins of the Peace Movement at Le Puy in 975." In Head and Landes, *The Peace of God*. Ithaca, forthcoming.

——. "Toward a Reappraisal of William the Great, Duke of Aquitaine (995–1030)." *Journal of Medieval History* 5 (1979): 11–21.

Barthélemy, Dominique. *Les deux âges de la seigneurie banale.* Paris, 1984.

Bates, David. *Normandy before 1066.* London, 1982.

Bautier, Robert-Henri. "L'hérésie d'Orléans et le mouvement intellectuel au début du XIᵉ siècle: Documents et hypothèses." In *95ᵉ Congrès des Sociétés savantes de Paris, Reims 1970, Section de philologie et d'histoire*, 1:63–88. Paris, 1975.

Bedos, Brigitte. "Signes et insignes du pouvoir royal et seigneuriale au Moyen Age: Le témoignage des sceaux." In *Actes du 105ᵉ Congrès national des sociétés savantes, Caen, 1980, Section de philologie et d'histoire*, 47–62. Paris, 1984.

Beech, George. "The Participation of Aquitanians in the Conquest of England, 1066–1100." *Anglo-Norman Studies* 9 (1986): 1–24.

Berbig, Hans Joachim. "Zur rechtlichen Relevanz von Ritus and Zeremoniell im römisch-deutschen Imperium." *Zeitschrift für Kirchengeschichte* 92 (1981): 204–49.

Besnier, Robert. "Actualité de la clameur de haro dans le droit de l'Ile de Guernesey." In *Droit privé et institutions régionales: Etudes historiques offertes à Jean Yver*, 63–68. Paris, 1976.

Biehl, Ludwig. *Das liturgische Gebet für Kaiser und Reich: Ein Beitrag zur Geschichte des Verhältnisses von Kirche und Staat.* Paderborn, 1937.

Bloch, Marc. *Les rois thaumaturges: Etude sur le caractère surnaturel attribué à la puissance royale, particulièrement en France et en Angleterre.* 1924; rpt. Paris, 1983. Published in English as *The Royal Touch: Sacred Monarchy and Scrofula in England and France*, trans. J. E. Anderson. London, 1973.

Bloch, Maurice, ed. *Political Language and Oratory in Traditional Society.* London, 1975.

Bonnaud-Delamare, R. "Les institutions de paix dans la province ecclésiastique de Reims au XIᵉ siècle." *Bulletin philologique et historique du Comité des travaux historiques et scientifiques, 1955–56*, 143–200. Paris, 1957.

——. "La paix d'Amiens et de Corbie au XIᵉ siècle." *Revue du Nord* 38 (1956): 167–78.

Bornscheuer, Lothar. *Miseriae regum: Untersuchungen zum Krisen- und Todesgedanken in der herrschaftstheologischen Vorstellung der ottonischsalischen Zeit.* Berlin, 1968.

Bouchard, Constance. *Sword, Miter, and Cloister: Nobility and the Church in Burgundy (980–1198).* Ithaca, 1987.

Bouman, C. A. *Sacring and Crowning: The Development of the Latin Ritual for the Anointing of Kings and the Coronation of an Emperor before the Eleventh Century.* Bijdragen van het instituut voor Middeleeuwse Geschiedenis der Rijks-Universiteit te Utrecht 30. Gröningen, 1957.

Bourdieu, Pierre. *Outline of a Theory of Practice.* Trans. Richard Nice. Cambridge, 1977.

Bourgin, G. *La commune de Soissons et le groupe communal soissonais*. Paris, 1908.

Bournazel, Eric. *Le gouvernement capétien au XIIe siècle (1108–1180)*. Paris, 1975.

Boussard, Jacques. "Le droit de *vicaria* à la lumière de quelques documents angevins et tourangeaux." In *Etudes de civilisation médiévale (IXe–XIIe siècles): Mélanges offertes à Edmond-René Labande*, 39–54. Poitiers, 1974.

———. "L'origine des familles seigneuriales dans la région de la Loire moyenne." *Cahiers de civilisation médiévale* 5 (1962): 303–22.

Bresslau, H. *Handbuch der Urkundenlehre für Deutschland und Italien*. 2 vols. Berlin, 1968, 1969.

Brühl, Carlrichard. "Fränkischer Krönungsbrauch und das Problem der 'Festkrönungen.'" *Historische Zeitschrift* 194 (1962): 265–326.

———. "Kronen- und Krönungsbrauch im frühen und höhen Mittelalter." *Historische Zeitschrift* 234 (1982): 1–31.

Brunner, Karl. "Der fränkische Fürstentitel im neunten und zehnten Jahrhundert." In Wolfram, *Intitulatio II*, 179–340.

Buchda, Gerhard. "Klage." In *Handwörterbuch zur deutschen Rechtsgeschichte* 2:837–45.

Bur, Michel. "A propos de la *Chronique de Mouzon*." I, "Les trois ordres dans la *Chronique de Mouzon*." II, "Architecture et liturgie à Reims au temps d'Adalberon (v. 976)." *Cahiers de civilisation médiévale* 26 (1983): 287–96; 27 (1984): 297–302.

———. *La formation du comté de Champagne, v. 950–v. 1150*. Nancy, 1977.

Canal, J.-M. "De clamoribus liturgicis et de antiphona Salve Regina." *Ephemerides liturgicae* 72 (1958): 199–212.

Cannadine, David, and Simon Price, eds. *Rituals of Royalty: Power and Ceremonial in Traditional Societies*. Cambridge, 1987.

Carlyle, R. W., and A. J. Carlyle. *A History of Mediaeval Political Theory in the West*. 6 vols. New York, 1903–1936.

Carozzi, Claude. "Le roi et la liturgie chez Helgaud de Fleury." In *Hagiographie, cultures et sociétés*, 417–32.

———. "La *Vie du roi Robert* par Helgaud de Fleury: Historiographie et hagiographie." In *L'Historiographie en Occident du Ve au XVe siècles*. Actes du Congrès de la Société des historiens médiévistes de l'enseignement supérieur public, Tours, June 10–12, 1977. *Annales de Bretagne et des Pays de l'Ouest* 87 (1980): 219–35.

Cazelles, Henri. "Gestes et paroles de prières dans l'Ancien Testament." In *Gestes et paroles*, 87–94.

Chaume, Maurice. "Observations sur la chronologie des chartes de l'abbaye de Cluny." *Revue Mabillon* 16 (1926): 44–48; 29 (1939): 81–89, 133–42; 31 (1941): 14–19, 42–45, 69–82; 32 (1942): 15–20, 133–36; 38 (1948): 1–6; 39 (1949): 41–43; 42 (1952): 1–4.

Chédeville, A. *Chartres et ses campagnes (XIe–XIIIe s.)*. Paris, 1973.

Classen, Peter. "Fortleben und Wanzel, spätrömischen Urkundenwesens im frühen Mittelalter." In *Recht und Schrift im Mittelalter*, ed. P. Classen, 13–54. *Vorträge und Forschungen* 23. Sigmaringen, 1977.

——. *Kaiserreskript und Königsurkunde: Diplomatische Studien zum Problem der Kontinuität zwischen Altertum und Mittelalter.* Thessalonica, 1977.

Corbet, Patrick. *Les saints ottoniens: Sainteté dynastique, sainteté royale, et sainteté féminine autour de l'an mil.* Sigmaringen, 1986.

Cowdrey, H. E. J. "The Anglo-Norman *Laudes Regiae*." *Viator* 12 (1981): 39–78.

——. *The Cluniacs and the Gregorian Reform.* Oxford, 1970.

Crick, Malcolm. *Explorations in Language and Meaning: Towards a Semantic Anthropology.* London, 1976.

Cutler, Anthony. *Transfigurations: Studies in the Dynamics of Byzantine Iconography.* Philadelphia, 1975.

Dauphin, Hubert. *Le bienheureux Richard, abbé de Saint-Vanne de Verdun.* Bibliothèque de la Revue d'histoire écclésiastique 24. Paris/Louvain, 1946.

Deshman, Robert. "*Christus rex et magi reges*: Kingship and Christology in Ottonian and Anglo-Saxon Art." *Frühmittelalterliche Studien* 10 (1976): 367–405.

——. "The Exalted Servant: The Ruler Theology of the Prayerbook of Charles the Bald." *Viator* 11 (1980): 384–417.

Devisse, Jean. *Hincmar, archevêque de Reims, 845–882.* 3 vols. Geneva, 1975–76.

De Vogüé, Adalbert. "L'abbé, vicaire du Christ, chez Saint Benoît et chez le Maître." *Collectanea Cisterciensia* 44/2 (1982): 89–100.

DeWald, Ernest T. *The Illustrations of the Utrecht Psalter.* Princeton, 1932.

Dhondt, Jan. *Les origines de la Flandre et de l'Artois.* Arras, 1944.

Duby, Georges. *The Chivalrous Society.* Trans. Cynthia Postan. Berkeley, 1977.

——. "Gérard de Cambrai, la paix et les trois fonctions sociales, 1024." In *Comptes-rendus des séances de l'Académie des Inscriptions et Belles-Lettres,* 136–46. Paris, 1976.

——. "L'image du prince en France au début du XIᵉ siècle." *Cahiers d'histoire* 17 (1972): 211–16.

——. *The Knight, the Lady, and the Priest: The Makings of Modern Marriage in Medieval France.* Trans. Barbara Bray. New York, 1983.

——. *Les trois ordres ou l'imaginaire du féodalisme.* Paris, 1978. Published in English as *The Three Orders: Feudal Society Imagined,* trans. Arthur Goldhammer. Chicago, 1978.

Dunbabin, Jean. *France in the Making (843–1180).* New York, 1985.

——. "The Maccabees as Exemplars in the Tenth and Eleventh Centuries." In *The Bible in the Medieval World: Essays in Honour of Beryl Smalley,* ed. Katherine Walsh and Diana Wood, 31–41. Oxford, 1985.

Ewig, Eugen. "Die Gebetsklausel für König und Reich in den merowingischen Königsurkunden." In *Tradition als historische Kraft,* ed. Norbert Kamp and Joachim Wollasch, 87–99. Berlin, 1982.

——. "La prière pour le roi et le royaume dans les privilèges épiscopaux de l'époque mérovingienne." In *Mélanges offerts à Jean Dauvillier,* 255–67. Toulouse, 1979.

——. "Zum christlichen Königsgedanken im Frühmittelalter." In *Spätantikes und Fränkisches Gallien: Gesammelte Schriften,* 1:3–71. Munich, 1976.

Fälschungen im Mittelalter. Internationaler Kongress der Monumenta Germaniae Historica, Munich, September 16–19, 1986. 5 vols. Hanover, 1988.

Fernandez, James W. "The Dark at the Bottom of the Stairs: The Inchoate in Symbolic Inquiry and Some Strategies for Coping with It." In *On Symbols in Anthropology: Essays in Honor of Harry Hoijer*, ed. Jacques Maquet. *Other Realities* 3 (1982): 13–43.

Feuchère, Pierre. "Une tentative manquée de concentration territoriale entre Somme et Seine: La principauté d'Amiens-Valois." *Moyen Age* 60 (1954): 1–34.

Fichtenau, Heinrich. *Arenga: Spätantike und Mittelalter im Spiegel von Urkundenformeln*. Mitteilungen des Instituts für österreichische Geschichtsforschung 18. Graz/Cologne, 1957.

——. *Lebensordnungen des 10. Jahrhunderts: Studien über Denkart und Existenz im einstigen Karolingerreich*. 2 vols. Stuttgart, 1984.

Fink, A. "Knien." *Handwörterbuch zur deutschen Rechtsgeschichte* 2:901–4.

Firth, Raymond. "Postures and Gestures of Respect." In *Echanges et Communications: Mélanges offertes à Claude Lévi-Strauss à l'occasion de son 60ème anniversaire*, ed. Jean Pouillon and Pierre Maranda, 188–209. The Hague, 1970.

Flori, Jean. *L'essor de la chevalerie, XIe–XIIe siècles*. Geneva, 1986.

Font-Réaulx, Jacques de. "Propos sur les diplômes des derniers Carolingiens." In *Recueil de travaux offerts à M. Clovis Brunel*, 1:425–35. Paris, 1955.

Fossier, Robert. *La terre et les hommes en Picardie jusqu'à la fin du XIIIe siècle*. 2 vols. Paris, 1968.

Frantzen, Allen J. *The Literature of Penance in Anglo-Saxon England*. New Brunswick, N.J., 1983.

Galtier, Paul. *L'église et la rémission des péchés aux premiers siècles*. Paris, 1932.

——. "Satisfaction." In *Dictionnaire de théologie catholique* 14/1:1129–1210.

Ganshof, François-Louis. *La Flandre sous les premiers comtes*. Brussels, 1949.

——. "Les origines de la Flandre impériale: Contribution à l'histoire de l'ancien Brabant." *Annales de la Société royale d'archéologie de Bruxelles: Mémoires* 46 (1942–43): 99–171.

Garel, Jean. "La prière du plus grand péril." In *Mélanges de langue et littérature médiévales offertes à Pierre le Gentile*, 311–18. Paris, 1973.

Garnier, François. *Le langage de l'image au Moyen Age: Signification et symbolique*. Paris, 1982.

Gawlik, Alfred. "Zur Bedeutung von Intervention und Petition: Beobachtungen zu Urkunden aus der Kanzlei König Heinrichs IV." In *Grundwissenschaften und Geschichte: Festschrift für Peter Acht*, 73–77. Munich, 1976.

Geary, Patrick. "Humiliation of Saints." In *Saints and Their Cults: Studies in Religious Sociology, Folklore, and History*, ed. Stephen Wilson, 123–40. Cambridge, 1983.

Génestal, Robert. *Le rôle des monastères comme établissements de crédit, étudié en Normandie du XIe siècle à la fin du XIIIe siècle*. Paris, 1901.

Genicot, Léopold. *Les actes publics*. Typologie des sources du Moyen Age occidentale 3. Turnhout, 1972.

Gerberto: Scienza, storia e mito. Atti del Gerberti Symposium, July 25–27, 1983. Bobbio, 1985.

Gestes et paroles dans les diverses familles liturgiques. Centro Liturgico Vincenziano, Bibliotheca Ephemerides liturgicae, subsidia 14. Rome, 1978.

Giry, Arthur. *Manuel de diplomatique.* Paris, 1894.

Goetz, Hans-Werner. "Kirchenschutz, Rechtswahrung und Reform: Zu den Zielen und zum Wesen der frühen Gottesfriedensbewegung in Frankreich." *Francia* 11 (1983): 193–239.

———. "Der letzte 'Karolinger'? Die Regierung Konrads I. im Spiegel seiner Urkunden." *Archiv für Diplomatik* 26 (1980): 56–125.

Goody, Esther. "'Greeting,' 'Begging,' and the Presentation of Respect." In *The Interpretation of Ritual: Essays in Honour of A. I. Richards,* ed. J. S. La Fontaine, 39–71. London, 1927.

Gougaud, Louis. "Attitudes of Prayer." In *Devotional and Ascetic Practices in the Middle Ages,* 1–43. London, 1927.

Grierson, Philip. "L'origine des comtes d'Amiens, Valois et Vexin." *Moyen Age* 49 (1939): 93–123.

Guillot, Olivier. "Les actes de Henri Ier et la chancellerie royale dans les années 1020–1060." In *Comptes-rendus des séances de l'Académie des Inscriptions et Belles-Lettres,* 81–97. Paris, 1988.

———. "Administration et gouvernement dans les états du comte d'Anjou au milieu du XIe siècle." In *Histoire comparée de l'administration,* 311–32.

———. *Le comte d'Anjou et son entourage au XIe siècle.* 2 vols. Paris, 1972.

———. "Le concept d'autorité dans l'ordre politique français issu de l'an mil." In Makdisi et al., *La notion d'autorité au Moyen Age,* 127–40.

Guyotjeannin, Olivier. *"Episcopus" et "comes": Affirmation et déclin de la seigneurie épiscopale au nord du royaume de France (Beauvais-Noyon, X^e–début XIIIe siècle).* Paris, 1987.

———. "Une interpolation datant des alentours de l'an mil et provenant de Marmoutier d'une notice perdue de 912, souscrite par le comte Robert, abbé de Saint-Martin de Tours et de Marmoutier." *Francia* 13 (1985): 680–86.

———. "Recherches sur le développement de la seigneurie épiscopale du nord du royaume de France (Xème–début XIIIème siècle): Les exemples de Beauvais et Noyon." Thèse doctorat. Université de Sorbonne (Paris IV), 1981.

Hagiographie, cultures et sociétés, IVe–XIIe siècles. Actes du colloque organisé à Nanterre et à Paris, May 2–5, 1979. Etudes Augustiennes. Paris, 1979.

Hallam, Elizabeth M. *Capetian France (987–1328).* London, 1980.

———. "The Kings and Princes in Eleventh-Century France." *Bulletin of the Institute of Historical Research* 53 (1980): 143–56.

———. "Royal Burial and the Cult of Kingship in France and England, 1060–1330." *Journal of Medieval History* 8 (1982): 359–80.

Halphen, Louis. *Le comté d'Anjou au XIe siècle.* Paris, 1906.

Hännig, Jürgen. *Consensus fidelium: Frühfeudale Interpretationen des Verhältnisses von Königtum und Adel am Beispiel des Frankenreichs.* Stuttgart, 1982.

Hausmann, Friedrich, and Alfred Gawlik, eds. *Arengenverzeichnis zu den Königs- und Kaiserurkunden von den Merowingern bis Heinrich VI.* Munich, 1987.

Head, Thomas, and Richard Landes, eds. *The Peace of God: Religion and Violence in Tenth- and Eleventh-Century France.* Ithaca, forthcoming.

Hilpisch, Stephen. "Der Rat der Brüder in den Benediktinerklöstern des Mittelalters." *Studien und Mitteilungen zur Geschichte des Benediktiner-Ordens und seiner Zweige, Bayerische Benediktinerakademie* 67 (1956): 221–36.

Histoire comparée de l'administration (IVᵉ–XVIIIᵉ siècles). Actes du XIVᵉ colloque historique franco-allemand, Tours, March 27–April 1, 1977. *Francia,* Supplement 9. Munich/Zurich, 1980.

Hobsbawm, Eric, and Terence Ranger, eds. *The Invention of Tradition.* Cambridge, 1983.

Hodüm, A. "La réforme monastique d'Arnoul le Grand, comte de Flandre." *Bulletin trimestriel de la Société académique des antiquaires de la Morinie* 18 (1957): 577–603.

Hoffmann, Hartmut. *Gottesfriede und Treuga Dei.* Stuttgart, 1964.

Horst, Johannes. *Proskynein: Zur Anbetung im Urchristentum nach ihrer religionsgeschichtlichen Eigenart.* Neutestamentliche Forschungen 3/2. Gütersloh, 1932.

Hülle, Werner. "Das Supplikenwesen in Rechtssachen: Anlagenplan für eine Dissertation." *Zeitschrift der Savigny-Stiftung für Rechtsgeschichte,* Germanistische Abteilung 90 (1973): 194–212.

Jäschke, Kurt-Ulrich. "Frühmittelalterliche Festkrönungen? Überlegungen zu Terminologie und Methode." *Historische Zeitschrift* 211 (1970): 556–88.

Johnson, Penelope D. *Prayer, Patronage, and Power: The Abbey of La Trinité, Vendôme (1032–1187).* New York, 1981.

Jungmann, Joseph A. *The Mass of the Roman Rite: Its Origins and Development.* Trans. Francis A. Brunner. 2 vols. Westminster, Md., 1986.

Kaiser, Reinhold. *Bischofsherrschaft zwischen Königtum und Furstenmacht: Studien zur bischöflichen Stadtherrschaft im west-französischen Reich im frühen und höhen Mittelalter.* Bonn, 1981.

Kantorowicz, Ernst. *The King's Two Bodies: A Study in Medieval Political Theology.* Princeton, 1957.

———. *Laudes Regiae: A Study in Liturgical Acclamations and Medieval Ruler Worship.* Berkeley, 1946.

Kaufmann, E. *Aequitatis Iudicium: Königsgericht und Billigkeit in der Rechtsordnung des frühen Mittelalters.* Frankfurter wissenschaftliche Beiträge, Rechts- und Staatswissenschaft, ser. 18. Frankfurt, 1959.

Kertzer, David. *Ritual, Politics, and Power.* New Haven, 1988.

Kienast, Walter. *Der Herzogstitel in Frankreich und Deutschland (9. bis 12. Jahrhundert).* Munich, 1968.

Klauser, Theodor. "Aurum coronarium." *Mitteilungen des deutschen archäologischen Instituts,* Römische Abteilung 59 (1944): 129–53.

———. *Kleine abendländische Liturgiegeschichte: Bericht und Besinnung.* Bonn, 1965. Published in English as *A Short History of the Western Liturgy,* trans. John Halliburton. 2d ed. Oxford, 1979.

———. *Der Ursprung der bischöflichen Insignien und Ehrenrechte.* Bonner Akademische Reden 1. Krefeld, 1948.

Köbler, Gerhard. "Klage, klagen, Kläger." *Zeitschrift der Savigny-Stiftung für Rechtsgeschichte,* Germanistische Abteilung 92 (1975): 1–20.

Koskenniemi, Heikki. *Studien zur Idee und Phraseologie des griechischen Briefes bis 400 n. Chr.* Helsinki, 1956.

Koziol, Geoffrey. "Monks, Feuds, and the Making of Peace in Eleventh-Century Flanders." In Head and Landes, *Peace of God.*

Kuttner, Stephan. "A Forgotten Definition of Justice." *Studia Gratiana* 20 (1976): 75–109.

Labande, Edmond-René. "Le *credo* epique, à propos des prières dans les chansons de geste." In *Recueil de travaux offert à M. Clovis Brunel,* 2:62–80. Paris, 1955.

Labande, L.-H. *Histoire de Beauvais et de ses institutions communales jusqu'au commencement du XVᵉ siècle.* Paris, 1892.

Ladner, G. B. "The Gestures of Prayer in Papal Iconography of the Thirteenth and Early Fourteenth Centuries." In *Images and Ideas in the Middle Ages,* 209–37. Rome, 1983.

Lanham, Carol D. "Prostrate at Your Feet: Toward a History of Latin Epistolography." Paper delivered to the Rocky Mountain Medieval and Renaissance Association, 1979.

Lauer, Philippe. *Le règne de Louis IV d'Outre-Mer.* Paris, 1900.

Lauranson-Rosaz, Christian. *L'Auvergne et ses marges (Velay, Gévaudan) du VIIIᵉ au XIᵉ siècle.* Le Puy-en-Velay, 1987.

Lechner, Josef. *Liturgik des römischen Ritus.* Freiburg, 1953.

Leclercq, Henri. "Génuflexion." *Dictionnaire d'archéologie chrétienne et de liturgie* 6/1:1017–21.

Lefranc, Abel. *Histoire de la ville de Noyon et de ses institutions jusqu'à la fin du XIIIᵉ siècle.* Paris, 1888.

Le Goff, Jacques. "The Symbolic Ritual of Vassalage." In *Time, Work, and Culture in the Middle Ages,* trans. Arthur Goldhammer, 237–87. Chicago, 1980.

Lemarignier, Jean-François. *Le gouvernement royal aux premiers temps capétiens (987–1108).* Paris, 1965.

———. "Paix et réforme monastique en Flandre et en Normandie autour de l'année 1023." In *Droit privé et institutions régionales: Etudes historiques offertes à Jean Yver,* 443–68. Paris, 1976.

———. *Recherches sur l'hommage en marche et les frontières féodales.* Lille, 1945.

Lesètre, H. "Prosternement." In *Dictionnaire de la Bible,* ed. F. Vigouroux, vol. 5, cols. 764–65. Paris, 1912.

Lévi-Strauss, Claude. *Structural Anthropology.* Trans. Claire Jacobson and Brooke Grundefest Schoepf. New York, 1963.

Leyser, Karl. *Rule and Conflict in an Early Medieval Society: Ottonian Saxony.* Bloomington, Ind., 1979.

Little, Lester K. "La morphologie des malédictions monastiques." *Annales: E.S.C.* 34 (1979): 49–60.

———. "Pride Goes before Avarice: Social Change and the Vices in Latin Christendom." *American Historical Review* 76 (1971): 16–49.

Lot, Ferdinand. *Les derniers carolingiens: Lothaire, Louis V, Charles de Lorraine (954–991).* Paris, 1891.

MacCormack, Sabine G. *Art and Ceremony in Late Antiquity.* Berkeley, 1981.

McCormick, Michael. *Eternal Victory: Triumphal Rulership in Late Antiquity, Byzantium, and the Early Medieval West.* Cambridge, 1986.

Magnou-Nortier, Elisabeth. *Foi et fidélité: Recherches sur l'évolution des liens personnels chez les Francs du VIIᵉ au IXᵉ siècle.* Toulouse, 1976.

Maillard-Luypaert, Monique. "Pouvoir et territoire dans la langue des actes royaux et princiers pour la Flandre et la Lotharingie (IXe–XIe siècles)." *Revue belge de philologie et d'histoire* 59 (1981): 810–27.

Makdisi, George, et al., eds. *La notion d'autorité au Moyen Age: Islam, Byzance, Occident.* Colloques internationaux de la Napoule, October 23–26, 1978. Paris, 1982.

Manz, Georg. *Ausdrucksformen der lateinischen Liturgiesprach bis ins elfte Jahrhundert.* Texte und Arbeiten 1/1. Beuron, 1941.

Martindale, Jane. "Conventum inter Guillelmum Aquitanorum comes et Hugonem Chiliarchum." *English Historical Review* 84 (1969): 528–48.

Meyers, A. R. "Parliamentary Petitions in the Fifteenth Century." *English Historical Review* 52 (1937): 385–404.

Michaud, Helène. *Les formulaires de grande chancellerie, 1500–1580.* Paris, 1972.

———. *La grande chancellerie et les écritures royales au XVIe siècle.* Paris, 1967.

Moore, R. I. *The Origins of European Dissent.* New York, 1977.

Moore, Sally Falk, and Barbara G. Myerhoff, eds. *Secular Ritual.* Assen, 1977.

Morel, Octave. *La grande chancellerie royale et l'expédition des lettres royaux, de l'avènement de Philippe de Valois à la fin du XIVe siècle (1328–1400).* Paris, 1900.

Mostert, Marco. *The Political Theology of Abbo of Fleury: A Study of Ideas about Society and Law of the Tenth-Century Monastic Reform Movement.* Hilversum, 1987.

Mulders, J. "Prostratie." In *Liturgisch Woordenboek* 2:2299–2302.

Nelson, Janet. "The Lord's Anointed and the People's Choice." In Cannadine and Price, *Rituals of Royalty*, 137–80.

———. "The Rites of the Conqueror." *Anglo-Norman Studies* 4 (1981): 117–32, 210–21.

———. "Ritual and Reality in the Early Medieval *Ordines*." *Studies in Church History* 11 (1975): 41–51.

Neumann, Ronald. "Die Arengen der Urkunden Ottos des Grossen." *Archiv für Diplomatik* 24 (1978): 292–358.

Neunheuser, Burkhard. "Les gestes de la prière à genoux et de la génuflexion dans les églises de rite romain." In *Gestes et paroles*, 153–65.

Newman, William Mendel. *Le domaine royal sous les premiers capétiens (987–1180).* Paris, 1937.

Ohm, Thomas. *Die Gebetsgebärden der Völker und das Christentum.* Leiden, 1948.

Ortigues, Edmond, and Dominique Iogna-Prat. "Raoul Glaber et l'historiographie clunisienne." *Studia medievali* 26 (1985): 537–72.

Peil, Dietmar. *Die Gebärde bei Chrétien, Hartmann und Wolfram.* Munich, 1975.

Pfister, Christian. *Etudes sur le règne de Robert le Pieux (996–1031).* Paris, 1885.

Pissard, H. *La clameur de haro en droit normand.* Caen, 1911.

Platelle, Henri. *La justice seigneuriale de l'abbaye de Saint-Amand, son organisation judiciaire, sa procédure et sa compétence du XIe au XVIe siècle.* Paris, 1965.

Poly, Jean-Pierre, and Eric Bournazel. *La mutation féodale, X^e–XIIIe siècles.* Paris, 1980.

Poschmann, Bernhard. *Der Ablass im Licht der Bussgeschichte.* Bonn, 1948.

La prière au Moyen Age: Litterature et civilisation. Sénéfiance 10. Aix-en-Provence, 1981.

Les Principautés au Moyen Age. Actes des Congrès de la Société des historiens médiévistes de l'enseignement supérieur public. Bordeaux, 1979.

Reuter, Timothy. "Plunder and Tribute in the Carolingian Empire." *Transactions of the Royal Historical Society* 35, 5th ser. (1985): 75–94.

Riché, Pierre. *Gerbert d'Aurillac: Le pape de l'an mil.* Paris, 1987.

Röhrich, Lutz. *Gebärde, Metapher, Parodie: Studien zur Sprache und Volksdichtung.* Düsseldorf, 1967.

Rordorf, W. "Les gestes accompagnant la prière, d'après Tertullien . . . et Origène . . ." In *Gestes et paroles,* 191–203.

Rosenwein, Barbara. *Rhinoceros Bound: Cluny in the Tenth Century.* Philadelphia, 1982.

Rossi, Marguerite. "La prière de demande dans l'épopée." In *La prière au Moyen Age,* 451–75.

Russell, Jeffrey Burton. *Dissent and Reform in the Early Middle Ages.* Berkeley, 1965.

Russo, François. "Pénitence et excommunication: Etude historique sur les rapports entre la théologie et le droit canon dans le domaine pénitentiel du XIᵉ au XIIIᵉ siècle." *Recherches des sciences religieuses* 33 (1946): 257–79, 431–61.

Sahlins, Marshall. *Islands of History.* Chicago, 1985.

Sassier, Yves. *Hugues Capet: Naissance d'une dynastie.* Paris, 1987.

Schäfer, Thomas. *Die Fusswaschung im monastischen Brauchtum und in der lateinischen Liturgie.* Texte und Arbeiten 1/47. Beuron, 1956.

Schmidt-Wiegand, Ruth. "Gebärden." In *Handwörterbuch zur deutschen Rechtsgeschichte* 1:1411–19.

——. "Gebärdensprache im mittelalterlichen Recht." *Frühmittelalterliche Studien* 16 (1982): 363–79.

Schmitt, Jean-Claude, ed. *Gestures.* In *History and Anthropology* 1/1 (1984).

Schneider, R. *Brüdergemeine und Schwurfreundschaft: Der Auflösungsprozess des Karolingerreiches im Spiegel der caritas-Terminologie in den Verträgen der karolingischen Teilkönige des 9. Jahrhunderts.* Lübeck/Hamburg, 1964.

Schneidmüller, Bernd. *Karolingische Tradition und frühes französisches Königtum: Untersuchungen zur Herrschaftslegitimation der westfränkisch-französischen Monarchie im 10. Jahrhundert.* Wiesbaden, 1979.

Schramm, P. E. *Die deutschen Kaiser und Könige in Bildern ihrer Zeit (751–1190).* Rev. F. Mütherich et al. Munich, 1983.

——. *Kaiser, Könige, und Päpste: Gesammelte Aufsätze zur Geschichte des Mittelalters.* 4 vols. Stuttgart, 1968–70.

——. *Der König von Frankreich: Das Wesen der Monarchie vom 9. zum 16. Jahrhundert.* 2 vols. Weimar, 1960.

Searle, Eleanor. "Frankish Rivalries and Norse Warriors." *Anglo-Norman Studies* 8 (1985): 198–213.

——. *Predatory Kinship and the Creation of Norman Power (840–1066).* Berkeley, 1988.

Sickel, Theodor. *Lehre von den Urkunden der ersten Karolinger (751–840).* 2 vols. Vienna, 1867.

Snijders, A. "Flectamus genua—levate." In *Liturgisch Woordenboek* 1:755–56.

———. "Knielen." In *Liturgisch Woordenboek* 2:1359–62.

Sperber, Dan. *Rethinking Symbolism*. Trans. Alice L. Morton. Cambridge, 1975.

Spiegel, Gabrielle. "Defense of the Realm: Evolution of a Capetian Propaganda Slogan." *Journal of Medieval History* 3 (1977): 115–33.

Stock, Brian. *The Implications of Literacy: Written Language and Models of Interpretation in the Eleventh and Twelfth Centuries*. Princeton, 1983.

Strecker, Ivo. *The Social Practice of Symbolization*. London, 1988.

Strubbe, E. I. "La paix de Dieu dans le nord de la France." *Recueils de la Société Jean Bodin* 14/1 (1961): 489–501.

Suntrup, Rudolf. *Die Bedeutung der liturgischen Gebärden und Bewegungen in lateinischen und deutschen Auslegungen des 9.–13. Jahrhunderts*. Munich, 1978.

Taylor, Lily Ross. "The *Proskynesis* and the Hellenistic Ruler Cult." *Journal of Hellenic Studies* 47 (1927): 53–62.

Teetaert, A. *La confession aux laïques dans l'église latine depuis le VIIIe jusqu'au XIVe siècle*. Paris, 1926.

Tellenbach, Gerd. "Römischer und christlicher Reichsgedanke in der Liturgie des frühen Mittelalters." In *Sitzungsberichte der Heidelberger Akademie der Wissenschaften*, Philologisch-historische Klasse (1934–35), 1. Heidelberg, 1934.

Tessier, Georges. "A propos de quelques actes toulousains du XIe siècle." In *Recueil de travaux offert à M. Clovis Brunel*, 2:566–80. Paris, 1955.

———. *Diplomatique royale française*. Paris, 1962.

Töpfer, Bernard. *Volk und Kirche zur Zeit den beginnenden Gottesfriedensbewegung in Frankreich*. Berlin, 1957.

Treitinger, Otto. *Die oströmischen Kaiser- und Reichsidee nach ihrer Gestaltung im höfischen Zeremoniell vom oströmischen Staats- und Reichsgedanken*. Darmstadt, 1956.

Trexler, Richard C. *Public Life in Renaissance Florence*. New York, 1980.

———, ed. *Persons in Groups: Social Behavior as Identity Formation in Medieval and Renaissance Europe*. Medieval and Renaissance Texts and Studies 36. Binghamton, N.Y., 1985.

Turner, Victor. *Dramas, Fields, and Metaphors: Symbolic Action in Human Society*. Ithaca, 1974.

———. *The Forest of Symbols: Aspects of Ndembu Ritual*. Ithaca, 1967.

Valenziano, Maria, and Crispino Valenziano. "La supplique des chanoines de la cathédral de Cefalú pour la sépulture du roi Roger." *Cahiers de civilisation médiévale* 21 (1978): 3–30.

Vancandard, E. "Absolution dans l'église latine, du VIIe au XIIe siècle." *Dictionnaire de théologie catholique* 1:161–68.

———. "Confession du Ier au XIIIe siècle." *Dictionnaire de théologie catholique* 3:838–94.

Van de Paverd, F. "Disciplinary Procedures in the Early Church." *Augustinianum* 21 (1981): 291–316.

Van Mingroot, E. "*Acta synodi Attrebatensis* (1025): Problèmes de critique de provenance." *Studia Gratiana* 20 (1976): 201–29.

Van Winter, J. M. "Uxorem de militari ordine sibi imparem." In *Miscellanea Mediaevalia in Memoriam J. F. Niermeyer*, 113–24. Gröningen, 1967.

Vaughn, Sally N. *The Abbey of Bec and the Anglo-Norman State (1034–1136)*. Woodbridge, Suff., 1981.

Vercauteren, Fernand. *Etude sur les "civitates" de la Belgique seconde*. Brussels, 1934.

Verhulst, Adriaan. "Note sur deux chartes de Lothaire, roi de France, pour l'abbaye de Saint-Bavon à Gand." *Bulletin de la Commission royale d'histoire* 155 (1989): 1–23.

Vezin, Jean. "L'influence des actes des hauts fonctionnaires romains sur les actes de Gaule et d'Espagne au VIIe siècle." In *Histoire comparée de l'administration,* 71–74.

Vogel, Cyrille. "La discipline pénitentielle en Gaule des origines au IXe siècle: Le dossier hagiographique." *Revue des sciences religieuses* 30 (1956): 1–26, 157–86.

——. "Les rites de la pénitence publique aux Xe et XIe siècles." In *Mélanges René Crozet*, 1:137–44. Poitiers, 1966.

Wallace-Hadrill, J. M. *Early Germanic Kingship in England and on the Continent*. Oxford, 1971.

——. "The *Via Regia* of the Carolingian Age." In *Trends in Medieval Political Thought*, ed. Beryl Smalley, 22–41. Oxford, 1965.

Werner, Karl Ferdinand. "Die Legitimität der Kapetinger und die Entstehung des *Reditus regni Francorum ad stirpem Karoli*." *Die Welt als Geschichte* 12 (1952): 214–15.

——. "Untersuchungen zur Frühzeit des französischen Fürstentums (9.–10. Jahrhundert)." *Die Welt als Geschichte* 18 (1958): 256–89; 19 (1959): 146–93; 20 (1960): 87–119.

——. "Westfranken-Frankreich unter den Spätkarolingern und frühen Kapetingern (888–1060)." In *Handbuch der europäischen Geschichte*, ed. Theodor Schieder, 1:731–83. Stuttgart, 1976.

White, Stephen D. *Custom, Kinship, and Gifts to Saints: The "Laudatio Parentum" in Western France, 1050–1150*. Durham, N.C., 1988.

——. "*Pactum Legem Vincit et Amor Judicium*: The Settlement of Disputes by Compromise in Eleventh-Century Western France." *American Journal of Legal History* 22 (1978): 281–308.

Wilentz, Sean, ed. *Rites of Power: Symbolism, Ritual, and Politics since the Middle Ages*. Philadelphia, 1985.

Willmes, Peter. *Der Herrscher-"Adventus" im Kloster des Frühmittelalters*. Munich, 1976.

Wolfram, Herwig, ed. *Intitulatio I: Lateinische Königs- und Fürstentitel bis zum Ende des 8. Jahrhunderts*. Mitteilungen des Instituts für österreichische Geschichtsforschung, Ergänzungsband 21. Vienna, 1967.

——, ed. *Intitulatio II: Lateinische Herrscher- und Fürstentitel im neunten und zehnten Jahrhundert*. Mitteilungen des Instituts für österreichische Geschichtsforschung, Ergänzungsband 24. Graz, 1973.

Zimmermann, Michel. "Protocoles et préambules dans les documents catalans du Xe au XIIe siècle: Evolution diplomatique et signification spirituelle." *Mélanges de la Casa de Velazquez* 10 (1974): 41–76.

Zoller-Devroey, Chantal. "Le domaine de l'abbaye Saint-Pierre de Corbie en Basse-Lotharingie et en Flandre au Moyen Age." *Revue belge de philologie et d'histoire* 54 (1976): 427–57, 1060–97.

Index

Aachen, 168, 233, 290

Abbéville, 139, 242, 246. *See also* Ponthieu: counts of

Abbo of Fleury, 122, 167, 169, 220–21

abbots: authority of, 31, 43, 78, 81, 135, 184, 189–93, 268, 306, 356n125; epithets and prerogatives, 27–28, 31–34, 41, 46, 49, 91, 184; as intercessors and petitioners, 28, 34–37, 41, 43–44, 46, 49, 54, 71–74, 189–90, 194, 249, 258; lay abbots, 28, 38–39, 46, 71, 90–91; petitions to, 27, 30–33, 36, 40–43, 49; relations with counts, 192, 207, 210, 245, 254

Acta synodi Atrebatensis. See Gerard, bishop of Cambrai

Adalbero, archbishop of Reims, 66, 113–16, 120–23, 125, 128, 132, 138, 161, 191–93, 242, 288, 362n20

Adalbero, bishop of Laon, 118–19, 121, 128–29, 159–60, 199, 220–21, 242, 244, 373n32

Adalhard, Saint, 102

Adelaide (queen, mother of Robert the Pious), 162–63, 168

Ademar of Chabannes, 145, 171

adventus, xii, 7, 13, 25, 84, 92, 114, 117–18, 120–21, 133–34, 137–39, 172, 299, 307. *See also occursus*

advocates, 5, 142–43, 207–8, 210–12, 225, 246, 278–79, 326–28, 333–35. *See also seigneurie banale*

Aimo of Fleury: *History of the Franks,* 145

Alberic of Coucy, 130, 205–6

Albert I, count of Vermandois, 149

Albert of Creil, 228

Alexander II, Pope, 61, 226

Amalric of Châteaufort, 75

Amboise, 253; lords of, 283–86 (*see also* Supplicius)

Amiens, 227, 238, 243, 275, 282, 326; bishops of, 43, 76, 135 (*see also* Fulk; Gui); cathedral of Notre-Dame, 224, 269–70; counts of, 76, 81, 135, 207–8, 224, 267–71 (*see also* Drogo; Guido; Ivo; Raoul; Simon; Walter)

Andrew of Fleury, 146, 186, 314

Angelran, abbot of Saint-Riquier, 190, 196, 210

Angelran I, count of Ponthieu, 43

Angelran II, count of Ponthieu, 43–44, 353n89

Angers, 250, 349n54; bishops of, 49, 55, 170, 366n75; cathedral of Saint-Maurice, 254. *See also* Saint-Aubin of Angers; Saint-Nicolas of Angers

Angoulême, 247; counts of, 134

Anjou, 17, 238, 262, 282, 358n134; counts of, 52–53, 250, 252–53, 283–84, 286, 297, 366n75, 372n20 (*see also* Fulk; Geoffrey; Henry Plantagenet)

anointings, xi, 5, 11, 24, 26, 46, 52, 84, 100–101, 109–10, 117, 120, 125–26, 131–32, 163, 168, 204, 288–90, 295–98, 310. *See also* coronations

Anscherus, abbot of Saint-Riquier, 387n46

Anselm of Laon, 182, 216

Anselm of Ribemont, 225, 410n139

Anselm of Saint-Quentin, 276

Aquitaine, xiii, 126, 135, 177; dukes of, 39, 40, 46, 50, 133–35, 247–48, 252, 283–84, 344n13, 357n129 (*see also* Ramnulf; William)

447

Library of Congress Cataloging-in-Publication Data
Koziol, Geoffrey.
    Begging pardon and favor : ritual and political order in early
medieval France / Geoffrey Koziol.
      p. cm.
    Includes bibliographical references and index.
    ISBN 978-0-8014-7753-9
    1. France—Politics and government—987–1328. 2. Dispute
resolution (Law)—France—History. 3. Pardon—France—History.
4. Petition, Right of—France—History. 5. Political customs and
rites—France—History. I. Title.
JN2337.K69 1992
944'.02—dc20
                                        91-55073